THE MUELLER REPORT

The Washington Post

Introduction and Analysis by
ROSALIND S. HELDERMAN
and MATT ZAPOTOSKY

PETER FINN
National Security Editor

SCRIBNER

New York   London   Toronto   Sydney   New Delhi

Scribner
An Imprint of Simon & Schuster, Inc.
1230 Avenue of the Americas
New York, NY 10020

First Scribner trade paperback edition April 2019

SCRIBNER and design are registered trademarks of The Gale Group, Inc.,
used under license by Simon & Schuster, Inc., the publisher of this work.

For information about special discounts for bulk purchases,
please contact Simon & Schuster Special Sales at 1-866-506-1949
or business@simonandschuster.com.

The Simon & Schuster Speakers Bureau can bring authors to your live event.
For more information or to book an event, contact the Simon & Schuster Speakers Bureau
at 1-866-248-3049 or visit our website at www.simonspeakers.com.

Manufactured in the United States of America

5   7   9   10   8   6   4

ISBN 978-1-9821-2973-6
ISBN 978-1-9821-2974-3 (ebook)

Contents

Contents

Introduction:
A President, a Prosecutor, and
the Protection of American Democracy

by Rosalind S. Helderman and
Matt Zapotosky of *The Washington Post*

The special counsel investigation that threatened Donald Trump's presidency was born of the commander-in-chief's rage.

In his first months in office, Trump had seethed over FBI director James B. Comey's refusal to tell the world that the president was not being scrutinized personally as part of the bureau's investigation of whether the Trump campaign had coordinated with Russia to interfere with the 2016 presidential race.

On May 9, 2017, Trump snapped. In a sharp break from Washington norms that afford FBI directors ten-year terms to give the bureau independence from politics, the president unceremoniously fired Comey. He conveyed the news in a terse letter, hand-delivered to FBI headquarters by his former personal bodyguard.

Trump's closest aides had warned him that the move could trigger a political uproar and lead to an expansion of the Russia inquiry—and it did.

Lawmakers on Capitol Hill cried foul. The FBI, already deep into its investigation of election interference, now feared that the most powerful man in the country was trying to obstruct its work. And Rod J. Rosenstein, the No. 2 official at the Justice Department, who had written a memo supporting Comey's dismissal, was incensed about the way the White House was pinning nearly all responsibility for the firing on him. He briefly considered resigning. Instead, Rosenstein turned to Robert S. Mueller III.

The deputy attorney general announced on May 17, 2017, that he had appointed the then-seventy-two-year-old Vietnam veteran and former FBI director to lead an independent investigation of interference in the 2016 election and other matters that might stem from the inquiry.

It was a broad mandate.

Over the next twenty-two months, Mueller, who had led the FBI through the attacks of September 11, 2001, and embodied the bureau's straight-arrow traditions, quietly and methodically investigated Trump and nearly everyone in his orbit, trying to determine whether any had conspired with the Kremlin to tilt the election, and whether the president himself had tried to obstruct justice.

That investigation culminated on March 22, 2019, when Mueller formally concluded his work and submitted a final report to Attorney General William P. Barr.

Barr held a press conference on April 18, less than two hours before the two-volume Mueller findings—*Report On The Investigation Into Russian Interference In The 2016 Presidential Election*—would be turned over to Congress. The attorney general noted repeatedly there was no "collusion"—a word Trump had popularized as he attacked the investigation—and revealed how the White House and Trump's personal lawyers had been given an advance look at the redacted document.

Barr's description of Mueller's report was favorable to Trump. In addition to finding no coordination between the Trump campaign and Russia, the attorney general said, Mueller had declined to reach a conclusion on whether the president had obstructed justice.

But the anodyne description belied what would soon be released. Mueller's report, despite redactions, offered a stunning account of how Russia worked to help the Trump campaign and how Trump's associates were willing to accept Russian assistance, and it presented an explosive and detailed narrative of how Trump sought to shut down the investigation as he worried about its impact.

"This is the end of my presidency," Trump said, by Mueller's account, when he learned of the special counsel's appointment. "I'm fucked."

Some—though not all—of what Mueller revealed had already been publicly known, although the report added layers of both facts and legal analysis. It told readers what the special counsel believed really happened at some meetings. Mueller's team, for example, described how in early August 2016, Trump's then–campaign chairman, Paul Manafort, met with a man whom the FBI had assessed as having ties to Russian intelligence and that that individual, Konstantin Kilimnik, wanted "to deliver in person a peace plan for Ukraine that Manafort acknowledged to the Special Counsel's Office was a 'backdoor' way for Russia to control part of eastern Ukraine."

"Both men believed the plan would require candidate Trump's assent to succeed (were he elected President)," the special counsel wrote. "They also discussed the status of the Trump Campaign and Manafort's strategy for winning Democratic votes in Midwestern states." Kilimnik in 2017 denied having ties to any intelligence service.

Mueller over and over again detailed moments when Russian government officials and others tried to make contacts with Trump's campaign, including a number of episodes not previously revealed in press coverage: a New York banker told the campaign about an outreach he'd received from "senior Kremlin officials" and one of them tried to invite Trump to Russia; Russian deputy prime minister Sergei Prikhodko emailed Trump's assistant to ask the then candidate to attend a Russian economic forum.

But the report confirmed, as Barr had suggested, that Mueller did not find a conspiracy between the Trump campaign and the Russians—though it suggested they had a shared motive.

"Although the investigation established that the Russian government perceived it would benefit from a Trump presidency and worked to secure that outcome, and that the Campaign expected it would benefit electorally from information stolen and released through Russian efforts, the investigation did not establish that members of the Trump Campaign conspired or coordinated with the Russian government in its election interference activities," Mueller's team wrote.

Mueller made clear that prosecutors did not consider "collusion" a legal term and never performed an analysis of that issue. They instead looked to see whether campaign aides made any agreements with Russians to assist in their effort to interfere in the election. Using that standard, they determined they could not establish that coordination took place between the campaign and Russia.

The report also confirmed Mueller had declined to reach a conclusion on obstruction, though it suggested that decision was heavily influenced by Justice Department legal guidance that says a sitting president can't be indicted. Mueller's team wrote that, based on that and other Justice Department policies, they decided "not to apply an approach that could potentially result in a judgment that the President committed crimes." In other words, they felt that because they could not charge the president, they should make no determination as to whether the president should be charged.

Barr felt no such compunction. He said he and Rosenstein reviewed the evidence themselves and determined it was not sufficient to make a case.

Mueller's report offered a less charitable version of Trump: describing how, more often than not, Trump's aides essentially saved their boss from his worst impulses by ignoring his directives to interfere with the Mueller investigation. In perhaps the most stark example, the report alleged that Trump called White House lawyer Don McGahn in June 2017 and told him to tell the acting attorney general that Mueller had to be removed.

"McGahn did not carry out the direction, however, deciding that he would resign rather than trigger what he regarded as a potential Saturday Night Massacre," Mueller's team wrote, referring to the night when President Nixon ordered his attorney general to fire a special prosecutor, triggering a cascade of resignations.

"The evidence we obtained about the President's actions and intent presents difficult issues that prevent us from conclusively determining that no criminal conduct occurred," Mueller's team wrote. "Accordingly, while this report does not conclude the President committed a crime, it also does not exonerate him."

Mueller's team wrote that their work was at times stymied by the lies witnesses told and the communications that they deleted or failed to maintain. And they said Trump himself, in resisting a sit-down interview, had provided "inadequate" written answers that stated more than thirty times he did not "'recall' or 'remember' or have an 'independent recollection'" of information investigators asked about.

While Mueller's team could have issued a subpoena to try to force his testimony, they wrote that it would have caused a "substantial delay," and they already had "sufficient evidence to understand relevant events and to make certain assessments."

The report was astonishing in part because, in a town fueled by leaks, Mueller largely kept his work under wraps. Until its release, Mueller had spoken almost entirely through indictments and other, often cryptic court filings.

In federal court, his team racked up an extraordinary record. His prosecutors charged thirty-four people, including twenty-six Russian nationals. They secured guilty pleas from seven people, including a former national security adviser and the chairman of Trump's campaign. They reconstructed the day-to-day interactions of Trump's closest aides and his adult children, exploring dozens of instances of Russian contacts with the Trump campaign. They documented the Russian attack on American democracy in breathtaking detail, even tracing individual keystrokes of Russian military officers in Moscow.

This introduction to the Mueller report is based on nearly three years of interviews by *Washington Post* reporters with the key figures in the saga at the White House, at the Justice Department, in the intelligence community, in the Trump campaign, in Moscow, and among the lawyers hired to defend those targeted by Mueller.

RUSSIAN FOOTSTEPS

The roots of the Mueller investigation were planted long before Trump was elected.

In the summer and fall of 2016, the FBI watched with alarm as the antisecrecy group WikiLeaks released Democratic Party emails that the bureau believed had been stolen by Russian government hackers. There were signs of foreign targeting of state voting systems. Also underway was a little-understood effort by Russian Internet trolls to influence American voters on social media through false news reports and incendiary political ads.

Meanwhile, Trump surrounded himself with campaign aides who had long-standing financial ties to Moscow. The candidate echoed Kremlin talking points about NATO and the European Union. Rather than condemning the Russian activity or calling on Russian president Vladimir Putin to stop it, he mocked the threat. "Russia, if you're listening, I hope you're able to find the thirty thousand emails that are missing," he said at a news conference in July 2016, referring to emails that Hillary Clinton, his Democratic opponent, had purged from a private server, saying they were personal communications and not related to her work while secretary of state. At that moment, WikiLeaks had just upended the Democratic National Convention by publishing thousands of internal party emails.

Soon after, the US government received a disturbing report from its ally Australia. Officials were told that George Papadopoulos, a young energy consultant chosen to advise Trump on foreign policy, had bragged to an Australian diplomat that he had been told that Russia had dirt on Clinton in the form of thousands of emails. Papadopoulos's boasts had come in May 2016, before the public even knew that the Democratic National Committee had been hacked.

In late July, the FBI opened "Crossfire Hurricane," a formal counterintelligence investigation of Russia's efforts that was focused in part on Papadopoulos. In October, as WikiLeaks published more stolen Democratic emails, a federal judge approved a secret order allowing the FBI to monitor Carter Page, another former Trump adviser. The bureau told the judge that it suspected Page was a Russian agent. It also was looking at Michael T. Flynn, a retired general who would become Trump's national security adviser, and Paul Manafort, his campaign chairman.

The investigation was charged from the start. It was highly unusual for the FBI to examine advisers of a leading presidential candidate in the middle of a campaign. Plus, the bureau had to sort out explosive but unverified allegations of Trump-Russia coordination slipped to agents in the summer of 2016 that came to be known as the "Steele Dossier."

The dossier had been commissioned by Fusion GPS, a Washington opposition research firm, and was funded by the Clinton campaign. It alleged that the Russians held salacious compromising material about Trump and that the Republican candidate had entered into a conspiracy with Russia to win the election. The FBI had worked previously with the dossier's author, former British intelligence officer Christopher Steele, and believed he was credible, although the document was a political product, commissioned by Trump's opponents. Trump and his allies would later argue that the FBI's investigation was tainted from the start by its reliance on Steele's work.

The inquiry also was marred by the texting between two FBI officials working on the case: agent Peter Strzok and Lisa Page, a bureau lawyer. Unbeknownst to many of their colleagues, the two had been having an extramarital affair and exchanged tens of thousands of text messages sharing their opinions of US political officials and expressing open disdain for Trump. One text from Strzok called the investigation of Trump's campaign an "insurance policy," while another declared "we'll stop" Trump from becoming president. Although the pair would assert that their personal views had no bearing on their work, the texts, when they later became public, gave Trump's supporters room to argue that the investigation was a set-up from the start. Strzok was later removed from the team and fired from the FBI; Page left the team and the bureau on her own.

If the FBI had wanted to stop Trump, a leak about the investigation might have done the trick. Instead, the bureau kept its work secret. That stood in contrast to the FBI's handling of its investigation of Clinton's use of a private email server, which Comey repeatedly addressed publicly in 2016, including in the final days of the campaign.

THE SESSIONS RECUSAL

On November 8, 2016, Trump was elected the nation's forty-fifth president. But as he prepared to take office, questions about Russia's role in the campaign only grew.

On December 29, President Barack Obama imposed new sanctions to punish the Kremlin for targeting the race. The next month, the US intelligence community formally concluded that Putin had ordered a covert operation to sow dissent in the American electorate, harm Clinton, and elect Trump.

In February, Flynn, Trump's newly installed national security adviser, was forced to resign after it was discovered that he had lied to Vice President Mike Pence when he said he had not spoken to a Russian envoy about the Obama sanctions. The next day, Trump pulled Comey aside in the Oval Office and, referring to the FBI's investigation of Flynn's activities, asked him to "let this go," according to Comey's account.

Shortly after, Attorney General Jeff Sessions announced that he would recuse himself from any investigation of the 2016 campaign.

The recusal came after *The Washington Post* reported that during the presidential campaign, Sessions, who was then a senator from Alabama, had twice met with Russia's ambassador to the United States. Sessions had not disclosed the meetings when he was asked at his confirmation hearing about contacts between Russians and the Trump campaign.

"I have been called a surrogate at a time or two in that campaign and I didn't have—did not have communications with the Russians," Sessions had said.

At a hastily arranged news conference, Sessions insisted that his recusal was not a reaction to the *Post*'s reporting, but instead the result of weeks of consultations with Justice Department ethics officials who had advised him to recuse.

When asked earlier in the day whether his attorney general should step aside, the president said, "I don't think so."

Sessions told advisers in the months that followed that he had no choice in the matter. The investigation was of Trump's campaign and its relationship with a foreign power. How could Sessions oversee that without raising questions about whether he had a conflict of interest?

Next, in the swirl of news roiling Washington, came the May 9, 2017, firing of Comey and the entry of Mueller.

Sessions happened to be at the White House for a meeting with Trump and others when word came that Rosenstein, the deputy attorney general, was appointing a special counsel.

"How could you let this happen, Jeff," he told Sessions, according to Mueller's report, amid a lengthy diatribe in the Oval Office.

Sessions left the White House shaken, according to people who spoke with him, and that night handed in a letter of resignation. Advisers convinced the president that he could not fire Sessions so soon after Comey without risking even more political fallout. Trump returned Sessions's letter with a curt handwritten note saying that he would not allow the attorney general to quit.

The president would never stop seething, however. Until the day Sessions stepped down in November 2018, Trump relentlessly attacked his attorney general and the department he commanded—raising fears that he would end Mueller's work.

Mueller, after all, was not an independent counsel, and thus not truly independent of Trump. The reason reached back to the 1990s. The lawyers who investigated the Iran-Contra scandal and the Bill Clinton/Monica Lewinsky affair worked under a now-defunct law, commonly known as the independent counsel act, which gave them wide latitude. These independent counsels were picked by a three-judge panel, and they did not answer directly to anyone in the executive branch.

That law was allowed to expire in 1999, after officials who worked under it—including independent counsel Kenneth W. Starr—came to believe it created an unelected, fourth branch of government to enforce the laws against the others. In its place, officials crafted the special counsel regulations, under which Mueller was appointed.

By design, Mueller was selected by the attorney general—or in this instance the acting attorney general, Rosenstein, because Sessions was recused—and subject to that official's oversight. The special counsel was required to notify the attorney general of significant steps he planned to take, not unlike any of the ninety-three US attorneys nationwide, and the attorney general was allowed to veto his decisions. Trump could have ordered Rosenstein to fire Mueller, although doing so would have caused a cascade of resignations at the Justice Department.

Rosenstein's decision to turn to an outsider to take over the politically charged investigation plucked the inquiry out of a toxic stew of internal Justice Department politics. Andrew McCabe, Comey's deputy, had been alarmed when his boss was fired. Wary of the president and Justice Department leaders, he began documenting his interactions with Rosenstein and others, including a meeting where he said Rosenstein had suggested wearing a wire to record the president. After Comey was fired, McCabe immediately authorized the FBI to open an investigation of Trump himself, something the bureau had declined to do for months.

Some at the Justice Department feared that McCabe was acting out of anger about Comey's removal. At a meeting shortly after Mueller's appointment, McCabe and Rosenstein each suggested that the other should recuse himself from any involvement with the case. Neither did.

THE G-MAN

At the time of his selection, Mueller was working as a partner at the white-shoe Washington law firm WilmerHale, but he had been employed in the private sector only since 2014. Before that, he had earned a reputation as a prosecutor of extraordinary discipline and intellect over a career in the nation's highest law enforcement jobs. Mueller, a Republican, had been appointed to top positions by four US presidents, two from each party.

Born into privilege, he graduated from Princeton University, then joined the Marines during the Vietnam War, at a time when many men his age, including Trump, looked to avoid service. Overseas, he led a rifle platoon and earned a Bronze Star Medal and a Purple Heart in combat.

Upon returning home, he enrolled at the University of Virginia Law School and after graduating, became a federal prosecutor in California and then Massachusetts. With only brief stints in private practice, he spent the next thirty years cycling through top jobs at the Justice Department until President George W. Bush appointed him to lead the FBI in July 2001. He was confirmed in August and had been on the job for less than a week when terrorists crashed planes into the World Trade Center and the Pentagon. For the next decade, he led the FBI through a tumultuous reorientation to focus on terrorist threats.

Mueller favored the G-Man's traditional uniform: business suits with starched white shirts, never colored. At the FBI, he was known for a punishing work ethic, and was often at his desk by 6 a.m. And he was famously press averse, with no tolerance for leaks by underlings.

Mueller quickly assembled a team of some of the most experienced lawyers in the country. He took with him from WilmerHale James Quarles, who had been an assistant special prosecutor on the Watergate Special Prosecution Force, and Aaron Zebley, who had been Mueller's chief of staff at the FBI. Quarles would come to work as a sort of senior executive in the office, handling many of the interactions with the White House, with Zebley again serving as Mueller's right-hand man.

As the summer of 2017 progressed, the group grew. Mueller added Andrew Weissmann, a prosecutor who had been involved in the high-profile Enron cases and was well known among defense lawyers as being aggressive; Zainab Ahmad, whose strong record of prosecuting terrorism cases earned her a glowing profile in *The New Yorker*; and Andrew Goldstein, a public-corruption specialist who had helped bring charges against prominent state officials in New York.

Signaling that he expected his work might generate cases worthy of consideration by the highest courts, Mueller also added several appellate specialists, including Michael Dreeben, who had argued more than a hundred cases before the Supreme Court and was considered one of the country's foremost experts in criminal law.

Trump, meanwhile, had trouble finding and keeping a lawyer to face down Mueller's dream team. Many of the nation's most prominent white-collar defense lawyers declined to represent the president of the United States, some citing conflicts and others privately confiding that they worried about the reputational harm that could come from an affiliation with an unpopular president.

When Mueller was appointed, Trump's legal team was led by Marc Kasowitz, a combative New York litigator who had defended Trump in business disputes but had little experience with Washington investigations. Trump soon replaced Kasowitz with John Dowd, a Washington fixture who had handled big cases but had a reputation as a bit of a loose cannon and was nearing the end of his career.

To deal with the inevitable crush of special counsel requests to interview White House staff members and review government documents, Trump named to the White House counsel's office Ty Cobb, who sported a walrus mustache and was a distant relative of the baseball great with whom he shared a name.

Working together, Dowd and Cobb devised a strategy of quiet accommodation to the special counsel. Instead of fighting his every request, they made more than twenty White House staff members available for interviews and turned over twenty thousand pages of official documents. Meanwhile, they made cheery but inaccurate pronouncements about the state of Mueller's inquiry. Cobb declared at one point that he was confident that the investigation would wrap up by Thanksgiving 2017. When the holiday came and went with no end, Cobb revised his prediction. The inquiry, he said, would be finished by Christmas, then soon after New Year's Day 2018. It was still underway in May 2018, when Cobb resigned and was replaced at the White House by Emmet T. Flood, a stern tactician who made no public pronouncements about anything at all.

ATTACKING MUELLER

Dowd and Cobb drew the line in their strategy of cooperation at allowing Mueller to interview the president. Trump repeatedly told the public that he would talk to Mueller's investigators, sparking a long-running will-he-or-won't-he drama. With his typical braggadocio, Trump believed he could talk his way out of anything Mueller might throw at him and, for a time, seemed open to a sit-down. His lawyers were adamantly opposed to the idea. They did not trust Mueller's team and feared that their client could not get through an interview session without being accused of perjury.

Disputes over the issue led to Dowd's resignation in March 2018. He was replaced by former New York mayor and federal prosecutor Rudolph W. Giuliani, who adopted a legal strategy more in keeping with the president's style. Confident that Mueller would abide by a long-standing Justice Department guideline that the Constitution does not allow for the criminal indictment of a sitting president, he believed Trump could face a political threat from impeachment but no true legal peril. In his view, the best legal defense was a political offense in the form of an unrelenting public campaign to undermine Mueller's credibility and convince voters that impeachment based on his findings would be unfair and unpalatable.

Giuliani's strategy had the added benefit of convincing Trump that there was no need to appear cooperative and sit for an interview. This approach suited Trump's lifelong ethos of responding to any threat by punching back harder. He amplified Giuliani's attacks, not just on the special counsel, but on the entire justice system.

People who spoke to Trump said that he derided Sessions privately as "Mr. Magoo," an elderly cartoon character popular in the 1960s and iconic for not acknowledging his poor eyesight, and Rosenstein as "Mr. Peepers," a bespectacled high school teacher from a 1950s sitcom. After word of the insults leaked, Trump denied using the nicknames. In public, he was nearly as insulting, asserting in September 2018 that "I don't have an attorney general." To witnesses involved in the Mueller investigation, Trump sent a clear message: Cooperate with investigators, and you will feel my wrath. Fight back, and you will have my support.

After Michael Cohen, his former lawyer and self-described fixer, pleaded guilty and implicated the president in a scheme to break campaign finance laws, Trump deemed him a "rat" and called for Cohen's father-in-law to be investigated for unnamed crimes.

In contrast, Trump had nothing but praise for Paul Manafort, his former campaign chairman, whose lawyers quietly assured Trump's team that he was not providing damaging information about the president, even after he pleaded guilty to crimes including tax fraud and began cooperating with Mueller.

"I feel very badly for Paul Manafort and his wonderful family," Trump wrote on Twitter. " 'Justice' took a 12 year old tax case, among other things, applied tremendous pressure on him and, unlike Michael Cohen, he refused to 'break'—make up stories in order to get a 'deal.' Such respect for a brave man!"

Legal analysts asserted that Trump might be obstructing justice in real time—using his presidential platform and pardon power to dissuade possible witnesses from cooperating with Mueller.

Trump's posture as president toward Russia also gave the law enforcement and intelligence communities cause for concern. He took great pains to conceal the details of his conversations with Putin, including at least once taking the notes of his own interpreter and demanding that the details of the discussion not be disclosed, even inside his administration. In a White House meeting in May 2017, he was said to have revealed highly classified information to the Russian foreign minister and ambassador—details so sensitive that they had been kept from close allies.

At a news conference in Helsinki the following year, Trump stood next to his Russian counterpart and seemed to cast doubt on whether Russia had been responsible for the election-related meddling at all—delivering a remarkable rebuke to those in the US intelligence community who had assessed the Kremlin was to blame.

"President Putin was extremely strong and powerful in his denial today," Trump said.

MUELLER'S FINDINGS

If Trump's goal was to derail the investigation, however, he failed. Mueller's team pushed forward, serving 2,800 subpoenas, executing nearly 500 search warrants, and questioning around 500 people. Witnesses who sat for those interviews said afterward that they were surprised by the prosecutors' careful, detailed work.

"The Mueller team knew more about what I did in 2016 than I knew myself," former Trump aide Michael Caputo said on CNN after emerging from his interview. "I think they know more about the Trump campaign than anyone who ever worked there."

Mueller's investigation accelerated in July 2017, after it emerged that Donald J. Trump Jr., the president's son, had attended a meeting at Trump Tower in New York during the campaign with a Russian lawyer who he was told would provide damaging information about Clinton. "If it's what you say, I love it," Trump Jr. had written in an email at the time.

Everyone who attended the meeting—including Manafort and Trump's son-in-law, Jared Kushner—said that it was a bust and that no dirt was provided. But the episode seemed to confirm that the Trump campaign was willing to accept Russian government help when offered. When Donald Trump Jr. was first asked about the meeting a year later, the president dictated a statement for his son that was misleading and incomplete. The meeting, it said, had been "primarily" about adoption.

Mueller's team toiled for long stretches in silence, emerging periodically to file bombshell indictments.

Two of the indictments appeared designed to explain to the American people exactly what the Russians did during the campaign. In February 2018, Mueller's team indicted thirteen Russian nationals and three Russian companies, alleging that they had engaged in a complex two-year scheme to interfere in US politics by posing as Americans and planting false news stories and divisive ads on social media. Working from a small office building in St. Petersburg, these trolls allegedly duped real Americans with whom they interacted online, amplifying tense debates about race, gun control, and sexual identity, pushing pro-Trump messages and even getting some Americans to organize and attend rallies they orchestrated. Yevgeniy Viktorovich Prigozhin, who the Russian news media has identified as the financial backer of the group, told Russia's state news agency of the indictment, "The Americans are very impressionable people, and they see what they want to see," adding, "I am not at all disappointed that I appear in this list. If they want to see the devil—let them." Then, in July 2018, Mueller's team indicted twelve Russian military intelligence officers, alleging that they hacked into the email accounts of the Democratic Party and Clinton campaign officials and posed online as an entity called Guccifer 2.0 to publish the material, including by passing it to WikiLeaks and others. The Russian Foreign Ministry rejected the indictment's allegations as lacking evidence and described the charges as a clear effort to derail an upcoming Trump-Putin summit in Helsinki. "It is unfortunate that distributing false information has become the norm in Washington, and that criminal cases are being initiated based on clearly political motives," the ministry said.

Among Trump's friends and aides, six men pleaded guilty or were indicted. Mostly, they were charged with lying to Congress and the FBI about a wide range of issues. None were accused of criminally coordinating with the Russians. But over and over again, they were accused of lying about efforts to develop inroads with Russia and leverage that country's hacking of Democratic emails.

Roger Stone, a Republican operative and longtime Trump friend, was charged in January 2019 with lying to Congress about his efforts to seek information from WikiLeaks as it was publishing hacked emails. He pleaded not guilty and vowed to beat the charges in court.

Cohen pleaded guilty to lying to Congress about efforts to build a Trump Tower in Moscow, including a phone call he had with an assistant to a top Putin aide.

Flynn admitted that he lied to the FBI about his contacts with the Russian ambassador during the presidential transition.

Papadopoulos said that he, too, had lied, hiding key details about his interaction with a London professor who had given him early warning about Russian hacking.

Manafort was convicted by a jury in Virginia in August 2018 of bank and tax fraud related to his handling of more than $60 million he earned consulting for Russia-friendly politicians in Ukraine before he joined the Trump campaign. He subsequently pleaded guilty to charges including not registering as a foreign agent for his Ukraine work.

Mueller's prosecutors later told a judge that Manafort continued to lie even after his plea. Notably, they said many of his lies were about his interactions with a Russian employee whom the FBI found to have ties to Russian intelligence. That employee has denied any such connection.

The release of Mueller's report thrust the case into the political arena, arming Democratic lawmakers with an array of new information to support their attacks on Trump and open possible new areas of inquiry for their own investigations.

Trump and his allies, in contrast, reacted with glee. "NO COLLUSION—NO OBSTRUCTION," the president tweeted, reprising a phrase he used throughout the investigation. Trump's supporters called for an investigation into the investigators, noting Mueller's report included no information about what had been learned about the Steele Dossier's salacious allegations or their role in initially launching the probe. Carter Page, who had been subject to nearly a year's worth of secret government monitoring, was never charged with any crime. The report said investigators did not establish that Page conspired with the Russian government.

Democrats noted Mueller's team wrote that they had not been able to solve every mystery they explored. Some witnesses lied. Others interacted using encrypted applications that left no record of their contemporaneous communications. According to the report, prosecutors were unable to figure out everything Page had done while visiting Moscow during the campaign. They also failed to determine what Paul Manafort's Russian employee did with internal Trump campaign polling data after Manafort slipped it to him during the campaign.

As Democrats sought to digest Mueller's voluminous findings, they also turned their fire on Barr, who many felt served as a shield for Trump by holding a press conference to summarize Mueller's findings in a way that was favorable for the president.

Barr also had announced the conclusion of the probe weeks before the report's release and revealed Mueller's top-line findings: that the special counsel could not prove coordination, and he would not reach a conclusion on obstruction. Though it would not be known for some time, Mueller privately complained to Barr about that characterization in a letter, asserting that the attorney general "did not fully capture the context, nature, and substance of this Office's work and conclusions." The missive was remarkable in its own right, and even more so because of the man who signed it. Mueller, rigid in his adherence to the bureaucratic chain of command, had rebuked his boss in writing, increasing the likelihood the disagreement would ultimately become public.

Democrats, too, felt Barr had set a pro-Trump narrative that was hard to shake—even if the report itself offered them a wealth of detail on Trump's actions that they could pursue in hearings. Some Democrats immediately said the report provided evidence the president had committed a crime. "Even in its incomplete form," Representative Jerry Nadler (D-New York), the chair of the House Judiciary Committee, said in a statement, "the Mueller report outlines disturbing evidence that President Trump engaged in obstruction of justice and other misconduct."

Nadler vowed to press on with investigations of Trump as Republicans called for them to end.

"Democrats who have been running around for the last two years making outlandish claims about the president and his family ought to apologize to the American people for misleading them and the press about this smear campaign," said Representative Steve Scalise (R-Louisiana), the Republican whip. "This report . . . delivered a death blow to their baseless conspiracy theories."

Mueller's investigation may have concluded, but Washington's political wars were as hot as ever.

List of Individuals, Arranged by Organizational Affiliation

THE SPECIAL COUNSEL'S OFFICE

Zainab Ahmad: Previously at the US Attorney's Office in Brooklyn, Zainab Ahmad was well-known as a terrorism prosecutor.

Greg Andres: Joining Robert S. Mueller III's team from the Davis Polk law firm, Greg Andres had previously worked as a Justice Department official and as chief of the criminal division at the US Attorney's Office in Brooklyn. He led the team that brought former Trump campaign chairman Paul Manafort to trial in federal court in Virginia.

Rush Atkinson: Previously at the Justice Department's fraud section, Rush Atkinson worked on economic crime cases.

Ryan Dickey: A veteran cyber prosecutor in the Justice Department's computer-crime and intellectual-property section, Ryan Dickey was brought onto Special Counsel Robert S. Mueller III's team late in 2017. At that time, he was the only attorney in the group known to specialize in cyber issues.

Michael Dreeben: Considered one of the Justice Department's foremost experts on criminal law, Michael Dreeben has argued more than a hundred cases before the Supreme Court. His early inclusion in the special counsel's office signaled that Robert S. Mueller III predicted from the start that his work might generate tough cases that would make their way through the highest levels of the US court system.

Kyle Freeny: Detailed from the Justice Department's criminal division, Kyle Freeny was considered an expert in money-laundering cases.

Andrew Goldstein: Previously at the US Attorney's Office in Manhattan, Andrew Goldstein was head of the public-corruption unit.

Adam Jed: Detailed from the Justice Department's Civil Division, Adam Jed worked on appeals cases.

Scott Meisler: Previously at the Justice Department's Criminal Division, Scott Meisler worked as an appellate lawyer.

Robert S. Mueller III: A Vietnam veteran, former Justice Department official, and former FBI director, Robert S. Mueller III was tapped in May 2017 to lead the investigation into whether the Trump campaign coordinated with the Kremlin to influence the 2016 election. Mueller also explored whether Trump obstructed justice. Amid one of the highest-profile cases in history, Mueller kept an astoundingly low profile, never holding any press conferences and barely providing any public statements beyond what his team said in court.

Elizabeth Prelogar: A former Supreme Court clerk detailed from the Solicitor General's Office, Elizabeth Prelogar specialized in appellate cases.

James Quarles: A former assistant special prosecutor for the Watergate Special Prosecution Force, James Quarles left the white-shoe law firm WilmerHale with Robert S. Mueller III to join the special counsel's office. He was one of Mueller's top deputies and often interacted with White House lawyers.

Jeannie Rhee: A former partner at the law firm WilmerHale, Jeannie Rhee, like Robert S. Mueller III and others, left the firm to join the special counsel's office. She had previously worked as a federal prosecutor in Washington and as a Justice Department official.

Brian M. Richardson: A former Supreme Court clerk and clerk for a judge serving on the US Court of Appeals in New York City, Brian M. Richardson was a relatively junior member of Mueller's team who worked on a variety of cases. He left the team and became a fellow at Columbia Law School.

Brandon Van Grack: A Justice Department lawyer, Brandon Van Grack had worked on Russia-related matters that preceded the creation of the special counsel's office. He was part of the team that brought former Trump campaign chairman Paul Manafort to trial and was also involved in the investigation into former Trump national security adviser Michael T. Flynn.

Andrew Weissmann: A lawyer who headed the Justice Department's fraud section and a key player in the high-profile Enron prosecutions, Andrew Weissmann was considered one of Robert S. Mueller III's top deputies and was deeply involved in the investigation of former Trump campaign chairman Paul Manafort.

Aaron Zebley: A former federal prosecutor and Robert S. Mueller III's chief of staff at the FBI, Aaron Zebley left the law firm of WilmerHale with his former boss to join the special counsel's office. He was considered one of Mueller's closest advisers.

Aaron Zelinsky: Detailed from the US Attorney's Office in Maryland, Aaron Zelinsky had worked with Rod J. Rosenstein, who had served as US attorney there before being named deputy attorney general.

THE DEPARTMENT OF JUSTICE

Uzo Asonye: An assistant US attorney in the Eastern District of Virginia, Uzo Asonye was part of the team that put former Trump campaign chairman Paul Manafort on trial there.

William P. Barr: President Trump's pick to succeed Jeff Sessions as attorney general, William Barr would come to supervise the special counsel probe as it approached its conclusion. Barr was friends with Robert S. Mueller III, both having worked together previously in the Justice Department. But before coming back into government, Barr had raised questions about Mueller's case and his team—even sending a memo to Justice Department leaders criticizing what he viewed as the special counsel's "fatally misconceived" theory of how the president might have obstructed justice.

Ed O'Callaghan: A top official in the deputy attorney general's office, Ed O'Callaghan was one of only a few Justice Department leaders to receive regular briefings on Special Counsel Robert S. Mueller III's closely held investigation.

Rod J. Rosenstein: The No. 2 official at the Justice Department, Rod J. Rosenstein appointed Robert S. Mueller III to lead the special counsel investigation and supervised him. Rosenstein was a complicated figure. A Trump appointee, he authored a memo laying the groundwork for James B. Comey to be fired, but he soon came to be a focus of the president's anger, and liberals came to view him as a protector of Mueller's work.

Jeff Sessions: The first US senator to endorse Trump for president and Trump's handpicked nominee to lead the Justice Department, Jeff Sessions was a key player for what he did not do in the Russia probe. After *The Washington Post* reported that Sessions had contacts with Russia's ambassador to the United States during the presidential campaign, contradicting what Sessions had told lawmakers during his confirmation hearing, Sessions recused himself from the investigation. That decision, which incensed Trump, ultimately led to Rod J. Rosenstein being put in charge of the probe.

THE FBI

James B. Comey: A veteran lawyer who was named FBI director by President Obama in 2013, James B. Comey was the face of the Russia probe until he was fired by President Trump from his ten-year position in May 2017. Comey's firing—and public disclosures about his interactions with President Trump—helped initiate the special counsel investigation, which took over cases the FBI had opened months earlier examining possible coordination between the Kremlin and the Trump campaign.

Andrew McCabe: The No. 2 official in the FBI under James B. Comey, Andrew McCabe became a frequent target of criticism from President Trump, especially after McCabe took command of the FBI in the wake of Comey's firing. McCabe, who was ultimately fired from the bureau amid allegations that he lied to investigators exploring a media disclosure, was in charge of the FBI when it opened a case into whether Trump had obstructed justice.

Lisa Page: An FBI lawyer and adviser to FBI deputy director Andrew McCabe, Lisa Page worked briefly on the special counsel team. She left after just months on the job, and it was later revealed that she had exchanged anti-Trump texts with Peter Strzok, an FBI agent and fellow member of the special counsel investigation with whom Page had an affair.

Peter Strzok: A veteran FBI counterintelligence agent, Peter Strzok was a key leader on the Russia investigation before Robert S. Mueller III was appointed special counsel, and Strzok was briefly the lead FBI agent on Mueller's team. Strzok was removed from the investigation and ultimately fired from the FBI after it was learned he had exchanged anti-Trump text messages with FBI lawyer Lisa Page.

THE DONALD TRUMP CAMPAIGN

Rick Gates: Deputy campaign manager for Donald Trump, Rick Gates was a longtime associate of Paul Manafort's and worked with Manafort in Ukraine prior to joining the Trump campaign. Gates pleaded guilty in February 2018 to conspiring against the United States, agreeing that he evaded taxes, helped Manafort commit bank fraud, and failed to register as a foreign lobbyist for his Ukraine work.

Paul Manafort: A longtime Republican political consultant, Paul Manafort joined the Trump campaign in March 2016 and served as its chairman from June to August. Prior to joining the campaign, Manafort had spent nearly a decade as a political consultant in Ukraine and doing business deals with Russian billionaire Oleg Deripaska. Manafort was convicted by a Virginia jury in August 2018 of eight counts of bank and tax fraud. A month later, he pleaded guilty to additional charges, including having failed to register as a foreign lobbyist while working for pro-Russian Ukrainian president Viktor Yanukovych.

Carter Page: An energy consultant with experience working in Moscow, Carter Page was named a national security adviser to Donald Trump's campaign in March 2016. In July, he traveled to Moscow, where he delivered a speech critical of US foreign policy and greeted a top Russian official. The FBI received secret permission to conduct surveillance of Page starting in October 2016, after convincing a federal judge that evidence suggested he might be a foreign agent.

George Papadopoulos: An energy consultant, George Papadopoulos was named a national security adviser to Donald Trump's campaign in March 2016. Papadopoulos said in his plea that he was told by a London-based professor that month that the Russians held damaging information about Democrat Hillary Clinton in the form of thousands of emails. Papadopoulos then spent months unsuccessfully trying to arrange meetings between Trump or his campaign aides with top Russian officials, according to court documents and campaign emails read to *The Washington Post*. Papadopoulos pleaded guilty in October 2017 to lying to the FBI about his Russia contacts and served fourteen days in prison.

Roger Stone: A longtime Republican campaign operative who has been friends with Donald Trump for thirty years, Roger Stone briefly worked for Trump's campaign in 2015 and then served as an informal adviser in 2016. Known for reveling in provocative political tricks, Stone cheered on WikiLeaks as it published emails stolen from the

Democratic National Committee and Hillary Clinton campaign chairman John Podesta. Stone also claimed before the election that he had advance knowledge of WikiLeaks' plans. Later, he insisted he had no contact with WikiLeaks nor exact knowledge of the group's plans. He was charged in January 2019 with false statements, witness tampering, and obstruction for trying to hide from Congress his efforts to learn about WikiLeaks' releases of hacked Democratic Party emails. He vowed to fight the charges.

THE TRUMP ORGANIZATION

Michael Cohen: A lawyer who served as executive vice president of the Trump Organization starting in 2007, Michael Cohen pleaded guilty in December 2018 to lying to Congress about the extent of efforts to build a Trump Tower in Moscow during the presidential campaign. Cohen also pleaded guilty to bank and tax fraud related to his personal finances and said that Donald Trump, identified in court documents as "Individual 1," instructed him to direct illegal payments to silence two women who said they had affairs with Trump.

Donald J. Trump Jr.: The eldest son of President Trump, Donald J. Trump Jr. is an executive at the real estate company founded by his father and served as an informal adviser to his campaign. In June 2016, Trump Jr. met with a Russian lawyer who, Trump Jr. was told, would share damaging information about Democratic candidate Hillary Clinton. "If it's what you say, I love it," Trump Jr. wrote in an email.

THE WHITE HOUSE

Steve Bannon: The White House's former chief strategist until August 2017, Steve Bannon was a witness in the Mueller probe, about which he expressed mixed views. After he was ousted as a formal adviser to President Trump, Bannon publicly pitched a plan that Trump cripple the Russia probe by firing Deputy Attorney General Rod J. Rosenstein, who oversaw it. Later, though, when news of his being interviewed by the special counsel became public, Bannon called Mueller's team "very professional and courteous."

Michael T. Flynn: A retired army lieutenant general, Michael I. Flynn briefly served as Donald Trump's first national security adviser before resigning in February 2017 after lying to the public and Vice President Mike Pence about his contacts with the Russian ambassador during the presidential transition. He pleaded guilty in December 2017 to lying to the FBI about those contacts as well and cooperated extensively with the special counsel's probe.

Jared Kushner: The husband of President Trump's daughter Ivanka, Jared Kushner drew the attention of investigators for meetings he had with a Russian banker and diplomat between the time when his father-in-law was elected and was sworn into office. When former Trump national security adviser Michael T. Flynn admitted lying about his own dealings with a Russian diplomat, Flynn said the interactions were done in consultation with senior Trump transition officials, including Kushner. In particular, Kushner directed Flynn to talk with the Russian ambassador about a UN resolution on Israel, people familiar with the investigation have told *The Washington Post*. Kushner has not publicly addressed the episode detailed in Flynn's plea.

K. T. McFarland: A deputy to former national security adviser Michael T. Flynn, K. T. McFarland was a key player in Flynn's fraught interactions with Sergey Kislyak, Russia's ambassador to the United States. Flynn admitted as part of a plea agreement that he spoke with McFarland at Trump's Mar-a-Lago resort before talking to the diplomat so they could "discuss what, if anything, to communicate to the Russian ambassador about the US sanctions." Flynn told FBI agents he did not discuss sanctions with the ambassador, though he would later admit that was a lie. McFarland was nominated to be the US ambassador to Singapore, though the nomination was later withdrawn amid the legal controversy surrounding her and Flynn.

Don McGahn: Don McGahn was the White House counsel from the start of Trump's administration until October 2018, giving him a front-row seat to some of President Trump's most problematic interactions with officials at his own Justice Department and to the turmoil induced by the special counsel's work. McGahn, who had also served as legal adviser to Trump's campaign, cooperated extensively with the special counsel investigation and frequently played the role of peacemaker when Trump bristled about the probe.

Mike Pence: The vice president of the United States, Mike Pence largely stayed away from the Russia probe, though he could not avoid it entirely. When Pence said on television in January 2017 that national security adviser Michael T. Flynn had not talked about sanctions with the Russian ambassador, that prompted alarm among federal law enforcement officials, who suspected Flynn might have lied to the vice president. Flynn would later admit that he did so.

Reince Priebus: The president's first chief of staff, Reince Priebus was a witness in the Mueller probe and shared valuable insights into Trump's position on the Justice Department and the special counsel investigation. Priebus talked with FBI director James B. Comey in the harried early days of the Trump administration and notably asked Comey whether the bureau had a secret warrant to surveil national security adviser Michael T. Flynn. Priebus, who served until July 2017, was also involved in confronting Flynn after it had become clear he had lied about his interactions with the Russian ambassador.

Donald J. Trump: The forty-fifth president of the United States, Donald J. Trump was a celebrity business mogul who defeated Democrat Hillary Clinton in 2016. In March 2017, the FBI announced that it was investigating Russian interference in the election and whether anyone associated with the Trump campaign coordinated with those efforts. Special Counsel Robert S. Mueller III took over the investigation in May 2017 with a mandate that included exploring whether Trump as president had attempted to obstruct the probe.

THE TRUMP LEGAL DEFENSE

Ty Cobb: A former partner at the law firm Hogan Lovells, Ty Cobb joined the White House in July 2017 to serve as the administration's point person in coordinating requests by the special counsel to interview White House staff or review official documents. Cobb advised the White House to cooperate with the effort and publicly offered inaccurate predictions that the investigation would soon be over. He resigned in May 2018.

John Dowd: A former marine and veteran white-collar-criminal defense attorney, John Dowd served as Donald Trump's lead personal attorney in the Mueller matter from June 2017 to March 2018. Dowd advised that Trump's White House and campaign should cooperate with the investigation, but Trump should avoid sitting for an interview, despite publicly promising to do so, *The Washington Post* has reported. Dowd quit after clashing with Trump over the issue.

Emmet T. Flood: A former partner at the Washington law firm Williams & Connolly, Emmet Flood was hired to serve in the White House counsel's office in May 2018, where he replaced Ty Cobb as the administration's point person in handling the Mueller probe. Flood steered clear of public attention but advised the White House to limit cooperation with the probe and researched ways to assert executive privilege to potentially prevent Mueller's report from being shared with Congress, *The Washington Post* has reported.

Rudolph W. Giuliani: The former mayor of New York City, Rudolph W. Giuliani was hired by President Trump to lead his personal legal team in April 2018. Giuliani waged an unrelenting public war on Mueller, seeming to believe that undermining public confidence in the investigation was the best way to make impeachment unpalatable to the American people.

Marc Kasowitz: A New York litigator who had helped Donald Trump handle business disputes, Marc Kasowitz served as President Trump's personal attorney during the investigation's earliest phases. He was minimized in his role in favor of John Dowd, who had far more Washington experience, after Robert S. Mueller III was appointed and the investigation picked up steam.

Jane and Marty Raskin: A husband-and-wife team who jointly ran a small Florida law firm and were hired to assist President Trump's legal efforts after John Dowd quit and Trump struggled to find someone else to take his case. While Rudolph W. Giuliani dominated airwaves and Trump's public message, the Raskins, particularly Jane, were credited with quietly devising his legal strategy.

Jay Sekulow: A conservative lawyer and activist with more experience dealing with religious-liberty and free-speech cases than criminal matters, Jay Sekulow was hired to serve as the public face of President Trump's personal legal team in the summer of 2017. His role expanded over time, as other lawyers came and went and he became the team's longest-serving member.

THE RUSSIANS

Aras Agalarov: An Azerbaijan-born billionaire and real estate developer based in Moscow, Aras Agalarov met Donald Trump in 2013, when Agalarov paid to sponsor the Miss Universe pageant in Moscow. Emails released by Donald Trump Jr. show that Agalarov asked his pop star son to get a meeting with members of the Trump campaign for Russian lawyer Natalia Veselnitskaya in June 2016.

Emin Agalarov: A Moscow-based pop star who also works in real estate alongside his father, billionaire Aras Agalarov. Emin Agalarov was involved with bringing Donald Trump's beauty pageant to Moscow in 2013, then Emin asked his publicist, Rob Goldstone, to get a meeting with the Trump campaign for lawyer Natalia Veselnitskaya in June 2016.

Maria Butina: A Russian gun-rights activist, Maria Butina pleaded guilty in December 2018 to conspiring to act as an unregistered agent of Russia for cozying up to American conservatives, notably leaders of the National Rifle Association. She asked Donald Trump a question about Russia at a public forum in 2015 and met Donald Trump Jr. at an NRA meeting in May 2016.

Oleg Deripaska: A Russian billionaire who is close to Russian president Vladimir Putin and has struggled to get visas to travel to the United States because of alleged ties to Russian organized crime, Oleg Deripaska employed Trump campaign chairman Paul Manafort as an investment consultant for years. At the time Manafort joined the Trump campaign in March 2016, Manafort owed Deripaska money and, through an aide, offered to give Deripaska "private briefings" about the campaign. Manafort and Deripaska have said the briefings never happened.

Kirill Dmitriev: The chief executive of the Russian sovereign wealth fund, the Russian Direct Investment Fund, Kirill Dmitriev met in the Seychelles in January 2017 with Erik Prince, a businessman and ally of Donald Trump's.

Sergey Gorkov: The chairman of the Russian state-owned Vnesh–econombank, better known as VEB, Sergey Gorkov met during the presidential transition with Jared Kushner, Donald Trump's son-in-law. The White House and the bank offered conflicting descriptions of the meeting, with the bank saying it was to discuss business strategy and the White House insisting it was unrelated to business, but instead was one of many diplomatic encounters Kushner had before Trump was sworn in as president.

Konstantin Kilimnik: A Russian army veteran who was hired by Paul Manafort to serve as his translator and manager of his political consulting business in Kiev. Konstantin Kilimnik served as Manafort's liaison to top Ukrainian and Russian politicians and businessmen, including Oleg Deripaska, according to people familiar with the business arrangement. A Deripaska spokesman has denied he ever interacted with Kilimnik. The FBI has assessed that Kilimnik had ties to Russian intelligence, and he was charged in 2018 with obstruction of justice. He was in contact with Manafort during his time with the Trump campaign, and Manafort was accused of passing Trump polling data to him. Kilimnik has denied having ties to Russian intelligence. As of April 2019, he was in Russia and had not addressed the obstruction charge, though court documents show that Manafort told prosecutors that Kilimnik didn't think he had suborned perjury and thought it was "crazy" that he was indicted.

Sergey Kislyak: The Russian ambassador to the United States from 2008 to 2017, Sergey Kislyak sat in the front row during a Donald Trump foreign policy speech in April 2016 and then interacted with several members of Trump's campaign, including Senator Jeff Sessions, in the months before the election. In December 2016, as Trump prepared to take office, Trump's incoming national security adviser, Michael T. Flynn, called Kislyak and asked that the Russians not respond to new sanctions imposed by President Barack Obama as a response to Russian election interference.

Viktor Netyksho: Viktor Netyksho is the Russian military intelligence officer US officials alleged in court documents was in command of Unit 26165, which is accused of hacking the Democratic National Committee, the Democratic Congressional Campaign Committee, and members of Hillary Clinton's campaign. The special counsel's office charged Netyksho, along with eleven other Russian nationals, in July 2018 with executing a hacking conspiracy to influence the 2016 election. Netyksho, who, as of April 2019, was in Russia and not expected to face the charges in a US courtroom, has not responded to the indictment.

Dmitry Peskov: Press secretary to Russian president Vladimir Putin, Dmitry Peskov is considered one of Putin's closest advisers. In January 2016, Trump lawyer Michael Cohen emailed Peskov to ask for his help advancing plans to build a Trump Tower in Moscow. Cohen later lied to Congress and said he received no response. In fact, a Peskov assistant responded and the two spoke by phone about the proposed project, according to Cohen's plea agreement.

Yevgeniy Prigozhin: A Russian businessman known as "Putin's chef" because he owned a catering business favored by the Russian president, Yevgeniy Prigozhin was accused by the special counsel's office of funding the St. Petersburg troll farm called the Internet Research Agency and its elaborate social media campaign to influence Americans prior to the 2016 election. He was charged in February 2018 along with twelve other Russian nationals with conspiring to defraud the United States for the social media plot. After his indictment, Prigozhin told a Russian state news agency that he was not upset to be charged. "Americans see what they want to see," he said.

Vladimir Putin: The president of Russia, a position he has held since 2012 and previously from 2000 to 2008. The US intelligence agencies announced in January 2017 that they had assessed that Vladimir Putin had personally ordered a multipronged operation during the 2016 presidential campaign intended to divide Americans, hurt the electoral prospects of Democrat Hillary Clinton, and elect Donald Trump.

Ivan Timofeev: Director of programs at the Moscow-based think tank the Russian International Affairs Council, Ivan Timofeev communicated with Trump campaign adviser George Papadopoulos in the spring of 2016 about arranging a meeting between Donald Trump and Vladimir Putin. Timofeev was referred to in Papadopoulos's plea deal as a "Russian national connected to the Russian Ministry of Foreign Affairs." Timofeev has not addressed that description but has said his think tank's interactions with Papadopoulos were routine academic outreach.

Alexander Torshin: A former Russian senator and deputy governor of the Russian central bank, Alexander Torshin is a lifetime member of the National Rifle Association and interacted with American conservatives, as did his assistant Maria Butina. In May 2016, a Republican operative asked Donald Trump's campaign to have the candidate meet with Torshin at an NRA meeting, referring to the banker as "Putin's emissary." The meeting did not take place, but Torshin has said he met Trump's son Donald Trump Jr.

Natalia Veselnitskaya: A Russian lawyer, Natalia Veselnitskaya has lobbied against the Magnitsky Act, a law passed in 2012 that imposed sanctions against top Russians for human rights abuses. The law has particularly vexed Vladimir Putin, and in retaliation for its passage Russia halted the adoption of Russian children by US families. Donald Trump Jr. agreed to meet with Veselnitskaya in June 2016 after being told she would provide damaging information about Hillary Clinton. Veselnitskaya was indicted in 2019 for obstruction of justice in connection with her work in an unrelated civil case. She denied the charges, telling Yahoo News that she would use "all methods" to defend herself from Russia but would not come to the United States to fight the charges in court.

OTHER RELEVANT INDIVIDUALS

Julian Assange: The founder of the antisecrecy organization known as WikiLeaks, which published hacked emails from the Democratic National Committee and Hillary Clinton's campaign, Julian Assange and his group were of great interest to special counsel investigators. Prosecutors mistakenly revealed in a court filing in late 2018 that Assange had been charged under seal, though it is unclear whether the charges relate to the special counsel investigation or the publication of other classified material. Assange was granted asylum by Ecuador and lived in the country's embassy in London for years. On April 11, 2019, Ecuador rescinded Assange's asylum and he was expelled from the embassy and arrested by British police on a US hacking charge. The legal battle over his extradition to the United States will likely take years.

John O. Brennan: The director of the CIA from March 2013 to January 2017, John Brennan's agency made critical assessments on the motive of the Russian election-influence operation, including that one of its goals was to help Donald Trump get elected president. Brennan was among the intelligence-community leaders to brief Trump on the Russian plot in January 2017. Since leaving government, Brennan has become a television commentator and is frequently critical of Trump.

James Clapper: The director of national intelligence from August 2010 to January 2017, James Clapper led intelligence-community efforts to determine the extent of Russian intervention during the 2016 US presidential election campaign. He was among the officials who briefed Donald Trump in January 2017 on the intelligence-community assessment of Russia's actions. In a book published after he left office, Clapper wrote that he had "no doubt" that Russia swung the election to Trump.

Jerome Corsi: A conservative writer and conspiracy theorist who helped popularize the false accusation that President Barack Obama was not born in the United States, Jerome Corsi corresponded with Trump associate Roger Stone about WikiLeaks before the election. Corsi announced in November 2018 that he had rejected a plea deal proposed by the special counsel's office in which he would have agreed he lied to investigators about some of his Stone contacts. Stone was charged in January 2019 with lying to Congress and witness tampering related to his dealings with Corsi over WikiLeaks. He vowed to fight the charges.

Randy Credico: A New York comedian and radio host, Randy Credico befriended Trump associate Roger Stone before the 2016 election. Stone told Congress that when he announced before the election that he had a back channel to WikiLeaks' founder Julian Assange, he was referencing Credico, who had interviewed Assange on his radio show. Credico denied serving as a back channel for Stone to Assange. Stone was charged in January 2019 with lying to Congress and witness tampering related to his dealings with Credico over WikiLeaks. He vowed to fight the charges.

Rob Goldstone: A British music promoter, Rob Goldstone had met Donald Trump when his Russian pop star client Emin Agalarov had helped bring Trump's Miss Universe pageant to Moscow in 2013. At Agalarov's request, Goldstone emailed Trump's son Donald Trump Jr. and asked if he would meet with a Russian lawyer who, Goldstone said, had information to share about Democrat Hillary Clinton. Goldstone attended the June 2016 meeting, along with Russian lawyer Natalia Veselnitskaya.

Joseph Mifsud: A Maltese academic who worked at the London Centre of International Law Practice, where Trump adviser George Papadopoulos was also employed when he was named to the campaign. Prosecutors said that Joseph Mifsud befriended Papadopoulos after he joined the campaign, introducing him to a Russian woman who said she was a niece of the Russian president and a Russian think tank director with ties to the Kremlin. According to Papadopoulos's plea, a London-based professor—later reported to be Mifsud—told the Trump adviser in April 2016 that the Russians held dirt about Democrat Hillary Clinton in the form of thousands of emails, a revelation that would later help spark the investigation into the Trump campaign and Russia. Mifsud has told *The Washington Post* he had no ties to Russia outside of academia and no contact with the Russian government. After Papadopoulos's plea, Mifsud denied wrongdoing and said he had had no knowledge of Clinton emails held by Russia. "I have a clear conscience," he told the *Telegraph*.

George Nader: A Lebanese American businessman who has acted as an adviser to the United Arab Emirates, George Nader cooperated with the special counsel's investigation as investigators sought to determine the purpose of a secret meeting in the Seychelles between Erik Prince and Kirill Dmitriev, the head of a Russian government-controlled wealth fund. Investigators gathered evidence that the meeting, which was brokered by Nader, was part of an effort to establish a back channel of communication between the Trump administration and the Kremlin, which Prince has denied. Nader's lawyer has declined to address the matter publicly. Nader has a checkered past, having been convicted years ago of transporting child pornography.

W. Samuel Patten: A Republican political consultant who pleaded guilty in August 2018 to failing to register as a foreign lobbyist while working for a Ukrainian political party from 2014 to 2018. He also acknowledged in his plea that he worked with a foreigner, who *The Washington Post* has identified as Paul Manafort's longtime aide Konstantin Kilimnik, to route an illegal foreign donation from a Ukrainian politician to Donald Trump's inaugural committee.

Richard Pinedo: A California man who pleaded guilty in October 2018 to identity theft for a scheme in which he sold bank account numbers online. Prosecutors said Russian nationals used the numbers to open PayPal accounts and fund a social media campaign to influence the American electorate.

Erik Prince: The founder of the now disbanded private security company Blackwater, Erik Prince participated in a secret meeting in the Seychelles just before Trump's inauguration with a Russian official close to Russian president Vladimir Putin. Investigators have explored whether the gathering was part of an effort to establish a back channel between the Kremlin and the incoming administration, though Prince has said it was an unplanned encounter when he was at a luxury hotel in the Indian Ocean island nation with officials from the United Arab Emirates.

Felix Sater: A New York real estate developer who emigrated from Russia as a child, Felix Sater was a former business associate of Donald Trump's. Sater worked during the presidential campaign with Trump lawyer Michael Cohen to try to build a Trump Tower in Moscow. As an executive at the Bayrock Group, Sater had licensed Trump's name to build towers around the world. In emails, Sater told Cohen that the ultimately unsuccessful building project could boost Trump's electoral chances and improve his relationship with Russian president Vladimir Putin.

Christopher Steele: A former officer with the British intelligence service MI6, Christopher Steele was hired by the private US political-intelligence firm Fusion GPS to research Donald Trump's ties to Russia. From June to December 2016, he submitted a series of reports that came to be known collectively as the "Steele Dossier," which alleged the Russians held compromising information about Trump and that Trump's campaign was conspiring with a Russian government effort to win him the election. The research, which was rejected by Trump, was funded by the Democratic National Committee and Hillary Clinton's campaign.

Alex van der Zwaan: A Dutch lawyer based in London, Alex van der Zwaan pleaded guilty in February 2018 to lying to the FBI about his work for the law firm Skadden, Arps, Slate, Meagher & Flom, where he helped produce a report regarding the jailing of a Ukrainian politician. Van der Zwaan lied during interviews about his contacts with Trump campaign aides Paul Manafort and Rick Gates, who had also worked in Ukraine. He served thirty days in prison.

Viktor Yanukovych: The former president of Ukraine, he was Paul Manafort's main client while Manafort was a political consultant in Kiev prior to joining the Trump campaign. Manafort was credited with professionalizing Yanukovych's political operation and helping him win his country's presidency in 2010. Manafort continued to advise Yanukovych and his party after his victory, earning millions of dollars. In 2014, Yanukovych was ousted from office by public protests and fled to Russia.

Note to the Reader:

The *Report On The Investigation Into Russian Interference In The 2016 Presidential Election* also includes a somewhat different list of referenced persons and entities that appears as Appendix B on page 453 in this volume.

Timeline of the Special Counsel's Investigation

May 17, 2017: Deputy Attorney General Rod J. Rosenstein appointed Robert S. Mueller III to serve as special counsel investigating any coordination between Russia and individuals associated with the Trump campaign, as well as any matters that might arise from the investigation.

October 5, 2017: George Papadopoulos, a former adviser to the Trump campaign, pleaded guilty to lying to the FBI about his Russia contacts during the presidential campaign. His plea was unsealed and made public at the end of October; he was arrested over the summer in secret and had been negotiating with prosecutors.

October 30, 2017: Former Trump campaign chairman Paul Manafort and his deputy, Rick Gates, were charged in Washington, DC, with conspiracy to defraud the United States and other crimes related to their work as political consultants in Ukraine prior to joining the Trump campaign.

December 1, 2017: Former national security adviser Michael T. Flynn pleaded guilty in federal court in Washington, DC, to lying to the FBI about his interactions during the presidential transition with Russian ambassador Sergey Kislyak.

February 16, 2018: Thirteen Russian nationals and three Russian companies were charged with conducting an elaborate two-year scheme to influence the US election by disseminating fake news and divisive advertising online and posing as Americans to inject toxic messages into online debate.

February 22, 2018: Manafort and Gates were charged again, this time in Alexandria, Virginia, with thirty-two counts related to tax and bank fraud.

February 23, 2018: Gates pleaded guilty to conspiracy to defraud the United States and lying to federal investigators and agreed to cooperate with Mueller.

June 8, 2018: Manafort was charged, along with Konstantin Kilimnik, a Russian with alleged ties to Russian intelligence who worked with Manafort in Ukraine, in a plot to obstruct justice by contacting potential witnesses against Manafort and suborning perjury. Kilimnik has denied having ties to Russian intelligence, but has not publicly addressed the obstruction charge.

July 13, 2018: Twelve Russian military intelligence officers were charged with participating in a scheme to hack email accounts of Democrats and publish correspondence stolen from the Democratic National Committee and Hillary Clinton's campaign chairman, John Podesta, via WikiLeaks.

July 16, 2018: Manafort's bail was revoked in the wake of witness-tampering accusations; the former Trump campaign chairman was jailed.

August 21, 2018: After a three-week trial, Manafort was convicted of eight counts of tax and bank fraud by a jury in Alexandria, Virginia. The star witness against Manafort was his former deputy Gates.

August 31, 2018: W. Samuel Patten, a political consultant, pleaded guilty to failing to register as a foreign lobbyist and admitted in an agreement with prosecutors that he steered $50,000 from a Ukrainian politician to Donald Trump's inaugural committee. Patten's case was technically handled by the US Attorney's Office in Washington, not Mueller's team, though it started with a referral from Mueller.

September 7, 2018: Papadopoulos was sentenced to serve fourteen days in prison for lying to investigators, becoming the first Trump adviser to be incarcerated as a result of the Mueller probe.

September 14, 2018: Avoiding a second trial in Washington, Manafort pleaded guilty to conspiracy against the United States and other crimes, admitting he committed bank and tax fraud, failed to properly register as a foreign agent while working as a political consultant in Ukraine, and attempted to tamper with witness testimony. He agreed to cooperate with Mueller.

November 7, 2018: After months of badgering Attorney General Jeff Sessions over his decision to recuse himself from the Russia investigation, President Trump requested Sessions's resignation. He was replaced by Acting Attorney General Matthew Whitaker, who assumed supervisory control of the Mueller investigation, and later rejected the advice of career ethics officials who thought he should recuse himself.

November 20, 2018: After months of negotiations over whether Trump would sit for an interview, lawyers for the president submitted answers in writing to questions about the campaign from prosecutors. The president's lawyers refused to answer questions about Trump's decisions after taking office.

November 26, 2018: Mueller's prosecutors informed a judge that Manafort had breached his plea agreement by lying to investigators during twelve interviews and two sessions in front of Mueller's grand jury.

November 29, 2018: Michael Cohen, a former personal attorney to Trump, pleaded guilty to lying to Congress about the extent of efforts to build a Trump Tower in Moscow during the campaign, including his contacts with the Kremlin about the project. He agreed to cooperate with Mueller. He had previously pleaded guilty in a separate investigation to campaign finance violations he said were directed by Trump.

December 7, 2018: President Trump confirmed he would nominate William P. Barr as the attorney general of the United States to take the spot vacated by Jeff Sessions. Barr, who had served as attorney general in the George H. W. Bush administration, won Senate confirmation on February 14, 2019, by a 54-45 vote and took over supervision of the special counsel investigation as it approached its conclusion.

December 12, 2018: Cohen was sentenced to three years in prison and said at an emotional hearing that he had "been living in a personal and mental incarceration" since going to work for Trump.

December 18, 2018: Flynn asked the court to hold off sentencing him for lying to the FBI after Judge Emmet G. Sullivan told the retired lieutenant general that he had sold out his country and suggested he was likely to sentence the former national security adviser to prison time, over a recommendation from Mueller's team.

January 24, 2019: Roger Stone, longtime Republican campaign operative and friend of Trump who briefly worked for the Trump campaign, was charged with trying to obstruct a congressional inquiry into the hacking of emails from the Democratic National Committee and John Podesta, Hillary Clinton's campaign chairman. Stone, who vowed to fight the charges, was accused of lying to Congress about his efforts to obtain information about WikiLeaks' releases of the material.

March 22, 2019: Attorney General William P. Barr informed Congress that Mueller had completed his investigation and submitted a final confidential report. A Justice Department official said there would be no more indictments as a result of the investigation.

March 24, 2019: Barr submitted to Congress a four-page summary of Mueller's principal conclusions. Barr indicated that Mueller found that the evidence did not establish that Trump or anyone associated with his campaign conspired with Russia to interfere in the election. Barr said that Mueller conducted a thorough finding of facts related to the issue of whether Trump had committed obstruction of justice but ultimately did not make a traditional recommendation as to whether to prosecute the president. In his report, Barr indicated that Mueller wrote, "while this report does not conclude that the President committed a crime, it also does not exonerate him." Barr told Congress that he and Rosenstein did not believe there was sufficient evidence to accuse Trump of obstruction.

March 27, 2019: Mueller submitted a letter to Barr, complaining that Barr's letter three days earlier had failed to "fully capture the context, nature, and substance" of Mueller's work. Mueller requested that Barr immediately release executive summaries of the report that had been written by his team. When the letter became public, several weeks later, Barr said he had declined, preferring to prepare the full report for release all at once.

April 18, 2019: Barr gave a press conference, again offering his summary of Mueller's conclusions, as well as his assessment that the president had not committed obstruction of justice. He then released publicly a 448-page redacted version of Mueller's final report.

May 1, 2019: Barr testified to the Senate Judiciary Committee about the report. Afterward, Senate Republicans declared they were done exploring Mueller's work, while Democrats in the House vowed to press forward with more investigations.

Report On The Investigation Into Russian Interference In The 2016 Presidential Election

Volume I of II

Special Counsel Robert S. Mueller, III

Submitted Pursuant to 28 C.F.R. § 600.8(c)

Washington, D.C.

March 2019

TABLE OF CONTENTS – VOLUME I

U.S. Department of Justice

~~Attorney Work Product // May Contain Material Protected Under Fed. R. Crim. P. 6(e)~~

ii

56

iii

U.S. Department of Justice

Attorney Work Product // May Contain Material Protected Under Fed. R. Crim. P. 6(e)

iv

U.S. Department of Justice

Attorney Work Product // May Contain Material Protected Under Fed. R. Crim. P. 6(e)

v

U.S. Department of Justice

~~Attorney Work Product // May Contain Material Protected Under Fed. R. Crim. P. 6(e)~~

INTRODUCTION TO VOLUME I

This report is submitted to the Attorney General pursuant to 28 C.F.R. § 600.8(c), which states that, "[a]t the conclusion of the Special Counsel's work, he . . . shall provide the Attorney General a confidential report explaining the prosecution or declination decisions [the Special Counsel] reached."

The Russian government interfered in the 2016 presidential election in sweeping and systematic fashion. Evidence of Russian government operations began to surface in mid-2016. In June, the Democratic National Committee and its cyber response team publicly announced that Russian hackers had compromised its computer network. Releases of hacked materials—hacks that public reporting soon attributed to the Russian government—began that same month. Additional releases followed in July through the organization WikiLeaks, with further releases in October and November.

In late July 2016, soon after WikiLeaks's first release of stolen documents, a foreign government contacted the FBI about a May 2016 encounter with Trump Campaign foreign policy advisor George Papadopoulos. Papadopoulos had suggested to a representative of that foreign government that the Trump Campaign had received indications from the Russian government that it could assist the Campaign through the anonymous release of information damaging to Democratic presidential candidate Hillary Clinton. That information prompted the FBI on July 31, 2016, to open an investigation into whether individuals associated with the Trump Campaign were coordinating with the Russian government in its interference activities.

That fall, two federal agencies jointly announced that the Russian government "directed recent compromises of e-mails from US persons and institutions, including US political organizations," and, "[t]hese thefts and disclosures are intended to interfere with the US election process." After the election, in late December 2016, the United States imposed sanctions on Russia for having interfered in the election. By early 2017, several congressional committees were examining Russia's interference in the election.

Within the Executive Branch, these investigatory efforts ultimately led to the May 2017 appointment of Special Counsel Robert S. Mueller, III. The order appointing the Special Counsel authorized him to investigate "the Russian government's efforts to interfere in the 2016 presidential election," including any links or coordination between the Russian government and individuals associated with the Trump Campaign.

As set forth in detail in this report, the Special Counsel's investigation established that Russia interfered in the 2016 presidential election principally through two operations. First, a Russian entity carried out a social media campaign that favored presidential candidate Donald J. Trump and disparaged presidential candidate Hillary Clinton. Second, a Russian intelligence service conducted computer-intrusion operations against entities, employees, and volunteers working on the Clinton Campaign and then released stolen documents. The investigation also identified numerous links between the Russian government and the Trump Campaign. Although the investigation established that the Russian government perceived it would benefit from a Trump presidency and worked to secure that outcome, and that the Campaign expected it would benefit

1

U.S. Department of Justice

~~Attorney-Work-Product~~ // ~~May-Contain-Material-Protected-Under-Fed. R. Crim. P. 6(e)~~

electorally from information stolen and released through Russian efforts, the investigation did not establish that members of the Trump Campaign conspired or coordinated with the Russian government in its election interference activities.

* * *

Below we describe the evidentiary considerations underpinning statements about the results of our investigation and the Special Counsel's charging decisions, and we then provide an overview of the two volumes of our report.

The report describes actions and events that the Special Counsel's Office found to be supported by the evidence collected in our investigation. In some instances, the report points out the absence of evidence or conflicts in the evidence about a particular fact or event. In other instances, when substantial, credible evidence enabled the Office to reach a conclusion with confidence, the report states that the investigation established that certain actions or events occurred. A statement that the investigation did not establish particular facts does not mean there was no evidence of those facts.

In evaluating whether evidence about collective action of multiple individuals constituted a crime, we applied the framework of conspiracy law, not the concept of "collusion." In so doing, the Office recognized that the word "collud[e]" was used in communications with the Acting Attorney General confirming certain aspects of the investigation's scope and that the term has frequently been invoked in public reporting about the investigation. But collusion is not a specific offense or theory of liability found in the United States Code, nor is it a term of art in federal criminal law. For those reasons, the Office's focus in analyzing questions of joint criminal liability was on conspiracy as defined in federal law. In connection with that analysis, we addressed the factual question whether members of the Trump Campaign "coordinat[ed]"—a term that appears in the appointment order—with Russian election interference activities. Like collusion, "coordination" does not have a settled definition in federal criminal law. We understood coordination to require an agreement—tacit or express—between the Trump Campaign and the Russian government on election interference. That requires more than the two parties taking actions that were informed by or responsive to the other's actions or interests. We applied the term coordination in that sense when stating in the report that the investigation did not establish that the Trump Campaign coordinated with the Russian government in its election interference activities.

* * *

The report on our investigation consists of two volumes:

Volume I describes the factual results of the Special Counsel's investigation of Russia's interference in the 2016 presidential election and its interactions with the Trump Campaign. Section I describes the scope of the investigation. Sections II and III describe the principal ways Russia interfered in the 2016 presidential election. Section IV describes links between the Russian

2

government and individuals associated with the Trump Campaign. Section V sets forth the Special Counsel's charging decisions.

Volume II addresses the President's actions towards the FBI's investigation into Russia's interference in the 2016 presidential election and related matters, and his actions towards the Special Counsel's investigation. Volume II separately states its framework and the considerations that guided that investigation.

3

EXECUTIVE SUMMARY TO VOLUME I

RUSSIAN SOCIAL MEDIA CAMPAIGN

The Internet Research Agency (IRA) carried out the earliest Russian interference operations identified by the investigation—a social media campaign designed to provoke and amplify political and social discord in the United States. The IRA was based in St. Petersburg, Russia, and received funding from Russian oligarch Yevgeniy Prigozhin and companies he controlled. Prigozhin is widely reported to have ties to Russian President Vladimir Putin, Harm to Ongoing Matter

In mid-2014, the IRA sent employees to the United States on an intelligence-gathering mission with instructions Harm to Ongoing Matter

The IRA later used social media accounts and interest groups to sow discord in the U.S. political system through what it termed "information warfare." The campaign evolved from a generalized program designed in 2014 and 2015 to undermine the U.S. electoral system, to a targeted operation that by early 2016 favored candidate Trump and disparaged candidate Clinton. The IRA's operation also included the purchase of political advertisements on social media in the names of U.S. persons and entities, as well as the staging of political rallies inside the United States. To organize those rallies, IRA employees posed as U.S. grassroots entities and persons and made contact with Trump supporters and Trump Campaign officials in the United States. The investigation did not identify evidence that any U.S. persons conspired or coordinated with the IRA. Section II of this report details the Office's investigation of the Russian social media campaign.

RUSSIAN HACKING OPERATIONS

At the same time that the IRA operation began to focus on supporting candidate Trump in early 2016, the Russian government employed a second form of interference: cyber intrusions (hacking) and releases of hacked materials damaging to the Clinton Campaign. The Russian intelligence service known as the Main Intelligence Directorate of the General Staff of the Russian Army (GRU) carried out these operations.

In March 2016, the GRU began hacking the email accounts of Clinton Campaign volunteers and employees, including campaign chairman John Podesta. In April 2016, the GRU hacked into the computer networks of the Democratic Congressional Campaign Committee (DCCC) and the Democratic National Committee (DNC). The GRU stole hundreds of thousands of documents from the compromised email accounts and networks. Around the time that the DNC announced in mid-June 2016 the Russian government's role in hacking its network, the GRU began disseminating stolen materials through the fictitious online personas "DCLeaks" and "Guccifer 2.0." The GRU later released additional materials through the organization WikiLeaks.

4

The presidential campaign of Donald J. Trump ("Trump Campaign" or "Campaign") showed interest in WikiLeaks's releases of documents and welcomed their potential to damage candidate Clinton. Beginning in June 2016, Harm to Ongoing Matter forecast to senior Campaign officials that WikiLeaks would release information damaging to candidate Clinton. WikiLeaks's first release came in July 2016. Around the same time, candidate Trump announced that he hoped Russia would recover emails described as missing from a private server used by Clinton when she was Secretary of State (he later said that he was speaking sarcastically). Harm to Ongoing Matter

WikiLeaks began releasing Podesta's stolen emails on October 7, 2016, less than one hour after a U.S. media outlet released video considered damaging to candidate Trump. Section III of this Report details the Office's investigation into the Russian hacking operations, as well as other efforts by Trump Campaign supporters to obtain Clinton-related emails.

RUSSIAN CONTACTS WITH THE CAMPAIGN

The social media campaign and the GRU hacking operations coincided with a series of contacts between Trump Campaign officials and individuals with ties to the Russian government. The Office investigated whether those contacts reflected or resulted in the Campaign conspiring or coordinating with Russia in its election-interference activities. Although the investigation established that the Russian government perceived it would benefit from a Trump presidency and worked to secure that outcome, and that the Campaign expected it would benefit electorally from information stolen and released through Russian efforts, the investigation did not establish that members of the Trump Campaign conspired or coordinated with the Russian government in its election interference activities.

The Russian contacts consisted of business connections, offers of assistance to the Campaign, invitations for candidate Trump and Putin to meet in person, invitations for Campaign officials and representatives of the Russian government to meet, and policy positions seeking improved U.S.-Russian relations. Section IV of this Report details the contacts between Russia and the Trump Campaign during the campaign and transition periods, the most salient of which are summarized below in chronological order.

2015. Some of the earliest contacts were made in connection with a Trump Organization real-estate project in Russia known as Trump Tower Moscow. Candidate Trump signed a Letter of Intent for Trump Tower Moscow by November 2015, and in January 2016 Trump Organization executive Michael Cohen emailed and spoke about the project with the office of Russian government press secretary Dmitry Peskov. The Trump Organization pursued the project through at least June 2016, including by considering travel to Russia by Cohen and candidate Trump.

Spring 2016. Campaign foreign policy advisor George Papadopoulos made early contact with Joseph Mifsud, a London-based professor who had connections to Russia and traveled to Moscow in April 2016. Immediately upon his return to London from that trip, Mifsud told Papadopoulos that the Russian government had "dirt" on Hillary Clinton in the form of thousands

5

of emails. One week later, in the first week of May 2016, Papadopoulos suggested to a representative of a foreign government that the Trump Campaign had received indications from the Russian government that it could assist the Campaign through the anonymous release of information damaging to candidate Clinton. Throughout that period of time and for several months thereafter, Papadopoulos worked with Mifsud and two Russian nationals to arrange a meeting between the Campaign and the Russian government. No meeting took place.

Summer 2016. Russian outreach to the Trump Campaign continued into the summer of 2016, as candidate Trump was becoming the presumptive Republican nominee for President. On June 9, 2016, for example, a Russian lawyer met with senior Trump Campaign officials Donald Trump Jr., Jared Kushner, and campaign chairman Paul Manafort to deliver what the email proposing the meeting had described as "official documents and information that would incriminate Hillary." The materials were offered to Trump Jr. as "part of Russia and its government's support for Mr. Trump." The written communications setting up the meeting showed that the Campaign anticipated receiving information from Russia that could assist candidate Trump's electoral prospects, but the Russian lawyer's presentation did not provide such information.

Days after the June 9 meeting, on June 14, 2016, a cybersecurity firm and the DNC announced that Russian government hackers had infiltrated the DNC and obtained access to opposition research on candidate Trump, among other documents.

In July 2016, Campaign foreign policy advisor Carter Page traveled in his personal capacity to Moscow and gave the keynote address at the New Economic School. Page had lived and worked in Russia between 2003 and 2007. After returning to the United States, Page became acquainted with at least two Russian intelligence officers, one of whom was later charged in 2015 with conspiracy to act as an unregistered agent of Russia. Page's July 2016 trip to Moscow and his advocacy for pro-Russian foreign policy drew media attention. The Campaign then distanced itself from Page and, by late September 2016, removed him from the Campaign.

July 2016 was also the month WikiLeaks first released emails stolen by the GRU from the DNC. On July 22, 2016, WikiLeaks posted thousands of internal DNC documents revealing information about the Clinton Campaign. Within days, there was public reporting that U.S. intelligence agencies had "high confidence" that the Russian government was behind the theft of emails and documents from the DNC. And within a week of the release, a foreign government informed the FBI about its May 2016 interaction with Papadopoulos and his statement that the Russian government could assist the Trump Campaign. On July 31, 2016, based on the foreign government reporting, the FBI opened an investigation into potential coordination between the Russian government and individuals associated with the Trump Campaign.

Separately, on August 2, 2016, Trump campaign chairman Paul Manafort met in New York City with his long-time business associate Konstantin Kilimnik, who the FBI assesses to have ties to Russian intelligence. Kilimnik requested the meeting to deliver in person a peace plan for Ukraine that Manafort acknowledged to the Special Counsel's Office was a "backdoor" way for Russia to control part of eastern Ukraine; both men believed the plan would require candidate Trump's assent to succeed (were he to be elected President). They also discussed the status of the

6

Trump Campaign and Manafort's strategy for winning Democratic votes in Midwestern states. Months before that meeting, Manafort had caused internal polling data to be shared with Kilimnik, and the sharing continued for some period of time after their August meeting.

Fall 2016. On October 7, 2016, the media released video of candidate Trump speaking in graphic terms about women years earlier, which was considered damaging to his candidacy. Less than an hour later, WikiLeaks made its second release: thousands of John Podesta's emails that had been stolen by the GRU in late March 2016. The FBI and other U.S. government institutions were at the time continuing their investigation of suspected Russian government efforts to interfere in the presidential election. That same day, October 7, the Department of Homeland Security and the Office of the Director of National Intelligence issued a joint public statement "that the Russian Government directed the recent compromises of e-mails from US persons and institutions, including from US political organizations." Those "thefts" and the "disclosures" of the hacked materials through online platforms such as WikiLeaks, the statement continued, "are intended to interfere with the US election process."

Post-2016 Election. Immediately after the November 8 election, Russian government officials and prominent Russian businessmen began trying to make inroads into the new administration. The most senior levels of the Russian government encouraged these efforts. The Russian Embassy made contact hours after the election to congratulate the President-Elect and to arrange a call with President Putin. Several Russian businessmen picked up the effort from there.

Kirill Dmitriev, the chief executive officer of Russia's sovereign wealth fund, was among the Russians who tried to make contact with the incoming administration. In early December, a business associate steered Dmitriev to Erik Prince, a supporter of the Trump Campaign and an associate of senior Trump advisor Steve Bannon. Dmitriev and Prince later met face-to-face in January 2017 in the Seychelles and discussed U.S.-Russia relations. During the same period, another business associate introduced Dmitriev to a friend of Jared Kushner who had not served on the Campaign or the Transition Team. Dmitriev and Kushner's friend collaborated on a short written reconciliation plan for the United States and Russia, which Dmitriev implied had been cleared through Putin. The friend gave that proposal to Kushner before the inauguration, and Kushner later gave copies to Bannon and incoming Secretary of State Rex Tillerson.

On December 29, 2016, then-President Obama imposed sanctions on Russia for having interfered in the election. Incoming National Security Advisor Michael Flynn called Russian Ambassador Sergey Kislyak and asked Russia not to escalate the situation in response to the sanctions. The following day, Putin announced that Russia would not take retaliatory measures in response to the sanctions at that time. Hours later, President-Elect Trump tweeted, "Great move on delay (by V. Putin)." The next day, on December 31, 2016, Kislyak called Flynn and told him the request had been received at the highest levels and Russia had chosen not to retaliate as a result of Flynn's request.

* * *

On January 6, 2017, members of the intelligence community briefed President-Elect Trump on a joint assessment—drafted and coordinated among the Central Intelligence Agency, FBI, and

7

National Security Agency—that concluded with high confidence that Russia had intervened in the election through a variety of means to assist Trump's candidacy and harm Clinton's. A declassified version of the assessment was publicly released that same day.

Between mid-January 2017 and early February 2017, three congressional committees—the House Permanent Select Committee on Intelligence (HPSCI), the Senate Select Committee on Intelligence (SSCI), and the Senate Judiciary Committee (SJC)—announced that they would conduct inquiries, or had already been conducting inquiries, into Russian interference in the election. Then-FBI Director James Comey later confirmed to Congress the existence of the FBI's investigation into Russian interference that had begun before the election. On March 20, 2017, in open-session testimony before HPSCI, Comey stated:

> I have been authorized by the Department of Justice to confirm that the FBI, as part of our counterintelligence mission, is investigating the Russian government's efforts to interfere in the 2016 presidential election, and that includes investigating the nature of any links between individuals associated with the Trump campaign and the Russian government and whether there was any coordination between the campaign and Russia's efforts. . . . As with any counterintelligence investigation, this will also include an assessment of whether any crimes were committed.

The investigation continued under then-Director Comey for the next seven weeks until May 9, 2017, when President Trump fired Comey as FBI Director—an action which is analyzed in Volume II of the report.

On May 17, 2017, Acting Attorney General Rod Rosenstein appointed the Special Counsel and authorized him to conduct the investigation that Comey had confirmed in his congressional testimony, as well as matters arising directly from the investigation, and any other matters within the scope of 28 C.F.R. § 600.4(a), which generally covers efforts to interfere with or obstruct the investigation.

President Trump reacted negatively to the Special Counsel's appointment. He told advisors that it was the end of his presidency, sought to have Attorney General Jefferson (Jeff) Sessions unrecuse from the Russia investigation and to have the Special Counsel removed, and engaged in efforts to curtail the Special Counsel's investigation and prevent the disclosure of evidence to it, including through public and private contacts with potential witnesses. Those and related actions are described and analyzed in Volume II of the report.

* * *

THE SPECIAL COUNSEL'S CHARGING DECISIONS

In reaching the charging decisions described in Volume I of the report, the Office determined whether the conduct it found amounted to a violation of federal criminal law chargeable under the Principles of Federal Prosecution. *See* Justice Manual § 9-27.000 *et seq.* (2018). The standard set forth in the Justice Manual is whether the conduct constitutes a crime; if so, whether admissible evidence would probably be sufficient to obtain and sustain a conviction;

8

and whether prosecution would serve a substantial federal interest that could not be adequately served by prosecution elsewhere or through non-criminal alternatives. *See* Justice Manual § 9-27.220.

Section V of the report provides detailed explanations of the Office's charging decisions, which contain three main components.

First, the Office determined that Russia's two principal interference operations in the 2016 U.S. presidential election—the social media campaign and the hacking-and-dumping operations—violated U.S. criminal law. Many of the individuals and entities involved in the social media campaign have been charged with participating in a conspiracy to defraud the United States by undermining through deceptive acts the work of federal agencies charged with regulating foreign influence in U.S. elections, as well as related counts of identity theft. *See United States v. Internet Research Agency, et al.*, No. 18-cr-32 (D.D.C.). Separately, Russian intelligence officers who carried out the hacking into Democratic Party computers and the personal email accounts of individuals affiliated with the Clinton Campaign conspired to violate, among other federal laws, the federal computer-intrusion statute, and they have been so charged. *See United States v. Netyksho, et al.*, No. 18-cr-215 (D.D.C.). Harm to Ongoing Matter

Personal Privacy

Second, while the investigation identified numerous links between individuals with ties to the Russian government and individuals associated with the Trump Campaign, the evidence was not sufficient to support criminal charges. Among other things, the evidence was not sufficient to charge any Campaign official as an unregistered agent of the Russian government or other Russian principal. And our evidence about the June 9, 2016 meeting and WikiLeaks's releases of hacked materials was not sufficient to charge a criminal campaign-finance violation. Further, the evidence was not sufficient to charge that any member of the Trump Campaign conspired with representatives of the Russian government to interfere in the 2016 election.

Third, the investigation established that several individuals affiliated with the Trump Campaign lied to the Office, and to Congress, about their interactions with Russian-affiliated individuals and related matters. Those lies materially impaired the investigation of Russian election interference. The Office charged some of those lies as violations of the federal false-statements statute. Former National Security Advisor Michael Flynn pleaded guilty to lying about his interactions with Russian Ambassador Kislyak during the transition period. George Papadopoulos, a foreign policy advisor during the campaign period, pleaded guilty to lying to investigators about, *inter alia*, the nature and timing of his interactions with Joseph Mifsud, the professor who told Papadopoulos that the Russians had dirt on candidate Clinton in the form of thousands of emails. Former Trump Organization attorney Michael Cohen pleaded guilty to making false statements to Congress about the Trump Moscow project. Harm to Ongoing Matter

And in February 2019, the U.S. District Court for the District of Columbia found that

9

Manafort lied to the Office and the grand jury concerning his interactions and communications with Konstantin Kilimnik about Trump Campaign polling data and a peace plan for Ukraine.

* * *

The Office investigated several other events that have been publicly reported to involve potential Russia-related contacts. For example, the investigation established that interactions between Russian Ambassador Kislyak and Trump Campaign officials both at the candidate's April 2016 foreign policy speech in Washington, D.C., and during the week of the Republican National Convention were brief, public, and non-substantive. And the investigation did not establish that one Campaign official's efforts to dilute a portion of the Republican Party platform on providing assistance to Ukraine were undertaken at the behest of candidate Trump or Russia. The investigation also did not establish that a meeting between Kislyak and Sessions in September 2016 at Sessions's Senate office included any more than a passing mention of the presidential campaign.

The investigation did not always yield admissible information or testimony, or a complete picture of the activities undertaken by subjects of the investigation. Some individuals invoked their Fifth Amendment right against compelled self-incrimination and were not, in the Office's judgment, appropriate candidates for grants of immunity. The Office limited its pursuit of other witnesses and information—such as information known to attorneys or individuals claiming to be members of the media—in light of internal Department of Justice policies. *See, e.g.,* Justice Manual §§ 9-13.400, 13.410. Some of the information obtained via court process, moreover, was presumptively covered by legal privilege and was screened from investigators by a filter (or "taint") team. Even when individuals testified or agreed to be interviewed, they sometimes provided information that was false or incomplete, leading to some of the false-statements charges described above. And the Office faced practical limits on its ability to access relevant evidence as well—numerous witnesses and subjects lived abroad, and documents were held outside the United States.

Further, the Office learned that some of the individuals we interviewed or whose conduct we investigated—including some associated with the Trump Campaign—deleted relevant communications or communicated during the relevant period using applications that feature encryption or that do not provide for long-term retention of data or communications records. In such cases, the Office was not able to corroborate witness statements through comparison to contemporaneous communications or fully question witnesses about statements that appeared inconsistent with other known facts.

Accordingly, while this report embodies factual and legal determinations that the Office believes to be accurate and complete to the greatest extent possible, given these identified gaps, the Office cannot rule out the possibility that the unavailable information would shed additional light on (or cast in a new light) the events described in the report.

10

I. THE SPECIAL COUNSEL'S INVESTIGATION

On May 17, 2017, Deputy Attorney General Rod J. Rosenstein—then serving as Acting Attorney General for the Russia investigation following the recusal of former Attorney General Jeff Sessions on March 2, 2016—appointed the Special Counsel "to investigate Russian interference with the 2016 presidential election and related matters." Office of the Deputy Att'y Gen., Order No. 3915-2017, *Appointment of Special Counsel to Investigate Russian Interference with the 2016 Presidential Election and Related Matters*, May 17, 2017) ("Appointment Order"). Relying on "the authority vested" in the Acting Attorney General, "including 28 U.S.C. §§ 509, 510, and 515," the Acting Attorney General ordered the appointment of a Special Counsel "in order to discharge [the Acting Attorney General's] responsibility to provide supervision and management of the Department of Justice, and to ensure a full and thorough investigation of the Russian government's efforts to interfere in the 2016 presidential election." Appointment Order (introduction). "The Special Counsel," the Order stated, "is authorized to conduct the investigation confirmed by then-FBI Director James B. Comey in testimony before the House Permanent Select Committee on Intelligence on March 20, 2017," including:

> (i) any links and/or coordination between the Russian government and individuals associated with the campaign of President Donald Trump; and
>
> (ii) any matters that arose or may arise directly from the investigation; and
>
> (iii) any other matters within the scope of 28 C.F.R. § 600.4(a).

Appointment Order ¶ (b). Section 600.4 affords the Special Counsel "the authority to investigate and prosecute federal crimes committed in the course of, and with intent to interfere with, the Special Counsel's investigation, such as perjury, obstruction of justice, destruction of evidence, and intimidation of witnesses." 28 C.F.R. § 600.4(a). The authority to investigate "any matters that arose . . . directly from the investigation," Appointment Order ¶ (b)(ii), covers similar crimes that may have occurred during the course of the FBI's confirmed investigation before the Special Counsel's appointment. "If the Special Counsel believes it is necessary and appropriate," the Order further provided, "the Special Counsel is authorized to prosecute federal crimes arising from the investigation of these matters." *Id.* ¶ (c). Finally, the Acting Attorney General made applicable "Sections 600.4 through 600.10 of Title 28 of the Code of Federal Regulations." *Id.* ¶ (d).

The Acting Attorney General further clarified the scope of the Special Counsel's investigatory authority in two subsequent memoranda. A memorandum dated August 2, 2017, explained that the Appointment Order had been "worded categorically in order to permit its public release without confirming specific investigations involving specific individuals." It then confirmed that the Special Counsel had been authorized since his appointment to investigate allegations that three Trump campaign officials—Carter Page, Paul Manafort, and George Papadopoulos—"committed a crime or crimes by colluding with Russian government officials with respect to the Russian government's efforts to interfere with the 2016 presidential election." The memorandum also confirmed the Special Counsel's authority to investigate certain other matters, including two additional sets of allegations involving Manafort (crimes arising from payments he received from the Ukrainian government and crimes arising from his receipt of loans

11

from a bank whose CEO was then seeking a position in the Trump Administration); allegations that Papadopoulos committed a crime or crimes by acting as an unregistered agent of the Israeli government; and four sets of allegations involving Michael Flynn, the former National Security Advisor to President Trump.

On October 20, 2017, the Acting Attorney General confirmed in a memorandum the Special Counsel's investigative authority as to several individuals and entities. First, "as part of a full and thorough investigation of the Russian government's efforts to interfere in the 2016 presidential election," the Special Counsel was authorized to investigate "the pertinent activities of Michael Cohen, Richard Gates, ▓Personal Privacy▓, Roger Stone, and ▓PP ▓." "Confirmation of the authorization to investigate such individuals," the memorandum stressed, "does not suggest that the Special Counsel has made a determination that any of them has committed a crime." Second, with respect to Michael Cohen, the memorandum recognized the Special Counsel's authority to investigate "leads relate[d] to Cohen's establishment and use of Essential Consultants LLC to, *inter alia*, receive funds from Russian-backed entities." Third, the memorandum memorialized the Special Counsel's authority to investigate individuals and entities who were possibly engaged in "jointly undertaken activity" with existing subjects of the investigation, including Paul Manafort. Finally, the memorandum described an FBI investigation opened before the Special Counsel's appointment into "allegations that [then-Attorney General Jeff Sessions] made false statements to the United States Senate[,]" and confirmed the Special Counsel's authority to investigate that matter.

The Special Counsel structured the investigation in view of his power and authority "to exercise all investigative and prosecutorial functions of any United States Attorney." 28 C.F.R. § 600.6. Like a U.S. Attorney's Office, the Special Counsel's Office considered a range of classified and unclassified information available to the FBI in the course of the Office's Russia investigation, and the Office structured that work around evidence for possible use in prosecutions of federal crimes (assuming that one or more crimes were identified that warranted prosecution). There was substantial evidence immediately available to the Special Counsel at the inception of the investigation in May 2017 because the FBI had, by that time, already investigated Russian election interference for nearly 10 months. The Special Counsel's Office exercised its judgment regarding what to investigate and did not, for instance, investigate every public report of a contact between the Trump Campaign and Russian-affiliated individuals and entities.

The Office has concluded its investigation into links and coordination between the Russian government and individuals associated with the Trump Campaign. Certain proceedings associated with the Office's work remain ongoing. After consultation with the Office of the Deputy Attorney General, the Office has transferred responsibility for those remaining issues to other components of the Department of Justice and FBI. Appendix D lists those transfers.

Two district courts confirmed the breadth of the Special Counsel's authority to investigate Russia election interference and links and/or coordination with the Trump Campaign. *See United States v. Manafort*, 312 F. Supp. 3d 60, 79-83 (D.D.C. 2018); *United States v. Manafort*, 321 F. Supp. 3d 640, 650-655 (E.D. Va. 2018). In the course of conducting that investigation, the Office periodically identified evidence of potential criminal activity that was outside the scope of the Special Counsel's authority established by the Acting Attorney General. After consultation with

12

the Office of the Deputy Attorney General, the Office referred that evidence to appropriate law enforcement authorities, principally other components of the Department of Justice and to the FBI. Appendix D summarizes those referrals.

* * *

To carry out the investigation and prosecution of the matters assigned to him, the Special Counsel assembled a team that at its high point included 19 attorneys—five of whom joined the Office from private practice and 14 on detail or assigned from other Department of Justice components. These attorneys were assisted by a filter team of Department lawyers and FBI personnel who screened materials obtained via court process for privileged information before turning those materials over to investigators; a support staff of three paralegals on detail from the Department's Antitrust Division; and an administrative staff of nine responsible for budget, finance, purchasing, human resources, records, facilities, security, information technology, and administrative support. The Special Counsel attorneys and support staff were co-located with and worked alongside approximately 40 FBI agents, intelligence analysts, forensic accountants, a paralegal, and professional staff assigned by the FBI to assist the Special Counsel's investigation. Those "assigned" FBI employees remained under FBI supervision at all times; the matters on which they assisted were supervised by the Special Counsel.[1]

During its investigation the Office issued more than 2,800 subpoenas under the auspices of a grand jury sitting in the District of Columbia; executed nearly 500 search-and-seizure warrants; obtained more than 230 orders for communications records under 18 U.S.C. § 2703(d); obtained almost 50 orders authorizing use of pen registers; made 13 requests to foreign governments pursuant to Mutual Legal Assistance Treaties; and interviewed approximately 500 witnesses, including almost 80 before a grand jury.

* * *

From its inception, the Office recognized that its investigation could identify foreign intelligence and counterintelligence information relevant to the FBI's broader national security mission. FBI personnel who assisted the Office established procedures to identify and convey such information to the FBI. The FBI's Counterintelligence Division met with the Office regularly for that purpose for most of the Office's tenure. For more than the past year, the FBI also embedded personnel at the Office who did not work on the Special Counsel's investigation, but whose purpose was to review the results of the investigation and to send—in writing—summaries of foreign intelligence and counterintelligence information to FBIHQ and FBI Field Offices. Those communications and other correspondence between the Office and the FBI contain information derived from the investigation, not all of which is contained in this Volume. This Volume is a summary. It contains, in the Office's judgment, that information necessary to account for the Special Counsel's prosecution and declination decisions and to describe the investigation's main factual results.

---

[1] FBI personnel assigned to the Special Counsel's Office were required to adhere to all applicable federal law and all Department and FBI regulations, guidelines, and policies. An FBI attorney worked on FBI-related matters for the Office, such as FBI compliance with all FBI policies and procedures, including the FBI's Domestic Investigations and Operations Guide (DIOG). That FBI attorney worked under FBI legal supervision, not the Special Counsel's supervision.

II. RUSSIAN "ACTIVE MEASURES" SOCIAL MEDIA CAMPAIGN

The first form of Russian election influence came principally from the Internet Research Agency, LLC (IRA), a Russian organization funded by Yevgeniy Viktorovich Prigozhin and companies he controlled, including Concord Management and Consulting LLC and Concord Catering (collectively "Concord").[2] The IRA conducted social media operations targeted at large U.S. audiences with the goal of sowing discord in the U.S. political system.[3] These operations constituted "active measures" (активные мероприятия), a term that typically refers to operations conducted by Russian security services aimed at influencing the course of international affairs.[4]

The IRA and its employees began operations targeting the United States as early as 2014. Using fictitious U.S. personas, IRA employees operated social media accounts and group pages designed to attract U.S. audiences. These groups and accounts, which addressed divisive U.S. political and social issues, falsely claimed to be controlled by U.S. activists. Over time, these social media accounts became a means to reach large U.S. audiences. IRA employees travelled to the United States in mid-2014 on an intelligence-gathering mission to obtain information and photographs for use in their social media posts.

IRA employees posted derogatory information about a number of candidates in the 2016 U.S. presidential election. By early to mid-2016, IRA operations included supporting the Trump Campaign and disparaging candidate Hillary Clinton. The IRA made various expenditures to carry out those activities, including buying political advertisements on social media in the names of U.S. persons and entities. Some IRA employees, posing as U.S. persons and without revealing their Russian association, communicated electronically with individuals associated with the Trump Campaign and with other political activists to seek to coordinate political activities, including the staging of political rallies.[5] The investigation did not identify evidence that any U.S. persons knowingly or intentionally coordinated with the IRA's interference operation.

By the end of the 2016 U.S. election, the IRA had the ability to reach millions of U.S. persons through their social media accounts. Multiple IRA-controlled Facebook groups and

---

[2] The Office is aware of reports that other Russian entities engaged in similar active measures operations targeting the United States. Some evidence collected by the Office corroborates those reports, and the Office has shared that evidence with other offices in the Department of Justice and FBI.

[3] Harm to Ongoing Matter
see also SM-2230634, serial 44 (analysis). The FBI case number cited here, and other FBI case numbers identified in the report, should be treated as law enforcement sensitive given the context. The report contains additional law enforcement sensitive information.

[4] As discussed in Part V below, the active measures investigation has resulted in criminal charges against 13 individual Russian nationals and three Russian entities, principally for conspiracy to defraud the United States, in violation of 18 U.S.C. § 371. *See* Volume I, Section V.A, *infra*; Indictment, *United States v. Internet Research Agency, et al.*, 1:18-cr-32 (D.D.C. Feb. 16, 2018), Doc. 1 ("*Internet Research Agency* Indictment").

[5] *Internet Research Agency* Indictment ¶¶ 52, 54, 55(a), 56, 74; Harm to Ongoing Matter

14

U.S. Department of Justice

~~Attorney Work Product~~ // ~~May Contain Material Protected Under Fed. R. Crim. P. 6(e)~~

Instagram accounts had hundreds of thousands of U.S. participants. IRA-controlled Twitter accounts separately had tens of thousands of followers, including multiple U.S. political figures who retweeted IRA-created content. In November 2017, a Facebook representative testified that Facebook had identified 470 IRA-controlled Facebook accounts that collectively made 80,000 posts between January 2015 and August 2017. Facebook estimated the IRA reached as many as 126 million persons through its Facebook accounts.[6] In January 2018, Twitter announced that it had identified 3,814 IRA-controlled Twitter accounts and notified approximately 1.4 million people Twitter believed may have been in contact with an IRA-controlled account.[7]

A. Structure of the Internet Research Agency

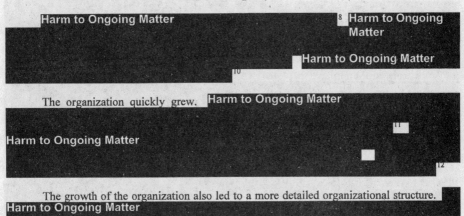

The organization quickly grew. Harm to Ongoing Matter

The growth of the organization also led to a more detailed organizational structure.

---

[6] *Social Media Influence in the 2016 U.S. Election, Hearing Before the Senate Select Committee on Intelligence*, 115th Cong. 13 (11/1/17) (testimony of Colin Stretch, General Counsel of Facebook) ("We estimate that roughly 29 million people were served content in their News Feeds directly from the IRA's 80,000 posts over the two years. Posts from these Pages were also shared, liked, and followed by people on Facebook, and, as a result, three times more people may have been exposed to a story that originated from the Russian operation. Our best estimate is that approximately 126 million people may have been served content from a Page associated with the IRA at some point during the two-year period."). The Facebook representative also testified that Facebook had identified 170 Instagram accounts that posted approximately 120,000 pieces of content during that time. Facebook did not offer an estimate of the audience reached via Instagram.

[7] Twitter, Update on Twitter's Review of the 2016 US Election (Jan. 31, 2018).

[8] *See* SM-2230634, serial 92.

[9] Harm to Ongoing Matter

[10] Harm to Ongoing Matter

[11] *See* SM-2230634, serial 86 Harm to Ongoing Matter

[12] Harm to Ongoing Matter

15

U.S. Department of Justice

~~Attorney Work Product // May Contain Material Protected Under Fed. R. Crim. P. 6(e)~~

Harm to Ongoing Matter

Two individuals headed the IRA's management: its general director, Mikhail Bystrov, and its executive director, Mikhail Burchik. **Harm to Ongoing Matter**

Harm to Ongoing Matter

As early as the spring of 2014, the IRA began to hide its funding and activities. **Harm to Ongoing Matter**

The IRA's U.S. operations are part of a larger set of interlocking operations known as "Project Lakhta," **Harm to Ongoing Matter**

Harm to Ongoing Matter

B. Funding and Oversight from Concord and Prigozhin

Until at least February 2018, Yevgeniy Viktorovich Prigozhin and two Concord companies funded the IRA. Prigozhin is a wealthy Russian businessman who served as the head of Concord.

---

[13] **Harm to Ongoing Matter**

[14] *See, e.g.*, SM-2230634, serials 9, 113 & 180 **Harm to Ongoing Matter**

[15] **Harm to Ongoing Matter**

[16] **Harm to Ongoing Matter**

See SM-2230634, serials 131 & 204.

[17] **Harm to Ongoing Matter**

[18] **Harm to Ongoing Matter**

16

U.S. Department of Justice

~~Attorney Work Product // May Contain Material Protected Under Fed. R. Crim. P. 6(e)~~

Harm to Ongoing Matter
    Prigozhin was sanctioned by the U.S. Treasury Department in December 2016,[19]
Harm to Ongoing Matter
                                [20] Harm to Ongoing Matter

                                                    Numerous media
sources have reported on Prigozhin's ties to Putin, and the two have appeared together in public
photographs.[22]

Harm to Ongoing Matter

                [23] Harm to Ongoing Matter

Harm to Ongoing Matter

                                                [4] Harm to Ongoing Matter

                                                [5] Harm to Ongoing Matter

Harm to Ongoing Matter

---

[19] U.S. Treasury Department, "Treasury Sanctions Individuals and Entities in Connection with Russia's Occupation of Crimea and the Conflict in Ukraine" (Dec. 20, 2016).

[20] Harm to Ongoing Matter

[21] Harm to Ongoing Matter

[22] *See, e.g.*, Neil MacFarquhar, *Yevgeny Prigozhin, Russian Oligarch Indicted by U.S., Is Known as "Putin's Cook"*, New York Times (Feb. 16, 2018).

[23] Harm to Ongoing Matter

[24] Harm to Ongoing Matter

[25] Harm to Ongoing Matter   *see also* SM-2230634, serial 113 HOM

17

U.S. Department of Justice

~~Attorney Work Product // May Contain Material Protected Under Fed. R. Crim. P. 6(e)~~

Harm to Ongoing Matter

Harm to Ongoing Matter

[26] Harm to Ongoing Matter

[27]

Harm to Ongoing Matter

Harm to Ongoing Matter

[28]

Harm to Ongoing Matter

---

[26] Harm to Ongoing Matter

[27] Harm to Ongoing Matter

[28] The term "troll" refers to internet users—in this context, paid operatives—who post inflammatory or otherwise disruptive content on social media or other websites.

18

IRA employees were aware that Prigozhin was involved in the IRA's U.S. operations,

Harm to Ongoing Matter

Harm to Ongoing Matter [29]

Harm to Ongoing Matter [30] In May 2016, IRA employees, claiming to be U.S. social activists and administrators of Facebook groups, recruited U.S. persons to hold signs (including one in front of the White House) that read "Happy 55th Birthday Dear Boss," as an homage to Prigozhin (whose 55th birthday was on June 1, 2016).[31]

Harm to Ongoing Matter [32]

Harm to Ongoing Matter

C. The IRA Targets U.S. Elections

1. The IRA Ramps Up U.S. Operations As Early As 2014

The IRA's U.S. operations sought to influence public opinion through online media and forums. By the spring of 2014, the IRA began to consolidate U.S. operations within a single general department, known internally as the "Translator" (Переводчик) department. **Harm to Ongoing Matter** IRA subdivided the Translator Department into different responsibilities, ranging from operations on different social media platforms to analytics to

---

[29] **Investigative Technique** *See* SM-2230634, serials 131 & 204.

[30] *See* SM-2230634, serial 156.

[31] *Internet Research Agency* Indictment ¶ 12(b); *see also* 5/26/16 Facebook Messages, ID 1479936895656747 (United Muslims of America) & **Personal Privacy**

[32] **Harm to Ongoing Matter** *see also* SM-2230634, serial 189. **Harm to Ongoing Matter**

graphics and IT.

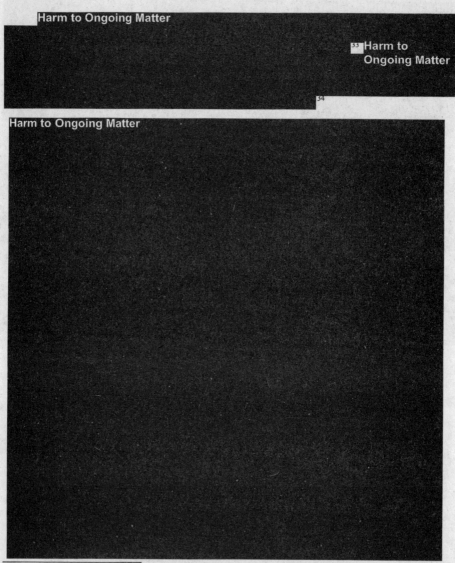

Harm to Ongoing Matter

[53] Harm to Ongoing Matter

[34]

Harm to Ongoing Matter

---

[33] Harm to Ongoing Matter

See SM-2230634, serial 205.

[34] *See* SM-2230634, serial 204 Harm to Ongoing Matter

20

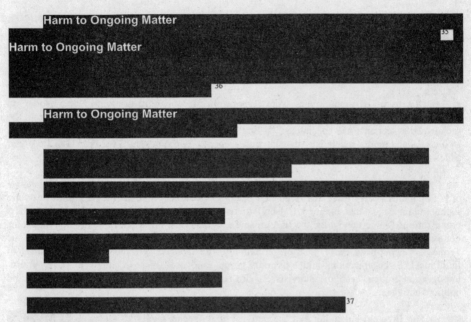

IRA employees also traveled to the United States on intelligence-gathering missions. In June 2014, four IRA employees applied to the U.S. Department of State to enter the United States, while lying about the purpose of their trip and claiming to be four friends who had met at a party.[38] Ultimately, two IRA employees—Anna Bogacheva and Aleksandra Krylova—received visas and entered the United States on June 4, 2014.

Prior to traveling, Krylova and Bogacheva compiled itineraries and instructions for the trip.

Harm to Ongoing Matter

Harm to Ongoing Matter

---

[35] Harm to Ongoing Matter

[36] Harm to Ongoing Matter

[37] Harm to Ongoing Matter

[38] See SM-2230634, serials 150 & 172 Harm to Ongoing Matter

[39] Harm to Ongoing Matter

U.S. Department of Justice

~~Attorney Work Product // May Contain Material Protected Under Fed. R. Crim. P. 6(e)~~

Harm to Ongoing Matter   [40]
Harm to Ongoing Matter
[41]

2. U.S. Operations Through IRA-Controlled Social Media Accounts

Dozens of IRA employees were responsible for operating accounts and personas on different U.S. social media platforms. The IRA referred to employees assigned to operate the social media accounts as "specialists."[42] Starting as early as 2014, the IRA's U.S. operations included social media specialists focusing on Facebook, YouTube, and Twitter.[43] The IRA later added specialists who operated on Tumblr and Instagram accounts.[44]

Initially, the IRA created social media accounts that pretended to be the personal accounts of U.S. persons.[45] By early 2015, the IRA began to create larger social media groups or public social media pages that claimed (falsely) to be affiliated with U.S. political and grassroots organizations. In certain cases, the IRA created accounts that mimicked real U.S. organizations. For example, one IRA-controlled Twitter account, @TEN_GOP, purported to be connected to the Tennessee Republican Party.[46] More commonly, the IRA created accounts in the names of fictitious U.S. organizations and grassroots groups and used these accounts to pose as anti-immigration groups, Tea Party activists, Black Lives Matter protestors, and other U.S. social and political activists.

The IRA closely monitored the activity of its social media accounts.
Harm to Ongoing Matter

Harm to Ongoing Matter

[40] Harm to Ongoing Matter

[41] Harm to Ongoing Matter

[42] Harm to Ongoing Matter

[43] Harm to Ongoing Matter

[44] *See, e.g.*, SM-2230634, serial 179 Harm to Ongoing Matter

[45] *See, e.g.*, Facebook ID 100011390466802 (Alex Anderson); Facebook ID 100009626173204 (Andrea Hansen); Facebook ID 100009728618427 (Gary Williams); Facebook ID 100013640043337 (Lakisha Richardson).

[46] The account claimed to be the "Unofficial Twitter of Tennessee Republicans" and made posts that appeared to be endorsements of the state political party. *See, e.g.*, @TEN_GOP, 4/3/16 Tweet ("Tennessee GOP backs @realDonaldTrump period #makeAmericagreatagain #tngop #tennessee #gop").

22

Harm to Ongoing Matter

Harm to Ongoing Matter

8

Harm to Ongoing Matter

By February 2016, internal IRA documents referred to support for the Trump Campaign and opposition to candidate Clinton.[49] For example, HOM   directions to IRA operators Harm to Ongoing Matter "Main idea: Use any opportunity to criticize Hillary [Clinton] and the rest (except Sanders and Trump - we support them)."[50] Harm to Ongoing Matter

The focus on the U.S. presidential campaign continued throughout 2016. In HOM 2016 internal HOM reviewing the IRA-controlled Facebook group "Secured Borders," the

---

[47] Harm to Ongoing Matter

[48] *See, e.g.*, SM-2230634 serial 131 HOM .

[49] The IRA posted content about the Clinton candidacy before Clinton officially announced her presidential campaign. IRA-controlled social media accounts criticized Clinton's record as Secretary of State and promoted various critiques of her candidacy. The IRA also used other techniques. Harm to Ongoing Matter *See* SM-2230634, serial 70.

[50] Harm to Ongoing Matter

23

author criticized the "lower number of posts dedicated to criticizing Hillary Clinton" and reminded the Facebook specialist "it is imperative to intensify criticizing Hillary Clinton."[51]

IRA employees also acknowledged that their work focused on influencing the U.S. presidential election. **Harm to Ongoing Matter**

Harm to Ongoing Matter

[52]

3. U.S. Operations Through Facebook

Many IRA operations used Facebook accounts created and operated by its specialists. **Harm to Ongoing Matter**

Harm to Ongoing Matter

[53]

Harm to Ongoing Matter

[4] IRA Facebook groups active during the 2016 campaign covered a range of political issues and included purported conservative

---

[51] **Harm to Ongoing Matter**

[52] **Harm to Ongoing Matter**

[53] **Harm to Ongoing Matter**

[54] **Harm to Ongoing Matter**

24

groups (with names such as "Being Patriotic," "Stop All Immigrants," "Secured Borders," and "Tea Party News"), purported Black social justice groups ("Black Matters," "Blacktivist," and "Don't Shoot Us"), LGBTQ groups ("LGBT United"), and religious groups ("United Muslims of America").

Throughout 2016, IRA accounts published an increasing number of materials supporting the Trump Campaign and opposing the Clinton Campaign. For example, on May 31, 2016, the operational account "Matt Skiber" began to privately message dozens of pro-Trump Facebook groups asking them to help plan a "pro-Trump rally near Trump Tower."[55]

To reach larger U.S. audiences, the IRA purchased advertisements from Facebook that promoted the IRA groups on the newsfeeds of U.S. audience members. According to Facebook, the IRA purchased over 3,500 advertisements, and the expenditures totaled approximately $100,000.[56]

During the U.S. presidential campaign, many IRA-purchased advertisements explicitly supported or opposed a presidential candidate or promoted U.S. rallies organized by the IRA (discussed below). As early as March 2016, the IRA purchased advertisements that overtly opposed the Clinton Campaign. For example, on March 18, 2016, the IRA purchased an advertisement depicting candidate Clinton and a caption that read in part, "If one day God lets this liar enter the White House as a president – that day would be a real national tragedy."[57] Similarly, on April 6, 2016, the IRA purchased advertisements for its account "Black Matters" calling for a "flashmob" of U.S. persons to "take a photo with #HillaryClintonForPrison2016 or #nohillary2016."[58] IRA-purchased advertisements featuring Clinton were, with very few exceptions, negative.[59]

IRA-purchased advertisements referencing candidate Trump largely supported his campaign. The first known IRA advertisement explicitly endorsing the Trump Campaign was purchased on April 19, 2016. The IRA bought an advertisement for its Instagram account "Tea Party News" asking U.S. persons to help them "make a patriotic team of young Trump supporters" by uploading photos with the hashtag "#KIDS4TRUMP."[60] In subsequent months, the IRA purchased dozens of advertisements supporting the Trump Campaign, predominantly through the Facebook groups "Being Patriotic," "Stop All Invaders," and "Secured Borders."

---

[55] 5/31/16 Facebook Message, ID 100009922908461 (Matt Skiber) to ID ▮▮ ▮▮▮▮▮
5/31/16 Facebook Message, ID 100009922908461 (Matt Skiber) to ID
Personal Privacy

[56] *Social Media Influence in the 2016 U.S. Election, Hearing Before the Senate Select Committee on Intelligence*, 115th Cong. 13 (11/1/17) (testimony of Colin Stretch, General Counsel of Facebook).

[57] 3/18/16 Facebook Advertisement ID 6045505152575.

[58] 4/6/16 Facebook Advertisement ID 6043740225319.

[59] *See* SM-2230634, serial 213 (documenting politically-oriented advertisements from the larger set provided by Facebook).

[60] 4/19/16 Facebook Advertisement ID 6045151094235.

Collectively, the IRA's social media accounts reached tens of millions of U.S. persons. Individual IRA social media accounts attracted hundreds of thousands of followers. For example, at the time they were deactivated by Facebook in mid-2017, the IRA's "United Muslims of America" Facebook group had over 300,000 followers, the "Don't Shoot Us" Facebook group had over 250,000 followers, the "Being Patriotic" Facebook group had over 200,000 followers, and the "Secured Borders" Facebook group had over 130,000 followers.[61] According to Facebook, in total the IRA-controlled accounts made over 80,000 posts before their deactivation in August 2017, and these posts reached at least 29 million U.S persons and "may have reached an estimated 126 million people."[62]

4. U.S. Operations Through Twitter

A number of IRA employees assigned to the Translator Department served as Twitter specialists. Harm to Ongoing Matter

[63]

The IRA's Twitter operations involved two strategies. First, IRA specialists operated certain Twitter accounts to create individual U.S. personas, Harm to Ongoing Matter

[4] Separately, the IRA operated a network of automated Twitter accounts (commonly referred to as a bot network) that enabled the IRA to amplify existing content on Twitter.

a. Individualized Accounts

Harm to Ongoing Matter

[65] Harm to Ongoing Matter

---

[61] *See* Facebook ID 1479936895656747 (United Muslims of America); Facebook ID 1157233400960126 (Don't Shoot); Facebook ID 1601685693432389 (Being Patriotic); Facebook ID 757183957716200 (Secured Borders). Harm to Ongoing Matter

Harm to Ongoing Matter

Harm to Ongoing Matter

[62] *Social Media Influence in the 2016 U.S. Election, Hearing Before the Senate Select Committee on Intelligence*, 115th Cong. 13 (11/1/17) (testimony of Colin Stretch, General Counsel of Facebook).

[63] Harm to Ongoing Matter

[64] Harm to Ongoing Matter

[65] Harm to Ongoing Matter

26

86

Harm to Ongoing Matter [66]

The IRA operated individualized Twitter accounts similar to the operation of its Facebook accounts, by continuously posting original content to the accounts while also communicating with U.S. Twitter users directly (through public tweeting or Twitter's private messaging).

The IRA used many of these accounts to attempt to influence U.S. audiences on the election. Individualized accounts used to influence the U.S. presidential election included @TEN_GOP (described above); @jenn_abrams (claiming to be a Virginian Trump supporter with 70,000 followers); @Pamela_Moore13 (claiming to be a Texan Trump supporter with 70,000 followers); and @America_1st_ (an anti-immigration persona with 24,000 followers).[67] In May 2016, the IRA created the Twitter account @march_for_trump, which promoted IRA-organized rallies in support of the Trump Campaign (described below).[68]

Using these accounts and others, the IRA provoked reactions from users and the media. Multiple IRA-posted tweets gained popularity.[70] U.S. media outlets also quoted tweets from IRA-controlled accounts and attributed them to the reactions of real U.S. persons.[71] Similarly, numerous high-

---

[66] **Harm to Ongoing Matter**

[67] Other individualized accounts included @MissouriNewsUS (an account with 3,800 followers that posted pro-Sanders and anti-Clinton material).

[68] *See* @march_for_trump, 5/30/16 Tweet (first post from account).

[69] **Harm to Ongoing Matter**

[70] For example, one IRA account tweeted, "To those people, who hate the Confederate flag. Did you know that the flag and the war wasn't about slavery, it was all about money." The tweet received over 40,000 responses. @Jenn_Abrams 4/24/17 (2:37 p.m.) Tweet.

[71] Josephine Lukito & Chris Wells, *Most Major Outlets Have Used Russian Tweets as Sources for Partisan Opinion: Study*, Columbia Journalism Review (Mar. 8, 2018); *see also Twitter Steps Up to Explain #NewYorkValues to Ted Cruz*, Washington Post (Jan. 15, 2016) (citing IRA tweet); *People Are Slamming the CIA for Claiming Russia Tried to Help Donald Trump*, U.S. News & World Report (Dec. 12, 2016).

27

87

U.S. Department of Justice

~~Attorney Work Product // May Contain Material Protected Under Fed. R. Crim. P. 6(e)~~

profile U.S. persons, including former Ambassador Michael McFaul,[72] Roger Stone,[73] Sean Hannity,[74] and Michael Flynn Jr.,[75] retweeted or responded to tweets posted to these IRA-controlled accounts. Multiple individuals affiliated with the Trump Campaign also promoted IRA tweets (discussed below).

b. IRA Botnet Activities

In January 2018, Twitter publicly identified 3,814 Twitter accounts associated with the IRA.[79] According to Twitter, in the ten weeks before the 2016 U.S. presidential election, these accounts posted approximately 175,993 tweets, "approximately 8.4% of which were election-

---

[72] @McFaul 4/30/16 Tweet (responding to tweet by @Jenn_Abrams).

[73] @RogerJStoneJr 5/30/16 Tweet (retweeting @Pamela_Moore13); @RogerJStoneJr 4/26/16 Tweet (same).

[74] @seanhannity 6/21/17 Tweet (retweeting @Pamela_Moore13).

[75] @mflynnJR 6/22/17 Tweet ("RT @Jenn_Abrams: This is what happens when you add the voice over of an old documentary about mental illness onto video of SJWs. . .").

[76] A botnet refers to a network of private computers or accounts controlled as a group to send specific automated messages. On the Twitter network, botnets can be used to promote and republish ("retweet") specific tweets or hashtags in order for them to gain larger audiences.

[77] Harm to Ongoing Matter

[78] Harm to Ongoing Matter

[79] Eli Rosenberg, *Twitter to Tell 677,000 Users they Were Had by the Russians. Some Signs Show the Problem Continues*, Washington Post (Jan. 19, 2019).

related."[80]   Twitter also announced that it had notified approximately 1.4 million people who Twitter believed may have been in contact with an IRA-controlled account.[81]

5. U.S. Operations Involving Political Rallies

The IRA organized and promoted political rallies inside the United States while posing as U.S. grassroots activists. First, the IRA used one of its preexisting social media personas (Facebook groups and Twitter accounts, for example) to announce and promote the event. The IRA then sent a large number of direct messages to followers of its social media account asking them to attend the event. From those who responded with interest in attending, the IRA then sought a U.S. person to serve as the event's coordinator. In most cases, the IRA account operator would tell the U.S. person that they personally could not attend the event due to some preexisting conflict or because they were somewhere else in the United States.[82] The IRA then further promoted the event by contacting U.S. media about the event and directing them to speak with the coordinator.[83] After the event, the IRA posted videos and photographs of the event to the IRA's social media accounts.[84]

The Office identified dozens of U.S. rallies organized by the IRA. The earliest evidence of a rally was a "confederate rally" in November 2015.[85] The IRA continued to organize rallies even after the 2016 U.S. presidential election. The attendance at rallies varied. Some rallies appear to have drawn few (if any) participants, while others drew hundreds. The reach and success of these rallies was closely monitored [Harm to Ongoing Matter]

---

[80] Twitter, "Update on Twitter's Review of the 2016 US Election" (updated Jan. 31, 2018). Twitter also reported identifying 50,258 automated accounts connected to the Russian government, which tweeted more than a million times in the ten weeks before the election.

[81] Twitter, "Update on Twitter's Review of the 2016 US Election" (updated Jan. 31, 2018).

[82] 8/20/16 Facebook Message, ID 100009922908461 (Matt Skiber) to ID [PP]

[83] *See, e.g.*, 7/21/16 Email, joshmilton024@gmail.com to [PP]; 7/21/16 Email, joshmilton024@gmail.com to [Personal Privacy]

[84] @march_for_trump 6/25/16 Tweet (posting photos from rally outside Trump Tower).

[85] Instagram ID 2228012168 (Stand For Freedom) 11/3/15 Post ("Good evening buds! Well I am planning to organize a confederate rally [. . .] in Houston on the 14 of November and I want more people to attend.").

Harm to Ongoing Matter

30

IRA Poster for Pennsylvania Rallies organized by the IRA

From June 2016 until the end of the presidential campaign, almost all of the U.S. rallies organized by the IRA focused on the U.S. election, often promoting the Trump Campaign and opposing the Clinton Campaign. Pro-Trump rallies included three in New York; a series of pro-Trump rallies in Florida in August 2016; and a series of pro-Trump rallies in October 2016 in Pennsylvania. The Florida rallies drew the attention of the Trump Campaign, which posted about the Miami rally on candidate Trump's Facebook account (as discussed below).[86]

Many of the same IRA employees who oversaw the IRA's social media accounts also conducted the day-to-day recruiting for political rallies inside the United States. **Harm to Ongoing Matter**

[87]

6. Targeting and Recruitment of U.S. Persons

As early as 2014, the IRA instructed its employees to target U.S. persons who could be used to advance its operational goals. Initially, recruitment focused on U.S. persons who could amplify the content posted by the IRA. **Harm to Ongoing Matter**

Harm to Ongoing Matter

[88]

IRA employees frequently used **Investigative Technique** Twitter, Facebook, and Instagram to contact and recruit U.S. persons who followed the group. The IRA recruited U.S. persons from across the political spectrum. For example, the IRA targeted the family of **Personal Privacy** and a number of black social justice activists

---

[86] The pro-Trump rallies were organized through multiple Facebook, Twitter, and email accounts. *See, e.g.*, Facebook ID 100009922908461 (Matt Skiber); Facebook ID 1601685693432389 (Being Patriotic); Twitter Account @march_for_trump; beingpatriotic@gmail.com. (Rallies were organized in New York on June 25, 2016; Florida on August 20, 2016; and Pennsylvania on October 2, 2016.)

[87] **Harm to Ongoing Matter**

[88] **Harm to Ongoing Matter**

while posing as a grassroots group called "Black Matters US."[89] In February 2017, the persona "Black Fist" (purporting to want to teach African-Americans to protect themselves when contacted by law enforcement) hired a self-defense instructor in New York to offer classes sponsored by Black Fist. The IRA also recruited moderators of conservative social media groups to promote IRA-generated content,[90] as well as recruited individuals to perform political acts (such as walking around New York City dressed up as Santa Claus with a Trump mask).[91]

Harm to Ongoing Matter

Harm to Ongoing Matter

[93] Harm to Ongoing Matter

[94]

HOM as the IRA's online audience became larger, the IRA tracked U.S. persons with whom they communicated and had successfully tasked (with tasks ranging from organizing rallies to taking pictures with certain political messages). Harm to Ongoing Matter

[95]

---

[89] 3/11/16 Facebook Advertisement ID 6045078289928, 5/6/16 Facebook Advertisement ID 6051652423528, 10/26/16 Facebook Advertisement ID 6055238604687; 10/27/16 Facebook Message, ID Personal Privacy & ID 100011698576461 (Taylor Brooks).

[90] 8/19/16 Facebook Message, ID 100009922908461 (Matt Skiber) to ID PP

[91] 12/8/16 Email, robot@craigslist.org to beingpatriotic@gmail.com (confirming Craigslist advertisement).

[92] 8/18-19/16 Twitter DMs, @march_for_trump & PP

[93] See, e.g., 11/11-27/16 Facebook Messages, ID 100011698576461 (Taylor Brooks) & ID Personal Privacy (arranging to pay for plane tickets and for a bull horn).

[94] See, e.g., 9/10/16 Facebook Message, ID 100009922908461 (Matt Skiber) & ID Personal Privacy (discussing payment for rally supplies); 8/18/16 Twitter DM, @march_for_trump to PP (discussing payment for construction materials).

[95] Harm to Ongoing Matter

Harm to Ongoing Matter

7. Interactions and Contacts with the Trump Campaign

The investigation identified two different forms of connections between the IRA and members of the Trump Campaign. (The investigation identified no similar connections between the IRA and the Clinton Campaign.) First, on multiple occasions, members and surrogates of the Trump Campaign promoted—typically by linking, retweeting, or similar methods of reposting—pro-Trump or anti-Clinton content published by the IRA through IRA-controlled social media accounts. Additionally, in a few instances, IRA employees represented themselves as U.S. persons to communicate with members of the Trump Campaign in an effort to seek assistance and coordination on IRA-organized political rallies inside the United States.

a. Trump Campaign Promotion of IRA Political Materials

Among the U.S. "leaders of public opinion" targeted by the IRA were various members and surrogates of the Trump Campaign. In total, Trump Campaign affiliates promoted dozens of tweets, posts, and other political content created by the IRA.

- Posts from the IRA-controlled Twitter account @TEN_GOP were cited or retweeted by multiple Trump Campaign officials and surrogates, including Donald J. Trump Jr.,[96] Eric

---

[96] *See, e.g.,* @DonaldJTrumpJr 10/26/16 Tweet ("RT @TEN_GOP: BREAKING Thousands of names changed on voter rolls in Indiana. Police investigating #VoterFraud. #DrainTheSwamp."); @DonaldJTrumpJr 11/2/16 Tweet ("RT @TEN_GOP: BREAKING: #VoterFraud by counting tens of thousands of ineligible mail in Hillary votes being reported in Broward County, Florida."); @DonaldJTrumpJr 11/8/16 Tweet ("RT @TEN_GOP: This vet passed away last month before he could vote for Trump. Here he is in his #MAGA hat. #voted #ElectionDay."). Trump Jr. retweeted additional @TEN_GOP content subsequent to the election.

33

U.S. Department of Justice

~~Attorney Work Product~~ // ~~May Contain Material Protected Under Fed. R. Crim. P. 6(e)~~

Trump,[97] Kellyanne Conway,[98] Brad Parscale,[99] and Michael T. Flynn.[100] These posts included allegations of voter fraud,[101] as well as allegations that Secretary Clinton had mishandled classified information.[102]

- A November 7, 2016 post from the IRA-controlled Twitter account @Pamela_Moore13 was retweeted by Donald J. Trump Jr.[103]

- On September 19, 2017, President Trump's personal account @realDonaldTrump responded to a tweet from the IRA-controlled account @10_gop (the backup account of @TEN_GOP, which had already been deactivated by Twitter). The tweet read: "We love you, Mr. President!"[104]

IRA employees monitored the reaction of the Trump Campaign and, later, Trump Administration officials to their tweets. For example, on August 23, 2016, the IRA-controlled persona "Matt Skiber" Facebook account sent a message to a U.S. Tea Party activist, writing that "Mr. Trump posted about our event in Miami! This is great!"[105] The IRA employee included a screenshot of candidate Trump's Facebook account, which included a post about the August 20, 2016 political rallies organized by the IRA.

Screenshot of Trump Facebook Account (from Matt Skiber)

---

[97] @EricTrump 10/20/16 Tweet ("RT @TEN_GOP: BREAKING Hillary shuts down press conference when asked about DNC Operatives corruption & #VoterFraud #debatenight #TrumpB").

[98] @KellyannePolls 11/6/16 Tweet ("RT @TEN_GOP: Mother of jailed sailor: 'Hold Hillary to same standards as my son on Classified info' #hillarysemail #WeinerGate.").

[99] @parscale 10/15/16 Tweet ("Thousands of deplorables chanting to the media: 'Tell The Truth!' RT if you are also done w/ biased Media! #FridayFeeling").

[100] @GenFlynn 11/7/16 (retweeting @TEN_GOP post that included in part "@realDonaldTrump & @mike_pence will be our next POTUS & VPOTUS.").

[101] @TEN_GOP 10/11/16 Tweet ("North Carolina finds 2,214 voters over the age of 110!!").

[102] @TEN_GOP 11/6/16 Tweet ("Mother of jailed sailor: 'Hold Hillary to same standards as my son on classified info #hillaryemail #WeinerGate.'").

[103] @DonaldJTrumpJr 11/7/16 Tweet ("RT @Pamela_Moore13: Detroit residents speak out against the failed policies of Obama, Hillary & democrats . . . .").

[104] @realDonaldTrump 9/19/17 (7:33 p.m.) Tweet ("THANK YOU for your support Miami! My team just shared photos from your TRUMP SIGN WAVING DAY, yesterday! I love you – and there is no question – TOGETHER, WE WILL MAKE AMERICA GREAT AGAIN!").

[105] 8/23/16 Facebook Message, ID 100009922908461 (Matt Skiber) to ID PP ▮▮▮▮▮▮▮▮

Harm to Ongoing Matter

[106]

b. Contact with Trump Campaign Officials in Connection to Rallies

Starting in June 2016, the IRA contacted different U.S. persons affiliated with the Trump Campaign in an effort to coordinate pro-Trump IRA-organized rallies inside the United States. In all cases, the IRA contacted the Campaign while claiming to be U.S. political activists working on behalf of a conservative grassroots organization. The IRA's contacts included requests for signs and other materials to use at rallies,[107] as well as requests to promote the rallies and help coordinate logistics.[108] While certain campaign volunteers agreed to provide the requested support (for example, agreeing to set aside a number of signs), the investigation has not identified evidence that any Trump Campaign official understood the requests were coming from foreign nationals.

* * *

In sum, the investigation established that Russia interfered in the 2016 presidential election through the "active measures" social media campaign carried out by the IRA, an organization funded by Prigozhin and companies that he controlled. As explained further in Volume I, Section V.A, *infra*, the Office concluded (and a grand jury has alleged) that Prigozhin, his companies, and IRA employees violated U.S. law through these operations, principally by undermining through deceptive acts the work of federal agencies charged with regulating foreign influence in U.S. elections.

---

[106] **Harm to Ongoing Matter**

[107] *See, e.g.*, 8/16/16 Email, joshmilton024@gmail.com to **PP** @donaldtrump.com (asking for Trump/Pence signs for Florida rally); 8/18/16 Email, joshmilton024@gmail.com to **PP** @donaldtrump.com (asking for Trump/Pence signs for Florida rally); 8/12/16 Email, joshmilton024@gmail.com to **PP** @donaldtrump.com (asking for "contact phone numbers for Trump Campaign affiliates" in various Florida cities and signs).

[108] 8/15/16 Email, **Personal Privacy** to joshmilton024@gmail.com (asking to add to locations to the "Florida Goes Trump," list); 8/16/16 Email, **Personal Privacy** to joshmilton024@gmail.com (volunteering to send an email blast to followers).

35

U.S. Department of Justice

~~Attorney Work Product // May Contain Material Protected Under Fed. R. Crim. P. 6(e)~~

III. RUSSIAN HACKING AND DUMPING OPERATIONS

Beginning in March 2016, units of the Russian Federation's Main Intelligence Directorate of the General Staff (GRU) hacked the computers and email accounts of organizations, employees, and volunteers supporting the Clinton Campaign, including the email account of campaign chairman John Podesta. Starting in April 2016, the GRU hacked into the computer networks of the Democratic Congressional Campaign Committee (DCCC) and the Democratic National Committee (DNC). The GRU targeted hundreds of email accounts used by Clinton Campaign employees, advisors, and volunteers. In total, the GRU stole hundreds of thousands of documents from the compromised email accounts and networks.[109] The GRU later released stolen Clinton Campaign and DNC documents through online personas, "DCLeaks" and "Guccifer 2.0," and later through the organization WikiLeaks. The release of the documents was designed and timed to interfere with the 2016 U.S. presidential election and undermine the Clinton Campaign.

The Trump Campaign showed interest in the WikiLeaks releases and, in the summer and fall of 2016, **Harm to Ongoing Matter**
After **HOM** WikiLeaks's first Clinton-related release **HOM**, the Trump Campaign stayed in contact **HOM** about WikiLeaks's activities. The investigation was unable to resolve **Harm to Ongoing Matter** WikiLeaks's release of the stolen Podesta emails on October 7, 2016, the same day a video from years earlier was published of Trump using graphic language about women.

A. GRU Hacking Directed at the Clinton Campaign

1. GRU Units Target the Clinton Campaign

Two military units of the GRU carried out the computer intrusions into the Clinton Campaign, DNC, and DCCC: Military Units 26165 and 74455.[110] Military Unit 26165 is a GRU cyber unit dedicated to targeting military, political, governmental, and non-governmental organizations outside of Russia, including in the United States.[111] The unit was sub-divided into departments with different specialties. One department, for example, developed specialized malicious software ("malware"), while another department conducted large-scale spearphishing campaigns.[112] **Investigative Technique** a bitcoin mining operation to

---

[109] As discussed in Section V below, our Office charged 12 GRU officers for crimes arising from the hacking of these computers, principally with conspiring to commit computer intrusions, in violation of 18 U.S.C. §§1030 and 371. *See* Volume I, Section V.B, *infra*; Indictment, *United States v. Netyksho*, No. 1:18-cr-215 (D.D.C. July 13, 2018), Doc. 1 ("*Netyksho* Indictment").

[110] *Netyksho* Indictment ¶ 1.

[111] Separate from this Office's indictment of GRU officers, in October 2018 a grand jury sitting in the Western District of Pennsylvania returned an indictment charging certain members of Unit 26165 with hacking the U.S. Anti-Doping Agency, the World Anti-Doping Agency, and other international sport associations. *United States v. Aleksei Sergeyevich Morenets*, No. 18-263 (W.D. Pa.).

[112] A spearphishing email is designed to appear as though it originates from a trusted source, and solicits information to enable the sender to gain access to an account or network, or causes the recipient to

secure bitcoins used to purchase computer infrastructure used in hacking operations.[113]

Military Unit 74455 is a related GRU unit with multiple departments that engaged in cyber operations. Unit 74455 assisted in the release of documents stolen by Unit 26165, the promotion of those releases, and the publication of anti-Clinton content on social media accounts operated by the GRU. Officers from Unit 74455 separately hacked computers belonging to state boards of elections, secretaries of state, and U.S. companies that supplied software and other technology related to the administration of U.S. elections.[114]

Beginning in mid-March 2016, Unit 26165 had primary responsibility for hacking the DCCC and DNC, as well as email accounts of individuals affiliated with the Clinton Campaign:[115]

- Unit 26165 used IT ▮▮▮▮▮▮▮▮▮▮ to learn about Investigative Technique different Democratic websites, including democrats.org, hillaryclinton.com, dnc.org, and dccc.org. Investigative Technique ▮▮▮▮▮▮▮▮▮▮▮▮▮▮▮ began before the GRU had obtained any credentials or gained access to these networks, indicating that the later DCCC and DNC intrusions were not crimes of opportunity but rather the result of targeting.[116]

- GRU officers also sent hundreds of spearphishing emails to the work and personal email accounts of Clinton Campaign employees and volunteers. Between March 10, 2016 and March 15, 2016, Unit 26165 appears to have sent approximately 90 spearphishing emails to email accounts at hillaryclinton.com. Starting on March 15, 2016, the GRU began targeting Google email accounts used by Clinton Campaign employees, along with a smaller number of dnc.org email accounts.[117]

The GRU spearphishing operation enabled it to gain access to numerous email accounts of Clinton Campaign employees and volunteers, including campaign chairman John Podesta, junior volunteers assigned to the Clinton Campaign's advance team, informal Clinton Campaign advisors, and a DNC employee.[118] GRU officers stole tens of thousands of emails from spearphishing victims, including various Clinton Campaign-related communications.

---

download malware that enables the sender to gain access to an account or network. *Netyksho* Indictment ¶ 10.

[113] Bitcoin mining consists of unlocking new bitcoins by solving computational problems. IT ▮▮▮▮▮ kept its newly mined coins in an account on the bitcoin exchange platform CEX.io. To make purchases, the GRU routed funds into other accounts through transactions designed to obscure the source of funds. *Netyksho* Indictment ¶ 62.

[114] *Netyksho* Indictment ¶ 69.

[115] *Netyksho* Indictment ¶ 9.

[116] *See* SM-2589105, serials 144 & 495.

[117] Investigative Technique ▮▮▮▮▮▮▮▮▮▮▮▮▮▮▮▮▮▮▮▮▮▮▮

[118] Investigative Technique ▮▮▮▮▮▮▮▮▮

37

2. Intrusions into the DCCC and DNC Networks

a. *Initial Access*

By no later than April 12, 2016, the GRU had gained access to the DCCC computer network using the credentials stolen from a DCCC employee who had been successfully spearphished the week before. Over the ensuing weeks, the GRU traversed the network, identifying different computers connected to the DCCC network. By stealing network access credentials along the way (including those of IT administrators with unrestricted access to the system), the GRU compromised approximately 29 different computers on the DCCC network.[119]

Approximately six days after first hacking into the DCCC network, on April 18, 2016, GRU officers gained access to the DNC network via a virtual private network (VPN) connection[120] between the DCCC and DNC networks.[121] Between April 18, 2016 and June 8, 2016, Unit 26165 compromised more than 30 computers on the DNC network, including the DNC mail server and shared file server.[122]

b. *Implantation of Malware on DCCC and DNC Networks*

Unit 26165 implanted on the DCCC and DNC networks two types of customized malware,[123] known as "X-Agent" and "X-Tunnel"; Mimikatz, a credential-harvesting tool; and rar.exe, a tool used in these intrusions to compile and compress materials for exfiltration. X-Agent was a multi-function hacking tool that allowed Unit 26165 to log keystrokes, take screenshots, and gather other data about the infected computers (*e.g.*, file directories, operating systems).[124] X-Tunnel was a hacking tool that created an encrypted connection between the victim DCCC/DNC computers and GRU-controlled computers outside the DCCC and DNC networks that was capable of large-scale data transfers.[125] GRU officers then used X-Tunnel to exfiltrate stolen data from the victim computers.

---

[119] Investigative Technique

[120] A VPN extends a private network, allowing users to send and receive data across public networks (such as the internet) as if the connecting computer was directly connected to the private network. The VPN in this case had been created to give a small number of DCCC employees access to certain databases housed on the DNC network. Therefore, while the DCCC employees were outside the DNC's private network, they could access parts of the DNC network from their DCCC computers.

[121] Investigative Technique SM-2589105-HACK, serial 5.

[122] Investigative Technique M-2589105-HACK, serial 5.

[123] "Malware" is short for malicious software, and here refers to software designed to allow a third party to infiltrate a computer without the consent or knowledge of the computer's user or operator.

[124] Investigative Technique

[125] Investigative Technique

To operate X-Agent and X-Tunnel on the DCCC and DNC networks, Unit 26165 officers set up a group of computers outside those networks to communicate with the implanted malware.[126] The first set of GRU-controlled computers, known by the GRU as "middle servers," sent and received messages to and from malware on the DNC/DCCC networks. The middle servers, in turn, relayed messages to a second set of GRU-controlled computers, labeled internally by the GRU as an "AMS Panel." The AMS Panel ▓Investigative Technique▓ served as a nerve center through which GRU officers monitored and directed the malware's operations on the DNC/DCCC networks.[127]

The AMS Panel used to control X-Agent during the DCCC and DNC intrusions was housed on a leased computer located near ▓ Arizona.[128] ▓Investigative Technique▓

[129]

▓Investigative Technique▓

▓Investigative Technique▓

---

[126] In connection with these intrusions, the GRU used computers (virtual private networks, dedicated servers operated by hosting companies, etc.) that it leased from third-party providers located all over the world. The investigation identified rental agreements and payments for computers located in, *inter alia,* ▓Investigative Technique▓ all of which were used in the operations targeting the U.S. election.

[127] *Netyksho* Indictment ¶ 25.

[128] *Netyksho* Indictment ¶ 24(c).

[129] *Netyksho* Indictment ¶ 24(b).

U.S. Department of Justice

~~Attorney-Work Product // May Contain Material Protected Under Fed. R. Crim. P. 6(e)~~

The Arizona-based AMS Panel also stored thousands of files containing keylogging sessions captured through X-Agent. These sessions were captured as GRU officers monitored DCCC and DNC employees' work on infected computers regularly between April 2016 and June 2016. Data captured in these keylogging sessions included passwords, internal communications between employees, banking information, and sensitive personal information.

c. Theft of Documents from DNC and DCCC Networks

Officers from Unit 26165 stole thousands of documents from the DCCC and DNC networks, including significant amounts of data pertaining to the 2016 U.S. federal elections. Stolen documents included internal strategy documents, fundraising data, opposition research, and emails from the work inboxes of DNC employees.[130]

The GRU began stealing DCCC data shortly after it gained access to the network. On April 14, 2016 (approximately three days after the initial intrusion) GRU officers downloaded rar.exe onto the DCCC's document server. The following day, the GRU searched one compromised DCCC computer for files containing search terms that included "Hillary," "DNC," "Cruz," and "Trump."[131] On April 25, 2016, the GRU collected and compressed PDF and Microsoft documents from folders on the DCCC's shared file server that pertained to the 2016 election.[132] The GRU appears to have compressed and exfiltrated over 70 gigabytes of data from this file server.[133]

The GRU also stole documents from the DNC network shortly after gaining access. On April 22, 2016, the GRU copied files from the DNC network to GRU-controlled computers. Stolen documents included the DNC's opposition research into candidate Trump.[134] Between approximately May 25, 2016 and June 1, 2016, GRU officers accessed the DNC's mail server from a GRU-controlled computer leased inside the United States.[135] During these connections,

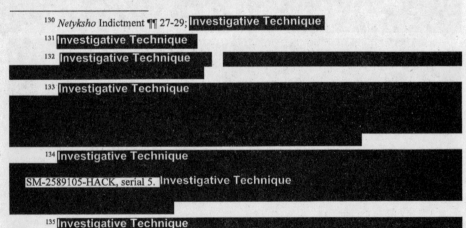

[130] *Netyksho* Indictment ¶¶ 27-29; Investigative Technique

[131] Investigative Technique

[132] Investigative Technique

[133] Investigative Technique

[134] Investigative Technique

SM-2589105-HACK, serial 5. Investigative Technique

[135] Investigative Technique

See SM-2589105-GJ, serial 649. As part of its investigation, the FBI later received images of DNC servers and copies of relevant traffic logs. *Netyksho* Indictment ¶¶ 28-29.

U.S. Department of Justice

~~Attorney-Work Product~~ // ~~May Contain Material Protected Under Fed. R. Crim. P. 6(e)~~

Unit 26165 officers appear to have stolen thousands of emails and attachments, which were later released by WikiLeaks in July 2016.[136]

B. Dissemination of the Hacked Materials

The GRU's operations extended beyond stealing materials, and included releasing documents stolen from the Clinton Campaign and its supporters. The GRU carried out the anonymous release through two fictitious online personas that it created—DCLeaks and Guccifer 2.0—and later through the organization WikiLeaks.

1. DCLeaks

The GRU began planning the releases at least as early as April 19, 2016, when Unit 26165 registered the domain dcleaks.com through a service that anonymized the registrant.[137] Unit 26165 paid for the registration using a pool of bitcoin that it had mined.[138] The dcleaks.com landing page pointed to different tranches of stolen documents, arranged by victim or subject matter. Other dcleaks.com pages contained indexes of the stolen emails that were being released (bearing the sender, recipient, and date of the email). To control access and the timing of releases, pages were sometimes password-protected for a period of time and later made unrestricted to the public.

Starting in June 2016, the GRU posted stolen documents onto the website dcleaks.com, including documents stolen from a number of individuals associated with the Clinton Campaign. These documents appeared to have originated from personal email accounts (in particular, Google and Microsoft accounts), rather than the DNC and DCCC computer networks. DCLeaks victims included an advisor to the Clinton Campaign, a former DNC employee and Clinton Campaign employee, and four other campaign volunteers.[139] The GRU released through dcleaks.com thousands of documents, including personal identifying and financial information, internal correspondence related to the Clinton Campaign and prior political jobs, and fundraising files and information.[140]

---

[136] *Netyksho* Indictment ¶ 29. The last-in-time DNC email released by WikiLeaks was dated May 25, 2016, the same period of time during which the GRU gained access to the DNC's email server. *Netyksho* Indictment ¶ 45.

[137] *Netyksho* Indictment ¶ 35. Approximately a week before the registration of dcleaks.com, the same actors attempted to register the website electionleaks.com using the same domain registration service. Investigative Technique

[138] *See* SM-2589105, serial 181; *Netyksho* Indictment ¶ 21(a).

[139] Investigative Technique

[140] *See, e.g.*, Internet Archive, "https://dcleaks.com/" (archive date Nov. 10, 2016). Additionally, DCLeaks released documents relating to Personal Privacy , emails belonging to PP , and emails from 2015 relating to Republican Party employees (under the portfolio name "The United States Republican Party"). "The United States Republican Party" portfolio contained approximately 300 emails from a variety of GOP members, PACs, campaigns, state parties, and businesses dated between May and October 2015. According to open-source reporting, these victims shared the same

U.S. Department of Justice

~~Attorney Work Product~~ // ~~May Contain Material Protected Under Fed. R. Crim. P. 6(e)~~

GRU officers operated a Facebook page under the DCLeaks moniker, which they primarily used to promote releases of materials.[141] The Facebook page was administered through a small number of preexisting GRU-controlled Facebook accounts.[142]

GRU officers also used the DCLeaks Facebook account, the Twitter account @dcleaks_, and the email account dcleaksproject@gmail.com to communicate privately with reporters and other U.S. persons. GRU officers using the DCLeaks persona gave certain reporters early access to archives of leaked files by sending them links and passwords to pages on the dcleaks.com website that had not yet become public. For example, on July 14, 2016, GRU officers operating under the DCLeaks persona sent a link and password for a non-public DCLeaks webpage to a U.S. reporter via the Facebook account.[143] Similarly, on September 14, 2016, GRU officers sent reporters Twitter direct messages from @dcleaks_, with a password to another non-public part of the dcleaks.com website.[144]

The DCLeaks.com website remained operational and public until March 2017.

2. Guccifer 2.0

On June 14, 2016, the DNC and its cyber-response team announced the breach of the DNC network and suspected theft of DNC documents. In the statements, the cyber-response team alleged that Russian state-sponsored actors (which they referred to as "Fancy Bear") were responsible for the breach.[145] Apparently in response to that announcement, on June 15, 2016, GRU officers using the persona Guccifer 2.0 created a WordPress blog. In the hours leading up to the launch of that WordPress blog, GRU officers logged into a Moscow-based server used and managed by Unit 74455 and searched for a number of specific words and phrases in English, including "some hundred sheets," "illuminati," and "worldwide known." Approximately two hours after the last of those searches, Guccifer 2.0 published its first post, attributing the DNC server hack to a lone Romanian hacker and using several of the unique English words and phrases that the GRU officers had searched for that day.[146]

Tennessee-based web-hosting company, called Smartech Corporation. William Bastone, *RNC E-Mail Was, In Fact, Hacked By Russians*, The Smoking Gun (Dec. 13, 2016).

[141] *Netyksho* Indictment ¶ 38.

[142] *See, e.g.*, Facebook Account 100008825623541 (Alice Donovan).

[143] 7/14/16 Facebook Message, ID 793058100795341 (DC Leaks) to ID Personal Privacy

[144] *See, e.g.,* 9/14/16 Twitter DM, @dcleaks_ to Personal Privacy ; 9/14/16 Twitter DM, @dcleaks_ to Personal Privacy . The messages read: "Hi https://t.co/QTvKUjQcOx pass: KvFsg%*14@gPgu& enjoy ;)."

[145] Dmitri Alperovitch, *Bears in the Midst: Intrusion into the Democratic National Committee*, CrowdStrike Blog (June 14, 2016). CrowdStrike updated its post after the June 15, 2016 post by Guccifer 2.0 claiming responsibility for the intrusion.

[146] *Netyksho* Indictment ¶¶ 41-42.

That same day, June 15, 2016, the GRU also used the Guccifer 2.0 WordPress blog to begin releasing to the public documents stolen from the DNC and DCCC computer networks. The Guccifer 2.0 persona ultimately released thousands of documents stolen from the DNC and DCCC in a series of blog posts between June 15, 2016 and October 18, 2016.[147] Released documents included opposition research performed by the DNC (including a memorandum analyzing potential criticisms of candidate Trump), internal policy documents (such as recommendations on how to address politically sensitive issues), analyses of specific congressional races, and fundraising documents. Releases were organized around thematic issues, such as specific states (*e.g.*, Florida and Pennsylvania) that were perceived as competitive in the 2016 U.S. presidential election.

Beginning in late June 2016, the GRU also used the Guccifer 2.0 persona to release documents directly to reporters and other interested individuals. Specifically, on June 27, 2016, Guccifer 2.0 sent an email to the news outlet The Smoking Gun offering to provide "exclusive access to some leaked emails linked [to] Hillary Clinton's staff."[148] The GRU later sent the reporter a password and link to a locked portion of the dcleaks.com website that contained an archive of emails stolen by Unit 26165 from a Clinton Campaign volunteer in March 2016.[149] That the Guccifer 2.0 persona provided reporters access to a restricted portion of the DCLeaks website tends to indicate that both personas were operated by the same or a closely-related group of people.[150]

The GRU continued its release efforts through Guccifer 2.0 into August 2016. For example, on August 15, 2016, the Guccifer 2.0 persona sent a candidate for the U.S. Congress documents related to the candidate's opponent.[151] On August 22, 2016, the Guccifer 2.0 persona transferred approximately 2.5 gigabytes of Florida-related data stolen from the DCCC to a U.S. blogger covering Florida politics.[152] On August 22, 2016, the Guccifer 2.0 persona sent a U.S. reporter documents stolen from the DCCC pertaining to the Black Lives Matter movement.[153]

---

[147] Releases of documents on the Guccifer 2.0 blog occurred on June 15, 2016; June 20, 2016; June 21, 2016; July 6, 2016; July 14, 2016; August 12, 2016; August 15, 2016; August 21, 2016; August 31, 2016; September 15, 2016; September 23, 2016; October 4, 2016; and October 18, 2016.

[148] 6/27/16 Email, guccifer20@aol.fr to ███████████ (subject "leaked emails"); ███

[149] 6/27/16 Email, guccifer20@aol.fr to ███████████ (subject "leaked emails"); ███ ; *see also* 6/27/16 Email, guccifer20@aol.fr to ███████████ (subject "leaked emails"); ███████████ (claiming DCLeaks was a "Wikileaks sub project").

[150] Before sending the reporter the link and password to the closed DCLeaks website, and in an apparent effort to deflect attention from the fact that DCLeaks and Guccifer 2.0 were operated by the same organization, the Guccifer 2.0 persona sent the reporter an email stating that DCLeaks was a "Wikileaks sub project" and that Guccifer 2.0 had asked DCLeaks to release the leaked emails with "closed access" to give reporters a preview of them.

[151] *Netyksho* Indictment ¶ 43(a).

[152] *Netyksho* Indictment ¶ 43(b).

[153] *Netyksho* Indictment ¶ 43(c).

The GRU was also in contact through the Guccifer 2.0 persona with HOM   a former Trump Campaign member Harm to Ongoing Matter

■

[154] In early August 2016, HOM   Twitter's suspension of the Guccifer 2.0 Twitter account. After it was reinstated, GRU officers posing as Guccifer 2.0 wrote HOM via private message, "thank u for writing back . . . do u find anyt[h]ing interesting in the docs i posted?" On August 17, 2016, the GRU added, "please tell me if i can help u anyhow . . . it would be a great pleasure to me." On September 9, 2016, the GRU—again posing as Guccifer 2.0—referred to a stolen DCCC document posted online and asked HOM "what do u think of the info on the turnout model for the democrats entire presidential campaign." HOM responded, "pretty standard."[155] The investigation did not identify evidence of other communications between HOM and Guccifer 2.0.

3. Use of WikiLeaks

In order to expand its interference in the 2016 U.S. presidential election, the GRU units transferred many of the documents they stole from the DNC and the chairman of the Clinton Campaign to WikiLeaks. GRU officers used both the DCLeaks and Guccifer 2.0 personas to communicate with WikiLeaks through Twitter private messaging and through encrypted channels, including possibly through WikiLeaks's private communication system.

a. WikiLeaks's Expressed Opposition Toward the Clinton Campaign

WikiLeaks, and particularly its founder Julian Assange, privately expressed opposition to candidate Clinton well before the first release of stolen documents. In November 2015, Assange wrote to other members and associates of WikiLeaks that "[w]e believe it would be much better for GOP to win . . . Dems+Media+liberals woudl [sic] then form a block to reign in their worst qualities. . . . With Hillary in charge, GOP will be pushing for her worst qualities., dems+media+neoliberals will be mute. . . . She's a bright, well connected, sadisitic sociopath."[156]

In March 2016, WikiLeaks released a searchable archive of approximately 30,000 Clinton emails that had been obtained through FOIA litigation.[157] While designing the archive, one WikiLeaks member explained the reason for building the archive to another associate:

---

[154] HOM

[155] Harm to Ongoing Matter

[156] 11/19/15 Twitter Group Chat, Group ID 594242937858486276, @WikiLeaks et al. Assange also wrote that, "GOP will generate a lot oposition [sic], including through dumb moves. Hillary will do the same thing, but co-opt the liberal opposition and the GOP opposition. Hence hillary has greater freedom to start wars than the GOP and has the will to do so." *Id.*

[157] WikiLeaks, "Hillary Clinton Email Archive," *available at* https://wikileaks.org/clinton-emails/.

44

[W]e want this repository to become "the place" to search for background on hillary's plotting at the state department during 2009-2013. . . . Firstly because its useful and will annoy Hillary, but secondly because we want to be seen to be a resource/player in the US election, because eit [sic] may en[]courage people to send us even more important leaks.[158]

b. WikiLeaks's First Contact with Guccifer 2.0 and DCLeaks

Shortly after the GRU's first release of stolen documents through dcleaks.com in June 2016, GRU officers also used the DCLeaks persona to contact WikiLeaks about possible coordination in the future release of stolen emails. On June 14, 2016, @dcleaks_ sent a direct message to @WikiLeaks, noting, "You announced your organization was preparing to publish more Hillary's emails. We are ready to support you. We have some sensitive information too, in particular, her financial documents. Let's do it together. What do you think about publishing our info at the same moment? Thank you."[159] ▉Investigative Technique▉

Around the same time, WikiLeaks initiated communications with the GRU persona Guccifer 2.0 shortly after it was used to release documents stolen from the DNC. On June 22, 2016, seven days after Guccifer 2.0's first releases of stolen DNC documents, WikiLeaks used Twitter's direct message function to contact the Guccifer 2.0 Twitter account and suggest that Guccifer 2.0 "[s]end any new material [stolen from the DNC] here for us to review and it will have a much higher impact than what you are doing."[160]

On July 6, 2016, WikiLeaks again contacted Guccifer 2.0 through Twitter's private messaging function, writing, "if you have anything hillary related we want it in the next tweo [sic] days prefable [sic] because the DNC is approaching and she will solidify bernie supporters behind her after." The Guccifer 2.0 persona responded, "ok . . . i see." WikiLeaks also explained, "we think trump has only a 25% chance of winning against hillary . . . so conflict between bernie and hillary is interesting."[161]

c. The GRU's Transfer of Stolen Materials to WikiLeaks

Both the GRU and WikiLeaks sought to hide their communications, which has limited the Office's ability to collect all of the communications between them. Thus, although it is clear that the stolen DNC and Podesta documents were transferred from the GRU to WikiLeaks, ▉▉▉ ▉Investigative Technique▉

---

[158] 3/14/16 Twitter DM, @WikiLeaks to ▉PP▉ Less than two weeks earlier, the same account had been used to send a private message opposing the idea of Clinton "in whitehouse with her bloodlutt and amitions [sic] of empire with hawkish liberal-interventionist appointees." 11/19/15 Twitter Group Chat, Group ID 594242937858486276, @WikiLeaks et al.

[159] 6/14/16 Twitter DM, @dcleaks_ to @WikiLeaks.

[160] *Netyksho* Indictment ¶ 47(a).

[161] 7/6/16 Twitter DMs, @WikiLeaks & @guccifer_2.

The Office was able to identify when the GRU (operating through its personas Guccifer 2.0 and DCLeaks) transferred some of the stolen documents to WikiLeaks through online archives set up by the GRU. Assange had access to the internet from the Ecuadorian Embassy in London, England. ▇▇Investigative Technique▇▇▇[62]

On July 14, 2016, GRU officers used a Guccifer 2.0 email account to send WikiLeaks an email bearing the subject "big archive" and the message "a new attempt."[163] The email contained an encrypted attachment with the name "wk dnc link1.txt.gpg."[164] Using the Guccifer 2.0 Twitter account, GRU officers sent WikiLeaks an encrypted file and instructions on how to open it.[165] On July 18, 2016, WikiLeaks confirmed in a direct message to the Guccifer 2.0 account that it had "the 1Gb or so archive" and would make a release of the stolen documents "this week."[166] On July 22, 2016, WikiLeaks released over 20,000 emails and other documents stolen from the DNC computer networks.[167] The Democratic National Convention began three days later.

Similar communications occurred between WikiLeaks and the GRU-operated persona DCLeaks. On September 15, 2016, @dcleaks wrote to @WikiLeaks, "hi there! I'm from DC Leaks. How could we discuss some submission-related issues? Am trying to reach out to you via your secured chat but getting no response. I've got something that might interest you. You won't be disappointed, I promise."[168] The WikiLeaks account responded, "Hi there," without further elaboration. The @dcleaks_ account did not respond immediately.

The same day, the Twitter account @guccifer_2 sent @dcleaks_ a direct message, which is the first known contact between the personas.[169] During subsequent communications, the

---

[162]▇▇Investigative Technique▇▇▇

[163] This was not the GRU's first attempt at transferring data to WikiLeaks. On June 29, 2016, the GRU used a Guccifer 2.0 email account to send a large encrypted file to a WikiLeaks email account. 6/29/16 Email, guccifer2@mail.com ▇T▇▇▇▇▇▇▇▇▇▇▇▇▇▇▇▇▇ (The email appears to have been undelivered.)

[164] See SM-2589105-DCLEAKS, serial 28 (analysis).

[165] 6/27/16 Twitter DM, @Guccifer_2 to @WikiLeaks.

[166] 7/18/16 Twitter DM, @Guccifer_2 & @WikiLeaks.

[167] "DNC Email Archive," WikiLeaks (Jul. 22, 2016), *available at* https://wikileaks.org/dnc-emails.

[168] 9/15/16 Twitter DM, @dcleaks_ to @WikiLeaks.

[169] 9/15/16 Twitter DM, @guccifer_2 to @dcleaks_.

Guccifer 2.0 persona informed DCLeaks that WikiLeaks was trying to contact DCLeaks and arrange for a way to speak through encrypted emails.[170]

An analysis of the metadata collected from the WikiLeaks site revealed that the stolen Podesta emails show a creation date of September 19, 2016.[171] Based on information about Assange's computer and its possible operating system, this date may be when the GRU staged the stolen Podesta emails for transfer to WikiLeaks (as the GRU had previously done in July 2016 for the DNC emails).[172] The WikiLeaks site also released PDFs and other documents taken from Podesta that were attachments to emails in his account; these documents had a creation date of October 2, 2016, which appears to be the date the attachments were separately staged by WikiLeaks on its site.[173]

Beginning on September 20, 2016, WikiLeaks and DCLeaks resumed communications in a brief exchange. On September 22, 2016, a DCLeaks email account dcleaksproject@gmail.com sent an email to a WikiLeaks account with the subject "Submission" and the message "Hi from DCLeaks." The email contained a PGP-encrypted message with the filename "wiki_mail.txt.gpg."[174] ▓Investigative Technique▓. The email, however, bears a number of similarities to the July 14, 2016 email in which GRU officers used the Guccifer 2.0 persona to give WikiLeaks access to the archive of DNC files. On September 22, 2016 (the same day of DCLeaks' email to WikiLeaks), the Twitter account @dcleaks_ sent a single message to @WikiLeaks with the string of characters ▓Investigative Technique▓

The Office cannot rule out that stolen documents were transferred to WikiLeaks through intermediaries who visited during the summer of 2016. For example, public reporting identified Andrew Müller-Maguhn as a WikiLeaks associate who may have assisted with the transfer of these stolen documents to WikiLeaks.[175] ▓Investigative Technique▓

---

[170] *See* SM-2589105-DCLEAKS, serial 28; 9/15/16 Twitter DM, @Guccifer_2 & @WikiLeaks.

[171] *See* SM-2284941, serials 63 & 64 ▓Investigative Technique▓

[172] ▓Investigative Technique▓ At the time, certain Apple operating systems used a setting that left a downloaded file's creation date the same as the creation date shown on the host computer. This would explain why the creation date on WikiLeaks's version of the files was still September 19, 2016. *See* SM-2284941, serial 62 ▓Investigative Technique▓

[173] When WikiLeaks saved attachments separately from the stolen emails, its computer system appears to have treated each attachment as a new file and given it a new creation date. *See* SM-2284941, serials 63 & 64.

[174] *See* 9/22/16 Email, dcleaksproject@gmail.com ▓IT▓

[175] Ellen Nakashima et al., *A German Hacker Offers a Rare Look Inside the Secretive World of Julian Assange and WikiLeaks*, Washington Post (Jan. 17, 2018).

Investigative Technique [176]

On October 7, 2016, WikiLeaks released the first emails stolen from the Podesta email account. In total, WikiLeaks released 33 tranches of stolen emails between October 7, 2016 and November 7, 2016. The releases included private speeches given by Clinton;[177] internal communications between Podesta and other high-ranking members of the Clinton Campaign;[178] and correspondence related to the Clinton Foundation.[179] In total, WikiLeaks released over 50,000 documents stolen from Podesta's personal email account. The last-in-time email released from Podesta's account was dated March 21, 2016, two days after Podesta received a spearphishing email sent by the GRU.

d. WikiLeaks Statements Dissembling About the Source of Stolen Materials

As reports attributing the DNC and DCCC hacks to the Russian government emerged, WikiLeaks and Assange made several public statements apparently designed to obscure the source of the materials that WikiLeaks was releasing. The file-transfer evidence described above and other information uncovered during the investigation discredit WikiLeaks's claims about the source of material that it posted.

Beginning in the summer of 2016, Assange and WikiLeaks made a number of statements about Seth Rich, a former DNC staff member who was killed in July 2016. The statements about Rich implied falsely that he had been the source of the stolen DNC emails. On August 9, 2016, the @WikiLeaks Twitter account posted: "ANNOUNCE: WikiLeaks has decided to issue a US$20k reward for information leading to conviction for the murder of DNC staffer Seth Rich."[180] Likewise, on August 25, 2016, Assange was asked in an interview, "Why are you so interested in Seth Rich's killer?" and responded, "We're very interested in anything that might be a threat to alleged Wikileaks sources." The interviewer responded to Assange's statement by commenting, "I know you don't want to reveal your source, but it certainly sounds like you're suggesting a man who leaked information to WikiLeaks was then murdered." Assange replied, "If there's someone who's potentially connected to our publication, and that person has been murdered in suspicious

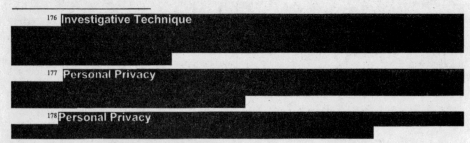

[176] Investigative Technique

[177] Personal Privacy

[178] Personal Privacy

[179] *Netyksho* Indictment ¶ 43.

[180] @WikiLeaks 8/9/16 Tweet.

circumstances, it doesn't necessarily mean that the two are connected. But it is a very serious matter…that type of allegation is very serious, as it's taken very seriously by us."[181]

After the U.S. intelligence community publicly announced its assessment that Russia was behind the hacking operation, Assange continued to deny that the Clinton materials released by WikiLeaks had come from Russian hacking. According to media reports, Assange told a U.S. congressman that the DNC hack was an "inside job," and purported to have "physical proof" that Russians did not give materials to Assange.[182]

C. Additional GRU Cyber Operations

While releasing the stolen emails and documents through DCLeaks, Guccifer 2.0, and WikiLeaks, GRU officers continued to target and hack victims linked to the Democratic campaign and, eventually, to target entities responsible for election administration in several states.

1. Summer and Fall 2016 Operations Targeting Democrat-Linked Victims

On July 27, 2016, Unit 26165 targeted email accounts connected to candidate Clinton's personal office PP███████. Earlier that day, candidate Trump made public statements that included the following: "Russia, if you're listening, I hope you're able to find the 30,000 emails that are missing. I think you will probably be rewarded mightily by our press."[183] The "30,000 emails" were apparently a reference to emails described in media accounts as having been stored on a personal server that candidate Clinton had used while serving as Secretary of State.

Within approximately five hours of Trump's statement, GRU officers targeted for the first time Clinton's personal office. After candidate Trump's remarks, Unit 26165 created and sent malicious links targeting 15 email accounts at the domain PP███████ including an email account belonging to Clinton aide PP███████ The investigation did not find evidence of earlier GRU attempts to compromise accounts hosted on this domain. It is unclear how the GRU was able to identify these email accounts, which were not public.[184]

Unit 26165 officers also hacked into a DNC account hosted on a cloud-computing service Personal Privacy ███████ On September 20, 2016, the GRU began to generate copies of the DNC data using PP███ function designed to allow users to produce backups of databases (referred to PP███ as "snapshots"). The GRU then stole those snapshots by moving

---

[181] See Assange: "Murdered DNC Staffer Was 'Potential' WikiLeaks Source," Fox News (Aug. 25, 2016)(containing video of Assange interview by Megyn Kelly).

[182] M. Raju & Z. Cohen, A GOP Congressman's Lonely Quest Defending Julian Assange, CNN (May 23, 2018).

[183] "Donald Trump on Russian & Missing Hillary Clinton Emails," YouTube Channel C-SPAN, Posted 7/27/16, available at https://www.youtube.com/watch?v=3kxG8uJUsWU (starting at 0:41).

[184] Investigative Technique ████████████████████████████

U.S. Department of Justice

~~Attorney Work Product // May Contain Material Protected Under Fed. R. Crim. P. 6(e)~~

them to ▓PP▓ account that they controlled; from there, the copies were moved to GRU-controlled computers. The GRU stole approximately 300 gigabytes of data from the DNC cloud-based account.[185]

2. Intrusions Targeting the Administration of U.S. Elections

In addition to targeting individuals involved in the Clinton Campaign, GRU officers also targeted individuals and entities involved in the administration of the elections. Victims included U.S. state and local entities, such as state boards of elections (SBOEs), secretaries of state, and county governments, as well as individuals who worked for those entities.[186] The GRU also targeted private technology firms responsible for manufacturing and administering election-related software and hardware, such as voter registration software and electronic polling stations.[187] The GRU continued to target these victims through the elections in November 2016. While the investigation identified evidence that the GRU targeted these individuals and entities, the Office did not investigate further. The Office did not, for instance, obtain or examine servers or other relevant items belonging to these victims. The Office understands that the FBI, the U.S. Department of Homeland Security, and the states have separately investigated that activity.

By at least the summer of 2016, GRU officers sought access to state and local computer networks by exploiting known software vulnerabilities on websites of state and local governmental entities. GRU officers, for example, targeted state and local databases of registered voters using a technique known as "SQL injection," by which malicious code was sent to the state or local website in order to run commands (such as exfiltrating the database contents).[188] In one instance in approximately June 2016, the GRU compromised the computer network of the Illinois State Board of Elections by exploiting a vulnerability in the SBOE's website. The GRU then gained access to a database containing information on millions of registered Illinois voters,[189] and extracted data related to thousands of U.S. voters before the malicious activity was identified.[190]

GRU officers ▓Investigative Technique▓ scanned state and local websites for vulnerabilities. For example, over a two-day period in July 2016, GRU officers ▓Investigative Technique▓ for vulnerabilities on websites of more than two dozen states. ▓Investigative Technique▓

---

[185] *Netyksho* Indictment ¶ 34; *see also* SM-2589105-HACK, serial 29 ▓Investigative Technique▓

[186] *Netyksho* Indictment ¶ 69.

[187] *Netyksho* Indictment ¶ 69; ▓Investigative Technique▓

[188] ▓Investigative Technique▓

[189] ▓Investigative Technique▓

[190] ▓Investigative Technique▓

Investigative Technique

Similar |T | for vulnerabilities continued through the election.

Unit 74455 also sent spearphishing emails to public officials involved in election administration and personnel at companies involved in voting technology. In August 2016, GRU officers targeted employees of **PP**   , a voting technology company that developed software used by numerous U.S. counties to manage voter rolls, and installed malware on the company network. Similarly, in November 2016, the GRU sent spearphishing emails to over 120 email accounts used by Florida county officials responsible for administering the 2016 U.S. election.[191] The spearphishing emails contained an attached Word document coded with malicious software (commonly referred to as a Trojan) that permitted the GRU to access the infected computer.[192] The FBI was separately responsible for this investigation. We understand the FBI believes that this operation enabled the GRU to gain access to the network of at least one Florida county government. The Office did not independently verify that belief and, as explained above, did not undertake the investigative steps that would have been necessary to do so.

D. Trump Campaign and the Dissemination of Hacked Materials

The Trump Campaign showed interest in WikiLeaks's releases of hacked materials throughout the summer and fall of 2016. **Harm to Ongoing Matter**

1. **HOM**

   a. Background

Harm to Ongoing Matter

---

[191] *Netyksho* Indictment ¶ 76; **Investigative Technique**

[192] **Investigative Technique**

51

111

b. Contacts with the Campaign about WikiLeaks

Harm to Ongoing Matter

Harm to Ongoing Matter

[93]

On June 12, 2016, Assange claimed in a televised interview to "have emails relating to Hillary Clinton which are pending publication,"[194] but provided no additional context.

In debriefings with the Office, former deputy campaign chairman Rick Gates said that, **Harm to Ongoing Matter**

Harm to Ongoing Matter

[195]

Gates recalled candidate Trump being generally frustrated that the Clinton emails had not been found.[196]

Paul Manafort, who would later become campaign chairman, **Harm to Ongoing Matter** [197] **Harm to Ongoing Matter**

[198]

---

[193] **Harm to Ongoing Matter**

[194] *See* Mahita Gajanan, *Julian Assange Timed DNC Email Release for Democratic Convention,* Time (July 27, 2016) (quoting the June 12, 2016 television interview).

[195] In February 2018, Gates pleaded guilty, pursuant to a plea agreement, to a superseding criminal information charging him with conspiring to defraud and commit multiple offenses (*i.e.*, tax fraud, failure to report foreign bank accounts, and acting as an unregistered agent of a foreign principal) against the United States, as well as making false statements to our Office. Superseding Criminal Information, *United States v. Richard W. Gates III*, 1:17-cr-201 (D.D.C. Feb. 23, 2018), Doc. 195 ("*Gates* Superseding Criminal Information"); Plea Agreement, *United States v. Richard W. Gates III*, 1:17-cr-201 (D.D.C. Feb. 23, 2018), Doc. 205 ("*Gates* Plea Agreement"). Gates has provided information and in-court testimony that the Office has deemed to be reliable.

[196] Gates 10/25/18 302, at 1-2.

[197] As explained further in Volume I, Section IV.A.8, *infra*, Manafort entered into a plea agreement with our Office. We determined that he breached the agreement by being untruthful in proffer sessions and before the grand jury. We have generally recounted his version of events in this report only when his statements are sufficiently corroborated to be trustworthy; to identify issues on which Manafort's untruthful responses may themselves be of evidentiary value; or to provide Manafort's explanations for certain events, even when we were unable to determine whether that explanation was credible. His account appears here principally because it aligns with those of other witnesses.

[198] **Grand Jury**

Michael Cohen, former executive vice president of the Trump Organization and special counsel to Donald J. Trump,[199] told the Office that he recalled an incident in which he was in candidate Trump's office in Trump Tower Harm to Ongoing Matter

[200]

Harm to Ongoing Matter

[201] Cohen further told the Office that, after WikiLeaks's subsequent release of stolen DNC emails in July 2016, candidate Trump said to Cohen something to the effect of, HOM

[202]

Harm to Ongoing Matter

According to Gates, Manafort expressed excitement about the release HOM [203] Manafort, for his part, told the Office that, shortly after WikiLeaks's July 22 release, Manafort also spoke with candidate Trump

Harm to Ongoing Matter

[204] Harm to Ongoing Matter

[205] Manafort also HOM wanted to be kept apprised of any

---

[199] In November 2018, Cohen pleaded guilty pursuant to a plea agreement to a single-count information charging him with making false statements to Congress, in violation of 18 U.S.C. § 1001(a) & (c). He had previously pleaded guilty to several other criminal charges brought by the U.S. Attorney's Office in the Southern District of New York, after a referral from this Office. In the months leading up to his false-statements guilty plea, Cohen met with our Office on multiple occasions for interviews and provided information that the Office has generally assessed to be reliable and that is included in this report.

[200] HOM

[201] Harm to Ongoing Matter

[202] Cohen 9/18/18 302, at 10. Harm to Ongoing Matter

Harm to Ongoing Matter

Harm to Ongoing Matter

[203] Gates 10/25/18 302 (serial 241), at 4.

[204] Grand Jury

[205] Grand Jury

developments with WikiLeaks and separately told Gates to keep in touch HOM about future WikiLeaks releases.[206]

 According to Gates, by the late summer of 2016, the Trump Campaign was planning a press strategy, a communications campaign, and messaging based on the possible release of Clinton emails by WikiLeaks.[207] Harm to Ongoing Matter [208] Harm to Ongoing Matter while Trump and Gates were driving to LaGuardia Airport. Harm to Ongoing Matter , shortly after the call candidate Trump told Gates that more releases of damaging information would be coming.[209]

Harm to Ongoing Matter [10]

c. Harm to Ongoing Matter

Harm to Ongoing Matter [11]

Corsi is an author who holds a doctorate in political science.[212] In 2016, Corsi also worked for the media outlet WorldNetDaily (WND). Harm to Ongoing Matter [13]

---

[206] Grand Jury

[207] Gates 4/10/18 302, at 3; Gates 4/11/18 302, at 1-2 (SM-2180998); Gates 10/25/18 302, at 2.

[208] HOM

[209] Gates 10/25/18 302 (serial 241), at 4.

[210] HOM

[211] HOM

[212] Corsi first rose to public prominence in August 2004 when he published his book *Unfit for Command: Swift Boat Veterans Speak Out Against John Kerry.* In the 2008 election cycle, Corsi gained prominence for being a leading proponent of the allegation that Barack Obama was not born in the United States. Corsi told the Office that Donald Trump expressed interest in his writings, and that he spoke with Trump on the phone on at least six occasions. Corsi 9/6/18 302, at 3.

[213] Corsi 10/31/18 302, at 2; Grand Jury Corsi was first interviewed on September 6, 2018 at the Special Counsel's offices in Washington, D.C. He was accompanied by counsel throughout the interview. Corsi was subsequently interviewed on September 17, 2018; September 21, 2018; October 31, 2018; November 1, 2018; and November 2, 2018. Counsel was

Harm to Ongoing Matter

[14] Corsi told the Office during interviews that he "must have" previously discussed Assange with Malloch.[215]

Harm to Ongoing Matter

[216] **Harm to Ongoing Matter**

[217]

Grand Jury

According to Malloch, Corsi asked him to put Corsi in touch with Assange, whom Corsi wished to interview. Malloch recalled that Corsi also suggested that individuals in the "orbit" of U.K. politician Nigel Farage might be able to contact Assange and asked if Malloch knew them. Malloch told Corsi that he would think about the request but made no actual attempt to connect Corsi with Assange.[218]

Harm to Ongoing Matter

[19]

Harm to Ongoing Matter

[20]

---

present for all interviews, and the interviews beginning on September 21, 2018 were conducted pursuant to a proffer agreement that precluded affirmative use of his statements against him in limited circumstances.

[214] HOM

[215] Corsi 10/31/18 302, at 4.

[216] HOM

[217] HOM

[218] Grand Jury Malloch denied ever communicating with Assange or WikiLeaks, stating that he did not pursue the request to contact Assange because he believed he had no connections to Assange. Grand Jury

[219] HOM

[220] **Harm to Ongoing Matter**

Malloch stated to investigators that beginning in or about August 2016, he and Corsi had multiple FaceTime discussions about WikiLeaks Harm to Ongoing Matter had made a connection to Assange and that the hacked emails of John Podesta would be released prior to Election Day and would be helpful to the Trump Campaign. In one conversation in or around August or September 2016, Corsi told Malloch that the release of the Podesta emails was coming, after which "we" were going to be in the driver's seat.[221]

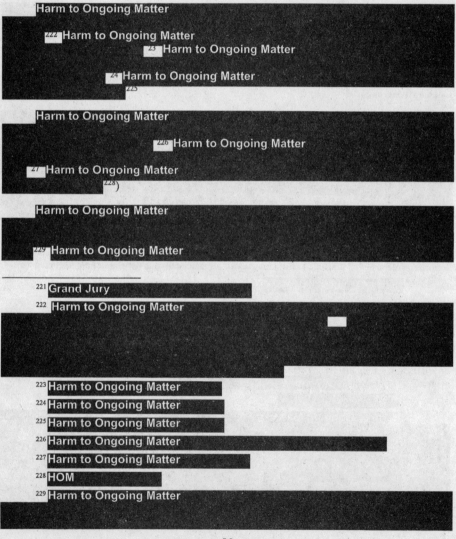

Harm to Ongoing Matter

[222] Harm to Ongoing Matter
[23] Harm to Ongoing Matter

[24] Harm to Ongoing Matter
225

Harm to Ongoing Matter

[226] Harm to Ongoing Matter

[27] Harm to Ongoing Matter
228)

Harm to Ongoing Matter

[229] Harm to Ongoing Matter

---

[221] Grand Jury
[222] Harm to Ongoing Matter

[223] Harm to Ongoing Matter
[224] Harm to Ongoing Matter
[225] Harm to Ongoing Matter
[226] Harm to Ongoing Matter
[227] Harm to Ongoing Matter
[228] HOM
[229] Harm to Ongoing Matter

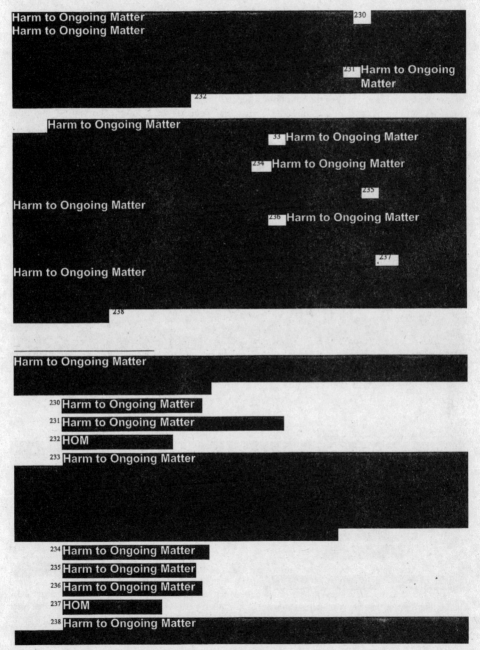

Harm to Ongoing Matter
Harm to Ongoing Matter

[230]

[231] Harm to Ongoing Matter

[232]

Harm to Ongoing Matter

[33] Harm to Ongoing Matter

[234] Harm to Ongoing Matter

[235]

Harm to Ongoing Matter

[236] Harm to Ongoing Matter

[237]

Harm to Ongoing Matter

[238]

Harm to Ongoing Matter

[230] Harm to Ongoing Matter
[231] Harm to Ongoing Matter
[232] HOM
[233] Harm to Ongoing Matter

[234] Harm to Ongoing Matter
[235] Harm to Ongoing Matter
[236] Harm to Ongoing Matter
[237] HOM
[238] Harm to Ongoing Matter

57

117

d. WikiLeaks's October 7, 2016 Release of Stolen Podesta Emails

On October 7, 2016, four days after the Assange press conference HOM ██████████████████████, the Washington Post published an *Access Hollywood* video that captured comments by candidate Trump some years earlier and that was expected to adversely affect the Campaign.[239] Less than an hour after the video's publication, WikiLeaks released the first set of emails stolen by the GRU from the account of Clinton Campaign chairman John Podesta.

Harm to Ongoing Matter

[240] Harm to Ongoing Matter

[241] Harm to Ongoing Matter

[242]

Harm to Ongoing Matter
[43] Harm to Ongoing Matter

Corsi said that, because he had no direct means of communicating with WikiLeaks, he told members of the news site WND—who were participating on a conference call with him that day—to reach Assange immediately.[244] Corsi claimed that the pressure was

---

Harm to Ongoing Matter

[239] Candidate Trump can be heard off camera making graphic statements about women.

[240] HOM ████████

[241] HOM ████████

[242] HOM ████████

[243] HOM ████████

[244] In a later November 2018 interview, Corsi stated Harm to Ongoing Matter ██████████████ that he believed Malloch was on the call but then focused on other individuals who were on the call-invitation, which Malloch was not. (Separate travel records show that at the time of the call, Malloch was aboard a transatlantic flight). Corsi at one point stated that after WikiLeaks's release of stolen emails on October 7, 2016, he concluded Malloch had gotten in contact with Assange. Corsi 11/1/18 302, at 6.

U.S. Department of Justice

Attorney Work Product // May Contain Material Protected Under Fed. R. Crim. P. 6(e)

enormous and recalled telling the conference call the *Access Hollywood* tape was coming.[245] Corsi stated that he was convinced that his efforts had caused WikiLeaks to release the emails when they did.[246] In a later November 2018 interview, Corsi stated that he thought that he had told people on a WND conference call about the forthcoming tape and had sent out a tweet asking whether anyone could contact Assange, but then said that maybe he had done nothing.[247]

The Office investigated Corsi's allegations about the events of October 7, 2016 but found little corroboration for his allegations about the day.[248] Harm to Ongoing Matter
[249] Harm to Ongoing Matter

[50] However, the phone records themselves do not indicate that the conversation was with any of the reporters who broke the *Access Hollywood* story, and the Office has not otherwise been able to identify the substance of the conversation. Harm to Ongoing Matter

.[251] However, the Office has not identified any conference call participant, or anyone who spoke to Corsi that day, who says that they received non-public information about the tape from Corsi or acknowledged having contacted a member of WikiLeaks on October 7, 2016 after a conversation with Corsi.

e. Donald Trump Jr. Interaction with WikiLeaks

Donald Trump Jr. had direct electronic communications with WikiLeaks during the campaign period. On September 20, 2016, an individual named Jason Fishbein sent WikiLeaks the password for an unlaunched website focused on Trump's "unprecedented and dangerous" ties

---

[245] During the same interview, Corsi also suggested that he may have sent out public tweets because he knew Assange was reading his tweets. Our Office was unable to find evidence of any such tweets.

[246] Corsi 9/21/18 302, at 6-7.

[247] Corsi 11/1/18 302, at 6.

[248] Harm to Ongoing Matter
Grand Jury

[249] Harm to Ongoing Matter

[250] HOM   Grand Jury   Harm to Ongoing Matter

[251] HOM   Grand Jury   Harm to Ongoing Matter
Grand Jury
Harm to Ongoing Matter

59

U.S. Department of Justice

~~Attorney Work Product~~ // ~~May Contain Material Protected Under Fed. R. Crim. P. 6(e)~~

to Russia, PutinTrump.org.[252] WikiLeaks publicly tweeted: "'Let's bomb Iraq' Progress for America PAC to launch "PutinTrump.org' at 9:30am. Oops pw is 'putintrump' putintrump.org." Several hours later, WikiLeaks sent a Twitter direct message to Donald Trump Jr., "A PAC run anti-Trump site putintrump.org is about to launch. The PAC is a recycled pro-Iraq war PAC. We have guessed the password. It is 'putintrump.' See 'About' for who is behind it. Any comments?"[253].

Several hours later, Trump Jr. emailed a variety of senior campaign staff:

Guys I got a weird Twitter DM from wikileaks. See below. I tried the password and it works and the about section they reference contains the next pic in terms of who is behind it. Not sure if this is anything but it seems like it's really wikileaks asking me as I follow them and it is a DM. Do you know the people mentioned and what the conspiracy they are looking for could be? These are just screen shots but it's a fully built out page claiming to be a PAC let me know your thoughts and if we want to look into it.[254]

Trump Jr. attached a screenshot of the "About" page for the unlaunched site PutinTrump.org. The next day (after the website had launched publicly), Trump Jr. sent a direct message to WikiLeaks: "Off the record, I don't know who that is but I'll ask around. Thanks."[255]

On October 3, 2016, WikiLeaks sent another direct message to Trump Jr., asking "you guys" to help disseminate a link alleging candidate Clinton had advocated using a drone to target Julian Assange. Trump Jr. responded that he already "had done so," and asked, "what's behind this Wednesday leak I keep reading about?"[256] WikiLeaks did not respond.

On October 12, 2016, WikiLeaks wrote again that it was "great to see you and your dad talking about our publications. Strongly suggest your dad tweets this link if he mentions us wlsearch.tk."[257] WikiLeaks wrote that the link would help Trump in "digging through" leaked emails and stated, "we just released Podesta emails Part 4."[258] Two days later, Trump Jr. publicly tweeted the wlsearch.tk link.[259]

---

[252] 9/20/16 Twitter DM, @JasonFishbein to @WikiLeaks; see JF00587 (9/21/16 Messages, ██ @jabber.cryptoparty.is & ██ @jabber.cryptoparty.is); Fishbein 9/5/18 302, at 4. When interviewed by our Office, Fishbein produced what he claimed to be logs from a chatroom in which the participants discussed U.S. politics; one of the other participants had posted the website and password that Fishbein sent to WikiLeaks.

[253] 9/20/16 Twitter DM, @WikiLeaks to @DonaldJTrumpJr.

[254] TRUMPORG_28_000629-33 (9/21/16 Email, Trump Jr. to Conway et al. (subject "Wikileaks")).

[255] 9/21/16 Twitter DM, @DonaldJTrumpJr to @WikiLeaks.

[256] 10/3/16 Twitter DMs, @DonaldJTrumpJr & @WikiLeaks.

[257] At the time, the link took users to a WikiLeaks archive of stolen Clinton Campaign documents.

[258] 10/12/16 Twitter DM, @WikiLeaks to @DonaldJTrumpJr.

[259] @DonaldJTrumpJr 10/14/16 (6:34 a.m.) Tweet.

2. Other Potential Campaign Interest in Russian Hacked Materials

Throughout 2016, the Trump Campaign expressed interest in Hillary Clinton's private email server and whether approximately 30,000 emails from that server had in fact been permanently destroyed, as reported by the media. Several individuals associated with the Campaign were contacted in 2016 about various efforts to obtain the missing Clinton emails and other stolen material in support of the Trump Campaign. Some of these contacts were met with skepticism, and nothing came of them; others were pursued to some degree. The investigation did not find evidence that the Trump Campaign recovered any such Clinton emails, or that these contacts were part of a coordinated effort between Russia and the Trump Campaign.

a. Henry Oknyansky (a/k/a Henry Greenberg)

In the spring of 2016, Trump Campaign advisor Michael Caputo learned through a Florida-based Russian business partner that another Florida-based Russian, Henry Oknyansky (who also went by the name Henry Greenberg), claimed to have information pertaining to Hillary Clinton. Caputo notified Roger Stone and brokered communication between Stone and Oknyansky. Oknyansky and Stone set up a May 2016 in-person meeting.[260]

Oknyansky was accompanied to the meeting by Alexei Rasin, a Ukrainian associate involved in Florida real estate. At the meeting, Rasin offered to sell Stone derogatory information on Clinton that Rasin claimed to have obtained while working for Clinton. Rasin claimed to possess financial statements demonstrating Clinton's involvement in money laundering with Rasin's companies. According to Oknyansky, Stone asked if the amounts in question totaled millions of dollars but was told it was closer to hundreds of thousands. Stone refused the offer, stating that Trump would not pay for opposition research.[261]

Oknyansky claimed to the Office that Rasin's motivation was financial. According to Oknyansky, Rasin had tried unsuccessfully to shop the Clinton information around to other interested parties, and Oknyansky would receive a cut if the information was sold.[262] Rasin is noted in public source documents as the director and/or registered agent for a number of Florida companies, none of which appears to be connected to Clinton. The Office found no other evidence that Rasin worked for Clinton or any Clinton-related entities.

In their statements to investigators, Oknyansky and Caputo had contradictory recollections about the meeting. Oknyansky claimed that Caputo accompanied Stone to the meeting and provided an introduction, whereas Caputo did not tell us that he had attended and claimed that he was never told what information Oknyansky offered. Caputo also stated that he was unaware Oknyansky sought to be paid for the information until Stone informed him after the fact.[263]

---

[260] Caputo 5/2/18 302, at 4; Oknyansky 7/13/18 302, at 1.

[261] Oknyansky 7/13/18 302, at 1-2.

[262] Oknyansky 7/13/18 302, at 2.

[263] Caputo 5/2/18 302, at 4; Oknyansky 7/13/18 302, at 1.

U.S. Department of Justice
Attorney Work Product // May Contain Material Protected Under Fed. R. Crim. P. 6(e)

The Office did not locate Rasin in the United States, although the Office confirmed Rasin had been issued a Florida driver's license. The Office otherwise was unable to determine the content and origin of the information he purportedly offered to Stone. Finally, the investigation did not identify evidence of a connection between the outreach or the meeting and Russian interference efforts.

b. Campaign Efforts to Obtain Deleted Clinton Emails

After candidate Trump stated on July 27, 2016, that he hoped Russia would "find the 30,000 emails that are missing," Trump asked individuals affiliated with his Campaign to find the deleted Clinton emails.[264] Michael Flynn—who would later serve as National Security Advisor in the Trump Administration—recalled that Trump made this request repeatedly, and Flynn subsequently contacted multiple people in an effort to obtain the emails.[265]

Barbara Ledeen and Peter Smith were among the people contacted by Flynn. Ledeen, a long-time Senate staffer who had previously sought the Clinton emails, provided updates to Flynn about her efforts throughout the summer of 2016.[266] Smith, an investment advisor who was active in Republican politics, also attempted to locate and obtain the deleted Clinton emails.[267]

Ledeen began her efforts to obtain the Clinton emails before Flynn's request, as early as December 2015.[268] On December 3, 2015, she emailed Smith a proposal to obtain the emails, stating, "Here is the proposal I briefly mentioned to you. The person I described to you would be happy to talk with you either in person or over the phone. The person can get the emails which 1. Were classified and 2. Were purloined by our enemies. That would demonstrate what needs to be demonstrated."[269]

Attached to the email was a 25-page proposal stating that the "Clinton email server was, in all likelihood, breached long ago," and that the Chinese, Russian, and Iranian intelligence services could "re-assemble the server's email content."[270] The proposal called for a three-phase approach. The first two phases consisted of open-source analysis. The third phase consisted of checking with certain intelligence sources "that have access through liaison work with various foreign services" to determine if any of those services had gotten to the server. The proposal noted, "Even if a single email was recovered and the providence [sic] of that email was a foreign service, it would be catastrophic to the Clinton campaign[.]" Smith forwarded the email to two colleagues and

---

[264] Flynn 4/25/18 302, at 5-6; Flynn 5/1/18 302, at 1-3.

[265] Flynn 5/1/18 302, at 1-3.

[266] Flynn 4/25/18 302, at 7; Flynn 5/4/18 302, at 1-2; Flynn 11/29/17 302, at 7-8.

[267] Flynn 11/29/17 302, at 7.

[268] Szobocsan 3/29/17 302, at 1.

[269] 12/3/15 Email, Ledeen to Smith.

[270] 12/3/15 Email, Ledeen to Smith (attachment).

62

U.S. Department of Justice

~~Attorney Work Product // May Contain Material Protected Under Fed. R. Crim. P. 6(e)~~

wrote, "we can discuss to whom it should be referred."[271] On December 16, 2015, Smith informed Ledeen that he declined to participate in her "initiative." According to one of Smith's business associates, Smith believed Ledeen's initiative was not viable at that time.[272]

Just weeks after Trump's July 2016 request to find the Clinton emails, however, Smith tried to locate and obtain the emails himself. He created a company, raised tens of thousands of dollars, and recruited security experts and business associates. Smith made claims to others involved in the effort (and those from whom he sought funding) that he was in contact with hackers with "ties and affiliations to Russia" who had access to the emails, and that his efforts were coordinated with the Trump Campaign.[273]

On August 28, 2016, Smith sent an email from an encrypted account with the subject "Sec. Clinton's unsecured private email server" to an undisclosed list of recipients, including Campaign co-chairman Sam Clovis. The email stated that Smith was "[j]ust finishing two days of sensitive meetings here in DC with involved groups to poke and probe on the above. It is clear that the Clinton's home-based, unprotected server was hacked with ease by both State-related players, and private mercenaries. Parties with varying interests, are circling to release ahead of the election."[274]

On September 2, 2016, Smith directed a business associate to establish KLS Research LLC in furtherance of his search for the deleted Clinton emails.[275] One of the purposes of KLS Research was to manage the funds Smith raised in support of his initiative.[276] KLS Research received over $30,000 during the presidential campaign, although Smith represented that he raised even more money.[277]

Smith recruited multiple people for his initiative, including security experts to search for and authenticate the emails.[278] In early September 2016, as part of his recruitment and fundraising effort, Smith circulated a document stating that his initiative was "in coordination" with the Trump Campaign, "to the extent permitted as an independent expenditure organization."[279] The document listed multiple individuals affiliated with the Trump Campaign, including Flynn, Clovis, Bannon,

---

[271] 12/3/15 Email, Smith to Szobocsan & Safron.

[272] Szobocsan 3/29/18 302, at 1.

[273] 8/31/16 Email, Smith to Smith.

[274] 8/28/16 Email, Smith to Smith.

[275] Incorporation papers of KLS Research LLC, 7/26/17 ██Grand Jury██ Szobocsan 3/29/18 302, at 2.

[276] Szobocsan 3/29/18 302, at 3.

[277] Financial Institution Record of Peter Smith and KLS Research LLC, 10/31/17 ████ ██Grand Jury██ 10/11/16 Email, Smith to ██Personal Privacy██

[278] Tait 8/22/17 302, at 3; York 7/12/17 302, at 1-2; York 11/22/17 302, at 1.

[279] York 7/13/17 302 (attachment KLS Research, LLC, "Clinton Email Reconnaissance Initiative," Sept. 9, 2016).

U.S. Department of Justice

~~Attorney Work Product // May Contain Material Protected Under Fed. R. Crim. P. 6(e)~~

and Kellyanne Conway.[280] The investigation established that Smith communicated with at least Flynn and Clovis about his search for the deleted Clinton emails,[281] but the Office did not identify evidence that any of the listed individuals initiated or directed Smith's efforts.

In September 2016, Smith and Ledeen got back in touch with each other about their respective efforts. Ledeen wrote to Smith, "wondering if you had some more detailed reports or memos or other data you could share because we have come a long way in our efforts since we last visited. . . . We would need as much technical discussion as possible so we could marry it against the new data we have found and then could share it back to you 'your eyes only.'"[282]

Ledeen claimed to have obtained a trove of emails (from what she described as the "dark web") that purported to be the deleted Clinton emails. Ledeen wanted to authenticate the emails and solicited contributions to fund that effort. Erik Prince provided funding to hire a tech advisor to ascertain the authenticity of the emails. According to Prince, the tech advisor determined that the emails were not authentic.[283]

A backup of Smith's computer contained two files that had been downloaded from WikiLeaks and that were originally attached to emails received by John Podesta. The files on Smith's computer had creation dates of October 2, 2016, which was prior to the date of their release by WikiLeaks. Forensic examination, however, established that the creation date did not reflect when the files were downloaded to Smith's computer. (It appears the creation date was when WikiLeaks staged the document for release, as discussed in Volume I, Section III.B.3.c, *supra*.[284]) The investigation did not otherwise identify evidence that Smith obtained the files before their release by WikiLeaks.

Smith continued to send emails to an undisclosed recipient list about Clinton's deleted emails until shortly before the election. For example, on October 28, 2016, Smith wrote that there was a "tug-of-war going on within WikiLeaks over its planned releases in the next few days," and that WikiLeaks "has maintained that it will save its best revelations for last, under the theory this allows little time for response prior to the U.S. election November 8."[285] An attachment to the

---

[280] The same recruitment document listed Jerome Corsi under "Independent Groups/Organizations/Individuals," and described him as an "established author and writer from the right on President Obama and Sec. Clinton."

[281] Flynn 11/29/17 302, at 7-8; 10/15/16 Email, Smith to Flynn et al.; 8/28/16 Email, Smith to Smith (bcc: Clovis et al.).

[282] 9/16/16 Email, Ledeen to Smith.

[283] Prince 4/4/18 302, at 4-5.

[284] The forensic analysis of Smith's computer devices found that Smith used an older Apple operating system that would have preserved that October 2, 2016 creation date when it was downloaded (no matter what day it was in fact downloaded by Smith). *See* Volume I, Section III.B.3.c, *supra*. The Office tested this theory in March 2019 by downloading the two files found on Smith's computer from WikiLeaks's site using the same Apple operating system on Smith's computer; both files were successfully downloaded and retained the October 2, 2016 creation date. *See* SM-2284941, serial 62.

[285] 10/28/16 Email, Smith to Smith.

U.S. Department of Justice

~~Attorney Work Product // May Contain Material Protected Under Fed. R. Crim. P. 6(e)~~

email claimed that WikiLeaks would release "All 33k deleted Emails" by "November 1st." No emails obtained from Clinton's server were subsequently released.

Smith drafted multiple emails stating or intimating that he was in contact with Russian hackers. For example, in one such email, Smith claimed that, in August 2016, KLS Research had organized meetings with parties who had access to the deleted Clinton emails, including parties with "ties and affiliations to Russia."[286] The investigation did not identify evidence that any such meetings occurred. Associates and security experts who worked with Smith on the initiative did not believe that Smith was in contact with Russian hackers and were aware of no such connection.[287] The investigation did not establish that Smith was in contact with Russian hackers or that Smith, Ledeen, or other individuals in touch with the Trump Campaign ultimately obtained the deleted Clinton emails.

* * *

In sum, the investigation established that the GRU hacked into email accounts of persons affiliated with the Clinton Campaign, as well as the computers of the DNC and DCCC. The GRU then exfiltrated data related to the 2016 election from these accounts and computers, and disseminated that data through fictitious online personas (DCLeaks and Guccifer 2.0) and later through WikiLeaks. The investigation also established that the Trump Campaign displayed interest in the WikiLeaks releases, and that Harm to Ongoing Matter

As explained in Volume I, Section V.B, *infra*, the evidence was sufficient to support computer-intrusion (and other) charges against GRU officers for their role in election-related hacking. Harm to Ongoing Matter

---

[286] 8/31/16 Email, Smith to Smith.

[287] Safron 3/20/18 302, at 3; Szobocsan 3/29/18 302, at 6.

125

U.S. Department of Justice

~~Attorney Work Product~~ // ~~May Contain Material Protected Under Fed. R. Crim. P. 6(e)~~

IV. RUSSIAN GOVERNMENT LINKS TO AND CONTACTS WITH THE TRUMP CAMPAIGN

The Office identified multiple contacts—"links," in the words of the Appointment Order—between Trump Campaign officials and individuals with ties to the Russian government. The Office investigated whether those contacts constituted a third avenue of attempted Russian interference with or influence on the 2016 presidential election. In particular, the investigation examined whether these contacts involved or resulted in coordination or a conspiracy with the Trump Campaign and Russia, including with respect to Russia providing assistance to the Campaign in exchange for any sort of favorable treatment in the future. Based on the available information, the investigation did not establish such coordination.

This Section describes the principal links between the Trump Campaign and individuals with ties to the Russian government, including some contacts with Campaign officials or associates that have been publicly reported to involve Russian contacts. Each subsection begins with an overview of the Russian contact at issue and then describes in detail the relevant facts, which are generally presented in chronological order, beginning with the early months of the Campaign and extending through the post-election, transition period.

A. Campaign Period (September 2015 – November 8, 2016)

Russian-government-connected individuals and media entities began showing interest in Trump's campaign in the months after he announced his candidacy in June 2015.[288] Because Trump's status as a public figure at the time was attributable in large part to his prior business and entertainment dealings, this Office investigated whether a business contact with Russia-linked individuals and entities during the campaign period—the Trump Tower Moscow project, *see* Volume I, Section IV.A.1, *infra*—led to or involved coordination of election assistance.

Outreach from individuals with ties to Russia continued in the spring and summer of 2016, when Trump was moving toward—and eventually becoming—the Republican nominee for President. As set forth below, the Office also evaluated a series of links during this period: outreach to two of Trump's then-recently named foreign policy advisors, including a representation that Russia had "dirt" on Clinton in the form of thousands of emails (Volume I, Sections IV.A.2 & IV.A.3); dealings with a D.C.-based think tank that specializes in Russia and has connections with its government (Volume I, Section IV.A.4); a meeting at Trump Tower between the Campaign and a Russian lawyer promising dirt on candidate Clinton that was "part of Russia and its government's support for [Trump]" (Volume I, Section IV.A.5); events at the Republican National Convention (Volume I, Section IV.A.6); post-Convention contacts between Trump Campaign officials and Russia's ambassador to the United States (Volume I, Section IV.A.7); and contacts through campaign chairman Paul Manafort, who had previously worked for a Russian oligarch and a pro-Russian political party in Ukraine (Volume I, Section IV.A.8).

---

[288] For example, on August 18, 2015, on behalf of the editor-in-chief of the internet newspaper *Vzglyad*, Georgi Asatryan emailed campaign press secretary Hope Hicks asking for a phone or in-person candidate interview. 8/18/15 Email, Asatryan to Hicks. One day earlier, the publication's founder (and former Russian parliamentarian) Konstantin Rykov had registered two Russian websites—Trump2016.ru and DonaldTrump2016.ru. No interview took place.

1. Trump Tower Moscow Project

The Trump Organization has pursued and completed projects outside the United States as part of its real estate portfolio. Some projects have involved the acquisition and ownership (through subsidiary corporate structures) of property. In other cases, the Trump Organization has executed licensing deals with real estate developers and management companies, often local to the country where the project was located.[289]

Between at least 2013 and 2016, the Trump Organization explored a similar licensing deal in Russia involving the construction of a Trump-branded property in Moscow. The project, commonly referred to as a "Trump Tower Moscow" or "Trump Moscow" project, anticipated a combination of commercial, hotel, and residential properties all within the same building. Between 2013 and June 2016, several employees of the Trump Organization, including then-president of the organization Donald J. Trump, pursued a Moscow deal with several Russian counterparties. From the fall of 2015 until the middle of 2016, Michael Cohen spearheaded the Trump Organization's pursuit of a Trump Tower Moscow project, including by reporting on the project's status to candidate Trump and other executives in the Trump Organization.[290]

a. *Trump Tower Moscow Venture with the Crocus Group (2013-2014)*

The Trump Organization and the Crocus Group, a Russian real estate conglomerate owned and controlled by Aras Agalarov, began discussing a Russia-based real estate project shortly after the conclusion of the 2013 Miss Universe pageant in Moscow.[291] Donald J. Trump Jr. served as the primary negotiator on behalf of the Trump Organization; Emin Agalarov (son of Aras Agalarov) and Irakli "Ike" Kaveladze represented the Crocus Group during negotiations,[292] with the occasional assistance of Robert Goldstone.[293]

In December 2013, Kaveladze and Trump Jr. negotiated and signed preliminary terms of

---

[289] *See, e.g., Interview of: Donald J. Trump, Jr, Senate Judiciary Committee*, 115th Cong. 151-52 (Sept. 7, 2017) (discussing licensing deals of specific projects).

[290] As noted in Volume I, Section III.D.1, *supra*, in November 2018, Cohen pleaded guilty to making false statements to Congress concerning, among other things, the duration of the Trump Tower Moscow project. *See* Information ¶ 7(a), *United States v. Michael Cohen*, 1:18-cr-850 (S.D.N.Y. Nov. 29, 2018), Doc. 2 ("*Cohen* Information").

[291] *See Interview of: Donald J. Trump, Jr, Senate Judiciary Committee*, 115th Cong. 13 (Sept. 7, 2017) ("Following the pageant the Trump Organization and Mr. Agalarov's company, Crocus Group, began preliminarily discussion [sic] potential real estate projects in Moscow."). As has been widely reported, the Miss Universe pageant—which Trump co-owned at the time—was held at the Agalarov-owned Crocus City Hall in Moscow in November 2013. Both groups were involved in organizing the pageant, and Aras Agalarov's son Emin was a musical performer at the event, which Trump attended.

[292] Kaveladze 11/16/17 302, at 2, 4-6; Grand Jury ▮▮▮▮▮▮ OSC-KAV_00385 (12/6/13 Email, Trump Jr. to Kaveladze & E. Agalarov).

[293] Grand Jury ▮▮▮▮▮▮

an agreement for the Trump Tower Moscow project.[294] On December 23, 2013, after discussions with Donald J. Trump, the Trump Organization agreed to accept an arrangement whereby the organization received a flat 3.5% commission on all sales, with no licensing fees or incentives.[295] The parties negotiated a letter of intent during January and February 2014.[296]

From January 2014 through November 2014, the Trump Organization and Crocus Group discussed development plans for the Moscow project. Some time before January 24, 2014, the Crocus Group sent the Trump Organization a proposal for a 800-unit, 194-meter building to be constructed at an Agalarov-owned site in Moscow called "Crocus City," which had also been the site of the Miss Universe pageant.[297] In February 2014, Ivanka Trump met with Emin Agalarov and toured the Crocus City site during a visit to Moscow.[298] From March 2014 through July 2014, the groups discussed "design standards" and other architectural elements.[299] For example, in July 2014, members of the Trump Organization sent Crocus Group counterparties questions about the "demographics of these prospective buyers" in the Crocus City area, the development of neighboring parcels in Crocus City, and concepts for redesigning portions of the building.[300] In August 2014, the Trump Organization requested specifications for a competing Marriott-branded tower being built in Crocus City.[301]

Beginning in September 2014, the Trump Organization stopped responding in a timely fashion to correspondence and proposals from the Crocus Group.[302] Communications between the two groups continued through November 2014 with decreasing frequency; what appears to be the last communication is dated November 24, 2014.[303] The project appears not to have developed past the planning stage, and no construction occurred.

---

[294] Grand Jury

[295] OSC-KAV_00452 (12/23/13 Email, Trump Jr. to Kaveladze & E. Agalarov).

[296] See, e.g., OSC-KAV_01158 (Letter agreement signed by Trump Jr. & E. Agalarov); OSC-KAV_01147 (1/20/14 Email, Kaveladze to Trump Jr. et al.).

[297] See, e.g., OSC-KAV_00972 (10/14/14 Email, McGee to Khoo et al.) (email from Crocus Group contractor about specifications); OSC-KAV_00540 (1/24/14 Email, McGee to Trump Jr. et al.).

[298] See OSC-KAV_00631 (2/5/14 Email, E. Agalarov to Ivanka Trump, Trump Jr. & Kaveladze); Goldstone Facebook post, 2/4/14 (8:01 a.m.) Investigative Technique

[299] See, e.g., OSC-KAV_00791 (6/3/14 Email, Kaveladze to Trump Jr. et al.; OSC-KAV_00799 (6/10/14 Email, Trump Jr. to Kaveladze et al.); OSC-KAV_00817 (6/16/14 Email, Trump Jr. to Kaveladze et al.).

[300] OSC-KAV_00870 (7/17/14 Email, Khoo to McGee et al.).

[301] OSC-KAV_00855 (8/4/14 Email, Khoo to McGee et al.).

[302] OSC-KAV_00903 (9/29/14 Email, Tropea to McGee & Kaveladze (noting last response was on August 26, 2014)); OSC-KAV_00906 (9/29/14 Email, Kaveladze to Tropea & McGee (suggesting silence "proves my fear that those guys are bailing out of the project")); OSC-KAV_00972 (10/14/14 Email, McGee to Khoo et al.) (email from Crocus Group contractor about development specifications)).

[303] OSC-KAV_01140 (11/24/14 Email, Khoo to McGee et al.).

b. Communications with I.C. Expert Investment Company and Giorgi Rtskhiladze (Summer and Fall 2015)

In the late summer of 2015, the Trump Organization received a new inquiry about pursuing a Trump Tower project in Moscow. In approximately September 2015, Felix Sater, a New York-based real estate advisor, contacted Michael Cohen, then-executive vice president of the Trump Organization and special counsel to Donald J. Trump.[304] Sater had previously worked with the Trump Organization and advised it on a number of domestic and international projects. Sater had explored the possibility of a Trump Tower project in Moscow while working with the Trump Organization and therefore knew of the organization's general interest in completing a deal there.[305] Sater had also served as an informal agent of the Trump Organization in Moscow previously and had accompanied Ivanka Trump and Donald Trump Jr. to Moscow in the mid-2000s.[306]

Sater contacted Cohen on behalf of I.C. Expert Investment Company (I.C. Expert), a Russian real-estate development corporation controlled by Andrei Vladimirovich Rozov.[307] Sater had known Rozov since approximately 2007 and, in 2014, had served as an agent on behalf of Rozov during Rozov's purchase of a building in New York City.[308] Sater later contacted Rozov and proposed that I.C. Expert pursue a Trump Tower Moscow project in which I.C. Expert would license the name and brand from the Trump Organization but construct the building on its own. Sater worked on the deal with Rozov and another employee of I.C. Expert.[309]

Cohen was the only Trump Organization representative to negotiate directly with I.C. Expert or its agents. In approximately September 2015, Cohen obtained approval to negotiate with I.C. Expert from candidate Trump, who was then president of the Trump Organization. Cohen provided updates directly to Trump about the project throughout 2015 and into 2016, assuring him the project was continuing.[310] Cohen also discussed the Trump Moscow project with Ivanka Trump as to design elements (such as possible architects to use for the project[311]) and Donald J. Trump Jr. (about his experience in Moscow and possible involvement in the project[312]) during the fall of 2015.

---

[304] Sater provided information to our Office in two 2017 interviews conducted under a proffer agreement. Grand Jury

[305] Grand Jury

[306] Sater 9/19/17 302, at 1-2, 5.

[307] Sater 9/19/17 302, at 3.

[308] Rozov 1/25/18 302, at 1.

[309] Rozov 1/25/18 302, at 1; see also 11/2/15 Email, Cohen to Rozov et al. (sending letter of intent).

[310] Cohen 9/12/18 302, at 1-2, 4-6.

[311] Cohen 9/12/18 302, at 5.

[312] Cohen 9/12/18 302, at 4-5.

Also during the fall of 2015, Cohen communicated about the Trump Moscow proposal with Giorgi Rtskhiladze, a business executive who previously had been involved in a development deal with the Trump Organization in Batumi, Georgia.[313] Cohen stated that he spoke to Rtskhiladze in part because Rtskhiladze had pursued business ventures in Moscow, including a licensing deal with the Agalarov-owned Crocus Group.[314] On September 22, 2015, Cohen forwarded a preliminary design study for the Trump Moscow project to Rtskhiladze, adding "I look forward to your reply about this spectacular project in Moscow." Rtskhiladze forwarded Cohen's email to an associate and wrote, "[i]f we could organize the meeting in New York at the highest level of the Russian Government and Mr. Trump this project would definitely receive the worldwide attention."[315]

On September 24, 2015, Rtskhiladze sent Cohen an attachment that he described as a proposed "[l]etter to the Mayor of Moscow from Trump org," explaining that "[w]e need to send this letter to the Mayor of Moscow (second guy in Russia) he is aware of the potential project and will pledge his support."[316] In a second email to Cohen sent the same day, Rtskhiladze provided a translation of the letter, which described the Trump Moscow project as a "symbol of stronger economic, business and cultural relationships between New York and Moscow and therefore United States and the Russian Federation."[317] On September 27, 2015, Rtskhiladze sent another email to Cohen, proposing that the Trump Organization partner on the Trump Moscow project with "Global Development Group LLC," which he described as being controlled by Michail Posikhin, a Russian architect, and Simon Nizharadze.[318] Cohen told the Office that he ultimately declined the proposal and instead continued to work with I.C. Expert, the company represented by Felix Sater.[319]

c. Letter of Intent and Contacts to Russian Government (October 2015-January 2016)

i. Trump Signs the Letter of Intent on behalf of the Trump Organization

Between approximately October 13, 2015 and November 2, 2015, the Trump Organization (through its subsidiary Trump Acquisition, LLC) and I.C. Expert completed a letter of intent (LOI) for a Trump Moscow property. The LOI, signed by Trump for the Trump Organization and Rozov on behalf of I.C. Expert, was "intended to facilitate further discussions" in order to "attempt to

---

[313] Rtskhiladze was a U.S.-based executive of the Georgian company Silk Road Group. In approximately 2011, Silk Road Group and the Trump Organization entered into a licensing agreement to build a Trump-branded property in Batumi, Georgia. Rtskhiladze was also involved in discussions for a Trump-branded project in Astana, Kazakhstan. The Office twice interviewed Rtskhiladze, **Grand Jury**

[314] Cohen 9/12/18 302, at 12; *see also* Rtskhiladze 5/10/18 302, at 1.

[315] 9/22/15 Email, Rtskhiladze to Nizharadze.

[316] 9/24/15 Email, Rtskhiladze to Cohen.

[317] 9/24/15 Email, Rtskhiladze to Cohen.

[318] 9/27/15 Email, Rtskhiladze to Cohen.

[319] Cohen 9/12/18 302, at 12.

enter into a mutually acceptable agreement" related to the Trump-branded project in Moscow.[320] The LOI contemplated a development with residential, hotel, commercial, and office components, and called for "[a]pproximately 250 first class, luxury residential condominiums," as well as "[o]ne first class, luxury hotel consisting of approximately 15 floors and containing not fewer than 150 hotel rooms."[321]   For the residential and commercial portions of the project, the Trump Organization would receive between 1% and 5% of all condominium sales,[322] plus 3% of all rental and other revenue.[323] For the project's hotel portion, the Trump Organization would receive a base fee of 3% of gross operating revenues for the first five years and 4% thereafter, plus a separate incentive fee of 20% of operating profit.[324] Under the LOI, the Trump Organization also would receive a $4 million "up-front fee" prior to groundbreaking.[325] Under these terms, the Trump Organization stood to earn substantial sums over the lifetime of the project, without assuming significant liabilities or financing commitments.[326]

On November 3, 2015, the day after the Trump Organization transmitted the LOI, Sater emailed Cohen suggesting that the Trump Moscow project could be used to increase candidate Trump's chances at being elected, writing:

> Buddy our boy can become President of the USA and we can engineer it. I will get all of Putins team to buy in on this, I will manage this process. . . . Michael, Putin gets on stage with Donald for a ribbon cutting for Trump Moscow, and Donald owns the republican nomination. And possibly beats Hillary and our boy is in. . . . We will manage this process better than anyone. You and I will get Donald and Vladimir on a stage together very shortly. That the game changer.[327]

Later that day, Sater followed up:

> Donald doesn't stare down, he negotiates and understands the economic issues and Putin only want to deal with a pragmatic leader, and a successful business man is a good candidate for someone who knows how to negotiate. "Business, politics, whatever it all is the same for someone who knows how to deal"

---

[320] 11/2/15 Email, Cohen to Rozov et al. (attachment) (hereinafter "LOI"); *see also* 10/13/15 Email, Sater to Cohen & Davis (attaching proposed letter of intent).

[321] LOI, p. 2.

[322] The LOI called for the Trump Organization to receive 5% of all gross sales up to $100 million; 4% of all gross sales from $100 million to $250 million; 3% of all gross sales from $250 million to $500 million; 2% of all gross sales from $500 million to $1 billion; and 1% of all gross sales over $1 billion. LOI, Schedule 2.

[323] LOI, Schedule 2.

[324] LOI, Schedule 1.

[325] LOI, Schedule 2.

[326] Cohen 9/12/18 302, at 3.

[327] 11/3/15 Email, Sater to Cohen (12:14 p.m.).

I think I can get Putin to say that at the Trump Moscow press conference.
If he says it we own this election. Americas most difficult adversary agreeing that Donald is a good guy to negotiate. . . .
We can own this election.
Michael my next steps are very sensitive with Putins very very close people, we can pull this off.
Michael lets go. 2 boys from Brooklyn getting a USA president elected. This is good really good.[328]

According to Cohen, he did not consider the political import of the Trump Moscow project to the 2016 U.S. presidential election at the time. Cohen also did not recall candidate Trump or anyone affiliated with the Trump Campaign discussing the political implications of the Trump Moscow project with him. However, Cohen recalled conversations with Trump in which the candidate suggested that his campaign would be a significant "infomercial" for Trump-branded properties.[329]

ii. Post-LOI Contacts with Individuals in Russia

Given the size of the Trump Moscow project, Sater and Cohen believed the project required approval (whether express or implicit) from the Russian national government, including from the Presidential Administration of Russia.[330] Sater stated that he therefore began to contact the Presidential Administration through another Russian business contact.[331] In early negotiations with the Trump Organization, Sater had alluded to the need for government approval and his attempts to set up meetings with Russian officials. On October 12, 2015, for example, Sater wrote to Cohen that "all we need is Putin on board and we are golden," and that a "meeting with Putin and top deputy is tentatively set for the 14th [of October]."[332] Grand Jury this meeting was being coordinated by associates in Russia and that he had no direct interaction with the Russian government.[333]

Approximately a month later, after the LOI had been signed, Lana Erchova emailed Ivanka Trump on behalf of Erchova's then-husband Dmitry Klokov, to offer Klokov's assistance to the Trump Campaign.[334] Klokov was at that time Director of External Communications for PJSC Federal Grid Company of Unified Energy System, a large Russian electricity transmission

---

[328] 11/3/15 Email, Sater to Cohen (12:40 p.m.).

[329] Cohen 9/12/18 302, at 3-4; Cohen 8/7/18 302, at 15.

[330] Grand Jury Sater 12/15/17 302, at 2.

[331] Sater 12/15/17 302, at 3-4.

[332] 10/12/15 Email, Sater to Cohen (8:07 a.m.).

[333] Grand Jury

[334] Ivanka Trump received an email from a woman who identified herself as "Lana E. Alexander," which said in part, "If you ask anyone who knows Russian to google my husband Dmitry Klokov, you'll see who he is close to and that he has done Putin's political campaigns." 11/16/15 Email, Erchova to I. Trump.

U.S. Department of Justice

~~Attorney Work Product // May Contain Material Protected Under Fed. R. Crim. P. 6(e)~~

company, and had been previously employed as an aide and press secretary to Russia's energy minister. Ivanka Trump forwarded the email to Cohen.[335] He told the Office that, after receiving this inquiry, he had conducted an internet search for Klokov's name and concluded (incorrectly) that Klokov was a former Olympic weightlifter.[336]

Between November 18 and 19, 2015, Klokov and Cohen had at least one telephone call and exchanged several emails. Describing himself in emails to Cohen as a "trusted person" who could offer the Campaign "political synergy" and "synergy on a government level," Klokov recommended that Cohen travel to Russia to speak with him and an unidentified intermediary. Klokov said that those conversations could facilitate a later meeting in Russia between the candidate and an individual Klokov described as "our person of interest."[337] In an email to the Office, Erchova later identified the "person of interest" as Russian President Vladimir Putin.[338]

In the telephone call and follow-on emails with Klokov, Cohen discussed his desire to use a near-term trip to Russia to do site surveys and talk over the Trump Moscow project with local developers. Cohen registered his willingness also to meet with Klokov and the unidentified intermediary, but was emphatic that all meetings in Russia involving him or candidate Trump—including a possible meeting between candidate Trump and Putin—would need to be "in conjunction with the development and an official visit" with the Trump Organization receiving a formal invitation to visit.[339] (Klokov had written previously that "the visit [by candidate Trump to Russia] has to be informal.")[340]

Klokov had also previously recommended to Cohen that he separate their negotiations over a possible meeting between Trump and "the person of interest" from any existing business track.[341] Re-emphasizing that his outreach was not done on behalf of any business, Klokov added in second email to Cohen that, if publicized well, such a meeting could have "phenomenal" impact "in a business dimension" and that the "person of interest['s]" "most important support" could have significant ramifications for the "level of projects and their capacity." Klokov concluded by telling

---

[335] 11/16/15 Email, I. Trump to Cohen.

[336] Cohen 8/7/18 302, at 17. During his interviews with the Office, Cohen still appeared to believe that the Klokov he spoke with was that Olympian. The investigation, however, established that the email address used to communicate with Cohen belongs to a different Dmitry Klokov, as described above.

[337] 11/18/15 Email, Klokov to Cohen (6:51 a.m.).

[338] In July 2018, the Office received an unsolicited email purporting to be from Erchova, in which she wrote that "[a]t the end of 2015 and beginning of 2016 I was asked by my ex-husband to contact Ivanka Trump . . . and offer cooperation to Trump's team on behalf of the Russian officials." 7/27/18 Email, Erchova to Special Counsel's Office. The email claimed that the officials wanted to offer candidate Trump "land in Crimea among other things and unofficial meeting with Putin." *Id.* In order to vet the email's claims, the Office responded requesting more details. The Office did not receive any reply.

[339] 11/18/15 Email, Cohen to Klokov (7:15 a.m.).

[340] 11/18/15 Email, Klokov to Cohen (6:51 a.m.).

[341] 11/18/15 Email, Klokov to Cohen (6:51 a.m.) ("I would suggest separating your negotiations and our proposal to meet. I assure you, after the meeting level of projects and their capacity can be completely different, having the most important support.").

73

Cohen that there was "no bigger warranty in any project than [the] consent of the person of interest."[342] Cohen rejected the proposal, saying that "[c]urrently our LOI developer is in talks with VP's Chief of Staff and arranging a formal invite for the two to meet."[343] This email appears to be their final exchange, and the investigation did not identify evidence that Cohen brought Klokov's initial offer of assistance to the Campaign's attention or that anyone associated with the Trump Organization or the Campaign dealt with Klokov at a later date. Cohen explained that he did not pursue the proposed meeting because he was already working on the Moscow Project with Sater, who Cohen understood to have his own connections to the Russian government.[344]

By late December 2015, however, Cohen was complaining that Sater had not been able to use those connections to set up the promised meeting with Russian government officials. Cohen told Sater that he was "setting up the meeting myself."[345] On January 11, 2016, Cohen emailed the office of Dmitry Peskov, the Russian government's press secretary, indicating that he desired contact with Sergei Ivanov, Putin's chief of staff. Cohen erroneously used the email address "Pr_peskova@prpress.**gof**.ru" instead of "Pr_peskova@prpress.**gov**.ru," so the email apparently did not go through.[346] On January 14, 2016, Cohen emailed a different address (info@prpress.gov.ru) with the following message:

> Dear Mr. Peskov,
> Over the past few months, I have been working with a company based in Russia regarding the development of a Trump Tower-Moscow project in Moscow City.
> Without getting into lengthy specifics, the communication between our two sides has stalled. As this project is too important, I am hereby requesting your assistance.
> I respectfully request someone, preferably you; contact me so that I might discuss the specifics as well as arranging meetings with the appropriate individuals.
> I thank you in advance for your assistance and look forward to hearing from you soon.[347]

Two days later, Cohen sent an email to Pr_peskova@prpress.**gov**.ru, repeating his request to speak with Sergei Ivanov.[348]

Cohen testified to Congress, and initially told the Office, that he did not recall receiving a response to this email inquiry and that he decided to terminate any further work on the Trump Moscow project as of January 2016. Cohen later admitted that these statements were false. In

---

[342] 11/19/15 Email, Klokov to Cohen (7:40 a.m.).

[343] 11/19/15 Email, Cohen to Klokov (12:56 p.m.).

[344] Cohen 9/18/18 302, at 12.

[345] FS00004 (12/30/15 Text Message, Cohen to Sater (6:17 p.m.)).

[346] 1/11/16 Email, Cohen to pr_peskova@prpress.gof.ru (9:12 a.m.).

[347] 1/14/16 Email, Cohen to info@prpress.gov.ru (9:21 a.m.).

[348] 1/16/16 Email, Cohen to pr_peskova@prpress.gov.ru (10:28 a.m.).

fact, Cohen had received (and recalled receiving) a response to his inquiry, and he continued to work on and update candidate Trump on the project through as late as June 2016.[349]

On January 20, 2016, Cohen received an email from Elena Poliakova, Peskov's personal assistant. Writing from her personal email account, Poliakova stated that she had been trying to reach Cohen and asked that he call her on the personal number that she provided.[350] Shortly after receiving Poliakova's email, Cohen called and spoke to her for 20 minutes.[351] Cohen described to Poliakova his position at the Trump Organization and outlined the proposed Trump Moscow project, including information about the Russian counterparty with which the Trump Organization had partnered. Cohen requested assistance in moving the project forward, both in securing land to build the project and with financing. According to Cohen, Poliakova asked detailed questions and took notes, stating that she would need to follow up with others in Russia.[352]

Cohen could not recall any direct follow-up from Poliakova or from any other representative of the Russian government, nor did the Office identify any evidence of direct follow-up. However, the day after Cohen's call with Poliakova, Sater texted Cohen, asking him to "[c]all me when you have a few minutes to chat . . . It's about Putin they called today."[353] Sater then sent a draft invitation for Cohen to visit Moscow to discuss the Trump Moscow project,[354] along with a note to "[t]ell me if the letter is good as amended by me or make whatever changes you want and send it back to me."[355] After a further round of edits, on January 25, 2016, Sater sent Cohen an invitation—signed by Andrey Ryabinskiy of the company MHJ—to travel to "Moscow for a working visit" about the "prospects of development and the construction business in Russia," "the various land plots available suited for construction of this enormous Tower," and "the opportunity to co-ordinate a follow up visit to Moscow by Mr. Donald Trump."[356] According

---

[349] *Cohen* Information ¶¶ 4, 7. Cohen's interactions with President Trump and the President's lawyers when preparing his congressional testimony are discussed further in Volume II. *See* Vol. II, Section II.K.3, *infra*.

[350] 1/20/16 Email, Poliakova to Cohen (5:57 a.m.) ("Mr. Cohen[,] I can't get through to both your phones. Pls, call me.").

[351] Telephone records show a 20-minute call on January 20, 2016 between Cohen and the number Poliakova provided in her email. Call Records of Michael Cohen ▮Grand Jury▮ After the call, Cohen saved Poliakova's contact information in his Trump Organization Outlook contact list. 1/20/16 Cohen Microsoft Outlook Entry (6:22 a.m.).

[352] Cohen 9/12/18 302, at 2-3.

[353] FS00011 (1/21/16 Text Messages, Sater to Cohen).

[354] The invitation purported to be from Genbank, a Russian bank that was, according to Sater, working at the behest of a larger bank, VTB, and would consider providing financing. FS00008 (12/31/15 Text Messages, Sater & Cohen). Additional information about Genbank can be found *infra*.

[355] FS00011 (1/21/16 Text Message, Sater to Cohen (7:44 p.m.)); 1/21/16 Email, Sater to Cohen (6:49 p.m.).

[356] 1/25/16 Email, Sater to Cohen (12:01 p.m.) (attachment).

75

135

U.S. Department of Justice

~~Attorney Work Product~~ // ~~May Contain Material Protected Under Fed. R. Crim. P. 6(e)~~

to Cohen, he elected not to travel at the time because of concerns about the lack of concrete proposals about land plots that could be considered as options for the project.[357]

d. Discussions about Russia Travel by Michael Cohen or Candidate Trump (December 2015-June 2016)

i. Sater's Overtures to Cohen to Travel to Russia

The late January communication was neither the first nor the last time that Cohen contemplated visiting Russia in pursuit of the Trump Moscow project. Beginning in late 2015, Sater repeatedly tried to arrange for Cohen and candidate Trump, as representatives of the Trump Organization, to travel to Russia to meet with Russian government officials and possible financing partners. In December 2015, Sater sent Cohen a number of emails about logistics for traveling to Russia for meetings.[358] On December 19, 2015, Sater wrote:

> Please call me I have Evgeney [Dvoskin] on the other line.[[359]] He needs a copy of your and Donald's passports they need a scan of every page of the passports. Invitations & Visas will be issued this week by VTB Bank to discuss financing for Trump Tower Moscow. Politically neither Putins office nor Ministry of Foreign Affairs cannot issue invite, so they are inviting commercially/ business. VTB is Russia's 2 biggest bank and VTB Bank CEO Andrey Kostin, will be at all meetings with Putin so that it is a business meeting not political. We will be invited to Russian consulate this week to receive invite & have visa issued.[360]

In response, Cohen texted Sater an image of his own passport.[361] Cohen told the Office that at one point he requested a copy of candidate Trump's passport from Rhona Graff, Trump's executive assistant at the Trump Organization, and that Graff later brought Trump's passport to Cohen's

---

[357] Cohen 9/12/18 302, at 6-7.

[358] *See, e.g.,* 12/1/15 Email, Sater to Cohen (12:41 p.m.) ("Please scan and send me a copy of your passport for the Russian Ministry of Foreign Affairs.").

[359] Toll records show that Sater was speaking to Evgeny Dvoskin. Call Records of Felix Sater Grand Jury Dvoskin is an executive of Genbank, a large bank with lending focused in Crimea, Ukraine. At the time that Sater provided this financing letter to Cohen, Genbank was subject to U.S. government sanctions, *see Russia/Ukraine-related Sanctions and Identifications,* Office of Foreign Assets Control (Dec. 22, 2015), *available at* https://www.treasury.gov/resource-center/sanctions/OFAC-Enforcement/Pages/20151222.aspx. Dvoskin, who had been deported from the United States in 2000 for criminal activity, was under indictment in the United States for stock fraud under the aliases Eugene Slusker and Gene Shustar. *See United States v. Rizzo, et al.,* 2:03-cr-63 (E.D.N.Y. Feb. 6, 2003).

[360] 12/19/15 Email, Sater to Cohen (10:50 a.m.); FS00002 (12/19/15 Text Messages, Sater to Cohen, (10:53 a.m.).

[361] FS00004 (12/19/15 Text Message, Cohen to Sater); ERT_0198-256 (12/19/15 Text Messages, Cohen & Sater).

U.S. Department of Justice

~~Attorney Work Product~~ // ~~May Contain Material Protected Under Fed. R. Crim. P. 6(e)~~

office.[362] The investigation did not, however, establish that the passport was forwarded to Sater.[363]

Into the spring of 2016, Sater and Cohen continued to discuss a trip to Moscow in connection with the Trump Moscow project. On April 20, 2016, Sater wrote Cohen, "[t]he People wanted to know when you are coming?"[364] On May 4, 2016, Sater followed up:

> I had a chat with Moscow. ASSUMING the trip does happen the question is before or after the convention. I said I believe, but don't know for sure, that's it's probably after the convention. Obviously the pre-meeting trip (you only) can happen anytime you want but the 2 big guys where [sic] the question. I said I would confirm and revert. . . . Let me know about If I was right by saying I believe after Cleveland and also when you want to speak to them and possibly fly over.[365]

Cohen responded, "My trip before Cleveland. Trump once he becomes the nominee after the convention."[366]

The day after this exchange, Sater tied Cohen's travel to Russia to the St. Petersburg International Economic Forum ("Forum"), an annual event attended by prominent Russian politicians and businessmen. Sater told the Office that he was informed by a business associate that Peskov wanted to invite Cohen to the Forum.[367] On May 5, 2016, Sater wrote to Cohen:

> Peskov would like to invite you as his guest to the St. Petersburg Forum which is Russia's Davos it's June 16-19. He wants to meet there with you and possibly introduce you to either Putin or Medvedev, as they are not sure if 1 or both will be there.
> This is perfect. The entire business class of Russia will be there as well.
> He said anything you want to discuss including dates and subjects are on the table to discuss[.][368]

The following day, Sater asked Cohen to confirm those dates would work for him to travel; Cohen wrote back, "[w]orks for me."[369]

---

[362] Cohen 9/12/18 302, at 5.

[363] On December 21, 2015, Sater sent Cohen a text message that read, "They need a copy of DJT passport," to which Cohen responded, "After I return from Moscow with you with a date for him." FS00004 (12/21/15 Text Messages, Cohen & Sater).

[364] FS00014 (4/20/16 Text Message, Sater to Cohen (9:06 p.m.)).

[365] FS00015 (5/4/16 Text Message, Sater to Cohen (7:38 p.m.)).

[366] FS00015 (5/4/16 Text Message, Cohen to Sater (8:03 p.m.)).

[367] Sater 12/15/17 302, at 4.

[368] FS00016 (5/5/16 Text Messages, Sater to Cohen (6:26 & 6:27 a.m.)).

[369] FS00016 (5/6/16 Text Messages, Cohen & Sater).

77

On June 9, 2016, Sater sent Cohen a notice that he (Sater) was completing the badges for the Forum, adding, "Putin is there on the 17th very strong chance you will meet him as well."[370] On June 13, 2016, Sater forwarded Cohen an invitation to the Forum signed by the Director of the Roscongress Foundation, the Russian entity organizing the Forum.[371] Sater also sent Cohen a Russian visa application and asked him to send two passport photos.[372] According to Cohen, the invitation gave no indication that Peskov had been involved in inviting him. Cohen was concerned that Russian officials were not actually involved or were not interested in meeting with him (as Sater had alleged), and so he decided not to go to the Forum.[373] On June 14, 2016, Cohen met Sater in the lobby of the Trump Tower in New York and informed him that he would not be traveling at that time.[374]

ii. Candidate Trump's Opportunities to Travel to Russia

The investigation identified evidence that, during the period the Trump Moscow project was under consideration, the possibility of candidate Trump visiting Russia arose in two contexts.

First, in interviews with the Office, Cohen stated that he discussed the subject of traveling to Russia with Trump twice: once in late 2015; and again in spring 2016.[375] According to Cohen, Trump indicated a willingness to travel if it would assist the project significantly. On one occasion, Trump told Cohen to speak with then-campaign manager Corey Lewandowski to coordinate the candidate's schedule. Cohen recalled that he spoke with Lewandowski, who suggested that they speak again when Cohen had actual dates to evaluate. Cohen indicated, however, that he knew that travel prior to the Republican National Convention would be impossible given the candidate's preexisting commitments to the Campaign.[376]

Second, like Cohen, Trump received and turned down an invitation to the St. Petersburg International Economic Forum. In late December 2015, Mira Duma—a contact of Ivanka Trump's from the fashion industry—first passed along invitations for Ivanka Trump and candidate Trump from Sergei Prikhodko, a Deputy Prime Minister of the Russian Federation.[377] On January 14, 2016, Rhona Graff sent an email to Duma stating that Trump was "honored to be asked to participate in the highly prestigious" Forum event, but that he would "have to decline" the invitation given his "very grueling and full travel schedule" as a presidential candidate.[378] Graff

---

[370] FS00018 (6/9/16 Text Messages, Sater & Cohen).

[371] 6/13/16 Email, Sater to Cohen (2:10 p.m.).

[372] FS00018 (6/13/16 Text Message, Sater to Cohen (2:20 p.m.)); 6/13/16 Email, Sater to Cohen.

[373] Cohen 9/12/18 302, at 6-8.

[374] FS00019 (6/14/16 Text Messages, Cohen & Sater (12:06 and 2:50 p.m.)).

[375] Cohen 9/12/18 302, at 2.

[376] Cohen 9/12/18 302, at 7.

[377] 12/21/15 Email, Mira to Ivanka Trump (6:57 a.m.) (attachments); TRUMPORG_16_000057 (1/7/16 Email, I. Trump to Graff (9:18 a.m.)).

[378] 1/14/16 Email, Graff to Mira.

asked Duma whether she recommended that Graff "send a formal note to the Deputy Prime Minister" declining his invitation; Duma replied that a formal note would be "great."[379]

It does not appear that Graff prepared that note immediately. According to written answers from President Trump,[380] Graff received an email from Deputy Prime Minister Prikhodko on March 17, 2016, again inviting Trump to participate in the 2016 Forum in St. Petersburg.[381] Two weeks later, on March 31, 2016, Graff prepared for Trump's signature a two-paragraph letter declining the invitation.[382] The letter stated that Trump's "schedule has become extremely demanding" because of the presidential campaign, that he "already ha[d] several commitments in the United States" for the time of the Forum, but that he otherwise "would have gladly given every consideration to attending such an important event."[383] Graff forwarded the letter to another executive assistant at the Trump Organization with instructions to print the document on letterhead for Trump to sign.[384]

At approximately the same time that the letter was being prepared, Robert Foresman—a New York-based investment banker—began reaching out to Graff to secure an in-person meeting with candidate Trump. According to Foresman, he had been asked by Anton Kobyakov, a Russian presidential aide involved with the Roscongress Foundation, to see if Trump could speak at the Forum.[385] Foresman first emailed Graff on March 31, 2016, following a phone introduction brokered through Trump business associate Mark Burnett (who produced the television show *The Apprentice*). In his email, Foresman referenced his long-standing personal and professional expertise in Russia and Ukraine, his work setting up an early "private channel" between Vladimir Putin and former U.S. President George W. Bush, and an "approach" he had received from "senior Kremlin officials" about the candidate. Foresman asked Graff for a meeting with the candidate, Corey Lewandowski, or "another relevant person" to discuss this and other "concrete things" Foresman felt uncomfortable discussing over "unsecure email."[386] On April 4, 2016, Graff forwarded Foresman's meeting request to Jessica Macchia, another executive assistant to Trump.[387]

---

[379] 1/15/16 Email, Mira to Graff.

[380] As explained in Volume II and Appendix C, on September 17, 2018, the Office sent written questions to the President's counsel. On November 20, 2018, the President provided written answers to those questions through counsel.

[381] Written Responses of Donald J. Trump (Nov. 20, 2018), at 17 (Response to Question IV, Part (e)) ("[D]ocuments show that Ms. Graff prepared for my signature a brief response declining the invitation.").

[382] Written Responses of Donald J. Trump (Nov. 20, 2018), at 17 (Response to Question IV, Part (e)); *see also* TRUMPORG_16_000134 (unsigned letter dated March 31, 2016).

[383] TRUMPORG_16_000134 (unsigned letter).

[384] TRUMPORG_16_000133 (3/31/16 Email, Graff to Macchia).

[385] Foresman 10/17/18 302, at 3-4.

[386] *See* TRUMPORG_16_00136 (3/31/16 Email, Foresman to Graff); *see also* Foresman 10/17/18 302, at 3-4.

[387] *See* TRUMPORG_16_00136 (4/4/16 Email, Graff to Macchia).

With no response forthcoming, Foresman twice sent reminders to Graff—first on April 26 and again on April 30, 2016.[388] Graff sent an apology to Foresman and forwarded his April 26 email (as well as his initial March 2016 email) to Lewandowski.[389] On May 2, 2016, Graff forwarded Foresman's April 30 email—which suggested an alternative meeting with Donald Trump Jr. or Eric Trump so that Foresman could convey to them information that "should be conveyed to [the candidate] personally or [to] someone [the candidate] absolutely trusts"—to policy advisor Stephen Miller.[390]

No communications or other evidence obtained by the Office indicate that the Trump Campaign learned that Foresman was reaching out to invite the candidate to the Forum or that the Campaign otherwise followed up with Foresman until after the election, when he interacted with the Transition Team as he pursued a possible position in the incoming Administration.[391] When interviewed by the Office, Foresman denied that the specific "approach" from "senior Kremlin officials" noted in his March 31, 2016 email was anything other than Kobyakov's invitation to Roscongress. According to Foresman, the "concrete things" he referenced in the same email were a combination of the invitation itself, Foresman's personal perspectives on the invitation and Russia policy in general, and details of a Ukraine plan supported by a U.S. think tank (EastWest Institute). Foresman told the Office that Kobyakov had extended similar invitations through him to another Republican presidential candidate and one other politician. Foresman also said that Kobyakov had asked Foresman to invite Trump to speak after that other presidential candidate withdrew from the race and the other politician's participation did not work out.[392] Finally, Foresman claimed to have no plans to establish a back channel involving Trump, stating the reference to his involvement in the Bush-Putin back channel was meant to burnish his credentials to the Campaign. Foresman commented that he had not recognized any of the experts announced as Trump's foreign policy team in March 2016, and wanted to secure an in-person meeting with the candidate to share his professional background and policy views, including that Trump should decline Kobyakov's invitation to speak at the Forum.[393]

2. George Papadopoulos

George Papadopoulos was a foreign policy advisor to the Trump Campaign from March

---

[388] *See* TRUMPORG_16_00137 (4/26/16 Email, Foresman to Graff); TRUMPORG_16_00141 (4/30/16 Email, Foresman to Graff).

[389] *See* TRUMPORG_16_00139 (4/27/16 Email, Graff to Foresman); TRUMPORG_16_00137 (4/27/16 Email, Graff to Lewandowski).

[390] TRUMPORG_16_00142 (5/2/16 Email, Graff to S. Miller); *see also* TRUMPORG_16_00143 (5/2/16 Email, Graff to S. Miller) (forwarding March 2016 email from Foresman).

[391] Foresman's contacts during the transition period are discussed further in Volume I, Section IV.B.3, *infra*.

[392] Foresman 10/17/18 302, at 4.

[393] Foresman 10/17/18 302, at 8-9.

U.S. Department of Justice

Attorney Work Product // May Contain Material Protected Under Fed. R. Crim. P. 6(e)

2016 to early October 2016.[394] In late April 2016, Papadopoulos was told by London-based professor Joseph Mifsud, immediately after Mifsud's return from a trip to Moscow, that the Russian government had obtained "dirt" on candidate Clinton in the form of thousands of emails. One week later, on May 6, 2016, Papadopoulos suggested to a representative of a foreign government that the Trump Campaign had received indications from the Russian government that it could assist the Campaign through the anonymous release of information that would be damaging to candidate Clinton.

Papadopoulos shared information about Russian "dirt" with people outside of the Campaign, and the Office investigated whether he also provided it to a Campaign official. Papadopoulos and the Campaign officials with whom he interacted told the Office that they did not recall that Papadopoulos passed them the information. Throughout the relevant period of time and for several months thereafter, Papadopoulos worked with Mifsud and two Russian nationals to arrange a meeting between the Campaign and the Russian government. That meeting never came to pass.

a. Origins of Campaign Work

In March 2016, Papadopoulos became a foreign policy advisor to the Trump Campaign.[395] As early as the summer of 2015, he had sought a role as a policy advisor to the Campaign but, in a September 30, 2015 email, he was told that the Campaign was not hiring policy advisors.[396] In late 2015, Papadopoulos obtained a paid position on the campaign of Republican presidential candidate Ben Carson.[397]

Although Carson remained in the presidential race until early March 2016, Papadopoulos had stopped actively working for his campaign by early February 2016.[398] At that time, Papadopoulos reached out to a contact at the London Centre of International Law Practice (LCILP), which billed itself as a "unique institution . . . comprising high-level professional international law practitioners, dedicated to the advancement of global legal knowledge and the practice of international law."[399] Papadopoulos said that he had finished his role with the Carson

---

[394] Papadopoulos met with our Office for debriefings on several occasions in the summer and fall of 2017, after he was arrested and charged in a sealed criminal complaint with making false statements in a January 2017 FBI interview about, *inter alia*, the timing, extent, and nature of his interactions and communications with Joseph Mifsud and two Russian nationals: Olga Polonskaya and Ivan Timofeev. Papadopoulos later pleaded guilty, pursuant to a plea agreement, to an information charging him with making false statements to the FBI, in violation of 18 U.S.C. § 1001(a).

[395] *A Transcript of Donald Trump's Meeting with the Washington Post Editorial Board*, Washington Post (Mar. 21, 2016).

[396] 7/15/15 LinkedIn Message, Papadopoulos to Lewandowski (6:57 a.m.); 9/30/15 Email, Glassner to Papadopoulos (7:42:21 a.m.).

[397] Papadopoulos 8/10/17 302, at 2.

[398] Papadopoulos 8/10/17 302, at 2; 2/4/16 Email, Papadopoulos to Idris.

[399] London Centre of International Law Practice, at https://www.lcilp.org/ (via web.archive.org).

campaign and asked if LCILP was hiring.[400] In early February, Papadopoulos agreed to join LCILP and arrived in London to begin work.[401]

As he was taking his position at LCILP, Papadopoulos contacted Trump campaign manager Corey Lewandowski via LinkedIn and emailed campaign official Michael Glassner about his interest in joining the Trump Campaign.[402] On March 2, 2016, Papadopoulos sent Glassner another message reiterating his interest.[403] Glassner passed along word of Papadopoulos's interest to another campaign official, Joy Lutes, who notified Papadopoulos by email that she had been told by Glassner to introduce Papadopoulos to Sam Clovis, the Trump Campaign's national co-chair and chief policy advisor.[404]

At the time of Papadopoulos's March 2 email, the media was criticizing the Trump Campaign for lack of experienced foreign policy or national security advisors within its ranks.[405] To address that issue, senior Campaign officials asked Clovis to put a foreign policy team together on short notice.[406] After receiving Papadopoulos's name from Lutes, Clovis performed a Google search on Papadopoulos, learned that he had worked at the Hudson Institute, and believed that he had credibility on energy issues.[407] On March 3, 2016, Clovis arranged to speak with Papadopoulos by phone to discuss Papadopoulos joining the Campaign as a foreign policy advisor, and on March 6, 2016, the two spoke.[408] Papadopoulos recalled that Russia was mentioned as a topic, and he understood from the conversation that Russia would be an important aspect of the Campaign's foreign policy.[409] At the end of the conversation, Clovis offered Papadopoulos a role as a foreign policy advisor to the Campaign, and Papadopoulos accepted the offer.[410]

b. Initial Russia-Related Contacts

Approximately a week after signing on as a foreign policy advisor, Papadopoulos traveled

---

[400] 2/4/16 Email, Papadopoulos to Idris.

[401] 2/5/16 Email, Idris to Papadopoulos (6:11:25 p.m.); 2/6/16 Email, Idris to Papadopoulos (5:34:15 p.m.).

[402] 2/4/16 LinkedIn Message, Papadopoulos to Lewandowski (1:28 p.m.); 2/4/16 Email, Papadopoulos to Glassner (2:10:36 p.m.).

[403] 3/2/16 Email, Papadopoulos to Glassner (11:17:23 a.m.).

[404] 3/2/16 Email, Lutes to Papadopoulos (10:08:15 p.m.).

[405] Clovis 10/3/17 302 (1 of 2), at 4.

[406] Clovis 10/3/17 302 (1 of 2), at 4.

[407] Grand Jury ; 3/3/16 Email, Lutes to Clovis & Papadopoulos (6:05:47 p.m.).

[408] 3/6/16 Email, Papadopoulos to Clovis (4:24:21 p.m.).

[409] Statement of Offense ¶ 4, *United States v. George Papadopoulos*, 1:17-cr-182 (D.D.C. Oct. 5, 2017), Doc. 19 ("*Papadopoulos* Statement of Offense").

[410] Papadopoulos 8/10/17 302, at 2.

to Rome, Italy, as part of his duties with LCILP.[411] The purpose of the trip was to meet officials affiliated with Link Campus University, a for-profit institution headed by a former Italian government official.[412] During the visit, Papadopoulos was introduced to Joseph Mifsud.

Mifsud is a Maltese national who worked as a professor at the London Academy of Diplomacy in London, England.[413] Although Mifsud worked out of London and was also affiliated with LCILP, the encounter in Rome was the first time that Papadopoulos met him.[414] Mifsud maintained various Russian contacts while living in London, as described further below. Among his contacts was ▓▓▓▓▓▓▓▓,[415] a one-time employee of the IRA, the entity that carried out the Russian social media campaign (*see* Volume I, Section II, *supra*). In January and February 2016, Mifsud and ▓▓▓▓ discussed ▓▓▓▓▓▓▓▓ possibly meeting in Russia. The investigation did not identify evidence of them meeting. Later, in the spring of 2016, ▓▓▓▓▓ was also in contact ▓▓▓▓▓▓▓▓ that was linked to an employee of the Russian Ministry of Defense, and that account had overlapping contacts with a group of Russian military-controlled Facebook accounts that included accounts used to promote the DCLeaks releases in the course of the GRU's hack-and-release operations (*see* Volume I, Section III.B.1, *supra*).

According to Papadopoulos, Mifsud at first seemed uninterested in Papadopoulos when they met in Rome.[416] After Papadopoulos informed Mifsud about his role in the Trump Campaign, however, Mifsud appeared to take greater interest in Papadopoulos.[417] The two discussed Mifsud's European and Russian contacts and had a general discussion about Russia; Mifsud also offered to introduce Papadopoulos to European leaders and others with contacts to the Russian government.[418] Papadopoulos told the Office that Mifsud's claim of substantial connections with Russian government officials interested Papadopoulos, who thought that such connections could increase his importance as a policy advisor to the Trump Campaign.[419]

---

[411] Papadopoulos 8/10/17 302, at 2-3; *Papadopoulos* Statement of Offense ¶ 5.

[412] Papadopoulos 8/10/17 302, at 2-3; Stephanie Kirchgaessner et al., *Joseph Mifsud: more questions than answers about mystery professor linked to Russia*, The Guardian (Oct. 31, 2017) ("Link Campus University . . . is headed by a former Italian interior minister named Vincenzo Scotti.").

[413] *Papadopoulos* Statement of Offense ¶ 5.

[414] Papadopoulos 8/10/17 302, at 3.

[415] *See, e.g.,* Investigative Technique ▓▓▓▓▓▓▓▓▓▓▓▓
Harm to Ongoing Matter ▓▓▓▓▓▓▓▓▓▓▓▓

[416] *Papadopoulos* Statement of Offense ¶ 5.

[417] *Papadopoulos* Statement of Offense ¶ 5.

[418] Papadopoulos 8/10/17 302, at 3; Papadopoulos 8/11/17 302, at 2.

[419] *Papadopoulos* Statement of Offense ¶ 5.

U.S. Department of Justice

~~Attorney-Work-Product~~ // ~~May Contain Material Protected Under Fed. R. Crim. P. 6(e)~~

On March 17, 2016, Papadopoulos returned to London.[420] Four days later, candidate Trump publicly named him as a member of the foreign policy and national security advisory team chaired by Senator Jeff Sessions, describing Papadopoulos as "an oil and energy consultant" and an "[e]xcellent guy."[421]

On March 24, 2016, Papadopoulos met with Mifsud in London.[422] Mifsud was accompanied by a Russian female named Olga Polonskaya. Mifsud introduced Polonskaya as a former student of his who had connections to Vladimir Putin.[423] Papadopoulos understood at the time that Polonskaya may have been Putin's niece but later learned that this was not true.[424] During the meeting, Polonskaya offered to help Papadopoulos establish contacts in Russia and stated that the Russian ambassador in London was a friend of hers.[425] Based on this interaction, Papadopoulos expected Mifsud and Polonskaya to introduce him to the Russian ambassador in London, but that did not occur.[426]

Following his meeting with Mifsud, Papadopoulos sent an email to members of the Trump Campaign's foreign policy advisory team. The subject line of the message was "Meeting with Russian leadership--including Putin."[427] The message stated in pertinent part:

I just finished a very productive lunch with a good friend of mine, Joseph Mifsud, the director of the London Academy of Diplomacy--who introduced me to both Putin's niece and the Russian Ambassador in London--who also acts as the Deputy Foreign Minister.[428]

The topic of the lunch was to arrange a meeting between us and the Russian leadership to discuss U.S.-Russia ties under President Trump. They are keen to host us in a "neutral" city, or directly in Moscow. They said the leadership, including Putin, is ready to meet with us and Mr. Trump should there be interest. Waiting for everyone's thoughts on moving forward with this very important issue.[429]

---

[420] Papadopoulos 8/10/17 302, at 2.

[421] Phillip Rucker & Robert Costa, *Trump Questions Need for NATO, Outlines Noninterventionist Foreign Policy*, Washington Post (Mar. 21, 2016).

[422] Papadopoulos 8/10/17 302, at 3; 3/24/16 Text Messages, Mifsud & Papadopoulos.

[423] Papadopoulos 8/10/17 302, at 3.

[424] Papadopoulos 8/10/17 302, at 3; Papadopoulos 2/10/17 302, at 2-3; Papadopoulos Internet Search History (3/24/16) (revealing late-morning and early-afternoon searches on March 24, 2016 for "putin's niece," "olga putin," and "russian president niece olga," among other terms).

[425] Papadopoulos 8/10/17 302, at 3.

[426] *Papadopoulos* Statement of Offense ¶ 8 n.1.

[427] 3/24/16 Email, Papadopoulos to Page et al. (8:48:21 a.m.).

[428] Papadopoulos's statements to the Campaign were false. As noted above, the woman he met was not Putin's niece, he had not met the Russian Ambassador in London, and the Ambassador did not also serve as Russia's Deputy Foreign Minister.

[429] 3/24/16 Email, Papadopoulos to Page et al. (8:48:21 a.m.).

U.S. Department of Justice

Attorney Work Product // May Contain Material Protected Under Fed. R. Crim. P. 6(e)

Papadopoulos's message came at a time when Clovis perceived a shift in the Campaign's approach toward Russia—from one of engaging with Russia through the NATO framework and taking a strong stance on Russian aggression in Ukraine, Grand Jury [430]

Clovis's response to Papadopoulos, however, did not reflect that shift. Replying to Papadopoulos and the other members of the foreign policy advisory team copied on the initial email, Clovis wrote:

> This is most informative. Let me work it through the campaign. No commitments until we see how this plays out. My thought is that we probably should not go forward with any meetings with the Russians until we have had occasion to sit with our NATO allies, especially France, Germany and Great Britain. We need to reassure our allies that we are not going to advance anything with Russia until we have everyone on the same page.

> More thoughts later today. Great work.[431]

c. March 31 Foreign Policy Team Meeting

The Campaign held a meeting of the foreign policy advisory team with Senator Sessions and candidate Trump approximately one week later, on March 31, 2016, in Washington, D.C.[432] The meeting—which was intended to generate press coverage for the Campaign[433]—took place at the Trump International Hotel.[434] Papadopoulos flew to Washington for the event. At the meeting, Senator Sessions sat at one end of an oval table, while Trump sat at the other. As reflected in the photograph below (which was posted to Trump's Instagram account), Papadopoulos sat between the two, two seats to Sessions's left:

---

[430] Grand Jury

[431] 3/24/16 Email, Clovis to Papadopoulos et al. (8:55:04 a.m.).

[432] Papadopoulos 8/10/17 302, at 4; Papadopoulos 8/11/17 302, at 3.

[433] Sessions 1/17/18 302, at 16-17.

[434] Papadopoulos 8/10/17 302, at 4.

March 31, 2016 Meeting of Foreign Policy Team, with Papadopoulos (Fourth from Right of Candidate Trump)

During the meeting, each of the newly announced foreign policy advisors introduced themselves and briefly described their areas of experience or expertise.[435] Papadopoulos spoke about his previous work in the energy sector and then brought up a potential meeting with Russian officials.[436] Specifically, Papadopoulos told the group that he had learned through his contacts in London that Putin wanted to meet with candidate Trump and that these connections could help arrange that meeting.[437]

Trump and Sessions both reacted to Papadopoulos's statement. Papadopoulos and Campaign advisor J.D. Gordon—who told investigators in an interview that he had a "crystal clear" recollection of the meeting—have stated that Trump was interested in and receptive to the idea of a meeting with Putin.[438] Papadopoulos understood Sessions to be similarly supportive of his efforts to arrange a meeting.[439] Gordon and two other attendees, however, recall that Sessions generally opposed the proposal, though they differ in their accounts of the concerns he voiced or the strength of the opposition he expressed.[440]

d. George Papadopoulos Learns That Russia Has "Dirt" in the Form of Clinton Emails

Whatever Sessions's precise words at the March 31 meeting, Papadopoulos did not understand Sessions or anyone else in the Trump Campaign to have directed that he refrain from

---

[435] Papadopoulos 8/10/17 302, at 4.

[436] Papadopoulos 8/10/17 302, at 4.

[437] *Papadopoulos* Statement of Offense ¶ 9; *see* Gordon 8/29/17 302, at 14; Carafano 9/12/17 302, at 2; Hoskins 9/14/17 302, at 1.

[438] Papadopoulos 8/10/17 302, at 4-5; Gordon 9/7/17 302, at 4-5.

[439] Papadopoulos 8/10/17 302, at 5; Papadopoulos 8/11/17 302, at 3.

[440] Sessions 1/17/18 302, at 17; Gordon 9/7/17 302, at 5; Hoskins 9/14/17 302, at 1; Carafano 9/12/17 302, at 2.

making further efforts to arrange a meeting between the Campaign and the Russian government. To the contrary, Papadopoulos told the Office that he understood the Campaign to be supportive of his efforts to arrange such a meeting.[441] Accordingly, when he returned to London, Papadopoulos resumed those efforts.[442]

Throughout April 2016, Papadopoulos continued to correspond with, meet with, and seek Russia contacts through Mifsud and, at times, Polonskaya.[443] For example, within a week of her initial March 24 meeting with him, Polonskaya attempted to send Papadopoulos a text message—which email exchanges show to have been drafted or edited by Mifsud—addressing Papadopoulos's "wish to engage with the Russian Federation."[444] When Papadopoulos learned from Mifsud that Polonskaya had tried to message him, he sent her an email seeking another meeting.[445] Polonskaya responded the next day that she was "back in St. Petersburg" but "would be very pleased to support [Papadopoulos's] initiatives between our two countries" and "to meet [him] again."[446] Papadopoulos stated in reply that he thought "a good step" would be to introduce him to "the Russian Ambassador in London," and that he would like to talk to the ambassador, "or anyone else you recommend, about a potential foreign policy trip to Russia."[447]

Mifsud, who had been copied on the email exchanges, replied on the morning of April 11, 2016. He wrote, "This is already been agreed. I am flying to Moscow on the 18th for a Valdai meeting, plus other meetings at the Duma. We will talk tomorrow."[448] The two bodies referenced by Mifsud are part of or associated with the Russian government: the Duma is a Russian legislative assembly,[449] while "Valdai" refers to the Valdai Discussion Club, a Moscow-based group that "is close to Russia's foreign-policy establishment."[450] Papadopoulos thanked Mifsud and said that he would see him "tomorrow."[451] For her part, Polonskaya responded that she had "already alerted my personal links to our conversation and your request," that "we are all very excited the possibility of a good relationship with Mr. Trump," and that "[t]he Russian Federation would love to welcome him once his candidature would be officially announced."[452]

---

[441] Papadopoulos 8/10/17 302, at 4-5; Papadopoulos 8/11/17 302, at 3; Papadopoulos 9/20/17 302, at 2.

[442] *Papadopoulos* Statement of Offense ¶ 10.

[443] *Papadopoulos* Statement of Offense ¶¶ 10-15.

[444] 3/29/16 Emails, Mifsud to Polonskaya (3:39 a.m. and 5:36 a.m.).

[445] 4/10/16 Email, Papadopoulos to Polonskaya (2:45:59 p.m.).

[446] 4/11/16 Email, Polonskaya to Papadopoulos (3:11:24 a.m.).

[447] 4/11/16 Email, Papadopoulos to Polonskaya (9:21:56 a.m.).

[448] 4/11/16 Email, Mifsud to Papadopoulos (11:43:53).

[449] *Papadopoulos* Statement of Offense ¶ 10(c).

[450] Anton Troianovski, *Putin Ally Warns of Arms Race as Russia Considers Response to U.S. Nuclear Stance*, Washington Post (Feb. 10, 2018).

[451] 4/11/16 Email, Papadopoulos to Mifsud (11:51:53 a.m.).

[452] 4/12/16 Email, Polonskaya to Papadopoulos (4:47:06 a.m.).

Papadopoulos's and Mifsud's mentions of seeing each other "tomorrow" referenced a meeting that the two had scheduled for the next morning, April 12, 2016, at the Andaz Hotel in London. Papadopoulos acknowledged the meeting during interviews with the Office,[453] and records from Papadopoulos's UK cellphone and his internet-search history all indicate that the meeting took place.[454]

Following the meeting, Mifsud traveled as planned to Moscow.[455] On April 18, 2016, while in Russia, Mifsud introduced Papadopoulos over email to Ivan Timofeev, a member of the Russian International Affairs Council (RIAC).[456] Mifsud had described Timofeev as having connections with the Russian Ministry of Foreign Affairs (MFA),[457] the executive entity in Russia responsible for Russian foreign relations.[458] Over the next several weeks, Papadopoulos and Timofeev had multiple conversations over Skype and email about setting "the groundwork" for a "potential" meeting between the Campaign and Russian government officials.[459] Papadopoulos told the Office that, on one Skype call, he believed that his conversation with Timofeev was being monitored or supervised by an unknown third party, because Timofeev spoke in an official manner and Papadopoulos heard odd noises on the line.[460] Timofeev also told Papadopoulos in an April 25, 2016 email that he had just spoken "to Igor Ivanov[,] the President of RIAC and former Foreign Minister of Russia," and conveyed Ivanov's advice about how best to arrange a "Moscow visit."[461]

After a stop in Rome, Mifsud returned to England on April 25, 2016.[462] The next day, Papadopoulos met Mifsud for breakfast at the Andaz Hotel (the same location as their last

---

[453] Papadopoulos 9/19/17 302, at 7.

[454] 4/12/16 Email, Mifsud to Papadopoulos (5:44:39 a.m.) (forwarding Libya-related document); 4/12/16 Email, Mifsud to Papadopoulos & Obaid (10:28:20 a.m.); Papadopoulos Internet Search History (Apr. 11, 2016 10:56:49 p.m.) (search for "andaz hotel liverpool street"); 4/12/16 Text Messages, Mifsud & Papadopoulos.

[455] See, e.g., 4/18/16 Email, Mifsud to Papadopoulos (8:04:54 a.m.).

[456] Papadopoulos 8/10/17 302, at 5.

[457] *Papadopoulos* Statement of Offense ¶ 11.

[458] During the campaign period, Papadopoulos connected over LinkedIn with several MFA-affiliated individuals in addition to Timofeev. On April 25, 2016, he connected with Dmitry Andreyko, publicly identified as a First Secretary at the Russian Embassy in Ireland. In July 2016, he connected with Yuriy Melnik, the spokesperson for the Russian Embassy in Washington and with Alexey Krasilnikov, publicly identified as a counselor with the MFA. And on September 16, 2016, he connected with Sergei Nalobin, also identified as an MFA official. *See* Papadopoulos LinkedIn Connections ██████████

[459] *Papadopoulos* Statement of Offense ¶ 11.

[460] Papadopoulos 8/10/17 302, at 5; Papadopoulos 9/19/17 302, at 10.

[461] 4/25/16 Email, Timofeev to Papadopoulos (8:16:35 a.m.).

[462] 4/22/16 Email, Mifsud to Papadopoulos (12:41:01 a.m.).

meeting).[463] During that meeting, Mifsud told Papadopoulos that he had met with high-level Russian government officials during his recent trip to Moscow. Mifsud also said that, on the trip, he learned that the Russians had obtained "dirt" on candidate Hillary Clinton. As Papadopoulos later stated to the FBI, Mifsud said that the "dirt" was in the form of "emails of Clinton," and that they "have thousands of emails."[464] On May 6, 2016, 10 days after that meeting with Mifsud, Papadopoulos suggested to a representative of a foreign government that the Trump Campaign had received indications from the Russian government that it could assist the Campaign through the anonymous release of information that would be damaging to Hillary Clinton.[465]

e. Russia-Related Communications With The Campaign

While he was discussing with his foreign contacts a potential meeting of campaign officials with Russian government officials, Papadopoulos kept campaign officials apprised of his efforts. On April 25, 2016, the day before Mifsud told Papadopoulos about the emails, Papadopoulos wrote to senior policy advisor Stephen Miller that "[t]he Russian government has an open invitation by Putin for Mr. Trump to meet him when he is ready," and that "[t]he advantage of being in London is that these governments tend to speak a bit more openly in 'neutral' cities."[466] On April 27, 2016, after his meeting with Mifsud, Papadopoulos wrote a second message to Miller stating that "some interesting messages [were] coming in from Moscow about a trip when the time is right."[467] The same day, Papadopoulos sent a similar email to campaign manager Corey Lewandowski, telling Lewandowski that Papadopoulos had "been receiving a lot of calls over the last month about Putin wanting to host [Trump] and the team when the time is right."[468]

Papadopoulos's Russia-related communications with Campaign officials continued throughout the spring and summer of 2016. On May 4, 2016, he forwarded to Lewandowski an email from Timofeev raising the possibility of a meeting in Moscow, asking Lewandowski whether that was "something we want to move forward with."[469] The next day, Papadopoulos forwarded the same Timofeev email to Sam Clovis, adding to the top of the email "Russia update."[470] He included the same email in a May 21, 2016 message to senior Campaign official Paul Manafort, under the subject line "Request from Russia to meet Mr. Trump," stating that "Russia has been eager to meet Mr. Trump for quite sometime and have been reaching out to me

---

[463] *Papadopoulos* Statement of Offense ¶ 14; 4/25/16 Text Messages, Mifsud & Papadopoulos.

[464] *Papadopoulos* Statement of Offense ¶ 14.

[465] This information is contained in the FBI case-opening document and related materials. ~~The information is law-enforcement sensitive (LES) and must be treated accordingly in any external dissemination.~~ The foreign government conveyed this information to the U.S. government on July 26, 2016, a few days after WikiLeaks's release of Clinton-related emails. The FBI opened its investigation of potential coordination between Russia and the Trump Campaign a few days later based on the information.

[466] 4/25/16 Email, Papadopoulos to S. Miller (8:12:44 p.m.).

[467] 4/27/16 Email, Papadopoulos to S. Miller (6:55:58 p.m.).

[468] 4/27/16 Email, Papadopoulos to Lewandowski (7:15:14 p.m.).

[469] 5/4/16 Email, Papadopoulos to Lewandowski (8:14:49 a.m.).

[470] 5/5/16 Email, Papadopoulos to Clovis (7:15:21 p.m.).

U.S. Department of Justice

~~Attorney Work Product // May Contain Material Protected Under Fed. R. Crim. P. 6(e)~~

to discuss."[471] Manafort forwarded the message to another Campaign official, without including Papadopoulos, and stated: "Let[']s discuss. We need someone to communicate that [Trump] is not doing these trips. It should be someone low level in the Campaign so as not to send any signal."[472]

On June 1, 2016, Papadopoulos replied to an earlier email chain with Lewandowski about a Russia visit, asking if Lewandowski "want[ed] to have a call about this topic" and whether "we were following up with it."[473] After Lewandowski told Papadopoulos to "connect with" Clovis because he was "running point," Papadopoulos emailed Clovis that "the Russian MFA" was asking him "if Mr. Trump is interested in visiting Russia at some point."[474] Papadopoulos wrote in an email that he "[w]anted to pass this info along to you for you to decide what's best to do with it and what message I should send (or to ignore)."[475]

After several email and Skype exchanges with Timofeev,[476] Papadopoulos sent one more email to Lewandowski on June 19, 2016, Lewandowski's last day as campaign manager.[477] The email stated that "[t]he Russian ministry of foreign affairs" had contacted him and asked whether, if Mr. Trump could not travel to Russia, a campaign representative such as Papadopoulos could attend meetings.[478] Papadopoulos told Lewandowski that he was "willing to make the trip off the record if it's in the interest of Mr. Trump and the campaign to meet specific people."[479]

Following Lewandowski's departure from the Campaign, Papadopoulos communicated with Clovis and Walid Phares, another member of the foreign policy advisory team, about an off-the-record meeting between the Campaign and Russian government officials or with Papadopoulos's other Russia connections, Mifsud and Timofeev.[480] Papadopoulos also interacted

---

[471] 5/21/16 Email, Papadopoulos to Manafort (2:30:14 p.m.).

[472] *Papadopoulos* Statement of Offense ¶ 19 n.2.

[473] 6/1/16 Email, Papadopoulos to Lewandowski (3:08:18 p.m.).

[474] 6/1/16 Email, Lewandowski to Papadopoulos (3:20:03 p.m.); 6/1/16 Email, Papadopoulos to Clovis (3:29:14 p.m.).

[475] 6/1/16 Email, Papadopoulos to Clovis (3:29:14 p.m.). Papadopoulos's email coincided in time with another message to Clovis suggesting a Trump-Putin meeting. First, on May 15, 2016, David Klein— a distant relative of then-Trump Organization lawyer Jason Greenblatt—emailed Clovis about a potential Campaign meeting with Berel Lazar, the Chief Rabbi of Russia. The email stated that Klein had contacted Lazar in February about a possible Trump-Putin meeting and that Lazar was "a very close confidante of Putin." DJTFP00011547 (5/15/16 Email, Klein to Clovis (5:45:24 p.m.)). The investigation did not find evidence that Clovis responded to Klein's email or that any further contacts of significance came out of Klein's subsequent meeting with Greenblatt and Rabbi Lazar at Trump Tower. Klein 8/30/18 302, at 2.

[476] *Papadopoulos* Statement of Offense ¶ 21(a).

[477] Grand Jury

[478] 6/19/16 Email, Papadopoulos to Lewandowski (1:11:11 p.m.).

[479] 6/19/16 Email, Papadopoulos to Lewandowski (1:11:11 p.m.).

[480] *Papadopoulos* Statement of Offense ¶ 21; 7/14/16 Email, Papadopoulos to Timofeev (11:57:24 p.m.); 7/15/16 Email, Papadopoulos to Mifsud; 7/27/16 Email, Papadopoulos to Mifsud (2:14:18 p.m.).

directly with Clovis and Phares in connection with the summit of the Transatlantic Parliamentary Group on Counterterrorism (TAG), a group for which Phares was co-secretary general.[481] On July 16, 2016, Papadopoulos attended the TAG summit in Washington, D.C., where he sat next to Clovis (as reflected in the photograph below).[482]

George Papadopoulos (far right) and Sam Clovis (second from right)

Although Clovis claimed to have no recollection of attending the TAG summit,[483] Papadopoulos remembered discussing Russia and a foreign policy trip with Clovis and Phares during the event.[484] Papadopoulos's recollection is consistent with emails sent before and after the TAG summit. The pre-summit messages included a July 11, 2016 email in which Phares suggested meeting Papadopoulos the day after the summit to chat,[485] and a July 12 message in the same chain in which Phares advised Papadopoulos that other summit attendees "are very nervous about Russia. So be aware."[486] Ten days after the summit, Papadopoulos sent an email to Mifsud listing Phares and Clovis as other "participants" in a potential meeting at the London Academy of Diplomacy.[487]

Finally, Papadopoulos's recollection is also consistent with handwritten notes from a

---

[481] Papadopoulos 9/19/17 302, at 16-17; *9th TAG Summit in Washington DC*, Transatlantic Parliament Group on Counter Terrorism.

[482] *9th TAG Summit in Washington DC*, Transatlantic Parliament Group on Counter Terrorism.

[483] Grand Jury

[484] Papadopoulos 9/19/17 302, at 16-17.

[485] 7/11/16 Email, Phares to Papadopoulos.

[486] 7/12/16 Email, Phares to Papadopoulos (14:52:29).

[487] 7/27/16 Email, Papadopoulos to Mifsud (14:14:18).

U.S. Department of Justice

~~Attorney Work Product // May Contain Material Protected Under Fed. R. Crim. P. 6(e)~~

journal that he kept at the time.[488] Those notes, which are reprinted in part below, appear to refer to potential September 2016 meetings in London with representatives of the "office of Putin," and suggest that Phares, Clovis, and Papadopoulos ("Walid/Sam me") would attend without the official backing of the Campaign ("no official letter/no message from Trump").[489]

September: Have an exploratory meeting to or lose. In September – if allowed they will blast Mr. Trump. We want the meeting in London/England Walid/Sam me No official letter/no message from Trump They are talking to us. -It is a lot of risk. -Office of Putin. -Explore: we are a campaign. off Israel! EGYPT Willingness to meet the FM sp with Walid/Sam -FM coming -Useful to have a session with him.	*(handwritten notes corresponding to the transcription at left)*

Later communications indicate that Clovis determined that he (Clovis) could not travel. On August 15, 2016, Papadopoulos emailed Clovis that he had received requests from multiple foreign governments, "even Russia[]," for "closed door workshops/consultations abroad," and asked whether there was still interest for Clovis, Phares, and Papadopoulos "to go on that trip."[490] Clovis copied Phares on his response, which said that he could not "travel before the election" but that he "would encourage [Papadopoulos] and Walid to make the trips, if it is feasible."[491]

---

[488] Papadopoulos 9/20/17 302, at 3.

[489] Papadopoulos declined to assist in deciphering his notes, telling investigators that he could not read his own handwriting from the journal. Papadopoulos 9/19/17 302, at 21. The notes, however, appear to read as listed in the column to the left of the image above.

[490] 8/15/16 Email, Papadopoulos to Clovis (11:59:07 a.m.).

[491] 8/15/16 Email, Clovis to Papadopoulos (12:01:45 p.m.).

Papadopoulos was dismissed from the Trump Campaign in early October 2016, after an interview he gave to the Russian news agency *Interfax* generated adverse publicity.[492]

f. Trump Campaign Knowledge of "Dirt"

Papadopoulos admitted telling at least one individual outside of the Campaign—specifically, the then-Greek foreign minister—about Russia's obtaining Clinton-related emails.[493] In addition, a different foreign government informed the FBI that, 10 days after meeting with Mifsud in late April 2016, Papadopoulos suggested that the Trump Campaign had received indications from the Russian government that it could assist the Campaign through the anonymous release of information that would be damaging to Hillary Clinton.[494] (This conversation occurred after the GRU spearphished Clinton Campaign chairman John Podesta and stole his emails, and the GRU hacked into the DCCC and DNC, *see* Volume I, Sections III.A & III.B, *supra*.) Such disclosures raised questions about whether Papadopoulos informed any Trump Campaign official about the emails.

When interviewed, Papadopoulos and the Campaign officials who interacted with him told the Office that they could not recall Papadopoulos's sharing the information that Russia had obtained "dirt" on candidate Clinton in the form of emails or that Russia could assist the Campaign through the anonymous release of information about Clinton. Papadopoulos stated that he could not clearly recall having told anyone on the Campaign and wavered about whether he accurately remembered an incident in which Clovis had been upset after hearing Papadopoulos tell Clovis that Papadopoulos thought "they have her emails."[495] The Campaign officials who interacted or corresponded with Papadopoulos have similarly stated, with varying degrees of certainty, that he did not tell them. Senior policy advisor Stephen Miller, for example, did not remember hearing anything from Papadopoulos or Clovis about Russia having emails of or dirt on candidate Clinton.[496] Clovis stated that he did not recall anyone, including Papadopoulos, having given him non-public information that a foreign government might be in possession of material damaging to Hillary Clinton.[497] Grand Jury

[98] Grand Jury

---

[492] *George Papadopoulos: Sanctions Have Done Little More Than to Turn Russia Towards China*, Interfax (Sept. 30, 2016).

[493] Papadopoulos 9/19/17 302, at 14-15; Def. Sent. Mem., *United States v. George Papadopoulos*, 1:17-cr-182 (D.D.C. Aug. 31, 2018), Doc. 45.

[494] *See* footnote 465 of Volume I, Section IV.A.2.d, *supra*.

[495] Papadopoulos 8/10/17 302, at 5; Papadopoulos 8/11/17 302, at 5; Papadopoulos 9/20/17 302, at 2.

[496] S. Miller 12/14/17 302, at 10.

[497] Grand Jury

[498] Grand Jury

93

████████ Grand Jury ██
████████████████████████ .[499] No documentary evidence, and nothing in the email accounts or other communications facilities reviewed by the Office, shows that Papadopoulos shared this information with the Campaign.

g. Additional George Papadopoulos Contact

The Office investigated another Russia-related contact with Papadopoulos. The Office was not fully able to explore the contact because the individual at issue—Sergei Millian—remained out of the country since the inception of our investigation and declined to meet with members of the Office despite our repeated efforts to obtain an interview.

Papadopoulos first connected with Millian via LinkedIn on July 15, 2016, shortly after Papadopoulos had attended the TAG Summit with Clovis.[500] Millian, an American citizen who is a native of Belarus, introduced himself "as president of [the] New York-based Russian American Chamber of Commerce," and claimed that through that position he had "insider knowledge and direct access to the top hierarchy in Russian politics."[501] Papadopoulos asked Timofeev whether he had heard of Millian.[502] Although Timofeev said no,[503] Papadopoulos met Millian in New York City.[504] The meetings took place on July 30 and August 1, 2016.[505] Afterwards, Millian invited Papadopoulos to attend—and potentially speak at—two international energy conferences, including one that was to be held in Moscow in September 2016.[506] Papadopoulos ultimately did not attend either conference.

On July 31, 2016, following his first in-person meeting with Millian, Papadopoulos emailed Trump Campaign official Bo Denysyk to say that he had been contacted "by some leaders of Russian-American voters here in the US about their interest in voting for Mr. Trump," and to ask whether he should "put you in touch with their group (US-Russia chamber of commerce)."[507] Denysyk thanked Papadopoulos "for taking the initiative," but asked him to "hold off with

---

[499] ████ Grand Jury ████████████

[500] 7/15/16 LinkedIn Message, Millian to Papadopoulos.

[501] 7/15/16 LinkedIn Message, Millian to Papadopoulos.

[502] 7/22/16 Facebook Message, Papadopoulos to Timofeev (7:40:23 p.m.); 7/26/16 Facebook Message, Papadopoulos to Timofeev (3:08:57 p.m.).

[503] 7/23/16 Facebook Message, Timofeev to Papadopoulos (4:31:37 a.m.); 7/26/16 Facebook Message, Timofeev to Papadopoulos (3:37:16 p.m.).

[504] 7/16/16 Text Messages, Papadopoulos & Millian (7:55:43 p.m.).

[505] 7/30/16 Text Messages, Papadopoulos & Millian (5:38 & 6:05 p.m.); 7/31/16 Text Messages, Millian & Papadopoulos (3:48 & 4:18 p.m.); 8/1/16 Text Message, Millian to Papadopoulos (8:19 p.m.).

[506] 8/2/16 Text Messages, Millian & Papadopoulos (3:04 & 3:05 p.m.); 8/3/16 Facebook Messages, Papadopoulos & Millian (4:07:37 a.m. & 1:11:58 p.m.).

[507] 7/31/16 Email, Papadopoulos to Denysyk (12:29:59 p.m.).

outreach to Russian-Americans" because "too many articles" had already portrayed the Campaign, then-campaign chairman Paul Manafort, and candidate Trump as "being pro-Russian."[508]

On August 23, 2016, Millian sent a Facebook message to Papadopoulos promising that he would "share with you a disruptive technology that might be instrumental in your political work for the campaign."[509] Papadopoulos claimed to have no recollection of this matter.[510]

On November 9, 2016, shortly after the election, Papadopoulos arranged to meet Millian in Chicago to discuss business opportunities, including potential work with Russian "billionaires who are not under sanctions."[511] The meeting took place on November 14, 2016, at the Trump Hotel and Tower in Chicago.[512] According to Papadopoulos, the two men discussed partnering on business deals, but Papadopoulos perceived that Millian's attitude toward him changed when Papadopoulos stated that he was only pursuing private-sector opportunities and was not interested in a job in the Administration.[513] The two remained in contact, however, and had extended online discussions about possible business opportunities in Russia.[514] The two also arranged to meet at a Washington, D.C. bar when both attended Trump's inauguration in late January 2017.[515]

3. Carter Page

Carter Page worked for the Trump Campaign from January 2016 to September 2016. He was formally and publicly announced as a foreign policy advisor by the candidate in March 2016.[516] Page had lived and worked in Russia, and he had been approached by Russian intelligence officers several years before he volunteered for the Trump Campaign. During his time with the Campaign, Page advocated pro-Russia foreign policy positions and traveled to Moscow in his personal capacity. Russian intelligence officials had formed relationships with Page in 2008 and 2013 and Russian officials may have focused on Page in 2016 because of his affiliation with the Campaign. However, the investigation did not establish that Page coordinated with the Russian government in its efforts to interfere with the 2016 presidential election.

---

[508] 7/31/16 Email, Denysyk to Papadopoulos (21:54:52).

[509] 8/23/16 Facebook Message, Millian to Papadopoulos (2:55:36 a.m.).

[510] Papadopoulos 9/20/17 302, at 2.

[511] 11/10/16 Facebook Message, Millian to Papadopoulos (9:35:05 p.m.).

[512] 11/14/16 Facebook Message, Millian to Papadopoulos (1:32:11 a.m.).

[513] Papadopoulos 9/19/17 302, at 19.

[514] E.g., 11/29/16 Facebook Messages, Papadopoulos & Millian (5:09 - 5:11 p.m.); 12/7/16 Facebook Message, Millian to Papadopoulos (5:10:54 p.m.).

[515] 1/20/17 Facebook Messages, Papadopoulos & Millian (4:37-4:39 a.m.).

[516] Page was interviewed by the FBI during five meetings in March 2017, before the Special Counsel's appointment. Grand Jury

95

a. Background

Before he began working for the Campaign in January 2016, Page had substantial prior experience studying Russian policy issues and living and working in Moscow. From 2004 to 2007, Page was the deputy branch manager of Merrill Lynch's Moscow office.[517] There, he worked on transactions involving the Russian energy company Gazprom and came to know Gazprom's deputy chief financial officer, Sergey Yatsenko.[518]

In 2008, Page founded Global Energy Capital LLC (GEC), an investment management and advisory firm focused on the energy sector in emerging markets.[519] Grand Jury ████████████████████████████████████[520] The company otherwise had no sources of income, and Page was forced to draw down his life savings to support himself and pursue his business venture.[521] Page asked Yatsenko to work with him at GEC as a senior advisor on a contingency basis, Grand Jury ████████████████[522]

In 2008, Page met Alexander Bulatov, a Russian government official who worked at the Russian Consulate in New York.[523] Page later learned that Bulatov was a Russian intelligence officer, Grand Jury ████████████████████████████████████[524]

In 2013, Victor Podobnyy, another Russian intelligence officer working covertly in the United States under diplomatic cover, formed a relationship with Page.[525] Podobnyy met Page at an energy symposium in New York City and began exchanging emails with him.[526] Podobnyy and Page also met in person on multiple occasions, during which Page offered his outlook on the future of the energy industry and provided documents to Podobnyy about the energy business.[527] In a recorded conversation on April 8, 2013, Podobnyy told another intelligence officer that Page was interested in business opportunities in Russia.[528] In Podobnyy's words, Page "got hooked on

---

[517] *Testimony of Carter Page, Hearing Before the U.S. House of Representatives, Permanent Select Committee on Intelligence*, 115th Cong. 40 (Nov. 2, 2017) (exhibit).

[518] Page 3/30/17 302, at 10.

[519] Grand Jury ██████████████████

[520] Grand Jury ██████████████████

[521] Grand Jury ██████████████████████

[522] Page 3/30/17 302, at 10; Grand Jury ██████████████████

[523] Grand Jury ██████████████████

[524] Grand Jury ██████████████

[525] Grand Jury ████████████████ Complaint ¶¶ 22, 24, 32, *United States v. Buryakov*, 1:15-mj-215 (S.D.N.Y. Jan. 23, 2015), Doc. 1 ("*Buryakov* Complaint").

[526] *Buryakov* Complaint ¶ 34.

[527] *Buryakov* Complaint ¶ 34.

[528] *Buryakov* Complaint ¶ 32.

Gazprom thinking that if they have a project, he could . . . rise up. Maybe he can. . . . [I]t's obvious that he wants to earn lots of money."[529] Podobnyy said that he had led Page on by "feed[ing] him empty promises" that Podobnyy would use his Russian business connections to help Page.[530] Podobnyy told the other intelligence officer that his method of recruiting foreign sources was to promise them favors and then discard them once he obtained relevant information from them.[531]

In 2015, Podobnyy and two other Russian intelligence officers were charged with conspiracy to act as an unregistered agent of a foreign government.[532] The criminal complaint detailed Podobnyy's interactions with and conversations about Page, who was identified only as "Male-1."[533] Based on the criminal complaint's description of the interactions, Page was aware that he was the individual described as "Male-1."[534] Page later spoke with a Russian government official at the United Nations General Assembly and identified himself so that the official would understand he was "Male-1" from the Podobnyy complaint.[535] Page told the official that he "didn't do anything" Grand Jury .[536]

In interviews with the FBI before the Office's opening, Page acknowledged that he understood that the individuals he had associated with were members of the Russian intelligence services, but he stated that he had only provided immaterial non-public information to them and that he did not view this relationship as a backchannel.[537] Page told investigating agents that "the more immaterial non-public information I give them, the better for this country."[538]

b. Origins of and Early Campaign Work

In January 2016, Page began volunteering on an informal, unpaid basis for the Trump Campaign after Ed Cox, a state Republican Party official, introduced Page to Trump Campaign officials.[539] Page told the Office that his goal in working on the Campaign was to help candidate Trump improve relations with Russia.[540] To that end, Page emailed Campaign officials offering his thoughts on U.S.-Russia relations, prepared talking points and briefing memos on Russia, and

---

[529] *Buryakov* Complaint.

[530] *Buryakov* Complaint.

[531] *Buryakov* Complaint.

[532] *See Buryakov* Complaint; *see also* Indictment, *United States v. Buryakov*, 1:15-cr-73 (S.D.N.Y. Feb. 9, 2015), Doc. 10; Grand Jury

[533] *Buryakov* Complaint ¶¶ 32-34; Grand Jury

[534] Grand Jury

[535] Page 3/16/17 302, at 4; Grand Jury

[536] Page 3/16/17 302, at 4; Grand Jury

[537] Page 3/30/17 302, at 6; Page 3/31/17 302, at 1.

[538] Page 3/31/17 302, at 1.

[539] Page 3/16/17 302, at 1; Grand Jury

[540] Page 3/10/17 302, at 2.

proposed that candidate Trump meet with President Vladimir Putin in Moscow.[541]

In communications with Campaign officials, Page also repeatedly touted his high-level contacts in Russia and his ability to forge connections between candidate Trump and senior Russian governmental officials. For example, on January 30, 2016, Page sent an email to senior Campaign officials stating that he had "spent the past week in Europe and ha[d] been in discussions with some individuals with close ties to the Kremlin" who recognized that Trump could have a "game-changing effect . . . in bringing the end of the new Cold War."[542] The email stated that "[t]hrough [his] discussions with these high level contacts," Page believed that "a direct meeting in Moscow between Mr[.] Trump and Putin could be arranged."[543] Page closed the email by criticizing U.S. sanctions on Russia.[544] **Grand Jury**

[545]

On March 21, 2016, candidate Trump formally and publicly identified Page as a member of his foreign policy team to advise on Russia and the energy sector.[546] Over the next several months, Page continued providing policy-related work product to Campaign officials. For example, in April 2016, Page provided feedback on an outline for a foreign policy speech that the candidate gave at the Mayflower Hotel,[547] *see* Volume I, Section IV.A.4, *infra*. In May 2016, Page prepared an outline of an energy policy speech for the Campaign and then traveled to Bismarck, North Dakota, to watch the candidate deliver the speech.[548] Chief policy advisor Sam Clovis expressed appreciation for Page's work and praised his work to other Campaign officials.[549]

c. Carter Page's July 2016 Trip To Moscow

Page's affiliation with the Trump Campaign took on a higher profile and drew the attention of Russian officials after the candidate named him a foreign policy advisor. As a result, in late April 2016, Page was invited to give a speech at the July 2016 commencement ceremony at the

---

[541] *See, e.g.*, 1/30/16 Email, Page to Glassner et al.; 3/17/16 Email, Page to Clovis (attaching a "President's Daily Brief" prepared by Page that discussed the "severe degradation of U.S.-Russia relations following Washington's meddling" in Ukraine); **Grand Jury**

[542] 1/30/16 Email, Page to Glassner et al.

[543] 1/30/16 Email, Page to Glassner et al.

[544] 1/30/16 Email, Page to Glassner et al.

[545] **Grand Jury**

[546] *A Transcript of Donald Trump's Meeting with the Washington Post Editorial Board*, Washington Post (Mar. 21, 2016); **Grand Jury**

[547] **Grand Jury**

[548] **Grand Jury**

[549] *See, e.g.*, 3/28/16 Email, Clovis to Lewandowski et al. (forwarding notes prepared by Page and stating, "I wanted to let you know the type of work some of our advisors are capable of.").

New Economic School (NES) in Moscow.[550] The NES commencement ceremony generally featured high-profile speakers; for example, President Barack Obama delivered a commencement address at the school in 2009.[551] NES officials told the Office that the interest in inviting Page to speak at NES was based entirely on his status as a Trump Campaign advisor who served as the candidate's Russia expert.[552] Andrej Krickovic, an associate of Page's and assistant professor at the Higher School of Economics in Russia, recommended that NES rector Shlomo Weber invite Page to give the commencement address based on his connection to the Trump Campaign.[553] Denis Klimentov, an employee of NES, said that when Russians learned of Page's involvement in the Trump Campaign in March 2016, the excitement was palpable.[554] Weber recalled that in summer 2016 there was substantial interest in the Trump Campaign in Moscow, and he felt that bringing a member of the Campaign to the school would be beneficial.[555]

Page was eager to accept the invitation to speak at NES, and he sought approval from Trump Campaign officials to make the trip to Russia.[556] On May 16, 2016, while that request was still under consideration, Page emailed Clovis, J.D. Gordon, and Walid Phares and suggested that candidate Trump take his place speaking at the commencement ceremony in Moscow.[557] On June 19, 2016, Page followed up again to request approval to speak at the NES event and to reiterate that NES "would love to have Mr. Trump speak at this annual celebration" in Page's place.[558] Campaign manager Corey Lewandowski responded the same day, saying, "If you want to do this, it would be out side [sic] of your role with the DJT for President campaign. I am certain Mr. Trump will not be able to attend."[559]

In early July 2016, Page traveled to Russia for the NES events. On July 5, 2016, Denis Klimentov, copying his brother, Dmitri Klimentov,[560] emailed Maria Zakharova, the Director of the Russian Ministry of Foreign Affairs' Information and Press Department, about Page's visit and his connection to the Trump Campaign.[561] Denis Klimentov said in the email that he wanted to draw the Russian government's attention to Page's visit in Moscow.[562] His message to Zakharova

---

[550] Page 3/16/17 302, at 2-3; Page 3/10/17 302, at 3.

[551] S. Weber 7/28/17 302, at 3.

[552] Y. Weber 6/1/17 302, at 4-5; S. Weber 7/28/17 302, at 3.

[553] See Y. Weber 6/1/17 302, at 4; S. Weber 7/28/17 302, at 3.

[554] De. Klimentov 6/9/17 302, at 2.

[555] S. Weber 7/28/17 302, at 3.

[556] See 5/16/16 Email, Page to Phares et al. (referring to submission of a "campaign advisor request form").

[557] Grand Jury ; 5/16/16 Email, Page to Phares et al.

[558] 6/19/16 Email, Page to Gordon et al.

[559] 6/19/16 Email, Lewandowski to Page et al.

[560] Dmitri Klimentov is a New York-based public relations consultant.

[561] 7/5/16 Email, Klimentov to Zakharova (translated).

[562] 7/5/16 Email, Klimentov to Zakharova (translated).

~~Attorney Work Product // May Contain Material Protected Under Fed. R. Crim. P. 6(e)~~

continued: "Page is Trump's adviser on foreign policy. He is a known businessman; he used to work in Russia. . . . If you have any questions, I will be happy to help contact him."[563] Dmitri Klimentov then contacted Russian Press Secretary Dmitry Peskov about Page's visit to see if Peskov wanted to introduce Page to any Russian government officials.[564] The following day, Peskov responded to what appears to have been the same Denis Klimentov-Zakharova email thread. Peskov wrote, "I have read about [Page]. Specialists say that he is far from being the main one. So I better not initiate a meeting in the Kremlin."[565]

On July 7, 2016, Page delivered the first of his two speeches in Moscow at NES.[566] In the speech, Page criticized the U.S. government's foreign policy toward Russia, stating that "Washington and other Western capitals have impeded potential progress through their often hypocritical focus on ideas such as democratization, inequality, corruption and regime change."[567] On July 8, 2016, Page delivered a speech during the NES commencement.[568] After Page delivered his commencement address, Russian Deputy Prime Minister and NES board member Arkady Dvorkovich spoke at the ceremony and stated that the sanctions the United States had imposed on Russia had hurt the NES.[569] Page and Dvorkovich shook hands at the commencement ceremony, and Weber recalled that Dvorkovich made statements to Page about working together in the future.[570] Grand Jury [571]

Page said that, during his time in Moscow, he met with friends and associates he knew from when he lived in Russia, including Andrey Baranov, a former Gazprom employee who had become the head of investor relations at Rosneft, a Russian energy company.[572] Page stated that he and Baranov talked about "immaterial non-public" information.[573] Page believed he and Baranov discussed Rosneft president Igor Sechin, and he thought Baranov might have mentioned

---

[563] 7/5/16 Email, Klimentov to Zakharova (translated).

[564] Dm. Klimentov 11/27/18 302, at 1-2.

[565] 7/6/16 Email, Peskov to Klimentov (translated).

[566] Page 3/10/17 302, at 3.

[567] *See* Carter W. Page, *The Lecture of Trump's Advisor Carter Page in Moscow*, YouTube Channel Katehon Think Tank, Posted July 7, 2016, *available at* https://www.youtube.com/watch?time_continue=28&v=1CYF29saA9w. Page also provided the FBI with a copy of his speech and slides from the speech. *See* Carter Page, "The Evolution of the World Economy: Trends and Potential," Speech at National Economic Speech (July 7, 2016).

[568] Page 3/10/17 302, at 3.

[569] Page 3/16/17 302, at 3.

[570] S. Weber 7/28/17 302, at 4.

[571] Grand Jury

[572] Page 3/10/17 302, at 3; Page 3/30/17 302, at 3; Page 3/31/17 302, at 2.

[573] Page 3/30/17 302, at 3.

the possibility of a sale of a stake in Rosneft in passing.[574] Page recalled mentioning his involvement in the Trump Campaign with Baranov, although he did not remember details of the conversation.[575] Page also met with individuals from Tatneft, a Russian energy company, to discuss possible business deals, including having Page work as a consultant.[576]

On July 8, 2016, while he was in Moscow, Page emailed several Campaign officials and stated he would send "a readout soon regarding some incredible insights and outreach I've received from a few Russian legislators and senior members of the Presidential Administration here."[577] On July 9, 2016, Page emailed Clovis, writing in pertinent part:

> Russian Deputy Prime minister and NES board member Arkady Dvorkovich also spoke before the event. In a private conversation, Dvorkovich expressed strong support for Mr. Trump and a desire to work together toward devising better solutions in response to the vast range of current international problems. Based on feedback from a diverse array of other sources close to the Presidential Administration, it was readily apparent that this sentiment is widely held at all levels of government.[578]

Despite these representations to the Campaign, Grand Jury

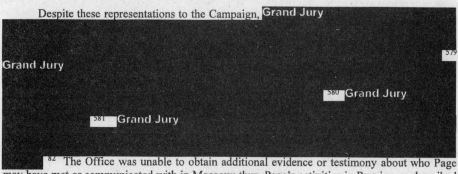

[82] The Office was unable to obtain additional evidence or testimony about who Page may have met or communicated with in Moscow; thus, Page's activities in Russia—as described in his emails with the Campaign—were not fully explained.

---

[574] Page 3/30/17 302, at 9. Grand Jury

[575] Grand Jury   Page 3/30/17 302, at 3.

[576] Page 3/10/17 302, at 3; Page 3/30/17 302, at 7; Page 3/31/17 302, at 2.

[577] Grand Jury   7/8/16 Email, Page to Dahl & Gordon.

[578] Grand Jury   7/9/16 Email, Page to Clovis.

[579] Grand Jury

[580] Grand Jury

[581] Grand Jury

[582] Grand Jury

101

U.S. Department of Justice

~~Attorney Work Product // May Contain Material Protected Under Fed. R. Crim. P. 6(e)~~

d. Later Campaign Work and Removal from the Campaign

In July 2016, after returning from Russia, Page traveled to the Republican National Convention in Cleveland.[583] While there, Page met Russian Ambassador to the United States Sergey Kislyak; that interaction is described in Volume I, Section IV.A.6.a, *infra*.[584] Page later emailed Campaign officials with feedback he said he received from ambassadors he had met at the Convention, and he wrote that Ambassador Kislyak was very worried about candidate Clinton's world views.[585] Grand Jury

.[586]

Following the Convention, Page's trip to Moscow and his advocacy for pro-Russia foreign policy drew the media's attention and began to generate substantial press coverage. The Campaign responded by distancing itself from Page, describing him as an "informal foreign policy advisor" who did "not speak for Mr. Trump or the campaign."[587] On September 23, 2016, Yahoo! News reported that U.S. intelligence officials were investigating whether Page had opened private communications with senior Russian officials to discuss U.S. sanctions policy under a possible Trump Administration.[588] A Campaign spokesman told Yahoo! News that Page had "no role" in the Campaign and that the Campaign was "not aware of any of his activities, past or present."[589] On September 24, 2016, Page was formally removed from the Campaign.[590]

Although Page had been removed from the Campaign, after the election he sought a position in the Trump Administration.[591] On November 14, 2016, he submitted an application to the Transition Team that inflated his credentials and experiences, stating that in his capacity as a Trump Campaign foreign policy advisor he had met with "top world leaders" and "effectively

---

[583] Page 3/10/17 302, at 4; Page 3/16/17 302, at 3.

[584] Page 3/10/17 302, at 4; Page 3/16/17 302, at 3.

[585] Grand Jury ; 7/23/16 Email, Page to Clovis; 7/25/16 Email, Page to Gordon & Schmitz.

[586] Grand Jury

[587] *See, e.g.*, Steven Mufson & Tom Hamburger, *Trump Advisor's Public Comments, Ties to Moscow Stir Unease in Both Parties*, Washington Post (Aug. 5, 2016).

[588] Michael Isikoff, *U.S. Intel Officials Probe Ties Between Trump Adviser and Kremlin*, Yahoo! News (Sept. 23, 2016).

[589] Michael Isikoff, *U.S. Intel Officials Probe Ties Between Trump Adviser and Kremlin*, Yahoo! News (Sept. 23, 2016); *see also* 9/25/16 Email, Hicks to Conway & Bannon (instructing that inquiries about Page should be answered with "[h]e was announced as an informal adviser in March. Since then he has had no role or official contact with the campaign. We have no knowledge of activities past or present and he now officially has been removed from all lists etc.").

[590] Page 3/16/17 302, at 2; *see, e.g.*, 9/23/16 Email, J. Miller to Bannon & S. Miller (discussing plans to remove Page from the campaign).

[591] Grand Jury , "Transition Online Form," 11/14/16 (Grand Jury

responded to diplomatic outreach efforts from senior government officials in Asia, Europe, the Middle East, Africa, [and] the Americas."[592] Page received no response from the Transition Team. When Page took a personal trip to Moscow in December 2016, he met again with at least one Russian government official. That interaction and a discussion of the December trip are set forth in Volume I, Section IV.B.6, *infra*.

4. Dimitri Simes and the Center for the National Interest

Members of the Trump Campaign interacted on several occasions with the Center for the National Interest (CNI), principally through its President and Chief Executive Officer, Dimitri Simes. CNI is a think tank with expertise in and connections to the Russian government. Simes was born in the former Soviet Union and immigrated to the United States in the 1970s. In April 2016, candidate Trump delivered his first speech on foreign policy and national security at an event hosted by the *National Interest*, a publication affiliated with CNI. Then-Senator Jeff Sessions and Russian Ambassador Kislyak both attended the event and, as a result, it gained some attention in relation to Sessions's confirmation hearings to become Attorney General. Sessions had various other contacts with CNI during the campaign period on foreign-policy matters, including Russia. Jared Kushner also interacted with Simes about Russian issues during the campaign. The investigation did not identify evidence that the Campaign passed or received any messages to or from the Russian government through CNI or Simes.

a. CNI and Dimitri Simes Connect with the Trump Campaign

CNI is a Washington-based non-profit organization that grew out of a center founded by former President Richard Nixon.[593] CNI describes itself "as a voice for strategic realism in U.S. foreign policy," and publishes a bi-monthly foreign policy magazine, the *National Interest*.[594] CNI is overseen by a board of directors and an advisory council that is largely honorary and whose members at the relevant time included Sessions, who served as an advisor to candidate Trump on national security and foreign policy issues.[595]

Dimitri Simes is president and CEO of CNI and the publisher and CEO of the *National Interest*.[596] Simes was born in the former Soviet Union, emigrated to the United States in the early 1970s, and joined CNI's predecessor after working at the Carnegie Endowment for International

---

[592] Grand Jury
Grand Jury , "Transition Online Form," 11/14/16

[593] Simes 3/8/18 302, at 1-2.

[594] *About the Center*, CNI, *available at* https://cftni.org/about/.

[595] *Advisory Counsel*, CNI, *available at* https://web.archive.org/web/20161030025331/ http://cftni.org/about/advisory-council/; Simes 3/8/18 302, at 3-4; Saunders 2/15/18 302, at 4; Sessions 1/17/18 302, at 16.

[596] Simes 3/8/18 302, at 2.

U.S. Department of Justice

~~Attorney Work Product // May Contain Material Protected Under Fed. R. Crim. P. 6(e)~~

Peace.[597] Simes personally has many contacts with current and former Russian government officials,[598] as does CNI collectively. As CNI stated when seeking a grant from the Carnegie Corporation in 2015, CNI has "unparalleled access to Russian officials and politicians among Washington think tanks,"[599] in part because CNI has arranged for U.S. delegations to visit Russia and for Russian delegations to visit the United States as part of so-called "Track II" diplomatic efforts.[600]

On March 14, 2016, CNI board member Richard Plepler organized a luncheon for CNI and its honorary chairman, Henry Kissinger, at the Time Warner Building in New York.[601] The idea behind the event was to generate interest in CNI's work and recruit new board members for CNI.[602] Along with Simes, attendees at the event included Jared Kushner, son-in-law of candidate Trump.[603] Kushner told the Office that the event came at a time when the Trump Campaign was having trouble securing support from experienced foreign policy professionals and that, as a result, he decided to seek Simes's assistance during the March 14 event.[604]

Simes and Kushner spoke again on a March 24, 2016 telephone call,[605] three days after Trump had publicly named the team of foreign policy advisors that had been put together on short notice.[606] On March 31, 2016, Simes and Kushner had an in-person, one-on-one meeting in Kushner's New York office.[607] During that meeting, Simes told Kushner that the best way to handle foreign-policy issues for the Trump Campaign would be to organize an advisory group of experts to meet with candidate Trump and develop a foreign policy approach that was consistent with Trump's voice.[608] Simes believed that Kushner was receptive to that suggestion.[609]

Simes also had contact with other individuals associated with the Trump Campaign regarding the Campaign's foreign policy positions. For example, on June 17, 2016, Simes sent J.D. Gordon an email with a "memo to Senator Sessions that we discussed at our recent meeting"

---

[597] Simes 3/8/18 302, at 1-2; Simes 3/27/18 302, at 19.

[598] Simes 3/27/18 302, at 10-15.

[599] C00011656 (*Rethinking U.S.-Russia Relations*, CNI (Apr. 18, 2015)).

[600] Simes 3/8/18 302, at 5; Saunders 2/15/18 302, at 29-30; Zakheim 1/25/18 302, at 3.

[601] Simes 3/8/18 302, at 6; C00006784 (3/11/16 Email, Gilbride to Saunders (3:43:12 p.m.); *cf.* Zakheim 1/25/18 302, at 1 (Kissinger was CNI's "Honorary Chairman of the Board"); Boyd 1/24/18 302, at 2; P. Sanders 2/15/18 302, at 5.

[602] Simes 3/8/18 302, at 5-6; Simes 3/27/18 302, at 2.

[603] Simes 3/8/18 302, at 6; Kushner 4/11/18 302 at 2.

[604] Kushner 4/11/18 302, at 2.

[605] Simes 3/8/18 302, at 6-7.

[606] Grand Jury ▮▮▮▮▮▮▮▮▮▮ *see* Volume I, Section IV.A.2, *supra*.

[607] Simes 3/8/18 302, at 7-9.

[608] Simes 3/8/18 302, at 7-8.

[609] Simes 3/8/18 302, at 8; *see also* Boyd 1/24/18 302, at 2.

164

U.S. Department of Justice

~~Attorney Work Product // May Contain Material Protected Under Fed. R. Crim. P. 6(e)~~

and asked Gordon to both read it and share it with Sessions. The memorandum proposed building a "small and carefully selected group of experts" to assist Sessions with the Campaign, operating under the assumption "that Hillary Clinton is very vulnerable on national security and foreign policy issues." The memorandum outlined key issues for the Campaign, including a "new beginning with Russia."[610]

b. National Interest Hosts a Foreign Policy Speech at the Mayflower Hotel

During both their March 24 phone call and their March 31 in-person meeting, Simes and Kushner discussed the possibility of CNI hosting a foreign policy speech by candidate Trump.[611] Following those conversations, Simes agreed that he and others associated with CNI would provide behind-the-scenes input on the substance of the foreign-policy speech and that CNI officials would coordinate the logistics of the speech with Sessions and his staff, including Sessions's chief of staff, Rick Dearborn.[612]

In mid-April 2016, Kushner put Simes in contact with senior policy advisor Stephen Miller and forwarded to Simes an outline of the foreign-policy speech that Miller had prepared.[613] Simes sent back to the Campaign bullet points with ideas for the speech that he had drafted with CNI Executive Director Paul Saunders and board member Richard Burt.[614] Simes received subsequent draft outlines from Miller, and he and Saunders spoke to Miller by phone about substantive changes to the speech.[615] It is not clear, however, whether CNI officials received an actual draft of the speech for comment; while Saunders recalled having received an actual draft, Simes did not, and the emails that CNI produced to this Office do not contain such a draft.[616]

After board members expressed concern to Simes that CNI's hosting the speech could be perceived as an endorsement of a particular candidate, CNI decided to have its publication, the National Interest, serve as the host and to have the event at the National Press Club.[617] Kushner later requested that the event be moved to the Mayflower Hotel, which was another venue that Simes had mentioned during initial discussions with the Campaign, in order to address concerns about security and capacity.[618]

---

[610] C00008187 (6/17/16 Email, Simes to Gordon (3:35:45 p.m.)).

[611] Simes 3/8/18 302, at 7.

[612] Simes 3/8/18 302, at 8-11; C00008923 (4/6/16 Email, Simes to Burt (2:22:28 p.m.)); Burt 2/9/18 302, at 7.

[613] C00008551 (4/17/16 Email, Kushner to Simes (2:44:25 p.m.)); C00006759 (4/14/16 Email Kushner to Simes & S. Miller (12:30 p.m.)).

[614] Burt 2/9/18 302, at 7; Saunders 2/15/18 302, at 7-8.

[615] Simes 3/8/18 302, at 13; Saunders 2/15/18 302, at 7-8.

[616] Simes 3/8/18 302, at 13; Saunders 2/15/18 302, at 7-8.

[617] Saunders 2/15/18 302, at 8; Simes 3/8/18 302, at 12; C00003834-43 (4/22/16 Email, Simes to Boyd et al. (8:47 a.m.)).

[618] Simes 3/8/18 302, at 12, 18; Saunders 2/15/18 302, at 11.

On April 25, 2016, Saunders booked event rooms at the Mayflower to host both the speech and a VIP reception that was to be held beforehand.[619] Saunders understood that the reception—at which invitees would have the chance to meet candidate Trump—would be a small event.[620] Saunders decided who would attend by looking at the list of CNI's invitees to the speech itself and then choosing a subset for the reception.[621] CNI's invitees to the reception included Sessions and Kislyak.[622] The week before the speech Simes had informed Kislyak that he would be invited to the speech, and that he would have the opportunity to meet Trump.[623]

When the pre-speech reception began on April 27, a receiving line was quickly organized so that attendees could meet Trump.[624] Sessions first stood next to Trump to introduce him to the members of Congress who were in attendance.[625] After those members had been introduced, Simes stood next to Trump and introduced him to the CNI invitees in attendance, including Kislyak.[626] Simes perceived the introduction to be positive and friendly, but thought it clear that Kislyak and Trump had just met for the first time.[627] Kislyak also met Kushner during the pre-speech reception. The two shook hands and chatted for a minute or two, during which Kushner recalled Kislyak saying, "we like what your candidate is saying . . . it's refreshing."[628]

Several public reports state that, in addition to speaking to Kushner at the pre-speech reception, Kislyak also met or conversed with Sessions at that time.[629] Sessions stated to investigators, however, that he did not remember any such conversation.[630] Nor did anyone else affiliated with CNI or the *National Interest* specifically recall a conversation or meeting between Sessions and Kislyak at the pre-speech reception.[631] It appears that, if a conversation occurred at the pre-speech reception, it was a brief one conducted in public view, similar to the exchange between Kushner and Kislyak.

---

[619] Saunders 2/15/18 302, at 11-12; C00006651-57 (Mayflower Group Sales Agreement).

[620] Saunders 2/15/18 302, at 12-13.

[621] Saunders 2/15/18 302, at 12.

[622] C00002575 (Attendee List); C00008536 (4/25/16 Email, Simes to Kushner (4:53:45 p.m.)).

[623] Simes 3/8/18 302, at 19-20.

[624] Simes 3/8/18 302, at 21.

[625] Simes 3/8/18 302, at 21.

[626] Simes 3/8/18 302, at 21.

[627] Simes 3/8/18 302, at 21.

[628] Kushner 4/11/18 302, at 4.

[629] *See, e.g.*, Ken Dilanian, *Did Trump, Kushner, Sessions Have an Undisclosed Meeting With Russian?*, NBC News (June 1, 2016); Julia Ioffe, *Why Did Jeff Sessions Really Meet With Sergey Kislyak*, The Atlantic (June 13, 2017).

[630] Sessions 1/17/18 302, at 22.

[631] Simes 3/8/18 302, at 21; Saunders 2/15/18 302, at 14, 21; Boyd 1/24/18 302, at 3-4; Heilbrunn 2/1/18 302, at 6; *Statement Regarding President Trump's April 27, 2016 Foreign Policy Speech at the Center for the National Interest*, CNI (Mar. 8, 2017).

106

The Office found no evidence that Kislyak conversed with either Trump or Sessions after the speech, or would have had the opportunity to do so. Simes, for example, did not recall seeing Kislyak at the post-speech luncheon,[632] and the only witness who accounted for Sessions's whereabouts stated that Sessions may have spoken to the press after the event but then departed for Capitol Hill.[633] Saunders recalled, based in part on a food-related request he received from a Campaign staff member, that Trump left the hotel a few minutes after the speech to go to the airport.[634]

c. Jeff Sessions's Post-Speech Interactions with CNI

In the wake of Sessions's confirmation hearings as Attorney General, questions arose about whether Sessions's campaign-period interactions with CNI apart from the Mayflower speech included any additional meetings with Ambassador Kislyak or involved Russian-related matters. With respect to Kislyak contacts, on May 23, 2016, Sessions attended CNI's Distinguished Service Award dinner at the Four Seasons Hotel in Washington, D.C.[635] Sessions attended a pre-dinner reception and was seated at one of two head tables for the event.[636] A seating chart prepared by Saunders indicates that Sessions was scheduled to be seated next to Kislyak, who appears to have responded to the invitation by indicating he would attend the event.[637] Sessions, however, did not remember seeing, speaking with, or sitting next to Kislyak at the dinner.[638] Although CNI board member Charles Boyd said he may have seen Kislyak at the dinner,[639] Simes, Saunders, and Jacob Heilbrunn—editor of the *National Interest*—all had no recollection of seeing Kislyak at the May 23 event.[640] Kislyak also does not appear in any of the photos from the event that the Office obtained.

In the summer of 2016, CNI organized at least two dinners in Washington, D.C. for Sessions to meet with experienced foreign policy professionals.[641] The dinners included CNI-affiliated individuals, such as Richard Burt and Zalmay Khalilzad, a former U.S. ambassador to Afghanistan and Iraq and the person who had introduced Trump before the April 27, 2016 foreign-

---

[632] Simes 3/8/18 302, at 22; Heilbrunn 2/1/18 302, at 7.

[633] Luff 1/30/18 302, at 4.

[634] Saunders 2/15/18 302, at 15.

[635] Sessions 1/17/18 302, at 22; Saunders 2/15/18 302, at 17.

[636] Saunders 2/15/18 302, at 17; C00004779-80 (5/23/16 Email, Cantelmo to Saunders & Hagberg (9:30:12 a.m.); C00004362 (5/23/16 Email, Bauman to Cantelmo et al. (2:02:32 a.m.).

[637] C00004362 (5/23/16 Email Bauman to Cantelmo et al. (2:02:32 a.m.).

[638] Sessions 1/17/18 302, at 22.

[639] Boyd 1/24/18 302, at 4.

[640] Simes 3/8/18 302, at 23; Saunders 2/15/18 302, at 18; Heilbrunn 2/1/18 302, at 7.

[641] Simes 3/8/18 302, at 31; Saunders 2/15/18 302, at 19; Burt 2/9/18 302, at 9-10; Khalilzad 1/9/18 302, at 5.

policy speech.[642] Khalilzad also met with Sessions one-on-one separately from the dinners.[643] At the dinners and in the meetings, the participants addressed U.S. relations with Russia, including how U.S. relations with NATO and European countries affected U.S. policy toward Russia.[644] But the discussions were not exclusively focused on Russia.[645] Khalilzad, for example, recalled discussing "nation-building" and violent extremism with Sessions.[646] In addition, Sessions asked Saunders (of CNI) to draft two memoranda not specific to Russia: one on Hillary Clinton's foreign policy shortcomings and another on Egypt.[647]

d. Jared Kushner's Continuing Contacts with Simes

Between the April 2016 speech at the Mayflower Hotel and the presidential election, Jared Kushner had periodic contacts with Simes.[648] Those contacts consisted of both in-person meetings and phone conversations, which concerned how to address issues relating to Russia in the Campaign and how to move forward with the advisory group of foreign policy experts that Simes had proposed.[649] Simes recalled that he, not Kushner, initiated all conversations about Russia, and that Kushner never asked him to set up back-channel conversations with Russians.[650] According to Simes, after the Mayflower speech in late April, Simes raised the issue of Russian contacts with Kushner, advised that it was bad optics for the Campaign to develop hidden Russian contacts, and told Kushner both that the Campaign should not highlight Russia as an issue and should handle any contacts with Russians with care.[651] Kushner generally provided a similar account of his interactions with Simes.[652]

Among the Kushner-Simes meetings was one held on August 17, 2016, at Simes's request, in Kushner's New York office. The meeting was to address foreign policy advice that CNI was providing and how to respond to the Clinton Campaign's Russia-related attacks on candidate

---

[642] Burt 2/9/18 302, at 9-10; Khalilzad 1/9/18 302, at 1-2, 5.

[643] Khalilzad 1/9/18 302, at 5-6.

[644] Simes 3/8/18 302, at 31; Burt 2/9/18 302, at 9-10; Khalilzad 1/9/18 302, at 5.

[645] Saunders 2/15/18 302, at 20.

[646] Khalilzad 1/9/18 302, at 6.

[647] Saunders 2/15/18 302, at 19-20.

[648] Simes 3/8/18 302, at 27.

[649] Simes 3/8/18 302, at 27.

[650] Simes 3/8/18 302, at 27.

[651] Simes 3/8/18 302, at 27. During this period of time, the Campaign received a request for a high-level Campaign official to meet with an officer at a Russian state-owned bank "to discuss an offer [that officer] claims to be carrying from President Putin to meet with" candidate Trump. NOSC00005653 (5/17/16 Email, Dearborn to Kushner (8:12 a.m.)). Copying Manafort and Gates, Kushner responded, "Pass on this. A lot of people come claiming to carry messages. Very few are able to verify. For now I think we decline such meetings. Most likely these people go back home and claim they have special access to gain importance for themselves. Be careful." NOSC00005653 (5/17/16 Email, Kushner to Dearborn).

[652] Kushner 4/11/18 302, at 11-13.

Trump.[653] In advance of the meeting, Simes sent Kushner a "Russia Policy Memo" laying out "what Mr. Trump may want to say about Russia."[654] In a cover email transmitting that memo and a phone call to set up the meeting, Simes mentioned "a well-documented story of highly questionable connections between Bill Clinton" and the Russian government, "parts of [which]" (according to Simes) had even been "discussed with the CIA and the FBI in the late 1990s and shared with the [Independent Counsel] at the end of the Clinton presidency."[655] Kushner forwarded the email to senior Trump Campaign officials Stephen Miller, Paul Manafort, and Rick Gates, with the note "suggestion only."[656] Manafort subsequently forwarded the email to his assistant and scheduled a meeting with Simes.[657] (Manafort was on the verge of leaving the Campaign by the time of the scheduled meeting with Simes, and Simes ended up meeting only with Kushner).

During the August 17 meeting, Simes provided Kushner the Clinton-related information that he had promised.[658] Simes told Kushner that, Personal Privacy

[659] Simes claimed that he had received this information from former CIA and Reagan White House official Fritz Ermarth, who claimed to have learned it from U.S. intelligence sources, not from Russians.[660]

Simes perceived that Kushner did not find the information to be of interest or use to the Campaign because it was, in Simes's words, "old news."[661] When interviewed by the Office, Kushner stated that he believed that there was little chance of something new being revealed about the Clintons given their long career as public figures, and that he never received from Simes information that could be "operationalized" for the Trump Campaign.[662] Despite Kushner's

---

[653] Simes 3/8/18 302, at 29-30; Simes 3/27/18 302, at 6; Kushner 4/11/18 302, at 12; C00007269 (8/10/16 Meeting Invitation, Vargas to Simes et al.); DJTFP00023484 (8/11/16 Email, Hagan to Manafort (5:57:15 p.m.)).

[654] C00007981-84 (8/9/16 Email, Simes to Kushner (6:09:21 p.m.)). The memorandum recommended "downplaying Russia as a U.S. foreign policy priority at this time" and suggested that "some tend to exaggerate Putin's flaws." The memorandum also recommended approaching general Russian-related questions in the framework of "how to work with Russia to advance important U.S. national interests" and that a Trump Administration "not go abroad in search of monsters to destroy." The memorandum did not discuss sanctions but did address how to handle Ukraine-related questions, including questions about Russia's invasion and annexation of Crimea.

[655] C00007981 (8/9/16 Email, Simes to Kushner (6:09:21 p.m.)).

[656] DJTFP00023459 (8/10/16 Email, Kushner to S. Miller et al. (11:30:13 a.m.)).

[657] DJTFP00023484 (8/11/16 Email, Hagan to Manafort (5:57:15 p.m.)).

[658] Simes 3/8/18 302, at 29-30; Simes 3/27/18 302, at 6; Kushner 4/11/18 302, at 12.

[659] Simes 3/8/18 302, at 30; Simes 3/27/18 302, at 6.

[660] Simes 3/8/18 302, at 30.

[661] Simes 3/8/18 302, at 30; Simes 3/27/18 302, at 6.

[662] Kushner 4/11/18 302, at 12.

reaction, Simes believed that he provided the same information at a small group meeting of foreign policy experts that CNI organized for Sessions.[663]

5. June 9, 2016 Meeting at Trump Tower

On June 9, 2016, senior representatives of the Trump Campaign met in Trump Tower with a Russian attorney expecting to receive derogatory information about Hillary Clinton from the Russian government. The meeting was proposed to Donald Trump Jr. in an email from Robert Goldstone, at the request of his then-client Emin Agalarov, the son of Russian real-estate developer Aras Agalarov. Goldstone relayed to Trump Jr. that the "Crown prosecutor of Russia . . . offered to provide the Trump Campaign with some official documents and information that would incriminate Hillary and her dealings with Russia" as "part of Russia and its government's support for Mr. Trump." Trump Jr. immediately responded that "if it's what you say I love it," and arranged the meeting through a series of emails and telephone calls.

Trump Jr. invited campaign chairman Paul Manafort and senior advisor Jared Kushner to attend the meeting, and both attended. Members of the Campaign discussed the meeting before it occurred, and Michael Cohen recalled that Trump Jr. may have told candidate Trump about an upcoming meeting to receive adverse information about Clinton, without linking the meeting to Russia. According to written answers submitted by President Trump, he has no recollection of learning of the meeting at the time, and the Office found no documentary evidence showing that he was made aware of the meeting—or its Russian connection—before it occurred.

The Russian attorney who spoke at the meeting, Natalia Veselnitskaya, had previously worked for the Russian government and maintained a relationship with that government throughout this period of time. She claimed that funds derived from illegal activities in Russia were provided to Hillary Clinton and other Democrats. Trump Jr. requested evidence to support those claims, but Veselnitskaya did not provide such information. She and her associates then turned to a critique of the origins of the Magnitsky Act, a 2012 statute that imposed financial and travel sanctions on Russian officials and that resulted in a retaliatory ban on adoptions of Russian children. Trump Jr. suggested that the issue could be revisited when and if candidate Trump was elected. After the election, Veselnitskaya made additional efforts to follow up on the meeting, but the Trump Transition Team did not engage.

a. Setting Up the June 9 Meeting

i. Outreach to Donald Trump Jr.

Aras Agalarov is a Russian real-estate developer with ties to Putin and other members of the Russian government, including Russia's Prosecutor General, Yuri Chaika.[664] Aras Agalarov is the president of the Crocus Group, a Russian enterprise that holds substantial Russian government construction contracts and that—as discussed above, Volume I, Section IV.A.1, *supra*

---

[663] Simes 3/8/18 302, at 30.

[664] **Grand Jury** ████████████ Goldstone 2/8/18 302, at 4.

—worked with Trump in connection with the 2013 Miss Universe pageant in Moscow and a potential Trump Moscow real-estate project.[665] The relationship continued over time, as the parties pursued the Trump Moscow project in 2013-2014 and exchanged gifts and letters in 2016.[666] For example, in April 2016, Trump responded to a letter from Aras Agalarov with a handwritten note.[667] Aras Agalarov expressed interest in Trump's campaign, passed on "congratulations" for winning in the primary and—according to one email drafted by Goldstone—an "offer" of his "support and that of many of his important Russian friends and colleagues[,] especially with reference to U.S./Russian relations."[668]

On June 3, 2016, Emin Agalarov called Goldstone, Emin's then-publicist.[669] Goldstone is a music and events promoter who represented Emin Agalarov from approximately late 2012 until late 2016.[670] While representing Emin Agalarov, Goldstone facilitated the ongoing contact between the Trumps and the Agalarovs—including an invitation that Trump sent to Putin to attend the 2013 Miss Universe Pageant in Moscow.[671] Grand Jury

.[672] Goldstone understood Grand Jury a Russian political connection, and Emin Agalarov indicated that the attorney was a prosecutor.[673] Goldstone recalled that the information that might interest the Trumps involved Hillary Clinton Grand Jury [674] Grand Jury

---

[665] Grand Jury Kaveladze 11/16/17 302, at 3; Shugart 9/25/17 302, at 2-3; Grand Jury

[666] Grand Jury Goldstone 2/8/18 302, at 10; Grand Jury Kaveladze 11/16/17 302, at 5-6; 4/25/16 Email, Graff to Goldstone.

[667] RG000033-34 (4/25/16 Email, Graff to Goldstone (attachment)).

[668] DJTJR00008 (2/29/16 Email, Goldstone to Trump Jr. et al.); Grand Jury

[669] Call Records of Robert Goldstone Grand Jury Goldstone 2/8/18 302, at 6.

[670] Goldstone 2/8/18 302, at 1-2; Grand Jury Beniaminov 1/6/18 302, at 3.

[671] Goldstone 2/8/18 302, at 1-5; Grand Jury DJTJR00008 (2/29/19 Email, Goldstone to Trump Jr.); Beniaminov 1/6/18 302, at 3; Shugart 9/25/17 302, at 2; TRUMPORG_18_001325 (6/21/13 Email, Goldstone to Graff); TRUMPORG_18_001013 (6/24/13 Email, Goldstone to Graff); TRUMPORG_18_001014 (6/24/13 Email, Graff to Shugart); TRUMPORG_18_001018 (6/26/13 Email, Graff to Goldstone); TRUMPORG_18_001022 (6/27/13 Email, Graff to L. Kelly); TRUMPORG_18_001333 (9/12/13 Email, Goldstone to Graff, Shugart); MUO00004289 (7/27/13 Email, Goldstone to Graff, Shugart).

[672] Grand Jury see Goldstone 2/8/18 302, at 6-7.

[673] Grand Jury

[674] Grand Jury

111

171

████ Grand Jury ████ [675]

The ███ Grand Jury ███ mentioned by Emin Agalarov was Natalia
Veselnitskaya.[676] From approximately 1998 until 2001, Veselnitskaya worked as a prosecutor for
the Central Administrative District of the Russian Prosecutor's Office,[677] and she continued to
perform government-related work and maintain ties to the Russian government following her
departure.[678] She lobbied and testified about the Magnitsky Act, which imposed financial
sanctions and travel restrictions on Russian officials and which was named for a Russian tax
specialist who exposed a fraud and later died in a Russian prison.[679] Putin called the statute "a
purely political, unfriendly act," and Russia responded by barring a list of current and former U.S.
officials from entering Russia and by halting the adoption of Russian children by U.S. citizens.[680]
Veselnitskaya performed legal work for Denis Katsyv,[681] the son of Russian businessman Peter
Katsyv, and for his company Prevezon Holdings Ltd., which was a defendant in a civil-forfeiture
action alleging the laundering of proceeds from the fraud exposed by Magnitsky.[682] She also

---

[675] ███ Grand Jury ███

[676] In December 2018, a grand jury in the Southern District of New York returned an indictment
charging Veselnitskaya with obstructing the *Prevezon* litigation discussed in the text above. *See* Indictment,
United States v. Natalia Vladimirovna Veselnitskaya, No. 18-cr-904 (S.D.N.Y.). The indictment alleges,
among other things, that Veselnitskaya lied to the district court about her relationship to the Russian
Prosecutor General's Office and her involvement in responding to a U.S. document request sent to the
Russian government.

[677] Veselnitskaya 11/20/17 Statement to the Senate Committee on the Judiciary, at 2; ████
███ Grand Jury ███

[678] Testimony of Natalia Veselnitskaya Before the Senate Committee on Judiciary (Nov. 20, 2017)
at 33; Keir Simmons & Rachel Elbaum, *Russian Lawyer Veselnitskaya Says She Didn't Give Trump Jr.
Info on Clinton*, NBC News (July 11, 2017); Maria Tsvetkova & Jack Stubbs, *Moscow Lawyer Who Met
Trump Jr. Had Russian Spy Agency As Client*, Reuters (July 21, 2017); Andrew E. Kramer & Sharon
LaFraniere, *Lawyer Who Was Said to Have Dirt on Clinton Had Closer Ties to Kremlin than She Let On*,
New York Times (Apr. 27, 2018).

[679] *See* Pub. L. No. 112-208 §§ 402, 404(a)(1), 126 Stat. 1502, 1502-1506. Sergei Magnitsky was
a Russian tax specialist who worked for William Browder, a former investment fund manager in Russia.
Browder hired Magnitsky to investigate tax fraud by Russian officials, and Magnitsky was charged with
helping Browder embezzle money. After Magnitsky died in a Russian prison, Browder lobbied Congress
to pass the Magnitsky Act. *See, e.g.*, Andrew E. Kramer, *Turning Tables in Magnitsky Case, Russia
Accuses Nemesis of Murder*, New York Times (Oct. 22, 2017); Testimony of Natalia Veselnitskaya Before
the Senate Committee on Judiciary (Nov. 20, 2017), Exhibits at 1-4; Rosie Gray, *Bill Browder's Testimony
to the Senate Judiciary Committee*, The Atlantic (July 25, 2017).

[680] Ellen Barry, *Russia Bars 18 Americans After Sanctions by US*, New York Times (Apr. 13, 2013);
Tom Porter, *Supporters of the Magnitsky Act Claim They've Been Targets of Russian Assassination and
Kidnapping Bids*, Newsweek (July 16, 2017).

[681] Testimony of Natalia Veselnitskaya Before the Senate Committee on Judiciary (Nov. 20, 2017),
at 21.

[682] *See* Veselnitskaya Decl., *United States v. Prevezon Holdings, Ltd.*, No. 13-cv-6326 (S.D.N.Y.);
see Prevezon Holdings, Second Amended Complaint; *Prevezon Holdings*, Mem. and Order; *Prevezon
Holdings*, Deposition of Oleg Lurie.

U.S. Department of Justice

~~Attorney Work Product // May Contain Material Protected Under Fed. R. Crim. P. 6(e)~~

appears to have been involved in an April 2016 approach to a U.S. congressional delegation in Moscow offering "confidential information" from "the Prosecutor General of Russia" about "interactions between certain political forces in our two countries."[683]

Shortly after his June 3 call with Emin Agalarov, Goldstone emailed Trump Jr.[684] The email stated:

> Good morning
> Emin just called and asked me to contact you with something very interesting.
> The Crown prosecutor of Russia met with his father Aras this morning and in their meeting offered to provide the Trump campaign with some official documents and information that would incriminate Hillary and her dealings with Russia and would be very useful to your father. This is obviously very high level and sensitive information but is part of Russia and its government's support for Mr. Trump - helped along by Aras and Emin.
> What do you think is the best way to handle this information and would you be able to speak to Emin about it directly?
> I can also send this info to your father via Rhona, but it is ultra sensitive so wanted to send to you first.
> Best
> Rob Goldstone

Within minutes of this email, Trump Jr. responded, emailing back: "Thanks Rob I appreciate that. I am on the road at the moment but perhaps I just speak to Emin first. Seems we have some time and if it's what you say I love it especially later in the summer. Could we do a call first thing next week when I am back?"[685] Goldstone conveyed Trump Jr.'s interest to Emin Agalarov, emailing that Trump Jr. "wants to speak personally on the issue."[686]

On June 6, 2016, Emin Agalarov asked Goldstone if there was "[a]ny news," and Goldstone explained that Trump Jr. was likely still traveling for the "final elections . . . where [T]rump will be 'crowned' the official nominee."[687] On the same day, Goldstone again emailed Trump Jr. and asked when Trump Jr. was "free to talk with Emin about this Hillary info."[688] Trump Jr. asked if

---

[683] *See* Gribbin 8/31/17 302, at 1-2 & 1A (undated one-page document given to congressional delegation). The Russian Prosecutor General is an official with broad national responsibilities in the Russian legal system. *See Federal Law on the Prosecutor's Office of the Russian Federation* (1992, amended 2004).

[684] RG000061 (6/3/16 Email, Goldstone to Trump Jr.); DJTJR00446 (6/3/16 Email, Goldstone to Donald Trump Jr.); @DonaldJTrumpJr 07/11/17 (11:00) Tweet.

[685] DJTJR00446 (6/3/16 Email, Trump Jr. to Goldstone); @DonaldJTrumpJr 07/11/17 (11:00) Tweet; RG000061 (6/3/16 Email, Trump Jr. to Goldstone).

[686] Grand Jury RG000062 (6/3/16 Email, Goldstone & Trump Jr.).

[687] RG000063 (6/6/16 Email, A. Agalarov to Goldstone); RG000064 (6/6/16 Email, Goldstone to A. Agalarov).

[688] RG000065 (6/6/16 Email, Goldstone to Trump Jr.); DJTJR00446 (6/6/16 Email, Goldstone to Trump Jr.).

they could "speak now," and Goldstone arranged a call between Trump Jr. and Emin Agalarov.[689] On June 6 and June 7, Trump Jr. and Emin Agalarov had multiple brief calls.[690]

Also on June 6, 2016, Aras Agalarov called Ike Kaveladze and asked him to attend a meeting in New York with the Trump Organization.[691] Kaveladze is a Georgia-born, naturalized U.S. citizen who worked in the United States for the Crocus Group and reported to Aras Agalarov.[692] Kaveladze told the Office that, in a second phone call on June 6, 2016, Aras Agalarov asked Kaveladze if he knew anything about the Magnitsky Act, and Aras sent him a short synopsis for the meeting and Veselnitskaya's business card. According to Kaveladze, Aras Agalarov said the purpose of the meeting was to discuss the Magnitsky Act, and he asked Kaveladze to translate.[693]

ii. Awareness of the Meeting Within the Campaign

On June 7, Goldstone emailed Trump Jr. and said that "Emin asked that I schedule a meeting with you and [t]he Russian government attorney who is flying over from Moscow."[694] Trump Jr. replied that Manafort (identified as the "campaign boss"), Jared Kushner, and Trump Jr. would likely attend.[695] Goldstone was surprised to learn that Trump Jr., Manafort, and Kushner would attend.[696] Kaveladze Grand Jury "puzzled" by the list of attendees and that he checked with one of Emin Agalarov's assistants, Roman Beniaminov, who said that the purpose of the meeting was for Veselnitskaya to convey "negative information on Hillary Clinton."[697] Beniaminov, however, stated that he did not recall having known or said that.[698]

Early on June 8, 2016 Kushner emailed his assistant, asking her to discuss a 3:00 p.m.

---

[689] DJTJR00445 (6/6/16 Email, Goldstone and Trump Jr.); RG000065-67 (6/6/16 Email, Goldstone and Trump Jr.); Grand Jury

[690] DJTJR00499 (Call Records of Donald Trump Jr. Grand Jury); Call Records of Donald Trump Jr. Grand Jury

[691] Kaveladze 11/16/17 302, at 6; Grand Jury

[692] Kaveladze 11/16/17 302, at 1-2; Grand Jury Beniaminov 1/6/18 302, at 2-3; Grand Jury

[693] Kaveladze 11/16/17 302, at 6.

[694] DJTJR00467 (6/7/16 Email, Goldstone to Trump Jr.); @DonaldJTrumpJr 07/11/17 (11:00) Tweet; RG000068 (6/7/16 Email, Goldstone to Trump Jr.); Grand Jury

[695] DJTJR00469 (6/7/16 Email, Trump Jr. to Goldstone); @DonaldJTrumpJr 07/11/17 (11:00) Tweet; RG000071 (6/7/16 Email, Trump Jr. to Goldstone); OSC-KAV_00048 (6/7/16 Email, Goldstone to Kaveladze); Grand Jury

[696] Goldstone 2/8/18 302, at 7; Grand Jury

[697] Grand Jury see Kaveladze 11/16/17 302 at 7; OSC-KAV_00048 (6/7/16 Email, Goldstone to Kaveladze).

[698] Beniaminov 1/6/18 302, at 3.

114

174

meeting the following day with Trump Jr.[699] Later that day, Trump Jr. forwarded the entirety of his email correspondence regarding the meeting with Goldstone to Manafort and Kushner, under the subject line "FW: Russia - Clinton – private and confidential," adding a note that the "[m]eeting got moved to 4 tomorrow at my offices."[700] Kushner then sent his assistant a second email, informing her that the "[m]eeting with don jr is 4pm now."[701] Manafort responded, "See you then. P."[702]

Rick Gates, who was the deputy campaign chairman, stated during interviews with the Office that in the days before June 9, 2016 Trump Jr. announced at a regular morning meeting of senior campaign staff and Trump family members that he had a lead on negative information about the Clinton Foundation.[703] Gates believed that Trump Jr. said the information was coming from a group in Kyrgyzstan and that he was introduced to the group by a friend.[704] Gates recalled that the meeting was attended by Trump Jr., Eric Trump, Paul Manafort, Hope Hicks, and, joining late, Ivanka Trump and Jared Kushner. According to Gates, Manafort warned the group that the meeting likely would not yield vital information and they should be careful.[705] Hicks denied any knowledge of the June 9 meeting before 2017,[706] and Kushner did not recall if the planned June 9 meeting came up at all earlier that week.[707]

Michael Cohen recalled being in Donald J. Trump's office on June 6 or 7 when Trump Jr. told his father that a meeting to obtain adverse information about Clinton was going forward.[708] Cohen did not recall Trump Jr. stating that the meeting was connected to Russia.[709] From the tenor of the conversation, Cohen believed that Trump Jr. had previously discussed the meeting with his father, although Cohen was not involved in any such conversation.[710] In an interview with the Senate Judiciary Committee, however, Trump Jr. stated that he did not inform his father about the

---

[699] NOSC0000007-08 (6/8/18 Email, Kushner to Vargas).

[700] NOSC00000039-42 (6/8/16 Email, Trump Jr. to Kushner & Manafort); DJTJR00485 (6/8/16 Email, Trump Jr. to Kushner & Manafort).

[701] NOSC0000004 (6/8/16 Email, Kushner to Vargas).

[702] 6/8/16 Email, Manafort to Trump Jr.

[703] Gates 1/30/18 302, at 7; Gates 3/1/18 302, at 3-4. Although the March 1 302 refers to "June 19," that is likely a typographical error; external emails indicate that a meeting with those participants occurred on June 6. See NOSC00023603 (6/6/16 Email, Gates to Trump Jr. et al.).

[704] Gates 1/30/18 302, at 7. Aras Agalarov is originally from Azerbaijan, and public reporting indicates that his company, the Crocus Group, has done substantial work in Kyrgyzstan. See Neil MacFarquhar, *A Russian Developer Helps Out the Kremlin on Occasion. Was He a Conduit to Trump?*, New York Times (July 16, 2017).

[705] Gates 3/1/18 302, at 3-4.

[706] Hicks 12/7/17 302, at 6.

[707] Kushner 4/11/18 302, at 8.

[708] Cohen 8/7/18 302, at 4-6.

[709] Cohen 8/7/18 302, at 4-5.

[710] Cohen 9/12/18 302, at 15-16.

U.S. Department of Justice

Attorney Work Product // May Contain Material Protected Under Fed. R. Crim. P. 6(e)

emails or the upcoming meeting.[711] Similarly, neither Manafort nor Kushner recalled anyone informing candidate Trump of the meeting, including Trump Jr.[712] President Trump has stated to this Office, in written answers to questions, that he has "no recollection of learning at the time" that his son, Manafort, or "Kushner was considering participating in a meeting in June 2016 concerning potentially negative information about Hillary Clinton."[713]

b. The Events of June 9, 2016

i. Arrangements for the Meeting

Veselnitskaya was in New York on June 9, 2016, for appellate proceedings in the *Prevezon* civil forfeiture litigation.[714] That day, Veselnitskaya called Rinat Akhmetshin, a Soviet-born U.S. lobbyist, Grand Jury and when she learned that he was in New York, invited him to lunch.[715] Akhmetshin told the Office that he had worked on issues relating to the Magnitsky Act and had worked on the *Prevezon* litigation.[716] Kaveladze and Anatoli Samochornov, a

---

[711] *Interview of: Donald J. Trump, Jr., Senate Judiciary Committee,* 115th Cong. 28-29, 84, 94-95 (Sept. 7, 2017). The Senate Judiciary Committee interview was not under oath, but Trump Jr. was advised that it is a violation of 18 U.S.C. § 1001 to make materially false statements in a congressional investigation. *Id.* at 10-11.

[712] Manafort 9/11/18 302, at 3-4; Kushner 4/11/18 302, at 10.

[713] Written Responses of Donald J. Trump (Nov. 20, 2018), at 8 (Response to Question I, Parts (a)-(c)). We considered whether one sequence of events suggested that candidate Trump had contemporaneous knowledge of the June 9 meeting. On June 7, 2016 Trump announced his intention to give "a major speech" "probably Monday of next week"—which would have been June 13—about "all of the things that have taken place with the Clintons." *See, e.g.,* Phillip Bump, *What we know about the Trump Tower meeting,* Washington Post (Aug. 7, 2018). Following the June 9 meeting, Trump changed the subject of his planned speech to national security. But the Office did not find evidence that the original idea for the speech was connected to the anticipated June 9 meeting or that the change of topic was attributable to the failure of that meeting to produce concrete evidence about Clinton. Other events, such as the Pulse nightclub shooting on June 12, could well have caused the change. The President's written answers to our questions state that the speech's focus was altered "[i]n light of" the Pulse nightclub shooting. *See* Written Responses, *supra.* As for the original topic of the June 13 speech, Trump has said that "he expected to give a speech referencing the publicly available, negative information about the Clintons," and that the draft of the speech prepared by Campaign staff "was based on publicly available material, including, in particular, information from the book *Clinton Cash* by Peter Schweizer." Written Responses, *supra.* In a later June 22 speech, Trump did speak extensively about allegations that Clinton was corrupt, drawing from the *Clinton Cash* book. *See Full Transcript: Donald Trump NYC Speech on Stakes of the Election,* politico.com (June 22, 2016).

[714] Testimony of Natalia Veselnitskaya Before the Senate Committee on Judiciary (Nov. 20, 2017) at 41, 42; Alison Frankel, *How Did Russian Lawyer Veselnitskaya Get into U.S. for Trump Tower Meeting?* Reuters, (Nov. 6, 2017); Michael Kranish et al., *Russian Lawyer who Met with Trump Jr. Has Long History Fighting Sanctions,* Washington Post (July 11, 2017); *see* OSC-KAV00113 (6/8/16 Email, Goldstone to Kaveladze); RG000073 (6/8/16 Email, Goldstone to Trump Jr.); Lieberman 12/13/17 302, at 5; *see also Prevezon Holdings* Order (Oct. 17, 2016).

[715] Grand Jury

[716] Akhmetshin 11/14/17 302, at 4-6; Grand Jury

116

176

Russian-born translator who had assisted Veselnitskaya with Magnitsky-related lobbying and the *Prevezon* case, also attended the lunch.[717] Grand Jury Veselnitskaya said she was meeting Grand Jury and asked Akhmetshin what she should tell him.[718] According to several participants in the lunch, Veselnitskaya showed Akhmetshin a document alleging financial misconduct by Bill Browder and the Ziff brothers (Americans with business in Russia), and those individuals subsequently making political donations to the DNC.[719] Grand Jury

[20]

The group then went to Trump Tower for the meeting.[721]

ii. Conduct of the Meeting

Trump Jr., Manafort, and Kushner participated on the Trump side, while Kaveladze, Samochornov, Akhmetshin, and Goldstone attended with Veselnitskaya.[722] The Office spoke to every participant except Veselnitskaya and Trump Jr., the latter of whom declined to be voluntarily interviewed by the Office Grand Jury

The meeting lasted approximately 20 minutes.[723] Grand Jury

[24] Goldstone recalled that Trump Jr. invited Veselnitskaya to begin but did not say anything about the subject of the meeting.[725] Participants agreed that Veselnitskaya stated that the Ziff brothers had broken Russian laws and had donated their profits to the DNC or the Clinton Campaign.[726] She asserted that the Ziff brothers had engaged in tax evasion and money laundering

---

[717] Kaveladze 11/16/17 302, at 7; Grand Jury Samochornov 7/13/17 302, at 2, 4; Grand Jury

[718] Grand Jury .

[719] Grand Jury Kaveladze 11/16/17 302, at 7; Grand Jury Samochornov did not recall the planned subject matter of the Trump Tower meeting coming up at lunch. Grand Jury Samochornov 7/12/17 302, at 4. In her later Senate statement and interactions with the press, Veselnitskaya produced what she claimed were the talking points that she brought to the June 9 meeting.

[720] Grand Jury

[721] *E.g.*, Samochornov 7/12/17 302, at 4.

[722] *E.g.*, Samochornov 7/12/17 302, at 4.

[723] *E.g.*, Samochornov 7/12/17 302, at 4; Goldstone 2/8/18 302, at 9.

[724] Grand Jury

[725] Grand Jury

[726] Grand Jury

117

in both the United States and Russia,[727] Grand Jury
[728] According to Akhmetshin, Trump Jr. asked follow-up questions about how the alleged payments could be tied specifically to the Clinton Campaign, but Veselnitskaya indicated that she could not trace the money once it entered the United States.[729] Kaveladze similarly recalled that Trump Jr. asked what they have on Clinton, and Kushner became aggravated and asked "[w]hat are we doing here?"[730]

Akhmetshin then spoke about U.S. sanctions imposed under the Magnitsky Act and Russia's response prohibiting U.S. adoption of Russian children.[731] Several participants recalled that Trump Jr. commented that Trump is a private citizen, and there was nothing they could do at that time.[732] Trump Jr. also said that they could revisit the issue if and when they were in government.[733] Notes that Manafort took on his phone reflect the general flow of the conversation, although not all of its details.[734]

At some point in the meeting, Kushner sent an iMessage to Manafort stating "waste of time," followed immediately by two separate emails to assistants at Kushner Companies with requests that

---

[727] Grand Jury

[728] Grand Jury

[729] Grand Jury Akhmetshin 11/14/17 302, at 12.

[730] Kaveladze 11/16/17 302, at 8; Grand Jury

[731] Samochornov 7/13/17 302, at 3; Grand Jury

[732] *E.g.*, Akhmetshin 11/14/17 302, at 12-13; Grand Jury

[733] Akhmetshin 11/14/17 302, at 12-13; Grand Jury Samochornov 7/13/17 302, at 3. Trump Jr. confirmed this in a statement he made in July 2017 after news of the June 2016 meeting broke. *Interview of: Donald J. Trump, Jr., Senate Judiciary Committee U.S. Senate Washington DC*, 115th Cong. 57 (Sept. 7, 2017).

[734] Manafort's notes state:

Bill browder
Offshore - Cyprus
133m shares
Companies
Not invest - loan
Value in Cyprus as inter
Illici
Active sponsors of RNC
Browder hired Joanna Glover
Tied into Cheney
Russian adoption by American families

PJM-SJC-00000001-02 (Notes Produced to Senate Judiciary Committee).

118

U.S. Department of Justice

~~Attorney Work Product // May Contain Material Protected Under Fed. R. Crim. P. 6(e)~~

they call him to give him an excuse to leave.[735] Samochornov recalled that Kushner departed the meeting before it concluded; Veselnitskaya recalled the same when interviewed by the press in July 2017.[736]

Veselnitskaya's press interviews and written statements to Congress differ materially from other accounts. In a July 2017 press interview, Veselnitskaya claimed that she has no connection to the Russian government and had not referred to any derogatory information concerning the Clinton Campaign when she met with Trump Campaign officials.[737] Veselnitskaya's November 2017 written submission to the Senate Judiciary Committee stated that the purpose of the June 9 meeting was not to connect with "the Trump Campaign" but rather to have "a private meeting with Donald Trump Jr.—a friend of my good acquaintance's son on the matter of assisting me or my colleagues in informing the Congress members as to the criminal nature of manipulation and interference with the legislative activities of the US Congress."[738] In other words, Veselnitskaya claimed her focus was on Congress and not the Campaign. No witness, however, recalled any reference to Congress during the meeting. Veselnitskaya also maintained that she "attended the meeting as a lawyer of Denis Katsyv," the previously mentioned owner of Prevezon Holdings, but she did not "introduce [her]self in this capacity."[739]

In a July 2017 television interview, Trump Jr. stated that while he had no way to gauge the reliability, credibility, or accuracy of what Goldstone had stated was the purpose of the meeting, if "someone has information on our opponent . . . maybe this is something. I should hear them out."[740] Trump Jr. further stated in September 2017 congressional testimony that he thought he should "listen to what Rob and his colleagues had to say."[741] Depending on what, if any, information was provided, Trump Jr. stated he could then "consult with counsel to make an informed decision as to whether to give it any further consideration."[742]

---

[735] NOSC00003992 (6/9/16 Text Message, Kushner to Manafort); Kushner 4/11/18 302, at 9; Vargas 4/4/18 302, at 7; NOSC00000044 (6/9/16 Email, Kushner to Vargas); NOSC00000045 (6/9/16 Email, Kushner to Cain).

[736] Samochornov 7/12/17 302, at 4; ▮Grand Jury▮▮▮▮▮▮▮ Kushner 4/11/18 302, at 9-10; *see also Interview of: Donald J. Trump, Jr., Senate Judiciary Committee*, 115th Cong. 48-49 (Sept. 7, 2017).

[737] *Russian Lawyer Veselnitskaya Says She Didn't Give Trump Jr. Info on Clinton*, NBC News (July 11, 2017).

[738] *Testimony of Natalia Veselnitskaya before the United States Senate Committee on the Judiciary*, 115th Cong. 10 (Nov 20, 2017).

[739] *Testimony of Natalia Veselnitskaya before the United States Senate Committee on the Judiciary*, 115th Cong. 21 (Nov. 20, 2017).

[740] Sean Hannity, *Transcript-Donald Trump Jr*, Fox News (July 11, 2017).

[741] *Interview of: Donald J. Trump, Jr, Senate Judiciary Committee*, 115th Cong. 16 (Sept. 7, 2017).

[742] *Interview of: Donald J. Trump, Jr, Senate Judiciary Committee*, 115th Cong. 16-17 (Sept. 7, 2017).

After the June 9 meeting concluded, Goldstone apologized to Trump Jr.[743] According to Goldstone, he told Trump Jr. ███████████ [744] and told Emin Agalarov in a phone call that the meeting was about adoption ████ [745] ███████ [46] Aras Agalarov asked Kaveladze to report in after the meeting, but before Kaveladze could call, Aras Agalarov called him.[747] With Veselnitskaya next to him, Kaveladze reported that the meeting had gone well, but he later told Aras Agalarov that the meeting about the Magnitsky Act had been a waste of time because it was not with lawyers and they were "preaching to the wrong crowd."[748]

c. Post-June 9 Events

Veselnitskaya and Aras Agalarov made at least two unsuccessful attempts after the election to meet with Trump representatives to convey similar information about Browder and the Magnitsky Act.[749] On November 23, 2016, Kaveladze emailed Goldstone about setting up another meeting "with T people" and sent a document bearing allegations similar to those conveyed on June 9.[750] Kaveladze followed up with Goldstone, stating that "Mr. A," which Goldstone understood to mean Aras Agalarov, called to ask about the meeting.[751] Goldstone emailed the document to Rhona Graff, saying that "Aras Agalarov has asked me to pass on this document in the hope it can be passed on to the appropriate team. If needed, a lawyer representing the case is

---

[743] Kaveladze 11/16/17 302, at 8; ███████ Goldstone 2/8/18 302, at 9; ███████

[744] ███████

[745] ███████ The week after the June 9 meeting, a cybersecurity firm and the DNC announced the Russian hack of the DNC. *See* Volume I, Section III.B.2, *supra*. ███████ (and one text message shows) that, shortly after the DNC announcement, Goldstone made comments connecting the DNC hacking announcement to the June 9 meeting. ███████ OSC-KAV_00029 (6/14/16 Email, Goldstone to E. Agalarov & Kaveladze (10:09 a.m.)). The investigation did not identify evidence connecting the events of June 9 to the GRU's hack-and-dump operation. OSC-KAV_00029-30 (6/14/16 Email, Goldstone to E. Agalarov).

[746] ███████

[747] Kaveladze 11/16/17 302, at 8; Call Records of Ike Kaveladze ███████

[748] Kaveladze 11/16/17 302, at 8; Call Records of Ike Kaveladze ███████ On June 14, 2016 Kaveladze's teenage daughter emailed asking how the June 9 meeting had gone, and Kaveladze responded, "meeting was boring. The Russians did not have any bad info on Hilary." OSC-KAV_00257 (6/14/16 Email, I. Kaveladze to A. Kaveladze; ███████

[749] Goldstone 2/8/18 302, at 11; ███████

[750] OSC-KAV_00138 (11/23/16 Email, Goldstone to Kaveladze); ███████

[751] RG000196 (11/26-29/16 Text Messages, Goldstone & Kaveladze); ███████

120

in New York currently and happy to meet with any member of his transition team."[752] According to Goldstone, around January 2017, Kaveladze contacted him again to set up another meeting, but Goldstone did not make the request.[753] The investigation did not identify evidence of the transition team following up.

Participants in the June 9, 2016 meeting began receiving inquiries from attorneys representing the Trump Organization starting in approximately June 2017.[754] On approximately June 2, 2017, Goldstone spoke with Alan Garten, general counsel of the Trump Organization, about his participation in the June 9 meeting.[755] The same day, Goldstone emailed Veselnitskaya's name to Garten, identifying her as the "woman who was the attorney who spoke at the meeting from Moscow."[756] Later in June 2017, Goldstone participated in a lengthier call with Garten and Alan Futerfas, outside counsel for the Trump Organization (and, subsequently, personal counsel for Trump Jr.).[757] On June 27, 2017, Goldstone emailed Emin Agalarov with the subject "Trump attorneys" and stated that he was "interviewed by attorneys" about the June 9 meeting who were "concerned because it links Don Jr. to officials from Russia—which he has always denied meeting."[758] Goldstone stressed that he "did say at the time this was an awful idea and a terrible meeting."[759] Emin Agalarov sent a screenshot of the message to Kaveladze.[760]

The June 9 meeting became public in July 2017. In a July 9, 2017 text message to Emin Agalarov, Goldstone wrote "I made sure I kept you and your father out of [t]his story,"[761] and "[i]f contacted I can do a dance and keep you out of it."[762] Goldstone added, "FBI now investigating," and "I hope this favor was worth for your dad—it could blow up."[763] On July 12, 2017 Emin Agalarov complained to Kaveladze that his father, Aras, "never listens" to him and that their

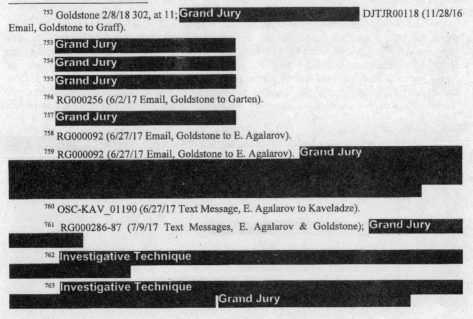

[752] Goldstone 2/8/18 302, at 11; Grand Jury _____ DJTJR00118 (11/28/16 Email, Goldstone to Graff).

[753] Grand Jury

[754] Grand Jury

[755] Grand Jury

[756] RG000256 (6/2/17 Email, Goldstone to Garten).

[757] Grand Jury

[758] RG000092 (6/27/17 Email, Goldstone to E. Agalarov).

[759] RG000092 (6/27/17 Email, Goldstone to E. Agalarov). Grand Jury

[760] OSC-KAV_01190 (6/27/17 Text Message, E. Agalarov to Kaveladze).

[761] RG000286-87 (7/9/17 Text Messages, E. Agalarov & Goldstone); Grand Jury

[762] Investigative Technique

[763] Investigative Technique
Grand Jury

121

U.S. Department of Justice

~~Attorney Work Product // May Contain Material Protected Under Fed. R. Crim. P. 6(e)~~

relationship with "mr T has been thrown down the drain."[764] The next month, Goldstone commented to Emin Agalarov about the volume of publicity the June 9 meeting had generated, stating that his "reputation [was] basically destroyed by this dumb meeting which your father insisted on even though Ike and Me told him would be bad news and not to do."[765] Goldstone added, "I am not able to respond out of courtesy to you and your father. So am painted as some mysterious link to Putin."[766]

After public reporting on the June 9 meeting began, representatives from the Trump Organization again reached out to participants. On July 10, 2017, Futerfas sent Goldstone an email with a proposed statement for Goldstone to issue, which read:

> As the person who arranged the meeting, I can definitively state that the statements I have read by Donald Trump Jr. are 100% accurate. The meeting was a complete waste of time and Don was never told Ms. Veselnitskaya's name prior to the meeting. Ms. Veselnitskaya mostly talked about the Magnitsky Act and Russian adoption laws and the meeting lasted 20 to 30 minutes at most. There was never any follow up and nothing ever came of the meeting.[767]

Grand Jury ▮▮▮ the statement drafted by Trump Organization representatives was Grand Jury ▮▮▮ [768] He proposed a different statement, asserting that he had been asked "by [his] client in Moscow – Emin Agalarov – to facilitate a meeting between a Russian attorney (Natalia Veselnitzkaya [sic]) and Donald Trump Jr. The lawyer had apparently stated that she had some information regarding funding to the DNC from Russia, which she believed Mr. Trump Jr. might find interesting."[769] Goldstone never released either statement.[770]

On the Russian end, there were also communications about what participants should say about the June 9 meeting. Specifically, the organization that hired Samochornov—an anti-Magnitsky Act group controlled by Veselnitskaya and the owner of Prevezon—offered to pay $90,000 of Samochornov's legal fees.[771] At Veselnitskaya's request, the organization sent Samochornov a transcript of a Veselnitskaya press interview, and Samochornov understood that the organization would pay his legal fees only if he made statements consistent with Veselnitskaya's.[772] Samochornov declined, telling the Office that he did not want to perjure

---

[764] OSC-KAV_01197 (7/11-12/17 Text Messages, Kaveladze & E. Agalarov); Grand Jury ▮▮▮

[765] Investigative Technique

[766] Investigative Technique

[767] 7/10/17 Email, Goldstone to Futerfas & Garten.

[768] Grand Jury

[769] 7/10/17 Email, Goldstone to Futerfas & Garten.

[770] Grand Jury

[771] Samochornov 7/13/17 302, at 1; Grand Jury

[772] Grand Jury ▮▮▮ Samochornov 7/13/17 302, at 1.

himself.[773] The individual who conveyed Veselnitskaya's request to Samochornov stated that he did not expressly condition payment on following Veselnitskaya's answers but, in hindsight, recognized that by sending the transcript, Samochornov could have interpreted the offer of assistance to be conditioned on his not contradicting Veselnitskaya's account.[774]

Volume II, Section II.G, *infra*, discusses interactions between President Trump, Trump Jr., and others in June and July 2017 regarding the June 9 meeting.

6. Events at the Republican National Convention

Trump Campaign officials met with Russian Ambassador Sergey Kislyak during the week of the Republican National Convention. The evidence indicates that those interactions were brief and non-substantive. During platform committee meetings immediately before the Convention, J.D. Gordon, a senior Campaign advisor on policy and national security, diluted a proposed amendment to the Republican Party platform expressing support for providing "lethal" assistance to Ukraine in response to Russian aggression. Gordon requested that platform committee personnel revise the proposed amendment to state that only "appropriate" assistance be provided to Ukraine. The original sponsor of the "lethal" assistance amendment stated that Gordon told her (the sponsor) that he was on the phone with candidate Trump in connection with his request to dilute the language. Gordon denied making that statement to the sponsor, although he acknowledged it was possible he mentioned having previously spoken to the candidate about the subject matter. The investigation did not establish that Gordon spoke to or was directed by the candidate to make that proposal. Gordon said that he sought the change because he believed the proposed language was inconsistent with Trump's position on Ukraine.

a. Ambassador Kislyak's Encounters with Senator Sessions and J.D. Gordon the Week of the RNC

In July 2016, Senator Sessions and Gordon spoke at the Global Partners in Diplomacy event, a conference co-sponsored by the State Department and the Heritage Foundation held in Cleveland, Ohio the same week as the Republican National Convention (RNC or "Convention").[775] Approximately 80 foreign ambassadors to the United States, including Kislyak, were invited to the conference.[776]

On July 20, 2016, Gordon and Sessions delivered their speeches at the conference.[777] In his speech, Gordon stated in pertinent part that the United States should have better relations with

---

[773] Samochornov 7/13/17 302, at 1.

[774] Grand Jury

[775] Gordon 8/29/17 302, at 9; Sessions 1/17/18 302, at 22; Allan Smith, *We Now Know More About why Jeff Sessions and a Russian Ambassador Crossed Paths at the Republican Convention*, Business Insider (Mar. 2, 2017).

[776] Gordon 8/29/17 302, at 9; Laura DeMarco, *Global Cleveland and Sen. Bob Corker Welcome International Republican National Convention Guests*, Cleveland Plain Dealer (July 20, 2016).

[777] Gordon 8/29/17 302, at 9; Sessions 1/17/18 302, at 22.

123

U.S. Department of Justice

~~Attorney Work Product~~ // ~~May Contain Material Protected Under Fed. R. Crim. P. 6(e)~~

Russia.[778] During Sessions's speech, he took questions from the audience, one of which may have been asked by Kislyak.[779] When the speeches concluded, several ambassadors lined up to greet the speakers.[780] Gordon shook hands with Kislyak and reiterated that he had meant what he said in the speech about improving U.S.-Russia relations.[781] Sessions separately spoke with between six and 12 ambassadors, including Kislyak.[782] Although Sessions stated during interviews with the Office that he had no specific recollection of what he discussed with Kislyak, he believed that the two spoke for only a few minutes and that they would have exchanged pleasantries and said some things about U.S.-Russia relations.[783]

Later that evening, Gordon attended a reception as part of the conference.[784] Gordon ran into Kislyak as the two prepared plates of food, and they decided to sit at the same table to eat.[785] They were joined at that table by the ambassadors from Azerbaijan and Kazakhstan, and by Trump Campaign advisor Carter Page.[786] As they ate, Gordon and Kislyak talked for what Gordon estimated to have been three to five minutes, during which Gordon again mentioned that he meant what he said in his speech about improving U.S.-Russia relations.[787]

b. Change to Republican Party Platform

In preparation for the 2016 Convention, foreign policy advisors to the Trump Campaign, working with the Republican National Committee, reviewed the 2012 Convention's foreign policy platform to identify divergence between the earlier platform and candidate Trump's positions.[788] The Campaign team discussed toning down language from the 2012 platform that identified Russia as the country's number one threat, given the candidate's belief that there needed to be better U.S. relations with Russia.[789] The RNC Platform Committee sent the 2016 draft platform to the National Security and Defense Platform Subcommittee on July 10, 2016, the evening before its

---

[778] Gordon 8/29/17 302, at 9.

[779] Sessions 1/17/18 302, at 22; Luff 1/30/18 302, at 3.

[780] Gordon 8/29/17 302, at 9; Luff 1/30/18 302, at 3.

[781] Gordon 8/29/17 302, at 9.

[782] Sessions 1/17/18 302, at 22; Luff 1/30/18 302, at 3; *see also* Volume I, Section IV.A.4.b, *supra* (explaining that Sessions and Kislyak may have met three months before this encounter during a reception held on April 26, 2016, at the Mayflower Hotel).

[783] Sessions 1/17/18 302, at 22.

[784] Gordon 8/29/17 302, at 9-10.

[785] Gordon 8/29/17 302, at 9-10.

[786] Gordon 8/29/17 302, at 10; *see also* Volume I, Section IV.A.3.d, *supra* (explaining that Page acknowledged meeting Kislyak at this event).

[787] Gordon 8/29/17 302, at 10.

[788] Gordon 8/29/17 302, at 10.

[789] Gordon 8/29/17 302, at 10.

first meeting to propose amendments.[790]

Although only delegates could participate in formal discussions and vote on the platform, the Trump Campaign could request changes, and members of the Trump Campaign attended committee meetings.[791] John Mashburn, the Campaign's policy director, helped oversee the Campaign's involvement in the platform committee meetings.[792] He told the Office that he directed Campaign staff at the Convention, including J.D. Gordon, to take a hands-off approach and only to challenge platform planks if they directly contradicted Trump's wishes.[793]

On July 11, 2016, delegate Diana Denman submitted a proposed platform amendment that included provision of armed support for Ukraine.[794] The amendment described Russia's "ongoing military aggression" in Ukraine and announced "support" for "maintaining (and, if warranted, increasing) sanctions against Russia until Ukraine's sovereignty and territorial integrity are fully restored" and for "providing lethal defensive weapons to Ukraine's armed forces and greater coordination with NATO on defense planning."[795] Gordon reviewed the proposed platform changes, including Denman's.[796] Gordon stated that he flagged this amendment because of Trump's stated position on Ukraine, which Gordon personally heard the candidate say at the March 31 foreign policy meeting—namely, that the Europeans should take primary responsibility for any assistance to Ukraine, that there should be improved U.S.-Russia relations, and that he did not want to start World War III over that region.[797] Gordon told the Office that Trump's statements on the campaign trail following the March meeting underscored those positions to the point where Gordon felt obliged to object to the proposed platform change and seek its dilution.[798]

On July 11, 2016, at a meeting of the National Security and Defense Platform Subcommittee, Denman offered her amendment.[799] Gordon and another Campaign staffer, Matt Miller, approached a committee co-chair and asked him to table the amendment to permit further discussion.[800] Gordon's concern with the amendment was the language about providing "lethal

---

[790] Gordon 8/29/17 302, at 10; Hoff 5/26/17 302, at 1-2.

[791] Hoff 5/26/17 302, at 1; Gordon 9/7/17 302, at 10.

[792] Mashburn 6/25/18 302, at 4; Manafort 9/20/18 302, at 7-8.

[793] Mashburn 6/25/18 302, at 4; Gordon 8/29/17 302, at 10.

[794] DENMAN 000001-02, DENMAN 000012, DENMAN 000021-22; Denman 12/4/17 302, at 1; Denman 6/7/17 302, at 2.

[795] DENMAN 000001-02, DENMAN 000012, DENMAN 000021-22.

[796] Gordon 8/29/17 302, at 10-11.

[797] Gordon 8/29/17 302, at 11; Gordon 9/7/17 302, at 11; Gordon 2/14/19 302, at 1-2, 5-6.

[798] Gordon 2/14/19 302, at 5-6.

[799] Denman 6/7/17 302, at 2; see DENMAN 000014.

[800] Denman 6/7/17 302, at 2; Denman 12/4/17 302, at 2; Gordon 9/7/17 302, at 11-12; see Hoff 5/26/17 302, at 2.

U.S. Department of Justice

~~Attorney Work Product~~ // ~~May Contain Material Protected Under Fed. R. Crim. P. 6(e)~~

defensive weapons to Ukraine."[801] Miller did not have any independent basis to believe that this language contradicted Trump's views and relied on Gordon's recollection of the candidate's views.[802]

According to Denman, she spoke with Gordon and Matt Miller, and they told her that they had to clear the language and that Gordon was "talking to New York."[803] Denman told others that she was asked by the two Trump Campaign staffers to strike "lethal defense weapons" from the proposal but that she refused.[804] Denman recalled Gordon saying that he was on the phone with candidate Trump, but she was skeptical whether that was true.[805] Gordon denied having told Denman that he was on the phone with Trump, although he acknowledged it was possible that he mentioned having previously spoken to the candidate about the subject matter.[806] Gordon's phone records reveal a call to Sessions's office in Washington that afternoon, but do not include calls directly to a number associated with Trump.[807] And according to the President's written answers to the Office's questions, he does not recall being involved in the change in language of the platform amendment.[808]

Gordon stated that he tried to reach Rick Dearborn, a senior foreign policy advisor, and Mashburn, the Campaign policy director. Gordon stated that he connected with both of them (he could not recall if by phone or in person) and apprised them of the language he took issue with in the proposed amendment. Gordon recalled no objection by either Dearborn or Mashburn and that all three Campaign advisors supported the alternative formulation ("appropriate assistance").[809] Dearborn recalled Gordon warning them about the amendment, but not weighing in because Gordon was more familiar with the Campaign's foreign policy stance.[810] Mashburn stated that Gordon reached him, and he told Gordon that Trump had not taken a stance on the issue and that the Campaign should not intervene.[811]

When the amendment came up again in the committee's proceedings, the subcommittee changed the amendment by striking the "lethal defense weapons" language and replacing it with

---

[801] Denman 6/7/17 302, at 3.

[802] M. Miller 10/25/17 302 at 3.

[803] Denman 12/4/17 302, at 2; Denman 6/7/17 302, at 2.

[804] Hoff 5/26/17 302, at 2.

[805] Denman 6/7/17 302, at 2-3, 3-4; Denman 12/4/17 302, at 2.

[806] Gordon 2/14/19 302, at 7.

[807] Call Records of J.D. Gordon Grand Jury   . Gordon stated to the Office that his calls with Sessions were unrelated to the platform change. Gordon 2/14/19 302, at 7.

[808] Written Responses of Donald J. Trump (Nov. 20, 2018), at 17 (Response to Question IV, Part (f)).

[809] Gordon 2/14/19 302, at 6-7; Gordon 9/7/17 302, at 11-12; see Gordon 8/29/17 302, at 11.

[810] Dearborn 11/28/17 302, at 7-8.

[811] Mashburn 6/25/18 302, at 4.

U.S. Department of Justice

~~Attorney Work Product // May Contain Material Protected Under Fed. R. Crim. P. 6(e)~~

"appropriate assistance."[812] Gordon stated that he and the subcommittee co-chair ultimately agreed to replace the language about armed assistance with "appropriate assistance."[813] The subcommittee accordingly approved Denman's amendment but with the term "appropriate assistance."[814] Gordon stated that, to his recollection, this was the only change sought by the Campaign.[815] Sam Clovis, the Campaign's national co-chair and chief policy advisor, stated he was surprised by the change and did not believe it was in line with Trump's stance.[816] Mashburn stated that when he saw the word "appropriate assistance," he believed that Gordon had violated Mashburn's directive not to intervene.[817]

7. Post-Convention Contacts with Kislyak

Ambassador Kislyak continued his efforts to interact with Campaign officials with responsibility for the foreign-policy portfolio—among them Sessions and Gordon—in the weeks after the Convention. The Office did not identify evidence in those interactions of coordination between the Campaign and the Russian government.

a. *Ambassador Kislyak Invites J.D. Gordon to Breakfast at the Ambassador's Residence*

On August 3, 2016, an official from the Embassy of the Russian Federation in the United States wrote to Gordon "[o]n behalf of" Ambassador Kislyak inviting Gordon "to have breakfast/tea with the Ambassador at his residence" in Washington, D.C. the following week.[818] Gordon responded five days later to decline the invitation. He wrote, "[t]hese days are not optimal for us, as we are busily knocking down a constant stream of false media stories while also preparing for the first debate with HRC. Hope to take a raincheck for another time when things quiet down a bit. Please pass along my regards to the Ambassador."[819] The investigation did not identify evidence that Gordon made any other arrangements to meet (or met) with Kislyak after this email.

b. *Senator Sessions's September 2016 Meeting with Ambassador Kislyak*

Also in August 2016, a representative of the Russian Embassy contacted Sessions's Senate office about setting up a meeting with Kislyak.[820] At the time, Sessions was a member of the

---

[812] Hoff 5/26/17 302, at 2-3; *see* Denman 12/4/17 302, at 2-3; Gordon 8/29/17 302, at 11.

[813] Gordon 8/29/17 302, at 11; Gordon 9/7/17 302, at 12.

[814] Hoff 5/26/17 302, at 2-3.

[815] Gordon 2/14/19 302, at 6.

[816] Clovis 10/3/17 302, at 10-11.

[817] Mashburn 6/25/18 302, at 4.

[818] DJTFP00004828 (8/3/16 Email, Pchelyakov [embassy@russianembassy.org] to Gordon).

[819] DJTFP00004953 (8/8/16 Email, Gordon to embassy@russianembassy.org).

[820] Luff 1/30/18 302, at 5.

Senate Foreign Relations Committee and would meet with foreign officials in that capacity.[821] But Sessions's staff reported, and Sessions himself acknowledged, that meeting requests from ambassadors increased substantially in 2016, as Sessions assumed a prominent role in the Trump Campaign and his name was mentioned for potential cabinet-level positions in a future Trump Administration.[822]

On September 8, 2016, Sessions met with Kislyak in his Senate office.[823] Sessions said that he believed he was doing the Campaign a service by meeting with foreign ambassadors, including Kislyak.[824] He was accompanied in the meeting by at least two of his Senate staff: Sandra Luff, his legislative director; and Pete Landrum, who handled military affairs.[825] The meeting lasted less than 30 minutes.[826] Sessions voiced concerns about Russia's sale of a missile-defense system to Iran, Russian planes buzzing U.S. military assets in the Middle East, and Russian aggression in emerging democracies such as Ukraine and Moldova.[827] Kislyak offered explanations on these issues and complained about NATO land forces in former Soviet-bloc countries that border Russia.[828] Landrum recalled that Kislyak referred to the presidential campaign as "an interesting campaign,"[829] and Sessions also recalled Kislyak saying that the Russian government was receptive to the overtures Trump had laid out during his campaign.[830] None of the attendees, though, remembered any discussion of Russian election interference or any request that Sessions convey information from the Russian government to the Trump Campaign.[831]

During the meeting, Kislyak invited Sessions to further discuss U.S.-Russia relations with him over a meal at the ambassador's residence.[832] Sessions was non-committal when Kislyak extended the invitation. After the meeting ended, Luff advised Sessions against accepting the one-on-one meeting with Kislyak, whom she assessed to be an "old school KGB guy."[833] Neither Luff nor Landrum recalled that Sessions followed up on the invitation or made any further effort to dine

---

[821] Sessions 1/17/18 302, at 23-24; Luff 1/30/18 302, at 5.

[822] Sessions 1/17/18 302, at 23-24; Luff 1/30/18 302, at 5; Landrum 2/27/18 302, at 3-5.

[823] Sessions 1/17/18 302, at 23.

[824] Sessions 1/17/18 302, at 23.

[825] Sessions 1/17/18 302, at 23; Luff 1/30/18 302, at 5-6; Landrum 2/27/18 302, at 4-5 (stating he could not remember if election was discussed).

[826] Luff 1/30/18 302, at 6; Landrum 2/27/18 302, at 5.

[827] Luff 1/30/18 302, at 6; Landrum 2/27/18 302, at 4-5.

[828] Luff 1/30/18 302, at 6; Landrum 2/27/18 302 at 4-5.

[829] Landrum 2/27/18 302, at 5.

[830] Sessions 1/17/18 302, at 23. Sessions also noted that ambassadors came to him for information about Trump and hoped he would pass along information to Trump. Sessions 1/17/18 302, at 23-24.

[831] Sessions 1/17/18 302, at 23; Luff 1/30/18 302, at 6; Landrum 2/27/18 302, at 5.

[832] Luff 1/30/18 302, at 5; Landrum 2/27/18 302, at 4.

[833] Luff 1/30/18 302, at 5.

or meet with Kislyak before the November 2016 election.[834] Sessions and Landrum recalled that, after the election, some efforts were made to arrange a meeting between Sessions and Kislyak.[835] According to Sessions, the request came through CNI and would have involved a meeting between Sessions and Kislyak, two other ambassadors, and the Governor of Alabama.[836] Sessions, however, was in New York on the day of the anticipated meeting and was unable to attend.[837] The investigation did not identify evidence that the two men met at any point after their September 8 meeting.

8. Paul Manafort

Paul Manafort served on the Trump Campaign, including a period as campaign chairman, from March to August 2016.[838] Manafort had connections to Russia through his prior work for Russian oligarch Oleg Deripaska and later through his work for a pro-Russian regime in Ukraine. Manafort stayed in touch with these contacts during the campaign period through Konstantin Kilimnik, a longtime Manafort employee who previously ran Manafort's office in Kiev and who the FBI assesses to have ties to Russian intelligence.

Manafort instructed Rick Gates, his deputy on the Campaign and a longtime employee,[839] to provide Kilimnik with updates on the Trump Campaign—including internal polling data, although Manafort claims not to recall that specific instruction. Manafort expected Kilimnik to share that information with others in Ukraine and with Deripaska. Gates periodically sent such polling data to Kilimnik during the campaign.

---

[834] Luff 1/30/18 302, at 6; Landrum 2/27/18 302, at 4-5.

[835] Sessions 1/17/18 302, at 23.

[836] Sessions 1/17/18 302, at 23.

[837] Sessions 1/17/18 302, at 23.

[838] On August 21, 2018, Manafort was convicted in the Eastern District of Virginia on eight tax, Foreign Bank Account Registration (FBAR), and bank fraud charges. On September 14, 2018, Manafort pleaded guilty in the District of Columbia to (1) conspiracy to defraud the United States and conspiracy to commit offenses against the United States (money laundering, tax fraud, FBAR, Foreign Agents Registration Act (FARA), and FARA false statements), and (2) conspiracy to obstruct justice (witness tampering). Manafort also admitted criminal conduct with which he had been charged in the Eastern District of Virginia, but as to which the jury hung. The conduct at issue in both cases involved Manafort's work in Ukraine and the money he earned for that work, as well as crimes after the Ukraine work ended. On March 7, 2019, Manafort was sentenced to 47 months of imprisonment in the Virginia prosecution. On March 13, the district court in D.C. sentenced Manafort to a total term of 73 months: 60 months on the Count 1 conspiracy (with 30 of those months to run concurrent to the Virginia sentence), and 13 months on the Count 1 conspiracy, to be served consecutive to the other two sentences. The two sentences resulted in a total term of 90 months.

[839] As noted in Volume I, Section III.D.1.b, *supra*, Gates pleaded guilty to two criminal charges in the District of Columbia, including making a false statement to the FBI, pursuant to a plea agreement. He has provided information and in-court testimony that the Office has deemed to be reliable. *See also* Transcript at 16, *United States v. Paul J. Manafort, Jr.*, 1:17-cr-201 (D.D.C. Feb. 13, 2019), Doc. 514 ("*Manafort* 2/13/19 Transcript") (court's explanation of reasons to credit Gates's statements in one instance).

Manafort also twice met Kilimnik in the United States during the campaign period and conveyed campaign information. The second meeting took place on August 2, 2016, in New York City. Kilimnik requested the meeting to deliver in person a message from former Ukrainian President Viktor Yanukovych, who was then living in Russia. The message was about a peace plan for Ukraine that Manafort has since acknowledged was a "backdoor" means for Russia to control eastern Ukraine. Several months later, after the presidential election, Kilimnik wrote an email to Manafort expressing the view—which Manafort later said he shared—that the plan's success would require U.S. support to succeed: "all that is required to start the process is a very minor 'wink' (or slight push) from [Donald Trump]."[840] The email also stated that if Manafort were designated as the U.S. representative and started the process, Yanukovych would ensure his reception in Russia "at the very top level."

Manafort communicated with Kilimnik about peace plans for Ukraine on at least four occasions after their first discussion of the topic on August 2: December 2016 (the Kilimnik email described above); January 2017; February 2017; and again in the spring of 2018. The Office reviewed numerous Manafort email and text communications, and asked President Trump about the plan in written questions.[841] The investigation did not uncover evidence of Manafort's passing along information about Ukrainian peace plans to the candidate or anyone else in the Campaign or the Administration. The Office was not, however, able to gain access to all of Manafort's electronic communications (in some instances, messages were sent using encryption applications). And while Manafort denied that he spoke to members of the Trump Campaign or the new Administration about the peace plan, he lied to the Office and the grand jury about the peace plan and his meetings with Kilimnik, and his unreliability on this subject was among the reasons that the district judge found that he breached his cooperation agreement.[842]

The Office could not reliably determine Manafort's purpose in sharing internal polling data with Kilimnik during the campaign period. Manafort Grand Jury did not see a downside to sharing campaign information, and told Gates that his role in the Campaign would

---

[840] The email was drafted in Kilimnik's DMP email account (in English) Investigative Technique

[841] According to the President's written answers, he does not remember Manafort communicating to him any particular positions that Ukraine or Russia would want the United States to support. Written Responses of Donald J. Trump (Nov. 20, 2018), at 16-17 (Response to Question IV, Part (d)).

[842] Manafort made several false statements during debriefings. Based on that conduct, the Office determined that Manafort had breached his plea agreement and could not be a cooperating witness. The judge presiding in Manafort's D.C. criminal case found by a preponderance of the evidence that Manafort intentionally made multiple false statements to the FBI, the Office, and the grand jury concerning his interactions and communications with Kilimnik (and concerning two other issues). Although the report refers at times to Manafort's statements, it does so only when those statements are sufficiently corroborated to be trustworthy, to identify issues on which Manafort's untruthful responses may themselves be of evidentiary value, or to provide Manafort's explanations for certain events, even when we were unable to determine whether that explanation was credible.

130

190

U.S. Department of Justice

~~Attorney Work Product // May Contain Material Protected Under Fed. R. Crim. P. 6(e)~~

be "good for business" and potentially a way to be made whole for work he previously completed in the Ukraine. As to Deripaska, Manafort claimed that by sharing campaign information with him, Deripaska might see value in their relationship and resolve a "disagreement"—a reference to one or more outstanding lawsuits. Because of questions about Manafort's credibility and our limited ability to gather evidence on what happened to the polling data after it was sent to Kilimnik, the Office could not assess what Kilimnik (or others he may have given it to) did with it. The Office did not identify evidence of a connection between Manafort's sharing polling data and Russia's interference in the election, which had already been reported by U.S. media outlets at the time of the August 2 meeting. The investigation did not establish that Manafort otherwise coordinated with the Russian government on its election-interference efforts.

a. Paul Manafort's Ties to Russia and Ukraine

Manafort's Russian contacts during the campaign and transition periods stem from his consulting work for Deripaska from approximately 2005 to 2009 and his separate political consulting work in Ukraine from 2005 to 2015, including through his company DMP International LLC (DMI). Kilimnik worked for Manafort in Kiev during this entire period and continued to communicate with Manafort through at least June 2018. Kilimnik, who speaks and writes Ukrainian and Russian, facilitated many of Manafort's communications with Deripaska and Ukrainian oligarchs.

i.   Oleg Deripaska Consulting Work

In approximately 2005, Manafort began working for Deripaska, a Russian oligarch who has a global empire involving aluminum and power companies and who is closely aligned with Vladimir Putin.[843] A memorandum describing work that Manafort performed for Deripaska in 2005 regarding the post-Soviet republics referenced the need to brief the Kremlin and the benefits that the work could confer on "the Putin Government."[844] Gates described the work Manafort did for Deripaska as "political risk insurance," and explained that Deripaska used Manafort to install friendly political officials in countries where Deripaska had business interests.[845] Manafort's company earned tens of millions of dollars from its work for Deripaska and was loaned millions of dollars by Deripaska as well.[846]

In 2007, Deripaska invested through another entity in Pericles Emerging Market Partners L.P. ("Pericles"), an investment fund created by Manafort and former Manafort business partner Richard Davis. The Pericles fund was established to pursue investments in Eastern Europe.[847] Deripaska was the sole investor.[848] Gates stated in interviews with the Office that the venture led

---

[843] Pinchuk et al., *Russian Tycoon Deripaska in Putin Delegation to China*, Reuters (June 8, 2018).

[844] 6/23/05 Memo, Manafort & Davis to Deripaska & Rothchild.

[845] Gates 2/2/18 302, at 7.

[846] Manafort 9/20/18 302, at 2-5; Manafort Income by Year, 2005 – 2015; Manafort Loans from Wire Transfers, 2005 – 2015.

[847] Gates 3/12/18 302, at 5.

[848] Manafort 12/16/15 Dep., at 157:8-11.

131

191

U.S. Department of Justice

~~Attorney Work Product // May Contain Material Protected Under Fed. R. Crim. P. 6(e)~~

to a deterioration of the relationship between Manafort and Deripaska.[849] In particular, when the fund failed, litigation between Manafort and Deripaska ensued. Gates stated that, by 2009, Manafort's business relationship with Deripaska had "dried up."[850] According to Gates, various interactions with Deripaska and his intermediaries over the past few years have involved trying to resolve the legal dispute.[851] As described below, in 2016, Manafort, Gates, Kilimnik, and others engaged in efforts to revive the Deripaska relationship and resolve the litigation.

ii.   Political Consulting Work

Through Deripaska, Manafort was introduced to Rinat Akhmetov, a Ukrainian oligarch who hired Manafort as a political consultant.[852] In 2005, Akhmetov hired Manafort to engage in political work supporting the Party of Regions,[853] a political party in Ukraine that was generally understood to align with Russia. Manafort assisted the Party of Regions in regaining power, and its candidate, Viktor Yanukovych, won the presidency in 2010. Manafort became a close and trusted political advisor to Yanukovych during his time as President of Ukraine. Yanukovych served in that role until 2014, when he fled to Russia amidst popular protests.[854]

iii.   Konstantin Kilimnik

Kilimnik is a Russian national who has lived in both Russia and Ukraine and was a longtime Manafort employee.[855] Kilimnik had direct and close access to Yanukovych and his senior entourage, and he facilitated communications between Manafort and his clients, including Yanukovych and multiple Ukrainian oligarchs.[856] Kilimnik also maintained a relationship with Deripaska's deputy, Viktor Boyarkin,[857] a Russian national who previously served in the defense attaché office of the Russian Embassy to the United States.[858]

---

[849] Gates 2/2/18 302, at 9.

[850] Gates 2/2/18 302, at 6.

[851] Gates 2/2/18 302, at 9-10.

[852] Manafort 7/30/14 302, at 1; Manafort 9/20/18 302, at 2.

[853] Manafort 9/11/18 302, at 5-6.

[854] Gates 3/16/18 302, at 1; Davis 2/8/18 302, at 9; Devine 7/6/18 302, at 2-3.

[855] Patten 5/22/18 302, at 5; Gates 1/29/18 302, at 18-19; 10/28/97 Kilimnik Visa Record, U.S. Department of State.

[856] Gates 1/29/18 302, at 18-19; Patten 5/22/18 302, at 8; Gates 1/31/18 302, at 4-5; Gates 1/30/18 302, at 2; Gates 2/2/18 302, at 11.

[857] Gates 1/29/18 302, at 18; Patten 5/22/18 302, at 8.

[858] Boyarkin Visa Record, U.S. Department of State.

Manafort told the Office that he did not believe Kilimnik was working as a Russian "spy."[859] The FBI, however, assesses that Kilimnik has ties to Russian intelligence.[860] Several pieces of the Office's evidence—including witness interviews and emails obtained through court-authorized search warrants—support that assessment:

- Kilimnik was born on April 27, 1970, in Dnipropetrovsk Oblast, then of the Soviet Union, and attended the Military Institute of the Ministry of Defense from 1987 until 1992.[861] Sam Patten, a business partner to Kilimnik,[862] stated that Kilimnik told him that he was a translator in the Russian army for seven years and that he later worked in the Russian armament industry selling arms and military equipment.[863]

- U.S. government visa records reveal that Kilimnik obtained a visa to travel to the United States with a Russian diplomatic passport in 1997.[864]

- Kilimnik worked for the International Republican Institute's (IRI) Moscow office, where he did translation work and general office management from 1998 to 2005.[865] While another official recalled the incident differently,[866] one former associate of Kilimnik's at IRI told the FBI that Kilimnik was fired from his post because his links to Russian intelligence were too strong. The same individual stated that it was well known at IRI that Kilimnik had links to the Russian government.[867]

- Jonathan Hawker, a British national who was a public relations consultant at FTI Consulting, worked with DMI on a public relations campaign for Yanukovych. After Hawker's work for DMI ended, Kilimnik contacted Hawker about working for a Russian

---

[859] Manafort 9/11/18 302, at 5.

[860] The Office has noted Kilimnik's assessed ties to Russian intelligence in public court filings. *E.g.*, Gov't Opp. to Mot. to Modify, *United States v. Paul J. Manafort, Jr.*, 1:17-cr-201 (D.D.C. Dec. 4, 2017), Doc. 73, at 2 ("*Manafort* (D.D.C.) Gov't Opp. to Mot. to Modify").

[861] 12/17/16 Kilimnik Visa Record, U.S. Department of State.

[862] In August 2018, Patten pleaded guilty pursuant to a plea agreement to violating the Foreign Agents Registration Act, and admitted in his Statement of Offense that he also misled and withheld documents from the Senate Select Committee on Intelligence in the course of its investigation of Russian election interference. Plea Agreement, *United States v. W. Samuel Patten*, 1:18-cr-260 (D.D.C. Aug. 31, 2018), Doc. 6; Statement of Offense, *United States v. W. Samuel Patten*, 1:18-cr-260 (D.D.C. Aug. 31, 2018), Doc. 7.

[863] Patten 5/22/18 302, at 5-6.

[864] 10/28/97 Kilimnik Visa Record, U.S. Department of State.

[865] Nix 3/30/18 302, at 1-2.

[866] Nix 3/30/18 302, at 2.

[867] Lenzi 1/30/18 302, at 2.

government entity on a public-relations project that would promote, in Western and Ukrainian media, Russia's position on its 2014 invasion of Crimea.[868]

- Gates suspected that Kilimnik was a "spy," a view that he shared with Manafort, Hawker, and Alexander van der Zwaan,[869] an attorney who had worked with DMI on a report for the Ukrainian Ministry of Foreign Affairs.[870]

Investigative Technique

b. Contacts during Paul Manafort's Time with the Trump Campaign

i. Paul Manafort Joins the Campaign

Manafort served on the Trump Campaign from late March to August 19, 2016. On March 29, 2016, the Campaign announced that Manafort would serve as the Campaign's "Convention Manager."[871] On May 19, 2016, Manafort was promoted to campaign chairman and chief strategist, and Gates, who had been assisting Manafort on the Campaign, was appointed deputy campaign chairman.[872]

Thomas Barrack and Roger Stone both recommended Manafort to candidate Trump.[873] In early 2016, at Manafort's request, Barrack suggested to Trump that Manafort join the Campaign to manage the Republican Convention.[874] Stone had worked with Manafort from approximately 1980 until the mid-1990s through various consulting and lobbying firms. Manafort met Trump in 1982 when Trump hired the Black, Manafort, Stone and Kelly lobbying firm.[875] Over the years, Manafort saw Trump at political and social events in New York City and at Stone's wedding, and Trump requested VIP status at the 1988 and 1996 Republican conventions worked by Manafort.[876]

---

[868] Hawker 1/9/18 302, at 13; 3/18/14 Email, Hawker & Tulukbaev.

[869] van der Zwaan pleaded guilty in the U.S. District Court for the District of Columbia to making false statements to the Special Counsel's Office. Plea Agreement, *United States v. Alex van der Zwaan*, 1:18-cr-31 (D.D.C. Feb. 20, 2018), Doc. 8.

[870] Hawker 6/9/18 302, at 4; van der Zwaan 11/3/17 302, at 22. Manafort said in an interview that Gates had joked with Kilimnik about Kilimnik's going to meet with his KGB handler. Manafort 10/16/18 302, at 7.

[871] *Press Release – Donald J. Trump Announces Campaign Convention Manager Paul J. Manafort*, The American Presidency Project – U.C. Santa Barbara (Mar. 29, 2016).

[872] Gates 1/29/18 302, at 8; Meghan Keneally, *Timeline of Manafort's role in the Trump Campaign*, ABC News (Oct. 20, 2017).

[873] Gates 1/29/18 302, at 7-8; Manafort 9/11/18 302, at 1-2; Barrack 12/12/17 302, at 3.

[874] Barrack 12/12/17 302, at 3; Gates 1/29/18 302, at 7-8.

[875] Manafort 10/16/18 302, at 6.

[876] Manafort 10/16/18 302, at 6.

134

U.S. Department of Justice

~~Attorney Work Product // May Contain Material Protected Under Fed. R. Crim. P. 6(e)~~

According to Gates, in March 2016, Manafort traveled to Trump's Mar-a-Lago estate in Florida to meet with Trump. Trump hired him at that time.[877] Manafort agreed to work on the Campaign without pay. Manafort had no meaningful income at this point in time, but resuscitating his domestic political campaign career could be financially beneficial in the future. Gates reported that Manafort intended, if Trump won the Presidency, to remain outside the Administration and monetize his relationship with the Administration.[878]

ii. Paul Manafort's Campaign-Period Contacts

Immediately upon joining the Campaign, Manafort directed Gates to prepare for his review separate memoranda addressed to Deripaska, Akhmetov, Serhiy Lyovochkin, and Boris Kolesnikov,[879] the last three being Ukrainian oligarchs who were senior Opposition Bloc officials.[880] The memoranda described Manafort's appointment to the Trump Campaign and indicated his willingness to consult on Ukrainian politics in the future. On March 30, 2016, Gates emailed the memoranda and a press release announcing Manafort's appointment to Kilimnik for translation and dissemination.[881] Manafort later followed up with Kilimnik to ensure his messages had been delivered, emailing on April 11, 2016 to ask whether Kilimnik had shown "our friends" the media coverage of his new role.[882] Kilimnik replied, "Absolutely. Every article." Manafort further asked: "How do we use to get whole. Has Ovd [Oleg Vladimirovich Deripaska] operation seen?" Kilimnik wrote back the same day, "Yes, I have been sending everything to Victor [Boyarkin, Deripaska's deputy], who has been forwarding the coverage directly to OVD."[883]

Gates reported that Manafort said that being hired on the Campaign would be "good for business" and increase the likelihood that Manafort would be paid the approximately $2 million he was owed for previous political consulting work in Ukraine.[884] Gates also explained to the Office that Manafort thought his role on the Campaign could help "confirm" that Deripaska had dropped the Pericles lawsuit, and that Gates believed Manafort sent polling data to Deripaska (as

---

[877] Gates 2/2/18 302, at 10.

[878] Gates 1/30/18 302, at 4.

[879] Gates 2/2/18 302, at 11.

[880] See Sharon LaFraniere, Manafort's Trial Isn't About Russia, but It Will Be in the Air, New York Times (July 30, 2018); Tierney Sneed, Prosecutors Believe Manafort Made $60 Million Consulting in Ukraine, Talking Points Memo (July 30, 2018); Mykola Vorobiov, How Pro-Russian Forces Will Take Revenge on Ukraine, Atlantic Council (Sept. 23, 2018); Sergii Leshchenko, Ukraine's Oligarchs Are Still Calling the Shots, Foreign Policy (Aug. 14, 2014); Interfax-Ukraine, Kolesnikov: Inevitability of Punishment Needed for Real Fight Against Smuggling in Ukraine, Kyiv Post (June 23, 2018); Igor Kossov, Kyiv Hotel Industry Makes Room for New Entrants, Kyiv Post (Mar. 7, 2019); Markian Kuzmowycz, How the Kremlin Can Win Ukraine's Elections, Atlantic Council (Nov. 19, 2018). The Opposition Bloc is a Ukraine political party that largely reconstituted the Party of Regions.

[881] 3/30/16 Email, Gates to Kilimnik.

[882] 4/11/16 Email, Manafort & Kilimnik.

[883] 4/11/16 Email, Manafort & Kilimnik.

[884] Gates 2/2/18 302, at 10.

135

discussed further below) so that Deripaska would not move forward with his lawsuit against Manafort.[885] Gates further stated that Deripaska wanted a visa to the United States, that Deripaska could believe that having Manafort in a position inside the Campaign or Administration might be helpful to Deripaska, and that Manafort's relationship with Trump could help Deripaska in other ways as well.[886] Gates stated, however, that Manafort never told him anything specific about what, if anything, Manafort might be offering Deripaska.[887]

Gates also reported that Manafort instructed him in April 2016 or early May 2016 to send Kilimnik Campaign internal polling data and other updates so that Kilimnik, in turn, could share it with Ukrainian oligarchs.[888] Gates understood that the information would also be shared with Deripaska. Grand Jury ███████████████████████████████.[889] Gates reported to the Office that he did not know why Manafort wanted him to send polling information, but Gates thought it was a way to showcase Manafort's work, and Manafort wanted to open doors to jobs after the Trump Campaign ended.[890] Gates said that Manafort's instruction included sending internal polling data prepared for the Trump Campaign by pollster Tony Fabrizio.[891] Fabrizio had worked with Manafort for years and was brought into the Campaign by Manafort. Gates stated that, in accordance with Manafort's instruction, he periodically sent Kilimnik polling data via WhatsApp; Gates then deleted the communications on a daily basis.[892] Gates further told the Office that, after Manafort left the Campaign in mid-August, Gates sent Kilimnik polling data less frequently and that the data he sent was more publicly available information and less internal data.[893]

Gates's account about polling data is consistent Grand Jury ███████████████████████████████[894] with multiple emails that Kilimnik sent to U.S. associates and press contacts between late July and mid-August of 2016. Those emails referenced "internal polling," described the status of the Trump Campaign and

---

[885] Gates 2/2/18 302, at 11; Gates 9/27/18 302 (serial 740), at 2.

[886] Gates 2/2/18 302, at 12.

[887] Gates 2/2/18 302, at 12.

[888] Gates 1/31/18 302, at 17; Gates 9/27/18 302 (serial 740), at 2. In a later interview with the Office, Gates stated that Manafort directed him to send polling data to Kilimnik after a May 7, 2016 meeting between Manafort and Kilimnik in New York, discussed in Volume I, Section IV.A.8.b.iii, *infra*. Gates 11/7/18 302, at 3.

[889] Gates 9/27/18 302, Part II, at 2; Grand Jury ██████████████.

[890] Gates 2/12/18 302, at 10; Gates 1/31/18 302, at 17.

[891] Gates 9/27/18 302 (serial 740), at 2; Gates 2/7/18 302, at 15.

[892] Gates 1/31/18 302, at 17.

[893] Gates 2/12/18 302, at 11-12. According to Gates, his access to internal polling data was more limited because Fabrizio was himself distanced from the Campaign at that point.

[894] Grand Jury ██████████████████

Manafort's role in it, and assessed Trump's prospects for victory.[895]   Manafort did not acknowledge instructing Gates to send Kilimnik internal data, Grand Jury
[896]

The Office also obtained contemporaneous emails that shed light on the purpose of the communications with Deripaska and that are consistent with Gates's account. For example, in response to a July 7, 2016, email from a Ukrainian reporter about Manafort's failed Deripaska-backed investment, Manafort asked Kilimnik whether there had been any movement on "this issue with our friend."[897]   Gates stated that "our friend" likely referred to Deripaska,[898] and Manafort told the Office that the "issue" (and "our biggest interest," as stated below) was a solution to the Deripaska-Pericles issue.[899] Kilimnik replied:

> I am carefully optimistic on the question of our biggest interest.

> Our friend [Boyarkin] said there is lately significantly more attention to the campaign in his boss' [Deripaska's] mind, and he will be most likely looking for ways to reach out to you pretty soon, understanding all the time sensitivity. I am more than sure that it will be resolved and we will get back to the original relationship with V.'s boss [Deripaska].[900]

Eight minutes later, Manafort replied that Kilimnik should tell Boyarkin's "boss," a reference to Deripaska, "that if he needs private briefings we can accommodate."[901] Manafort has alleged to the Office that he was willing to brief Deripaska only on public campaign matters and gave an example: why Trump selected Mike Pence as the Vice-Presidential running mate.[902] Manafort said he never gave Deripaska a briefing.[903] Manafort noted that if Trump won, Deripaska would want to use Manafort to advance whatever interests Deripaska had in the United States and elsewhere.[904]

---

[895] 8/18/16 Email, Kilimnik to Dirkse; 8/18/16 Email, Kilimnik to Schultz; 8/18/16 Email, Kilimnik to Marson; 7/27/16 Email, Kilimnik to Ash; 8/18/16 Email, Kilimnik to Ash; 8/18/16 Email, Kilimnik to Jackson; 8/18/16 Email, Kilimnik to Mendoza-Wilson; 8/19/16 Email, Kilimnik to Patten.

[896] Grand Jury

[897] 7/7/16 Email, Manafort to Kilimnik.

[898] Gates 2/2/18 302, at 13.

[899] Manafort 9/11/18 302, at 6.

[900] 7/8/16 Email, Kilimnik to Manafort.

[901] 7/8/16 Email, Kilimnik to Manafort; Gates 2/2/18 302, at 13.

[902] Manafort 9/11/18 302, at 6.

[903] Manafort 9/11/18 302, at 6.

[904] Manafort 9/11/18 302, at 6.

iii. *Paul Manafort's Two Campaign-Period Meetings with Konstantin Kilimnik in the United States*

Manafort twice met with Kilimnik in person during the campaign period—once in May and again in August 2016. The first meeting took place on May 7, 2016, in New York City.[905] In the days leading to the meeting, Kilimnik had been working to gather information about the political situation in Ukraine. That included information gleaned from a trip that former Party of Regions official Yuriy Boyko had recently taken to Moscow—a trip that likely included meetings between Boyko and high-ranking Russian officials.[906] Kilimnik then traveled to Washington, D.C. on or about May 5, 2016; while in Washington, Kilimnik had pre-arranged meetings with State Department employees.[907]

Late on the evening of May 6, Gates arranged for Kilimnik to take a 3:00 a.m. train to meet Manafort in New York for breakfast on May 7.[908] According to Manafort, during the meeting, he and Kilimnik talked about events in Ukraine, and Manafort briefed Kilimnik on the Trump Campaign, expecting Kilimnik to pass the information back to individuals in Ukraine and elsewhere.[909] Manafort stated that Opposition Bloc members recognized Manafort's position on the Campaign was an opportunity, but Kilimnik did not ask for anything.[910] Kilimnik spoke about a plan of Boyko to boost election participation in the eastern zone of Ukraine, which was the base for the Opposition Bloc.[911] Kilimnik returned to Washington, D.C. right after the meeting with Manafort.

Manafort met with Kilimnik a second time at the Grand Havana Club in New York City on the evening of August 2, 2016. The events leading to the meeting are as follows. On July 28, 2016, Kilimnik flew from Kiev to Moscow.[912] The next day, Kilimnik wrote to Manafort requesting that they meet, using coded language about a conversation he had that day.[913] In an email with a subject line "Black Caviar," Kilimnik wrote:

> I met today with the guy who gave you your biggest black caviar jar several years ago. We spent about 5 hours talking about his story, and I have several important messages from him to you. He asked me to go and brief you on our conversation. I said I have to run it by you first, but in principle I am prepared to do it. . . . It has to do about the future of his

---

[905] ████ Investigative Technique ████

[906] 4/26/16 Email, Kilimnik to Purcell, at 2; Gates 2/2/18 302, at 12; Patten 5/22/18 302, at 6-7; Gates 11/7/18 302, at 3.

[907] 5/7/16 Email, Kilimnik to Charap & Kimmage; 5/7/16 Email, Kasanof to Kilimnik.

[908] 5/6/16 Email, Manafort to Gates; 5/6/16 Email, Gates to Kilimnik.

[909] Manafort 10/11/18 302, at 1.

[910] Manafort 10/11/18 302, at 1.

[911] Manafort 10/11/18 302, at 1.

[912] 7/25/16 Email, Kilimnik to katrin@yana.kiev.ua (2:17:34 a.m.).

[913] 7/29/16 Email, Kilimnik to Manafort (10:51 a.m.).

country, and is quite interesting.[914]

Manafort identified "the guy who gave you your biggest black caviar jar" as Yanukovych. He explained that, in 2010, he and Yanukovych had lunch to celebrate the recent presidential election. Yanukovych gave Manafort a large jar of black caviar that was worth approximately $30,000 to $40,000.[915] Manafort's identification of Yanukovych as "the guy who gave you your biggest black caviar jar" is consistent with Kilimnik being in Moscow—where Yanukovych resided—when Kilimnik wrote "I met today with the guy," and with a December 2016 email in which Kilimnik referred to Yanukovych as "BG," Grand Jury [916] Manafort replied to Kilimnik's July 29 email, "Tuesday [August 2] is best . . . Tues or weds in NYC."[917]

Three days later, on July 31, 2016, Kilimnik flew back to Kiev from Moscow, and on that same day, wrote to Manafort that he needed "about 2 hours" for their meeting "because it is a long caviar story to tell."[918] Kilimnik wrote that he would arrive at JFK on August 2 at 7:30 p.m., and he and Manafort agreed to a late dinner that night.[919] Documentary evidence—including flight, phone, and hotel records, and the timing of text messages exchanged[920]—confirms the dinner took place as planned on August 2.[921]

As to the contents of the meeting itself, the accounts of Manafort and Gates—who arrived late to the dinner—differ in certain respects. But their versions of events, when assessed alongside available documentary evidence and what Kilimnik told business associate Sam Patten, indicate that at least three principal topics were discussed.

First, Manafort and Kilimnik discussed a plan to resolve the ongoing political problems in Ukraine by creating an autonomous republic in its more industrialized eastern region of Donbas,[922]

---

[914] 7/29/16 Email, Kilimnik to Manafort (10:51 a.m.).

[915] Manafort 9/12/18 302, at 3.

[916] 7/29/16 Email, Manafort to Kilimnik; Investigative Technique ; Grand Jury

[917] 7/29/16 Email, Manafort to Kilimnik.

[918] 7/31/16 Email, Manafort to Kilimnik.

[919] 7/31/16 Email, Manafort to Kilimnik.

[920] Kilimnik 8/2/16 CBP Record; Call Records of Konstantin Kilimnik Grand Jury ; Call Records of Rick Gates Grand Jury ; 8/2-3/16, Kilimnik Park Lane Hotel Receipt.

[921] Deripaska's private plane also flew to Teterboro Airport in New Jersey on the evening of August 2, 2016. According to Customs and Border Protection records, the only passengers on the plane were Deripaska's wife, daughter, mother, and father-in-law, and separate records obtained by our Office confirm that Kilimnik flew on a commercial flight to New York.

[922] The Luhansk and Donetsk People's Republics, which are located in the Donbas region of Ukraine, declared themselves independent in response to the popular unrest in 2014 that removed President Yanukovych from power. Pro-Russian Ukrainian militia forces, with backing from the Russian military, have occupied the region since 2014. Under the Yanukovych-backed plan, Russia would assist in withdrawing the military, and Donbas would become an autonomous region within Ukraine with its own

and having Yanukovych, the Ukrainian President ousted in 2014, elected to head that republic.[923] That plan, Manafort later acknowledged, constituted a "backdoor" means for Russia to control eastern Ukraine.[924] Manafort initially said that, if he had not cut off the discussion, Kilimnik would have asked Manafort in the August 2 meeting to convince Trump to come out in favor of the peace plan, and Yanukovych would have expected Manafort to use his connections in Europe and Ukraine to support the plan.[925] Manafort also initially told the Office that he had said to Kilimnik that the plan was crazy, that the discussion ended, and that he did not recall Kilimnik asking Manafort to reconsider the plan after their August 2 meeting.[926] Manafort said Grand Jury

that he reacted negatively to Yanukovych sending—years later—an "urgent" request when Yanukovych needed him.[927] When confronted with an email written by Kilimnik on or about December 8, 2016, however, Manafort acknowledged Kilimnik raised the peace plan again in that email.[928] Manafort ultimately acknowledged Kilimnik also raised the peace plan in January and February 2017 meetings with Manafort. Grand Jury
[929]

Second, Manafort briefed Kilimnik on the state of the Trump Campaign and Manafort's plan to win the election.[930] That briefing encompassed the Campaign's messaging and its internal polling data. According to Gates, it also included discussion of "battleground" states, which Manafort identified as Michigan, Wisconsin, Pennsylvania, and Minnesota.[931] Manafort did not refer explicitly to "battleground" states in his telling of the August 2 discussion, Grand Jury
[32]

---

prime minister. The plan emphasized that Yanukovych would be an ideal candidate to bring peace to the region as prime minister of the republic, and facilitate the reintegration of the region into Ukraine with the support of the U.S. and Russian presidents. As noted above, according to GJ the written documentation describing the plan, for the plan to work, both U.S. and Russian support were necessary. Grand Jury 2/21/18 Email, Manafort, Ward, & Fabrizio, at 3-5.

[923] Manafort 9/11/18 302, at 4; Grand Jury

[924] Grand Jury

[925] Manafort 9/11/18 302, at 4.

[926] Manafort 9/12/18 302, at 4.

[927] Grand Jury Manafort 9/11/18 302, at 5; Manafort 9/12/18 302, at 4.

[928] Manafort 9/12/18 302, at 4; Investigative Technique

[929] Grand Jury Documentary evidence confirms the peace-plan discussions in 2018. 2/19/18 Email, Fabrizio to Ward (forwarding email from Manafort); 2/21/18 Email, Manafort to Ward & Fabrizio.

[930] Manafort 9/11/18 302, at 5.

[931] Gates 1/30/18 302, at 3, 5.

[932] Grand Jury

Third, according to Gates and what Kilimnik told Patten, Manafort and Kilimnik discussed two sets of financial disputes related to Manafort's previous work in the region. Those consisted of the unresolved Deripaska lawsuit and the funds that the Opposition Bloc owed to Manafort for his political consulting work and how Manafort might be able to obtain payment.[933]

After the meeting, Gates and Manafort both stated that they left separately from Kilimnik because they knew the media was tracking Manafort and wanted to avoid media reporting on his connections to Kilimnik.[934]

c. Post-Resignation Activities

Manafort resigned from the Trump Campaign in mid-August 2016, approximately two weeks after his second meeting with Kilimnik, amidst negative media reporting about his political consulting work for the pro-Russian Party of Regions in Ukraine. Despite his resignation, Manafort continued to offer advice to various Campaign officials through the November election. Manafort told Gates that he still spoke with Kushner, Bannon, and candidate Trump,[935] and some of those post-resignation contacts are documented in emails. For example, on October 21, 2016, Manafort sent Kushner an email and attached a strategy memorandum proposing that the Campaign make the case against Clinton "as the failed and corrupt champion of the establishment" and that "Wikileaks provides the Trump campaign the ability to make the case in a very credible way – by using the words of Clinton, its campaign officials and DNC members."[936] Later, in a November 5, 2016 email to Kushner entitled "Securing the Victory," Manafort stated that he was "really feeling good about our prospects on Tuesday and focusing on preserving the victory," and that he was concerned the Clinton Campaign would respond to a loss by "mov[ing] immediately to discredit the [Trump] victory and claim voter fraud and cyber-fraud, including the claim that the Russians have hacked into the voting machines and tampered with the results."[937]

Trump was elected President on November 8, 2016. Manafort told the Office that, in the wake of Trump's victory, he was not interested in an Administration job. Manafort instead preferred to stay on the "outside," and monetize his campaign position to generate business given his familiarity and relationship with Trump and the incoming Administration.[938] Manafort appeared to follow that plan, as he traveled to the Middle East, Cuba, South Korea, Japan, and China and was paid to explain what a Trump presidency would entail.[939]

Manafort's activities in early 2017 included meetings relating to Ukraine and Russia. The

[933] Gates 1/30/18 302, at 2-4; Patten 5/22/18 302, at 7.

[934] Gates 1/30/18 302, at 5; Manafort 9/11/18 302, at 5.

[935] Gates 2/12/18 302, at 12.

[936] NOSC00021517-20 (10/21/16 Email, Manafort to Kushner).

[937] NOSC00021573-75 (11/5/16 Email, Manafort to Kushner).

[938] Manafort 9/12/18 302, at 1, 4-5; Gates 1/30/18 302, at 4.

[939] Manafort 9/12/18 302, at 1.

141

201

first meeting, which took place in Madrid, Spain in January 2017, was with Georgiy Oganov. Oganov, who had previously worked at the Russian Embassy in the United States, was a senior executive at a Deripaska company and was believed to report directly to Deripaska.[940] Manafort initially denied attending the meeting. When he later acknowledged it, he claimed that the meeting had been arranged by his lawyers and concerned only the Pericles lawsuit.[941] Other evidence, however, provides reason to doubt Manafort's statement that the sole topic of the meeting was the Pericles lawsuit. In particular, text messages to Manafort from a number associated with Kilimnik suggest that Kilimnik and Boyarkin—not Manafort's counsel—had arranged the meeting between Manafort and Oganov.[942] Kilimnik's message states that the meeting was supposed to be "not about money or Pericles" but instead "about recreating [the] old friendship"—ostensibly between Manafort and Deripaska—"and talking about global politics."[943] Manafort also replied by text that he "need[s] this finished before Jan. 20,"[944] which appears to be a reference to resolving Pericles before the inauguration.

On January 15, 2017, three days after his return from Madrid, Manafort emailed K.T. McFarland, who was at that time designated to be Deputy National Security Advisor and was formally appointed to that position on January 20, 2017.[945] Manafort's January 15 email to McFarland stated: "I have some important information I want to share that I picked up on my travels over the last month."[946] Manafort told the Office that the email referred to an issue regarding Cuba, not Russia or Ukraine, and Manafort had traveled to Cuba in the past month.[947] Either way, McFarland—who was advised by Flynn not to respond to the Manafort inquiry—appears not to have responded to Manafort.[948]

Manafort told the Office that around the time of the Presidential Inauguration in January, he met with Kilimnik and Ukrainian oligarch Serhiy Lyovochkin at the Westin Hotel in Alexandria, Virginia.[949] During this meeting, Kilimnik again discussed the Yanukovych peace plan that he had broached at the August 2 meeting and in a detailed December 8, 2016 message found in Kilimnik's DMP email account.[950] In that December 8 email, which Manafort

---

[940] Kalashnikova 5/17/18 302, at 4; Gary Lee, *Soviet Embassy's Identity Crisis*, Washington Post (Dec. 20, 1991); *Georgy S. Oganov Executive Profile & Biography*, Bloomberg (Mar. 12, 2019).

[941] Manafort 9/11/18 302, at 7.

[942] Text Message, Manafort & Kilimnik.

[943] Text Message, Manafort & Kilimnik; Manafort 9/12/18 302, at 5.

[944] Text Message, Manafort & Kilimnik.

[945] 1/15/17 Email, Manafort, McFarland, & Flynn.

[946] 1/15/17 Email, Manafort, McFarland, & Flynn.

[947] Manafort 9/11/18 302, at 7.

[948] 1/15/17 Email, Manafort, McFarland, & Flynn; McFarland 12/22/17 302, at 18-19.

[949] Grand Jury Manafort 9/11/18 302, at 7; Manafort 9/21/18 302, at 3; 1/19/17 & 1/22/17 Kilimnik CBP Records, Jan. 19 and 22, 2017; 2016-17 Text Messages, Kilimnik & Patten, at 1-2.

[950] Investigative Technique

142

acknowledged having read,[951] Kilimnik wrote, "[a]ll that is required to start the process is a very minor 'wink' (or slight push) from DT"—an apparent reference to President-elect Trump—"and a decision to authorize you to be a 'special representative' and manage this process." Kilimnik assured Manafort, with that authority, he "could start the process and within 10 days visit Russia [Yanukovych] guarantees your reception at the very top level," and that "DT could have peace in Ukraine basically within a few months after inauguration."[952]

As noted above, Grand Jury   and statements to the Office, Manafort sought to qualify his engagement on and support for the plan. Grand Jury

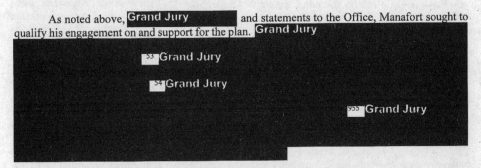

[53] Grand Jury

[54] Grand Jury

[955] Grand Jury

On February 26, 2017, Manafort met Kilimnik in Madrid, where Kilimnik had flown from Moscow.[956] In his first two interviews with the Office, Manafort denied meeting with Kilimnik on his Madrid trip and then—after being confronted with documentary evidence that Kilimnik was in Madrid at the same time as him—recognized that he met him in Madrid. Manafort said that Kilimnik had updated him on a criminal investigation into so-called "black ledger" payments to Manafort that was being conducted by Ukraine's National Anti-Corruption Bureau.[957] Grand Jury

[958]

Manafort remained in contact with Kilimnik throughout 2017 and into the spring of 2018.

---

[951] Manafort 9/11/18 302, at 6; Grand Jury

[952] Investigative Technique

[953] Grand Jury

[954] Grand Jury .

[955] Grand Jury

[956] 2/21/17 Email, Zatynaiko to Kilimnik.

[957] Manafort 9/13/18 302, at 1.

[958] Grand Jury   In resolving whether Manafort breached his cooperation plea agreement by lying to the Office, the district court found that Manafort lied about, among other things, his contacts with Kilimnik regarding the peace plan, including the meeting in Madrid. *Manafort* 2/13/19 Transcript, at 29-31, 40.

143

U.S. Department of Justice

~~Attorney Work Product // May Contain Material Protected Under Fed. R. Crim. P. 6(e)~~

Those contacts included matters pertaining to the criminal charges brought by the Office,[959] and the Ukraine peace plan. In early 2018, Manafort retained his longtime polling firm to craft a draft poll in Ukraine, sent the pollsters a three-page primer on the plan sent by Kilimnik, and worked with Kilimnik to formulate the polling questions.[960] The primer sent to the pollsters specifically called for the United States and President Trump to support the Autonomous Republic of Donbas with Yanukovych as Prime Minister,[961] and a series of questions in the draft poll asked for opinions on Yanukovych's role in resolving the conflict in Donbas.[962] (The poll was not solely about Donbas; it also sought participants' views on leaders apart from Yanukovych as they pertained to the 2019 Ukraine presidential election.)

The Office has not uncovered evidence that Manafort brought the Ukraine peace plan to the attention of the Trump Campaign or the Trump Administration. Kilimnik continued his efforts to promote the peace plan to the Executive Branch (*e.g.*, U.S. Department of State) into the summer of 2018.[963]

B. Post-Election and Transition-Period Contacts

Trump was elected President on November 8, 2016. Beginning immediately after the election, individuals connected to the Russian government started contacting officials on the Trump Campaign and Transition Team through multiple channels—sometimes through Russian Ambassador Kislyak and at other times through individuals who sought reliable contacts through U.S. persons not formally tied to the Campaign or Transition Team. The most senior levels of the Russian government encouraged these efforts. The investigation did not establish that these efforts reflected or constituted coordination between the Trump Campaign and Russia in its election-interference activities.

1. Immediate Post-Election Activity

As soon as news broke that Trump had been elected President, Russian government officials and prominent Russian businessmen began trying to make inroads into the new Administration. They appeared not to have preexisting contacts and struggled to connect with senior officials around the President-Elect. As explained below, those efforts entailed both official contact through the Russian Embassy in the United States and outreaches—sanctioned at high levels of the Russian government—through business rather than political contacts.

---

[959] *Manafort* (D.D.C.) Gov't Opp. to Mot. to Modify, at 2; Superseding Indictment ¶¶ 48-51, *United States v. Paul J. Manafort, Jr.*, 1:17-cr-201 (D.D.C. June 8, 2018), Doc. 318.

[960] 2/12/18 Email, Fabrizio to Manafort & Ward; 2/16/18 Email, Fabrizio to Manafort; 2/19/18 Email, Fabrizio to Ward; 2/21/18 Email, Manafort to Ward & Fabrizio.

[961] 2/21/18 Email, Manafort to Ward & Fabrizio (7:16:49 a.m.) (attachment).

[962] 3/9/18 Email, Ward to Manafort & Fabrizio (attachment).

[963] Investigative Technique

U.S. Department of Justice

~~Attorney Work Product~~ // ~~May Contain Material Protected Under Fed. R. Crim. P. 6(e)~~

a. Outreach from the Russian Government

At approximately 3 a.m. on election night, Trump Campaign press secretary Hope Hicks received a telephone call on her personal cell phone from a person who sounded foreign but was calling from a number with a DC area code.[964] Although Hicks had a hard time understanding the person, she could make out the words "Putin call."[965] Hicks told the caller to send her an email.[966]

The following morning, on November 9, 2016, Sergey Kuznetsov, an official at the Russian Embassy to the United States, emailed Hicks from his Gmail address with the subject line, "Message from Putin."[967] Attached to the email was a message from Putin, in both English and Russian, which Kuznetsov asked Hicks to convey to the President-Elect.[968] In the message, Putin offered his congratulations to Trump for his electoral victory, stating he "look[ed] forward to working with [Trump] on leading Russian-American relations out of crisis."[969]

Hicks forwarded the email to Kushner, asking, "Can you look into this? Don't want to get duped but don't want to blow off Putin!"[970] Kushner stated in Congressional testimony that he believed that it would be possible to verify the authenticity of the forwarded email through the Russian Ambassador, whom Kushner had previously met in April 2016.[971] Unable to recall the Russian Ambassador's name, Kushner emailed Dimitri Simes of CNI, whom he had consulted previously about Russia, see Volume I, Section IV.A.4, supra, and asked, "What is the name of Russian ambassador?"[972] Kushner forwarded Simes's response—which identified Kislyak by name—to Hicks.[973] After checking with Kushner to see what he had learned, Hicks conveyed Putin's letter to transition officials.[974] Five days later, on November 14, 2016, Trump and Putin spoke by phone in the presence of Transition Team members, including incoming National Security Advisor Michael Flynn.[975]

---

[964] Hicks 12/8/17 302, at 3.

[965] Hicks 12/8/17 302, at 3.

[966] Hicks 12/8/17 302, at 3.

[967] NOSC00044381 (11/9/16 Email, Kuznetsov to Hicks (5:27 a.m.)).

[968] NOSC00044381-82 (11/9/16 Email, Kuznetsov to Hicks (5:27 a.m.)).

[969] NOSC00044382 (11/9/16 Letter from Putin to President-Elect Trump (Nov. 9, 2016) (translation)).

[970] NOSC00044381 (11/9/16 Email, Hicks to Kushner (10:26 a.m.)).

[971] Statement of Jared C. Kushner to Congressional Committees, at 4 (Jul. 24, 2017).

[972] NOSC00000058 (11/9/16 Email, Kushner to Simes (10:28 a.m.)); Statement of Jared Kushner to Congressional Committees, at 4 (Jul. 24, 2017).

[973] NOSC00000058 (11/9/16 Email, Kushner to Hicks (11:05:44 a.m.)).

[974] Hicks 12/8/17 302, at 3-4.

[975] Flynn 11/16/17 302, at 8-10; see Doug G. Ware, *Trump, Russia's Putin Talk about Syria, Icy Relations in Phone Call*, UPI (Nov. 14, 2016).

U.S. Department of Justice

~~Attorney-Work Product~~ // ~~May Contain Material Protected Under Fed. R. Crim. P. 6(e)~~

b. High-Level Encouragement of Contacts through Alternative Channels

As Russian officials in the United States reached out to the President-Elect and his team, a number of Russian individuals working in the private sector began their own efforts to make contact. Petr Aven, a Russian national who heads Alfa-Bank, Russia's largest commercial bank, described to the Office interactions with Putin during this time period that might account for the flurry of Russian activity.[976]

Aven told the Office that he is one of approximately 50 wealthy Russian businessmen who regularly meet with Putin in the Kremlin; these 50 men are often referred to as "oligarchs."[977] Aven told the Office that he met on a quarterly basis with Putin, including in the fourth quarter (Q4) of 2016, shortly after the U.S. presidential election.[978] Aven said that he took these meetings seriously and understood that any suggestions or critiques that Putin made during these meetings were implicit directives, and that there would be consequences for Aven if he did not follow through.[979] As was typical, the 2016 Q4 meeting with Putin was preceded by a preparatory meeting with Putin's chief of staff, Anton Vaino.[980]

According to Aven, at his Q4 2016 one-on-one meeting with Putin,[981] Putin raised the prospect that the United States would impose additional sanctions on Russian interests, including sanctions against Aven and/or Alfa-Bank.[982] Putin suggested that Aven needed to take steps to protect himself and Alfa-Bank.[983] Aven also testified that Putin spoke of the difficulty faced by the Russian government in getting in touch with the incoming Trump Administration.[984] According to Aven, Putin indicated that he did not know with whom formally to speak and generally did not know the people around the President-Elect.[985]

---

[976] Aven provided information to the Office in an interview and through an attorney proffer, ▆▆ Grand Jury

[977] Aven 8/2/18 302, at 7.

[978] Grand Jury

[979] Aven 8/2/18 302, at 2-3.

[980] Grand Jury and interview with the Office, Aven referred to the high-ranking Russian government officials using numbers (e.g., Official 1, Official 2). Aven separately confirmed through an attorney proffer that Official 1 was Putin and Official 2 was Putin's chief of staff, Vaino. See Affidavit of Ryan Junck (Aug. 2, 2018) (hard copy on file).

[981] At the time of his Q4 2016 meeting with Putin, Aven was generally aware of the press coverage about Russian interference in the U.S. election. According to Aven, he did not discuss that topic with Putin at any point, and Putin did not mention the rationale behind the threat of new sanctions. Aven 8/2/18 302, at 5-7.

[982] Grand Jury

[983] Grand Jury

[984] Grand Jury

[985] Grand Jury

146

206

Aven ▮Grand Jury▮ told Putin he would take steps to protect himself and the Alfa-Bank shareholders from potential sanctions, and one of those steps would be to try to reach out to the incoming Administration to establish a line of communication.[986] Aven described Putin responding with skepticism about Aven's prospect for success.[987] According to Aven, although Putin did not expressly direct him to reach out to the Trump Transition Team, Aven understood that Putin expected him to try to respond to the concerns he had raised.[988] Aven's efforts are described in Volume I, Section IV.B.5, *infra*.

2. Kirill Dmitriev's Transition-Era Outreach to the Incoming Administration

Aven's description of his interactions with Putin is consistent with the behavior of Kirill Dmitriev, a Russian national who heads Russia's sovereign wealth fund and is closely connected to Putin. Dmitriev undertook efforts to meet members of the incoming Trump Administration in the months after the election. Dmitriev asked a close business associate who worked for the United Arab Emirates (UAE) royal court, George Nader, to introduce him to Trump transition officials, and Nader eventually arranged a meeting in the Seychelles between Dmitriev and Erik Prince, a Trump Campaign supporter and an associate of Steve Bannon.[989] In addition, the UAE national security advisor introduced Dmitriev to a hedge fund manager and friend of Jared Kushner, Rick Gerson, in late November 2016. In December 2016 and January 2017, Dmitriev and Gerson worked on a proposal for reconciliation between the United States and Russia, which Dmitriev implied he cleared through Putin. Gerson provided that proposal to Kushner before the inauguration, and Kushner later gave copies to Bannon and Secretary of State Rex Tillerson.

a. Background

Dmitriev is a Russian national who was appointed CEO of Russia's sovereign wealth fund, the Russian Direct Investment Fund (RDIF), when it was founded in 2011.[990] Dmitriev reported directly to Putin and frequently referred to Putin as his "boss."[991]

RDIF has co-invested in various projects with UAE sovereign wealth funds.[992] Dmitriev regularly interacted with Nader, a senior advisor to UAE Crown Prince Mohammed bin Zayed

---

[986] ▮Grand Jury▮

[987] ▮Grand Jury▮ Aven 8/2/18 302, at 6.

[988] Aven 8/2/18 302, at 4-8; ▮Grand Jury▮

[989] Nader provided information to the Office in multiple interviews, all but one of which were conducted under a proffer agreement.▮Grand Jury▮. The investigators also interviewed Prince under a proffer agreement. Bannon was interviewed by the Office, ▮Grand Jury▮ under a proffer agreement.

[990] Kirill Dmitriev Biography, Russian Direct Investment Fund, *available at* https://rdif.ru/Eng_person_dmitriev_kirill/. *See also* Overview, Russian Direct Investment Fund, *available at* https://rdif.ru/Eng_About/.

[991] Gerson 6/15/18 302, at 1. *See also, e.g.,* 12/14/16 Text Message, Dmitriev to Gerson; 1/9/17 Text Message, Dmitriev to Gerson.

[992] ▮Grand Jury▮

U.S. Department of Justice

~~Attorney Work Product~~ // ~~May Contain Material Protected Under Fed. R. Crim. P. 6(e)~~

(Crown Prince Mohammed), in connection with RDIF's dealings with the UAE.[993] Putin wanted Dmitriev to be in charge of both the financial and the political relationship between Russia and the Gulf states, in part because Dmitriev had been educated in the West and spoke English fluently.[994] Nader considered Dmitriev to be Putin's interlocutor in the Gulf region, and would relay Dmitriev's views directly to Crown Prince Mohammed.[995]

Nader developed contacts with both U.S. presidential campaigns during the 2016 election, and kept Dmitriev abreast of his efforts to do so.[996] According to Nader, Dmitriev said that his and the government of Russia's preference was for candidate Trump to win, and asked Nader to assist him in meeting members of the Trump Campaign.[997] Grand Jury [998] Nader did not introduce Dmitriev to anyone associated with the Trump Campaign before the election.[999]

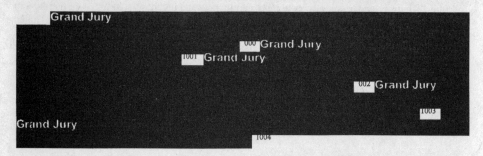

Erik Prince is a businessman who had relationships with various individuals associated with the Trump Campaign, including Steve Bannon, Donald Trump Jr., and Roger Stone.[1005] Prince did not have a formal role in the Campaign, although he offered to host a fundraiser for

---

[993] Nader 1/22/18 302, at 1-2; Nader 1/23/18 302, at 2-3; 5/3/16 Email, Nader to Phares; Grand Jury

[994] Nader 1/22/18 302, at 1-2.

[995] Nader 1/22/18 302, at 3.

[996] Nader 1/22/18 302, at 3; Grand Jury

[997] Nader 1/22/18 302, at 3; Grand Jury

[998] Grand Jury

[999] Nader 1/22/18 302, at 3.

[1000] Grand Jury

[1001] Grand Jury

[1002] Grand Jury

[1003] Grand Jury

[1004] Grand Jury

[1005] Prince 4/4/18 302, at 1-5; Bannon 2/14/18 302, at 21.

Trump and sent unsolicited policy papers on issues such as foreign policy, trade, and Russian election interference to Bannon.[1006]

After the election, Prince frequently visited transition offices at Trump Tower, primarily to meet with Bannon but on occasion to meet Michael Flynn and others.[1007] Prince and Bannon would discuss, *inter alia*, foreign policy issues and Prince's recommendations regarding who should be appointed to fill key national security positions.[1008] Although Prince was not formally affiliated with the transition, Nader ▮Grand Jury▮ received assurances ▮Grand Jury▮ that the incoming Administration considered Prince a trusted associate.[1009]

b. Kirill Dmitriev's Post-Election Contacts With the Incoming Administration

Soon after midnight on election night, Dmitriev messaged ▮Investigative Technique▮ who was traveling to New York to attend the 2016 World Chess Championship. ▮Investigative Technique▮ Dmitry Peskov, the Russian Federation's press secretary, who was also attending the World Chess Championship.[1010] ▮Investigative Technique▮ [1011] ▮Investigative Technique▮ [1012] ▮Investigative Technique▮ [1013]

At approximately 2:40 a.m. on November 9, 2016, news reports stated that candidate Clinton had called President-Elect Trump to concede. At ▮Investigative Technique▮ [1014] ▮Investigative Technique▮ wrote to Dmitriev, "Putin has won."[1015]

[1006] Prince 4/4/18 302, at 1, 3-4; Prince 5/3/18 302, at 2; Bannon 2/14/18 302, at 19-20; 10/18/16 Email, Prince to Bannon.

[1007] Flynn 11/20/17 302, at 6; Flynn 1/11/18 302, at 5; Flynn 1/24/18 302, at 5-6; Flynn 5/1/18 302, at 11; Prince 4/4/18 302, at 5, 8; Bannon 2/14/18 302, at 20-21; 11/12/16 Email, Prince to Corallo.

[1008] Prince 4/4/18 302, at 5; Bannon 2/14/18 302, at 21.

[1009] ▮Grand Jury▮

[1010] ▮Investigative Technique▮ Nader 1/22/18 302, at 5-6; ▮▮ ▮Grand Jury▮

[1011] ▮Investigative Technique▮

[1012] ▮Investigative Technique▮

[1013] ▮Investigative Technique▮

[1014] ▮Investigative Technique▮

[1015] ▮Investigative Technique▮

Later that morning, Dmitriev contacted Nader, who was in New York, to request a meeting with the "key people" in the incoming Administration as soon as possible in light of the "[g]reat results."[1016] He asked Nader to convey to the incoming Administration that "we want to start rebuilding the relationship in whatever is a comfortable pace for them. We understand all of the sensitivities and are not in a rush."[1017] Dmitriev and Nader had previously discussed Nader introducing him to the contacts Nader had made within the Trump Campaign.[1018] Dmitriev also told Nader that he would ask Putin for permission to travel to the United States, where he would be able to speak to media outlets about the positive impact of Trump's election and the need for reconciliation between the United States and Russia.[1019]

Later that day, Dmitriev flew to New York, where Peskov was separately traveling to attend the chess tournament.[1020] Dmitriev invited Nader to the opening of the tournament and noted that, if there was "a chance to see anyone key from Trump camp," he "would love to start building for the future."[1021] Dmitriev also asked Nader to invite Kushner to the event so that he (Dmitriev) could meet him.[1022] Nader did not pass along Dmitriev's invitation to anyone connected with the incoming Administration.[1023] Although one World Chess Federation official recalled hearing from an attendee that President-Elect Trump had stopped by the tournament, the investigation did not establish that Trump or any Campaign or Transition Team official attended the event.[1024] And the President's written answers denied that he had.[1025]

Nader stated that Dmitriev continued to press him to set up a meeting with transition officials, and was particularly focused on Kushner and Trump Jr.[1026] Dmitriev told Nader that Putin would be very grateful to Nader and that a meeting would make history.[1027] Grand Jury

---

[1016] 11/9/16 Text Message, Dmitriev to Nader (9:34 a.m.); Nader 1/22/18 302, at 4.

[1017] 11/9/16 Text Message, Dmitriev to Nader (11:58 p.m.).

[1018] Nader 1/22/18 302, at 3.

[1019] 11/9/16 Text Message, Dmitriev to Nader (10:06 a.m.); 11/9/16 Text Message, Dmitriev to Nader (10:10 a.m.); Grand Jury

[1020] 11/9/16 Text Message, Dmitriev to Nader (10:08 a.m.); 11/9/16 Text Message, Dmitriev to Nader (3:40 p.m.); Nader 1/22/18 302, at 5.

[1021] 11/9/16 Text Message, Dmitriev to Nader (7:10 p.m.).

[1022] 11/10/16 Text Message, Dmitriev to Nader (5:20 a.m.).

[1023] Nader 1/22/18 302, at 5-6.

[1024] Marinello 5/31/18 302, at 2-3; Nader 1/22/18 302, at 5-6.

[1025] Written Responses of Donald J. Trump (Nov. 20, 2018), at 17-18 (Response to Question V, Part (a).

[1026] Nader 1/22/18 302, at 6; Grand Jury

[1027] Nader 1/22/18 302, at 6; Grand Jury

U.S. Department of Justice

~~Attorney Work Product // May Contain Material Protected Under Fed. R. Crim. P. 6(e)~~

GJ [1028] Grand Jury

[029] According to Nader, Dmitriev was very anxious to connect with the incoming Administration and told Nader that he would try other routes to do so besides Nader himself.[1030] Nader did not ultimately introduce Dmitriev to anyone associated with the incoming Administration during Dmitriev's post-election trip to New York.[1031]

In early December 2016, Dmitriev again broached the topic of meeting incoming Administration officials with Nader in January or February.[1032] Dmitriev sent Nader a list of publicly available quotes of Dmitriev speaking positively about Donald Trump "in case they [were] helpful."[1033]

c. Erik Prince and Kirill Dmitriev Meet in the Seychelles

i. George Nader and Erik Prince Arrange Seychelles Meeting with Dmitriev

Nader traveled to New York in early January 2017 and had lunchtime and dinner meetings with Erik Prince on January 3, 2017.[1034] Nader and Prince discussed Dmitriev.[1035] Nader informed Prince that the Russians were looking to build a link with the incoming Trump Administration.[1036] Grand Jury he told Prince that Dmitriev had been pushing Nader to introduce him to someone from the incoming Administration Grand Jury .[1037] Nader suggested, in light of Prince's relationship with Transition Team officials, that Prince and Dmitriev meet to discuss issues of mutual concern.[1038] Grand Jury Prince told Nader that he needed to think further about it and to check with Transition Team officials.[1039]

After his dinner with Prince, Nader sent Prince a link to a Wikipedia entry about Dmitriev, and sent Dmitriev a message stating that he had just met "with some key people within the family and inner circle"—a reference to Prince—and that he had spoken at length and positively about

---

[1028] Grand Jury

[1029] Grand Jury

[1030] Nader 1/22/18 302, at 6.

[1031] Nader 1/22/18 302, at 5-7.

[1032] 12/8/16 Text Messages, Dmitriev to Nader (12:10:31 a.m.); Nader 1/22/18 302, at 11.

[1033] 12/8/16 Text Message, Dmitriev to Nader (12:10:31 a.m.); 12/8/16 Text Message, Dmitriev to Nader (12:10:57 a.m.).

[1034] Prince 4/4/18 302, at 8.

[1035] Prince 5/3/18 302, at 3; Grand Jury

[1036] Grand Jury

[1037] Grand Jury

[1038] Grand Jury

[1039] Grand Jury

151

Dmitriev.[1040] Nader told Dmitriev that the people he met had asked for Dmitriev's bio, and Dmitriev replied that he would update and send it.[1041] Nader later received from Dmitriev two files concerning Dmitriev: one was a two-page biography, and the other was a list of Dmitriev's positive quotes about Donald Trump.[1042]

The next morning, Nader forwarded the message and attachments Dmitriev had sent him to Prince.[1043] Nader wrote to Prince that these documents were the versions "to be used with some additional details for them" (with "them" referring to members of the incoming Administration).[1044] Prince opened the attachments at Trump Tower within an hour of receiving them.[1045] Prince stated that, while he was at Trump Tower that day, he spoke with Kellyanne Conway, Wilbur Ross, Steve Mnuchin, and others while waiting to see Bannon.[1046] Cell-site location data for Prince's mobile phone indicates that Prince remained at Trump Tower for approximately three hours.[1047] Prince said that he could not recall whether, during those three hours, he met with Bannon and discussed Dmitriev with him.[1048] Grand Jury
[1049]

Prince booked a ticket to the Seychelles on January 7, 2017.[1050] The following day, Nader wrote to Dmitriev that he had a "pleasant surprise" for him, namely that he had arranged for Dmitriev to meet "a Special Guest" from "the New Team," referring to Prince.[1051] Nader asked Dmitriev if he could come to the Seychelles for the meeting on January 12, 2017, and Dmitriev agreed.[1052]

The following day, Dmitriev sought assurance from Nader that the Seychelles meeting would be worthwhile.[1053] Grand Jury Dmitriev was not enthusiastic about the idea of meeting with Prince, and that Nader assured him that Prince wielded influence with the incoming

---

[1040] 1/4/17 Text Message, Nader to Prince; 1/4/17 Text Messages, Nader to Dmitriev (5:24 a.m. – 5:26 a.m.); Nader 1/22/18 302, at 8-9; Grand Jury

[1041] 1/4/17 Text Messages, Nader & Dmitriev (7:24:27 a.m.).

[1042] 1/4/17 Text Messages, Dmitriev to Nader (7:25-7:29 a.m.)

[1043] 1/4/17 Text Messages, Nader to Prince.

[1044] 1/4/17 Text Messages, Nader to Prince; Grand Jury

[1045] Prince 5/3/18 302, at 1-3.

[1046] Prince 5/3/18 302, at 2-3.

[1047] Cell-site location data for Prince's mobile phone Investigative Technique

[1048] Prince 5/3/18 302, at 3.

[1049] Grand Jury

[1050] 1/5/17 Email, Kasbo to Prince.

[1051] 1/8/17 Text Messages, Nader to Dmitriev (6:05 – 6:10 p.m.).

[1052] 1/8/17 Text Messages, Nader & Dmitriev (6:10 – 7:27 p.m.).

[1053] 1/9/17 Text Message, Dmitriev to Nader.

U.S. Department of Justice

~~Attorney Work Product // May Contain Material Protected Under Fed. R. Crim. P. 6(e)~~

Administration.[1054] Nader wrote to Dmitriev, "This guy [Prince] is designated by Steve [Bannon] to meet you! I know him and he is very very well connected and trusted by the New Team. His sister is now a Minister of Education."[1055] According to Nader, Prince had led him to believe that Bannon was aware of Prince's upcoming meeting with Dmitriev, and Prince acknowledged that it was fair for Nader to think that Prince would pass information on to the Transition Team.[1056] Bannon, however, told the Office that Prince did not tell him in advance about his meeting with Dmitriev.[1057]

ii. The Seychelles Meetings

Dmitriev arrived with his wife in the Seychelles on January 11, 2017, and checked into the Four Seasons Resort where Crown Prince Mohammed and Nader were staying.[1058] Prince arrived that same day.[1059] Prince and Dmitriev met for the first time that afternoon in Nader's villa, with Nader present.[1060] The initial meeting lasted approximately 30-45 minutes.[1061]

Grand Jury

[1062] Prince described the eight years of the Obama Administration in negative terms, and stated that he was looking forward to a new era of cooperation and conflict resolution.[1063] According to Prince, he told Dmitriev that Bannon was effective if not conventional, and that Prince provided policy papers to Bannon.[1064]

Grand Jury

[1065] Grand Jury

[1054] Grand Jury

[1055] 1/9/17 Text Message, Nader to Dmitriev (2:12:56 p.m.); Nader 1/19/18 302, at 13; Grand Jury

[1056] Nader 1/19/18 302, at 13; Grand Jury Prince 5/3/18 302, at 3.

[1057] Bannon 2/14/18 302, at 25-26.

[1058] 1/10/17 Text Messages, Dmitriev & Nader (2:05:54 – 3:30:25 p.m.); 1/11/17 Text Messages, Dmitriev & Nader (2:16:16 – 5:17:59 p.m.).

[1059] 1/7/17 Email, Kasbo to Prince.

[1060] 1/11/17 Text Messages, Nader & Dmitriev (5:18:24 – 5:37:14 p.m.); Grand Jury

[1061] Prince 5/3/18 302, at 4; Grand Jury

[1062] Grand Jury

[1063] Grand Jury

[1064] Prince 5/3/18 302, at 4.

[1065] Grand Jury

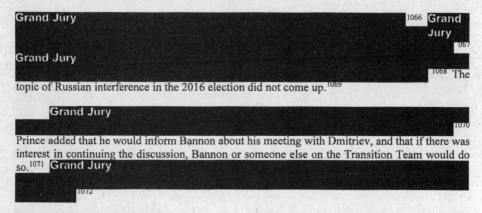

topic of Russian interference in the 2016 election did not come up.[1069]

Prince added that he would inform Bannon about his meeting with Dmitriev, and that if there was interest in continuing the discussion, Bannon or someone else on the Transition Team would do so.[1071] Grand Jury

Afterwards, Prince returned to his room, where he learned that a Russian aircraft carrier had sailed to Libya, which led him to call Nader and ask him to set up another meeting with Dmitriev.[1073] According to Nader, Prince called and said he had checked with his associates back home and needed to convey to Dmitriev that Libya was "off the table."[1074] Nader wrote to Dmitriev that Prince had "received an urgent message that he needs to convey to you immediately," and arranged for himself, Dmitriev, and Prince to meet at a restaurant on the Four Seasons property.[1075]

At the second meeting, Prince told Dmitriev that the United States could not accept any Russian involvement in Libya because it would make the situation there much worse.[1076] Grand Jury

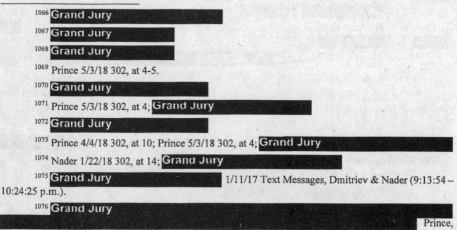

[1066] Grand Jury

[1067] Grand Jury

[1068] Grand Jury

[1069] Prince 5/3/18 302, at 4-5.

[1070] Grand Jury

[1071] Prince 5/3/18 302, at 4; Grand Jury

[1072] Grand Jury

[1073] Prince 4/4/18 302, at 10; Prince 5/3/18 302, at 4; Grand Jury

[1074] Nader 1/22/18 302, at 14; Grand Jury

[1075] Grand Jury   1/11/17 Text Messages, Dmitriev & Nader (9:13:54 – 10:24:25 p.m.).

[1076] Grand Jury

Prince, however, denied that and recalled that he was making these remarks to Dmitriev not in an official capacity for the transition but based on his experience as a former naval officer. Prince 5/3/18 302, at 4.

███████ Grand Jury ███████ [1077]

After the brief second meeting concluded, Nader and Dmitriev discussed what had transpired.[1078] Dmitriev told Nader that he was disappointed in his meetings with Prince for two reasons: first, he believed the Russians needed to be communicating with someone who had more authority within the incoming Administration than Prince had.[1079] Second, he had hoped to have a discussion of greater substance, such as outlining a strategic roadmap for both countries to follow.[1080] Dmitriev told Nader that ███ Grand Jury ███ Prince's comments ███ Grand Jury ███ were insulting ███ Grand Jury ███ [1081]

Hours after the second meeting, Prince sent two text messages to Bannon from the Seychelles.[1082] As described further below, investigators were unable to obtain the content of these or other messages between Prince and Bannon, and the investigation also did not identify evidence of any further communication between Prince and Dmitriev after their meetings in the Seychelles.

iii. Erik Prince's Meeting with Steve Bannon after the Seychelles Trip

After the Seychelles meetings, Prince told Nader that he would inform Bannon about his discussion with Dmitriev and would convey that someone within the Russian power structure was interested in seeking better relations with the incoming Administration.[1083] On January 12, 2017, Prince contacted Bannon's personal assistant to set up a meeting for the following week.[1084] Several days later, Prince messaged her again asking about Bannon's schedule.[1085]

Prince said that he met Bannon at Bannon's home after returning to the United States in mid-January and briefed him about several topics, including his meeting with Dmitriev.[1086] Prince told the Office that he explained to Bannon that Dmitriev was the head of a Russian sovereign wealth fund and was interested in improving relations between the United States and Russia.[1087] Prince had on his cellphone a screenshot of Dmitriev's Wikipedia page dated January 16, 2017,

---

[1077] ███ Grand Jury ███

[1078] Nader 1/22/18 302, at 15; ███ Grand Jury ███

[1079] Nader 1/22/18 302, at 9, 15; ███ Grand Jury ███

[1080] Nader 1/22/18 302, at 15.

[1081] ███ Grand Jury ███ Nader 1/22/18 302, at 15.

[1082] Call Records of Erik Prince ███ Grand Jury ███ .

[1083] Prince 4/4/18 302, at 10; Prince 5/3/18 302, at 4; ███ Grand Jury ███

[1084] 1/12/17 Text Messages, Prince to Preate.

[1085] 1/15/17 Text Message, Prince to Preate.

[1086] Prince 4/4/18 302, at 11; Prince 5/3/18 302, at 5.

[1087] Prince 4/4/18 302, at 11; Prince 5/3/18 302, at 5.

and Prince told the Office that he likely showed that image to Bannon.[1088] Prince also believed he provided Bannon with Dmitriev's contact information.[1089] According to Prince, Bannon instructed Prince not to follow up with Dmitriev, and Prince had the impression that the issue was not a priority for Bannon.[1090] Prince related that Bannon did not appear angry, just relatively uninterested.[1091]

Bannon, by contrast, told the Office that he never discussed with Prince anything regarding Dmitriev, RDIF, or any meetings with Russian individuals or people associated with Putin.[1092] Bannon also stated that had Prince mentioned such a meeting, Bannon would have remembered it, and Bannon would have objected to such a meeting having taken place.[1093]

The conflicting accounts provided by Bannon and Prince could not be independently clarified by reviewing their communications, because neither one was able to produce any of the messages they exchanged in the time period surrounding the Seychelles meeting. Prince's phone contained no text messages prior to March 2017, though provider records indicate that he and Bannon exchanged dozens of messages.[1094] Prince denied deleting any messages but claimed he did not know why there were no messages on his device before March 2017.[1095] Bannon's devices similarly contained no messages in the relevant time period, and Bannon also stated he did not know why messages did not appear on his device.[1096] Bannon told the Office that, during both the months before and after the Seychelles meeting, he regularly used his personal Blackberry and personal email for work-related communications (including those with Prince), and he took no steps to preserve these work communications.[1097]

d. Kirill Dmitriev's Post-Election Contact with Rick Gerson Regarding U.S.-Russia Relations

Dmitriev's contacts during the transition period were not limited to those facilitated by Nader. In approximately late November 2016, the UAE national security advisor introduced Dmitriev to Rick Gerson, a friend of Jared Kushner who runs a hedge fund in New York.[1098] Gerson stated he had no formal role in the transition and had no involvement in the Trump

---

[1088] Prince 5/3/18 302, at 5; 1/16/17 Image on Prince Phone (on file with the Office).

[1089] Prince 5/3/18 302, at 5.

[1090] Prince 5/3/18 302, at 5.

[1091] Prince 5/3/18 302, at 5.

[1092] Bannon 10/26/18 302, at 10-11.

[1093] Bannon 10/26/18 302, at 10-11.

[1094] Call Records of Erik Prince Grand Jury

[1095] Prince 4/4/18 302, at 6.

[1096] Bannon 10/26/18 302, at 11; Bannon 2/14/18 302, at 36.

[1097] Bannon 10/26/18 302, at 11.

[1098] Gerson 6/5/18 302, at 1, 3; 11/26/16 Text Message, Dmitriev to Gerson; 1/25/17 Text Message, Dmitriev to Nader.

Campaign other than occasional casual discussions about the Campaign with Kushner.[1099] After the election, Gerson assisted the transition by arranging meetings for transition officials with former UK prime minister Tony Blair and a UAE delegation led by Crown Prince Mohammed.[1100]

When Dmitriev and Gerson met, they principally discussed potential joint ventures between Gerson's hedge fund and RDIF.[1101] Dmitriev was interested in improved economic cooperation between the United States and Russia and asked Gerson who he should meet with in the incoming Administration who would be helpful towards this goal.[1102] Gerson replied that he would try to figure out the best way to arrange appropriate introductions, but noted that confidentiality would be required because of the sensitivity of holding such meetings before the new Administration took power, and before Cabinet nominees had been confirmed by the Senate.[1103] Gerson said he would ask Kushner and Michael Flynn who the "key person or people" were on the topics of reconciliation with Russia, joint security concerns, and economic matters.[1104]

Dmitriev told Gerson that he had been tasked by Putin to develop and execute a reconciliation plan between the United States and Russia. He noted in a text message to Gerson that if Russia was "approached with respect and willingness to understand our position, we can have Major Breakthroughs quickly."[1105] Gerson and Dmitriev exchanged ideas in December 2016 about what such a reconciliation plan would include.[1106] Gerson told the Office that the Transition Team had not asked him to engage in these discussions with Dmitriev, and that he did so on his own initiative and as a private citizen.[1107]

On January 9, 2017, the same day he asked Nader whether meeting Prince would be worthwhile, Dmitriev sent his biography to Gerson and asked him if he could "share it with Jared (or somebody else very senior in the team) – so that they know that we are focused from our side on improving the relationship and my boss asked me to play a key role in that."[1108] Dmitriev also asked Gerson if he knew Prince, and if Prince was somebody important or worth spending time

---

[1099] Gerson 6/5/18 302, at 1.

[1100] Gerson 6/5/18 302, at 1-2; Kushner 4/11/18 302, at 21.

[1101] Gerson 6/5/18 302, at 3-4; *see, e.g.*, 12/2/16 Text Messages, Dmitriev & Gerson; 12/14/16 Text Messages, Dmitriev & Gerson; 1/3/17 Text Message, Gerson to Dmitriev; 12/2/16 Email, Tolokonnikov to Gerson.

[1102] Gerson 6/5/18 302, at 3; 12/14/16 Text Message, Dmitriev to Gerson.

[1103] 12/14/16 Text Message, Gerson to Dmitriev.

[1104] 12/14/16 Text Message, Gerson to Dmitriev.

[1105] 12/14/16 Text Messages, Dmitriev & Gerson; Gerson 6/15/18 302, at 1.

[1106] 12/14/16 Text Messages, Dmitriev & Gerson.

[1107] Gerson 6/15/18 302, at 1.

[1108] 1/9/17 Text Messages, Dmitriev to Gerson; 1/9/17 Text Message, Dmitriev to Nader.

U.S. Department of Justice

~~Attorney Work Product // May Contain Material Protected Under Fed. R. Crim. P. 6(e)~~

with.[1109]   After his trip to the Seychelles, Dmitriev told Gerson that Bannon had asked Prince to meet with Dmitriev and that the two had had a positive meeting.[1110]

On January 16, 2017, Dmitriev consolidated the ideas for U.S.-Russia reconciliation that he and Gerson had been discussing into a two-page document that listed five main points: (1) jointly fighting terrorism; (2) jointly engaging in anti-weapons of mass destruction efforts; (3) developing "win-win" economic and investment initiatives; (4) maintaining an honest, open, and continual dialogue regarding issues of disagreement; and (5) ensuring proper communication and trust by "key people" from each country.[1111]   On January 18, 2017, Gerson gave a copy of the document to Kushner.[1112]   Kushner had not heard of Dmitriev at that time.[1113]   Gerson explained that Dmitriev was the head of RDIF, and Gerson may have alluded to Dmitriev's being well connected.[1114]   Kushner placed the document in a file and said he would get it to the right people.[1115]   Kushner ultimately gave one copy of the document to Bannon and another to Rex Tillerson; according to Kushner, neither of them followed up with Kushner about it.[1116]   On January 19, 2017, Dmitriev sent Nader a copy of the two-page document, telling him that this was "a view from our side that I discussed in my meeting on the islands and with you and with our friends. Please share with them – we believe this is a good foundation to start from."[1117]

Gerson informed Dmitriev that he had given the document to Kushner soon after delivering it.[1118]   On January 26, 2017, Dmitriev wrote to Gerson that his "boss"—an apparent reference to Putin—was asking if there had been any feedback on the proposal.[1119]   Dmitriev said, "[w]e do not want to rush things and move at a comfortable speed. At the same time, my boss asked me to try to have the key US meetings in the next two weeks if possible."[1120]   He informed Gerson that Putin and President Trump would speak by phone that Saturday, and noted that that information was "very confidential."[1121]

The same day, Dmitriev wrote to Nader that he had seen his "boss" again yesterday who had "emphasized that this is a great priority for us and that we need to build this communication

---

[1109] Gerson 6/5/18 302, at 4.

[1110] 1/18/17 Text Messages, Dmitriev & Gerson.

[1111] 1/16/17 Text Messages, Dmitriev & Gerson.

[1112] Gerson 6/5/18 302, at 3; Gerson 6/15/18 302, at 2.

[1113] Gerson 6/5/18 302, at 3.

[1114] Gerson 6/5/18 302, at 3; Gerson 6/15/18 302, at 1-2; Kushner 4/11/18 302, at 22.

[1115] Gerson 6/5/18 302, at 3.

[1116] Kushner 4/11/18 302, at 32.

[1117] 1/19/17 Text Message, Dmitriev to Nader (11:11:56 a.m.).

[1118] 1/18/17 Text Message, Gerson to Dmitriev; Gerson 6/15/18 302, at 2.

[1119] 1/26/17 Text Message, Dmitriev to Gerson.

[1120] 1/26/17 Text Message, Dmitriev to Gerson.

[1121] 1/26/17 Text Message, Dmitriev to Gerson.

U.S. Department of Justice

~~Attorney Work Product~~ // ~~May Contain Material Protected Under Fed. R. Crim. P. 6(e)~~

channel to avoid bureaucracy."[1122] On January 28, 2017, Dmitriev texted Nader that he wanted "to see if I can confirm to my boss that your friends may use some of the ideas from the 2 pager I sent you in the telephone call that will happen at 12 EST,"[1123] an apparent reference to the call scheduled between President Trump and Putin. Nader replied, "Definitely paper was so submitted to Team by Rick and me. They took it seriously!"[1124] After the call between President Trump and Putin occurred, Dmitriev wrote to Nader that "the call went very well. My boss wants me to continue making some public statements that us [sic] Russia cooperation is good and important."[1125] Gerson also wrote to Dmitriev to say that the call had gone well, and Dmitriev replied that the document they had drafted together "played an important role."[1126]

Gerson and Dmitriev appeared to stop communicating with one another in approximately March 2017, when the investment deal they had been working on together showed no signs of progressing.[1127]

3. Ambassador Kislyak's Meeting with Jared Kushner and Michael Flynn in Trump Tower Following the Election

On November 16, 2016, Catherine Vargas, an executive assistant to Kushner, received a request for a meeting with Russian Ambassador Sergey Kislyak.[1128] That same day, Vargas sent Kushner an email with the subject, "MISSED CALL: Russian Ambassador to the US, Sergey Ivanovich Kislyak . . . ."[1129] The text of the email read, "RE: setting up a time to meet w/you on 12/1. LMK how to proceed." Kushner responded in relevant part, "I think I do this one -- confirm with Dimitri [Simes of CNI] that this is the right guy."[1130] After reaching out to a colleague of Simes at CNI, Vargas reported back to Kushner that Kislyak was "the best go-to guy for routine matters in the US," while Yuri Ushakov, a Russian foreign policy advisor, was the contact for "more direct/substantial matters."[1131]

Bob Foresman, the UBS investment bank executive who had previously tried to transmit to candidate Trump an invitation to speak at an economic forum in Russia, *see* Volume I, Section IV.A.1.d.ii, *supra*, may have provided similar information to the Transition Team. According to

---

[1122] 1/26/17 Text Message, Dmitriev to Nader (10:04:41 p.m.).

[1123] 1/28/17 Text Message, Dmitriev to Nader (11:05:39 a.m.).

[1124] 1/28/17 Text Message, Nader to Dmitriev (11:11:33 a.m.).

[1125] 1/29/17 Text Message, Dmitriev to Nader (11:06:35 a.m.).

[1126] 1/28/17 Text Message, Gerson to Dmitriev; 1/29/17 Text Message, Dmitriev to Gerson.

[1127] Gerson 6/15/18 302, at 4; 3/21/17 Text Message, Gerson to Dmitriev.

[1128] *Statement of Jared C. Kushner to Congressional Committees* ("Kushner Stmt."), at 6 (7/24/17) (written statement by Kushner to the Senate Judiciary Committee).

[1129] NOSC00004356 (11/16/16 Email, Vargas to Kushner (6:44 p.m.)).

[1130] NOSC00004356 (11/16/16 Email, Kushner to Vargas (9:54 p.m.)).

[1131] 11/17/16 Email, Brown to Simes (10:41 a.m.); Brown 10/13/17 302, at 4; 11/17/16 Email, Vargas to Kushner (12:31:18).

Foresman, at the end of an early December 2016 meeting with incoming National Security Advisor Michael Flynn and his designated deputy (K.T. McFarland) in New York, Flynn asked Foresman for his thoughts on Kislyak. Foresman had not met Kislyak but told Flynn that, while Kislyak was an important person, Kislyak did not have a direct line to Putin.[1132] Foresman subsequently traveled to Moscow, inquired of a source he believed to be close to Putin, and heard back from that source that Ushakov would be the official channel for the incoming U.S. national security advisor.[1133] Foresman acknowledged that Flynn had not asked him to undertake that inquiry in Russia but told the Office that he nonetheless felt obligated to report the information back to Flynn, and that he worked to get a face-to-face meeting with Flynn in January 2017 so that he could do so.[1134] Email correspondence suggests that the meeting ultimately went forward,[1135] but Flynn has no recollection of it or of the earlier December meeting.[1136] (The investigation did not identify evidence of Flynn or Kushner meeting with Ushakov after being given his name.[1137])

In the meantime, although he had already formed the impression that Kislyak was not necessarily the right point of contact,[1138] Kushner went forward with the meeting that Kislyak had requested on November 16. It took place at Trump Tower on November 30, 2016.[1139] At Kushner's invitation, Flynn also attended; Bannon was invited but did not attend.[1140] During the meeting, which lasted approximately 30 minutes, Kushner expressed a desire on the part of the incoming Administration to start afresh with U.S.-Russian relations.[1141] Kushner also asked Kislyak to identify the best person (whether Kislyak or someone else) with whom to direct future discussions—someone who had contact with Putin and the ability to speak for him.[1142]

The three men also discussed U.S. policy toward Syria, and Kislyak floated the idea of having Russian generals brief the Transition Team on the topic using a secure communications line.[1143] After Flynn explained that there was no secure line in the Transition Team offices,

---

[1132] Foresman 10/17/18 302, at 17.

[1133] Foresman 10/17/18 302, at 17-18.

[1134] Foresman 10/17/18 302, at 18.

[1135] RMF-SCO-00000015 (1/5/17 Email, Foresman to Atencio & Flaherty); RMF-SCO-00000015 (1/5/17 Email, Flaherty to Foresman & Atencio).

[1136] 9/26/18 Attorney Proffer from Covington & Burling LLP (reflected in email on file with the Office).

[1137] Vargas 4/4/18 302, at 5.

[1138] Kushner 11/1/17 302, at 4.

[1139] AKIN_GUMP_BERKOWITZ_0000016-019 (11/29/16 Email, Vargas to Kuznetsov).

[1140] Flynn 1/11/18 302, at 2; NOS00004240 (Calendar Invite, Vargas to Kushner & Flynn).

[1141] Kushner Stmt. at 6.

[1142] Kushner Stmt. at 6; Kushner 4/11/18 302, at 18.

[1143] Kushner Stmt. at 7; Kushner 4/11/18 302, at 18; Flynn 1/11/18 302, at 2.

Kushner asked Kislyak if they could communicate using secure facilities at the Russian Embassy.[1144] Kislyak quickly rejected that idea.[1145]

4. Jared Kushner's Meeting with Sergey Gorkov

On December 6, 2016, the Russian Embassy reached out to Kushner's assistant to set up a second meeting between Kislyak and Kushner.[1146] Kushner declined several proposed meeting dates, but Kushner's assistant indicated that Kislyak was very insistent about securing a second meeting.[1147] Kushner told the Office that he did not want to take another meeting because he had already decided Kislyak was not the right channel for him to communicate with Russia, so he arranged to have one of his assistants, Avi Berkowitz, meet with Kislyak in his stead.[1148] Although embassy official Sergey Kuznetsov wrote to Berkowitz that Kislyak thought it "important" to "continue the conversation with Mr. Kushner in person,"[1149] Kislyak nonetheless agreed to meet instead with Berkowitz once it became apparent that Kushner was unlikely to take a meeting.

Berkowitz met with Kislyak on December 12, 2016, at Trump Tower.[1150] The meeting lasted only a few minutes, during which Kislyak indicated that he wanted Kushner to meet someone who had a direct line to Putin: Sergey Gorkov, the head of the Russian-government-owned bank Vnesheconombank (VEB).

Kushner agreed to meet with Gorkov.[1151] The one-on-one meeting took place the next day, December 13, 2016, at the Colony Capital building in Manhattan, where Kushner had previously scheduled meetings.[1152] VEB was (and is) the subject of Department of Treasury economic sanctions imposed in response to Russia's annexation of Crimea.[1153] Kushner did not, however, recall any discussion during his meeting with Gorkov about the sanctions against VEB or sanctions more generally.[1154] Kushner stated in an interview that he did not engage in any preparation for

---

[1144] Kushner 4/11/18 302, at 18.

[1145] Kushner 4/11/18 302, at 18.

[1146] Kushner Stmt. at 7; NOSC00000123 (12/6/16 Email, Vargas to Kushner (12:11:40 p.m.)).

[1147] Kushner 4/11/18 302, at 19; NOSC00000130 (12/12/16 Email, Kushner to Vargas (10:41 p.m.)).

[1148] Kushner 4/11/18 302, at 19; Kushner Stmt. at 7; DJTFP_SCO_01442290 (12/6/16 Email, Berkowitz to ██ ███████).

[1149] DJTFP_SCO_01442290 (12/7/16 Email ██ ████████ to Berkowitz (12:31:39 p.m.)).

[1150] Berkowitz 1/12/18 302, at 7; AKIN_GUMP_BERKOWITZ_000001-04 (12/12/16 Text Messages, Berkowitz & 202-701-8532).

[1151] Kushner 4/11/18 302, at 19; NOSC00000130-135 (12/12/16 Email, Kushner to Berkowitz).

[1152] Kushner 4/11/18 302, at 19; NOSC00000130-135 (12/12/16 Email, Kushner to Berkowitz).

[1153] *Announcement of Treasury Sanctions on Entities Within the Financial Services and Energy Sectors of Russia, Against Arms or Related Materiel Entities, and those Undermining Ukraine's Sovereignty*, United States Department of the Treasury (Jul. 16, 2014).

[1154] Kushner 4/11/18 302, at 20.

the meeting and that no one on the Transition Team even did a Google search for Gorkov's name.[1155]

At the start of the meeting, Gorkov presented Kushner with two gifts: a painting and a bag of soil from the town in Belarus where Kushner's family originated.[1156]

The accounts from Kushner and Gorkov differ as to whether the meeting was diplomatic or business in nature. Kushner told the Office that the meeting was diplomatic, with Gorkov expressing disappointment with U.S.-Russia relations under President Obama and hopes for improved relations with the incoming Administration.[1157] According to Kushner, although Gorkov told Kushner a little bit about his bank and made some statements about the Russian economy, the two did not discuss Kushner's companies or private business dealings of any kind.[1158] (At the time of the meeting, Kushner Companies had a debt obligation coming due on the building it owned at 666 Fifth Avenue, and there had been public reporting both about efforts to secure lending on the property and possible conflicts of interest for Kushner arising out of his company's borrowing from foreign lenders.[1159])

In contrast, in a 2017 public statement, VEB suggested Gorkov met with Kushner in Kushner's capacity as CEO of Kushner Companies for the purpose of discussing business, rather than as part of a diplomatic effort. In particular, VEB characterized Gorkov's meeting with Kushner as part of a series of "roadshow meetings" with "representatives of major US banks and business circles," which included "negotiations" and discussion of the "most promising business lines and sectors."[1160]

Foresman, the investment bank executive mentioned in Volume I, Sections IV.A.1 and IV.B.3, *supra*, told the Office that he met with Gorkov and VEB deputy chairman Nikolay Tsekhomsky in Moscow just before Gorkov left for New York to meet Kushner.[1161] According to Foresman, Gorkov and Tsekhomsky told him that they were traveling to New York to discuss post-election issues with U.S. financial institutions, that their trip was sanctioned by Putin, and that they would be reporting back to Putin upon their return.[1162]

[1155] Kushner 4/11/18 302, at 19. Berkowitz, by contrast, stated to the Office that he had googled Gorkov's name and told Kushner that Gorkov appeared to be a banker. Berkowitz 1/12/18 302, at 8.

[1156] Kushner 4/11/18 302, at 19-20.

[1157] Kushner Stmt. at 8.

[1158] Kushner Stmt. at 8.

[1159] *See, e.g.*, Peter Grant, *Donald Trump Son-in-Law Jared Kushner Could Face His Own Conflict-of-Interest Questions*, Wall Street Journal (Nov. 29, 2016).

[1160] Patrick Reevell & Matthew Mosk, *Russian Banker Sergey Gorkov Brushes off Questions About Meeting with Jared Kushner*, ABC News (June 1, 2017).

[1161] Foresman 10/17/18 302, at 14-15.

[1162] Foresman 10/17/18 302, at 15-16.

The investigation did not resolve the apparent conflict in the accounts of Kushner and Gorkov or determine whether the meeting was diplomatic in nature (as Kushner stated), focused on business (as VEB's public statement indicated), or whether it involved some combination of those matters or other matters. Regardless, the investigation did not identify evidence that Kushner and Gorkov engaged in any substantive follow-up after the meeting.

Rather, a few days after the meeting, Gorkov's assistant texted Kushner's assistant, "Hi, please inform your side that the information about the meeting had a very positive response!"[1163] Over the following weeks, the two assistants exchanged a handful of additional cordial texts.[1164] On February 8, 2017, Gorkov's assistant texted Kushner's assistant (Berkowitz) to try to set up another meeting, and followed up by text at least twice in the days that followed.[1165] According to Berkowitz, he did not respond to the meeting request in light of the press coverage regarding the Russia investigation, and did not tell Kushner about the meeting request.[1166]

5. Petr Aven's Outreach Efforts to the Transition Team

In December 2016, weeks after the one-on-one meeting with Putin described in Volume I, Section IV.B.1.b, *supra*, Petr Aven attended what he described as a separate "all-hands" oligarch meeting between Putin and Russia's most prominent businessmen.[1167] As in Aven's one-on-one meeting, a main topic of discussion at the oligarch meeting in December 2016 was the prospect of forthcoming U.S. economic sanctions.[1168]

After the December 2016 all-hands meeting, Aven tried to establish a connection to the Trump team. Aven instructed Richard Burt to make contact with the incoming Trump Administration. Burt was on the board of directors for LetterOne (L1), another company headed by Aven, and had done work for Alfa-Bank.[1169] Burt had previously served as U.S. ambassador to Germany and Assistant Secretary of State for European and Canadian Affairs, and one of his primary roles with Alfa-Bank and L1 was to facilitate introductions to business contacts in the United States and other Western countries.[1170]

While at a L1 board meeting held in Luxembourg in late December 2016, Aven pulled Burt aside and told him that he had spoken to someone high in the Russian government who expressed

---

[1163] AKIN_GUMP_BERKOWITZ_0000011 (12/19/16 Text Message, Ivanchenko to Berkowitz (9:56 a.m.)).

[1164] AKIN_GUMP_BERKOWITZ_0000011-15 (12/19/16 – 2/16/17 Text Messages, Ivanchenko & Berkowitz).

[1165] AKIN_GUMP_BERKOWITZ_0000015 (2/8/17 Text Message, Ivanchenko to Berkowitz (10:41 a.m.)).

[1166] Berkowitz 3/22/18 302, at 4-5.

[1167] Aven 8/2/18 302, at 7; Grand Jury

[1168] Grand Jury

[1169] Grand Jury Aven 8/2/18 302, at 6.

[1170] Grand Jury Aven 8/2/18 302, at 6; Burt 2/9/18 302, at 2.

163

U.S. Department of Justice

~~Attorney Work Product~~ // ~~May Contain Material Protected Under Fed. R. Crim. P. 6(e)~~

interest in establishing a communications channel between the Kremlin and the Trump Transition Team.[1171] Aven asked for Burt's help in contacting members of the Transition Team.[1172] Although Burt had been responsible for helping Aven build connections in the past, Burt viewed Aven's request as unusual and outside the normal realm of his dealings with Aven.[1173]

Burt, who is a member of the board of CNI (discussed at Volume I, Section IV.A.4, *supra*),[1174] decided to approach CNI president Dimitri Simes for help facilitating Aven's request, recalling that Simes had some relationship with Kushner.[1175] At the time, Simes was lobbying the Trump Transition Team, on Burt's behalf, to appoint Burt U.S. ambassador to Russia.[1176]

Burt contacted Simes by telephone and asked if he could arrange a meeting with Kushner to discuss setting up a high-level communications channel between Putin and the incoming Administration.[1177] Simes told the Office that he declined and stated to Burt that setting up such a channel was not a good idea in light of the media attention surrounding Russian influence in the U.S. presidential election.[1178] According to Simes, he understood that Burt was seeking a secret channel, and Simes did not want CNI to be seen as an intermediary between the Russian government and the incoming Administration.[1179] Based on what Simes had read in the media, he stated that he already had concerns that Trump's business connections could be exploited by Russia, and Simes said that he did not want CNI to have any involvement or apparent involvement in facilitating any connection.[1180]

In an email dated December 22, 2016, Burt recounted for Aven his conversation with Simes:

> Through a trusted third party, I have reached out to the very influential person I mentioned in Luxembourg concerning Project A. There is an interest and an understanding for the need to establish such a channel. But the individual emphasized that at this moment, with so much intense interest in the Congress and the media over the question of cyber-hacking (and who ordered what), Project A was too explosive to discuss. The individual agreed to discuss it again after the New Year. I trust the individual's instincts on this.

[1171] Burt 2/9/18 302, at 2; Grand Jury

[1172] Grand Jury

[1173] Burt 2/9/18 302, at 4.

[1174] Burt 2/9/18 302, at 5.

[1175] Burt 2/9/18 302, at 3.

[1176] Burt 2/9/18 302, at 3.

[1177] Burt 2/9/18 302, at 3; Simes 3/27/18 302, at 4.

[1178] Burt 2/9/18 302, at 3; Simes 3/27/18 302, at 4.

[1179] Simes 3/27/18 302, at 5.

[1180] Simes 3/27/18 302, at 5.

If this is unclear or you would like to discuss, don't hesitate to call.[1181]

According to Burt, the "very influential person" referenced in his email was Simes, and the reference to a "trusted third party" was a fabrication, as no such third party existed. "Project A" was a term that Burt created for Aven's effort to help establish a communications channel between Russia and the Trump team, which he used in light of the sensitivities surrounding what Aven was requesting, especially in light of the recent attention to Russia's influence in the U.S. presidential election.[1182] According to Burt, his report that there was "interest" in a communications channel reflected Simes's views, not necessarily those of the Transition Team, and in any event, Burt acknowledged that he added some "hype" to that sentence to make it sound like there was more interest from the Transition Team than may have actually existed.[1183]

Aven replied to Burt's email on the same day, saying "Thank you. All clear."[1184] According to Aven, this statement indicated that he did not want the outreach to continue.[1185] Burt spoke to Aven some time thereafter about his attempt to make contact with the Trump team, explaining to Aven that the current environment made it impossible, ▓Grand Jury▓ ▓▓▓▓▓▓▓▓▓▓.[1186] Burt did not recall discussing Aven's request with Simes again, nor did he recall speaking to anyone else about the request.[1187]

In the first quarter of 2017, Aven met again with Putin and other Russian officials.[1188] At that meeting, Putin asked about Aven's attempt to build relations with the Trump Administration, and Aven recounted his lack of success.[1189] ▓Grand Jury▓ ▓▓▓▓[1190] Putin continued to inquire about Aven's efforts to connect to the Trump Administration in several subsequent quarterly meetings.[1191]

Aven also told Putin's chief of staff that he had been subpoenaed by the FBI.[1192] As part of that conversation, he reported that he had been asked by the FBI about whether he had worked to create a back channel between the Russian government and the Trump Administration.[1193]

[1181] 12/22/16 Email, Burt to Aven (7:23 p.m.).

[1182] Burt 2/9/18 302, at 3.

[1183] Burt 2/9/18 302, at 3-4.

[1184] 12/22/16 Email, Aven to Burt (4:58:22 p.m.).

[1185] Aven 8/2/18 302, at 7.

[1186] ▓Grand Jury▓

[1187] Burt 2/9/18 302, at 3-4.

[1188] ▓Grand Jury▓

[1189] ▓Grand Jury▓ Aven 8/2/18 302, at 7.

[1190] ▓Grand Jury▓

[1191] ▓Grand Jury▓

[1192] Aven 8/2/18 302, at 8.

[1193] Aven 8/2/18 302, at 8; ▓Grand Jury▓

According to Aven, the official showed no emotion in response to this report and did not appear to care.[1194]

6. Carter Page Contact with Deputy Prime Minister Arkady Dvorkovich

In December 2016, more than two months after he was removed from the Trump Campaign, former Campaign foreign policy advisor Carter Page again visited Moscow in an attempt to pursue business opportunities.[1195] ▆▆Grand Jury▆▆

▆▆▆▆▆▆▆▆▆▆▆▆▆▆▆▆▆▆▆▆▆▆▆▆▆▆▆[1196] According to Konstantin Kilimnik, Paul Manafort's associate, Page also gave some individuals in Russia the impression that he had maintained his connections to President-Elect Trump. In a December 8, 2016 email intended for Manafort, Kilimnik wrote, "Carter Page is in Moscow today, sending messages he is authorized to talk to Russia on behalf of DT on a range of issues of mutual interest, including Ukraine."[1197]

On December 9, 2016, Page went to dinner with NES employees Shlomo Weber and Andrej Krickovic.[1198] Weber had contacted Dvorkovich to let him know that Page was in town and to invite him to stop by the dinner if he wished to do so, and Dvorkovich came to the restaurant for a few minutes to meet with Page.[1199] Dvorkovich congratulated Page on Trump's election and expressed interest in starting a dialogue between the United States and Russia.[1200] Dvorkovich asked Page if he could facilitate connecting Dvorkovich with individuals involved in the transition to begin a discussion of future cooperation.[1201] ▆▆Grand Jury▆▆

▆▆▆▆▆▆[1202]▆▆Grand Jury▆▆

▆▆▆▆▆▆▆▆▆▆▆▆▆▆▆▆▆▆▆▆▆▆▆▆▆[1203]

[1194] Aven 8/2/18 302, at 8; ▆▆Grand Jury▆▆

[1195] Page 3/10/17 302, at 4; Page 3/16/17 302, at 3; ▆▆Grand Jury▆▆ Among other meetings, Page contacted Andrey Baranov, head of investor relations at Rosneft, and they discussed the sale of Rosneft and meetings Baranov had attended with Rosneft CEO Igor Sechin. ▆▆Grand Jury▆▆ ▆▆▆▆▆▆

[1196] ▆▆Grand Jury▆▆

[1197] ▆▆Investigative Technique▆▆

[1198] Page 3/16/17 302, at 3; Page 3/30/17 302, at 8.

[1199] Weber 7/28/17 302, at 4; Page 3/16/17 302, at 3; ▆▆Grand Jury▆▆

[1200] Page 3/16/17 302, at 3; ▆▆Grand Jury▆▆

[1201] Page 3/16/17 302, at 3; ▆▆Grand Jury▆▆

[1202] ▆▆Grand Jury▆▆

[1203] ▆▆Grand Jury▆▆

166

Grand Jury Dvorkovich separately discussed working together in the future by forming an academic partnership.[1204] Grand Jury

[1205] Grand Jury

206

7. Contacts With and Through Michael T. Flynn

Incoming National Security Advisor Michael Flynn was the Transition Team's primary conduit for communications with the Russian Ambassador and dealt with Russia on two sensitive matters during the transition period: a United Nations Security Council vote and the Russian government's reaction to the United States's imposition of sanctions for Russian interference in the 2016 election.[1207] Despite Kushner's conclusion that Kislyak did not wield influence inside the Russian government, the Transition Team turned to Flynn's relationship with Kislyak on both issues. As to the sanctions, Flynn spoke by phone to K.T. McFarland, his incoming deputy, to prepare for his call to Kislyak; McFarland was with the President-Elect and other senior members of the Transition Team at Mar-a-Lago at the time. Although transition officials at Mar-a-Lago had some concern about possible Russian reactions to the sanctions, the investigation did not identify evidence that the President-Elect asked Flynn to make any request to Kislyak. Flynn asked Kislyak not to escalate the situation in response to U.S. sanctions imposed on December 29, 2016, and Kislyak later reported to Flynn that Russia acceded to that request.

a. United Nations Vote on Israeli Settlements

On December 21, 2016, Egypt submitted a resolution to the United Nations Security Council calling on Israel to cease settlement activities in Palestinian territory.[1208] The Security Council, which includes Russia, was scheduled to vote on the resolution the following day.[1209] There was speculation in the media that the Obama Administration would not oppose the resolution.[1210]

[1204] Grand Jury

[1205] Grand Jury

[1206] Grand Jury

[1207] As discussed further in Volume I, Section V.C.4, *infra*, Flynn pleaded guilty to making false statements to the FBI, in violation of 18 U.S.C. § 1001, about these communications with Ambassador Kislyak. Plea Agreement, *United States v. Michael T. Flynn*, No. 1:17-cr-232 (D.D.C. Dec. 1, 2017), Doc. 3. Flynn's plea agreement required that he cooperate with this Office, and the statements from Flynn in this report reflect his cooperation over the course of multiple debriefings in 2017 and 2018.

[1208] Karen DeYoung, *How the U.S. Came to Abstain on a U.N. Resolution Condemning Israeli Settlements*, Washington Post (Dec. 28, 2016).

[1209] Karen DeYoung, *How the U.S. Came to Abstain on a U.N. Resolution Condemning Israeli Settlements*, Washington Post (Dec. 28, 2016).

[1210] Michelle Nichols & Lesley Wroughton, *U.S. Intended to Allow Passage of U.N. Draft Critical of Israel*, Reuters (Dec. 21, 2016).

According to Flynn, the Transition Team regarded the vote as a significant issue and wanted to support Israel by opposing the resolution.[1211] On December 22, 2016, multiple members of the Transition Team, as well as President-Elect Trump, communicated with foreign government officials to determine their views on the resolution and to rally support to delay the vote or defeat the resolution.[1212] Kushner led the effort for the Transition Team; Flynn was responsible for the Russian government.[1213] Minutes after an early morning phone call with Kushner on December 22, Flynn called Kislyak.[1214] According to Flynn, he informed Kislyak about the vote and the Transition Team's opposition to the resolution, and requested that Russia vote against or delay the resolution.[1215] Later that day, President-Elect Trump spoke with Egyptian President Abdel Fattah al-Sisi about the vote.[1216] Ultimately, Egypt postponed the vote.[1217]

On December 23, 2016, Malaysia, New Zealand, Senegal, and Venezuela resubmitted the resolution.[1218] Throughout the day, members of the Transition Team continued to talk with foreign leaders about the resolution, with Flynn continuing to lead the outreach with the Russian government through Kislyak.[1219] When Flynn again spoke with Kislyak, Kislyak informed Flynn that if the resolution came to a vote, Russia would not vote against it.[1220] The resolution later passed 14-0, with the United States abstaining.[1221]

b. U.S. Sanctions Against Russia

Flynn was also the Transition Team member who spoke with the Russian government when the Obama Administration imposed sanctions and other measures against Russia in response to Russia's interference in the 2016 presidential election. On December 28, 2016, then-President Obama signed Executive Order 13757, which took effect at 12:01 a.m. the following day and

---

[1211] Flynn 11/16/17 302, at 12; Flynn 11/17/17 302, at 2.

[1212] Flynn 11/16/17 302, at 12-14; Flynn 11/17/17 302, at 2.

[1213] Flynn 11/16/17 302, at 12-14; Flynn 11/17/17 302, at 2; Kushner 11/1/17 302, at 3; 12/22/16 Email, Kushner to Flynn; 12/22/16 Email, McFarland to Personal Privacy et al.

[1214] Flynn 11/16/17 302, at 13; Call Records of Michael T. Flynn Grand Jury .

[1215] Statement of Offense ¶ 3(d), *United States v. Michael T. Flynn*, No. 1:17-cr-232 (D.D.C. Dec. 1, 2017), Doc. 4 ("*Flynn* Statement of Offense"); Flynn 11/16/17 302, at 12-13.

[1216] Flynn 11/17/17 302, at 2; Flynn 11/16/17 302, at 13.

[1217] *U.N. Vote on Israeli Settlement Postponed, "Potentially Indefinitely"*, Reuters (Dec. 22, 2016).

[1218] Somini Sengupta & Rick Gladstone, *Rebuffing Israel, U.S. Allows Censure Over Settlements*, New York Times (Dec. 23, 2016).

[1219] Flynn 11/16/17 302, at 12-14; Kushner 11/1/17 302, at 3; 12/23/16 Email, Flynn to Kushner et al.

[1220] *Flynn* Statement of Offense ¶ 3(g).

[1221] *Israel's Settlements Have No Legal Validity, Constitute Flagrant Violation of International Law, Security Council Reaffirms*, 7853rd Meeting (PM), United Nations Security Council (Dec. 23, 2016).

imposed sanctions on nine Russian individuals and entities.[1222] On December 29, 2016, the Obama Administration also expelled 35 Russian government officials and closed two Russian government-owned compounds in the United States.[1223]

During the rollout of the sanctions, President-Elect Trump and multiple Transition Team senior officials, including McFarland, Steve Bannon, and Reince Priebus, were staying at the Mar-a-Lago club in Palm Beach, Florida. Flynn was on vacation in the Dominican Republic,[1224] but was in daily contact with McFarland.[1225]

The Transition Team and President-Elect Trump were concerned that these sanctions would harm the United States's relationship with Russia.[1226] Although the details and timing of sanctions were unknown on December 28, 2016, the media began reporting that retaliatory measures from the Obama Administration against Russia were forthcoming.[1227] When asked about imposing sanctions on Russia for its alleged interference in the 2016 presidential election, President-Elect Trump told the media, "I think we ought to get on with our lives."[1228]

Russia initiated the outreach to the Transition Team. On the evening of December 28, 2016, Kislyak texted Flynn, "can you kindly call me back at your convenience."[1229] Flynn did not respond to the text message that evening. Someone from the Russian Embassy also called Flynn the next morning, at 10:38 a.m., but they did not talk.[1230]

The sanctions were announced publicly on December 29, 2016.[1231] At 1:53 p.m. that day, McFarland began exchanging emails with multiple Transition Team members and advisors about the impact the sanctions would have on the incoming Administration.[1232] At 2:07 p.m., a Transition Team member texted Flynn a link to a New York Times article about the sanctions.[1233] At 2:29

[1222] *Taking Additional Steps to Address the National Emergency With Respect to Significant Malicious Cyber-Enabled Activities*, The White House, Office of the Press Secretary (Dec. 29, 2016).

[1223] *Statement by the President on Actions in Response to Russian Malicious Cyber Activity and Harassment*, The White House, Office of the Press Secretary (Dec. 29, 2016).

[1224] Flynn 11/16/17 302, at 14; McFarland 12/22/17 302, at 3-8; Bannon 2/12/18 302, at 5.

[1225] Flynn 11/17/17 302, at 5; Flynn 1/19/18 302, at 1; McFarland 11/22/17 302, at 3-9.

[1226] Flynn 11/17/17 302, at 3.

[1227] Christine Wang, *US to announce new sanctions against Russia in response to election hacking*, CNBC (Dec. 28, 2016).

[1228] John Wagner, *Trump on alleged election interference by Russia: "Get on with our lives"*, Washington Post (Dec. 29, 2016).

[1229] SF000006 (12/28/16 Text Message, Kislyak to Flynn).

[1230] Call Records of Michael T. Flynn Grand Jury

[1231] Flynn 11/17/17 302, at 2-3; McFarland 12/22/17 302, at 4-5.

[1232] 12/29/16 Email, McFarland to O'Brien et al.; 12/29/16 Email, McFarland to Flynn et al.

[1233] SF000001 (12/29/16 Text Message, Flaherty to Flynn).

p.m., McFarland called Flynn, but they did not talk.[1234] Shortly thereafter, McFarland and Bannon discussed the sanctions.[1235] According to McFarland, Bannon remarked that the sanctions would hurt their ability to have good relations with Russia, and that Russian escalation would make things more difficult.[1236] McFarland believed she told Bannon that Flynn was scheduled to talk to Kislyak later that night.[1237] McFarland also believed she may have discussed the sanctions with Priebus, and likewise told him that Flynn was scheduled to talk to Kislyak that night.[1238] At 3:14 p.m., Flynn texted a Transition Team member who was assisting McFarland, "Time for a call???"[1239] The Transition Team member responded that McFarland was on the phone with Tom Bossert, a Transition Team senior official, to which Flynn responded, "Tit for tat w Russia not good. Russian AMBO reaching out to me today."[1240]

Flynn recalled that he chose not to communicate with Kislyak about the sanctions until he had heard from the team at Mar-a-Lago.[1241] He first spoke with Michael Ledeen,[1242] a Transition Team member who advised on foreign policy and national security matters, for 20 minutes.[1243] Flynn then spoke with McFarland for almost 20 minutes to discuss what, if anything, to communicate to Kislyak about the sanctions.[1244] On that call, McFarland and Flynn discussed the sanctions, including their potential impact on the incoming Trump Administration's foreign policy goals.[1245] McFarland and Flynn also discussed that Transition Team members in Mar-a-Lago did not want Russia to escalate the situation.[1246] They both understood that Flynn would relay a message to Kislyak in hopes of making sure the situation would not get out of hand.[1247]

[1234] Call Records of K.T. McFarland **Grand Jury** .

[1235] McFarland 12/22/17 302, at 5-6.

[1236] McFarland 12/22/17 302, at 5-6.

[1237] McFarland 12/22/17 302, at 6.

[1238] McFarland 12/22/17 302, at 6.

[1239] SF000001 (12/29/16 Text Message, Flynn to Flaherty).

[1240] SF000001 (12/29/16 Text Message, Flynn to Flaherty).

[1241] Flynn 11/20/17 302, at 3.

[1242] Michael Ledeen is married to Barbara Ledeen, the Senate staffer whose 2016 efforts to locate Hillary Clinton's missing emails are described in Volume I, Section III.D.2, *supra*.

[1243] Flynn 11/17/17 302, at 3; Call Records of Michael Ledeen **Grand Jury** .

[1244] Flynn 11/17/17 302, at 3-4; *Flynn* Statement of Offense ¶ 3(c); Call Records of K.T. McFarland **Grand Jury** ; Call Records of Michael T. Flynn **Grand Jury** .

[1245] Flynn 11/17/17 302, at 3-4

[1246] Flynn 11/17/17 302, at 3-4; *Flynn* Statement of Offense ¶ 3(c); McFarland 12/22/17 302, at 6-7.

[1247] Flynn 11/17/17 302, at 4; McFarland 12/22/17 302, at 6-7.

Immediately after speaking with McFarland, Flynn called and spoke with Kislyak.[1248] Flynn discussed multiple topics with Kislyak, including the sanctions, scheduling a video teleconference between President-Elect Trump and Putin, an upcoming terrorism conference, and Russia's views about the Middle East.[1249] With respect to the sanctions, Flynn requested that Russia not escalate the situation, not get into a "tit for tat," and only respond to the sanctions in a reciprocal manner.[1250]

Multiple Transition Team members were aware that Flynn was speaking with Kislyak that day. In addition to her conversations with Bannon and Reince Priebus, at 4:43 p.m., McFarland sent an email to Transition Team members about the sanctions, informing the group that "Gen [F]lynn is talking to russian ambassador this evening."[1251] Less than an hour later, McFarland briefed President-Elect Trump. Bannon, Priebus, Sean Spicer, and other Transition Team members were present.[1252] During the briefing, President-Elect Trump asked McFarland if the Russians did "it," meaning the intrusions intended to influence the presidential election.[1253] McFarland said yes, and President-Elect Trump expressed doubt that it was the Russians.[1254] McFarland also discussed potential Russian responses to the sanctions, and said Russia's response would be an indicator of what the Russians wanted going forward.[1255] President-Elect Trump opined that the sanctions provided him with leverage to use with the Russians.[1256] McFarland recalled that at the end of the meeting, someone may have mentioned to President-Elect Trump that Flynn was speaking to the Russian ambassador that evening.[1257]

After the briefing, Flynn and McFarland spoke over the phone.[1258] Flynn reported on the substance of his call with Kislyak, including their discussion of the sanctions.[1259] According to McFarland, Flynn mentioned that the Russian response to the sanctions was not going to be escalatory because they wanted a good relationship with the incoming Administration.[1260] McFarland also gave Flynn a summary of her recent briefing with President-Elect Trump.[1261]

[1248] Flynn Statement of Offense ¶ 3(d).

[1249] Flynn 11/17/17 302, at 3-4; *Flynn* Statement of Offense ¶ 3(c); 12/30/16 Email, Flynn to McFarland.

[1250] Flynn 11/17/17 302, at 1; *Flynn* Statement of Offense ¶ 3(d).

[1251] 12/29/16 Email, McFarland to Flynn et al.

[1252] 12/29/16 Email, Westerhout to Flaherty; McFarland 12/22/17 302, at 7.

[1253] McFarland 12/22/17 302, at 7.

[1254] McFarland 12/22/17 302, at 7.

[1255] McFarland 12/22/17 302, at 7.

[1256] McFarland 12/22/17 302, at 7.

[1257] McFarland 12/22/17 302, at 7.

[1258] McFarland 12/22/17 302, at 7.

[1259] Flynn 11/17/17 302, at 4; *Flynn* Statement of Offense ¶ 3(e).

[1260] McFarland 12/22/17 302, at 8.

[1261] McFarland 12/22/17 302, at 8.

The next day, December 30, 2016, Russian Foreign Minister Sergey Lavrov remarked that Russia would respond in kind to the sanctions.[1262] Putin superseded that comment two hours later, releasing a statement that Russia would not take retaliatory measures in response to the sanctions at that time.[1263] Hours later President-Elect Trump tweeted, "Great move on delay (by V. Putin)."[1264] Shortly thereafter, Flynn sent a text message to McFarland summarizing his call with Kislyak from the day before, which she emailed to Kushner, Bannon, Priebus, and other Transition Team members.[1265] The text message and email did not include sanctions as one of the topics discussed with Kislyak.[1266] Flynn told the Office that he did not document his discussion of sanctions because it could be perceived as getting in the way of the Obama Administration's foreign policy.[1267]

On December 31, 2016, Kislyak called Flynn and told him the request had been received at the highest levels and that Russia had chosen not to retaliate to the sanctions in response to the request.[1268] Two hours later, Flynn spoke with McFarland and relayed his conversation with Kislyak.[1269] According to McFarland, Flynn remarked that the Russians wanted a better relationship and that the relationship was back on track.[1270] Flynn also told McFarland that he believed his phone call had made a difference.[1271] McFarland recalled congratulating Flynn in response.[1272] Flynn spoke with other Transition Team members that day, but does not recall whether they discussed the sanctions.[1273] Flynn recalled discussing the sanctions with Bannon the next day and that Bannon appeared to know about Flynn's conversation with Kislyak.[1274] Bannon,

---

[1262] *Comment by Foreign Minister Sergey Lavrov on recent US sanctions and the expulsion of Russian diplomats, Moscow, December 20, 2016*, The Ministry of Foreign Affairs of the Russian Federation (Dec. 30, 2016 (5:32 a.m.)).

[1263] *Statement of the President of the Russian Federation*, Kremlin, Office of the President (Dec. 30, 2016 (7:15 a.m.)).

[1264] @realDonaldTrump 12/30/16 (11:41 a.m.) Tweet.

[1265] 12/30/16 Email, Flynn to McFarland; 12/30/16 Email, McFarland to Kushner et al.

[1266] 12/30/16 Email, McFarland to Kushner et al.

[1267] Flynn 11/17/17 302, at 4.

[1268] Call Records of Michael T. Flynn ▮Grand Jury▮ ; Flynn 11/17/17 302, at 1; Flynn 1/19/17 302, at 3; Flynn Statement of Offense ¶ 3(g).

[1269] Call Records of Michael T. Flynn ▮Grand Jury▮ ; Flynn 11/17/17 302, at 5; Flynn 1/19/17 302, at 3; McFarland 12/22/17 302, at 10.

[1270] McFarland 12/22/17 302, at 10.

[1271] McFarland 12/22/17 302, at 10.

[1272] McFarland 12/22/17 302, at 10.

[1273] Flynn 11/17/17 302, at 5-6.

[1274] Flynn 11/21/17 302, at 1; Flynn 11/20/17 302, at 3; Flynn 1/19/17 302, at 5; *Flynn* Statement of Offense ¶ 3(h).

U.S. Department of Justice

Attorney Work Product // May Contain Material Protected Under Fed. R. Crim. P. 6(e)

for his part, recalled meeting with Flynn that day, but said that he did not remember discussing sanctions with him.[1275]

Additional information about Flynn's sanctions-related discussions with Kislyak, and the handling of those discussions by the Transition Team and the Trump Administration, is provided in Volume II of this report.

* * *

In sum, the investigation established multiple links between Trump Campaign officials and individuals tied to the Russian government. Those links included Russian offers of assistance to the Campaign. In some instances, the Campaign was receptive to the offer, while in other instances the Campaign officials shied away. Ultimately, the investigation did not establish that the Campaign coordinated or conspired with the Russian government in its election-interference activities.

[1275] Bannon 2/12/18 302, at 9.

V. PROSECUTION AND DECLINATION DECISIONS

The Appointment Order authorized the Special Counsel's Office "to prosecute federal crimes arising from [its] investigation" of the matters assigned to it. In deciding whether to exercise this prosecutorial authority, the Office has been guided by the Principles of Federal Prosecution set forth in the Justice (formerly U.S. Attorney's) Manual. In particular, the Office has evaluated whether the conduct of the individuals considered for prosecution constituted a federal offense and whether admissible evidence would probably be sufficient to obtain and sustain a conviction for such an offense. Justice Manual § 9-27.220 (2018). Where the answer to those questions was yes, the Office further considered whether the prosecution would serve a substantial federal interest, the individuals were subject to effective prosecution in another jurisdiction, and there existed an adequate non-criminal alternative to prosecution. *Id.*

As explained below, those considerations led the Office to seek charges against two sets of Russian nationals for their roles in perpetrating the active-measures social media campaign and computer-intrusion operations. Harm to Ongoing Matter

The Office similarly determined that the contacts between Campaign officials and Russia-linked individuals either did not involve the commission of a federal crime or, in the case of campaign-finance offenses, that our evidence was not sufficient to obtain and sustain a criminal conviction. At the same time, the Office concluded that the Principles of Federal Prosecution supported charging certain individuals connected to the Campaign with making false statements or otherwise obstructing this investigation or parallel congressional investigations.

A. Russian "Active Measures" Social Media Campaign

On February 16, 2018, a federal grand jury in the District of Columbia returned an indictment charging 13 Russian nationals and three Russian entities—including the Internet Research Agency (IRA) and Concord Management and Consulting LLC (Concord)—with violating U.S. criminal laws in order to interfere with U.S. elections and political processes.[1276] The indictment charges all of the defendants with conspiracy to defraud the United States (Count One), three defendants with conspiracy to commit wire fraud and bank fraud (Count Two), and five defendants with aggravated identity theft (Counts Three through Eight). *Internet Research Agency* Indictment. Concord, which is one of the entities charged in the Count One conspiracy, entered an appearance through U.S. counsel and moved to dismiss the charge on multiple grounds. In orders and memorandum opinions issued on August 13 and November 15, 2018, the district court denied Concord's motions to dismiss. *United States v. Concord Management & Consulting LLC*, 347 F. Supp. 3d 38 (D.D.C. 2018). *United States v. Concord Management & Consulting LLC*, 317 F. Supp. 3d 598 (D.D.C. 2018). As of this writing, the prosecution of Concord remains ongoing before the U.S. District Court for the District of Columbia. The other defendants remain at large.

[1276] A more detailed explanation of the charging decision in this case is set forth in a separate memorandum provided to the Acting Attorney General before the indictment.

174

U.S. Department of Justice

~~Attorney Work Product // May Contain Material Protected Under Fed. R. Crim. P. 6(e)~~

Although members of the IRA had contact with individuals affiliated with the Trump Campaign, the indictment does not charge any Trump Campaign official or any other U.S. person with participating in the conspiracy. That is because the investigation did not identify evidence that any U.S. person who coordinated or communicated with the IRA knew that he or she was speaking with Russian nationals engaged in the criminal conspiracy. The Office therefore determined that such persons did not have the knowledge or criminal purpose required to charge them in the conspiracy to defraud the United States (Count One) or in the separate count alleging a wire- and bank-fraud conspiracy involving the IRA and two individual Russian nationals (Count Two).

The Office did, however, charge one U.S. national for his role in supplying false or stolen bank account numbers that allowed the IRA conspirators to access U.S. online payment systems by circumventing those systems' security features. On February 12, 2018, Richard Pinedo pleaded guilty, pursuant to a single-count information, to identity fraud, in violation of 18 U.S.C. § 1028(a)(7) and (b)(1)(D). Plea Agreement, *United States v. Richard Pinedo*, No. 1:18-cr-24 (D.D.C. Feb. 12, 2018), Doc. 10. The investigation did not establish that Pinedo was aware of the identity of the IRA members who purchased bank account numbers from him. Pinedo's sales of account numbers enabled the IRA members to anonymously access a financial network through which they transacted with U.S. persons and companies. *See* Gov't Sent. Mem. at 3, *United States v. Richard Pinedo*, No. 1:18-cr-24 (D.D.C. Sept. 26, 2018), Doc. 24. On October 10, 2018, Pinedo was sentenced to six months of imprisonment, to be followed by six months of home confinement, and was ordered to complete 100 hours of community service.

B. Russian Hacking and Dumping Operations

1. Section 1030 Computer-Intrusion Conspiracy

a. Background

On July 13, 2018, a federal grand jury in the District of Columbia returned an indictment charging Russian military intelligence officers from the GRU with conspiring to hack into various U.S. computers used by the Clinton Campaign, DNC, DCCC, and other U.S. persons, in violation of 18 U.S.C. §§ 1030 and 371 (Count One); committing identity theft and conspiring to commit money laundering in furtherance of that hacking conspiracy, in violation of 18 U.S.C. §§ 1028A and 1956(h) (Counts Two through Ten); and a separate conspiracy to hack into the computers of U.S. persons and entities responsible for the administration of the 2016 U.S. election, in violation of 18 U.S.C. §§ 1030 and 371 (Count Eleven). *Netyksho* Indictment.[1277] As of this writing, all 12 defendants remain at large.

The *Netyksho* indictment alleges that the defendants conspired with one another and with others to hack into the computers of U.S. persons and entities involved in the 2016 U.S. presidential election, steal documents from those computers, and stage releases of the stolen documents to interfere in the election. *Netyksho* Indictment ¶ 2. The indictment also describes how, in staging

---

[1277] The Office provided a more detailed explanation of the charging decision in this case in meetings with the Office of the Acting Attorney General before the indictment.

the releases, the defendants used the Guccifer 2.0 persona to disseminate documents through WikiLeaks. On July 22, 2016, WikiLeaks released over 20,000 emails and other documents that the hacking conspirators had stolen from the DNC. *Netyksho* Indictment ¶ 48. In addition, on October 7, 2016, WikiLeaks began releasing emails that some conspirators had stolen from Clinton Campaign chairman John Podesta after a successful spearphishing operation. *Netyksho* Indictment ¶ 49.

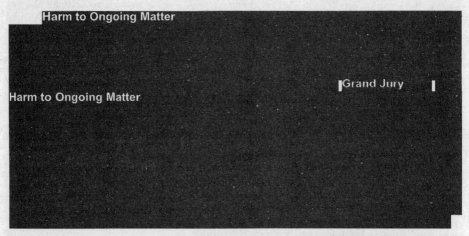

b. *Charging Decision As to* Harm to Ongoing Matter

[1278] The Office also considered, but ruled out, charges on the theory that the post-hacking sharing and dissemination of emails could constitute trafficking in or receipt of stolen property under the National Stolen Property Act (NSPA), 18 U.S.C. §§ 2314 and 2315. The statutes comprising the NSPA cover "goods, wares, or merchandise," and lower courts have largely understood that phrase to be limited to tangible items since the Supreme Court's decision in *Dowling v. United States*, 473 U.S. 207 (1985). *See United States v. Yijia Zhang*, 995 F. Supp. 2d 340, 344-48 (E.D. Pa. 2014) (collecting cases). One of those post-*Dowling* decisions—*United States v. Brown*, 925 F.2d 1301 (10th Cir. 1991)—specifically held that the NSPA does not reach "a computer program in source code form," even though that code was stored in tangible items (*i.e.*, a hard disk and in a three-ring notebook). *Id.* at 1302-03. Congress, in turn, cited the *Brown* opinion in explaining the need for amendments to 18 U.S.C. § 1030(a)(2) that "would ensure that the theft of intangible information by the unauthorized use of a computer is prohibited in the same way theft of physical items [is] protected." S. Rep. 104-357, at 7 (1996). That sequence of events would make it difficult to argue that hacked emails in electronic form, which are the relevant stolen items here, constitute "goods, wares, or merchandise" within the meaning of the NSPA.

Harm to Ongoing Matter

Harm to Ongoing Matter

Harm to Ongoing Matter

Harm to Ongoing Matter

Harm to Ongoing Matter

[279] Harm to Ongoing Matter

Harm to Ongoing Matter

Harm to Ongoing Matter

[1279] Harm to Ongoing Matter

Harm to Ongoing Matter

2. <u>Potential Section 1030 Violation By</u> PP

Personal Privacy

Personal Privacy

See United States v. Willis, 476 F.3d 1121, 1125 n.1 (10th Cir. 2007) (explaining that the 1986 amendments to Section 1030 reflect Congress's desire to reach "'intentional acts of unauthorized access—rather than mistaken, inadvertent, or careless ones'") (quoting S. Rep. 99-432, at 5 (1986)). In addition, the computer Personal Privacy likely qualifies as a "protected" one under the statute, which reaches "effectively all computers with Internet access." *United States v. Nosal*, 676 F.3d 854, 859 (9th Cir. 2012) (en banc). Personal Privacy

Applying the Principles of Federal Prosecution, however, the Office determined that prosecution of this potential violation was not warranted. Those Principles instruct prosecutors to consider, among other things, the nature and seriousness of the offense, the person's culpability in connection with the offense, and the probable sentence to be imposed if the prosecution is successful. Justice Manual § 9-27.230. Personal Privacy

U.S. Department of Justice

~~Attorney Work Product~~ // ~~May Contain Material Protected Under Fed. R. Crim. P. 6(e)~~

Personal Privacy

C. Russian Government Outreach and Contacts

As explained in Section IV above, the Office's investigation uncovered evidence of numerous links (*i.e.*, contacts) between Trump Campaign officials and individuals having or claiming to have ties to the Russian government. The Office evaluated the contacts under several sets of federal laws, including conspiracy laws and statutes governing foreign agents who operate in the United States. After considering the available evidence, the Office did not pursue charges under these statutes against any of the individuals discussed in Section IV above—with the exception of FARA charges against Paul Manafort and Richard Gates based on their activities on behalf of Ukraine.

One of the interactions between the Trump Campaign and Russian-affiliated individuals—the June 9, 2016 meeting between high-ranking campaign officials and Russians promising derogatory information on Hillary Clinton—implicates an additional body of law: campaign-finance statutes. Schemes involving the solicitation or receipt of assistance from foreign sources raise difficult statutory and constitutional questions. As explained below, the Office evaluated those questions in connection with the June 9 meeting Harm to Ongoing Matter . The Office ultimately concluded that, even if the principal legal questions were resolved favorably to the government, a prosecution would encounter difficulties proving that Campaign officials or individuals connected to the Campaign willfully violated the law.

Finally, although the evidence of contacts between Campaign officials and Russia-affiliated individuals may not have been sufficient to establish or sustain criminal charges, several U.S. persons connected to the Campaign made false statements about those contacts and took other steps to obstruct the Office's investigation and those of Congress. This Office has therefore charged some of those individuals with making false statements and obstructing justice.

1. Potential Coordination: Conspiracy and Collusion

As an initial matter, this Office evaluated potentially criminal conduct that involved the collective action of multiple individuals not under the rubric of "collusion," but through the lens of conspiracy law. In so doing, the Office recognized that the word "collud[e]" appears in the Acting Attorney General's August 2, 2017 memorandum; it has frequently been invoked in public reporting; and it is sometimes referenced in antitrust law, *see, e.g., Brooke Group v. Brown & Williamson Tobacco Corp.*, 509 U.S. 209, 227 (1993). But collusion is not a specific offense or theory of liability found in the U.S. Code; nor is it a term of art in federal criminal law. To the contrary, even as defined in legal dictionaries, collusion is largely synonymous with conspiracy as that crime is set forth in the general federal conspiracy statute, 18 U.S.C. § 371. *See Black's Law Dictionary* 321 (10th ed. 2014) (collusion is "[a]n agreement to defraud another or to do or obtain something forbidden by law"); 1 Alexander Burrill, *A Law Dictionary and Glossary* 311 (1871) ("An agreement between two or more persons to defraud another by the forms of law, or to employ such forms as means of accomplishing some unlawful object."); 1 *Bouvier's Law Dictionary* 352

U.S. Department of Justice

~~Attorney Work Product // May Contain Material Protected Under Fed. R. Crim. P. 6(e)~~

(1897) ("An agreement between two or more persons to defraud a person of his rights by the forms of law, or to obtain an object forbidden by law.").

For that reason, this Office's focus in resolving the question of joint criminal liability was on conspiracy as defined in federal law, not the commonly discussed term "collusion." The Office considered in particular whether contacts between Trump Campaign officials and Russia-linked individuals could trigger liability for the crime of conspiracy—either under statutes that have their own conspiracy language (*e.g.*, 18 U.S.C. §§ 1349, 1951(a)), or under the general conspiracy statute (18 U.S.C. § 371). The investigation did not establish that the contacts described in Volume I, Section IV, *supra*, amounted to an agreement to commit any substantive violation of federal criminal law—including foreign-influence and campaign-finance laws, both of which are discussed further below. The Office therefore did not charge any individual associated with the Trump Campaign with conspiracy to commit a federal offense arising from Russia contacts, either under a specific statute or under Section 371's offenses clause.

The Office also did not charge any campaign official or associate with a conspiracy under Section 371's defraud clause. That clause criminalizes participating in an agreement to obstruct a lawful function of the U.S. government or its agencies through deceitful or dishonest means. *See Dennis v. United States*, 384 U.S. 855, 861 (1966); *Hammerschmidt v. United States*, 265 U.S. 182, 188 (1924); *see also United States v. Concord Mgmt. & Consulting LLC*, 347 F. Supp. 3d 38, 46 (D.D.C. 2018). The investigation did not establish any agreement among Campaign officials— or between such officials and Russia-linked individuals—to interfere with or obstruct a lawful function of a government agency during the campaign or transition period. And, as discussed in Volume I, Section V.A, *supra*, the investigation did not identify evidence that any Campaign official or associate knowingly and intentionally participated in the conspiracy to defraud that the Office charged, namely, the active-measures conspiracy described in Volume I, Section II, *supra*. Accordingly, the Office did not charge any Campaign associate or other U.S. person with conspiracy to defraud the United States based on the Russia-related contacts described in Section IV above.

2. Potential Coordination: Foreign Agent Statutes (FARA and 18 U.S.C. § 951)

The Office next assessed the potential liability of Campaign-affiliated individuals under federal statutes regulating actions on behalf of, or work done for, a foreign government.

a. *Governing Law*

Under 18 U.S.C. § 951, it is generally illegal to act in the United States as an agent of a foreign government without providing notice to the Attorney General. Although the defendant must act on behalf of a foreign government (as opposed to other kinds of foreign entities), the acts need not involve espionage; rather, acts of any type suffice for liability. *See United States v. Duran*, 596 F.3d 1283, 1293-94 (11th Cir. 2010); *United States v. Latchin*, 554 F.3d 709, 715 (7th Cir. 2009); *United States v. Dumeisi*, 424 F.3d 566, 581 (7th Cir. 2005). An "agent of a foreign government" is an "individual" who "agrees to operate" in the United States "subject to the direction or control of a foreign government or official." 18 U.S.C. § 951(d).

181

The crime defined by Section 951 is complete upon knowingly acting in the United States as an unregistered foreign-government agent. 18 U.S.C. § 951(a). The statute does not require willfulness, and knowledge of the notification requirement is not an element of the offense. *United States v. Campa*, 529 F.3d 980, 998-99 (11th Cir. 2008); *Duran*, 596 F.3d at 1291-94; *Dumeisi*, 424 F.3d at 581.

The Foreign Agents Registration Act (FARA) generally makes it illegal to act as an agent of a foreign principal by engaging in certain (largely political) activities in the United States without registering with the Attorney General. 22 U.S.C. §§ 611-621. The triggering agency relationship must be with a foreign principal or "a person any of whose activities are directly or indirectly supervised, directed, controlled, financed, or subsidized in whole or in major part by a foreign principal." 22 U.S.C. § 611(c)(1). That includes a foreign government or political party and various foreign individuals and entities. 22 U.S.C. § 611(b). A covered relationship exists if a person "acts as an agent, representative, employee, or servant" or "in any other capacity at the order, request, or under the [foreign principal's] direction or control." 22 U.S.C. § 611(c)(1). It is sufficient if the person "agrees, consents, assumes or purports to act as, or who is or holds himself out to be, whether or not pursuant to contractual relationship, an agent of a foreign principal." 22 U.S.C. § 611(c)(2).

The triggering activity is that the agent "directly or through any other person" in the United States (1) engages in "political activities for or in the interests of [the] foreign principal," which includes attempts to influence federal officials or the public; (2) acts as "public relations counsel, publicity agent, information-service employee or political consultant for or in the interests of such foreign principal"; (3) "solicits, collects, disburses, or dispenses contributions, loans, money, or other things of value for or in the interest of such foreign principal"; or (4) "represents the interests of such foreign principal" before any federal agency or official. 22 U.S.C. § 611(c)(1).

It is a crime to engage in a "[w]illful violation of any provision of the Act or any regulation thereunder." 22 U.S.C. § 618(a)(1). It is also a crime willfully to make false statements or omissions of material facts in FARA registration statements or supplements. 22 U.S.C. § 618(a)(2). Most violations have a maximum penalty of five years of imprisonment and a $10,000 fine. 22 U.S.C. § 618.

b. Application

The investigation uncovered extensive evidence that Paul Manafort's and Richard Gates's pre-campaign work for the government of Ukraine violated FARA. Manafort and Gates were charged for that conduct and admitted to it when they pleaded guilty to superseding criminal informations in the District of Columbia prosecution.[1280] The evidence underlying those charges is not addressed in this report because it was discussed in public court documents and in a separate

---

[1280] *Gates* Superseding Criminal Information; Waiver of Indictment, *United States v. Richard W. Gates III*, 1:17-cr-201 (D.D.C. Feb. 23, 2018), Doc. 203; Waiver of Trial by Jury, *United States v. Richard W. Gates III*, 1:17-cr-201 (D.D.C. Feb. 23, 2018), Doc. 204; *Gates* Plea Agreement; Statement of Offense, *United States v. Richard W. Gates III*, 1:17-cr-201 (D.D.C. Feb. 23, 2018), Doc. 206; Plea Agreement, *United States v. Paul J. Manafort, Jr.*, 1:17-cr-201 (D.D.C. Sept. 14, 2018), Doc. 422; Statement of Offense, *United States v. Paul J. Manafort, Jr.*, 1:17-cr-201 (D.D.C. Sept. 14, 2018), Doc. 423.

U.S. Department of Justice

~~Attorney Work Product~~ // ~~May Contain Material Protected Under Fed. R. Crim. P. 6(e)~~

prosecution memorandum submitted to the Acting Attorney General before the original indictment in that case.

In addition, the investigation produced evidence of FARA violations involving Michael Flynn. Those potential violations, however, concerned a country other than Russia (*i.e.*, Turkey) and were resolved when Flynn admitted to the underlying facts in the Statement of Offense that accompanied his guilty plea to a false-statements charge. Statement of Offense, *United States v. Michael T. Flynn*, No. 1:17-cr-232 (D.D.C. Dec. 1, 2017), Doc. 4 ("*Flynn* Statement of Offense").[1281]

The investigation did not, however, yield evidence sufficient to sustain any charge that any individual affiliated with the Trump Campaign acted as an agent of a foreign principal within the meaning of FARA or, in terms of Section 951, subject to the direction or control of the government of Russia, or any official thereof. In particular, the Office did not find evidence likely to prove beyond a reasonable doubt that Campaign officials such as Paul Manafort, George Papadopoulos, and Carter Page acted as agents of the Russian government—or at its direction, control, or request—during the relevant time period.[1282] Personal Privacy

As a result, the Office did not charge PP any other Trump Campaign official with violating FARA or Section 951, or attempting or conspiring to do so, based on contacts with the Russian government or a Russian principal.

Finally, the Office investigated whether one of the above campaign advisors—George Papadopoulos—acted as an agent of, or at the direction and control of, the government of Israel. While the investigation revealed significant ties between Papadopoulos and Israel (and search warrants were obtained in part on that basis), the Office ultimately determined that the evidence was not sufficient to obtain and sustain a conviction under FARA or Section 951.

3. Campaign Finance

Several areas of the Office's investigation involved efforts or offers by foreign nationals to provide negative information about candidate Clinton to the Trump Campaign or to distribute that information to the public, to the anticipated benefit of the Campaign. As explained below, the Office considered whether two of those efforts in particular—the June 9, 2016 meeting at Trump

---

[1281] Harm to Ongoing Matter

[1282] On four occasions, the Foreign Intelligence Surveillance Court (FISC) issued warrants based on a finding of probable cause to believe that Page was an agent of a foreign power. 50 U.S.C. §§ 1801(b), 1805(a)(2)(A). The FISC's probable-cause finding was based on a different (and lower) standard than the one governing the Office's decision whether to bring charges against Page, which is whether admissible evidence would likely be sufficient to prove beyond a reasonable doubt that Page acted as an agent of the Russian Federation during the period at issue. *Cf. United States v. Cardoza*, 713 F.3d 656, 660 (D.C. Cir. 2013) (explaining that probable cause requires only "a fair probability," and not "certainty, or proof beyond a reasonable doubt, or proof by a preponderance of the evidence").

Tower ███Harm to Ongoing Matter███████████████████—constituted prosecutable violations of the campaign-finance laws. The Office determined that the evidence was not sufficient to charge either incident as a criminal violation.

a. Overview Of Governing Law

"[T]he United States has a compelling interest . . . in limiting the participation of foreign citizens in activities of democratic self-government, and in thereby preventing foreign influence over the U.S. political process." *Bluman v. FEC*, 800 F. Supp. 2d 281, 288 (D.D.C. 2011) (Kavanaugh, J., for three-judge court), *aff'd*, 565 U.S. 1104 (2012). To that end, federal campaign-finance law broadly prohibits foreign nationals from making contributions, donations, expenditures, or other disbursements in connection with federal, state, or local candidate elections, and prohibits anyone from soliciting, accepting, or receiving such contributions or donations. As relevant here, foreign nationals may not make—and no one may "solicit, accept, or receive" from them—"a contribution or donation of money or other thing of value" or "an express or implied promise to make a contribution or donation, in connection with a Federal, State, or local election." 52 U.S.C. § 30121(a)(1)(A), (a)(2).[1283] The term "contribution," which is used throughout the campaign-finance law, "includes" "any gift, subscription, loan, advance, or deposit of money or anything of value made by any person for the purpose of influencing any election for Federal office." 52 U.S.C. § 30101(8)(A)(i). It excludes, among other things, "the value of [volunteer] services." 52 U.S.C. § 30101(8)(B)(i).

Foreign nationals are also barred from making "an expenditure, independent expenditure, or disbursement for an electioneering communication." 52 U.S.C. § 30121(a)(1)(C). The term "expenditure" "includes" "any purchase, payment, distribution, loan, advance, deposit, or gift of money or anything of value, made by any person for the purpose of influencing any election for Federal office." 52 U.S.C. § 30101(9)(A)(i). It excludes, among other things, news stories and non-partisan get-out-the-vote activities. 52 U.S.C. § 30101(9)(B)(i)-(ii). An "independent expenditure" is an expenditure "expressly advocating the election or defeat of a clearly identified candidate" and made independently of the campaign. 52 U.S.C. § 30101(17). An "electioneering communication" is a broadcast communication that "refers to a clearly identified candidate for Federal office" and is made within specified time periods and targeted at the relevant electorate. 52 U.S.C. § 30104(f)(3).

The statute defines "foreign national" by reference to FARA and the Immigration and Nationality Act, with minor modification. 52 U.S.C. § 30121(b) (cross-referencing 22 U.S.C. § 611(b)(1)-(3) and 8 U.S.C. § 1101(a)(20), (22)). That definition yields five, sometimes-overlapping categories of foreign nationals, which include all of the individuals and entities relevant for present purposes—namely, foreign governments and political parties, individuals

---

[1283] Campaign-finance law also places financial limits on contributions, 52 U.S.C. § 30116(a), and prohibits contributions from corporations, banks, and labor unions, 52 U.S.C. § 30118(a); *see Citizens United v. FEC*, 558 U.S. 310, 320 (2010). Because the conduct that the Office investigated involved possible electoral activity by foreign nationals, the foreign-contributions ban is the most readily applicable provision.

outside of the U.S. who are not legal permanent residents, and certain non-U.S. entities located outside of the U.S.

A "knowing[] and willful[]" violation involving an aggregate of $25,000 or more in a calendar year is a felony. 52 U.S.C. § 30109(d)(1)(A)(i); *see Bluman*, 800 F. Supp. 2d at 292 (noting that a willful violation will require some "proof of the defendant's knowledge of the law"); *United States v. Danielczyk*, 917 F. Supp. 2d 573, 577 (E.D. Va. 2013) (applying willfulness standard drawn from *Bryan v. United States*, 524 U.S. 184, 191-92 (1998)); *see also Wagner v. FEC*, 793 F.3d 1, 19 n.23 (D.C. Cir. 2015) (en banc) (same). A "knowing[] and willful[]" violation involving an aggregate of $2,000 or more in a calendar year, but less than $25,000, is a misdemeanor. 52 U.S.C. § 30109(d)(1)(A)(ii).

b. Application to June 9 Trump Tower Meeting

The Office considered whether to charge Trump Campaign officials with crimes in connection with the June 9 meeting described in Volume I, Section IV.A.5, *supra*. The Office concluded that, in light of the government's substantial burden of proof on issues of intent ("knowing" and "willful"), and the difficulty of establishing the value of the offered information, criminal charges would not meet the Justice Manual standard that "the admissible evidence will probably be sufficient to obtain and sustain a conviction." Justice Manual § 9-27.220.

In brief, the key facts are that, on June 3, 2016, Robert Goldstone emailed Donald Trump Jr., to pass along from Emin and Aras Agalarov an "offer" from Russia's "Crown prosecutor" to "the Trump campaign" of "official documents and information that would incriminate Hillary and her dealings with Russia and would be very useful to [Trump Jr.'s] father." The email described this as "very high level and sensitive information" that is "part of Russia and its government's support to Mr. Trump-helped along by Aras and Emin." Trump Jr. responded: "if it's what you say I love it especially later in the summer." Trump Jr. and Emin Agalarov had follow-up conversations and, within days, scheduled a meeting with Russian representatives that was attended by Trump Jr., Manafort, and Kushner. The communications setting up the meeting and the attendance by high-level Campaign representatives support an inference that the Campaign anticipated receiving derogatory documents and information from official Russian sources that could assist candidate Trump's electoral prospects.

This series of events could implicate the federal election-law ban on contributions and donations by foreign nationals, 52 U.S.C. § 30121(a)(1)(A). Specifically, Goldstone passed along an offer purportedly from a Russian government official to provide "official documents and information" to the Trump Campaign for the purposes of influencing the presidential election. Trump Jr. appears to have accepted that offer and to have arranged a meeting to receive those materials. Documentary evidence in the form of email chains supports the inference that Kushner and Manafort were aware of that purpose and attended the June 9 meeting anticipating the receipt of helpful information to the Campaign from Russian sources.

The Office considered whether this evidence would establish a conspiracy to violate the foreign contributions ban, in violation of 18 U.S.C. § 371; the solicitation of an illegal foreign-source contribution; or the acceptance or receipt of "an express or implied promise to make a

185

[foreign-source] contribution," both in violation of 52 U.S.C. § 30121(a)(1)(A), (a)(2). There are reasonable arguments that the offered information would constitute a "thing of value" within the meaning of these provisions, but the Office determined that the government would not be likely to obtain and sustain a conviction for two other reasons: first, the Office did not obtain admissible evidence likely to meet the government's burden to prove beyond a reasonable doubt that these individuals acted "willfully," *i.e.*, with general knowledge of the illegality of their conduct; and, second, the government would likely encounter difficulty in proving beyond a reasonable doubt that the value of the promised information exceeded the threshold for a criminal violation, *see* 52 U.S.C. § 30109(d)(1)(A)(i).

i. Thing-of-Value Element

A threshold legal question is whether providing to a campaign "documents and information" of the type involved here would constitute a prohibited campaign contribution. The foreign contribution ban is not limited to contributions of money. It expressly prohibits "a contribution or donation of money or *other thing of value*." 52 U.S.C. § 30121(a)(1)(A), (a)(2) (emphasis added). And the term "contribution" is defined throughout the campaign-finance laws to "include[]" "any gift, subscription, loan, advance, or deposit of money or *anything of value*." 52 U.S.C. § 30101(8)(A)(i) (emphasis added).

The phrases "thing of value" and "anything of value" are broad and inclusive enough to encompass at least some forms of valuable information. Throughout the United States Code, these phrases serve as "term[s] of art" that are construed "broad[ly]." *United States v. Nilsen*, 967 F.2d 539, 542 (11th Cir. 1992) (per curiam) ("thing of value" includes "both tangibles and intangibles"); *see also, e.g.*, 18 U.S.C. §§ 201(b)(1), 666(a)(2) (bribery statutes); *id.* § 641 (theft of government property). For example, the term "thing of value" encompasses law enforcement reports that would reveal the identity of informants, *United States v. Girard*, 601 F.2d 69, 71 (2d Cir. 1979); classified materials, *United States v. Fowler*, 932 F.2d 306, 310 (4th Cir. 1991); confidential information about a competitive bid, *United States v. Matzkin*, 14 F.3d 1014, 1020 (4th Cir. 1994); secret grand jury information, *United States v. Jeter*, 775 F.2d 670, 680 (6th Cir. 1985); and information about a witness's whereabouts, *United States v. Sheker*, 618 F.2d 607, 609 (9th Cir. 1980) (per curiam). And in the public corruption context, "'thing of value' is defined broadly to include the value which the defendant subjectively attaches to the items received." *United States v. Renzi*, 769 F.3d 731, 744 (9th Cir. 2014) (internal quotation marks omitted).

Federal Election Commission (FEC) regulations recognize the value to a campaign of at least some forms of information, stating that the term "anything of value" includes "the provision of any goods or services without charge," such as "membership lists" and "mailing lists." 11 C.F.R. § 100.52(d)(1). The FEC has concluded that the phrase includes a state-by-state list of activists. *See Citizens for Responsibility and Ethics in Washington v. FEC*, 475 F.3d 337, 338 (D.C. Cir. 2007) (describing the FEC's findings). Likewise, polling data provided to a campaign constitutes a "contribution." FEC Advisory Opinion 1990-12 (Strub), 1990 WL 153454 (citing 11 C.F.R. § 106.4(b)). And in the specific context of the foreign-contributions ban, the FEC has concluded that "election materials used in previous Canadian campaigns," including "flyers, advertisements, door hangers, tri-folds, signs, and other printed material," constitute "anything of

186

U.S. Department of Justice

~~Attorney Work Product~~ // ~~May Contain Material Protected Under Fed. R. Crim. P. 6(e)~~

value," even though "the value of these materials may be nominal or difficult to ascertain." FEC Advisory Opinion 2007-22 (Hurysz), 2007 WL 5172375, at *5.

These authorities would support the view that candidate-related opposition research given to a campaign for the purpose of influencing an election could constitute a contribution to which the foreign-source ban could apply. A campaign can be assisted not only by the provision of funds, but also by the provision of derogatory information about an opponent. Political campaigns frequently conduct and pay for opposition research. A foreign entity that engaged in such research and provided resulting information to a campaign could exert a greater effect on an election, and a greater tendency to ingratiate the donor to the candidate, than a gift of money or tangible things of value. At the same time, no judicial decision has treated the voluntary provision of uncompensated opposition research or similar information as a thing of value that could amount to a contribution under campaign-finance law. Such an interpretation could have implications beyond the foreign-source ban, *see* 52 U.S.C. § 30116(a) (imposing monetary limits on campaign contributions), and raise First Amendment questions. Those questions could be especially difficult where the information consisted simply of the recounting of historically accurate facts. It is uncertain how courts would resolve those issues.

ii. Willfulness

Even assuming that the promised "documents and information that would incriminate Hillary" constitute a "thing of value" under campaign-finance law, the government would encounter other challenges in seeking to obtain and sustain a conviction. Most significantly, the government has not obtained admissible evidence that is likely to establish the scienter requirement beyond a reasonable doubt. To prove that a defendant acted "knowingly and willfully," the government would have to show that the defendant had general knowledge that his conduct was unlawful. U.S. Department of Justice, *Federal Prosecution of Election Offenses* 123 (8th ed. Dec. 2017) ("*Election Offenses*"); *see Bluman*, 800 F. Supp. 2d at 292 (noting that a willful violation requires "proof of the defendant's knowledge of the law"); *Danielczyk*, 917 F. Supp. 2d at 577 ("knowledge of general unlawfulness"). "This standard creates an elevated scienter element requiring, at the very least, that application of the law to the facts in question be fairly clear. When there is substantial doubt concerning whether the law applies to the facts of a particular matter, the offender is more likely to have an intent defense." *Election Offenses* 123.

On the facts here, the government would unlikely be able to prove beyond a reasonable doubt that the June 9 meeting participants had general knowledge that their conduct was unlawful. The investigation has not developed evidence that the participants in the meeting were familiar with the foreign-contribution ban or the application of federal law to the relevant factual context. The government does not have strong evidence of surreptitious behavior or efforts at concealment at the time of the June 9 meeting. While the government has evidence of later efforts to prevent disclosure of the nature of the June 9 meeting that could circumstantially provide support for a showing of scienter, *see* Volume II, Section II.G, *infra*, that concealment occurred more than a year later, involved individuals who did not attend the June 9 meeting, and may reflect an intention to avoid political consequences rather than any prior knowledge of illegality. Additionally, in light of the unresolved legal questions about whether giving "documents and information" of the sort offered here constitutes a campaign contribution, Trump Jr. could mount a factual defense that he

187

did not believe his response to the offer and the June 9 meeting itself violated the law. Given his less direct involvement in arranging the June 9 meeting, Kushner could likely mount a similar defense. And, while Manafort is experienced with political campaigns, the Office has not developed evidence showing that he had relevant knowledge of these legal issues.

iii. Difficulties in Valuing Promised Information

The Office would also encounter difficulty proving beyond a reasonable doubt that the value of the promised documents and information exceeds the $2,000 threshold for a criminal violation, as well as the $25,000 threshold for felony punishment. *See* 52 U.S.C. § 30109(d)(1). The type of evidence commonly used to establish the value of non-monetary contributions—such as pricing the contribution on a commercial market or determining the upstream acquisition cost or the cost of distribution—would likely be unavailable or ineffective in this factual setting. Although damaging opposition research is surely valuable to a campaign, it appears that the information ultimately delivered in the meeting was not valuable. And while value in a conspiracy may well be measured by what the participants expected to receive at the time of the agreement, *see, e.g.*, *United States v. Tombrello*, 666 F.2d 485, 489 (11th Cir. 1982), Goldstone's description of the offered material here was quite general. His suggestion of the information's value—*i.e.*, that it would "incriminate Hillary" and "would be very useful to [Trump Jr.'s] father"—was non-specific and may have been understood as being of uncertain worth or reliability, given Goldstone's lack of direct access to the original source. The uncertainty over what would be delivered could be reflected in Trump Jr.'s response ("*if it's what you say* I love it") (emphasis added).

Accordingly, taking into account the high burden to establish a culpable mental state in a campaign-finance prosecution and the difficulty in establishing the required valuation, the Office decided not to pursue criminal campaign-finance charges against Trump Jr. or other campaign officials for the events culminating in the June 9 meeting.

c. Application to Harm to Ongoing Matter

Harm to Ongoing Matter

Harm to Ongoing Matter

188

248

Harm to Ongoing Matter

i. *Questions Over Whether* Harm to Ongoing Matter

Harm to Ongoing Matter

Harm to Ongoing Matter

Harm to Ongoing Matter

189

ii. Willfulness

As discussed, to establish a criminal campaign-finance violation, the government must prove that the defendant acted "knowingly and willfully." 52 U.S.C. § 30109(d)(1)(A)(i). That standard requires proof that the defendant knew generally that his conduct was unlawful. *Election Offenses* 123. Given the uncertainties noted above, the "willfulness" requirement would pose a substantial barrier to prosecution.

iii. Constitutional Considerations

Finally, the First Amendment could pose constraints on a prosecution. Harm to Ongoing Matter

iv. Analysis as to HOM

4. False Statements and Obstruction of the Investigation

The Office determined that certain individuals associated with the Campaign lied to investigators about Campaign contacts with Russia and have taken other actions to interfere with the investigation. As explained below, the Office therefore charged some U.S. persons connected to the Campaign with false statements and obstruction offenses.

a. *Overview Of Governing Law*

False Statements. The principal federal statute criminalizing false statements to government investigators is 18 U.S.C. § 1001. As relevant here, under Section 1001(a)(2), it is a crime to knowingly and willfully "make[] any materially false, fictitious, or fraudulent statement or representation" "in any matter within the jurisdiction of the executive . . . branch of the Government." An FBI investigation is a matter within the Executive Branch's jurisdiction. *United States v. Rodgers*, 466 U.S. 475, 479 (1984). The statute also applies to a subset of legislative branch actions—*viz.*, administrative matters and "investigation[s] or review[s]" conducted by a congressional committee or subcommittee. 18 U.S.C. § 1001(c)(1) and (2); *see United States v. Pickett*, 353 F.3d 62, 66 (D.C. Cir. 2004).

Whether the statement was made to law enforcement or congressional investigators, the government must prove beyond a reasonable doubt the same basic non-jurisdictional elements: the statement was false, fictitious, or fraudulent; the defendant knew both that it was false and that it was unlawful to make a false statement; and the false statement was material. *See, e.g., United States v. Smith*, 831 F.3d 1207, 1222 n.27 (9th Cir. 2017) (listing elements); *see also* Ninth Circuit Pattern Instruction 8.73 & cmt. (explaining that the Section 1001 jury instruction was modified in light of the Department of Justice's position that the phrase "knowingly and willfully" in the statute requires the defendant's knowledge that his or her conduct was unlawful). In the D.C. Circuit, the government must prove that the statement was actually false; a statement that is misleading but "literally true" does not satisfy Section 1001(a)(2). *See United States v. Milton*, 8 F.3d 39, 45

(D.C. Cir. 1993); *United States v. Dale*, 991 F.2d 819, 832-33 & n.22 (D.C. Cir. 1993). For that false statement to qualify as "material," it must have a natural tendency to influence, or be capable of influencing, a discrete decision or any other function of the agency to which it is addressed. *See United States v. Gaudin*, 515 U.S. 506, 509 (1995); *United States v. Moore*, 612 F.3d 698, 701 (D.C. Cir. 2010).

Perjury. Under the federal perjury statutes, it is a crime for a witness testifying under oath before a grand jury to knowingly make any false material declaration. *See* 18 U.S.C. § 1623. The government must prove four elements beyond a reasonable doubt to obtain a conviction under Section 1623(a): the defendant testified under oath before a federal grand jury; the defendant's testimony was false in one or more respects; the false testimony concerned matters that were material to the grand jury investigation; and the false testimony was knowingly given. *United States v. Bridges*, 717 F.2d 1444, 1449 n.30 (D.C. Cir. 1983). The general perjury statute, 18 U.S.C. § 1621, also applies to grand jury testimony and has similar elements, except that it requires that the witness have acted willfully and that the government satisfy "strict common-law requirements for establishing falsity." *See Dunn v. United States*, 442 U.S. 100, 106 & n.6 (1979) (explaining "the two-witness rule" and the corroboration that it demands).

Obstruction of Justice. Three basic elements are common to the obstruction statutes pertinent to this Office's charging decisions: an obstructive act; some form of nexus between the obstructive act and an official proceeding; and criminal (*i.e.*, corrupt) intent. A detailed discussion of those elements, and the law governing obstruction of justice more generally, is included in Volume II of the report.

b. Application to Certain Individuals

i. George Papadopoulos

Investigators approached Papadopoulos for an interview based on his role as a foreign policy advisor to the Trump Campaign and his suggestion to a foreign government representative that Russia had indicated that it could assist the Campaign through the anonymous release of information damaging to candidate Clinton. On January 27, 2017, Papadopoulos agreed to be interviewed by FBI agents, who informed him that the interview was part of the investigation into potential Russian government interference in the 2016 presidential election.

During the interview, Papadopoulos lied about the timing, extent, and nature of his communications with Joseph Mifsud, Olga Polonskaya, and Ivan Timofeev. With respect to timing, Papadopoulos acknowledged that he had met Mifsud and that Mifsud told him the Russians had "dirt" on Clinton in the form of "thousands of emails." But Papadopoulos stated multiple times that those communications occurred before he joined the Trump Campaign and that it was a "very strange coincidence" to be told of the "dirt" before he started working for the Campaign. This account was false. Papadopoulos met Mifsud for the first time on approximately March 14, 2016, after Papadopoulos had already learned he would be a foreign policy advisor for the Campaign. Mifsud showed interest in Papadopoulos only after learning of his role on the Campaign. And Mifsud told Papadopoulos about the Russians possessing "dirt" on candidate Clinton in late April 2016, more than a month after Papadopoulos had joined the Campaign and been publicly announced by candidate Trump. Statement of Offense ¶¶ 25-26, *United States v. George Papadopoulos*, No. 1:17-cr-182 (D.D.C. Oct. 5, 2017), Doc. 19 ("*Papadopoulos* Statement of Offense").

Papadopoulos also made false statements in an effort to minimize the extent and importance of his communications with Mifsud. For example, Papadopoulos stated that "[Mifsud]'s a nothing," that he thought Mifsud was "just a guy talk[ing] up connections or something," and that he believed Mifsud was "BS'ing to be completely honest with you." In fact, however, Papadopoulos understood Mifsud to have substantial connections to high-level Russian government officials and that Mifsud spoke with some of those officials in Moscow before telling Papadopoulos about the "dirt." Papadopoulos also engaged in extensive communications over a period of months with Mifsud about foreign policy issues for the Campaign, including efforts to arrange a "history making" meeting between the Campaign and Russian government officials. In addition, Papadopoulos failed to inform investigators that Mifsud had introduced him to Timofeev, the Russian national who Papadopoulos understood to be connected to the Russian Ministry of Foreign Affairs, despite being asked if he had met with Russian nationals or "[a]nyone with a Russian accent" during the campaign. *Papadopoulos* Statement of Offense ¶¶ 27-29.

Papadopoulos also falsely claimed that he met Polonskaya before he joined the Campaign, and falsely told the FBI that he had "no" relationship at all with her. He stated that the extent of their communications was her sending emails—"Just, 'Hi, how are you?' That's it." In truth, however, Papadopoulos met Polonskaya on March 24, 2016, after he had joined the Campaign; he believed that she had connections to high-level Russian government officials and could help him arrange a potential foreign policy trip to Russia. During the campaign he emailed and spoke with her over Skype on numerous occasions about the potential foreign policy trip to Russia. *Papadopoulos* Statement of Offense ¶¶ 30-31.

Papadopoulos's false statements in January 2017 impeded the FBI's investigation into Russian interference in the 2016 presidential election. Most immediately, those statements hindered investigators' ability to effectively question Mifsud when he was interviewed in the lobby of a Washington, D.C. hotel on February 10, 2017. *See* Gov't Sent. Mem. at 6, *United States v. George Papadopoulos*, No. 1:17-cr-182 (D.D.C. Aug. 18, 2017), Doc. 44. During that interview, Mifsud admitted to knowing Papadopoulos and to having introduced him to Polonskaya and Timofeev. But Mifsud denied that he had advance knowledge that Russia was in possession of emails damaging to candidate Clinton, stating that he and Papadopoulos had discussed cybersecurity and hacking as a larger issue and that Papadopoulos must have misunderstood their conversation. Mifsud also falsely stated that he had not seen Papadopoulos since the meeting at which Mifsud introduced him to Polonskaya, even though emails, text messages, and other information show that Mifsud met with Papadopoulos on at least two other occasions—April 12 and April 26, 2016. In addition, Mifsud omitted that he had drafted (or edited) the follow-up message that Polonskaya sent to Papadopoulos following the initial meeting and that, as reflected in the language of that email chain ("Baby, thank you!"), Mifsud may have been involved in a personal relationship with Polonskaya at the time. The false information and omissions in Papadopoulos's January 2017 interview undermined investigators' ability to challenge Mifsud when he made these inaccurate statements.

Given the seriousness of the lies and omissions and their effect on the FBI's investigation, the Office charged Papadopoulos with making false statements to the FBI, in violation of 18 U.S.C. § 1001. Information, *United States v. George Papadopoulos*, No. 1:17-cr-182 (D.D.C. Oct. 3, 2017), Doc. 8. On October 7, 2017, Papadopoulos pleaded guilty to that charge pursuant to a plea agreement. On September 7, 2018, he was sentenced to 14 days of imprisonment, a $9,500 fine, and 200 hours of community service.

ii. PP

iii. Michael Flynn

Michael Flynn agreed to be interviewed by the FBI on January 24, 2017, four days after he had officially assumed his duties as National Security Advisor to the President. During the interview, Flynn made several false statements pertaining to his communications with the Russian ambassador.

First, Flynn made two false statements about his conversations with Russian Ambassador Kislyak in late December 2016, at a time when the United States had imposed sanctions on Russia for interfering with the 2016 presidential election and Russia was considering its response. *See Flynn* Statement of Offense. Flynn told the agents that he did not ask Kislyak to refrain from escalating the situation in response to the United States's imposition of sanctions. That statement was false. On December 29, 2016, Flynn called Kislyak to request Russian restraint. Flynn made the call immediately after speaking to a senior Transition Team official (K.T. McFarland) about what to communicate to Kislyak. Flynn then spoke with McFarland again after the Kislyak call to report on the substance of that conversation. Flynn also falsely told the FBI that he did not remember a follow-up conversation in which Kislyak stated that Russia had chosen to moderate its response to the U.S. sanctions as a result of Flynn's request. On December 31, 2016, Flynn in fact had such a conversation with Kislyak, and he again spoke with McFarland within hours of the call to relay the substance of his conversation with Kislyak. *See Flynn* Statement of Offense ¶ 3.

194

Second, Flynn made false statements about calls he had previously made to representatives of Russia and other countries regarding a resolution submitted by Egypt to the United Nations Security Council on December 21, 2016. Specifically, Flynn stated that he only asked the countries' positions on how they would vote on the resolution and that he did not request that any of the countries take any particular action on the resolution. That statement was false. On December 22, 2016, Flynn called Kislyak, informed him of the incoming Trump Administration's opposition to the resolution, and requested that Russia vote against or delay the resolution. Flynn also falsely stated that Kislyak never described Russia's response to his December 22 request regarding the resolution. Kislyak in fact told Flynn in a conversation on December 23, 2016, that Russia would not vote against the resolution if it came to a vote. *See Flynn* Statement of Offense ¶ 4.

Flynn made these false statements to the FBI at a time when he was serving as National Security Advisor and when the FBI had an open investigation into Russian interference in the 2016 presidential election, including the nature of any links between the Trump Campaign and Russia. Flynn's false statements and omissions impeded and otherwise had a material impact on that ongoing investigation. *Flynn* Statement of Offense ¶¶ 1-2. They also came shortly before Flynn made separate submissions to the Department of Justice, pursuant to FARA, that also contained materially false statements and omissions. *Id.* ¶ 5. Based on the totality of that conduct, the Office decided to charge Flynn with making false statements to the FBI, in violation of 18 U.S.C. § 1001(a). On December 1, 2017, and pursuant to a plea agreement, Flynn pleaded guilty to that charge and also admitted his false statements to the Department in his FARA filing. *See id.*; Plea Agreement, *United States v. Michael T. Flynn*, No. 1:17-cr-232 (D.D.C. Dec. 1, 2017), Doc. 3. Flynn is awaiting sentencing.

iv. Michael Cohen

Michael Cohen was the executive vice president and special counsel to the Trump Organization when Trump was president of the Trump Organization. Information ¶ 1, *United States v. Cohen*, No. 1:18-cr-850 (S.D.N.Y. Nov. 29, 2018), Doc. 2 ("*Cohen* Information"). From the fall of 2015 through approximately June 2016, Cohen was involved in a project to build a Trump-branded tower and adjoining development in Moscow. The project was known as Trump Tower Moscow.

In 2017, Cohen was called to testify before the House Permanent Select Committee on Intelligence (HPSCI) and the Senate Select Committee on Intelligence (SSCI), both of which were investigating Russian interference in the 2016 presidential election and possible links between Russia and the presidential campaigns. In late August 2017, in advance of his testimony, Cohen caused a two-page statement to be sent to SSCI and HPSCI addressing Trump Tower Moscow. *Cohen* Information ¶¶ 2-3. The letter contained three representations relevant here. First, Cohen stated that the Trump Moscow project had ended in January 2016 and that he had briefed candidate Trump on the project only three times before making the unilateral decision to terminate it. Second, Cohen represented that he never agreed to travel to Russia in connection with the project and never considered asking Trump to travel for the project. Third, Cohen stated that he did not recall any Russian government contact about the project, including any response to an email that

195

he had sent to a Russian government email account. *Cohen* Information ¶ 4. Cohen later asked that his two-page statement be incorporated into his testimony's transcript before SSCI, and he ultimately gave testimony to SSCI that was consistent with that statement. *Cohen* Information ¶ 5.

Each of the foregoing representations in Cohen's two-page statement was false and misleading. Consideration of the project had extended through approximately June 2016 and included more than three progress reports from Cohen to Trump. Cohen had discussed with Felix Sater his own travel to Russia as part of the project, and he had inquired about the possibility of Trump traveling there—both with the candidate himself and with senior campaign official Corey Lewandowski. Cohen did recall that he had received a response to the email that he sent to Russian government spokesman Dmitry Peskov—in particular, that he received an email reply and had a follow-up phone conversation with an English-speaking assistant to Peskov in mid-January 2016. *Cohen* Information ¶ 7. Cohen knew the statements in the letter to be false at the time, and admitted that he made them in an effort (1) to minimize the links between the project and Trump (who by this time was President), and (2) to give the false impression that the project had ended before the first vote in the Republican Party primary process, in the hopes of limiting the ongoing Russia investigations. *Id.*

Given the nature of the false statements and the fact that he repeated them during his initial interview with the Office, we charged Cohen with violating Section 1001. On November 29, 2018, Cohen pleaded guilty pursuant to a plea agreement to a single-count information charging him with making false statements in a matter within the jurisdiction of the legislative branch, in violation of 18 U.S.C. § 1001(a)(2) and (c). *Cohen* Information. The case was transferred to the district judge presiding over the separate prosecution of Cohen pursued by the Southern District of New York (after a referral from our Office). On December 7, 2018, this Office submitted a letter to that judge recommending that Cohen's cooperation with our investigation be taken into account in sentencing Cohen on both the false-statements charge and the offenses in the Southern District prosecution. On December 12, 2018, the judge sentenced Cohen to two months of imprisonment on the false-statements count, to run concurrently with a 36-month sentence imposed on the other counts.

v. HOM

Harm to Ongoing Matter

196

256

Harm to Ongoing Matter

Harm to Ongoing Matter

Harm to Ongoing Matter

vi. Jeff Sessions

As set forth in Volume I, Section IV.A.6, *supra*, the investigation established that, while a U.S. Senator and a Trump Campaign advisor, former Attorney General Jeff Sessions interacted with Russian Ambassador Kislyak during the week of the Republican National Convention in July 2016 and again at a meeting in Sessions's Senate office in September 2016. The investigation also established that Sessions and Kislyak both attended a reception held before candidate Trump's

197

foreign policy speech at the Mayflower Hotel in Washington, D.C., in April 2016, and that it is possible that they met briefly at that reception.

The Office considered whether, in light of these interactions, Sessions committed perjury before, or made false statements to, Congress in connection with his confirmation as Attorney General. In January 2017 testimony during his confirmation hearing, Sessions stated in response to a question about Trump Campaign communications with the Russian government that he had "been called a surrogate at a time or two in that campaign and I didn't have – did not have communications with the Russians." In written responses submitted on January 17, 2017, Sessions answered "[n]o" to a question asking whether he had "been in contact with anyone connected to any part of the Russian government about the 2016 election, either before or after election day." And, in a March 2017 supplement to his testimony, Sessions identified two of the campaign-period contacts with Ambassador Kislyak noted above, which had been reported in the media following the January 2017 confirmation hearing. Sessions stated in the supplemental response that he did "not recall any discussions with the Russian Ambassador, or any other representatives of the Russian government, regarding the political campaign on these occasions or any other occasion."

Although the investigation established that Sessions interacted with Kislyak on the occasions described above and that Kislyak mentioned the presidential campaign on at least one occasion, the evidence is not sufficient to prove that Sessions gave knowingly false answers to Russia-related questions in light of the wording and context of those questions. With respect to Sessions's statements that he did "not recall any discussions with the Russian Ambassador . . . regarding the political campaign" and he had not been in contact with any Russian official "about the 2016 election," the evidence concerning the nature of Sessions's interactions with Kislyak makes it plausible that Sessions did not recall discussing the campaign with Kislyak at the time of his statements. Similarly, while Sessions stated in his January 2017 oral testimony that he "did not have communications with Russians," he did so in response to a question that had linked such communications to an alleged "continuing exchange of information" between the Trump Campaign and Russian government intermediaries. Sessions later explained to the Senate and to the Office that he understood the question as narrowly calling for disclosure of interactions with Russians that involved the exchange of campaign information, as distinguished from more routine contacts with Russian nationals. Given the context in which the question was asked, that understanding is plausible.

Accordingly, the Office concluded that the evidence was insufficient to prove that Sessions was willfully untruthful in his answers and thus insufficient to obtain or sustain a conviction for perjury or false statements. Consistent with the Principles of Federal Prosecution, the Office therefore determined not to pursue charges against Sessions and informed his counsel of that decision in March 2018.

vii. Others Interviewed During the Investigation

The Office considered whether, during the course of the investigation, other individuals interviewed either omitted material information or provided information determined to be false. Applying the Principles of Federal Prosecution, the Office did not seek criminal charges against any individuals other than those listed above. In some instances, that decision was due to

198

evidentiary hurdles to proving falsity. In others, the Office determined that the witness ultimately provided truthful information and that considerations of culpability, deterrence, and resource-preservation weighed against prosecution. *See* Justice Manual §§ 9-27.220, 9-27.230.

Personal Privacy

PP

Personal Privacy

Grand Jury
Personal Privacy
Grand Jury
Personal Privacy

PP

Grand Jury

Personal Privacy

PP

Personal Privacy

U.S. Department of Justice

~~Attorney Work Product // May Contain Material Protected Under Fed. R. Crim. P. 6(e)~~

Report On The Investigation Into Russian Interference In The 2016 Presidential Election

Volume II of II

Special Counsel Robert S. Mueller, III

Submitted Pursuant to 28 C.F.R. § 600.8(c)

Washington, D.C.

March 2019

U.S. Department of Justice

~~Attorney Work Product // May Contain Material Protected Under Fed. R. Crim. P. 6(e)~~

TABLE OF CONTENTS – VOLUME II

i

ii

iii

U.S. Department of Justice

~~Attorney Work Product~~ // ~~May Contain Material Protected Under Fed. R. Crim. P. 6(e)~~

U.S. Department of Justice

~~Attorney Work Product // May Contain Material Protected Under Fed. R. Crim. P. 6(e)~~

INTRODUCTION TO VOLUME II

This report is submitted to the Attorney General pursuant to 28 C.F.R. § 600.8(c), which states that, "[a]t the conclusion of the Special Counsel's work, he . . . shall provide the Attorney General a confidential report explaining the prosecution or declination decisions [the Special Counsel] reached."

Beginning in 2017, the President of the United States took a variety of actions towards the ongoing FBI investigation into Russia's interference in the 2016 presidential election and related matters that raised questions about whether he had obstructed justice. The Order appointing the Special Counsel gave this Office jurisdiction to investigate matters that arose directly from the FBI's Russia investigation, including whether the President had obstructed justice in connection with Russia-related investigations. The Special Counsel's jurisdiction also covered potentially obstructive acts related to the Special Counsel's investigation itself. This Volume of our report summarizes our obstruction-of-justice investigation of the President.

We first describe the considerations that guided our obstruction-of-justice investigation, and then provide an overview of this Volume:

First, a traditional prosecution or declination decision entails a binary determination to initiate or decline a prosecution, but we determined not to make a traditional prosecutorial judgment. The Office of Legal Counsel (OLC) has issued an opinion finding that "the indictment or criminal prosecution of a sitting President would impermissibly undermine the capacity of the executive branch to perform its constitutionally assigned functions" in violation of "the constitutional separation of powers."[1] Given the role of the Special Counsel as an attorney in the Department of Justice and the framework of the Special Counsel regulations, *see* 28 U.S.C. § 515; 28 C.F.R. § 600.7(a), this Office accepted OLC's legal conclusion for the purpose of exercising prosecutorial jurisdiction. And apart from OLC's constitutional view, we recognized that a federal criminal accusation against a sitting President would place burdens on the President's capacity to govern and potentially preempt constitutional processes for addressing presidential misconduct.[2]

Second, while the OLC opinion concludes that a sitting President may not be prosecuted, it recognizes that a criminal investigation during the President's term is permissible.[3] The OLC opinion also recognizes that a President does not have immunity after he leaves office.[4] And if individuals other than the President committed an obstruction offense, they may be prosecuted at this time. Given those considerations, the facts known to us, and the strong public interest in

[1] *A Sitting President's Amenability to Indictment and Criminal Prosecution*, 24 Op. O.L.C. 222, 222, 260 (2000) (OLC Op.).

[2] *See* U.S. CONST. Art. I § 2, cl. 5; § 3, cl. 6; *cf.* OLC Op. at 257-258 (discussing relationship between impeachment and criminal prosecution of a sitting President).

[3] OLC Op. at 257 n.36 ("A grand jury could continue to gather evidence throughout the period of immunity").

[4] OLC Op. at 255 ("Recognizing an immunity from prosecution for a sitting President would not preclude such prosecution once the President's term is over or he is otherwise removed from office by resignation or impeachment").

1

safeguarding the integrity of the criminal justice system, we conducted a thorough factual investigation in order to preserve the evidence when memories were fresh and documentary materials were available.

Third, we considered whether to evaluate the conduct we investigated under the Justice Manual standards governing prosecution and declination decisions, but we determined not to apply an approach that could potentially result in a judgment that the President committed crimes. The threshold step under the Justice Manual standards is to assess whether a person's conduct "constitutes a federal offense." U.S. Dep't of Justice, Justice Manual § 9-27.220 (2018) (Justice Manual). Fairness concerns counseled against potentially reaching that judgment when no charges can be brought. The ordinary means for an individual to respond to an accusation is through a speedy and public trial, with all the procedural protections that surround a criminal case. An individual who believes he was wrongly accused can use that process to seek to clear his name. In contrast, a prosecutor's judgment that crimes were committed, but that no charges will be brought, affords no such adversarial opportunity for public name-clearing before an impartial adjudicator.[5]

The concerns about the fairness of such a determination would be heightened in the case of a sitting President, where a federal prosecutor's accusation of a crime, even in an internal report, could carry consequences that extend beyond the realm of criminal justice. OLC noted similar concerns about sealed indictments. Even if an indictment were sealed during the President's term, OLC reasoned, "it would be very difficult to preserve [an indictment's] secrecy," and if an indictment became public, "[t]he stigma and opprobrium" could imperil the President's ability to govern."[6] Although a prosecutor's internal report would not represent a formal public accusation akin to an indictment, the possibility of the report's public disclosure and the absence of a neutral adjudicatory forum to review its findings counseled against potentially determining "that the person's conduct constitutes a federal offense." Justice Manual § 9-27.220.

Fourth, if we had confidence after a thorough investigation of the facts that the President clearly did not commit obstruction of justice, we would so state. Based on the facts and the applicable legal standards, however, we are unable to reach that judgment. The evidence we obtained about the President's actions and intent presents difficult issues that prevent us from conclusively determining that no criminal conduct occurred. Accordingly, while this report does not conclude that the President committed a crime, it also does not exonerate him.

*   *   *

This report on our investigation consists of four parts. Section I provides an overview of obstruction-of-justice principles and summarizes certain investigatory and evidentiary considerations. Section II sets forth the factual results of our obstruction investigation and analyzes the evidence. Section III addresses statutory and constitutional defenses. Section IV states our conclusion.

---

[5] For that reason, criticisms have been lodged against the practice of naming unindicted co-conspirators in an indictment. *See United States v. Briggs*, 514 F.2d 794, 802 (5th Cir. 1975) ("The courts have struck down with strong language efforts by grand juries to accuse persons of crime while affording them no forum in which to vindicate themselves."); *see also* Justice Manual § 9-11.130.

[6] OLC Op. at 259 & n.38 (citation omitted).

2

EXECUTIVE SUMMARY TO VOLUME II

Our obstruction-of-justice inquiry focused on a series of actions by the President that related to the Russian-interference investigations, including the President's conduct towards the law enforcement officials overseeing the investigations and the witnesses to relevant events.

FACTUAL RESULTS OF THE OBSTRUCTION INVESTIGATION

The key issues and events we examined include the following:

The Campaign's response to reports about Russian support for Trump. During the 2016 presidential campaign, questions arose about the Russian government's apparent support for candidate Trump. After WikiLeaks released politically damaging Democratic Party emails that were reported to have been hacked by Russia, Trump publicly expressed skepticism that Russia was responsible for the hacks at the same time that he and other Campaign officials privately sought information ▮Harm to Ongoing Matter▮ about any further planned WikiLeaks releases. Trump also denied having any business in or connections to Russia, even though as late as June 2016 the Trump Organization had been pursuing a licensing deal for a skyscraper to be built in Russia called Trump Tower Moscow. After the election, the President expressed concerns to advisors that reports of Russia's election interference might lead the public to question the legitimacy of his election.

Conduct involving FBI Director Comey and Michael Flynn. In mid-January 2017, incoming National Security Advisor Michael Flynn falsely denied to the Vice President, other administration officials, and FBI agents that he had talked to Russian Ambassador Sergey Kislyak about Russia's response to U.S. sanctions on Russia for its election interference. On January 27, the day after the President was told that Flynn had lied to the Vice President and had made similar statements to the FBI, the President invited FBI Director Comey to a private dinner at the White House and told Comey that he needed loyalty. On February 14, the day after the President requested Flynn's resignation, the President told an outside advisor, "Now that we fired Flynn, the Russia thing is over." The advisor disagreed and said the investigations would continue.

Later that afternoon, the President cleared the Oval Office to have a one-on-one meeting with Comey. Referring to the FBI's investigation of Flynn, the President said, "I hope you can see your way clear to letting this go, to letting Flynn go. He is a good guy. I hope you can let this go." Shortly after requesting Flynn's resignation and speaking privately to Comey, the President sought to have Deputy National Security Advisor K.T. McFarland draft an internal letter stating that the President had not directed Flynn to discuss sanctions with Kislyak. McFarland declined because she did not know whether that was true, and a White House Counsel's Office attorney thought that the request would look like a quid pro quo for an ambassadorship she had been offered.

The President's reaction to the continuing Russia investigation. In February 2017, Attorney General Jeff Sessions began to assess whether he had to recuse himself from campaign-related investigations because of his role in the Trump Campaign. In early March, the President told White House Counsel Donald McGahn to stop Sessions from recusing. And after Sessions announced his recusal on March 2, the President expressed anger at the decision and told advisors that he should have an Attorney General who would protect him. That weekend, the President took Sessions aside at an event and urged him to "unrecuse." Later in March, Comey publicly

3

disclosed at a congressional hearing that the FBI was investigating "the Russian government's efforts to interfere in the 2016 presidential election," including any links or coordination between the Russian government and the Trump Campaign. In the following days, the President reached out to the Director of National Intelligence and the leaders of the Central Intelligence Agency (CIA) and the National Security Agency (NSA) to ask them what they could do to publicly dispel the suggestion that the President had any connection to the Russian election-interference effort. The President also twice called Comey directly, notwithstanding guidance from McGahn to avoid direct contacts with the Department of Justice. Comey had previously assured the President that the FBI was not investigating him personally, and the President asked Comey to "lift the cloud" of the Russia investigation by saying that publicly.

The President's termination of Comey. On May 3, 2017, Comey testified in a congressional hearing, but declined to answer questions about whether the President was personally under investigation. Within days, the President decided to terminate Comey. The President insisted that the termination letter, which was written for public release, state that Comey had informed the President that he was not under investigation. The day of the firing, the White House maintained that Comey's termination resulted from independent recommendations from the Attorney General and Deputy Attorney General that Comey should be discharged for mishandling the Hillary Clinton email investigation. But the President had decided to fire Comey before hearing from the Department of Justice. The day after firing Comey, the President told Russian officials that he had "faced great pressure because of Russia," which had been "taken off" by Comey's firing. The next day, the President acknowledged in a television interview that he was going to fire Comey regardless of the Department of Justice's recommendation and that when he "decided to just do it," he was thinking that "this thing with Trump and Russia is a made-up story." In response to a question about whether he was angry with Comey about the Russia investigation, the President said, "As far as I'm concerned, I want that thing to be absolutely done properly," adding that firing Comey "might even lengthen out the investigation."

The appointment of a Special Counsel and efforts to remove him. On May 17, 2017, the Acting Attorney General for the Russia investigation appointed a Special Counsel to conduct the investigation and related matters. The President reacted to news that a Special Counsel had been appointed by telling advisors that it was "the end of his presidency" and demanding that Sessions resign. Sessions submitted his resignation, but the President ultimately did not accept it. The President told aides that the Special Counsel had conflicts of interest and suggested that the Special Counsel therefore could not serve. The President's advisors told him the asserted conflicts were meritless and had already been considered by the Department of Justice.

On June 14, 2017, the media reported that the Special Counsel's Office was investigating whether the President had obstructed justice. Press reports called this "a major turning point" in the investigation: while Comey had told the President he was not under investigation, following Comey's firing, the President now was under investigation. The President reacted to this news with a series of tweets criticizing the Department of Justice and the Special Counsel's investigation. On June 17, 2017, the President called McGahn at home and directed him to call the Acting Attorney General and say that the Special Counsel had conflicts of interest and must be removed. McGahn did not carry out the direction, however, deciding that he would resign rather than trigger what he regarded as a potential Saturday Night Massacre.

4

Efforts to curtail the Special Counsel's investigation. Two days after directing McGahn to have the Special Counsel removed, the President made another attempt to affect the course of the Russia investigation. On June 19, 2017, the President met one-on-one in the Oval Office with his former campaign manager Corey Lewandowski, a trusted advisor outside the government, and dictated a message for Lewandowski to deliver to Sessions. The message said that Sessions should publicly announce that, notwithstanding his recusal from the Russia investigation, the investigation was "very unfair" to the President, the President had done nothing wrong, and Sessions planned to meet with the Special Counsel and "let [him] move forward with investigating election meddling for future elections." Lewandowski said he understood what the President wanted Sessions to do.

One month later, in another private meeting with Lewandowski on July 19, 2017, the President asked about the status of his message for Sessions to limit the Special Counsel investigation to future election interference. Lewandowski told the President that the message would be delivered soon. Hours after that meeting, the President publicly criticized Sessions in an interview with the New York Times, and then issued a series of tweets making it clear that Sessions's job was in jeopardy. Lewandowski did not want to deliver the President's message personally, so he asked senior White House official Rick Dearborn to deliver it to Sessions. Dearborn was uncomfortable with the task and did not follow through.

Efforts to prevent public disclosure of evidence. In the summer of 2017, the President learned that media outlets were asking questions about the June 9, 2016 meeting at Trump Tower between senior campaign officials, including Donald Trump Jr., and a Russian lawyer who was said to be offering damaging information about Hillary Clinton as "part of Russia and its government's support for Mr. Trump." On several occasions, the President directed aides not to publicly disclose the emails setting up the June 9 meeting, suggesting that the emails would not leak and that the number of lawyers with access to them should be limited. Before the emails became public, the President edited a press statement for Trump Jr. by deleting a line that acknowledged that the meeting was with "an individual who [Trump Jr.] was told might have information helpful to the campaign" and instead said only that the meeting was about adoptions of Russian children. When the press asked questions about the President's involvement in Trump Jr.'s statement, the President's personal lawyer repeatedly denied the President had played any role.

Further efforts to have the Attorney General take control of the investigation. In early summer 2017, the President called Sessions at home and again asked him to reverse his recusal from the Russia investigation. Sessions did not reverse his recusal. In October 2017, the President met privately with Sessions in the Oval Office and asked him to "take [a] look" at investigating Clinton. In December 2017, shortly after Flynn pleaded guilty pursuant to a cooperation agreement, the President met with Sessions in the Oval Office and suggested, according to notes taken by a senior advisor, that if Sessions unrecused and took back supervision of the Russia investigation, he would be a "hero." The President told Sessions, "I'm not going to do anything or direct you to do anything. I just want to be treated fairly." In response, Sessions volunteered that he had never seen anything "improper" on the campaign and told the President there was a "whole new leadership team" in place. He did not unrecuse.

Efforts to have McGahn deny that the President had ordered him to have the Special Counsel removed. In early 2018, the press reported that the President had directed McGahn to

5

have the Special Counsel removed in June 2017 and that McGahn had threatened to resign rather than carry out the order. The President reacted to the news stories by directing White House officials to tell McGahn to dispute the story and create a record stating he had not been ordered to have the Special Counsel removed. McGahn told those officials that the media reports were accurate in stating that the President had directed McGahn to have the Special Counsel removed. The President then met with McGahn in the Oval Office and again pressured him to deny the reports. In the same meeting, the President also asked McGahn why he had told the Special Counsel about the President's effort to remove the Special Counsel and why McGahn took notes of his conversations with the President. McGahn refused to back away from what he remembered happening and perceived the President to be testing his mettle.

Conduct towards Flynn, Manafort, HOM . After Flynn withdrew from a joint defense agreement with the President and began cooperating with the government, the President's personal counsel left a message for Flynn's attorneys reminding them of the President's warm feelings towards Flynn, which he said "still remains," and asking for a "heads up" if Flynn knew "information that implicates the President." When Flynn's counsel reiterated that Flynn could no longer share information pursuant to a joint defense agreement, the President's personal counsel said he would make sure that the President knew that Flynn's actions reflected "hostility" towards the President. During Manafort's prosecution and when the jury in his criminal trial was deliberating, the President praised Manafort in public, said that Manafort was being treated unfairly, and declined to rule out a pardon. After Manafort was convicted, the President called Manafort "a brave man" for refusing to "break" and said that "flipping" "almost ought to be outlawed." Harm to Ongoing Matter

Conduct involving Michael Cohen. The President's conduct towards Michael Cohen, a former Trump Organization executive, changed from praise for Cohen when he falsely minimized the President's involvement in the Trump Tower Moscow project, to castigation of Cohen when he became a cooperating witness. From September 2015 to June 2016, Cohen had pursued the Trump Tower Moscow project on behalf of the Trump Organization and had briefed candidate Trump on the project numerous times, including discussing whether Trump should travel to Russia to advance the deal. In 2017, Cohen provided false testimony to Congress about the project, including stating that he had only briefed Trump on the project three times and never discussed travel to Russia with him, in an effort to adhere to a "party line" that Cohen said was developed to minimize the President's connections to Russia. While preparing for his congressional testimony, Cohen had extensive discussions with the President's personal counsel, who, according to Cohen, said that Cohen should "stay on message" and not contradict the President. After the FBI searched Cohen's home and office in April 2018, the President publicly asserted that Cohen would not "flip," contacted him directly to tell him to "stay strong," and privately passed messages of support to him. Cohen also discussed pardons with the President's personal counsel and believed that if he stayed on message he would be taken care of. But after Cohen began cooperating with the government in the summer of 2018, the President publicly criticized him, called him a "rat," and suggested that his family members had committed crimes.

6

270

Overarching factual issues. We did not make a traditional prosecution decision about these facts, but the evidence we obtained supports several general statements about the President's conduct.

Several features of the conduct we investigated distinguish it from typical obstruction-of-justice cases. First, the investigation concerned the President, and some of his actions, such as firing the FBI director, involved facially lawful acts within his Article II authority, which raises constitutional issues discussed below. At the same time, the President's position as the head of the Executive Branch provided him with unique and powerful means of influencing official proceedings, subordinate officers, and potential witnesses—all of which is relevant to a potential obstruction-of-justice analysis. Second, unlike cases in which a subject engages in obstruction of justice to cover up a crime, the evidence we obtained did not establish that the President was involved in an underlying crime related to Russian election interference. Although the obstruction statutes do not require proof of such a crime, the absence of that evidence affects the analysis of the President's intent and requires consideration of other possible motives for his conduct. Third, many of the President's acts directed at witnesses, including discouragement of cooperation with the government and suggestions of possible future pardons, took place in public view. That circumstance is unusual, but no principle of law excludes public acts from the reach of the obstruction laws. If the likely effect of public acts is to influence witnesses or alter their testimony, the harm to the justice system's integrity is the same.

Although the series of events we investigated involved discrete acts, the overall pattern of the President's conduct towards the investigations can shed light on the nature of the President's acts and the inferences that can be drawn about his intent. In particular, the actions we investigated can be divided into two phases, reflecting a possible shift in the President's motives. The first phase covered the period from the President's first interactions with Comey through the President's firing of Comey. During that time, the President had been repeatedly told he was not personally under investigation. Soon after the firing of Comey and the appointment of the Special Counsel, however, the President became aware that his own conduct was being investigated in an obstruction-of-justice inquiry. At that point, the President engaged in a second phase of conduct, involving public attacks on the investigation, non-public efforts to control it, and efforts in both public and private to encourage witnesses not to cooperate with the investigation. Judgments about the nature of the President's motives during each phase would be informed by the totality of the evidence.

STATUTORY AND CONSTITUTIONAL DEFENSES

The President's counsel raised statutory and constitutional defenses to a possible obstruction-of-justice analysis of the conduct we investigated. We concluded that none of those legal defenses provided a basis for declining to investigate the facts.

Statutory defenses. Consistent with precedent and the Department of Justice's general approach to interpreting obstruction statutes, we concluded that several statutes could apply here. *See* 18 U.S.C. §§ 1503, 1505, 1512(b)(3), 1512(c)(2). Section 1512(c)(2) is an omnibus obstruction-of-justice provision that covers a range of obstructive acts directed at pending or contemplated official proceedings. No principle of statutory construction justifies narrowing the provision to cover only conduct that impairs the integrity or availability of evidence. Sections 1503 and 1505 also offer broad protection against obstructive acts directed at pending grand jury,

7

judicial, administrative, and congressional proceedings, and they are supplemented by a provision in Section 1512(b) aimed specifically at conduct intended to prevent or hinder the communication to law enforcement of information related to a federal crime.

Constitutional defenses. As for constitutional defenses arising from the President's status as the head of the Executive Branch, we recognized that the Department of Justice and the courts have not definitively resolved these issues. We therefore examined those issues through the framework established by Supreme Court precedent governing separation-of-powers issues. The Department of Justice and the President's personal counsel have recognized that the President is subject to statutes that prohibit obstruction of justice by bribing a witness or suborning perjury because that conduct does not implicate his constitutional authority. With respect to whether the President can be found to have obstructed justice by exercising his powers under Article II of the Constitution, we concluded that Congress has authority to prohibit a President's corrupt use of his authority in order to protect the integrity of the administration of justice.

Under applicable Supreme Court precedent, the Constitution does not categorically and permanently immunize a President for obstructing justice through the use of his Article II powers. The separation-of-powers doctrine authorizes Congress to protect official proceedings, including those of courts and grand juries, from corrupt, obstructive acts regardless of their source. We also concluded that any inroad on presidential authority that would occur from prohibiting corrupt acts does not undermine the President's ability to fulfill his constitutional mission. The term "corruptly" sets a demanding standard. It requires a concrete showing that a person acted with an intent to obtain an improper advantage for himself or someone else, inconsistent with official duty and the rights of others. A preclusion of "corrupt" official action does not diminish the President's ability to exercise Article II powers. For example, the proper supervision of criminal law does not demand freedom for the President to act with a corrupt intention of shielding himself from criminal punishment, avoiding financial liability, or preventing personal embarrassment. To the contrary, a statute that prohibits official action undertaken for such corrupt purposes furthers, rather than hinders, the impartial and evenhanded administration of the law. It also aligns with the President's constitutional duty to faithfully execute the laws. Finally, we concluded that in the rare case in which a criminal investigation of the President's conduct is justified, inquiries to determine whether the President acted for a corrupt motive should not impermissibly chill his performance of his constitutionally assigned duties. The conclusion that Congress may apply the obstruction laws to the President's corrupt exercise of the powers of office accords with our constitutional system of checks and balances and the principle that no person is above the law.

CONCLUSION

Because we determined not to make a traditional prosecutorial judgment, we did not draw ultimate conclusions about the President's conduct. The evidence we obtained about the President's actions and intent presents difficult issues that would need to be resolved if we were making a traditional prosecutorial judgment. At the same time, if we had confidence after a thorough investigation of the facts that the President clearly did not commit obstruction of justice, we would so state. Based on the facts and the applicable legal standards, we are unable to reach that judgment. Accordingly, while this report does not conclude that the President committed a crime, it also does not exonerate him.

8

I. BACKGROUND LEGAL AND EVIDENTIARY PRINCIPLES

A.   Legal Framework of Obstruction of Justice

The May 17, 2017 Appointment Order and the Special Counsel regulations provide this Office with jurisdiction to investigate "federal crimes committed in the course of, and with intent to interfere with, the Special Counsel's investigation, such as perjury, obstruction of justice, destruction of evidence, and intimidation of witnesses." 28 C.F.R. § 600.4(a). Because of that description of our jurisdiction, we sought evidence for our obstruction-of-justice investigation with the elements of obstruction offenses in mind. Our evidentiary analysis is similarly focused on the elements of such offenses, although we do not draw conclusions on the ultimate questions that govern a prosecutorial decision under the Principles of Federal Prosecution. *See* Justice Manual § 9-27.000 *et seq.* (2018).

Here, we summarize the law interpreting the elements of potentially relevant obstruction statutes in an ordinary case. This discussion does not address the unique constitutional issues that arise in an inquiry into official acts by the President. Those issues are discussed in a later section of this report addressing constitutional defenses that the President's counsel have raised. *See* Volume II, Section III.B, *infra*.

Three basic elements are common to most of the relevant obstruction statutes: (1) an obstructive act; (2) a nexus between the obstructive act and an official proceeding; and (3) a corrupt intent. *See*, *e.g.*, 18 U.S.C. §§ 1503, 1505, 1512(c)(2). We describe those elements as they have been interpreted by the courts. We then discuss a more specific statute aimed at witness tampering, *see* 18 U.S.C. § 1512(b), and describe the requirements for attempted offenses and endeavors to obstruct justice, *see* 18 U.S.C. §§ 1503, 1512(c)(2).

Obstructive act.   Obstruction-of-justice law "reaches all corrupt conduct capable of producing an effect that prevents justice from being duly administered, regardless of the means employed." *United States v. Silverman*, 745 F.2d 1386, 1393 (11th Cir. 1984) (interpreting 18 U.S.C. § 1503). An "effort to influence" a proceeding can qualify as an endeavor to obstruct justice even if the effort was "subtle or circuitous" and "however cleverly or with whatever cloaking of purpose" it was made. *United States v. Roe*, 529 F.2d 629, 632 (4th Cir. 1975); *see also United States v. Quattrone*, 441 F.3d 153, 173 (2d Cir. 2006). The verbs "'obstruct or impede' are broad" and "can refer to anything that blocks, makes difficult, or hinders." *Marinello v. United States*, 138 S. Ct. 1101, 1106 (2018) (internal brackets and quotation marks omitted).

An improper motive can render an actor's conduct criminal even when the conduct would otherwise be lawful and within the actor's authority. *See United States v. Cueto*, 151 F.3d 620, 631 (7th Cir. 1998) (affirming obstruction conviction of a criminal defense attorney for "litigation-related conduct"); *United States v. Cintolo*, 818 F.2d 980, 992 (1st Cir. 1987) ("any act by any party—whether lawful or unlawful on its face—may abridge § 1503 if performed with a corrupt motive").

Nexus to a pending or contemplated official proceeding. Obstruction-of-justice law generally requires a nexus, or connection, to an official proceeding. In Section 1503, the nexus must be to pending "judicial or grand jury proceedings." *United States v. Aguilar*, 515 U.S. 593,

9

599 (1995). In Section 1505, the nexus can include a connection to a "pending" federal agency proceeding or a congressional inquiry or investigation. Under both statutes, the government must demonstrate "a relationship in time, causation, or logic" between the obstructive act and the proceeding or inquiry to be obstructed. *Id.* at 599; *see also Arthur Andersen LLP v. United States,* 544 U.S. 696, 707-708 (2005). Section 1512(c) prohibits obstructive efforts aimed at official proceedings including judicial or grand jury proceedings. 18 U.S.C. § 1515(a)(1)(A). "For purposes of" Section 1512, "an official proceeding need not be pending or about to be instituted at the time of the offense." 18 U.S.C. § 1512(f)(1). Although a proceeding need not already be in progress to trigger liability under Section 1512(c), a nexus to a contemplated proceeding still must be shown. *United States v. Young,* 916 F.3d 368, 386 (4th Cir. 2019); *United States v. Petruk,* 781 F.3d 438, 445 (8th Cir. 2015); *United States v. Phillips,* 583 F.3d 1261, 1264 (10th Cir. 2009); *United States v. Reich,* 479 F.3d 179, 186 (2d Cir. 2007). The nexus requirement narrows the scope of obstruction statutes to ensure that individuals have "fair warning" of what the law proscribes. *Aguilar,* 515 U.S. at 600 (internal quotation marks omitted).

The nexus showing has subjective and objective components. As an objective matter, a defendant must act "in a manner that is *likely* to obstruct justice," such that the statute "excludes defendants who have an evil purpose but use means that would only unnaturally and improbably be successful." *Aguilar,* 515 U.S. at 601-602 (emphasis added; internal quotation marks omitted). "[T]he endeavor must have the natural and probable effect of interfering with the due administration of justice." *Id.* at 599 (citation and internal quotation marks omitted). As a subjective matter, the actor must have "contemplated a particular, foreseeable proceeding." *Petruk,* 781 F.3d at 445-446. A defendant need not directly impede the proceeding. Rather, a nexus exists if "discretionary actions of a third person would be required to obstruct the judicial proceeding if it was foreseeable to the defendant that the third party would act on the [defendant's] communication in such a way as to obstruct the judicial proceeding." *United States v. Martinez,* 862 F.3d 223, 238 (2d Cir. 2017) (brackets, ellipses, and internal quotation marks omitted).

Corruptly. The word "corruptly" provides the intent element for obstruction of justice and means acting "knowingly and dishonestly" or "with an improper motive." *United States v. Richardson,* 676 F.3d 491, 508 (5th Cir. 2012); *United States v. Gordon,* 710 F.3d 1124, 1151 (10th Cir. 2013) (to act corruptly means to "act[] with an improper purpose and to engage in conduct knowingly and dishonestly with the specific intent to subvert, impede or obstruct" the relevant proceeding) (some quotation marks omitted); *see* 18 U.S.C. § 1515(b) ("As used in section 1505, the term 'corruptly' means acting with an improper purpose, personally or by influencing another."); *see also Arthur Andersen,* 544 U.S. at 705-706 (interpreting "corruptly" to mean "wrongful, immoral, depraved, or evil" and holding that acting "knowingly . . . corruptly" in 18 U.S.C. § 1512(b) requires "consciousness of wrongdoing"). The requisite showing is made when a person acted with an intent to obtain an "improper advantage for [him]self or someone else, inconsistent with official duty and the rights of others." BALLENTINE'S LAW DICTIONARY 276 (3d ed. 1969); *see United States v. Pasha,* 797 F.3d 1122, 1132 (D.C. Cir. 2015); *Aguilar,* 515 U.S. at 616 (Scalia, J., concurring in part and dissenting in part) (characterizing this definition as the "longstanding and well-accepted meaning" of "corruptly").

Witness tampering. A more specific provision in Section 1512 prohibits tampering with a witness. *See* 18 U.S.C. § 1512(b)(1), (3) (making it a crime to "knowingly use[] intimidation . . . or corruptly persuade[] another person," or "engage[] in misleading conduct towards another

10

274

person," with the intent to "influence, delay, or prevent the testimony of any person in an official proceeding" or to "hinder, delay, or prevent the communication to a law enforcement officer . . . of information relating to the commission or possible commission of a Federal offense"). To establish corrupt persuasion, it is sufficient that the defendant asked a potential witness to lie to investigators in contemplation of a likely federal investigation into his conduct. *United States v. Edlind*, 887 F.3d 166, 174 (4th Cir. 2018); *United States v. Sparks*, 791 F.3d 1188, 1191-1192 (10th Cir. 2015); *United States* v. *Byrne*, 435 F.3d 16, 23-26 (1st Cir. 2006); *United States v. LaShay*, 417 F.3d 715, 718-719 (7th Cir. 2005); *United States v. Burns*, 298 F.3d 523, 539-540 (6th Cir. 2002); *United States v. Pennington*, 168 F.3d 1060, 1066 (8th Cir. 1999). The "persuasion" need not be coercive, intimidating, or explicit; it is sufficient to "urge," "induce," "ask[]," "argu[e]," "giv[e] reasons," *Sparks*, 791 F.3d at 1192, or "coach[] or remind[] witnesses by planting misleading facts," *Edlind*, 887 F.3d at 174. Corrupt persuasion is shown "where a defendant tells a potential witness a false story as if the story were true, intending that the witness believe the story and testify to it." *United States v. Rodolitz*, 786 F.2d 77, 82 (2d Cir. 1986); *see United States v. Gabriel*, 125 F.3d 89, 102 (2d Cir. 1997). It also covers urging a witness to recall a fact that the witness did not know, even if the fact was actually true. *See LaShay*, 417 F.3d at 719. Corrupt persuasion also can be shown in certain circumstances when a person, with an improper motive, urges a witness not to cooperate with law enforcement. *See United States v. Shotts*, 145 F.3d 1289, 1301 (11th Cr. 1998) (telling Secretary "not to [say] anything [to the FBI] and [she] would not be bothered").

When the charge is acting with the intent to hinder, delay, or prevent the communication of information to law enforcement under Section 1512(b)(3), the "nexus" to a proceeding inquiry articulated in *Aguilar*—that an individual have "knowledge that his actions are likely to affect the judicial proceeding," 515 U.S. at 599—does not apply because the obstructive act is aimed at the communication of information to investigators, not at impeding an official proceeding.

Acting "knowingly . . . corruptly" requires proof that the individual was "conscious of wrongdoing." *Arthur Andersen*, 544 U.S. at 705-706 (declining to explore "[t]he outer limits of this element" but indicating that an instruction was infirm where it permitted conviction even if the defendant "honestly and sincerely believed that [the] conduct was lawful"). It is an affirmative defense that "the conduct consisted solely of lawful conduct and that the defendant's sole intention was to encourage, induce, or cause the other person to testify truthfully." 18 U.S.C. § 1512(e).

Attempts and endeavors. Section 1512(c)(2) covers both substantive obstruction offenses and attempts to obstruct justice. Under general principles of attempt law, a person is guilty of an attempt when he has the intent to commit a substantive offense and takes an overt act that constitutes a substantial step towards that goal. *See United States v. Resendiz-Ponce*, 549 U.S. 102, 106-107 (2007). "[T]he act [must be] substantial, in that it was strongly corroborative of the defendant's criminal purpose." *United States v. Pratt*, 351 F.3d 131, 135 (4th Cir. 2003). While "mere abstract talk" does not suffice, any "concrete and specific" acts that corroborate the defendant's intent can constitute a "substantial step." *United States v. Irving*, 665 F.3d 1184, 1198-1205 (10th Cir. 2011). Thus, "soliciting an innocent agent to engage in conduct constituting an element of the crime" may qualify as a substantial step. Model Penal Code § 5.01(2)(g); *see United States v. Lucas*, 499 F.3d 769, 781 (8th Cir. 2007).

11

The omnibus clause of 18 U.S.C. § 1503 prohibits an "endeavor" to obstruct justice, which sweeps more broadly than Section 1512's attempt provision. *See United States v. Sampson*, 898 F.3d 287, 302 (2d Cir. 2018); *United States v. Leisure*, 844 F.2d 1347, 1366-1367 (8th Cir. 1988) (collecting cases). "It is well established that a[n] [obstruction-of-justice] offense is complete when one corruptly endeavors to obstruct or impede the due administration of justice; the prosecution need not prove that the due administration of justice was actually obstructed or impeded." *United States v. Davis*, 854 F.3d 1276, 1292 (11th Cir. 2017) (internal quotation marks omitted).

B.   Investigative and Evidentiary Considerations

After the appointment of the Special Counsel, this Office obtained evidence about the following events relating to potential issues of obstruction of justice involving the President:

(a) The President's January 27, 2017 dinner with former FBI Director James Comey in which the President reportedly asked for Comey's loyalty, one day after the White House had been briefed by the Department of Justice on contacts between former National Security Advisor Michael Flynn and the Russian Ambassador;

(b) The President's February 14, 2017 meeting with Comey in which the President reportedly asked Comey not to pursue an investigation of Flynn;

(c) The President's private requests to Comey to make public the fact that the President was not the subject of an FBI investigation and to lift what the President regarded as a cloud;

(d) The President's outreach to the Director of National Intelligence and the Directors of the National Security Agency and the Central Intelligence Agency about the FBI's Russia investigation;

(e) The President's stated rationales for terminating Comey on May 9, 2017, including statements that could reasonably be understood as acknowledging that the FBI's Russia investigation was a factor in Comey's termination; and

(f) The President's reported involvement in issuing a statement about the June 9, 2016 Trump Tower meeting between Russians and senior Trump Campaign officials that said the meeting was about adoption and omitted that the Russians had offered to provide the Trump Campaign with derogatory information about Hillary Clinton.

Taking into account that information and our analysis of applicable statutory and constitutional principles (discussed below in Volume II, Section III, *infra*), we determined that there was a sufficient factual and legal basis to further investigate potential obstruction-of-justice issues involving the President.

Many of the core issues in an obstruction-of-justice investigation turn on an individual's actions and intent. We therefore requested that the White House provide us with documentary evidence in its possession on the relevant events. We also sought and obtained the White House's concurrence in our conducting interviews of White House personnel who had relevant information. And we interviewed other witnesses who had pertinent knowledge, obtained documents on a

12

voluntary basis when possible, and used legal process where appropriate. These investigative steps allowed us to gather a substantial amount of evidence.

We also sought a voluntary interview with the President. After more than a year of discussion, the President declined to be interviewed. Grand Jury

During the course of our discussions, the President did agree to answer written questions on certain Russia-related topics, and he provided us with answers. He did not similarly agree to provide written answers to questions on obstruction topics or questions on events during the transition. Ultimately, while we believed that we had the authority and legal justification to issue a grand jury subpoena to obtain the President's testimony, we chose not to do so. We made that decision in view of the substantial delay that such an investigative step would likely produce at a late stage in our investigation. We also assessed that based on the significant body of evidence we had already obtained of the President's actions and his public and private statements describing or explaining those actions, we had sufficient evidence to understand relevant events and to make certain assessments without the President's testimony. The Office's decision-making process on this issue is described in more detail in Appendix C, *infra*, in a note that precedes the President's written responses.

In assessing the evidence we obtained, we relied on common principles that apply in any investigation. The issue of criminal intent is often inferred from circumstantial evidence. *See, e.g., United States v. Croteau*, 819 F.3d 1293, 1305 (11th Cir. 2016) ("[G]uilty knowledge can rarely be established by direct evidence. . . . Therefore, mens rea elements such as knowledge or intent may be proved by circumstantial evidence.") (internal quotation marks omitted); *United States v. Robinson*, 702 F.3d 22, 36 (2d Cir. 2012) ("The government's case rested on circumstantial evidence, but the *mens rea* elements of knowledge and intent can often be proved through circumstantial evidence and the reasonable inferences drawn therefrom.") (internal quotation marks omitted). The principle that intent can be inferred from circumstantial evidence is a necessity in criminal cases, given the right of a subject to assert his privilege against compelled self-incrimination under the Fifth Amendment and therefore decline to testify. Accordingly, determinations on intent are frequently reached without the opportunity to interview an investigatory subject.

Obstruction-of-justice cases are consistent with this rule. *See, e.g., Edlind*, 887 F.3d at 174, 176 (relying on "significant circumstantial evidence that [the defendant] was conscious of her wrongdoing" in an obstruction case; "[b]ecause evidence of intent will almost always be circumstantial, a defendant may be found culpable where the reasonable and foreseeable consequences of her acts are the obstruction of justice") (internal quotation marks, ellipses, and punctuation omitted); *Quattrone*, 441 F.3d at 173-174. Circumstantial evidence that illuminates intent may include a pattern of potentially obstructive acts. Fed. R. Evid. 404(b) ("Evidence of a crime, wrong, or other act . . . may be admissible . . . [to] prov[e] motive, opportunity, intent, preparation, plan, knowledge, identity, absence of mistake, or lack of accident."); *see, e.g., United States v. Frankhauser*, 80 F.3d 641, 648-650 (1st Cir. 1996); *United States v. Arnold*, 773 F.2d 823, 832-834 (7th Cir. 1985); *Cintolo*, 818 F.2d at 1000.

Credibility judgments may also be made based on objective facts and circumstantial evidence. Standard jury instructions highlight a variety of factors that are often relevant in

13

assessing credibility. These include whether a witness had a reason not to tell the truth; whether the witness had a good memory; whether the witness had the opportunity to observe the events about which he testified; whether the witness's testimony was corroborated by other witnesses; and whether anything the witness said or wrote previously contradicts his testimony. *See, e.g., First Circuit Pattern Jury Instructions* § 1.06 (2018); *Fifth Circuit Pattern Jury Instructions (Criminal Cases)* § 1.08 (2012); *Seventh Circuit Pattern Jury Instruction* § 3.01 (2012).

In addition to those general factors, we took into account more specific factors in assessing the credibility of conflicting accounts of the facts. For example, contemporaneous written notes can provide strong corroborating evidence. *See United States v. Nobles*, 422 U.S. 225, 232 (1975) (the fact that a "statement appeared in the contemporaneously recorded report . . . would tend strongly to corroborate the investigator's version of the interview"). Similarly, a witness's recitation of his account before he had any motive to fabricate also supports the witness's credibility. *See Tome v. United States*, 513 U.S. 150, 158 (1995) ("A consistent statement that predates the motive is a square rebuttal of the charge that the testimony was contrived as a consequence of that motive."). Finally, a witness's false description of an encounter can imply consciousness of wrongdoing. *See Al-Adahi v. Obama*, 613 F.3d 1102, 1107 (D.C. Cir. 2010) (noting the "well-settled principle that false exculpatory statements are evidence—often strong evidence—of guilt"). We applied those settled legal principles in evaluating the factual results of our investigation.

14

II. FACTUAL RESULTS OF THE OBSTRUCTION INVESTIGATION

This section of the report details the evidence we obtained. We first provide an overview of how Russia became an issue in the 2016 presidential campaign, and how candidate Trump responded. We then turn to the key events that we investigated: the President's conduct concerning the FBI investigation of Michael Flynn; the President's reaction to public confirmation of the FBI's Russia investigation; events leading up to and surrounding the termination of FBI Director Comey; efforts to terminate the Special Counsel; efforts to curtail the scope of the Special Counsel's investigation; efforts to prevent disclosure of information about the June 9, 2016 Trump Tower meeting between Russians and senior campaign officials; efforts to have the Attorney General unrecuse; and conduct towards McGahn, Cohen, and other witnesses.

We summarize the evidence we found and then analyze it by reference to the three statutory obstruction-of-justice elements: obstructive act, nexus to a proceeding, and intent. We focus on elements because, by regulation, the Special Counsel has "jurisdiction . . . to investigate . . . federal crimes committed in the course of, and with intent to interfere with, the Special Counsel's investigation, such as perjury, obstruction of justice, destruction of evidence, and intimidation of witnesses." 28 C.F.R. § 600.4(a). Consistent with our jurisdiction to investigate federal obstruction crimes, we gathered evidence that is relevant to the elements of those crimes and analyzed them within an elements framework—while refraining from reaching ultimate conclusions about whether crimes were committed, for the reasons explained above. This section also does not address legal and constitutional defenses raised by counsel for the President; those defenses are analyzed in Volume II, Section III, *infra*.

A. The Campaign's Response to Reports About Russian Support for Trump

During the 2016 campaign, the media raised questions about a possible connection between the Trump Campaign and Russia.[7] The questions intensified after WikiLeaks released politically damaging Democratic Party emails that were reported to have been hacked by Russia. Trump responded to questions about possible connections to Russia by denying any business involvement in Russia—even though the Trump Organization had pursued a business project in Russia as late as June 2016. Trump also expressed skepticism that Russia had hacked the emails at the same time as he and other Campaign advisors privately sought information HOM ███████ about any further planned WikiLeaks releases. After the election, when questions persisted about possible links between Russia and the Trump Campaign, the President-Elect continued to deny any connections to Russia and privately expressed concerns that reports of Russian election interference might lead the public to question the legitimacy of his election.[8]

---

[7] This section summarizes and cites various news stories not for the truth of the information contained in the stories, but rather to place candidate Trump's response to those stories in context. Volume I of this report analyzes the underlying facts of several relevant events that were reported on by the media during the campaign.

[8] As discussed in Volume I, while the investigation identified numerous links between individuals with ties to the Russian government and individuals associated with the Trump Campaign, the evidence was not sufficient to charge that any member of the Trump Campaign conspired or coordinated with representatives of the Russian government to interfere in the 2016 election.

15

1. <u>Press Reports Allege Links Between the Trump Campaign and Russia</u>

On June 16, 2015, Donald J. Trump declared his intent to seek nomination as the Republican candidate for President.[9] By early 2016, he distinguished himself among Republican candidates by speaking of closer ties with Russia,[10] saying he would get along well with Russian President Vladimir Putin,[11] questioning whether the NATO alliance was obsolete,[12] and praising Putin as a "strong leader."[13] The press reported that Russian political analysts and commentators perceived Trump as favorable to Russia.[14]

Beginning in February 2016 and continuing through the summer, the media reported that several Trump campaign advisors appeared to have ties to Russia. For example, the press reported that campaign advisor Michael Flynn was seated next to Vladimir Putin at an RT gala in Moscow in December 2015 and that Flynn had appeared regularly on RT as an analyst.[15] The press also reported that foreign policy advisor Carter Page had ties to a Russian state-run gas company,[16] and that campaign chairman Paul Manafort had done work for the "Russian-backed former Ukrainian president Viktor Yanukovych."[17] In addition, the press raised questions during the Republican

---

[9] @realDonaldTrump 6/16/15 (11:57 a.m. ET) Tweet.

[10] *See, e.g.*, Meet the Press Interview with Donald J. Trump, NBC (Dec. 20, 2015) (Trump: "I think it would be a positive thing if Russia and the United States actually got along"); *Presidential Candidate Donald Trump News Conference, Hanahan, South Carolina*, C-SPAN (Feb. 15, 2016) ("You want to make a good deal for the country, you want to deal with Russia.").

[11] *See, e.g.*, *Anderson Cooper 360 Degrees*, CNN (July 8, 2015) ("I think I get along with [Putin] fine."); Andrew Rafferty, *Trump Says He Would "Get Along Very Well" With Putin*, NBC (July 30, 2015) (quoting Trump as saying, "I think I would get along very well with Vladimir Putin.").

[12] *See, e.g.*, @realDonaldTrump Tweet 3/24/16 (7:47 a.m. ET); @realDonaldTrump Tweet 3/24/16 (7:59 a.m. ET).

[13] *See, e.g.*, Meet the Press Interview with Donald J. Trump, NBC (Dec. 20, 2015) ("[Putin] is a strong leader. What am I gonna say, he's a weak leader? He's making mincemeat out of our President."); *Donald Trump Campaign Rally in Vandalia, Ohio*, C-SPAN (Mar. 12, 2016) ("I said [Putin] was a strong leader, which he is. I mean, he might be bad, he might be good. But he's a strong leader.").

[14] *See, e.g.*, Andrew Osborn, *From Russia with love: why the Kremlin backs Trump*, Reuters (Mar. 24, 2016); Robert Zubrin, *Trump: The Kremlin's Candidate*, National Review (Apr. 4, 2016).

[15] *See, e.g.*, Mark Hosenball & Steve Holland, *Trump being advised by ex-U.S. Lieutenant General who favors closer Russia ties*, Reuters (Feb. 26, 2016); Tom Hamburger et al., *Inside Trump's financial ties to Russia and his unusual flattery of Vladimir Putin*, Washington Post (June 17, 2016). Certain matters pertaining to Flynn are described in Volume I, Section IV.B.7, *supra*.

[16] *See, e.g.*, Zachary Mider, *Trump's New Russia Advisor Has Deep Ties to Kremlin's Gazprom*, Bloomberg (Mar. 30, 2016); Julia Iofee, *Who is Carter Page?*, Politico (Sep. 23, 2016). Certain matters pertaining to Page are described in Volume I, Section IV.A.3, *supra*.

[17] Tracy Wilkinson, *In a shift, Republican platform doesn't call for arming Ukraine against Russia, spurring outrage*, Los Angeles Times (July 21, 2016); Josh Rogin, *Trump campaign guts GOP's anti-Russia stance on Ukraine*, Washington Post (July 18, 2016).

16

U.S. Department of Justice

~~Attorney Work Product // May Contain Material Protected Under Fed. R. Crim. P. 6(e)~~

National Convention about the Trump Campaign's involvement in changing the Republican platform's stance on giving "weapons to Ukraine to fight Russian and rebel forces."[18]

2. The Trump Campaign Reacts to WikiLeaks's Release of Hacked Emails

On June 14, 2016, a cybersecurity firm that had conducted in-house analysis for the Democratic National Committee (DNC) posted an announcement that Russian government hackers had infiltrated the DNC's computer and obtained access to documents.[19]

On July 22, 2016, the day before the Democratic National Convention, WikiLeaks posted thousands of hacked DNC documents revealing sensitive internal deliberations.[20] Soon thereafter, Hillary Clinton's campaign manager publicly contended that Russia had hacked the DNC emails and arranged their release in order to help candidate Trump.[21] On July 26, 2016, the New York Times reported that U.S. "intelligence agencies ha[d] told the White House they now have 'high confidence' that the Russian government was behind the theft of emails and documents from the Democratic National Committee."[22]

Within the Trump Campaign, aides reacted with enthusiasm to reports of the hacks.[23] **Harm to Ongoing Matter** discussed with Campaign officials that WikiLeaks would release the hacked material.[24] Some witnesses said that Trump himself discussed the possibility of upcoming releases **HOM**. Michael Cohen, then-executive vice president of the Trump Organization and special counsel to Trump, recalled hearing **Harm to Ongoing Matter**.[25] Cohen recalled that Trump responded, "oh good, alright,"

---

[18] Josh Rogin, *Trump campaign guts GOP's anti-Russia stance on Ukraine,* Washington Post, Opinions (July 18, 2016). The Republican Platform events are described in Volume I, Section IV.A.6, *supra.*

[19] *Bears in the Midst: Intrusion into the Democratic National Committee*, CrowdStrike (June 15, 2016) (post originally appearing on June 14, 2016, according to records of the timing provided by CrowdStrike); Ellen Nakashima, *Russian government hackers penetrated DNC, stole opposition research on Trump,* Washington Post (June 14, 2016).

[20] Tom Hamburger and Karen Tumulty, *WikiLeaks releases thousands of documents about Clinton and internal deliberations*, Washington Post (July 22, 2016).

[21] Amber Phillips, *Clinton campaign manager: Russians leaked Democrats' emails to help Donald Trump,* Washington Post (July 24, 2016).

[22] David E. Sanger and Eric Schmitt, *Spy Agency Consensus Grows That Russia Hacked D.N.C.,* New York Times (July 26, 2016).

[23] Gates 4/10/18 302, at 5; Newman 8/23/18 302, at 1.

[24] Gates 4/11/18 302, at 2-3 (SM-2180998); Gates 10/25/18 302, at 2; *see also* Volume I, Section III.D.1, *supra.*

[25] Cohen 8/7/18 302, at 8; *see also* Volume I, Section III.D.1, *supra.* According to Cohen, after WikiLeaks's subsequent release of stolen DNC emails on July 22, 2016, Trump said to Cohen words to the effect of, **HOM** Cohen 9/18/18 302, at 10. Cohen's role in the candidate's and later

17

and ███Harm to Ongoing Matter███.[26] Manafort said that shortly after WikiLeaks's July 22, 2016 release of hacked documents, he spoke to Trump ███Harm to Ongoing Matter███; Manafort recalled that Trump responded that Manafort should ██HOM██ keep Trump updated.[27] Deputy campaign manager Rick Gates said that Manafort was getting pressure about ██HOM██ information and that Manafort instructed Gates ██HOM██ status updates on upcoming releases.[28] Around the same time, Gates was with Trump on a trip to an airport ██HOM██, and shortly after the call ended, Trump told Gates that more releases of damaging information would be coming.[29] ███Harm to Ongoing Matter███ were discussed within the Campaign,[30] and in the summer of 2016, the Campaign was planning a communications strategy based on the possible release of Clinton emails by WikiLeaks.[31]

3. The Trump Campaign Reacts to Allegations That Russia was Seeking to Aid Candidate Trump

In the days that followed WikiLeaks's July 22, 2016 release of hacked DNC emails, the Trump Campaign publicly rejected suggestions that Russia was seeking to aid candidate Trump. On July 26, 2016, Trump tweeted that it was "[c]razy" to suggest that Russia was "dealing with Trump"[32] and that "[f]or the record," he had "ZERO investments in Russia."[33]

In a press conference the next day, July 27, 2016, Trump characterized "this whole thing with Russia" as "a total deflection" and stated that it was "farfetched" and "ridiculous."[34] Trump said that the assertion that Russia had hacked the emails was unproven, but stated that it would give him "no pause" if Russia had Clinton's emails.[35] Trump added, "Russia, if you're listening, I hope you're able to find the 30,000 emails that are missing. I think you will probably be rewarded

---

President's activities, and his own criminal conduct, is described in Volume II, Section II.K, *infra*, and in Volume I, Section IV.A.1, *supra*.

[26] Cohen 8/7/18 302, at 8.

[27] ███Grand Jury███. As explained in footnote 197 of Volume I, Section III.D.1.b, *supra*, this Office has included Manafort's account of these events because it aligns with those of other witnesses and is corroborated to that extent.

[28] Gates 10/25/18 302, at 4.

[29] Gates 10/25/18 302, at 4.

[30] Bannon 1/18/19 302, at 3.

[31] Gates 4/11/18 302, at 1-2 (SM-2180998); Gates 10/25/18 302, at 2 (messaging strategy was being formed in June/July timeframe based on claims by Assange on June 12, 2016, ███████ ███Harm to Ongoing Matter███).

[32] @realDonaldTrump 7/26/16 (6:47 p.m. ET) Tweet.

[33] @realDonaldTrump 7/26/16 (6:50 p.m. ET) Tweet.

[34] *Donald Trump News Conference, Doral, Florida*, C-SPAN (July 27, 2016).

[35] *Donald Trump News Conference, Doral, Florida*, C-SPAN (July 27, 2016).

mightily by our press."[36] Trump also said that "there's nothing that I can think of that I'd rather do than have Russia friendly as opposed to the way they are right now," and in response to a question about whether he would recognize Crimea as Russian territory and consider lifting sanctions, Trump replied, "We'll be looking at that. Yeah, we'll be looking."[37]

During the press conference, Trump repeated "I have nothing to do with Russia" five times.[38] He stated that "the closest [he] came to Russia" was that Russians may have purchased a home or condos from him.[39] He said that after he held the Miss Universe pageant in Moscow in 2013 he had been interested in working with Russian companies that "wanted to put a lot of money into developments in Russia" but "it never worked out."[40] He explained, "[f]rankly, I didn't want to do it for a couple of different reasons. But we had a major developer . . . that wanted to develop property in Moscow and other places. But we decided not to do it."[41] The Trump Organization, however, had been pursuing a building project in Moscow—the Trump Tower Moscow project— from approximately September 2015 through June 2016, and the candidate was regularly updated on developments, including possible trips by Michael Cohen to Moscow to promote the deal and by Trump himself to finalize it.[42]

Cohen recalled speaking with Trump after the press conference about Trump's denial of any business dealings in Russia, which Cohen regarded as untrue.[43] Trump told Cohen that Trump Tower Moscow was not a deal yet and said, "Why mention it if it is not a deal?"[44] According to Cohen, at around this time, in response to Trump's disavowal of connections to Russia, campaign

---

[36] *Donald Trump News Conference, Doral, Florida*, C-SPAN (July 27, 2016). Within five hours of Trump's remark, a Russian intelligence service began targeting email accounts associated with Hillary Clinton for possible hacks. *See* Volume I, Section III, *supra*. In written answers submitted in this investigation, the President stated that he made the "Russia, if you're listening" statement "in jest and sarcastically, as was apparent to any objective observer." Written Responses of Donald J. Trump (Nov. 20, 2018), at 13 (Response to Question II, Part (d)).

[37] *Donald Trump News Conference, Doral, Florida*, C-SPAN (July 27, 2016). In his written answers submitted in this investigation, the President said that his statement that "we'll be looking" at Crimea and sanctions "did not communicate any position." Written Responses of Donald J. Trump (Nov. 20, 2018), at 17 (Response to Question IV, Part (g)).

[38] *Donald Trump News Conference, Doral, Florida*, C-SPAN (July 27, 2016).

[39] *Donald Trump News Conference, Doral, Florida*, C-SPAN (July 27, 2016).

[40] *Donald Trump News Conference, Doral, Florida*, C-SPAN (July 27, 2016).

[41] *Donald Trump News Conference, Doral, Florida*, C-SPAN (July 27, 2016).

[42] The Trump Tower Moscow project and Trump's involvement in it is discussed in detail in Volume I, Section IV.A.1, *supra*, and Volume II, Section II.K, *infra*.

[43] Cohen 9/18/18 302, at 4.

[44] Cohen 9/18/18 302, at 4-5.

19

283

advisors had developed a "party line" that Trump had no business with Russia and no connections to Russia.[45]

In addition to denying any connections with Russia, the Trump Campaign reacted to reports of Russian election interference in aid of the Campaign by seeking to distance itself from Russian contacts. For example, in August 2016, foreign policy advisor J.D. Gordon declined an invitation to Russian Ambassador Sergey Kislyak's residence because the timing was "not optimal" in view of media reports about Russian interference.[46] On August 19, 2016, Manafort was asked to resign amid media coverage scrutinizing his ties to a pro-Russian political party in Ukraine and links to Russian business.[47] And when the media published stories about Page's connections to Russia in September 2016, Trump Campaign officials terminated Page's association with the Campaign and told the press that he had played "no role" in the Campaign.[48]

On October 7, 2016, WikiLeaks released the first set of emails stolen by a Russian intelligence agency from Clinton Campaign chairman John Podesta.[49] The same day, the federal government announced that "the Russian Government directed the recent compromises of e-mails from US persons and institutions, including from US political organizations."[50] The government statement directly linked Russian hacking to the releases on WikiLeaks, with the goal of interfering with the presidential election, and concluded "that only Russia's senior-most officials could have authorized these activities" based on their "scope and sensitivity."[51]

On October 11, 2016, Podesta stated publicly that the FBI was investigating Russia's hacking and said that candidate Trump might have known in advance that the hacked emails were going to be released.[52] Vice Presidential Candidate Mike Pence was asked whether the Trump

---

[45] Cohen 11/20/18 302, at 1; Cohen 9/18/18 302, at 3-5. The formation of the "party line" is described in greater detail in Volume II, Section II.K, *infra*.

[46] DJTFP00004953 (8/8/16 Email, Gordon to Pchelyakov) (stating that "[t]hese days are not optimal for us, as we are busily knocking down a stream of false media stories"). The invitation and Gordon's response are discussed in Volume I, Section IV.A.7.*a*, *supra*.

[47] *See, e.g.*, Amber Phillips, *Paul Manafort's complicated ties to Ukraine, explained*, Washington Post (Aug. 19, 2016) ("There were also a wave of fresh headlines dealing with investigations into [Manafort's] ties to a pro-Russian political party in Ukraine."); Tom Winter & Ken Dilanian, *Donald Trump Aide Paul Manafort Scrutinized for Russian Business Ties*, NBC (Aug. 18, 2016). Relevant events involving Manafort are discussed in Volume I, Section IV.A.8, *supra*.

[48] Michael Isikoff, *U.S. intel officials probe ties between Trump adviser and Kremlin*, Yahoo News (Sep. 23, 2016); *see, e.g.*, 9/25/16 Email, Hicks to Conway & Bannon; 9/23/16 Email, J. Miller to Bannon & S. Miller; Page 3/16/17 302, at 2.

[49] @WikiLeaks 10/7/16 (4:32 p.m. ET) Tweet.

[50] Joint Statement from the Department Of Homeland Security and Office of the Director of National Intelligence on Election Security, DHS (Oct. 7, 2016).

[51] Joint Statement from the Department Of Homeland Security and Office of the Director of National Intelligence on Election Security, DHS (Oct. 7, 2016).

[52] John Wagner & Anne Gearan, *Clinton campaign chairman ties email hack to Russians, suggests Trump had early warning*, Washington Post (Oct. 11, 2016).

20

Campaign was "in cahoots" with WikiLeaks in releasing damaging Clinton-related information and responded, "Nothing could be further from the truth."[53]

4. After the Election, Trump Continues to Deny Any Contacts or Connections with Russia or That Russia Aided his Election

On November 8, 2016, Trump was elected President. Two days later, Russian officials told the press that the Russian government had maintained contacts with Trump's "immediate entourage" during the campaign.[54] In response, Hope Hicks, who had been the Trump Campaign spokesperson, said, "We are not aware of any campaign representatives that were in touch with any foreign entities before yesterday, when Mr. Trump spoke with many world leaders."[55] Hicks gave an additional statement denying any contacts between the Campaign and Russia: "It never happened. There was no communication between the campaign and any foreign entity during the campaign."[56]

On December 10, 2016, the press reported that U.S. intelligence agencies had "concluded that Russia interfered in last month's presidential election to boost Donald Trump's bid for the White House."[57] Reacting to the story the next day, President-Elect Trump stated, "I think it's ridiculous. I think it's just another excuse."[58] He continued that no one really knew who was responsible for the hacking, suggesting that the intelligence community had "no idea if it's Russia or China or somebody. It could be somebody sitting in a bed some place."[59] The President-Elect

---

[53] Louis Nelson, *Pence denies Trump camp in cahoots with WikiLeaks*, Politico (Oct. 14, 2016).

[54] Ivan Nechepurenko, *Russian Officials Were in Contact With Trump Allies, Diplomat Says*, New York Times (Nov. 10, 2016) (quoting Russian Deputy Foreign Minister Sergey Ryabkov saying, "[t]here were contacts" and "I cannot say that all, but a number of them maintained contacts with Russian representatives"); Jim Heintz & Matthew Lee, *Russia eyes better ties with Trump; says contacts underway*, Associated Press (Nov. 11, 2016) (quoting Ryabkov saying, "I don't say that all of them, but a whole array of them supported contacts with Russian representatives").

[55] Ivan Nechepurenko, *Russian Officials Were in Contact With Trump Allies, Diplomat Says*, New York Times (Nov. 11, 2016) (quoting Hicks).

[56] Jim Heintz & Matthew Lee, *Russia eyes better ties with Trump; says contacts underway*, Associated Press (Nov. 10, 2016) (quoting Hicks). Hicks recalled that after she made that statement, she spoke with Campaign advisors Kellyanne Conway, Stephen Miller, Jason Miller, and probably Kushner and Bannon to ensure it was accurate, and there was no hesitation or pushback from any of them. Hicks 12/8/17 302, at 4.

[57] Damien Gayle, *CIA concludes Russia interfered to help Trump win election, say reports*, Guardian (Dec. 10, 2016).

[58] *Chris Wallace Hosts "Fox News Sunday," Interview with President-Elect Donald Trump*, CQ Newsmaker Transcripts (Dec. 11, 2016).

[59] *Chris Wallace Hosts "Fox News Sunday," Interview with President-Elect Donald Trump*, CQ Newsmaker Transcripts (Dec. 11, 2016).

21

also said that Democrats were "putting [] out" the story of Russian interference "because they suffered one of the greatest defeats in the history of politics."[60]

On December 18, 2016, Podesta told the press that the election was "distorted by the Russian intervention" and questioned whether Trump Campaign officials had been "in touch with the Russians."[61] The same day, incoming Chief of Staff Reince Priebus appeared on Fox News Sunday and declined to say whether the President-Elect accepted the intelligence community's determination that Russia intervened in the election.[62] When asked about any contact or coordination between the Campaign and Russia, Priebus said, "Even this question is insane. Of course we didn't interface with the Russians."[63] Priebus added that "this whole thing is a spin job" and said, "the real question is, why the Democrats . . . are doing everything they can to delegitimize the outcome of the election?"[64]

On December 29, 2016, the Obama Administration announced that in response to Russian cyber operations aimed at the U.S. election, it was imposing sanctions and other measures on several Russian individuals and entities.[65] When first asked about the sanctions, President-Elect Trump said, "I think we ought to get on with our lives."[66] He then put out a statement that said "It's time for our country to move on to bigger and better things," but indicated that he would meet with intelligence community leaders the following week for a briefing on Russian interference.[67] The briefing occurred on January 6, 2017.[68] Following the briefing, the intelligence community released the public version of its assessment, which concluded with high confidence that Russia had intervened in the election through a variety of means with the goal of harming Clinton's

[60] *Chris Wallace Hosts "Fox News Sunday," Interview with President-Elect Donald Trump,* CQ Newsmaker Transcripts (Dec. 11, 2016).

[61] David Morgan, *Clinton campaign: It's an 'open question' if Trump team colluded with Russia,* Reuters Business Insider (Dec. 18, 2016).

[62] *Chris Wallace Hosts "Fox News Sunday," Interview with Incoming White House Chief of Staff Reince Priebus,* Fox News (Dec. 18, 2016).

[63] *Chris Wallace Hosts "Fox News Sunday," Interview with Incoming White House Chief of Staff Reince Priebus,* Fox News (Dec. 18, 2016).

[64] *Chris Wallace Hosts "Fox News Sunday," Interview with Incoming White House Chief of Staff Reince Priebus,* Fox News (Dec. 18, 2016).

[65] *Statement by the President on Actions in Response to Russian Malicious Cyber Activity and Harassment,* White House (Dec. 29, 2016); *see also* Missy Ryan et al., *Obama administration announces measures to punish Russia for 2016 election interference,* Washington Post (Dec. 29, 2016).

[66] John Wagner, *Trump on alleged election interference by Russia: 'Get on with our lives,'* Washington Post (Dec. 29, 2016).

[67] Missy Ryan et al., *Obama administration announces measures to punish Russia for 2016 election interference,* Washington Post (Dec. 29, 2016).

[68] Comey 11/15/17 302, at 3.

286

electability.[69]   The assessment further concluded with high confidence that Putin and the Russian government had developed a clear preference for Trump.[70]

Several days later, BuzzFeed published unverified allegations compiled by former British intelligence officer Christopher Steele during the campaign about candidate Trump's Russia connections under the headline "These Reports Allege Trump Has Deep Ties To Russia."[71]   In a press conference the next day, the President-Elect called the release "an absolute disgrace" and said, "I have no dealings with Russia. I have no deals that could happen in Russia, because we've stayed away. . . . So I have no deals, I have no loans and I have no dealings. We could make deals in Russia very easily if we wanted to, I just don't want to because I think that would be a conflict."[72]

Several advisors recalled that the President-Elect viewed stories about his Russian connections, the Russia investigations, and the intelligence community assessment of Russian interference as a threat to the legitimacy of his electoral victory.[73]   Hicks, for example, said that the President-Elect viewed the intelligence community assessment as his "Achilles heel" because, even if Russia had no impact on the election, people would think Russia helped him win, taking away from what he had accomplished.[74]   Sean Spicer, the first White House communications director, recalled that the President thought the Russia story was developed to undermine the legitimacy of his election.[75]   Gates said the President viewed the Russia investigation as an attack on the legitimacy of his win.[76]   And Priebus recalled that when the intelligence assessment came out, the President-Elect was concerned people would question the legitimacy of his win.[77]

---

[69] Office of the Director of National Intelligence, *Russia's Influence Campaign Targeting the 2016 US Presidential Election*, at 1 (Jan. 6, 2017).

[70] Office of the Director of National Intelligence, *Russia's Influence Campaign Targeting the 2016 US Presidential Election,* at 1 (Jan. 6, 2017).

[71] Ken Bensinger et al., *These Reports Allege Trump Has Deep Ties To Russia*, BuzzFeed (Jan. 10, 2017).

[72] *Donald Trump's News Conference: Full Transcript and Video*, New York Times (Jan. 11, 2017), *available at* https://www.nytimes.com/2017/01/11/us/politics/trump-press-conference-transcript.html.

[73] Priebus 10/13/17 302, at 7; Hicks 3/13/18 302, at 18; Spicer 10/16/17 302, at 6; Bannon 2/14/18 302, at 2; Gates 4/18/18 302, at 3; *see* Pompeo 6/28/17 302, at 2 (the President believed that the purpose of the Russia investigation was to delegitimize his presidency).

[74] Hicks 3/13/18 302, at 18.

[75] Spicer 10/17/17 302, at 6.

[76] Gates 4/18/18 302, at 3.

[77] Priebus 10/13/17 302, at 7.

23

B.   The President's Conduct Concerning the Investigation of Michael Flynn

Overview

During the presidential transition, incoming National Security Advisor Michael Flynn had two phone calls with the Russian Ambassador to the United States about the Russian response to U.S. sanctions imposed because of Russia's election interference. After the press reported on Flynn's contacts with the Russian Ambassador, Flynn lied to incoming Administration officials by saying he had not discussed sanctions on the calls. The officials publicly repeated those lies in press interviews. The FBI, which previously was investigating Flynn for other matters, interviewed him about the calls in the first week after the inauguration, and Flynn told similar lies to the FBI. On January 26, 2017, Department of Justice (DOJ) officials notified the White House that Flynn and the Russian Ambassador had discussed sanctions and that Flynn had been interviewed by the FBI. The next night, the President had a private dinner with FBI Director James Comey in which he asked for Comey's loyalty. On February 13, 2017, the President asked Flynn to resign. The following day, the President had a one-on-one conversation with Comey in which he said, "I hope you can see your way clear to letting this go, to letting Flynn go."

Evidence

1. Incoming National Security Advisor Flynn Discusses Sanctions on Russia with Russian Ambassador Sergey Kislyak

Shortly after the election, President-Elect Trump announced he would appoint Michael Flynn as his National Security Advisor.[78] For the next two months, Flynn played an active role on the Presidential Transition Team (PTT) coordinating policy positions and communicating with foreign government officials, including Russian Ambassador to the United States Sergey Kislyak.[79]

On December 29, 2016, as noted in Volume II, Section II.A.4, *supra*, the Obama Administration announced that it was imposing sanctions and other measures on several Russian individuals and entities.[80] That day, multiple members of the PTT exchanged emails about the sanctions and the impact they would have on the incoming Administration, and Flynn informed members of the PTT that he would be speaking to the Russian Ambassador later in the day.[81]

---

[78] Flynn 11/16/17 302, at 7; *President-Elect Donald J. Trump Selects U.S. Senator Jeff Sessions for Attorney General, Lt. Gen. Michael Flynn as Assistant to the President for National Security Affairs and U.S. Rep. Mike Pompeo as Director of the Central Intelligence Agency*, President-Elect Donald J. Trump Press Release (Nov. 18, 2016); *see also, e.g.*, Bryan Bender, *Trump names Mike Flynn national security adviser*, Politico, (Nov. 17, 2016).

[79] Flynn 11/16/17 302, at 8-14; Priebus 10/13/17 302, at 3-5.

[80] *Statement by the President on Actions in Response to Russian Malicious Cyber Activity and Harassment*, The White House, Office of the Press Secretary (Dec. 29, 2016).

[81] 12/29/16 Email, O'Brien to McFarland et al.; 12/29/16 Email, Bossert to Flynn et al.; 12/29/16 Email, McFarland to Flynn et al.; SF000001 (12/29/16 Text Message, Flynn to Flaherty) ("Tit for tat w Russia not good. Russian AMBO reaching out to me today."); Flynn 1/19/18 302, at 2.

24

Flynn, who was in the Dominican Republic at the time, and K.T. McFarland, who was slated to become the Deputy National Security Advisor and was at the Mar-a-Lago resort in Florida with the President-Elect and other senior staff, talked by phone about what, if anything, Flynn should communicate to Kislyak about the sanctions.[82] McFarland had spoken with incoming Administration officials about the sanctions and Russia's possible responses and thought she had mentioned in those conversations that Flynn was scheduled to speak with Kislyak.[83] Based on those conversations, McFarland informed Flynn that incoming Administration officials at Mar-a-Lago did not want Russia to escalate the situation.[84] At 4:43 p.m. that afternoon, McFarland sent an email to several officials about the sanctions and informed the group that "Gen [F]lynn is talking to russian ambassador this evening."[85]

Approximately one hour later, McFarland met with the President-Elect and senior officials and briefed them on the sanctions and Russia's possible responses.[86] Incoming Chief of Staff Reince Priebus recalled that McFarland may have mentioned at the meeting that the sanctions situation could be "cooled down" and not escalated.[87] McFarland recalled that at the end of the meeting, someone may have mentioned to the President-Elect that Flynn was speaking to the Russian Ambassador that evening.[88] McFarland did not recall any response by the President-Elect.[89] Priebus recalled that the President-Elect viewed the sanctions as an attempt by the Obama Administration to embarrass him by delegitimizing his election.[90]

Immediately after discussing the sanctions with McFarland on December 29, 2016, Flynn called Kislyak and requested that Russia respond to the sanctions only in a reciprocal manner, without escalating the situation.[91] After the call, Flynn briefed McFarland on its substance.[92] Flynn told McFarland that the Russian response to the sanctions was not going to be escalatory because Russia wanted a good relationship with the Trump Administration.[93] On December 30, 2016, Russian President Vladimir Putin announced that Russia would not take retaliatory measures

---

[82] Statement of Offense at 2-3, *United States v. Michael T. Flynn*, 1:17-cr-232 (D.D.C. Dec. 1, 2017), Doc. 4 (*Flynn* Statement of Offense); Flynn 11/17/17 302, at 3-4; Flynn 11/20/17 302, at 3; McFarland 12/22/17 302, at 6-7.

[83] McFarland 12/22/17 302, at 4-7 (recalling discussions about this issue with Bannon and Priebus).

[84] *Flynn* Statement of Offense, at 3; Flynn 11/17/17 302, at 3-4; McFarland 12/22/17 302, at 6-7.

[85] 12/29/16 Email, McFarland to Flynn et al.

[86] McFarland 12/22/17 302, at 7.

[87] Priebus 1/18/18 302, at 3.

[88] McFarland 12/22/17 302, at 7. Priebus thought it was possible that McFarland had mentioned Flynn's scheduled call with Kislyak at this meeting, although he was not certain. Priebus 1/18/18 302, at 3.

[89] McFarland 12/22/17 302, at 7.

[90] Priebus 1/18/18 302, at 3.

[91] *Flynn* Statement of Offense, at 3; Flynn 11/17/17 302, at 3-4.

[92] *Flynn* Statement of Offense, at 3; McFarland 12/22/17 302, at 7-8; Flynn 11/17/17 302, at 4.

[93] McFarland 12/22/17 302, at 8.

25

in response to the sanctions at that time and would instead "plan . . . further steps to restore Russian-US relations based on the policies of the Trump Administration."[94] Following that announcement, the President-Elect tweeted, "Great move on delay (by V. Putin) - I always knew he was very smart!"[95]

On December 31, 2016, Kislyak called Flynn and told him that Flynn's request had been received at the highest levels and Russia had chosen not to retaliate in response to the request.[96] Later that day, Flynn told McFarland about this follow-up conversation with Kislyak and Russia's decision not to escalate the sanctions situation based on Flynn's request.[97] McFarland recalled that Flynn thought his phone call had made a difference.[98] Flynn spoke with other incoming Administration officials that day, but does not recall whether they discussed the sanctions.[99]

Flynn recalled discussing the sanctions issue with incoming Administration official Stephen Bannon the next day.[100] Flynn said that Bannon appeared to know about Flynn's conversations with Kislyak, and he and Bannon agreed that they had "stopped the train on Russia's response" to the sanctions.[101] On January 3, 2017, Flynn saw the President-Elect in person and thought they discussed the Russian reaction to the sanctions, but Flynn did not have a specific recollection of telling the President-Elect about the substance of his calls with Kislyak.[102]

Members of the intelligence community were surprised by Russia's decision not to retaliate in response to the sanctions.[103] When analyzing Russia's response, they became aware of Flynn's discussion of sanctions with Kislyak.[104] Previously, the FBI had opened an investigation of Flynn based on his relationship with the Russian government.[105] Flynn's contacts with Kislyak became a key component of that investigation.[106]

---

[94] *Statement by the President of Russia*, President of Russia (Dec. 30, 2016) 12/30/16.

[95] @realDonaldTrump 12/30/16 (2:41 p.m. ET) Tweet.

[96] Flynn 1/19/18 302, at 3; *Flynn* Statement of Offense, at 3.

[97] Flynn 1/19/18 302, at 3; Flynn 11/17/17 302, at 6; McFarland 12/22/17 302, at 10; *Flynn* Statement of Offense, at 3.

[98] McFarland 12/22/17 302, at 10; *see* Flynn 1/19/18 302, at 4.

[99] Flynn 11/17/17 302, at 5-6.

[100] Flynn 1/19/18 302, at 4-5. Bannon recalled meeting with Flynn that day, but said he did not remember discussing sanctions with him. Bannon 2/12/18 302, at 9.

[101] Flynn 11/21/17 302, at 1; Flynn 1/19/18 302, at 5.

[102] Flynn 1/19/18 302, at 6; Flynn 11/17/17 302, at 6.

[103] McCord 7/17/17 302, at 2.

[104] McCord 7/17/17 302, at 2.

[105] McCord 7/17/17 302, at 2-3; Comey 11/15/17 302, at 5.

[106] McCord 7/17/17 302, at 2-3.

26

U.S. Department of Justice

~~Attorney Work Product // May Contain Material Protected Under Fed. R. Crim. P. 6(e)~~

2. President-Elect Trump is Briefed on the Intelligence Community's Assessment of Russian Interference in the Election and Congress Opens Election-Interference Investigations

On January 6, 2017, as noted in Volume II, Section II.A.4, *supra*, intelligence officials briefed President-Elect Trump and the incoming Administration on the intelligence community's assessment that Russia had interfered in the 2016 presidential election.[107] When the briefing concluded, Comey spoke with the President-Elect privately to brief him on unverified, personally sensitive allegations compiled by Steele.[108] According to a memorandum Comey drafted immediately after their private discussion, the President-Elect began the meeting by telling Comey he had conducted himself honorably over the prior year and had a great reputation.[109] The President-Elect stated that he thought highly of Comey, looked forward to working with him, and hoped that he planned to stay on as FBI director.[110] Comey responded that he intended to continue serving in that role.[111] Comey then briefed the President-Elect on the sensitive material in the Steele reporting.[112] Comey recalled that the President-Elect seemed defensive, so Comey decided

---

[107] *Hearing on Russian Election Interference Before the Senate Select Intelligence Committee*, 115th Cong. (June 8, 2017) (Statement for the Record of James B. Comey, former Director of the FBI, at 1-2).

[108] Comey 11/15/17 302, at 3; *Hearing on Russian Election Interference Before the Senate Select Intelligence Committee*, 115th Cong. (June 8, 2017) (Statement for the Record of James B. Comey, former Director of the FBI, at 1-2).

[109] Comey 1/7/17 Memorandum, at 1. Comey began drafting the memorandum summarizing the meeting immediately after it occurred. Comey 11/15/17 302, at 4. He finished the memorandum that evening and finalized it the following morning. Comey 11/15/17 302, at 4.

[110] Comey 1/7/17 Memorandum, at 1; Comey 11/15/17 302, at 3. Comey identified several other occasions in January 2017 when the President reiterated that he hoped Comey would stay on as FBI director. On January 11, President-Elect Trump called Comey to discuss the Steele reports and stated that he thought Comey was doing great and the President-Elect hoped he would remain in his position as FBI director. Comey 11/15/17 302, at 4; *Hearing on Russian Election Interference Before the Senate Select Intelligence Committee*, 115th Cong. (June 8, 2017) (testimony of James B. Comey, former Director of the FBI), CQ Cong. Transcripts, at 90. ("[D]uring that call, he asked me again, 'Hope you're going to stay, you're doing a great job.' And I told him that I intended to."). On January 22, at a White House reception honoring law enforcement, the President greeted Comey and said he looked forward to working with him. *Hearing on Russian Election Interference Before the Senate Select Intelligence Committee*, 115th Cong. (June 8, 2017) (testimony of James B. Comey, former Director of the FBI), CQ Cong. Transcripts, at 22. And as discussed in greater detail in Volume II, Section II.D, *infra*, on January 27, the President invited Comey to dinner at the White House and said he was glad Comey wanted to stay on as FBI Director.

[111] Comey 1/7/17 Memorandum, at 1; Comey 11/15/17 302, at 3.

[112] Comey 1/7/17 Memorandum, at 1-2; Comey 11/15/17 302, at 3. Comey's briefing included the Steele reporting's unverified allegation that the Russians had compromising tapes of the President involving conduct when he was a private citizen during a 2013 trip to Moscow for the Miss Universe Pageant. During the 2016 presidential campaign, a similar claim may have reached candidate Trump. On October 30, 2016, Michael Cohen received a text from Russian businessman Giorgi Rtskhiladze that said, "Stopped flow of tapes from Russia but not sure if there's anything else. Just so you know . . . ." 10/30/16 Text Message, Rtskhiladze to Cohen. Rtskhiladze said "tapes" referred to compromising tapes of Trump rumored to be held by persons associated with the Russian real estate conglomerate Crocus Group, which had helped host

27

to assure him that the FBI was not investigating him personally.[113] Comey recalled he did not want the President-Elect to think of the conversation as a "J. Edgar Hoover move."[114]

On January 10, 2017, the media reported that Comey had briefed the President-Elect on the Steele reporting,[115] and BuzzFeed News published information compiled by Steele online, stating that the information included "specific, unverified, and potentially unverifiable allegations of contact between Trump aides and Russian operatives."[116] The next day, the President-Elect expressed concern to intelligence community leaders about the fact that the information had leaked and asked whether they could make public statements refuting the allegations in the Steele reports.[117]

In the following weeks, three Congressional committees opened investigations to examine Russia's interference in the election and whether the Trump Campaign had colluded with Russia.[118] On January 13, 2017, the Senate Select Committee on Intelligence (SSCI) announced that it would conduct a bipartisan inquiry into Russian interference in the election, including any "links between Russia and individuals associated with political campaigns."[119] On January 25, 2017, the House Permanent Select Committee on Intelligence (HPSCI) announced that it had been conducting an investigation into Russian election interference and possible coordination with the political campaigns.[120] And on February 2, 2017, the Senate Judiciary Committee announced that it too would investigate Russian efforts to intervene in the election.[121]

---

the 2013 Miss Universe Pageant in Russia. Rtskhiladze 4/4/18 302, at 12. Cohen said he spoke to Trump about the issue after receiving the texts from Rtskhiladze. Cohen 9/12/18 302, at 13. Rtskhiladze said he was told the tapes were fake, but he did not communicate that to Cohen. Rtskhiladze 5/10/18 302, at 7.

[113] Comey 11/15/17 302, at 3-4; *Hearing on Russian Election Interference Before the Senate Select Intelligence Committee*, 115th Cong. (June 8, 2017) (Statement for the Record of James B. Comey, former Director of the FBI, at 2).

[114] Comey 11/15/17 302, at 3.

[115] *See, e.g.,* Evan Perez et al., *Intel chiefs presented Trump with claims of Russian efforts to compromise him*, CNN (Jan. 10, 2017; updated Jan. 12, 2017).

[116] Ken Bensinger et al., *These Reports Allege Trump Has Deep Ties To Russia*, BuzzFeed News (Jan. 10, 2017).

[117] *See* 1/11/17 Email, Clapper to Comey ("He asked if I could put out a statement. He would prefer of course that I say the documents are bogus, which, of course, I can't do."); 1/12/17 Email, Comey to Clapper ("He called me at 5 yesterday and we had a very similar conversation."); Comey 11/15/17 302, at 4-5.

[118] *See 2016 Presidential Election Investigation Fast Facts*, CNN (first published Oct. 12, 2017; updated Mar. 1, 2019) (summarizing starting dates of Russia-related investigations).

[119] *Joint Statement on Committee Inquiry into Russian Intelligence Activities*, SSCI (Jan. 13, 2017).

[120] *Joint Statement on Progress of Bipartisan HPSCI Inquiry into Russian Active Measures*, HPSCI (Jan. 25, 2017).

[121] *Joint Statement from Senators Graham and Whitehouse on Investigation into Russian Influence on Democratic Nations' Elections* (Feb. 2, 2017).

28

3. Flynn Makes False Statements About his Communications with Kislyak to Incoming Administration Officials, the Media, and the FBI

On January 12, 2017, a Washington Post columnist reported that Flynn and Kislyak communicated on the day the Obama Administration announced the Russia sanctions.[122] The column questioned whether Flynn had said something to "undercut the U.S. sanctions" and whether Flynn's communications had violated the letter or spirit of the Logan Act.[123]

President-Elect Trump called Priebus after the story was published and expressed anger about it.[124] Priebus recalled that the President-Elect asked, "What the hell is this all about?"[125] Priebus called Flynn and told him that the President-Elect was angry about the reporting on Flynn's conversations with Kislyak.[126] Flynn recalled that he felt a lot of pressure because Priebus had spoken to the "boss" and said Flynn needed to "kill the story."[127] Flynn directed McFarland to call the Washington Post columnist and inform him that no discussion of sanctions had occurred.[128] McFarland recalled that Flynn said words to the effect of, "I want to kill the story."[129] McFarland made the call as Flynn had requested although she knew she was providing false information, and the Washington Post updated the column to reflect that a "Trump official" had denied that Flynn and Kislyak discussed sanctions.[130]

When Priebus and other incoming Administration officials questioned Flynn internally about the Washington Post column, Flynn maintained that he had not discussed sanctions with Kislyak.[131] Flynn repeated that claim to Vice President-Elect Michael Pence and to incoming press secretary Sean Spicer.[132] In subsequent media interviews in mid-January, Pence, Priebus, and

---

[122] David Ignatius, *Why did Obama dawdle on Russia's hacking?*, Washington Post (Jan. 12, 2017).

[123] David Ignatius, *Why did Obama dawdle on Russia's hacking?*, Washington Post (Jan. 12, 2017). The Logan Act makes it a crime for "[a]ny citizen of the United States, wherever he may be" to "without authority of the United States, directly or indirectly commence[] or carr[y] on any correspondence or intercourse with any foreign government or any officer or agent thereof, in relation to any disputes or controversies with the United States, or to defeat the measures of the United States." 18 U.S.C. § 953.

[124] Priebus 1/18/18 302, at 6.

[125] Priebus 1/18/18 302, at 6.

[126] Priebus 1/18/18 302, at 6.

[127] Flynn 11/21/17 302, at 1; Flynn 11/20/17 302, at 6.

[128] McFarland 12/22/17 302, at 12-13.

[129] McFarland 12/22/17 302, at 12.

[130] McFarland 12/22/17 302, at 12-13; McFarland 8/29/17 302, at 8; *see* David Ignatius, *Why did Obama dawdle on Russia's hacking?*, Washington Post (Jan. 12, 2017).

[131] Flynn 11/17/17 302, at 1, 8; Flynn 1/19/18 302, at 7; Priebus 10/13/17 302, at 7-8; S. Miller 8/31/17 302, at 8-11.

[132] Flynn 11/17/17 302, at 1, 8; Flynn 1/19/18 302, at 7; S. Miller 8/31/17 302, at 10-11.

Spicer denied that Flynn and Kislyak had discussed sanctions, basing those denials on their conversations with Flynn.[133]

The public statements of incoming Administration officials denying that Flynn and Kislyak had discussed sanctions alarmed senior DOJ officials, who were aware that the statements were not true.[134] Those officials were concerned that Flynn had lied to his colleagues—who in turn had unwittingly misled the American public—creating a compromise situation for Flynn because the Department of Justice assessed that the Russian government could prove Flynn lied.[135] The FBI investigative team also believed that Flynn's calls with Kislyak and subsequent denials about discussing sanctions raised potential Logan Act issues and were relevant to the FBI's broader Russia investigation.[136]

On January 20, 2017, President Trump was inaugurated and Flynn was sworn in as National Security Advisor. On January 23, 2017, Spicer delivered his first press briefing and stated that he had spoken with Flynn the night before, who confirmed that the calls with Kislyak were about topics unrelated to sanctions.[137] Spicer's statements added to the Department of Justice's concerns that Russia had leverage over Flynn based on his lies and could use that derogatory information to compromise him.[138]

On January 24, 2017, Flynn agreed to be interviewed by agents from the FBI.[139] During the interview, which took place at the White House, Flynn falsely stated that he did not ask Kislyak to refrain from escalating the situation in response to the sanctions on Russia imposed by the Obama Administration.[140] Flynn also falsely stated that he did not remember a follow-up conversation in which Kislyak stated that Russia had chosen to moderate its response to those sanctions as a result of Flynn's request.[141]

---

[133] *Face the Nation Interview with Vice President-Elect Pence*, CBS (Jan. 15, 2017); Julie Hirschfield Davis et al., *Trump National Security Advisor Called Russian Envoy Day Before Sanctions Were Imposed*, Washington Post (Jan. 13, 2017); *Meet the Press Interview with Reince Priebus*, NBC (Jan. 15, 2017).

[134] Yates 8/15/17 302, at 2-3; McCord 7/17/17 302, at 3-4; McCabe 8/17/17 302, at 5 (DOJ officials were "really freaked out about it").

[135] Yates 8/15/17 302, at 3; McCord 7/17/17 302, at 4.

[136] McCord 7/17/17 302, at 4; McCabe 8/17/17 302, at 5-6.

[137] Sean Spicer, *White House Daily Briefing*, C-SPAN (Jan. 23, 2017).

[138] Yates 8/15/17 302, at 4; Axelrod 7/20/17 302, at 5.

[139] *Flynn* Statement of Offense, at 2.

[140] *Flynn* Statement of Offense, at 2.

[141] *Flynn* Statement of Offense, at 2. On December 1, 2017, Flynn admitted to making these false statements and pleaded guilty to violating 18 U.S.C. § 1001, which makes it a crime to knowingly and willfully "make[] any materially false, fictitious, or fraudulent statement or representation" to federal law enforcement officials. *See* Volume I, Section IV.A.7, *supra.*

30

4. DOJ Officials Notify the White House of Their Concerns About Flynn

On January 26, 2017, Acting Attorney General Sally Yates contacted White House Counsel Donald McGahn and informed him that she needed to discuss a sensitive matter with him in person.[142] Later that day, Yates and Mary McCord, a senior national security official at the Department of Justice, met at the White House with McGahn and White House Counsel's Office attorney James Burnham.[143] Yates said that the public statements made by the Vice President denying that Flynn and Kislyak discussed sanctions were not true and put Flynn in a potentially compromised position because the Russians would know he had lied.[144] Yates disclosed that Flynn had been interviewed by the FBI.[145] She declined to answer a specific question about how Flynn had performed during that interview,[146] but she indicated that Flynn's statements to the FBI were similar to the statements he had made to Pence and Spicer denying that he had discussed sanctions.[147] McGahn came away from the meeting with the impression that the FBI had not pinned Flynn down in lies,[148] but he asked John Eisenberg, who served as legal advisor to the National Security Council, to examine potential legal issues raised by Flynn's FBI interview and his contacts with Kislyak.[149]

That afternoon, McGahn notified the President that Yates had come to the White House to discuss concerns about Flynn.[150] McGahn described what Yates had told him, and the President asked him to repeat it, so he did.[151] McGahn recalled that when he described the FBI interview of Flynn, he said that Flynn did not disclose having discussed sanctions with Kislyak, but that there may not have been a clear violation of 18 U.S.C. § 1001.[152] The President asked about Section 1001, and McGahn explained the law to him, and also explained the Logan Act.[153] The President

---

[142] Yates 8/15/17 302, at 6.

[143] Yates 8/15/17 302, at 6; McCord 7/17/17 302, at 6; SCR015_000198 (2/15/17 Draft Memorandum to file from the Office of the Counsel to the President).

[144] Yates 8/15/17 302, at 6-8; McCord 7/17/17 302, at 6-7; Burnham 11/3/17 302, at 4; SCR015_000198 (2/15/17 Draft Memorandum to file from the Office of the Counsel to the President).

[145] McGahn 11/30/17 302, at 5; Yates 8/15/17 302, at 7; McCord 7/17/17 302, at 7; Burnham 11/3/17 302, at 4.

[146] Yates 8/15/17 302, at 7; McCord 7/17/17 302, at 7.

[147] SCR015_000198 (2/15/17 Draft Memorandum to file from the Office of the Counsel to the President); Burnham 11/3/17 302, at 4.

[148] McGahn 11/30/17 302, at 5.

[149] SCR015_000198 (2/15/17 Draft Memorandum to file from the Office of the Counsel to the President); McGahn 11/30/17 302, at 6, 8.

[150] McGahn 11/30/17 302, at 6; SCR015_000278 (White House Counsel's Office Memorandum re: "Flynn Tick Tock") (on January 26, "McGahn IMMEDIATELY advises POTUS"); SCR015_000198 (2/15/17 Draft Memorandum to file from the Office of the Counsel to the President).

[151] McGahn 11/30/17 302, at 6.

[152] McGahn 11/30/17 302, at 7.

[153] McGahn 11/30/17 302, at 7.

U.S. Department of Justice

~~Attorney Work Product // May Contain Material Protected Under Fed. R. Crim. P. 6(e)~~

instructed McGahn to work with Priebus and Bannon to look into the matter further and directed that they not discuss it with any other officials.[154] Priebus recalled that the President was angry with Flynn in light of what Yates had told the White House and said, "not again, this guy, this stuff."[155]

That evening, the President dined with several senior advisors and asked the group what they thought about FBI Director Comey.[156] According to Director of National Intelligence Dan Coats, who was at the dinner, no one openly advocated terminating Comey but the consensus on him was not positive.[157] Coats told the group that he thought Comey was a good director.[158] Coats encouraged the President to meet Comey face-to-face and spend time with him before making a decision about whether to retain him.[159]

5. McGahn has a Follow-Up Meeting About Flynn with Yates; President Trump has Dinner with FBI Director Comey

The next day, January 27, 2017, McGahn and Eisenberg discussed the results of Eisenberg's initial legal research into Flynn's conduct, and specifically whether Flynn may have violated the Espionage Act, the Logan Act, or 18 U.S.C. § 1001.[160] Based on his preliminary research, Eisenberg informed McGahn that there was a possibility that Flynn had violated 18 U.S.C. § 1001 and the Logan Act.[161] Eisenberg noted that the United States had never successfully prosecuted an individual under the Logan Act and that Flynn could have possible defenses, and

---

[154] McGahn 11/30/17 302, at 7; SCR015_000198-99 (2/15/17 Draft Memorandum to file from the Office of the Counsel to the President).

[155] Priebus 10/13/17 302, at 8. Several witnesses said that the President was unhappy with Flynn for other reasons at this time. Bannon said that Flynn's standing with the President was not good by December 2016. Bannon 2/12/18 302, at 12. The President-Elect had concerns because President Obama had warned him about Flynn shortly after the election. Bannon 2/12/18 302, at 4-5; Hicks 12/8/17 302, at 7 (President Obama's comment sat with President-Elect Trump more than Hicks expected). Priebus said that the President had become unhappy with Flynn even before the story of his calls with Kislyak broke and had become so upset with Flynn that he would not look at him during intelligence briefings. Priebus 1/18/18 302, at 8. Hicks said that the President thought Flynn had bad judgment and was angered by tweets sent by Flynn and his son, and she described Flynn as "being on thin ice" by early February 2017. Hicks 12/8/17 302, at 7, 10.

[156] Coats 6/14/17 302, at 2.

[157] Coats 6/14/17 302, at 2.

[158] Coats 6/14/17 302, at 2.

[159] Coats 6/14/17 302, at 2.

[160] SCR015_000199 (2/15/17 Draft Memorandum to file from the Office of the Counsel to the President); McGahn 11/30/17 302, at 8.

[161] SCR015_000199 (2/15/17 Draft Memorandum to file from the Office of the Counsel to the President); Eisenberg 11/29/17 302, at 9.

told McGahn that he believed it was unlikely that a prosecutor would pursue a Logan Act charge under the circumstances.[162]

That same morning, McGahn asked Yates to return to the White House to discuss Flynn again.[163] In that second meeting, McGahn expressed doubts that the Department of Justice would bring a Logan Act prosecution against Flynn, but stated that the White House did not want to take action that would interfere with an ongoing FBI investigation of Flynn.[164] Yates responded that Department of Justice had notified the White House so that it could take action in response to the information provided.[165] McGahn ended the meeting by asking Yates for access to the underlying information the Department of Justice possessed pertaining to Flynn's discussions with Kislyak.[166]

Also on January 27, the President called FBI Director Comey and invited him to dinner that evening.[167] Priebus recalled that before the dinner, he told the President something like, "don't talk about Russia, whatever you do," and the President promised he would not talk about Russia at the dinner.[168] McGahn had previously advised the President that he should not communicate directly with the Department of Justice to avoid the perception or reality of political interference in law enforcement.[169] When Bannon learned about the President's planned dinner with Comey, he suggested that he or Priebus also attend, but the President stated that he wanted to dine with Comey alone.[170] Comey said that when he arrived for the dinner that evening, he was surprised and concerned to see that no one else had been invited.[171]

---

[162] SCR015_000199 (2/15/17 Draft Memorandum to file from the Office of the Counsel to the President); Eisenberg 11/29/17 302, at 9.

[163] SCR015_000199 (2/15/17 Draft Memorandum to file from the Office of the Counsel to the President); McGahn 11/30/17 302, at 8; Yates 8/15/17 302, at 8.

[164] Yates 8/15/17 302, at 9; McGahn 11/30/17 302, at 8.

[165] Yates 8/15/17 302, at 9; Burnham 11/3/17 302, at 5; see SCR015_00199 (2/15/17 Draft Memorandum to file from the Office of the Counsel to the President) ("Yates was unwilling to confirm or deny that there was an ongoing investigation but did indicate that the Department of Justice would not object to the White House taking action against Flynn.").

[166] Yates 9/15/17 302, at 9; Burnham 11/3/17 302, at 5. In accordance with McGahn's request, the Department of Justice made the underlying information available and Eisenberg viewed the information in early February. Eisenberg 11/29/17 302, at 5; FBI 2/7/17 Electronic Communication, at 1 (documenting 2/2/17 meeting with Eisenberg).

[167] Comey 11/15/17 302, at 6; SCR012b_000001 (President's Daily Diary, 1/27/17); Hearing on Russian Election Interference Before the Senate Select Intelligence Committee, 115th Cong. (June 8, 2017) (Statement for the Record of James B. Comey, former Director of the FBI, at 2-3).

[168] Priebus 10/13/17 302, at 17.

[169] See McGahn 11/30/17 302, at 9; Dhillon 11/21/17 302, at 2; Bannon 2/12/18 302, at 17.

[170] Bannon 2/12/18 302, at 17.

[171] Hearing on Russian Election Interference Before the Senate Select Intelligence Committee, 115th Cong. (June 8, 2017) (Statement for the Record of James B. Comey, former Director of the FBI, at 3); see Comey 11/15/17 302, at 6.

Comey provided an account of the dinner in a contemporaneous memo, an interview with this Office, and congressional testimony. According to Comey's account of the dinner, the President repeatedly brought up Comey's future, asking whether he wanted to stay on as FBI director.[172] Because the President had previously said he wanted Comey to stay on as FBI director, Comey interpreted the President's comments as an effort to create a patronage relationship by having Comey ask for his job.[173] The President also brought up the Steele reporting that Comey had raised in the January 6, 2017 briefing and stated that he was thinking about ordering the FBI to investigate the allegations to prove they were false.[174] Comey responded that the President should think carefully about issuing such an order because it could create a narrative that the FBI was investigating him personally, which was incorrect.[175] Later in the dinner, the President brought up Flynn and said, "the guy has serious judgment issues."[176] Comey did not comment on Flynn and the President did not acknowledge any FBI interest in or contact with Flynn.[177]

According to Comey's account, at one point during the dinner the President stated, "I need loyalty, I expect loyalty."[178] Comey did not respond and the conversation moved on to other topics, but the President returned to the subject of Comey's job at the end of the dinner and repeated, "I need loyalty."[179] Comey responded, "You will always get honesty from me."[180] The

---

[172] Comey 11/15/17 302, at 7; Comey 1/28/17 Memorandum, at 1, 3; *Hearing on Russian Election Interference Before the Senate Select Intelligence Committee*, 115th Cong. (June 8, 2017) (Statement for the Record of James B. Comey, former Director of the FBI, at 3).

[173] Comey 11/15/17 302, at 7; *Hearing on Russian Election Interference Before the Senate Select Intelligence Committee*, 115th Cong. (June 8, 2017) (Statement for the Record of James B. Comey, former Director of the FBI, at 3).

[174] Comey 1/28/17 Memorandum, at 3; *Hearing on Russian Election Interference Before the Senate Select Intelligence Committee*, 115th Cong. (June 8, 2017) (Statement for the Record of James B. Comey, former Director of the FBI, at 4).

[175] Comey 1/28/17 Memorandum, at 3; *Hearing on Russian Election Interference Before the Senate Select Intelligence Committee*, 115th Cong. (June 8, 2017) (Statement for the Record of James B. Comey, former Director of the FBI, at 4).

[176] Comey 1/28/17 Memorandum, at 4; Comey 11/15/17 302, at 7.

[177] Comey 1/28/17 Memorandum, at 4; Comey 11/15/17 302, at 7.

[178] Comey 1/28/18 Memorandum, at 2; Comey 11/15/17 302, at 7; *Hearing on Russian Election Interference Before the Senate Select Intelligence Committee*, 115th Cong. (June 8, 2017) (Statement for the Record of James B. Comey, former Director of the FBI, at 3).

[179] Comey 1/28/17 Memorandum, at 3; Comey 11/15/17 302, at 7; *Hearing on Russian Election Interference Before the Senate Select Intelligence Committee*, 115th Cong. (June 8, 2017) (Statement for the Record of James B. Comey, former Director of the FBI, at 3-4).

[180] Comey 1/28/17 Memorandum, at 3; Comey 11/15/17 302, at 7; *Hearing on Russian Election Interference Before the Senate Select Intelligence Committee*, 115th Cong. (June 8, 2017) (Statement for the Record of James B. Comey, former Director of the FBI, at 4).

President said, "That's what I want, honest loyalty."[181] Comey said, "You will get that from me."[182]

After Comey's account of the dinner became public, the President and his advisors disputed that he had asked for Comey's loyalty.[183] The President also indicated that he had not invited Comey to dinner, telling a reporter that he thought Comey had "asked for the dinner" because "he wanted to stay on."[184] But substantial evidence corroborates Comey's account of the dinner invitation and the request for loyalty. The President's Daily Diary confirms that the President "extend[ed] a dinner invitation" to Comey on January 27.[185] With respect to the substance of the dinner conversation, Comey documented the President's request for loyalty in a memorandum he began drafting the night of the dinner;[186] senior FBI officials recall that Comey told them about the loyalty request shortly after the dinner occurred;[187] and Comey described the request while

---

[181] Comey 1/28/17 Memorandum, at 3; Comey 11/15/17 302, at 7; *Hearing on Russian Election Interference Before the Senate Select Intelligence Committee*, 115th Cong. (June 8, 2017) (Statement for the Record of James B. Comey, former Director of the FBI, at 4).

[182] Comey 1/28/17 Memorandum, at 3; Comey 11/15/17 302, at 7; *Hearing on Russian Election Interference Before the Senate Select Intelligence Committee*, 115th Cong. (June 8, 2017) (Statement for the Record of James B. Comey, former Director of the FBI, at 4).

[183] *See, e.g.*, Michael S. Schmidt, *In a Private Dinner, Trump Demanded Loyalty. Comey Demurred.*, New York Times (May 11, 2017) (quoting Sarah Sanders as saying, "[The President] would never even suggest the expectation of personal loyalty"); Ali Vitali, *Trump Never Asked for Comey's Loyalty, President's Personal Lawyer Says*, NBC (June 8, 2017) (quoting the President's personal counsel as saying, "The president also never told Mr. Comey, 'I need loyalty, I expect loyalty,' in form or substance."); Remarks by President Trump in Press Conference, White House (June 9, 2017) ("I hardly know the man. I'm not going to say 'I want you to pledge allegiance.' Who would do that? Who would ask a man to pledge allegiance under oath?"). In a private conversation with Spicer, the President stated that he had never asked for Comey's loyalty, but added that if he had asked for loyalty, "Who cares?" Spicer 10/16/17 302, at 4. The President also told McGahn that he never said what Comey said he had. McGahn 12/12/17 302, at 17.

[184] *Interview of Donald J. Trump*, NBC (May 11, 2017).

[185] SCR012b_000001 (President's Daily Diary, 1/27/17) (reflecting that the President called Comey in the morning on January 27 and "[t]he purpose of the call was to extend a dinner invitation"). In addition, two witnesses corroborate Comey's account that the President reached out to schedule the dinner, without Comey having asked for it. Priebus 10/13/17 302, at 17 (the President asked to schedule the January 27 dinner because he did not know much about Comey and intended to ask him whether he wanted to stay on as FBI Director); Rybicki 11/21/18 302, at 3 (recalling that Comey told him about the President's dinner invitation on the day of the dinner).

[186] Comey 11/15/17 302, at 8; *Hearing on Russian Election Interference Before the Senate Select Intelligence Committee*, 115th Cong. (June 8, 2017) (Statement for the Record of James B. Comey, former Director of the FBI, at 4).

[187] McCabe 8/17/17 302, at 9-10; Rybicki 11/21/18 302, at 3. After leaving the White House, Comey called Deputy Director of the FBI Andrew McCabe, summarized what he and the President had discussed, including the President's request for loyalty, and expressed shock over the President's request. McCabe 8/17/17 302, at 9. Comey also convened a meeting with his senior leadership team to discuss what the President had asked of him during the dinner and whether he had handled the request for loyalty properly. McCabe 8/17/17 302, at 10; Rybicki 11/21/18 302, at 3. In addition, Comey distributed his

35

U.S. Department of Justice

~~Attorney Work Product // May Contain Material Protected Under Fed. R. Crim. P. 6(e)~~

under oath in congressional proceedings and in a subsequent interview with investigators subject to penalties for lying under 18 U.S.C. § 1001. Comey's memory of the details of the dinner, including that the President requested loyalty, has remained consistent throughout.[188]

6. Flynn's Resignation

On February 2, 2017, Eisenberg reviewed the underlying information relating to Flynn's calls with Kislyak.[189] Eisenberg recalled that he prepared a memorandum about criminal statutes that could apply to Flynn's conduct, but he did not believe the White House had enough information to make a definitive recommendation to the President.[190] Eisenberg and McGahn discussed that Eisenberg's review of the underlying information confirmed his preliminary conclusion that Flynn was unlikely to be prosecuted for violating the Logan Act.[191] Because White House officials were uncertain what Flynn had told the FBI, however, they could not assess his exposure to prosecution for violating 18 U.S.C. § 1001.[192]

The week of February 6, Flynn had a one-on-one conversation with the President in the Oval Office about the negative media coverage of his contacts with Kislyak.[193] Flynn recalled that the President was upset and asked him for information on the conversations.[194] Flynn listed the specific dates on which he remembered speaking with Kislyak, but the President corrected one of the dates he listed.[195] The President asked Flynn what he and Kislyak discussed and Flynn responded that he might have talked about sanctions.[196]

---

memorandum documenting the dinner to his senior leadership team, and McCabe confirmed that the memorandum captured what Comey said on the telephone call immediately following the dinner. McCabe 8/17/17 302, at 9-10.

[188] There also is evidence that corroborates other aspects of the memoranda Comey wrote documenting his interactions with the President. For example, Comey recalled, and his memoranda reflect, that he told the President in his January 6, 2017 meeting, and on phone calls on March 30 and April 11, 2017, that the FBI was not investigating the President personally. On May 8, 2017, during White House discussions about firing Comey, the President told Rosenstein and others that Comey had told him three times that he was not under investigation, including once in person and twice on the phone. Gauhar-000058 (Gauhar 5/16/17 Notes).

[189] Eisenberg 11/29/17 302, at 5; FBI 2/7/17 Electronic Communication, at 1 (documenting 2/2/17 meeting with Eisenberg).

[190] Eisenberg 11/29/17 302, at 6.

[191] Eisenberg 11/29/17 302, at 9; SCR015_000200 (2/15/17 Draft Memorandum to file from the Office of the Counsel to the President).

[192] Eisenberg 11/29/17 302, at 9.

[193] Flynn 11/21/17 302, at 2.

[194] Flynn 11/21/17 302, at 2.

[195] Flynn 11/21/17 302, at 2.

[196] Flynn 11/21/17 302, at 2-3.

36

On February 9, 2017, the Washington Post reported that Flynn discussed sanctions with Kislyak the month before the President took office.[197] After the publication of that story, Vice President Pence learned of the Department of Justice's notification to the White House about the content of Flynn's calls.[198] He and other advisors then sought access to and reviewed the underlying information about Flynn's contacts with Kislyak.[199] FBI Deputy Director Andrew McCabe, who provided the White House officials access to the information and was present when they reviewed it, recalled the officials asking him whether Flynn's conduct violated the Logan Act.[200] McCabe responded that he did not know, but the FBI was investigating the matter because it was a possibility.[201] Based on the evidence of Flynn's contacts with Kislyak, McGahn and Priebus concluded that Flynn could not have forgotten the details of the discussions of sanctions and had instead been lying about what he discussed with Kislyak.[202] Flynn had also told White House officials that the FBI had told him that the FBI was closing out its investigation of him,[203] but Eisenberg did not believe him.[204] After reviewing the materials and speaking with Flynn, McGahn and Priebus concluded that Flynn should be terminated and recommended that course of action to the President.[205]

That weekend, Flynn accompanied the President to Mar-a-Lago.[206] Flynn recalled that on February 12, 2017, on the return flight to D.C. on Air Force One, the President asked him whether he had lied to the Vice President.[207] Flynn responded that he may have forgotten details of his calls, but he did not think he lied.[208] The President responded, "Okay. That's fine. I got it."[209]

---

[197] Greg Miller et al., *National security adviser Flynn discussed sanctions with Russian ambassador, despite denials, officials say*, Washington Post (Feb. 9, 2017).

[198] SCR015_000202 (2/15/17 Draft Memorandum to file from the Office of the Counsel to the President); McGahn 11/30/17 302, at 12.

[199] SCR015_000202 (2/15/17 Draft Memorandum to file from the Office of the Counsel to the President); McCabe 8/17/17 302, at 11-13; Priebus 10/13/17 302, at 10; McGahn 11/30/17 302, at 12.

[200] McCabe 8/17/17 302, at 13.

[201] McCabe 8/17/17 302, at 13.

[202] McGahn 11/30/17 302, at 12; Priebus 1/18/18 302, at 8; Priebus 10/13/17 302, at 10; SCR015_000202 (2/15/17 Draft Memorandum to file from the Office of the Counsel to the President).

[203] McGahn 11/30/17 302, at 11; Eisenberg 11/29/17 302, at 9; Priebus 10/13/17 302, at 11.

[204] Eisenberg 11/29/17 302, at 9.

[205] SCR015_000202 (2/15/17 Draft Memorandum to file from the Office of the Counsel to the President); Priebus 10/13/17 302, at 10; McGahn 11/30/17 302, at 12.

[206] Flynn 11/17/17 302, at 8.

[207] Flynn 1/19/18 302, at 9; Flynn 11/17/17 302, at 8.

[208] Flynn 11/17/17 302, at 8; Flynn 1/19/18 302, at 9.

[209] Flynn 1/19/18 302, at 9.

On February 13, 2017, Priebus told Flynn he had to resign.[210] Flynn said he wanted to say goodbye to the President, so Priebus brought him to the Oval Office.[211] Priebus recalled that the President hugged Flynn, shook his hand, and said, "We'll give you a good recommendation. You're a good guy. We'll take care of you."[212]

Talking points on the resignation prepared by the White House Counsel's Office and distributed to the White House communications team stated that McGahn had advised the President that Flynn was unlikely to be prosecuted, and the President had determined that the issue with Flynn was one of trust.[213] Spicer told the press the next day that Flynn was forced to resign "not based on a legal issue, but based on a trust issue, [where] a level of trust between the President and General Flynn had eroded to the point where [the President] felt he had to make a change."[214]

7. The President Discusses Flynn with FBI Director Comey

On February 14, 2017, the day after Flynn's resignation, the President had lunch at the White House with New Jersey Governor Chris Christie.[215] According to Christie, at one point during the lunch the President said, "Now that we fired Flynn, the Russia thing is over."[216] Christie laughed and responded, "No way."[217] He said, "this Russia thing is far from over" and "[w]e'll be here on Valentine's Day 2018 talking about this."[218] The President said, "[w]hat do you mean? Flynn met with the Russians. That was the problem. I fired Flynn. It's over."[219] Christie recalled responding that based on his experience both as a prosecutor and as someone who had been investigated, firing Flynn would not end the investigation.[220] Christie said there was no way to make an investigation shorter, but a lot of ways to make it longer.[221] The President asked Christie what he meant, and Christie told the President not to talk about the investigation even if he was

---

[210] Priebus 1/18/18 302, at 9.

[211] Priebus 1/18/18 302, at 9; Flynn 11/17/17 302, at 10.

[212] Priebus 1/18/18 302, at 9; Flynn 11/17/17 302, at 10.

[213] SCR004_00600 (2/16/17 Email, Burnham to Donaldson).

[214] Sean Spicer, *White House Daily Briefing*, C-SPAN (Feb. 14, 2017). After Flynn pleaded guilty to violating 18 U.S.C. § 1001 in December 2017, the President tweeted, "I had to fire General Flynn because he lied to the Vice President and the FBI." @realDonaldTrump 12/2/17 (12:14 p.m. ET) Tweet. The next day, the President's personal counsel told the press that he had drafted the tweet. Maegan Vazquez et al., *Trump's lawyer says he was behind President's tweet about firing Flynn*, CNN (Dec. 3, 2017).

[215] Christie 2/13/19 302, at 2-3; SCR012b_000022 (President's Daily Diary, 2/14/17).

[216] Christie 2/13/19 302, at 3.

[217] Christie 2/13/19 302, at 3.

[218] Christie 2/13/19 302, at 3. Christie said he thought when the President said "the Russia thing" he was referring to not just the investigations but also press coverage about Russia. Christie thought the more important thing was that there was an investigation. Christie 2/13/19 302, at 4.

[219] Christie 2/13/19 302, at 3.

[220] Christie 2/13/19 302, at 3.

[221] Christie 2/13/19 302, at 3.

frustrated at times.[222] Christie also told the President that he would never be able to get rid of Flynn, "like gum on the bottom of your shoe."[223]

Towards the end of the lunch, the President brought up Comey and asked if Christie was still friendly with him.[224] Christie said he was.[225] The President told Christie to call Comey and tell him that the President "really like[s] him. Tell him he's part of the team."[226] At the end of the lunch, the President repeated his request that Christie reach out to Comey.[227] Christie had no intention of complying with the President's request that he contact Comey.[228] He thought the President's request was "nonsensical" and Christie did not want to put Comey in the position of having to receive such a phone call.[229] Christie thought it would have been uncomfortable to pass on that message.[230]

At 4 p.m. that afternoon, the President met with Comey, Sessions, and other officials for a homeland security briefing.[231] At the end of the briefing, the President dismissed the other attendees and stated that he wanted to speak to Comey alone.[232] Sessions and senior advisor to the President Jared Kushner remained in the Oval Office as other participants left, but the President

---

[222] Christie 2/13/19 302, at 3-4.

[223] Christie 2/13/19 302, at 3. Christie also recalled that during the lunch, Flynn called Kushner, who was at the lunch, and complained about what Spicer had said about Flynn in his press briefing that day. Kushner told Flynn words to the effect of, "You know the President respects you. The President cares about you. I'll get the President to send out a positive tweet about you later." Kushner looked at the President when he mentioned the tweet, and the President nodded his assent. Christie 2/13/19 302, at 3. Flynn recalled getting upset at Spicer's comments in the press conference and calling Kushner to say he did not appreciate the comments. Flynn 1/19/18 302, at 9.

[224] Christie 2/13/19 302, at 4.

[225] Christie 2/13/19 302, at 4.

[226] Christie 2/13/19 302, at 4-5.

[227] Christie 2/13/19 302, at 5.

[228] Christie 2/13/19 302, at 5.

[229] Christie 2/13/19 302, at 5.

[230] Christie 2/13/19 302, at 5.

[231] SCR012b_000022 (President's Daily Diary, 2/14/17); Comey 11/15/17 302, at 9.

[232] Comey 11/15/17 302, at 10; 2/14/17 Comey Memorandum, at 1; *Hearing on Russian Election Interference Before the Senate Select Intelligence Committee*, 115th Cong. (June 8, 2017) (Statement for the Record of James B. Comey, former Director of the FBI, at 4); Priebus 10/13/17 302, at 18 (confirming that everyone was shooed out "like Comey said" in his June testimony).

excused them, repeating that he wanted to speak only with Comey.[233] At some point after others had left the Oval Office, Priebus opened the door, but the President sent him away.[234]

According to Comey's account of the meeting, once they were alone, the President began the conversation by saying, "I want to talk about Mike Flynn."[235] The President stated that Flynn had not done anything wrong in speaking with the Russians, but had to be terminated because he had misled the Vice President.[236] The conversation turned to the topic of leaks of classified information, but the President returned to Flynn, saying "he is a good guy and has been through a lot."[237] The President stated, "I hope you can see your way clear to letting this go, to letting Flynn go. He is a good guy. I hope you can let this go."[238] Comey agreed that Flynn "is a good guy," but did not commit to ending the investigation of Flynn.[239] Comey testified under oath that he took the President's statement "as a direction" because of the President's position and the circumstances of the one-on-one meeting.[240]

---

[233] Comey 11/15/17 302, at 10; Comey 2/14/17 Memorandum, at 1; *Hearing on Russian Election Interference Before the Senate Select Intelligence Committee*, 115th Cong. (June 8, 2017) (Statement for the Record of James B. Comey, former Director of the FBI, at 4). Sessions recalled that the President asked to speak to Comey alone and that Sessions was one of the last to leave the room; he described Comey's testimony about the events leading up to the private meeting with the President as "pretty accurate." Sessions 1/17/18 302, at 6. Kushner had no recollection of whether the President asked Comey to stay behind. Kushner 4/11/18 302, at 24.

[234] Comey 2/14/17 Memorandum, at 2; Priebus 10/13/17 302, at 18.

[235] Comey 11/15/17 302, at 10; Comey 2/14/17 Memorandum, at 1; *Hearing on Russian Election Interference Before the Senate Select Intelligence Committee*, 115th Cong. (June 8, 2017) (Statement for the Record of James B. Comey, former Director of the FBI, at 4).

[236] Comey 2/14/17 Memorandum, at 1; *Hearing on Russian Election Interference Before the Senate Select Intelligence Committee*, 115th Cong. (June 8, 2017) (Statement for the Record of James B. Comey, former Director of the FBI, at 5).

[237] Comey 11/15/17 302, at 10; Comey 2/14/17 Memorandum, at 2; *Hearing on Russian Election Interference Before the Senate Select Intelligence Committee*, 115th Cong. (June 8, 2017) (Statement for the Record of James B. Comey, former Director of the FBI, at 5).

[238] *Hearing on Russian Election Interference Before the Senate Select Intelligence Committee*, 115th Cong. (June 8, 2017) (Statement for the Record of James B. Comey, former Director of the FBI, at 5); Comey 2/14/17 Memorandum, at 2. Comey said he was highly confident that the words in quotations in his Memorandum documenting this meeting were the exact words used by the President. He said he knew from the outset of the meeting that he was about to have a conversation of consequence, and he remembered the words used by the President and wrote them down soon after the meeting. Comey 11/15/17 302, at 10-11.

[239] Comey 11/15/17 302, at 10; Comey 2/14/17 Memorandum, at 2.

[240] *Hearing on Russian Election Interference Before the Senate Select Intelligence Committee*, 115th Cong. (June 8, 2017) (CQ Cong. Transcripts, at 31) (testimony of James B. Comey, former Director of the FBI). Comey further stated, "I mean, this is the president of the United States, with me alone, saying, 'I hope' this. I took it as, this is what he wants me to do." *Id.*; *see also* Comey 11/15/17 302, at 10 (Comey took the statement as an order to shut down the Flynn investigation).

Shortly after meeting with the President, Comey began drafting a memorandum documenting their conversation.[241] Comey also met with his senior leadership team to discuss the President's request, and they agreed not to inform FBI officials working on the Flynn case of the President's statements so the officials would not be influenced by the request.[242] Comey also asked for a meeting with Sessions and requested that Sessions not leave Comey alone with the President again.[243]

8. The Media Raises Questions About the President's Delay in Terminating Flynn

After Flynn was forced to resign, the press raised questions about why the President waited more than two weeks after the DOJ notification to remove Flynn and whether the President had known about Flynn's contacts with Kislyak before the DOJ notification.[244] The press also continued to raise questions about connections between Russia and the President's campaign.[245] On February 15, 2017, the President told reporters, "General Flynn is a wonderful man. I think he's been treated very, very unfairly by the media."[246] On February 16, 2017, the President held

---

[241] Comey 11/15/17 302, at 11; *Hearing on Russian Election Interference Before the Senate Select Intelligence Committee*, 115th Cong. (June 8, 2017) (Statement for the record of James B. Comey, former Director of the FBI, at 5).

[242] Comey 11/15/17 302, at 11; Rybicki 6/9/17 302, at 4; Rybicki 6/22/17 302, at 1; *Hearing on Russian Election Interference Before the Senate Select Intelligence Committee*, 115th Cong. (June 8, 2017) (Statement for the record of James B. Comey, former Director of the FBI, at 5-6).

[243] Comey 11/15/17 302, at 11; Rybicki 6/9/17 302, at 4-5; Rybicki 6/22/17 302, at 1-2; Sessions 1/17/18 302, at 6 (confirming that later in the week following Comey's one-on-one meeting with the President in the Oval Office, Comey told the Attorney General that he did not want to be alone with the President); Hunt 2/1/18 302, at 6 (within days of the February 14 Oval Office meeting, Comey told Sessions he did not think it was appropriate for the FBI Director to meet alone with the President); Rybicki 11/21/18 302, at 4 (Rybicki helped to schedule the meeting with Sessions because Comey wanted to talk about his concerns about meeting with the President alone); *Hearing on Russian Election Interference Before the Senate Select Intelligence Committee*, 115th Cong. (June 8, 2017) (Statement for the record of James B. Comey, former Director of the FBI, at 6).

[244] *See, e.g.*, Sean Spicer, *White House Daily Briefing*, C-SPAN (Feb. 14, 2017) (questions from the press included, "if [the President] was notified 17 days ago that Flynn had misled the Vice President, other officials here, and that he was a potential threat to blackmail by the Russians, why would he be kept on for almost three weeks?" and "Did the President instruct [Flynn] to talk about sanctions with the [Russian ambassador]?"). Priebus recalled that the President initially equivocated on whether to fire Flynn because it would generate negative press to lose his National Security Advisor so early in his term. Priebus 1/18/18 302, at 8.

[245] *E.g.*, Sean Sullivan et al., *Senators from both parties pledge to deepen probe of Russia and the 2016 election*, Washington Post (Feb. 14, 2017); Aaron Blake, *5 times Donald Trump's team denied contact with Russia*, Washington Post (Feb. 15, 2017); Oren Dorell, *Donald Trump's ties to Russia go back 30 years*, USA Today (Feb. 15, 2017); Pamela Brown et al., *Trump aides were in constant touch with senior Russian officials during campaign*, CNN (Feb. 15, 2017); Austin Wright, *Comey briefs senators amid furor over Trump-Russia ties*, Politico (Feb. 17, 2017); Megan Twohey & Scott Shane, *A Back-Channel Plan for Ukraine and Russia, Courtesy of Trump Associates*, New York Times (Feb. 19, 2017).

[246] Remarks by President Trump and Prime Minister Netanyahu of Israel in Joint Press Conference, White House (Feb. 15, 2017).

41

a press conference and said that he removed Flynn because Flynn "didn't tell the Vice President of the United States the facts, and then he didn't remember. And that just wasn't acceptable to me."[247] The President said he did not direct Flynn to discuss sanctions with Kislyak, but "it certainly would have been okay with me if he did. I would have directed him to do it if I thought he wasn't doing it. I didn't direct him, but I would have directed him because that's his job."[248] In listing the reasons for terminating Flynn, the President did not say that Flynn had lied to him.[249] The President also denied having any connection to Russia, stating, "I have nothing to do with Russia. I told you, I have no deals there. I have no anything."[250] The President also said he "had nothing to do with" WikiLeaks's publication of information hacked from the Clinton campaign.[251]

9. The President Attempts to Have K.T. McFarland Create a Witness Statement Denying that he Directed Flynn's Discussions with Kislyak

On February 22, 2017, Priebus and Bannon told McFarland that the President wanted her to resign as Deputy National Security Advisor, but they suggested to her that the Administration could make her the ambassador to Singapore.[252] The next day, the President asked Priebus to have McFarland draft an internal email that would confirm that the President did not direct Flynn to call the Russian Ambassador about sanctions.[253] Priebus said he told the President he would only direct McFarland to write such a letter if she were comfortable with it.[254] Priebus called McFarland into his office to convey the President's request that she memorialize in writing that the President did not direct Flynn to talk to Kislyak.[255] McFarland told Priebus she did not know whether the President had directed Flynn to talk to Kislyak about sanctions, and she declined to say yes or no

---

[247] Remarks by President Trump in Press Conference, White House (Feb. 16, 2017).

[248] Remarks by President Trump in Press Conference, White House (Feb. 16, 2017). The President also said that Flynn's conduct "wasn't wrong – what he did in terms of the information he saw." The President said that Flynn was just "doing the job," and "if anything, he did something right."

[249] Remarks by President Trump in Press Conference, White House (Feb. 16, 2017); Priebus 1/18/18 302, at 9.

[250] Remarks by President Trump in Press Conference, White House (Feb. 16, 2017).

[251] Remarks by President Trump in Press Conference, White House (Feb. 16, 2017).

[252] KTMF_00000047 (McFarland 2/26/17 Memorandum for the Record); McFarland 12/22/17 302, at 16-17.

[253] See Priebus 1/18/18 302, at 11; see also KTMF_00000048 (McFarland 2/26/17 Memorandum for the Record); McFarland 12/22/17 302, at 17.

[254] Priebus 1/18/18 302, at 11.

[255] KTMF_00000048 (McFarland 2/26/17 Memorandum for the Record); McFarland 12/22/17 302, at 17.

to the request.[256] Priebus understood that McFarland was not comfortable with the President's request, and he recommended that she talk to attorneys in the White House Counsel's Office.[257]

McFarland then reached out to Eisenberg.[258] McFarland told him that she had been fired from her job as Deputy National Security Advisor and offered the ambassadorship in Singapore but that the President and Priebus wanted a letter from her denying that the President directed Flynn to discuss sanctions with Kislyak.[259] Eisenberg advised McFarland not to write the requested letter.[260] As documented by McFarland in a contemporaneous "Memorandum for the Record" that she wrote because she was concerned by the President's request: "Eisenberg . . . thought the requested email and letter would be a bad idea – from my side because the email would be awkward. Why would I be emailing Priebus to make a statement for the record? But it would also be a bad idea for the President because it looked as if my ambassadorial appointment was in some way a quid pro quo."[261] Later that evening, Priebus stopped by McFarland's office and told her not to write the email and to forget he even mentioned it.[262]

Around the same time, the President asked Priebus to reach out to Flynn and let him know that the President still cared about him.[263] Priebus called Flynn and said that he was checking in and that Flynn was an American hero.[264] Priebus thought the President did not want Flynn saying bad things about him.[265]

On March 31, 2017, following news that Flynn had offered to testify before the FBI and congressional investigators in exchange for immunity, the President tweeted, "Mike Flynn should ask for immunity in that this is a witch hunt (excuse for big election loss), by media & Dems, of

---

[256] KTMF_00000047 (McFarland 2/26/17 Memorandum for the Record) ("I said I did not know whether he did or didn't, but was in Maralago the week between Christmas and New Year's (while Flynn was on vacation in Carribean) and I was not aware of any Flynn-Trump, or Trump-Russian phone calls"); McFarland 12/22/17 302, at 17.

[257] Priebus 1/18/18 302, at 11.

[258] McFarland 12/22/17 302, at 17.

[259] McFarland 12/22/17 302, at 17.

[260] KTMF_00000048 (McFarland 2/26/17 Memorandum for the Record); McFarland 12/22/17 302, at 17.

[261] KTMF_00000048 (McFarland 2/26/17 Memorandum for the Record); see McFarland 12/22/17 302, at 17.

[262] McFarland 12/22/17 302, at 17; KTMF_00000048 (McFarland 2/26/17 Memorandum for the Record).

[263] Priebus 1/18/18 302, at 9.

[264] Priebus 1/18/18 302, at 9; Flynn 1/19/18 302, at 9.

[265] Priebus 1/18/18 302, at 9-10.

43

historic proportion!"[266] In late March or early April, the President asked McFarland to pass a message to Flynn telling him the President felt bad for him and that he should stay strong.[267]

Analysis

In analyzing the President's conduct related to the Flynn investigation, the following evidence is relevant to the elements of obstruction of justice:

a.　Obstructive act.　According to Comey's account of his February 14, 2017 meeting in the Oval Office, the President told him, "I hope you can see your way clear to letting this go, to letting Flynn go. . . . I hope you can let this go." In analyzing whether these statements constitute an obstructive act, a threshold question is whether Comey's account of the interaction is accurate, and, if so, whether the President's statements had the tendency to impede the administration of justice by shutting down an inquiry that could result in a grand jury investigation and a criminal charge.

After Comey's account of the President's request to "let[] Flynn go" became public, the President publicly disputed several aspects of the story. The President told the New York Times that he did not "shoo other people out of the room" when he talked to Comey and that he did not remember having a one-on-one conversation with Comey.[268] The President also publicly denied that he had asked Comey to "let[] Flynn go" or otherwise communicated that Comey should drop the investigation of Flynn.[269] In private, the President denied aspects of Comey's account to White House advisors, but acknowledged to Priebus that he brought Flynn up in the meeting with Comey and stated that Flynn was a good guy.[270] Despite those denials, substantial evidence corroborates Comey's account.

---

[266] @realDonaldTrump 3/31/17 (7:04 a.m. ET) Tweet; *see* Shane Harris at al., *Mike Flynn Offers to Testify in Exchange for Immunity*, Wall Street Journal (Mar. 30, 2017).

[267] McFarland 12/22/17 302, at 18.

[268] *Excerpts From The Times's Interview With Trump*, New York Times (July 19, 2017). Hicks recalled that the President told her he had never asked Comey to stay behind in his office. Hicks 12/8/17 302, at 12.

[269] In a statement on May 16, 2017, the White House said: "While the President has repeatedly expressed his view that General Flynn is a decent man who served and protected our country, the President has never asked Mr. Comey or anyone else to end any investigation, including any investigation involving General Flynn. . . . This is not a truthful or accurate portrayal of the conversation between the President and Mr. Comey." *See* Michael S. Schmidt, *Comey Memorandum Says Trump Asked Him to End Flynn Investigation*, New York Times (May 16, 2017) (quoting White House statement); @realDonaldTrump 12/3/17 (6:15 a.m. ET) Tweet ("I never asked Comey to stop investigating Flynn. Just more Fake News covering another Comey lie!").

[270] Priebus recalled that the President acknowledged telling Comey that Flynn was a good guy and he hoped "everything worked out for him." Priebus 10/13/17 302, at 19. McGahn recalled that the President denied saying to Comey that he hoped Comey would let Flynn go, but added that he was "allowed to hope." The President told McGahn he did not think he had crossed any lines. McGahn 12/14/17 302, at 8.

First, Comey wrote a detailed memorandum of his encounter with the President on the same day it occurred. Comey also told senior FBI officials about the meeting with the President that day, and their recollections of what Comey told them at the time are consistent with Comey's account.[271]

Second, Comey provided testimony about the President's request that he "let[] Flynn go" under oath in congressional proceedings and in interviews with federal investigators subject to penalties for lying under 18 U.S.C. § 1001. Comey's recollections of the encounter have remained consistent over time.

Third, the objective, corroborated circumstances of how the one-on-one meeting came to occur support Comey's description of the event. Comey recalled that the President cleared the room to speak with Comey alone after a homeland security briefing in the Oval Office, that Kushner and Sessions lingered and had to be shooed out by the President, and that Priebus briefly opened the door during the meeting, prompting the President to wave him away. While the President has publicly denied those details, other Administration officials who were present have confirmed Comey's account of how he ended up in a one-on-one meeting with the President.[272] And the President acknowledged to Priebus and McGahn that he in fact spoke to Comey about Flynn in their one-on-one meeting.

Fourth, the President's decision to clear the room and, in particular, to exclude the Attorney General from the meeting signals that the President wanted to be alone with Comey, which is consistent with the delivery of a message of the type that Comey recalls, rather than a more innocuous conversation that could have occurred in the presence of the Attorney General.

Finally, Comey's reaction to the President's statements is consistent with the President having asked him to "let[] Flynn go." Comey met with the FBI leadership team, which agreed to keep the President's statements closely held and not to inform the team working on the Flynn investigation so that they would not be influenced by the President's request. Comey also promptly met with the Attorney General to ask him not to be left alone with the President again, an account verified by Sessions, FBI Chief of Staff James Rybicki, and Jody Hunt, who was then the Attorney General's chief of staff.

A second question is whether the President's statements, which were not phrased as a direct order to Comey, could impede or interfere with the FBI's investigation of Flynn. While the President said he "hope[d]" Comey could "let[] Flynn go," rather than affirmatively directing him to do so, the circumstances of the conversation show that the President was asking Comey to close the FBI's investigation into Flynn. First, the President arranged the meeting with Comey so that they would be alone and purposely excluded the Attorney General, which suggests that the President meant to make a request to Comey that he did not want anyone else to hear. Second, because the President is the head of the Executive Branch, when he says that he "hopes" a subordinate will do something, it is reasonable to expect that the subordinate will do what the President wants. Indeed, the President repeated a version of "let this go" three times, and Comey

---

[271] Rybicki 11/21/18 302, at 4; McCabe 8/17/17 302, at 13-14.

[272] *See* Priebus 10/13/17 302, at 18; Sessions 1/17/18 302, at 6.

testified that he understood the President's statements as a directive, which is corroborated by the way Comey reacted at the time.

    b.   <u>Nexus to a proceeding</u>. To establish a nexus to a proceeding, it would be necessary to show that the President could reasonably foresee and actually contemplated that the investigation of Flynn was likely to lead to a grand jury investigation or prosecution.

    At the time of the President's one-on-one meeting with Comey, no grand jury subpoenas had been issued as part of the FBI's investigation into Flynn. But Flynn's lies to the FBI violated federal criminal law, Grand Jury , and resulted in Flynn's prosecution for violating 18 U.S.C. § 1001. By the time the President spoke to Comey about Flynn, DOJ officials had informed McGahn, who informed the President, that Flynn's statements to senior White House officials about his contacts with Kislyak were not true and that Flynn had told the same version of events to the FBI. McGahn also informed the President that Flynn's conduct could violate 18 U.S.C. § 1001. After the Vice President and senior White House officials reviewed the underlying information about Flynn's calls on February 10, 2017, they believed that Flynn could not have forgotten his conversations with Kislyak and concluded that he had been lying. In addition, the President's instruction to the FBI Director to "let[] Flynn go" suggests his awareness that Flynn could face criminal exposure for his conduct and was at risk of prosecution.

    c.   <u>Intent</u>. As part of our investigation, we examined whether the President had a personal stake in the outcome of an investigation into Flynn—for example, whether the President was aware of Flynn's communications with Kislyak close in time to when they occurred, such that the President knew that Flynn had lied to senior White House officials and that those lies had been passed on to the public. Some evidence suggests that the President knew about the existence and content of Flynn's calls when they occurred, but the evidence is inconclusive and could not be relied upon to establish the President's knowledge. In advance of Flynn's initial call with Kislyak, the President attended a meeting where the sanctions were discussed and an advisor may have mentioned that Flynn was scheduled to talk to Kislyak. Flynn told McFarland about the substance of his calls with Kislyak and said they may have made a difference in Russia's response, and Flynn recalled talking to Bannon in early January 2017 about how they had successfully "stopped the train on Russia's response" to the sanctions. It would have been reasonable for Flynn to have wanted the President to know of his communications with Kislyak because Kislyak told Flynn his request had been received at the highest levels in Russia and that Russia had chosen not to retaliate in response to the request, and the President was pleased by the Russian response, calling it a "[g]reat move." And the President never said publicly or internally that Flynn had lied to him about the calls with Kislyak.

    But McFarland did not recall providing the President-Elect with Flynn's read-out of his calls with Kislyak, and Flynn does not have a specific recollection of telling the President-Elect directly about the calls. Bannon also said he did not recall hearing about the calls from Flynn. And in February 2017, the President asked Flynn what was discussed on the calls and whether he had lied to the Vice President, suggesting that he did not already know. Our investigation accordingly did not produce evidence that established that the President knew about Flynn's discussions of sanctions before the Department of Justice notified the White House of those discussions in late January 2017. The evidence also does not establish that Flynn otherwise possessed information damaging to the President that would give the President a personal incentive to end the FBI's inquiry into Flynn's conduct.

Evidence does establish that the President connected the Flynn investigation to the FBI's broader Russia investigation and that he believed, as he told Christie, that terminating Flynn would end "the whole Russia thing." Flynn's firing occurred at a time when the media and Congress were raising questions about Russia's interference in the election and whether members of the President's campaign had colluded with Russia. Multiple witnesses recalled that the President viewed the Russia investigations as a challenge to the legitimacy of his election. The President paid careful attention to negative coverage of Flynn and reacted with annoyance and anger when the story broke disclosing that Flynn had discussed sanctions with Kislyak. Just hours before meeting one-on-one with Comey, the President told Christie that firing Flynn would put an end to the Russia inquiries. And after Christie pushed back, telling the President that firing Flynn would not end the Russia investigation, the President asked Christie to reach out to Comey and convey that the President liked him and he was part of "the team." That afternoon, the President cleared the room and asked Comey to "let[] Flynn go."

We also sought evidence relevant to assessing whether the President's direction to Comey was motivated by sympathy towards Flynn. In public statements the President repeatedly described Flynn as a good person who had been harmed by the Russia investigation, and the President directed advisors to reach out to Flynn to tell him the President "care[d]" about him and felt bad for him. At the same time, multiple senior advisors, including Bannon, Priebus, and Hicks, said that the President had become unhappy with Flynn well before Flynn was forced to resign and that the President was frequently irritated with Flynn. Priebus said he believed the President's initial reluctance to fire Flynn stemmed not from personal regard, but from concern about the negative press that would be generated by firing the National Security Advisor so early in the Administration. And Priebus indicated that the President's post-firing expressions of support for Flynn were motivated by the President's desire to keep Flynn from saying negative things about him.

The way in which the President communicated the request to Comey also is relevant to understanding the President's intent. When the President first learned about the FBI investigation into Flynn, he told McGahn, Bannon, and Priebus not to discuss the matter with anyone else in the White House. The next day, the President invited Comey for a one-on-one dinner against the advice of an aide who recommended that other White House officials also attend. At the dinner, the President asked Comey for "loyalty" and, at a different point in the conversation, mentioned that Flynn had judgment issues. When the President met with Comey the day after Flynn's termination—shortly after being told by Christie that firing Flynn would not end the Russia investigation—the President cleared the room, even excluding the Attorney General, so that he could again speak to Comey alone. The President's decision to meet one-on-one with Comey contravened the advice of the White House Counsel that the President should not communicate directly with the Department of Justice to avoid any appearance of interfering in law enforcement activities. And the President later denied that he cleared the room and asked Comey to "let[] Flynn go"—a denial that would have been unnecessary if he believed his request was a proper exercise of prosecutorial discretion.

47

Finally, the President's effort to have McFarland write an internal email denying that the President had directed Flynn to discuss sanctions with Kislyak highlights the President's concern about being associated with Flynn's conduct. The evidence does not establish that the President was trying to have McFarland lie. The President's request, however, was sufficiently irregular that McFarland—who did not know the full extent of Flynn's communications with the President and thus could not make the representation the President wanted—felt the need to draft an internal memorandum documenting the President's request, and Eisenberg was concerned that the request would look like a quid pro quo in exchange for an ambassadorship.

C.   The President's Reaction to Public Confirmation of the FBI's Russia Investigation

Overview

In early March 2017, the President learned that Sessions was considering recusing from the Russia investigation and tried to prevent the recusal. After Sessions announced his recusal on March 2, the President expressed anger at Sessions for the decision and then privately asked Sessions to "unrecuse." On March 20, 2017, Comey publicly disclosed the existence of the FBI's Russia investigation. In the days that followed, the President contacted Comey and other intelligence agency leaders and asked them to push back publicly on the suggestion that the President had any connection to the Russian election-interference effort in order to "lift the cloud" of the ongoing investigation.

Evidence

1. Attorney General Sessions Recuses From the Russia Investigation

In late February 2017, the Department of Justice began an internal analysis of whether Sessions should recuse from the Russia investigation based on his role in the 2016 Trump Campaign.[273] On March 1, 2017, the press reported that, in his January confirmation hearing to become Attorney General, Senator Sessions had not disclosed two meetings he had with Russian Ambassador Kislyak before the presidential election, leading to congressional calls for Sessions to recuse or for a special counsel to investigate Russia's interference in the presidential election.[274]

Also on March 1, the President called Comey and said he wanted to check in and see how Comey was doing.[275] According to an email Comey sent to his chief of staff after the call, the President "talked about Sessions a bit," said that he had heard Comey was "doing great," and said that he hoped Comey would come by to say hello when he was at the White House.[276] Comey

---

[273] Sessions 1/17/18 302, at 1; Hunt 2/1/18 302, at 3.

[274] *E.g.*, Adam Entous et al., *Sessions met with Russian envoy twice last year, encounters he later did not disclose*, Washington Post (Mar. 1, 2017).

[275] 3/1/17 Email, Comey to Rybicki; SCR012b_000030 (President's Daily Diary, 3/1/17, reflecting call with Comey at 11:55 am.)

[276] 3/1/17 Email, Comey to Rybicki; *see Hearing on Russian Election Interference Before the Senate Select Intelligence Committee*, 115th Cong. (June 8, 2017) (CQ Cong. Transcripts, at 86) (testimony

48

U.S. Department of Justice

Attorney Work Product // May Contain Material Protected Under Fed. R. Crim. P. 6(e)

interpreted the call as an effort by the President to "pull [him] in," but he did not perceive the call as an attempt by the President to find out what Comey was doing with the Flynn investigation.[277]

The next morning, the President called McGahn and urged him to contact Sessions to tell him not to recuse himself from the Russia investigation.[278] McGahn understood the President to be concerned that a recusal would make Sessions look guilty for omitting details in his confirmation hearing; leave the President unprotected from an investigation that could hobble the presidency and derail his policy objectives; and detract from favorable press coverage of a Presidential Address to Congress the President had delivered earlier in the week.[279] McGahn reached out to Sessions and reported that the President was not happy about the possibility of recusal.[280] Sessions replied that he intended to follow the rules on recusal.[281] McGahn reported back to the President about the call with Sessions, and the President reiterated that he did not want Sessions to recuse.[282] Throughout the day, McGahn continued trying on behalf of the President to avert Sessions's recusal by speaking to Sessions's personal counsel, Sessions's chief of staff, and Senate Majority Leader Mitch McConnell, and by contacting Sessions himself two more times.[283] Sessions recalled that other White House advisors also called him that day to argue against his recusal.[284]

That afternoon, Sessions announced his decision to recuse "from any existing or future investigations of any matters related in any way to the campaigns for President of the United States."[285] Sessions believed the decision to recuse was not a close call, given the applicable

---

of James B. Comey, former Director of the FBI) ("[H]e called me one day. . . . [H]e just called to check in and tell me I was doing an awesome job, and wanted to see how I was doing.").

[277] Comey 11/15/17 302, at 17-18.

[278] McGahn 11/30/17 302, at 16.

[279] McGahn 11/30/17 302, at 16-17; see SC_AD_00123 (Donaldson 3/2/17 Notes) ("Just in the middle of another Russia Fiasco.").

[280] Sessions 1/17/18 302, at 3.

[281] McGahn 11/30/17 302, at 17.

[282] McGahn 11/30/17 302, at 17.

[283] McGahn 11/30/17 302, at 18-19; Sessions 1/17/18 302, at 3; Hunt 2/1/18 302, at 4; Donaldson 11/6/17 302, at 8-10; see Hunt-000017; SC_AD_00121 (Donaldson 3/2/17 Notes).

[284] Sessions 1/17/18 302, at 3.

[285] Attorney General Sessions Statement on Recusal, Department of Justice Press Release (Mar. 2, 2017) ("During the course of the last several weeks, I have met with the relevant senior career Department officials to discuss whether I should recuse myself from any matters arising from the campaigns for President of the United States. Having concluded those meetings today, I have decided to recuse myself from any existing or future investigations of any matters related in any way to the campaigns for President of the United States."). At the time of Sessions's recusal, Dana Boente, then the Acting Deputy Attorney General and U.S. Attorney for the Eastern District of Virginia, became the Acting Attorney General for campaign-related matters pursuant to an executive order specifying the order of succession at the Department of Justice. Id. ("Consistent with the succession order for the Department of Justice, . . . Dana Boente shall act as and perform the functions of the Attorney General with respect to any matters from

49

language in the Code of Federal Regulations (CFR), which Sessions considered to be clear and decisive.[286] Sessions thought that any argument that the CFR did not apply to him was "very thin."[287] Sessions got the impression, based on calls he received from White House officials, that the President was very upset with him and did not think he had done his duty as Attorney General.[288]

Shortly after Sessions announced his recusal, the White House Counsel's Office directed that Sessions should not be contacted about the matter.[289] Internal White House Counsel's Office notes from March 2, 2017, state "No contact w/Sessions" and "No comms / Serious concerns about obstruction."[290]

On March 3, the day after Sessions's recusal, McGahn was called into the Oval Office.[291] Other advisors were there, including Priebus and Bannon.[292] The President opened the conversation by saying, "I don't have a lawyer."[293] The President expressed anger at McGahn about the recusal and brought up Roy Cohn, stating that he wished Cohn was his attorney.[294] McGahn interpreted this comment as directed at him, suggesting that Cohn would fight for the

---

which I have recused myself to the extent they exist."); *see* Exec. Order No. 13775, 82 Fed. Reg. 10697 (Feb. 14, 2017).

[286] Sessions 1/17/18 302, at 1-2. 28 C.F.R. § 45.2 provides that "no employee shall participate in a criminal investigation or prosecution if he has a personal or political relationship with . . . [a]ny person or organization substantially involved in the conduct that is the subject of the investigation or prosecution," and defines "political relationship" as "a close identification with an elected official, a candidate (whether or not successful) for elective, public office, a political party, or a campaign organization, arising from service as a principal adviser thereto or a principal official thereof."

[287] Sessions 1/17/18 302, at 2.

[288] Sessions 1/17/18 302, at 3.

[289] Donaldson 11/6/17 302, at 11; SC_AD_00123 (Donaldson 3/2/17 Notes). It is not clear whether the President was aware of the White House Counsel's Office direction not to contact Sessions about his recusal.

[290] SC_AD_00123 (Donaldson 3/2/17 Notes). McGahn said he believed the note "No comms / Serious concerns about obstruction" may have referred to concerns McGahn had about the press team saying "crazy things" and trying to spin Sessions's recusal in a way that would raise concerns about obstruction. McGahn 11/30/17 302, at 19. Donaldson recalled that "No comms" referred to the order that no one should contact Sessions. Donaldson 11/6/17 302, at 11.

[291] McGahn 12/12/17 302, at 2.

[292] McGahn 12/12/17 302, at 2.

[293] McGahn 12/12/17 302, at 2.

[294] McGahn 12/12/17 302, at 2. Cohn had previously served as a lawyer for the President during his career as a private businessman. Priebus recalled that when the President talked about Cohn, he said Cohn would win cases for him that had no chance, and that Cohn had done incredible things for him. Priebus 4/3/18 302, at 5. Bannon recalled the President describing Cohn as a winner and a fixer, someone who got things done. Bannon 2/14/18 302, at 6.

U.S. Department of Justice

~~Attorney Work Product // May Contain Material Protected Under Fed. R. Crim. P. 6(e)~~

President whereas McGahn would not.[295] The President wanted McGahn to talk to Sessions about the recusal, but McGahn told the President that DOJ ethics officials had weighed in on Sessions's decision to recuse.[296] The President then brought up former Attorneys General Robert Kennedy and Eric Holder and said that they had protected their presidents.[297] The President also pushed back on the DOJ contacts policy, and said words to the effect of, "You're telling me that Bobby and Jack didn't talk about investigations? Or Obama didn't tell Eric Holder who to investigate?"[298] Bannon recalled that the President was as mad as Bannon had ever seen him and that he screamed at McGahn about how weak Sessions was.[299] Bannon recalled telling the President that Sessions's recusal was not a surprise and that before the inauguration they had discussed that Sessions would have to recuse from campaign-related investigations because of his work on the Trump Campaign.[300]

That weekend, Sessions and McGahn flew to Mar-a-Lago to meet with the President.[301] Sessions recalled that the President pulled him aside to speak to him alone and suggested that Sessions should "unrecuse" from the Russia investigation.[302] The President contrasted Sessions with Attorneys General Holder and Kennedy, who had developed a strategy to help their presidents where Sessions had not.[303] Sessions said he had the impression that the President feared that the investigation could spin out of control and disrupt his ability to govern, which Sessions could have helped avert if he were still overseeing it.[304]

On March 5, 2017, the White House Counsel's Office was informed that the FBI was asking for transition-period records relating to Flynn—indicating that the FBI was still actively investigating him.[305] On March 6, the President told advisors he wanted to call the Acting Attorney

---

[295] McGahn 12/12/17 302, at 2.

[296] McGahn 12/12/17 302, at 2.

[297] McGahn 12/12/17 302, at 3. Bannon said the President saw Robert Kennedy and Eric Holder as Attorneys General who protected the presidents they served. The President thought Holder always stood up for President Obama and even took a contempt charge for him, and Robert Kennedy always had his brother's back. Bannon 2/14/18 302, at 5. Priebus recalled that the President said he had been told his entire life he needed to have a great lawyer, a "bulldog," and added that Holder had been willing to take a contempt-of-Congress charge for President Obama. Priebus 4/3/18 302, at 5.

[298] McGahn 12/12/17 302, at 3.

[299] Bannon 2/14/18 302, at 5.

[300] Bannon 2/14/18 302, at 5.

[301] Sessions 1/17/18 302, at 3; Hunt 2/1/18 302, at 5; McGahn 12/12/17 302, at 3.

[302] Sessions 1/17/18 302, at 3-4.

[303] Sessions 1/17/18 302, at 3-4

[304] Sessions 1/17/18 302, at 3-4. Hicks recalled that after Sessions recused, the President was angry and scolded Sessions in her presence, but she could not remember exactly when that conversation occurred. Hicks 12/8/17 302, at 13.

[305] SC_AD_000137 (Donaldson 3/5/17 Notes); *see* Donaldson 11/6/17 302, at 13.

General to find out whether the White House or the President was being investigated, although it is not clear whether the President knew at that time of the FBI's recent request concerning Flynn.[306]

2. FBI Director Comey Publicly Confirms the Existence of the Russia Investigation in Testimony Before HPSCI

On March 9, 2017, Comey briefed the "Gang of Eight" congressional leaders about the FBI's investigation of Russian interference, including an identification of the principal U.S. subjects of the investigation.[307] Although it is unclear whether the President knew of that briefing at the time, notes taken by Annie Donaldson, then McGahn's chief of staff, on March 12, 2017, state, "POTUS in panic/chaos . . . Need binders to put in front of POTUS. (1) All things related to Russia."[308] The week after Comey's briefing, the White House Counsel's Office was in contact with SSCI Chairman Senator Richard Burr about the Russia investigations and appears to have received information about the status of the FBI investigation.[309]

On March 20, 2017, Comey was scheduled to testify before HPSCI.[310] In advance of Comey's testimony, congressional officials made clear that they wanted Comey to provide information about the ongoing FBI investigation.[311] Dana Boente, who at that time was the Acting Attorney General for the Russia investigation, authorized Comey to confirm the existence of the Russia investigation and agreed that Comey should decline to comment on whether any particular individuals, including the President, were being investigated.[312]

---

[306] Donaldson 11/6/17 302, at 14; see SC_AD_000168 (Donaldson 3/6/17 Notes) ("POTUS wants to call Dana [then the Acting Attorney General for campaign-related investigations] / Is investigation / No / We know something on Flynn / GSA got contacted by FBI / There's something hot").

[307] Comey 11/15/17 302, at 13-14; SNS-Classified-0000140-44 (3/8/17 Email, Gauhar to Page et al.).

[308] SC_AD_00188 (Donaldson 3/12/18 Notes). Donaldson said she was not part of the conversation that led to these notes, and must have been told about it from others. Donaldson 11/6/17 302, at 13.

[309] Donaldson 11/6/17 302, at 14-15. On March 16, 2017, the White House Counsel's Office was briefed by Senator Burr on the existence of "4-5 targets." Donaldson 11/6/17 302, at 15. The "targets" were identified in notes taken by Donaldson as "Flynn (FBI was in—wrapping up)→DOJ looking for phone records"; "Comey→Manafort (Ukr + Russia, not campaign)"; HOM "Carter Page ($ game)"; and "Greek Guy" (potentially referring to George Papadopoulos, later charged with violating 18 U.S.C. § 1001 for lying to the FBI). SC_AD_00198 (Donaldson 3/16/17 Notes). Donaldson and McGahn both said they believed these were targets of SSCI. Donaldson 11/6/17 302, at 15; McGahn 12/12/17 302, at 4. But SSCI does not formally investigate individuals as "targets"; the notes on their face reference the FBI, the Department of Justice, and Comey; and the notes track the background materials prepared by the FBI for Comey's briefing to the Gang of 8 on March 9. See SNS-Classified-0000140-44 (3/8/17 Email, Gauhar to Page et al.); see also Donaldson 11/6/17 302, at 15 (Donaldson could not rule out that Burr had told McGahn those individuals were the FBI's targets).

[310] Hearing on Russian Election Tampering Before the House Permanent Select Intelligence Committee, 115th Cong. (Mar. 20, 2017).

[311] Comey 11/15/17 302, at 16; McCabe 8/17/17, at 15; McGahn 12/14/17 302, at 1.

[312] Boente 1/31/18 302, at 5; Comey 11/15/17 302, at 16-17.

In his opening remarks at the HPSCI hearing, which were drafted in consultation with the Department of Justice, Comey stated that he had "been authorized by the Department of Justice to confirm that the FBI, as part of [its] counterintelligence mission, is investigating the Russian government's efforts to interfere in the 2016 presidential election and that includes investigating the nature of any links between individuals associated with the Trump campaign and the Russian government and whether there was any coordination between the campaign and Russia's efforts. As with any counterintelligence investigation, this will also include an assessment of whether any crimes were committed."[313] Comey added that he would not comment further on what the FBI was "doing and whose conduct [it] [was] examining" because the investigation was ongoing and classified—but he observed that he had "taken the extraordinary step in consultation with the Department of Justice of briefing this Congress's leaders . . . in a classified setting in detail about the investigation."[314] Comey was specifically asked whether President Trump was "under investigation during the campaign" or "under investigation now."[315] Comey declined to answer, stating, "Please don't over interpret what I've said as—as the chair and ranking know, we have briefed him in great detail on the subjects of the investigation and what we're doing, but I'm not gonna answer about anybody in this forum."[316] Comey was also asked whether the FBI was investigating the information contained in the Steele reporting, and he declined to answer.[317]

According to McGahn and Donaldson, the President had expressed frustration with Comey before his March 20 testimony, and the testimony made matters worse.[318] The President had previously criticized Comey for too frequently making headlines and for not attending intelligence briefings at the White House, and the President suspected Comey of leaking certain information to the media.[319] McGahn said the President thought Comey was acting like "his own branch of government."[320]

---

[313] *Hearing on Russian Election Tampering Before the House Permanent Select Intelligence Committee*, 115th Cong. (Mar. 20, 2017) (CQ Cong. Transcripts, at 11) (testimony by FBI Director James B. Comey); Comey 11/15/17 302, at 17; Boente 1/31/18 302, at 5 (confirming that the Department of Justice authorized Comey's remarks).

[314] *Hearing on Russian Election Tampering Before the House Permanent Select Intelligence Committee*, 115th Cong. (Mar. 20, 2017) (CQ Cong. Transcripts, at 11) (testimony by FBI Director James B. Comey).

[315] *Hearing on Russian Election Tampering Before the House Permanent Select Intelligence Committee*, 115th Cong. (Mar. 20, 2017) (CQ Cong. Transcripts, at 130) (question by Rep. Swalwell).

[316] *Hearing on Russian Election Tampering Before the House Permanent Select Intelligence Committee*, 115th Cong. (Mar. 20, 2017) (CQ Cong. Transcripts, at 130) (testimony by FBI Director James B. Comey).

[317] *Hearing on Russian Election Tampering Before the House Permanent Select Intelligence Committee*, 115th Cong. (Mar. 20, 2017) (CQ Cong. Transcripts, at 143) (testimony by FBI Director James B. Comey).

[318] Donaldson 11/6/17 302, at 21; McGahn 12/12/17 302, at 7.

[319] Donaldson 11/6/17 302, at 21; McGahn 12/12/17 302, at 6-9.

[320] McGahn 12/12/17 302, at 7.

U.S. Department of Justice

~~Attorney Work Product // May Contain Material Protected Under Fed. R. Crim. P. 6(e)~~

Press reports following Comey's March 20 testimony suggested that the FBI was investigating the President, contrary to what Comey had told the President at the end of the January 6, 2017 intelligence assessment briefing.[321] McGahn, Donaldson, and senior advisor Stephen Miller recalled that the President was upset with Comey's testimony and the press coverage that followed because of the suggestion that the President was under investigation.[322] Notes from the White House Counsel's Office dated March 21, 2017, indicate that the President was "beside himself" over Comey's testimony.[323] The President called McGahn repeatedly that day to ask him to intervene with the Department of Justice, and, according to the notes, the President was "getting hotter and hotter, get rid?"[324] Officials in the White House Counsel's Office became so concerned that the President would fire Comey that they began drafting a memorandum that examined whether the President needed cause to terminate the FBI director.[325]

At the President's urging, McGahn contacted Boente several times on March 21, 2017, to seek Boente's assistance in having Comey or the Department of Justice correct the misperception that the President was under investigation.[326] Boente did not specifically recall the conversations, although he did remember one conversation with McGahn around this time where McGahn asked if there was a way to speed up or end the Russia investigation as quickly as possible.[327] Boente said McGahn told him the President was under a cloud and it made it hard for him to govern.[328] Boente recalled telling McGahn that there was no good way to shorten the investigation and attempting to do so could erode confidence in the investigation's conclusions.[329] Boente said McGahn agreed and dropped the issue.[330] The President also sought to speak with Boente directly, but McGahn told the President that Boente did not want to talk to the President about the request

---

[321] *E.g.*, Matt Apuzzo et al., *F.B.I. Is Investigating Trump's Russia Ties, Comey Confirms*, New York Times (Mar. 20, 2017); Andy Greenberg. *The FBI Has Been Investigating Trump's Russia Ties Since July*, Wired (Mar. 20, 2017); Julie Borger & Spencer Ackerman, *Trump-Russia collusion is being investigated by FBI, Comey confirms*, Guardian (Mar. 20, 2017); *see* Comey 1/6/17 Memorandum, at 2.

[322] Donaldson 11/6/17 302, at 16-17; S. Miller 10/31/17 302, at 4; McGahn 12/12/17 302, at 5-7.

[323] SC_AD_00213 (Donaldson 3/21/17 Notes). The notes from that day also indicate that the President referred to the "Comey bombshell" which "made [him] look like a fool." SC_AD_00206 (Donaldson 3/21/17 Notes).

[324] SC_AD_00210 (Donaldson 3/21/17 Notes).

[325] SCR016_000002-05 (White House Counsel's Office Memorandum). White House Counsel's Office attorney Uttam Dhillon did not recall a triggering event causing the White House Counsel's Office to begin this research. Dhillon 11/21/17 302, at 5. Metadata from the document, which was provided by the White House, establishes that it was created on March 21, 2017.

[326] Donaldson 11/6/17 302, at 16-21; McGahn 12/12/17 302, at 5-7.

[327] Boente 1/31/18 302, at 5.

[328] Boente 1/31/18 302, at 5.

[329] Boente 1/31/18 302, at 5.

[330] Boente 1/31/18 302, at 5.

to intervene with Comey.[331] McGahn recalled Boente telling him in calls that day that he did not think it was sustainable for Comey to stay on as FBI director for the next four years, which McGahn said he conveyed to the President.[332] Boente did not recall discussing with McGahn or anyone else the idea that Comey should not continue as FBI director.[333]

3. The President Asks Intelligence Community Leaders to Make Public Statements that he had No Connection to Russia

In the weeks following Comey's March 20, 2017 testimony, the President repeatedly asked intelligence community officials to push back publicly on any suggestion that the President had a connection to the Russian election-interference effort.

On March 22, 2017, the President asked Director of National Intelligence Daniel Coats and CIA Director Michael Pompeo to stay behind in the Oval Office after a Presidential Daily Briefing.[334] According to Coats, the President asked them whether they could say publicly that no link existed between him and Russia.[335] Coats responded that the Office of the Director of National Intelligence (ODNI) has nothing to do with investigations and it was not his role to make a public statement on the Russia investigation.[336] Pompeo had no recollection of being asked to stay behind after the March 22 briefing, but he recalled that the President regularly urged officials to get the word out that he had not done anything wrong related to Russia.[337]

Coats told this Office that the President never asked him to speak to Comey about the FBI investigation.[338] Some ODNI staffers, however, had a different recollection of how Coats described the meeting immediately after it occurred. According to senior ODNI official Michael Dempsey, Coats said after the meeting that the President had brought up the Russia investigation and asked him to contact Comey to see if there was a way to get past the investigation, get it over with, end it, or words to that effect.[339] Dempsey said that Coats described the President's comments as falling "somewhere between musing about hating the investigation" and wanting Coats to "do something to stop it."[340] Dempsey said Coats made it clear that he would not get involved with an ongoing FBI investigation.[341] Edward Gistaro, another ODNI official, recalled

---

[331] SC_AD_00210 (Donaldson 3/21/17 Notes); McGahn 12/12/17 302, at 7; Donaldson 11/6/17 302, at 19.

[332] McGahn 12/12/17 302, at 7; Burnham 11/03/17 302, at 11.

[333] Boente 1/31/18 302, at 3.

[334] Coats 6/14/17 302, at 3; Culver 6/14/17 302, at 2.

[335] Coats 6/14/17 302, at 3.

[336] Coats 6/14/17 302, at 3.

[337] Pompeo 6/28/17 302, at 1-3.

[338] Coats 6/14/17 302, at 3.

[339] Dempsey 6/14/17 302, at 2.

[340] Dempsey 6/14/17 302, at 2-3.

[341] Dempsey 6/14/17 302, at 3.

that right after Coats's meeting with the President, on the walk from the Oval Office back to the Eisenhower Executive Office Building, Coats said that the President had kept him behind to ask him what he could do to "help with the investigation."[342] Another ODNI staffer who had been waiting for Coats outside the Oval Office talked to Gistaro a few minutes later and recalled Gistaro reporting that Coats was upset because the President had asked him to contact Comey to convince him there was nothing to the Russia investigation.[343]

On Saturday, March 25, 2017, three days after the meeting in the Oval Office, the President called Coats and again complained about the Russia investigations, saying words to the effect of, "I can't do anything with Russia, there's things I'd like to do with Russia, with trade, with ISIS, they're all over me with this."[344] Coats told the President that the investigations were going to go on and the best thing to do was to let them run their course.[345] Coats later testified in a congressional hearing that he had "never felt pressure to intervene or interfere in any way and shape—with shaping intelligence in a political way, or in relationship . . . to an ongoing investigation."[346]

On March 26, 2017, the day after the President called Coats, the President called NSA Director Admiral Michael Rogers.[347] The President expressed frustration with the Russia investigation, saying that it made relations with the Russians difficult.[348] The President told Rogers "the thing with the Russians [wa]s messing up" his ability to get things done with Russia.[349] The President also said that the news stories linking him with Russia were not true and asked Rogers if he could do anything to refute the stories.[350] Deputy Director of the NSA Richard Ledgett, who was present for the call, said it was the most unusual thing he had experienced in 40 years of government service.[351] After the call concluded, Ledgett prepared a memorandum that he and Rogers both signed documenting the content of the conversation and the President's request, and they placed the memorandum in a safe.[352] But Rogers did not perceive the President's request to be an order, and the President did not ask Rogers to push back on the Russia

---

[342] Gistaro 6/14/17 302, at 2.

[343] Culver 6/14/17 302, at 2-3.

[344] Coats 6/14/17 302, at 4.

[345] Coats 6/14/17 302, at 4; Dempsey 6/14/17 302, at 3 (Coats relayed that the President had asked several times what Coats could do to help "get [the investigation] done," and Coats had repeatedly told the President that fastest way to "get it done" was to let it run its course).

[346] Hearing on Foreign Intelligence Surveillance Act Before the Senate Select Intelligence Committee, 115th Cong. (June 7, 2017) (CQ Cong. Transcripts, at 25) (testimony by Daniel Coats, Director of National Intelligence).

[347] Rogers 6/12/17 302, at 3-4.

[348] Rogers 6/12/17 302, at 4.

[349] Ledgett 6/13/17 302, at 1-2; see Rogers 6/12/17 302, at 4.

[350] Rogers 6/12/17 302, at 4-5; Ledgett 6/13/17 302, at 2.

[351] Ledgett 6/13/17 302, at 2.

[352] Ledgett 6/13/17 302, at 2-3; Rogers 6/12/17 302, at 4.

56

320

investigation itself.[353] Rogers later testified in a congressional hearing that as NSA Director he had "never been directed to do anything [he] believe[d] to be illegal, immoral, unethical or inappropriate" and did "not recall ever feeling pressured to do so."[354]

In addition to the specific comments made to Coats, Pompeo, and Rogers, the President spoke on other occasions in the presence of intelligence community officials about the Russia investigation and stated that it interfered with his ability to conduct foreign relations.[355] On at least two occasions, the President began Presidential Daily Briefings by stating that there was no collusion with Russia and he hoped a press statement to that effect could be issued.[356] Pompeo recalled that the President vented about the investigation on multiple occasions, complaining that there was no evidence against him and that nobody would publicly defend him.[357] Rogers recalled a private conversation with the President in which he "vent[ed]" about the investigation, said he had done nothing wrong, and said something like the "Russia thing has got to go away."[358] Coats recalled the President bringing up the Russia investigation several times, and Coats said he finally told the President that Coats's job was to provide intelligence and not get involved in investigations.[359]

4. The President Asks Comey to "Lift the Cloud" Created by the Russia Investigation

On the morning of March 30, 2017, the President reached out to Comey directly about the Russia investigation.[360] According to Comey's contemporaneous record of the conversation, the President said "he was trying to run the country and the cloud of this Russia business was making

---

[353] Rogers 6/12/17 302, at 5; Ledgett 6/13/17 302, at 2.

[354] *Hearing on Foreign Intelligence Surveillance Act Before the Senate Select Intelligence Committee*, 115th Cong. (June 7, 2017) (CQ Cong. Transcripts, at 20) (testimony by Admiral Michael Rogers, Director of the National Security Agency).

[355] Gistaro 6/14/17 302, at 1, 3; Pompeo 6/28/17 302, at 2-3.

[356] Gistaro 6/14/17 302, at 1.

[357] Pompeo 6/28/17 302, at 2.

[358] Rogers 6/12/17 302, at 6.

[359] Coats 6/14/17 302, at 3-4.

[360] SCR012b_000044 (President's Daily Diary, 3/30/17, reflecting call to Comey from 8:14 - 8:24 a.m.); Comey 3/30/17 Memorandum, at 1 ("The President called me on my CMS phone at 8:13 am today . . . . The call lasted 11 minutes (about 10 minutes when he was connected)."; *Hearing on Russian Election Interference Before the Senate Select Intelligence Committee*, 115th Cong. (June 8, 2017) (Statement for the Record of James B. Comey, former Director of the FBI, at 6).

U.S. Department of Justice

~~Attorney Work Product // May Contain Material Protected Under Fed. R. Crim. P. 6(e)~~

that difficult."[361] The President asked Comey what could be done to "lift the cloud."[362] Comey explained "that we were running it down as quickly as possible and that there would be great benefit, if we didn't find anything, to our Good Housekeeping seal of approval, but we had to do our work."[363] Comey also told the President that congressional leaders were aware that the FBI was not investigating the President personally.[364] The President said several times, "We need to get that fact out."[365] The President commented that if there was "some satellite" (which Comey took to mean an associate of the President's or the campaign) that did something, "it would be good to find that out" but that he himself had not done anything wrong and he hoped Comey "would find a way to get out that we weren't investigating him."[366] After the call ended, Comey called Boente and told him about the conversation, asked for guidance on how to respond, and said he was uncomfortable with direct contact from the President about the investigation.[367]

On the morning of April 11, 2017, the President called Comey again.[368] According to Comey's contemporaneous record of the conversation, the President said he was "following up to see if [Comey] did what [the President] had asked last time—getting out that he personally is not under investigation."[369] Comey responded that he had passed the request to Boente but not heard back, and he informed the President that the traditional channel for such a request would be to

---

[361] Comey 3/30/17 Memorandum, at 1. Comey subsequently testified before Congress about this conversation and described it to our Office; his recollections were consistent with his memorandum. *Hearing on Russian Election Interference Before the Senate Select Intelligence Committee*, 115th Cong. (June 8, 2017) (Statement for the Record of James B. Comey, former Director of the FBI, at 6); Comey 11/15/17 302, at 18.

[362] Comey 3/30/17 Memorandum, at 1; Comey 11/15/17 302, at 18.

[363] Comey 3/30/17 Memorandum, at 1; Comey 11/15/17 302, at 18.

[364] Comey 3/30/17 Memorandum, at 1; *Hearing on Russian Election Interference Before the Senate Select Intelligence Committee*, 115th Cong. (June 8, 2017) (Statement for the Record of James B. Comey, former Director of the FBI, at 6).

[365] Comey 3/30/17 Memorandum, at 1; *Hearing on Russian Election Interference Before the Senate Select Intelligence Committee*, 115th Cong. (June 8, 2017) (Statement for the Record of James B. Comey, former Director of the FBI, at 6).

[366] Comey 3/30/17 Memorandum, at 1; *Hearing on Russian Election Interference Before the Senate Select Intelligence Committee*, 115th Cong. (June 8, 2017) (Statement for the Record of James B. Comey, former Director of the FBI, at 6-7).

[367] Comey 3/30/17 Memorandum, at 2; Boente 1/31/18 302, at 6-7; *Hearing on Russian Election Interference Before the Senate Select Intelligence Committee*, 115th Cong. (June 8, 2017) (Statement for the Record of James B. Comey, former Director of the FBI, at 7).

[368] SCR012b_000053 (President's Daily Diary, 4/11/17, reflecting call to Comey from 8:27 – 8:31 a.m.); Comey 4/11/17 Memorandum, at 1 ("I returned the president's call this morning at 8:26 am EDT. We spoke for about four minutes.").

[369] Comey 4/11/17 Memorandum, at 1. Comey subsequently testified before Congress about this conversation and his recollections were consistent with his memo. *Hearing on Russian Election Interference Before the Senate Select Intelligence Committee*, 115th Cong. (June 8, 2017) (Statement for the Record of James B. Comey, former Director of the FBI, at 7).

have the White House Counsel contact DOJ leadership.[370] The President said he would take that step.[371] The President then added, "Because I have been very loyal to you, very loyal, we had that thing, you know."[372] In a televised interview that was taped early that afternoon, the President was asked if it was too late for him to ask Comey to step down; the President responded, "No, it's not too late, but you know, I have confidence in him. We'll see what happens. You know, it's going to be interesting."[373] After the interview, Hicks told the President she thought the President's comment about Comey should be removed from the broadcast of the interview, but the President wanted to keep it in, which Hicks thought was unusual.[374]

Later that day, the President told senior advisors, including McGahn and Priebus, that he had reached out to Comey twice in recent weeks.[375] The President acknowledged that McGahn would not approve of the outreach to Comey because McGahn had previously cautioned the President that he should not talk to Comey directly to prevent any perception that the White House was interfering with investigations.[376] The President told McGahn that Comey had indicated the FBI could make a public statement that the President was not under investigation if the Department of Justice approved that action.[377] After speaking with the President, McGahn followed up with Boente to relay the President's understanding that the FBI could make a public announcement if the Department of Justice cleared it.[378] McGahn recalled that Boente said Comey had told him there was nothing obstructive about the calls from the President, but they made Comey uncomfortable.[379] According to McGahn, Boente responded that he did not want to issue a statement about the President not being under investigation because of the potential political ramifications and did not want to order Comey to do it because that action could prompt the

[370] Comey 4/11/17 Memorandum, at 1.

[371] Comey 4/11/17 Memorandum, at 1.

[372] Comey 4/11/17 Memorandum, at 1. In a footnote to this statement in his memorandum, Comey wrote, "His use of these words did not fit with the flow of the call, which at that point had moved away from any request of me, but I have recorded it here as it happened."

[373] Maria Bartiromo, *Interview with President Trump*, Fox Business Network (Apr. 12, 2017); SCR012b_000054 (President's Daily Diary, 4/11/17, reflecting Bartiromo interview from 12:30 - 12:55 p.m.).

[374] Hicks 12/8/17 302, at 13.

[375] Priebus 10/13/17 302, at 23; McGahn 12/12/17 302, at 9.

[376] Priebus 10/13/17 302, at 23; McGahn 12/12/17 302, at 9; *see* McGahn 11/30/17 302, at 9; Dhillon 11/21/17 302, at 2 (stating that White House Counsel attorneys had advised the President not to contact the FBI Director directly because it could create a perception he was interfering with investigations). Later in April, the President told other attorneys in the White House Counsel's Office that he had called Comey even though he knew they had advised against direct contact. Dhillon 11/21/17 302, at 2 (recalling that the President said, "I know you told me not to, but I called Comey anyway.").

[377] McGahn 12/12/17 302, at 9.

[378] McGahn 12/12/17 302, at 9.

[379] McGahn 12/12/17 302, at 9; *see* Boente 1/31/18 302, at 6 (recalling that Comey told him after the March 30, 2017 call that it was not obstructive).

59

U.S. Department of Justice

~~Attorney Work Product~~ // ~~May Contain Material Protected Under Fed. R. Crim. P. 6(e)~~

appointment of a Special Counsel.[380] Boente did not recall that aspect of his conversation with McGahn, but did recall telling McGahn that the direct outreaches from the President to Comey were a problem.[381] Boente recalled that McGahn agreed and said he would do what he could to address that issue.[382]

Analysis

In analyzing the President's reaction to Sessions's recusal and the requests he made to Coats, Pompeo, Rogers, and Comey, the following evidence is relevant to the elements of obstruction of justice:

    a.   <u>Obstructive act</u>. The evidence shows that, after Comey's March 20, 2017 testimony, the President repeatedly reached out to intelligence agency leaders to discuss the FBI's investigation. But witnesses had different recollections of the precise content of those outreaches. Some ODNI officials recalled that Coats told them immediately after the March 22 Oval Office meeting that the President asked Coats to intervene with Comey and "stop" the investigation. But the first-hand witnesses to the encounter remember the conversation differently. Pompeo had no memory of the specific meeting, but generally recalled the President urging officials to get the word out that the President had not done anything wrong related to Russia. Coats recalled that the President asked that Coats state publicly that no link existed between the President and Russia, but did not ask him to speak with Comey or to help end the investigation. The other outreaches by the President during this period were similar in nature. The President asked Rogers if he could do anything to refute the stories linking the President to Russia, and the President asked Comey to make a public statement that would "lift the cloud" of the ongoing investigation by making clear that the President was not personally under investigation. These requests, while significant enough that Rogers thought it important to document the encounter in a written memorandum, were not interpreted by the officials who received them as directives to improperly interfere with the investigation.

    b.   <u>Nexus to a proceeding</u>. At the time of the President's outreaches to leaders of the intelligence agencies in late March and early April 2017, the FBI's Russia investigation did not yet involve grand jury proceedings. The outreaches, however, came after and were in response to Comey's March 20, 2017 announcement that the FBI, as a part of its counterintelligence mission, was conducting an investigation into Russian interference in the 2016 presidential election. Comey testified that the investigation included any links or coordination with Trump campaign officials and would "include an assessment of whether any crimes were committed."

    c.   <u>Intent</u>. As described above, the evidence does not establish that the President asked or directed intelligence agency leaders to stop or interfere with the FBI's Russia investigation— and the President affirmatively told Comey that if "some satellite" was involved in Russian election interference "it would be good to find that out." But the President's intent in trying to prevent Sessions's recusal, and in reaching out to Coats, Pompeo, Rogers, and Comey following

---

[380] McGahn 12/12/17 302, at 9-10.

[381] Boente 1/31/18 302, at 7; McGahn 12/12/17 302, at 9.

[382] Boente 1/31/18 302, at 7.

U.S. Department of Justice

~~Attorney Work Product // May Contain Material Protected Under Fed. R. Crim. P. 6(e)~~

Comey's public announcement of the FBI's Russia investigation, is nevertheless relevant to understanding what motivated the President's other actions towards the investigation.

The evidence shows that the President was focused on the Russia investigation's implications for his presidency—and, specifically, on dispelling any suggestion that he was under investigation or had links to Russia. In early March, the President attempted to prevent Sessions's recusal, even after being told that Sessions was following DOJ conflict-of-interest rules. After Sessions recused, the White House Counsel's Office tried to cut off further contact with Sessions about the matter, although it is not clear whether that direction was conveyed to the President. The President continued to raise the issue of Sessions's recusal and, when he had the opportunity, he pulled Sessions aside and urged him to unrecuse. The President also told advisors that he wanted an Attorney General who would protect him, the way he perceived Robert Kennedy and Eric Holder to have protected their presidents. The President made statements about being able to direct the course of criminal investigations, saying words to the effect of, "You're telling me that Bobby and Jack didn't talk about investigations? Or Obama didn't tell Eric Holder who to investigate?"

After Comey publicly confirmed the existence of the FBI's Russia investigation on March 20, 2017, the President was "beside himself" and expressed anger that Comey did not issue a statement correcting any misperception that the President himself was under investigation. The President sought to speak with Acting Attorney General Boente directly and told McGahn to contact Boente to request that Comey make a clarifying statement. The President then asked other intelligence community leaders to make public statements to refute the suggestion that the President had links to Russia, but the leaders told him they could not publicly comment on the investigation. On March 30 and April 11, against the advice of White House advisors who had informed him that any direct contact with the FBI could be perceived as improper interference in an ongoing investigation, the President made personal outreaches to Comey asking him to "lift the cloud" of the Russia investigation by making public the fact that the President was not personally under investigation.

Evidence indicates that the President was angered by both the existence of the Russia investigation and the public reporting that he was under investigation, which he knew was not true based on Comey's representations. The President complained to advisors that if people thought Russia helped him with the election, it would detract from what he had accomplished.

Other evidence indicates that the President was concerned about the impact of the Russia investigation on his ability to govern. The President complained that the perception that he was under investigation was hurting his ability to conduct foreign relations, particularly with Russia. The President told Coats he "can't do anything with Russia," he told Rogers that "the thing with the Russians" was interfering with his ability to conduct foreign affairs, and he told Comey that "he was trying to run the country and the cloud of this Russia business was making that difficult."

61

U.S. Department of Justice

~~Attorney Work Product // May Contain Material Protected Under Fed. R. Crim. P. 6(e)~~

D.   **Events Leading Up To and Surrounding the Termination of FBI Director Comey**

Overview

Comey was scheduled to testify before Congress on May 3, 2017. Leading up to that testimony, the President continued to tell advisors that he wanted Comey to make public that the President was not under investigation. At the hearing, Comey declined to answer questions about the scope or subjects of the Russia investigation and did not state publicly that the President was not under investigation. Two days later, on May 5, 2017, the President told close aides he was going to fire Comey, and on May 9, he did so, using his official termination letter to make public that Comey had on three occasions informed the President that he was not under investigation. The President decided to fire Comey before receiving advice or a recommendation from the Department of Justice, but he approved an initial public account of the termination that attributed it to a recommendation from the Department of Justice based on Comey's handling of the Clinton email investigation. After Deputy Attorney General Rod Rosenstein resisted attributing the firing to his recommendation, the President acknowledged that he intended to fire Comey regardless of the DOJ recommendation and was thinking of the Russia investigation when he made the decision. The President also told the Russian Foreign Minister, "I just fired the head of the F.B.I. He was crazy, a real nut job. I faced great pressure because of Russia. That's taken off. . . . . I'm not under investigation."

Evidence

1.   Comey Testifies Before the Senate Judiciary Committee and Declines to Answer Questions About Whether the President is Under Investigation

On May 3, 2017, Comey was scheduled to testify at an FBI oversight hearing before the Senate Judiciary Committee.[383] McGahn recalled that in the week leading up to the hearing, the President said that it would be the last straw if Comey did not take the opportunity to set the record straight by publicly announcing that the President was not under investigation.[384] The President had previously told McGahn that the perception that the President was under investigation was hurting his ability to carry out his presidential duties and deal with foreign leaders.[385] At the hearing, Comey declined to answer questions about the status of the Russia investigation, stating "[t]he Department of Justice ha[d] authorized [him] to confirm that [the Russia investigation] exists," but that he was "not going to say another word about it" until the investigation was completed.[386] Comey also declined to answer questions about whether investigators had "ruled

---

[383] *Hearing on Oversight of the FBI before the Senate Judiciary Committee*, 115th Cong. (May 3, 2017).

[384] McGahn 12/12/17 302, at 10-11.

[385] McGahn 12/12/17 302, at 7, 10-11 (McGahn believed that two foreign leaders had expressed sympathy to the President for being under investigation); SC_AD_00265 (Donaldson 4/11/17 Notes) ("P Called Comey – Day we told him not to? 'You are not under investigation' NK/China/Sapping Credibility").

[386] *Hearing on FBI Oversight Before the Senate Judiciary Committee*, 115th Cong. (CQ Cong. Transcripts, at 70) (May 3, 2017) (testimony by FBI Director James Comey). Comey repeated this point

62

U.S. Department of Justice

~~Attorney Work Product // May Contain Material Protected Under Fed. R. Crim. P. 6(e)~~

out anyone in the Trump campaign as potentially a target of th[e] criminal investigation," including whether the FBI had "ruled out the president of the United States."[387]

Comey was also asked at the hearing about his decision to announce 11 days before the presidential election that the FBI was reopening the Clinton email investigation.[388] Comey stated that it made him "mildly nauseous to think that we might have had some impact on the election," but added that "even in hindsight" he "would make the same decision."[389] He later repeated that he had no regrets about how he had handled the email investigation and believed he had "done the right thing at each turn."[390]

In the afternoon following Comey's testimony, the President met with McGahn, Sessions, and Sessions's Chief of Staff Jody Hunt.[391] At that meeting, the President asked McGahn how Comey had done in his testimony and McGahn relayed that Comey had declined to answer questions about whether the President was under investigation.[392] The President became very upset and directed his anger at Sessions.[393] According to notes written by Hunt, the President said, "This is terrible Jeff. It's all because you recused. AG is supposed to be most important appointment. Kennedy appointed his brother. Obama appointed Holder. I appointed you and you recused yourself. You left me on an island. I can't do anything."[394] The President said that the recusal was unfair and that it was interfering with his ability to govern and undermining his authority with foreign leaders.[395] Sessions responded that he had had no choice but to recuse, and it was a mandatory rather than discretionary decision.[396] Hunt recalled that Sessions also stated at

---

several times during his testimony. *See id.* at 26 (explaining that he was "not going to say another peep about [the investigation] until we're done"); *id.* at 90 (stating that he would not provide any updates about the status of investigation "before the matter is concluded").

[387] *Hearing on FBI Oversight Before the Senate Judiciary Committee*, 115th Cong. (May 3, 2017) (CQ Cong. Transcripts, at 87-88) (questions by Sen. Blumenthal and testimony by FBI Director James B. Comey).

[388] *Hearing on FBI Oversight Before the Senate Judiciary Committee*, 115th Cong. (May 3, 2017) (CQ Cong. Transcripts, at 15) (question by Sen. Feinstein).

[389] *Hearing on FBI Oversight Before the Senate Judiciary Committee*, 115th Cong. (May 3, 2017) (CQ Cong. Transcripts, at 17) (testimony by FBI Director James B. Comey).

[390] *Hearing on FBI Oversight Before the Senate Judiciary Committee*, 115th Cong. (May 3, 2017) (CQ Cong. Transcripts, at 92) (testimony by FBI Director James B. Comey).

[391] Sessions 1/17/18 302, at 8; Hunt 2/1/18 302, at 8.

[392] Sessions 1/17/18 302, at 8; Hunt-000021 (Hunt 5/3/17 Notes); McGahn 3/8/18 302, at 6.

[393] Sessions 1/17/18 302, at 8-9.

[394] Hunt-000021 (Hunt 5/3/17 Notes). Hunt said that he wrote down notes describing this meeting and others with the President after the events occurred. Hunt 2/1/17 302, at 2.

[395] Hunt-000021-22 (Hunt 5/3/17 Notes) ("I have foreign leaders saying they are sorry I am being investigated."); Sessions 1/17/18 302, at 8 (Sessions recalled that a Chinese leader had said to the President that he was sorry the President was under investigation, which the President interpreted as undermining his authority); Hunt 2/1/18 302, at 8.

[396] Sessions 1/17/18 302, at 8; Hunt-000022 (Hunt 5/3/17 Notes).

U.S. Department of Justice

~~Attorney Work Product // May Contain Material Protected Under Fed. R. Crim. P. 6(e)~~

some point during the conversation that a new start at the FBI would be appropriate and the President should consider replacing Comey as FBI director.[397] According to Sessions, when the meeting concluded, it was clear that the President was unhappy with Comey, but Sessions did not think the President had made the decision to terminate Comey.[398]

Bannon recalled that the President brought Comey up with him at least eight times on May 3 and May 4, 2017.[399] According to Bannon, the President said the same thing each time: "He told me three times I'm not under investigation. He's a showboater. He's a grandstander. I don't know any Russians. There was no collusion."[400] Bannon told the President that he could not fire Comey because "that ship had sailed."[401] Bannon also told the President that firing Comey was not going to stop the investigation, cautioning him that he could fire the FBI director but could not fire the FBI.[402]

2. The President Makes the Decision to Terminate Comey

The weekend following Comey's May 3, 2017 testimony, the President traveled to his resort in Bedminster, New Jersey.[403] At a dinner on Friday, May 5, attended by the President and various advisors and family members, including Jared Kushner and senior advisor Stephen Miller, the President stated that he wanted to remove Comey and had ideas for a letter that would be used to make the announcement.[404] The President dictated arguments and specific language for the letter, and Miller took notes.[405] As reflected in the notes, the President told Miller that the letter should start, "While I greatly appreciate you informing me that I am not under investigation concerning what I have often stated is a fabricated story on a Trump-Russia relationship – pertaining to the 2016 presidential election, please be informed that I, and I believe the American public – including Ds and Rs – have lost faith in you as Director of the FBI."[406] Following the dinner, Miller prepared a termination letter based on those notes and research he conducted to support the President's arguments.[407] Over the weekend, the President provided several rounds of

---

[397] Hunt-000022 (Hunt 5/3/17 Notes).

[398] Sessions 1/17/18 302, at 9.

[399] Bannon 2/12/18 302, at 20.

[400] Bannon 2/12/18 302, at 20.

[401] Bannon 2/12/18 302, at 20.

[402] Bannon 2/12/18 302, at 20-21; see Priebus 10/13/17 302, at 28.

[403] S. Miller 10/31/17 302, at 4-5; SCR025_000019 (President's Daily Diary, 5/4/17).

[404] S. Miller 10/31/17 302, at 5.

[405] S. Miller 10/31/17 302, at 5-6.

[406] S. Miller 5/5/17 Notes, at 1; see S. Miller 10/31/17 302, at 8.

[407] S. Miller 10/31/17 302, at 6.

edits on the draft letter.[408] Miller said the President was adamant that he not tell anyone at the White House what they were preparing because the President was worried about leaks.[409]

In his discussions with Miller, the President made clear that he wanted the letter to open with a reference to him not being under investigation.[410] Miller said he believed that fact was important to the President to show that Comey was not being terminated based on any such investigation.[411] According to Miller, the President wanted to establish as a factual matter that Comey had been under a "review period" and did not have assurance from the President that he would be permitted to keep his job.[412]

The final version of the termination letter prepared by Miller and the President began in a way that closely tracked what the President had dictated to Miller at the May 5 dinner: "Dear Director Comey, While I greatly appreciate your informing me, on three separate occasions, that I am not under investigation concerning the fabricated and politically-motivated allegations of a Trump-Russia relationship with respect to the 2016 Presidential Election, please be informed that I, along with members of both political parties and, most importantly, the American Public, have lost faith in you as the Director of the FBI and you are hereby terminated."[413] The four-page letter went on to critique Comey's judgment and conduct, including his May 3 testimony before the Senate Judiciary Committee, his handling of the Clinton email investigation, and his failure to hold leakers accountable.[414] The letter stated that Comey had "asked [the President] at dinner shortly after inauguration to let [Comey] stay on in the Director's role, and [the President] said that [he] would consider it," but the President had "concluded that [he] ha[d] no alternative but to find new leadership for the Bureau – a leader that restores confidence and trust."[415]

In the morning of Monday, May 8, 2017, the President met in the Oval Office with senior advisors, including McGahn, Priebus, and Miller, and informed them he had decided to terminate Comey.[416] The President read aloud the first paragraphs of the termination letter he wrote with

---

[408] S. Miller 10/31/17 302, at 6-8.

[409] S. Miller 10/31/17 302, at 7. Miller said he did not want Priebus to be blindsided, so on Sunday night he called Priebus to tell him that the President had been thinking about the "Comey situation" and there would be an important discussion on Monday. S. Miller 10/31/17 302, at 7.

[410] S. Miller 10/31/17 302, at 8.

[411] S. Miller 10/31/17 302, at 8.

[412] S. Miller 10/31/17 302, at 10.

[413] SCR013c_000003-06 (Draft Termination Letter to FBI Director Comey).

[414] SCR013c_000003-06 (Draft Termination Letter to FBI Director Comey). Kushner said that the termination letter reflected the reasons the President wanted to fire Comey and was the truest representation of what the President had said during the May 5 dinner. Kushner 4/11/18 302, at 25.

[415] SCR013c_000003 (Draft Termination Letter to FBI Director Comey).

[416] McGahn 12/12/17 302, at 11; Priebus 10/13/17 302, at 24; S. Miller 10/31/17 302, at 11; Dhillon 11/21/17 302, at 6; Eisenberg 11/29/17 302, at 13.

Miller and conveyed that the decision had been made and was not up for discussion.[417]   The President told the group that Miller had researched the issue and determined the President had the authority to terminate Comey without cause.[418]   In an effort to slow down the decision-making process, McGahn told the President that DOJ leadership was currently discussing Comey's status and suggested that White House Counsel's Office attorneys should talk with Sessions and Rod Rosenstein, who had recently been confirmed as the Deputy Attorney General.[419]   McGahn said that previously scheduled meetings with Sessions and Rosenstein that day would be an opportunity to find out what they thought about firing Comey.[420]

At noon, Sessions, Rosenstein, and Hunt met with McGahn and White House Counsel's Office attorney Uttam Dhillon at the White House.[421]   McGahn said that the President had decided to fire Comey and asked for Sessions's and Rosenstein's views.[422]   Sessions and Rosenstein criticized Comey and did not raise concerns about replacing him.[423]   McGahn and Dhillon said the fact that neither Sessions nor Rosenstein objected to replacing Comey gave them peace of mind that the President's decision to fire Comey was not an attempt to obstruct justice.[424]   An Oval Office meeting was scheduled later that day so that Sessions and Rosenstein could discuss the issue with the President.[425]

At around 5 p.m., the President and several White House officials met with Sessions and Rosenstein to discuss Comey.[426]   The President told the group that he had watched Comey's May

---

[417] S. Miller 10/31/17 302, at 11 (observing that the President started the meeting by saying, "I'm going to read you a letter. Don't talk me out of this. I've made my decision."); Dhillon 11/21/17 302, at 6 (the President announced in an irreversible way that he was firing Comey); Eisenberg 11/29/17 302, at 13 (the President did not leave whether or not to fire Comey up for discussion); Priebus 10/13/17 302, at 25; McGahn 12/12/17 302, at 11-12.

[418] Dhillon 302 11/21/17, at 6; Eisenberg 11/29/17 302, at 13; McGahn 12/12/17 302, at 11.

[419] McGahn 12/12/17 302, at 12, 13; S. Miller 10/31/17 302, at 11; Dhillon 11/21/17 302, at 7. Because of the Attorney General's recusal, Rosenstein became the Acting Attorney General for the Russia investigation upon his confirmation as Deputy Attorney General. See 28 U.S.C. § 508(a) ("In case of a vacancy in the office of Attorney General, or of his absence or disability, the Deputy Attorney General may exercise all the duties of that office").

[420] McGahn 12/12/17 302, at 12.

[421] Dhillon 11/21/17 302, at 7; McGahn 12/12/17 302, at 13; Gauhar-000056 (Gauhar 5/16/17 Notes); see Gauhar-000056-72 (2/11/19 Memorandum to File attaching Gauhar handwritten notes) ("Ms. Gauhar determined that she likely recorded all these notes during one or more meetings on Tuesday, May 16, 2017.").

[422] McGahn 12/12/17 302, at 13; see Gauhar-000056 (Gauhar 5/16/17 Notes).

[423] Dhillon 11/21/17 302, at 7-9; Sessions 1/17/18 302, at 9; McGahn 12/12/17 302, at 13.

[424] McGahn 12/12/17 302, at 13; Dhillon 11/21/17 302, at 9.

[425] Hunt-000026 (Hunt 5/8/17 Notes); see Gauhar-000057 (Gauhar 5/16/17 Notes).

[426] Rosenstein 5/23/17 302, at 2; McGahn 12/12/17 302, at 14; see Gauhar-000057 (Gauhar 5/16/17 Notes).

3 testimony over the weekend and thought that something was "not right" with Comey.[427] The President said that Comey should be removed and asked Sessions and Rosenstein for their views.[428] Hunt, who was in the room, recalled that Sessions responded that he had previously recommended that Comey be replaced.[429] McGahn and Dhillon said Rosenstein described his concerns about Comey's handling of the Clinton email investigation.[430]

The President then distributed copies of the termination letter he had drafted with Miller, and the discussion turned to the mechanics of how to fire Comey and whether the President's letter should be used.[431] McGahn and Dhillon urged the President to permit Comey to resign, but the President was adamant that he be fired.[432] The group discussed the possibility that Rosenstein and Sessions could provide a recommendation in writing that Comey should be removed.[433] The President agreed and told Rosenstein to draft a memorandum, but said he wanted to receive it first thing the next morning.[434] Hunt's notes reflect that the President told Rosenstein to include in his recommendation the fact that Comey had refused to confirm that the President was not personally under investigation.[435] According to notes taken by a senior DOJ official of Rosenstein's description of his meeting with the President, the President said, "Put the Russia stuff in the memo."[436] Rosenstein responded that the Russia investigation was not the basis of his recommendation, so he did not think Russia should be mentioned.[437] The President told Rosenstein he would appreciate it if Rosenstein put it in his letter anyway.[438] When Rosenstein

---

[427] Hunt-000026-27 (Hunt 5/8/17 Notes).

[428] Sessions 1/17/18 302, at 10; *see* Gauhar-000058 (Gauhar 5/16/17 Notes) ("POTUS to AG: What is your rec?").

[429] Hunt-000027 (Hunt 5/8/17 Notes).

[430] McGahn 12/12/17 302, at 14; Dhillon 11/21/17 302, at 7.

[431] Hunt-000028 (Hunt 5/8/17 Notes).

[432] McGahn 12/12/17 302, at 13.

[433] Hunt-000028-29 (Hunt 5/8/17 Notes).

[434] McCabe 9/26/17 302, at 13; Rosenstein 5/23/17 302, at 2; *see* Gauhar-000059 (Gauhar 5/16/17 Notes) ("POTUS tells DAG to write a memo").

[435] Hunt-000028-29 (Hunt 5/8/17 Notes) ("POTUS asked if Rod's recommendation would include the fact that although Comey talks about the investigation he refuses to say that the President is not under investigation. . . . So it would be good if your recommendation would make mention of the fact that Comey refuses to say public[ly] what he said privately 3 times.").

[436] Gauhar-000059 (Gauhar 5/16/17 Notes).

[437] Sessions 1/17/18 302 at 10; McCabe 9/26/17 302, at 13; *see* Gauhar-000059 (Gauhar 5/16/17 Notes).

[438] Gauhar-000059 (Gauhar 5/16/17 Notes); McCabe 5/16/17 Memorandum 1; McCabe 9/26/17 302, at 13.

U.S. Department of Justice

Attorney Work Product // May Contain Material Protected Under Fed. R. Crim. P. 6(e)

left the meeting, he knew that Comey would be terminated, and he told DOJ colleagues that his own reasons for replacing Comey were "not [the President's] reasons."[439]

On May 9, Hunt delivered to the White House a letter from Sessions recommending Comey's removal and a memorandum from Rosenstein, addressed to the Attorney General, titled "Restoring Public Confidence in the FBI."[440] McGahn recalled that the President liked the DOJ letters and agreed that they should provide the foundation for a new cover letter from the President accepting the recommendation to terminate Comey.[441] Notes taken by Donaldson on May 9 reflected the view of the White House Counsel's Office that the President's original termination letter should "[n]ot [see the] light of day" and that it would be better to offer "[n]o other rationales" for the firing than what was in Rosenstein's and Sessions's memoranda.[442] The President asked Miller to draft a new termination letter and directed Miller to say in the letter that Comey had informed the President three times that he was not under investigation.[443] McGahn, Priebus, and Dhillon objected to including that language, but the President insisted that it be included.[444] McGahn, Priebus, and others perceived that language to be the most important part of the letter to

---

[439] Rosenstein 5/23/17 302, at 2; Gauhar-000059 (Gauhar 5/16/17 Notes) ("DAG reasons not their reasons [POTUS]"); Gauhar-000060 (Gauhar 5/16/17 Notes) ("1st draft had a recommendation. Took it out b/c knew decision had already been made.").

[440] Rosenstein 5/23/17 302, at 4; McGahn 12/12/17 302, at 15; 5/9/17 Letter, Sessions to President Trump ("Based on my evaluation, and for the reasons expressed by the Deputy Attorney General in the attached memorandum, I have concluded that a fresh start is needed at the leadership of the FBI."); 5/9/17 Memorandum, Rosenstein to Sessions (concluding with, "The way the Director handled the conclusion of the email investigation was wrong. As a result, the FBI is unlikely to regain public and congressional trust until it has a Director who understands the gravity of the mistakes and pledges never to repeat them. Having refused to admit his errors, the Director cannot be expected to implement the necessary corrective actions.").

[441] S. Miller 10/31/17 302, at 12; McGahn 12/12/17 302, at 15; Hunt-000031 (Hunt 5/9/17 Notes).

[442] SC_AD_00342 (Donaldson 5/9/17 Notes). Donaldson also wrote "[i]s this the beginning of the end?" because she was worried that the decision to terminate Comey and the manner in which it was carried out would be the end of the presidency. Donaldson 11/6/17 302, at 25.

[443] S. Miller 10/31/17 302, at 12; McGahn 12/12/17 302, at 15; Hunt-000032 (Hunt 5/9/17 Notes).

[444] McGahn 12/12/17 302, at 15; S. Miller 10/31/17 302, at 12; Dhillon 11/21/17 302, at 8, 10; Priebus 10/13/17 302, at 27; Hunt 2/1/18 302, at 14-15; Hunt-000032 (Hunt 5/9/17 Notes).

U.S. Department of Justice

~~Attorney Work Product // May Contain Material Protected Under Fed. R. Crim. P. 6(e)~~

the President.[445] Dhillon made a final pitch to the President that Comey should be permitted to resign, but the President refused.[446]

Around the time the President's letter was finalized, Priebus summoned Spicer and the press team to the Oval Office, where they were told that Comey had been terminated for the reasons stated in the letters by Rosenstein and Sessions.[447] To announce Comey's termination, the White House released a statement, which Priebus thought had been dictated by the President.[448] In full, the statement read: "Today, President Donald J. Trump informed FBI Director James Comey that he has been terminated and removed from office. President Trump acted based on the clear recommendations of both Deputy Attorney General Rod Rosenstein and Attorney General Jeff Sessions."[449]

That evening, FBI Deputy Director Andrew McCabe was summoned to meet with the President at the White House.[450] The President told McCabe that he had fired Comey because of the decisions Comey had made in the Clinton email investigation and for many other reasons.[451] The President asked McCabe if he was aware that Comey had told the President three times that he was not under investigation.[452] The President also asked McCabe whether many people in the FBI disliked Comey and whether McCabe was part of the "resistance" that had disagreed with Comey's decisions in the Clinton investigation.[453] McCabe told the President that he knew Comey had told the President he was not under investigation, that most people in the FBI felt positively about Comey, and that McCabe worked "very closely" with Comey and was part of all the decisions that had been made in the Clinton investigation.[454]

---

[445] Dhillon 11/21/17 302, at 10; Eisenberg 11/29/17 302, at 15 (providing the view that the President's desire to include the language about not being under investigation was the "driving animus of the whole thing"); Burnham 11/3/17 302, at 16 (Burnham knew the only line the President cared about was the line that said Comey advised the President on three separate occasions that the President was not under investigation). According to Hunt's notes, the reference to Comey's statement would indicate that "notwithstanding" Comey's having informed the President that he was not under investigation, the President was terminating Comey. Hunt-000032 (Hunt 5/9/17 Notes). McGahn said he believed the President wanted the language included so that people would not think that the President had terminated Comey because the President was under investigation. McGahn 12/12/17 302, at 15.

[446] McGahn 12/12/17 302, at 15; Donaldson 11/6/17 302, at 25; see SC_AD_00342 (Donaldson 5/9/17 Notes) ("Resign vs. Removal. – POTUS/removal.").

[447] Spicer 10/16/17 302, at 9; McGahn 12/12/17 302, at 16.

[448] Priebus 10/13/17 302, at 28.

[449] *Statement of the Press Secretary,* The White House, Office of the Press Secretary (May 9, 2017).

[450] McCabe 9/26/17 302, at 4; SCR025_000044 (President's Daily Diary, 5/9/17); McCabe 5/10/17 Memorandum, at 1.

[451] McCabe 9/26/17 302, at 5; McCabe 5/10/17 Memorandum, at 1.

[452] McCabe 9/26/17 302, at 5; McCabe 5/10/17 Memorandum, at 1-2.

[453] McCabe 9/26/17 302, at 5; McCabe 5/10/17 Memorandum, at 1-2.

[454] McCabe 9/26/17 302, at 5; McCabe 5/10/17 Memorandum, at 1-2.

Later that evening, the President told his communications team he was unhappy with the press coverage of Comey's termination and ordered them to go out and defend him.[455] The President also called Chris Christie and, according to Christie, said he was getting "killed" in the press over Comey's termination.[456] The President asked what he should do.[457] Christie asked, "Did you fire [Comey] because of what Rod wrote in the memo?", and the President responded, "Yes."[458] Christie said that the President should "get Rod out there" and have him defend the decision.[459] The President told Christie that this was a "good idea" and said he was going to call Rosenstein right away.[460]

That night, the White House Press Office called the Department of Justice and said the White House wanted to put out a statement saying that it was Rosenstein's idea to fire Comey.[461] Rosenstein told other DOJ officials that he would not participate in putting out a "false story."[462] The President then called Rosenstein directly and said he was watching Fox News, that the coverage had been great, and that he wanted Rosenstein to do a press conference.[463] Rosenstein responded that this was not a good idea because if the press asked him, he would tell the truth that Comey's firing was not his idea.[464] Sessions also informed the White House Counsel's Office that evening that Rosenstein was upset that his memorandum was being portrayed as the reason for Comey's termination.[465]

In an unplanned press conference late in the evening of May 9, 2017, Spicer told reporters, "It was all [Rosenstein]. No one from the White House. It was a DOJ decision."[466] That evening and the next morning, White House officials and spokespeople continued to maintain that the

---

[455] Spicer 10/16/17 302, at 11; Hicks 12/8/17, at 18; Sanders 7/3/18 302, at 2.

[456] Christie 2/13/19 302, at 6.

[457] Christie 2/13/19 302, at 6.

[458] Christie 2/13/19 302, at 6.

[459] Christie 2/13/19 302, at 6.

[460] Christie 2/13/19 302, at 6.

[461] Gauhar-000071 (Gauhar 5/16/17 Notes); Page Memorandum, at 3 (recording events of 5/16/17); McCabe 9/26/17 302, at 14.

[462] Rosenstein 5/23/17 302, at 4-5; Gauhar-000059 (Gauhar 5/16/17 Notes).

[463] Rosenstein 5/23/17 302, at 4-5; Gauhar-000071 (Gauhar 5/16/17 Notes).

[464] Gauhar-000071 (Gauhar 5/16/17 Notes). DOJ notes from the week of Comey's firing indicate that Priebus was "screaming" at the DOJ public affairs office trying to get Rosenstein to do a press conference, and the DOJ public affairs office told Priebus that Rosenstein had told the President he was not doing it. Gauhar-000071-72 (Gauhar 5/16/17 Notes).

[465] McGahn 12/12/17 302, at 16-17; Donaldson 11/6/17 302, at 26-27; Dhillon 11/21/17 302, at 11.

[466] Jenna Johnson, *After Trump fired Comey, White House staff scrambled to explain why*, Washington Post (May 10, 2017) (quoting Spicer).

President's decision to terminate Comey was driven by the recommendations the President received from Rosenstein and Sessions.[467]

In the morning on May 10, 2017, President Trump met with Russian Foreign Minister Sergey Lavrov and Russian Ambassador Sergey Kislyak in the Oval Office.[468] The media subsequently reported that during the May 10 meeting the President brought up his decision the prior day to terminate Comey, telling Lavrov and Kislyak: "I just fired the head of the F.B.I. He was crazy, a real nut job. I faced great pressure because of Russia. That's taken off. . . . I'm not under investigation."[469] The President never denied making those statements, and the White House did not dispute the account, instead issuing a statement that said: "By grandstanding and politicizing the investigation into Russia's actions, James Comey created unnecessary pressure on our ability to engage and negotiate with Russia. The investigation would have always continued, and obviously, the termination of Comey would not have ended it. Once again, the real story is that our national security has been undermined by the leaking of private and highly classified information."[470] Hicks said that when she told the President about the reports on his meeting with Lavrov, he did not look concerned and said of Comey, "he *is* crazy."[471] When McGahn asked the President about his comments to Lavrov, the President said it was good that Comey was fired because that took the pressure off by making it clear that he was not under investigation so he could get more work done.[472]

That same morning, on May 10, 2017, the President called McCabe.[473] According to a memorandum McCabe wrote following the call, the President asked McCabe to come over to the White House to discuss whether the President should visit FBI headquarters and make a speech to

---

[467] *See, e.g.*, Sarah Sanders, *White House Daily Briefing*, C-SPAN (May 10, 2017); SCR013_001088 (5/10/17 Email, Hemming to Cheung et al.) (internal White House email describing comments on the Comey termination by Vice President Pence).

[468] SCR08_000353 (5/9/17 White House Document, "Working Visit with Foreign Minister Sergey Lavrov of Russia"); SCR08_001274 (5/10/17 Email, Ciaramella to Kelly et al.). The meeting had been planned on May 2, 2017, during a telephone call between the President and Russian President Vladimir Putin, and the meeting date was confirmed on May 5, 2017, the same day the President dictated ideas for the Comey termination letter to Stephen Miller. SCR08_001274 (5/10/17 Email, Ciaramella to Kelly et al.).

[469] Matt Apuzzo et al., *Trump Told Russians That Firing "Nut Job" Comey Eased Pressure From Investigation*, New York Times (May 19, 2017).

[470] SCR08_002117 (5/19/17 Email, Walters to Farhi (CBS News)); *see* Spicer 10/16/17 302, at 13 (noting he would have been told to "clean it up" if the reporting on the meeting with the Russian Foreign Minister was inaccurate, but he was never told to correct the reporting); Hicks 12/8/17 302, at 19 (recalling that the President never denied making the statements attributed to him in the Lavrov meeting and that the President had said similar things about Comey in an off-the-record meeting with reporters on May 18, 2017, calling Comey a "nut job" and "crazy").

[471] Hicks 12/8/17 302, at 19.

[472] McGahn 12/12/17 302, at 18.

[473] SCR025_000046 (President's Daily Diary, 5/10/17); McCabe 5/10/17 Memorandum, at 1.

employees.[474] The President said he had received "hundreds" of messages from FBI employees indicating their support for terminating Comey.[475] The President also told McCabe that Comey should not have been permitted to travel back to Washington, D.C. on the FBI's airplane after he had been terminated and that he did not want Comey "in the building again," even to collect his belongings.[476] When McCabe met with the President that afternoon, the President, without prompting, told McCabe that people in the FBI loved the President, estimated that at least 80% of the FBI had voted for him, and asked McCabe who he had voted for in the 2016 presidential election.[477]

In the afternoon of May 10, 2017, deputy press secretary Sarah Sanders spoke to the President about his decision to fire Comey and then spoke to reporters in a televised press conference.[478] Sanders told reporters that the President, the Department of Justice, and bipartisan members of Congress had lost confidence in Comey, "[a]nd most importantly, the rank and file of the FBI had lost confidence in their director. Accordingly, the President accepted the recommendation of his Deputy Attorney General to remove James Comey from his position."[479] In response to questions from reporters, Sanders said that Rosenstein decided "on his own" to review Comey's performance and that Rosenstein decided "on his own" to come to the President on Monday, May 8 to express his concerns about Comey. When a reporter indicated that the "vast majority" of FBI agents supported Comey, Sanders said, "Look, we've heard from countless members of the FBI that say very different things."[480] Following the press conference, Sanders spoke to the President, who told her she did a good job and did not point out any inaccuracies in her comments.[481] Sanders told this Office that her reference to hearing from "countless members of the FBI" was a "slip of the tongue."[482] She also recalled that her statement in a separate press interview that rank-and-file FBI agents had lost confidence in Comey was a comment she made "in the heat of the moment" that was not founded on anything.[483]

Also on May 10, 2017, Sessions and Rosenstein each spoke to McGahn and expressed concern that the White House was creating a narrative that Rosenstein had initiated the decision to

---

[474] McCabe 5/10/17 Memorandum, at 1.

[475] McCabe 5/10/17 Memorandum, at 1.

[476] McCabe 5/10/17 Memorandum, at 1; Rybicki 6/13/17 302, at 2. Comey had been visiting the FBI's Los Angeles office when he found out he had been terminated. Comey 11/15/17 302, at 22.

[477] McCabe 5/10/17 Memorandum, at 1-2. McCabe's memorandum documenting his meeting with the President is consistent with notes taken by the White House Counsel's Office. See SC_AD_00347 (Donaldson 5/10/17 Notes).

[478] Sanders 7/3/18 302, at 4; Sarah Sanders, White House Daily Briefing, C-SPAN (May 10, 2017).

[479] Sarah Sanders, White House Daily Briefing, C-SPAN (May 10, 2017); Sanders 7/3/18 302, at 4.

[480] Sarah Sanders, White House Daily Briefing, C-SPAN (May 10, 2017).

[481] Sanders 7/3/18 302, at 4.

[482] Sanders 7/3/18 302, at 4.

[483] Sanders 7/3/18 302, at 3.

fire Comey.[484] The White House Counsel's Office agreed that it was factually wrong to say that the Department of Justice had initiated Comey's termination,[485] and McGahn asked attorneys in the White House Counsel's Office to work with the press office to correct the narrative.[486]

The next day, on May 11, 2017, the President participated in an interview with Lester Holt. The President told White House Counsel's Office attorneys in advance of the interview that the communications team could not get the story right, so he was going on Lester Holt to say what really happened.[487] During the interview, the President stated that he had made the decision to fire Comey before the President met with Rosenstein and Sessions. The President told Holt, "I was going to fire regardless of recommendation . . . . [Rosenstein] made a recommendation. But regardless of recommendation, I was going to fire Comey knowing there was no good time to do it."[488] The President continued, "And in fact, when I decided to just do it, I said to myself—I said, you know, this Russia thing with Trump and Russia is a made-up story. It's an excuse by the Democrats for having lost an election that they should've won."[489]

In response to a question about whether he was angry with Comey about the Russia investigation, the President said, "As far as I'm concerned, I want that thing to be absolutely done properly."[490] The President added that he realized his termination of Comey "probably maybe will confuse people" with the result that it "might even lengthen out the investigation," but he "ha[d] to do the right thing for the American people" and Comey was "the wrong man for that position."[491] The President described Comey as "a showboat" and "a grandstander," said that "[t]he FBI has been in turmoil," and said he wanted "to have a really competent, capable director."[492] The President affirmed that he expected the new FBI director to continue the Russia investigation.[493]

On the evening of May 11, 2017, following the Lester Holt interview, the President tweeted, "Russia must be laughing up their sleeves watching as the U.S. tears itself apart over a Democrat EXCUSE for losing the election."[494] The same day, the media reported that the President had demanded that Comey pledge his loyalty to the President in a private dinner shortly

---

[484] McGahn 12/12/17 302, at 16-17; Donaldson 11/6/17 302, at 26; *see* Dhillon 11/21/17 302, at 11.

[485] Donaldson 11/6/17 302, at 27.

[486] McGahn 12/12/17 302, at 17.

[487] Dhillon 11/21/17 302, at 11.

[488] *Interview with President Donald Trump*, NBC (May 11, 2017) Transcript, at 2.

[489] *Interview with President Donald Trump*, NBC (May 11, 2017) Transcript, at 2.

[490] *Interview with President Donald Trump*, NBC (May 11, 2017) Transcript, at 3.

[491] *Interview with President Donald Trump*, NBC (May 11, 2017) Transcript, at 3.

[492] *Interview with President Donald Trump*, NBC (May 11, 2017) Transcript, at 1, 5.

[493] *Interview with President Donald Trump*, NBC (May 11, 2017) Transcript, at 7.

[494] @realDonaldTrump 5/11/17 (4:34 p.m. ET) Tweet.

after being sworn in.[495] Late in the morning of May 12, 2017, the President tweeted, "Again, the story that there was collusion between the Russians & Trump campaign was fabricated by Dems as an excuse for losing the election."[496] The President also tweeted, "James Comey better hope that there are no 'tapes' of our conversations before he starts leaking to the press!" and "When James Clapper himself, and virtually everyone else with knowledge of the witch hunt, says there is no collusion, when does it end?"[497]

Analysis

In analyzing the President's decision to fire Comey, the following evidence is relevant to the elements of obstruction of justice:

a.   Obstructive act. The act of firing Comey removed the individual overseeing the FBI's Russia investigation. The President knew that Comey was personally involved in the investigation based on Comey's briefing of the Gang of Eight, Comey's March 20, 2017 public testimony about the investigation, and the President's one-on-one conversations with Comey.

Firing Comey would qualify as an obstructive act if it had the natural and probable effect of interfering with or impeding the investigation—for example, if the termination would have the effect of delaying or disrupting the investigation or providing the President with the opportunity to appoint a director who would take a different approach to the investigation that the President perceived as more protective of his personal interests. Relevant circumstances bearing on that issue include whether the President's actions had the potential to discourage a successor director or other law enforcement officials in their conduct of the Russia investigation. The President fired Comey abruptly without offering him an opportunity to resign, banned him from the FBI building, and criticized him publicly, calling him a "showboat" and claiming that the FBI was "in turmoil" under his leadership. And the President followed the termination with public statements that were highly critical of the investigation; for example, three days after firing Comey, the President referred to the investigation as a "witch hunt" and asked, "when does it end?" Those actions had the potential to affect a successor director's conduct of the investigation.

The anticipated effect of removing the FBI director, however, would not necessarily be to prevent or impede the FBI from continuing its investigation. As a general matter, FBI investigations run under the operational direction of FBI personnel levels below the FBI director. Bannon made a similar point when he told the President that he could fire the FBI director, but could not fire the FBI. The White House issued a press statement the day after Comey was fired that said, "The investigation would have always continued, and obviously, the termination of Comey would not have ended it." In addition, in his May 11 interview with Lester Holt, the President stated that he understood when he made the decision to fire Comey that the action might prolong the investigation. And the President chose McCabe to serve as interim director, even

---

[495] Michael S. Schmidt, *In a Private Dinner, Trump Demanded Loyalty. Comey Demurred.*, New York Times (May 11, 2017).

[496] @realDonaldTrump 5/12/17 (7:51 a.m. ET) Tweet.

[497] @realDonaldTrump 5/12/17 (8:26 a.m. ET) Tweet; @realDonaldTrump 5/12/17 (8:54 a.m. ET) Tweet.

though McCabe told the President he had worked "very closely" with Comey and was part of all the decisions made in the Clinton investigation.

      b.   <u>Nexus to a proceeding</u>. The nexus element would be satisfied by evidence showing that a grand jury proceeding or criminal prosecution arising from an FBI investigation was objectively foreseeable and actually contemplated by the President when he terminated Comey.

      Several facts would be relevant to such a showing. At the time the President fired Comey, a grand jury had not begun to hear evidence related to the Russia investigation and no grand jury subpoenas had been issued. On March 20, 2017, however, Comey had announced that the FBI was investigating Russia's interference in the election, including "an assessment of whether any crimes were committed." It was widely known that the FBI, as part of the Russia investigation, was investigating the hacking of the DNC's computers—a clear criminal offense.

      In addition, at the time the President fired Comey, evidence indicates the President knew that Flynn was still under criminal investigation and could potentially be prosecuted, despite the President's February 14, 2017 request that Comey "let[] Flynn go." On March 5, 2017, the White House Counsel's Office was informed that the FBI was asking for transition-period records relating to Flynn—indicating that the FBI was still actively investigating him. The same day, the President told advisors he wanted to call Dana Boente, then the Acting Attorney General for the Russia investigation, to find out whether the White House or the President was being investigated. On March 31, 2017, the President signaled his awareness that Flynn remained in legal jeopardy by tweeting that "Mike Flynn should ask for immunity" before he agreed to provide testimony to the FBI or Congress. And in late March or early April, the President asked McFarland to pass a message to Flynn telling him that the President felt bad for him and that he should stay strong, further demonstrating the President's awareness of Flynn's criminal exposure.

      c.   <u>Intent</u>. Substantial evidence indicates that the catalyst for the President's decision to fire Comey was Comey's unwillingness to publicly state that the President was not personally under investigation, despite the President's repeated requests that Comey make such an announcement. In the week leading up to Comey's May 3, 2017 Senate Judiciary Committee testimony, the President told McGahn that it would be the last straw if Comey did not set the record straight and publicly announce that the President was not under investigation. But during his May 3 testimony, Comey refused to answer questions about whether the President was being investigated. Comey's refusal angered the President, who criticized Sessions for leaving him isolated and exposed, saying "You left me on an island." Two days later, the President told advisors he had decided to fire Comey and dictated a letter to Stephen Miller that began with a reference to the fact that the President was not being investigated: "While I greatly appreciate you informing me that I am not under investigation concerning what I have often stated is a fabricated story on a Trump-Russia relationship . . . ." The President later asked Rosenstein to include "Russia" in his memorandum and to say that Comey had told the President that he was not under investigation. And the President's final termination letter included a sentence, at the President's insistence and against McGahn's advice, stating that Comey had told the President on three separate occasions that he was not under investigation.

      The President's other stated rationales for why he fired Comey are not similarly supported by the evidence. The termination letter the President and Stephen Miller prepared in Bedminster

U.S. Department of Justice

Attorney Work Product // May Contain Material Protected Under Fed. R. Crim. P. 6(e)

cited Comey's handling of the Clinton email investigation, and the President told McCabe he fired Comey for that reason. But the facts surrounding Comey's handling of the Clinton email investigation were well known to the President at the time he assumed office, and the President had made it clear to both Comey and the President's senior staff in early 2017 that he wanted Comey to stay on as director. And Rosenstein articulated his criticism of Comey's handling of the Clinton investigation after the President had already decided to fire Comey. The President's draft termination letter also stated that morale in the FBI was at an all-time low and Sanders told the press after Comey's termination that the White House had heard from "countless" FBI agents who had lost confidence in Comey. But the evidence does not support those claims. The President told Comey at their January 27 dinner that "the people of the FBI really like [him]," no evidence suggests that the President heard otherwise before deciding to terminate Comey, and Sanders acknowledged to investigators that her comments were not founded on anything.

We also considered why it was important to the President that Comey announce publicly that he was not under investigation. Some evidence indicates that the President believed that the erroneous perception he was under investigation harmed his ability to manage domestic and foreign affairs, particularly in dealings with Russia. The President told Comey that the "cloud" of "this Russia business" was making it difficult to run the country. The President told Sessions and McGahn that foreign leaders had expressed sympathy to him for being under investigation and that the perception he was under investigation was hurting his ability to address foreign relations issues. The President complained to Rogers that "the thing with the Russians [was] messing up" his ability to get things done with Russia, and told Coats, "I can't do anything with Russia, there's things I'd like to do with Russia, with trade, with ISIS, they're all over me with this." The President also may have viewed Comey as insubordinate for his failure to make clear in the May 3 testimony that the President was not under investigation.

Other evidence, however, indicates that the President wanted to protect himself from an investigation into his campaign. The day after learning about the FBI's interview of Flynn, the President had a one-on-one dinner with Comey, against the advice of senior aides, and told Comey he needed Comey's "loyalty." When the President later asked Comey for a second time to make public that he was not under investigation, he brought up loyalty again, saying "Because I have been very loyal to you, very loyal, we had that thing, you know." After the President learned of Sessions's recusal from the Russia investigation, the President was furious and said he wanted an Attorney General who would protect him the way he perceived Robert Kennedy and Eric Holder to have protected their presidents. The President also said he wanted to be able to tell his Attorney General "who to investigate."

In addition, the President had a motive to put the FBI's Russia investigation behind him. The evidence does not establish that the termination of Comey was designed to cover up a conspiracy between the Trump Campaign and Russia: As described in Volume I, the evidence uncovered in the investigation did not establish that the President or those close to him were involved in the charged Russian computer-hacking or active-measure conspiracies, or that the President otherwise had an unlawful relationship with any Russian official. But the evidence does indicate that a thorough FBI investigation would uncover facts about the campaign and the President personally that the President could have understood to be crimes or that would give rise to personal and political concerns. Although the President publicly stated during and after the election that he had no connection to Russia, the Trump Organization, through Michael Cohen,

76

was pursuing the proposed Trump Tower Moscow project through June 2016 and candidate Trump was repeatedly briefed on the progress of those efforts.[498] In addition, some witnesses said that Trump was aware that ▮Harm to Ongoing Matter▮ ▮▮ at a time when public reports stated that Russian intelligence officials were behind the hacks, and that Trump privately sought information about future WikiLeaks releases.[499] More broadly, multiple witnesses described the President's preoccupation with press coverage of the Russia investigation and his persistent concern that it raised questions about the legitimacy of his election.[500]

Finally, the President and White House aides initially advanced a pretextual reason to the press and the public for Comey's termination. In the immediate aftermath of the firing, the President dictated a press statement suggesting that he had acted based on the DOJ recommendations, and White House press officials repeated that story. But the President had decided to fire Comey before the White House solicited those recommendations. Although the President ultimately acknowledged that he was going to fire Comey regardless of the Department of Justice's recommendations, he did so only after DOJ officials made clear to him that they would resist the White House's suggestion that they had prompted the process that led to Comey's termination. The initial reliance on a pretextual justification could support an inference that the President had concerns about providing the real reason for the firing, although the evidence does not resolve whether those concerns were personal, political, or both.

E. The President's Efforts to Remove the Special Counsel

Overview

The Acting Attorney General appointed a Special Counsel on May 17, 2017, prompting the President to state that it was the end of his presidency and that Attorney General Sessions had failed to protect him and should resign. Sessions submitted his resignation, which the President ultimately did not accept. The President told senior advisors that the Special Counsel had conflicts of interest, but they responded that those claims were "ridiculous" and posed no obstacle to the Special Counsel's service. Department of Justice ethics officials similarly cleared the Special Counsel's service. On June 14, 2017, the press reported that the President was being personally investigated for obstruction of justice and the President responded with a series of tweets

---

[498] *See* Volume II, Section II.K.1, *infra*.

[499] *See* Volume I, Section III.D.1, *supra*.

[500] In addition to whether the President had a motive related to Russia-related matters that an FBI investigation could uncover, we considered whether the President's intent in firing Comey was connected to other conduct that could come to light as a result of the FBI's Russian-interference investigation. In particular, Michael Cohen was a potential subject of investigation because of his pursuit of the Trump Tower Moscow project and involvement in other activities. And facts uncovered in the Russia investigation, which our Office referred to the U.S. Attorney's Office for the Southern District of New York, ultimately led to the conviction of Cohen in the Southern District of New York for campaign-finance offenses related to payments he said he made at the direction of the President. *See* Volume II, Section II.K.5, *infra*. The investigation, however, did not establish that when the President fired Comey, he was considering the possibility that the FBI's investigation would uncover these payments or that the President's intent in firing Comey was otherwise connected to a concern about these matters coming to light.

criticizing the Special Counsel's investigation. That weekend, the President called McGahn and directed him to have the Special Counsel removed because of asserted conflicts of interest. McGahn did not carry out the instruction for fear of being seen as triggering another Saturday Night Massacre and instead prepared to resign. McGahn ultimately did not quit and the President did not follow up with McGahn on his request to have the Special Counsel removed.

Evidence

1. The Appointment of the Special Counsel and the President's Reaction

On May 17, 2017, Acting Attorney General Rosenstein appointed Robert S. Mueller, III as Special Counsel and authorized him to conduct the Russia investigation and matters that arose from the investigation.[501] The President learned of the Special Counsel's appointment from Sessions, who was with the President, Hunt, and McGahn conducting interviews for a new FBI Director.[502] Sessions stepped out of the Oval Office to take a call from Rosenstein, who told him about the Special Counsel appointment, and Sessions then returned to inform the President of the news.[503] According to notes written by Hunt, when Sessions told the President that a Special Counsel had been appointed, the President slumped back in his chair and said, "Oh my God. This is terrible. This is the end of my Presidency. I'm fucked."[504] The President became angry and lambasted the Attorney General for his decision to recuse from the investigation, stating, "How could you let this happen, Jeff?"[505] The President said the position of Attorney General was his most important appointment and that Sessions had "let [him] down," contrasting him to Eric Holder and Robert Kennedy.[506] Sessions recalled that the President said to him, "you were supposed to protect me," or words to that effect.[507] The President returned to the consequences of the appointment and said, "Everyone tells me if you get one of these independent counsels it ruins your presidency. It takes years and years and I won't be able to do anything. This is the worst thing that ever happened to me."[508]

---

[501] Office of the Deputy Attorney General, Order No. 3915-2017, *Appointment of Special Counsel to Investigate Russian Interference with the 2016 Presidential Election and Related Matters* (May 17, 2017).

[502] Sessions 1/17/18 302, at 13; Hunt 2/1/18 302, at 18; McGahn 12/14/17 302, at 4; Hunt-000039 (Hunt 5/17/17 Notes).

[503] Sessions 1/17/18 302, at 13; Hunt 2/1/18 302, at 18; McGahn 12/14/17 302, at 4; Hunt-000039 (Hunt 5/17/17 Notes).

[504] Hunt-000039 (Hunt 5/17/17 Notes).

[505] Hunt-000039 (Hunt 5/17/17 Notes); Sessions 1/17/18 302, at 13-14.

[506] Hunt-000040; *see* Sessions 1/17/18 302, at 14.

[507] Sessions 1/17/18 302, at 14.

[508] Hunt-000040 (Hunt 5/17/17 Notes); *see* Sessions 1/17/18 302, at 14. Early the next morning, the President tweeted, "This is the single greatest witch hunt of a politician in American history!" @realDonaldTrump 5/18/17 (7:52 a.m. ET) Tweet.

The President then told Sessions he should resign as Attorney General.[509] Sessions agreed to submit his resignation and left the Oval Office.[510] Hicks saw the President shortly after Sessions departed and described the President as being extremely upset by the Special Counsel's appointment.[511] Hicks said that she had only seen the President like that one other time, when the Access Hollywood tape came out during the campaign.[512]

The next day, May 18, 2017, FBI agents delivered to McGahn a preservation notice that discussed an investigation related to Comey's termination and directed the White House to preserve all relevant documents.[513] When he received the letter, McGahn issued a document hold to White House staff and instructed them not to send out any burn bags over the weekend while he sorted things out.[514]

Also on May 18, Sessions finalized a resignation letter that stated, "Pursuant to our conversation of yesterday, and at your request, I hereby offer my resignation."[515] Sessions, accompanied by Hunt, brought the letter to the White House and handed it to the President.[516] The President put the resignation letter in his pocket and asked Sessions several times whether he wanted to continue serving as Attorney General.[517] Sessions ultimately told the President he wanted to stay, but it was up to the President.[518] The President said he wanted Sessions to stay.[519] At the conclusion of the meeting, the President shook Sessions's hand but did not return the resignation letter.[520]

When Priebus and Bannon learned that the President was holding onto Sessions's resignation letter, they became concerned that it could be used to influence the Department of Justice.[521] Priebus told Sessions it was not good for the President to have the letter because it

[509] Hunt-000041 (Hunt 5/17/17 Notes); Sessions 1/17/18 302, at 14.

[510] Hunt-000041 (Hunt 5/17/17 Notes); Sessions 1/17/18 302, at 14.

[511] Hicks 12/8/17 302, at 21.

[512] Hicks 12/8/17 302, at 21. The Access Hollywood tape was released on October 7, 2016, as discussed in Volume I, Section III.D.1, *supra*.

[513] McGahn 12/14/17 302, at 9; SCR015_000175-82 (Undated Draft Memoranda to White House Staff).

[514] McGahn 12/14/17 302, at 9; SCR015_000175-82 (Undated Draft Memoranda to White House Staff). The White House Counsel's Office had previously issued a document hold on February 27, 2017. SCR015_000171 (2/17/17 Memorandum from McGahn to Executive Office of the President Staff).

[515] Hunt-000047 (Hunt 5/18/17 Notes); 5/18/17 Letter, Sessions to President Trump (resigning as Attorney General).

[516] Hunt-000047-49 (Hunt 5/18/17 Notes); Sessions 1/17/18 302, at 14.

[517] Hunt-000047-49 (Hunt 5/18/17 Notes); Sessions 1/17/18 302, at 14.

[518] Hunt-000048-49 (Hunt 5/18/17 Notes); Sessions 1/17/18 302, at 14.

[519] Sessions 1/17/18 302, at 14.

[520] Hunt-000049 (Hunt 5/18/17 Notes).

[521] Hunt-000050-51 (Hunt 5/18/17 Notes).

U.S. Department of Justice

~~Attorney Work Product // May Contain Material Protected Under Fed. R. Crim. P. 6(e)~~

would function as a kind of "shock collar" that the President could use any time he wanted; Priebus said the President had "DOJ by the throat."[522] Priebus and Bannon told Sessions they would attempt to get the letter back from the President with a notation that he was not accepting Sessions's resignation.[523]

On May 19, 2017, the President left for a trip to the Middle East.[524] Hicks recalled that on the President's flight from Saudi Arabia to Tel Aviv, the President pulled Sessions's resignation letter from his pocket, showed it to a group of senior advisors, and asked them what he should do about it.[525] During the trip, Priebus asked about the resignation letter so he could return it to Sessions, but the President told him that the letter was back at the White House, somewhere in the residence.[526] It was not until May 30, three days after the President returned from the trip, that the President returned the letter to Sessions with a notation saying, "Not accepted."[527]

2. The President Asserts that the Special Counsel has Conflicts of Interest

In the days following the Special Counsel's appointment, the President repeatedly told advisors, including Priebus, Bannon, and McGahn, that Special Counsel Mueller had conflicts of interest.[528] The President cited as conflicts that Mueller had interviewed for the FBI Director position shortly before being appointed as Special Counsel, that he had worked for a law firm that represented people affiliated with the President, and that Mueller had disputed certain fees relating to his membership in a Trump golf course in Northern Virginia.[529] The President's advisors pushed

---

[522] Hunt-000050 (Hunt 5/18/17 Notes); Priebus 10/13/17 302, at 21; Hunt 2/1/18 302, at 21.

[523] Hunt-000051 (Hunt 5/18/17 Notes).

[524] SCR026_000110 (President's Daily Diary, 5/19/17).

[525] Hicks 12/8/17 302, at 22.

[526] Priebus 10/13/17 302, at 21. Hunt's notes state that when Priebus returned from the trip, Priebus told Hunt that the President was supposed to have given him the letter, but when he asked for it, the President "slapped the desk" and said he had forgotten it back at the hotel. Hunt-000052 (Hunt Notes, undated).

[527] Hunt-000052-53 (Hunt 5/30/17 Notes); 5/18/17 Letter, Sessions to President Trump (resignation letter). Robert Porter, who was the White House Staff Secretary at the time, said that in the days after the President returned from the Middle East trip, the President took Sessions's letter out of a drawer in the Oval Office and showed it to Porter. Porter 4/13/18 302, at 8. Personal Privacy

[528] Priebus 1/18/18 302, at 12; Bannon 2/14/18 302, at 10; McGahn 3/8/18 302, at 1; McGahn 12/14/17 302, at 10; Bannon 10/26/18 302, at 12.

[529] Priebus 1/18/18 302, at 12; Bannon 2/14/18 302, at 10. In October 2011, Mueller resigned his family's membership from Trump National Golf Club in Sterling, Virginia, in a letter that noted that "we live in the District and find that we are unable to make full use of the Club" and that inquired "whether we would be entitled to a refund of a portion of our initial membership fee," which was paid in 1994. 10/12/11 Letter, Muellers to Trump National Golf Club. About two weeks later, the controller of the club responded that the Muellers' resignation would be effective October 31, 2011, and that they would be "placed on a waitlist to be refunded on a first resigned / first refunded basis" in accordance with the club's legal

back on his assertion of conflicts, telling the President they did not count as true conflicts.[530] Bannon recalled telling the President that the purported conflicts were "ridiculous" and that none of them was real or could come close to justifying precluding Mueller from serving as Special Counsel.[531] As for Mueller's interview for FBI Director, Bannon recalled that the White House had invited Mueller to speak to the President to offer a perspective on the institution of the FBI.[532] Bannon said that, although the White House thought about beseeching Mueller to become Director again, he did not come in looking for the job.[533] Bannon also told the President that the law firm position did not amount to a conflict in the legal community.[534] And Bannon told the President that the golf course dispute did not rise to the level of a conflict and claiming one was "ridiculous and petty."[535] The President did not respond when Bannon pushed back on the stated conflicts of interest.[536]

On May 23, 2017, the Department of Justice announced that ethics officials had determined that the Special Counsel's prior law firm position did not bar his service, generating media reports that Mueller had been cleared to serve.[537] McGahn recalled that around the same time, the President complained about the asserted conflicts and prodded McGahn to reach out to Rosenstein about the issue.[538] McGahn said he responded that he could not make such a call and that the President should instead consult his personal lawyer because it was not a White House issue.[539] Contemporaneous notes of a May 23, 2017 conversation between McGahn and the President reflect that McGahn told the President that he would not call Rosenstein and that he would suggest that the President not make such a call either.[540] McGahn advised that the President could discuss the issue with his personal attorney but it would "look like still trying to meddle in [the] investigation" and "knocking out Mueller" would be "[a]nother fact used to claim obst[ruction] of

---

documents. 10/27/11 Letter, Muellers to Trump National Golf Club. The Muellers have not had further contact with the club.

[530] Priebus 4/3/18 302, at 3; Bannon 10/26/18 302, at 13 (confirming that he, Priebus, and McGahn pushed back on the asserted conflicts).

[531] Bannon 10/26/18 302, at 12-13.

[532] Bannon 10/26/18 302, at 12.

[533] Bannon 10/26/18 302, at 12.

[534] Bannon 10/26/18 302, at 12.

[535] Bannon 10/26/18 302, at 13.

[536] Bannon 10/26/18 302, at 12.

[537] Matt Zapotosky & Matea Gold, *Justice Department ethics experts clear Mueller to lead Russia probe*, Washington Post (May 23, 2017).

[538] McGahn 3/8/18 302, at 1; McGahn 12/14/17 302, at 10; Priebus 1/18/18 302, at 12.

[539] McGahn 3/8/18 302, at 1. McGahn and Donaldson said that after the appointment of the Special Counsel, they considered themselves potential fact witnesses and accordingly told the President that inquiries related to the investigation should be brought to his personal counsel. McGahn 12/14/17 302, at 7; Donaldson 4/2/18 302, at 5.

[540] SC_AD_00361 (Donaldson 5/31/17 Notes).

81

U.S. Department of Justice

Attorney Work Product // May Contain Material Protected Under Fed. R. Crim. P. 6(e)

just[ice]."[541] McGahn told the President that his "biggest exposure" was not his act of firing Comey but his "other contacts" and "calls," and his "ask re: Flynn."[542] By the time McGahn provided this advice to the President, there had been widespread reporting on the President's request for Comey's loyalty, which the President publicly denied; his request that Comey "let[] Flynn go," which the President also denied; and the President's statement to the Russian Foreign Minister that the termination of Comey had relieved "great pressure" related to Russia, which the President did not deny.[543]

On June 8, 2017, Comey testified before Congress about his interactions with the President before his termination, including the request for loyalty, the request that Comey "let[] Flynn go," and the request that Comey "lift the cloud" over the presidency caused by the ongoing investigation.[544] Comey's testimony led to a series of news reports about whether the President had obstructed justice.[545] On June 9, 2017, the Special Counsel's Office informed the White House Counsel's Office that investigators intended to interview intelligence community officials who had allegedly been asked by the President to push back against the Russia investigation.[546]

On Monday, June 12, 2017, Christopher Ruddy, the chief executive of Newsmax Media and a longtime friend of the President's, met at the White House with Priebus and Bannon.[547] Ruddy recalled that they told him the President was strongly considering firing the Special Counsel

---

[541] SC_AD_00361 (Donaldson 5/31/17 Notes).

[542] SC_AD_00361 (Donaldson 5/31/17 Notes).

[543] See, e.g., Michael S. Schmidt, In a Private Dinner, Trump Demanded Loyalty. Comey Demurred., New York Times (May 11, 2017); Michael S. Schmidt, Comey Memorandum Says Trump Asked Him to End Flynn Investigation, New York Times (May 16, 2017); Matt Apuzzo et al., Trump Told Russians That Firing 'Nut Job' Comey Eased Pressure From Investigation, New York Times (May 19, 2017).

[544] Hearing on Russian Election Interference Before the Senate Select Intelligence Committee, 115th Cong. (June 8, 2017) (Statement for the Record of James B. Comey, former Director of the FBI, at 5-6). Comey testified that he deliberately caused his memorandum documenting the February 14, 2017 meeting to be leaked to the New York Times in response to a tweet from the President, sent on May 12, 2017, that stated "James Comey better hope that there are no 'tapes' of our conversations before he starts leaking to the press!," and because he thought sharing the memorandum with a reporter "might prompt the appointment of a special counsel." Hearing on Russian Election Interference Before the Senate Select Intelligence Committee, 115th Cong. (June 8, 2017) (CQ Cong. Transcripts, at 55) (testimony by James B. Comey, former Director of the FBI).

[545] See, e.g., Matt Zapotosky, Comey lays out the case that Trump obstructed justice, Washington Post (June 8, 2017) ("Legal analysts said Comey's testimony clarified and bolstered the case that the president obstructed justice.").

[546] 6/9/17 Email, Special Counsel's Office to the White House Counsel's Office. This Office made the notification to give the White House an opportunity to invoke executive privilege in advance of the interviews. On June 12, 2017, the Special Counsel's Office interviewed Admiral Rogers in the presence of agency counsel. Rogers 6/12/17 302, at 1. On June 13, the Special Counsel's Office interviewed Ledgett. Ledgett 6/13/17 302, at 1. On June 14, the Office interviewed Coats and other personnel from his office. Coats 6/14/17 302, at 1; Gistaro 6/14/17 302, at 1; Culver 6/14/17 302, at 1.

[547] Ruddy 6/6/18 302, at 5.

and that he would do so precipitously, without vetting the decision through Administration officials.[548] Ruddy asked Priebus if Ruddy could talk publicly about the discussion they had about the Special Counsel, and Priebus said he could.[549] Priebus told Ruddy he hoped another blow up like the one that followed the termination of Comey did not happen.[550] Later that day, Ruddy stated in a televised interview that the President was "considering perhaps terminating the Special Counsel" based on purported conflicts of interest.[551] Ruddy later told another news outlet that "Trump is definitely considering" terminating the Special Counsel and "it's not something that's being dismissed."[552] Ruddy's comments led to extensive coverage in the media that the President was considering firing the Special Counsel.[553]

White House officials were unhappy with that press coverage and Ruddy heard from friends that the President was upset with him.[554] On June 13, 2017, Sanders asked the President for guidance on how to respond to press inquiries about the possible firing of the Special Counsel.[555] The President dictated an answer, which Sanders delivered, saying that "[w]hile the president has every right to" fire the Special Counsel, "he has no intention to do so."[556]

Also on June 13, 2017, the President's personal counsel contacted the Special Counsel's Office and raised concerns about possible conflicts.[557] The President's counsel cited Mueller's previous partnership in his law firm, his interview for the FBI Director position, and an asserted personal relationship he had with Comey.[558] That same day, Rosenstein had testified publicly before Congress and said he saw no evidence of good cause to terminate the Special Counsel, including for conflicts of interest.[559] Two days later, on June 15, 2017, the Special Counsel's

---

[548] Ruddy 6/6/18 302, at 5-6.

[549] Ruddy 6/6/18 302, at 6.

[550] Ruddy 6/6/18 302, at 6.

[551] *Trump Confidant Christopher Ruddy says Mueller has "real conflicts" as special counsel*, PBS (June 12, 2017); Michael D. Shear & Maggie Haberman, *Friend Says Trump Is Considering Firing Mueller as Special Counsel*, New York Times (June 12, 2017).

[552] Katherine Faulders & Veronica Stracqualursi, *Trump friend Chris Ruddy says Spicer's 'bizarre' statement doesn't deny claim Trump seeking Mueller firing*, ABC (June 13, 2017).

[553] *See, e.g.*, Michael D. Shear & Maggie Haberman, *Friend Says Trump Is Considering Firing Mueller as Special Counsel*, New York Times (June 12, 2017).

[554] Ruddy 6/6/18 302, at 6-7.

[555] Sanders 7/3/18 302, at 6-7.

[556] Glenn Thrush et al., *Trump Stews, Staff Steps In, and Mueller Is Safe for Now*, New York Times (June 13, 2017); *see* Sanders 7/3/18 302, at 6 (Sanders spoke with the President directly before speaking to the press on Air Force One and the answer she gave is the answer the President told her to give).

[557] Special Counsel's Office Attorney 6/13/17 Notes.

[558] Special Counsel's Office Attorney 6/13/17 Notes.

[559] *Hearing on Fiscal 2018 Justice Department Budget before the Senate Appropriations Subcommittee on Commerce, Justice, and Science*, 115th Cong. (June 13, 2017) (CQ Cong. Transcripts, at 14) (testimony by Rod Rosenstein, Deputy Attorney General).

U.S. Department of Justice

~~Attorney Work Product // May Contain Material Protected Under Fed. R. Crim. P. 6(e)~~

Office informed the Acting Attorney General's office about the areas of concern raised by the President's counsel and told the President's counsel that their concerns had been communicated to Rosenstein so that the Department of Justice could take any appropriate action.[560]

3. The Press Reports that the President is Being Investigated for Obstruction of Justice and the President Directs the White House Counsel to Have the Special Counsel Removed

On the evening of June 14, 2017, the Washington Post published an article stating that the Special Counsel was investigating whether the President had attempted to obstruct justice.[561] This was the first public report that the President himself was under investigation by the Special Counsel's Office, and cable news networks quickly picked up on the report.[562] The Post story stated that the Special Counsel was interviewing intelligence community leaders, including Coats and Rogers, about what the President had asked them to do in response to Comey's March 20, 2017 testimony; that the inquiry into obstruction marked "a major turning point" in the investigation; and that while "Trump had received private assurances from then-FBI Director James B. Comey starting in January that he was not personally under investigation," "[o]fficials say that changed shortly after Comey's firing."[563] That evening, at approximately 10:31 p.m., the President called McGahn on McGahn's personal cell phone and they spoke for about 15 minutes.[564] McGahn did not have a clear memory of the call but thought they might have discussed the stories reporting that the President was under investigation.[565]

Beginning early the next day, June 15, 2017, the President issued a series of tweets acknowledging the existence of the obstruction investigation and criticizing it. He wrote: "They made up a phony collusion with the Russians story, found zero proof, so now they go for obstruction of justice on the phony story. Nice",[566] "You are witnessing the single greatest WITCH HUNT in American political history—led by some very bad and conflicted people!",[567] and "Crooked H destroyed phones w/ hammer, 'bleached' emails, & had husband meet w/AG days

---

[560] Special Counsel's Office Attorney 6/15/17 Notes.

[561] Devlin Barrett et al., *Special counsel is investigating Trump for possible obstruction of justice, officials say*, Washington Post (June 14, 2017).

[562] CNN, for example, began running a chyron at 6:55 p.m. that stated: "WASH POST: MUELLER INVESTIGATING TRUMP FOR OBSTRUCTION OF JUSTICE." CNN, (June 14, 2017, published online at 7:15 p.m. ET).

[563] Devlin Barrett et al., *Special counsel is investigating Trump for possible obstruction of justice, officials say*, Washington Post (June 14, 2017).

[564] SCR026_000183 (President's Daily Diary, 6/14/17) (reflecting call from the President to McGahn on 6/14/17 with start time 10:31 p.m. and end time 10:46 p.m.); Call Records of Don McGahn.

[565] McGahn 2/28/19 302, at 1-2. McGahn thought he and the President also probably talked about the investiture ceremony for Supreme Court Justice Neil Gorsuch, which was scheduled for the following day. McGahn 2/28/18 302, at 2.

[566] @realDonaldTrump 6/15/17 (6:55 a.m. ET) Tweet.

[567] @realDonaldTrump 6/15/17 (7:57 a.m. ET) Tweet.

before she was cleared—& they talk about obstruction?"[568] The next day, June 16, 2017, the President wrote additional tweets criticizing the investigation: "After 7 months of investigations & committee hearings about my 'collusion with the Russians,' nobody has been able to show any proof. Sad!";[569] and "I am being investigated for firing the FBI Director by the man who told me to fire the FBI Director! Witch Hunt."[570]

On Saturday, June 17, 2017, the President called McGahn and directed him to have the Special Counsel removed.[571] McGahn was at home and the President was at Camp David.[572] In interviews with this Office, McGahn recalled that the President called him at home twice and on both occasions directed him to call Rosenstein and say that Mueller had conflicts that precluded him from serving as Special Counsel.[573]

On the first call, McGahn recalled that the President said something like, "You gotta do this. You gotta call Rod."[574] McGahn said he told the President that he would see what he could do.[575] McGahn was perturbed by the call and did not intend to act on the request.[576] He and other advisors believed the asserted conflicts were "silly" and "not real," and they had previously communicated that view to the President.[577] McGahn also had made clear to the President that the White House Counsel's Office should not be involved in any effort to press the issue of conflicts.[578] McGahn was concerned about having any role in asking the Acting Attorney General to fire the Special Counsel because he had grown up in the Reagan era and wanted to be more like Judge

---

[568] @realDonaldTrump 6/15/17 (3:56 p.m. ET) Tweet.

[569] @realDonaldTrump 6/16/17 (7:53 a.m. ET) Tweet.

[570] @realDonaldTrump 6/16/17 (9:07 a.m. ET) Tweet.

[571] McGahn 3/8/18 302, at 1-2; McGahn 12/14/17 302, at 10.

[572] McGahn 3/8/18 302, at 1, 3; SCR026_000196 (President's Daily Diary, 6/17/17) (records showing President departed the White House at 11:07 a.m. on June 17, 2017, and arrived at Camp David at 11:37 a.m.).

[573] McGahn 3/8/18 302, at 1-2; McGahn 12/14/17 302, at 10. Phone records show that the President called McGahn in the afternoon on June 17, 2017, and they spoke for approximately 23 minutes. SCR026_000196 (President's Daily Diary, 6/17/17) (reflecting call from the President to McGahn on 6/17/17 with start time 2:23 p.m. and end time 2:46 p.m.); (Call Records of Don McGahn). Phone records do not show another call between McGahn and the President that day. Although McGahn recalled receiving multiple calls from the President on the same day, in light of the phone records he thought it was possible that the first call instead occurred on June 14, 2017, shortly after the press reported that the President was under investigation for obstruction of justice. McGahn 2/28/19 302, at 1-3. While McGahn was not certain of the specific dates of the calls, McGahn was confident that he had at least two phone conversations with the President in which the President directed him to call the Acting Attorney General to have the Special Counsel removed. McGahn 2/28/19 302, at 1-3.

[574] McGahn 3/8/18 302, at 1.

[575] McGahn 3/8/18 302, at 1.

[576] McGahn 3/8/18 302, at 1.

[577] McGahn 3/8/18 302, at 1-2.

[578] McGahn 3/8/18 302, at 1-2.

85

U.S. Department of Justice

Attorney Work Product // May Contain Material Protected Under Fed. R. Crim. P. 6(e)

Robert Bork and not "Saturday Night Massacre Bork."[579] McGahn considered the President's request to be an inflection point and he wanted to hit the brakes.[580]

When the President called McGahn a second time to follow up on the order to call the Department of Justice, McGahn recalled that the President was more direct, saying something like, "Call Rod, tell Rod that Mueller has conflicts and can't be the Special Counsel."[581] McGahn recalled the President telling him "Mueller has to go" and "Call me back when you do it."[582] McGahn understood the President to be saying that the Special Counsel had to be removed by Rosenstein.[583] To end the conversation with the President, McGahn left the President with the impression that McGahn would call Rosenstein.[584] McGahn recalled that he had already said no to the President's request and he was worn down, so he just wanted to get off the phone.[585]

McGahn recalled feeling trapped because he did not plan to follow the President's directive but did not know what he would say the next time the President called.[586] McGahn decided he had to resign.[587] He called his personal lawyer and then called his chief of staff, Annie Donaldson, to inform her of his decision.[588] He then drove to the office to pack his belongings and submit his resignation letter.[589] Donaldson recalled that McGahn told her the President had called and demanded he contact the Department of Justice and that the President wanted him to do something that McGahn did not want to do.[590] McGahn told Donaldson that the President had called at least twice and in one of the calls asked "have you done it?"[591] McGahn did not tell Donaldson the specifics of the President's request because he was consciously trying not to involve her in the

---

[579] McGahn 3/8/18 302, at 2.

[580] McGahn 3/8/18 302, at 2.

[581] McGahn 3/8/18 302, at 5.

[582] McGahn 3/8/18 302, at 2, 5; McGahn 2/28/19 302, at 3.

[583] McGahn 3/8/18 302, at 1-2, 5.

[584] McGahn 3/8/18 302, at 2.

[585] McGahn 2/28/19 302, at 3; McGahn 3/8/18 302, at 2.

[586] McGahn 3/8/18 302, at 2.

[587] McGahn 3/8/18 302, at 2.

[588] McGahn 3/8/18 302, at 2-3; McGahn 2/28/19 302, at 3; Donaldson 4/2/18 302, at 4; Call Records of Don McGahn.

[589] McGahn 3/8/18 302, at 2; Donaldson 4/2/18 302, at 4.

[590] Donaldson 4/2/18 302, at 4.

[591] Donaldson 4/2/18 302, at 4.

investigation, but Donaldson inferred that the President's directive was related to the Russia investigation.[592] Donaldson prepared to resign along with McGahn.[593]

That evening, McGahn called both Priebus and Bannon and told them that he intended to resign.[594] McGahn recalled that, after speaking with his attorney and given the nature of the President's request, he decided not to share details of the President's request with other White House staff.[595] Priebus recalled that McGahn said that the President had asked him to "do crazy shit," but he thought McGahn did not tell him the specifics of the President's request because McGahn was trying to protect Priebus from what he did not need to know.[596] Priebus and Bannon both urged McGahn not to quit, and McGahn ultimately returned to work that Monday and remained in his position.[597] He had not told the President directly that he planned to resign, and when they next saw each other the President did not ask McGahn whether he had followed through with calling Rosenstein.[598]

Around the same time, Chris Christie recalled a telephone call with the President in which the President asked what Christie thought about the President firing the Special Counsel.[599] Christie advised against doing so because there was no substantive basis for the President to fire the Special Counsel, and because the President would lose support from Republicans in Congress if he did so.[600]

Analysis

In analyzing the President's direction to McGahn to have the Special Counsel removed, the following evidence is relevant to the elements of obstruction of justice:

a.   Obstructive act. As with the President's firing of Comey, the attempt to remove the Special Counsel would qualify as an obstructive act if it would naturally obstruct the

---

[592] McGahn 2/28/19 302, at 3-4; Donaldson 4/2/18 302, at 4-5. Donaldson said she believed McGahn consciously did not share details with her because he did not want to drag her into the investigation. Donaldson 4/2/18 302, at 5; see McGahn 2/28/19 302, at 3.

[593] Donaldson 4/2/18 302, at 5.

[594] McGahn 12/14/17 302, at 10; Call Records of Don McGahn; McGahn 2/28/19 302, at 3-4; Priebus 4/3/18 302, at 6-7.

[595] McGahn 2/28/19 302, at 4. Priebus and Bannon confirmed that McGahn did not tell them the specific details of the President's request. Priebus 4/3/18 302, at 7; Bannon 2/14/18 302, at 10.

[596] Priebus 4/3/18 302, at 7.

[597] McGahn 3/8/18 302, at 3; McGahn 2/28/19 302, at 3-4.

[598] McGahn 3/8/18 302, at 3.

[599] Christie 2/13/19 302, at 7. Christie did not recall the precise date of this call, but believed it was after Christopher Wray was announced as the nominee to be the new FBI director, which was on June 7, 2017. Christie 2/13/19 302, at 7. Telephone records show that the President called Christie twice after that time period, on July 4, 2017, and July 14, 2017. Call Records of Chris Christie.

[600] Christie 2/13/19 302, at 7.

87

351

investigation and any grand jury proceedings that might flow from the inquiry. Even if the removal of the lead prosecutor would not prevent the investigation from continuing under a new appointee, a factfinder would need to consider whether the act had the potential to delay further action in the investigation, chill the actions of any replacement Special Counsel, or otherwise impede the investigation.

A threshold question is whether the President in fact directed McGahn to have the Special Counsel removed. After news organizations reported that in June 2017 the President had ordered McGahn to have the Special Counsel removed, the President publicly disputed these accounts, and privately told McGahn that he had simply wanted McGahn to bring conflicts of interest to the Department of Justice's attention. *See* Volume II, Section II.I, *infra*. Some of the President's specific language that McGahn recalled from the calls is consistent with that explanation. Substantial evidence, however, supports the conclusion that the President went further and in fact directed McGahn to call Rosenstein to have the Special Counsel removed.

First, McGahn's clear recollection was that the President directed him to tell Rosenstein not only that conflicts existed but also that "Mueller has to go." McGahn is a credible witness with no motive to lie or exaggerate given the position he held in the White House.[601] McGahn spoke with the President twice and understood the directive the same way both times, making it unlikely that he misheard or misinterpreted the President's request. In response to that request, McGahn decided to quit because he did not want to participate in events that he described as akin to the Saturday Night Massacre. He called his lawyer, drove to the White House, packed up his office, prepared to submit a resignation letter with his chief of staff, told Priebus that the President had asked him to "do crazy shit," and informed Priebus and Bannon that he was leaving. Those acts would be a highly unusual reaction to a request to convey information to the Department of Justice.

Second, in the days before the calls to McGahn, the President, through his counsel, had already brought the asserted conflicts to the attention of the Department of Justice. Accordingly, the President had no reason to have McGahn call Rosenstein that weekend to raise conflicts issues that already had been raised.

Third, the President's sense of urgency and repeated requests to McGahn to take immediate action on a weekend—"You gotta do this. You gotta call Rod."—support McGahn's recollection that the President wanted the Department of Justice to take action to remove the Special Counsel. Had the President instead sought only to have the Department of Justice re-examine asserted conflicts to evaluate whether they posed an ethical bar, it would have been unnecessary to set the process in motion on a Saturday and to make repeated calls to McGahn.

Finally, the President had discussed "knocking out Mueller" and raised conflicts of interest in a May 23, 2017 call with McGahn, reflecting that the President connected the conflicts to a plan to remove the Special Counsel. And in the days leading up to June 17, 2017, the President made clear to Priebus and Bannon, who then told Ruddy, that the President was considering terminating

---

[601] When this Office first interviewed McGahn about this topic, he was reluctant to share detailed information about what had occurred and only did so after continued questioning. *See* McGahn 12/14/17 302 (agent notes).

U.S. Department of Justice

Attorney Work Product // May Contain Material Protected Under Fed. R. Crim. P. 6(e)

the Special Counsel. Also during this time period, the President reached out to Christie to get his thoughts on firing the Special Counsel. This evidence shows that the President was not just seeking an examination of whether conflicts existed but instead was looking to use asserted conflicts as a way to terminate the Special Counsel.

b.   Nexus to an official proceeding. To satisfy the proceeding requirement, it would be necessary to establish a nexus between the President's act of seeking to terminate the Special Counsel and a pending or foreseeable grand jury proceeding.

Substantial evidence indicates that by June 17, 2017, the President knew his conduct was under investigation by a federal prosecutor who could present any evidence of federal crimes to a grand jury. On May 23, 2017, McGahn explicitly warned the President that his "biggest exposure" was not his act of firing Comey but his "other contacts" and "calls," and his "ask re: Flynn." By early June, it was widely reported in the media that federal prosecutors had issued grand jury subpoenas in the Flynn inquiry and that the Special Counsel had taken over the Flynn investigation.[602] On June 9, 2017, the Special Counsel's Office informed the White House that investigators would be interviewing intelligence agency officials who allegedly had been asked by the President to push back against the Russia investigation. On June 14, 2017, news outlets began reporting that the President was himself being investigated for obstruction of justice. Based on widespread reporting, the President knew that such an investigation could include his request for Comey's loyalty; his request that Comey "let[] Flynn go"; his outreach to Coats and Rogers; and his termination of Comey and statement to the Russian Foreign Minister that the termination had relieved "great pressure" related to Russia. And on June 16, 2017, the day before he directed McGahn to have the Special Counsel removed, the President publicly acknowledged that his conduct was under investigation by a federal prosecutor, tweeting, "I am being investigated for firing the FBI Director by the man who told me to fire the FBI Director!"

c.   Intent. Substantial evidence indicates that the President's attempts to remove the Special Counsel were linked to the Special Counsel's oversight of investigations that involved the President's conduct—and, most immediately, to reports that the President was being investigated for potential obstruction of justice.

Before the President terminated Comey, the President considered it critically important that he was not under investigation and that the public not erroneously think he was being investigated. As described in Volume II, Section II.D, supra, advisors perceived the President, while he was drafting the Comey termination letter, to be concerned more than anything else about getting out that he was not personally under investigation. When the President learned of the appointment of the Special Counsel on May 17, 2017, he expressed further concern about the investigation, saying "[t]his is the end of my Presidency." The President also faulted Sessions for recusing, saying "you were supposed to protect me."

On June 14, 2017, when the Washington Post reported that the Special Counsel was investigating the President for obstruction of justice, the President was facing what he had wanted

---

[602] See, e.g., Evan Perez et al., *CNN exclusive: Grand jury subpoenas issued in FBI's Russia investigation*, CNN (May 9, 2017); Matt Ford, *Why Mueller Is Taking Over the Michael Flynn Grand Jury*, The Atlantic (June 2, 2017).

89

to avoid: a criminal investigation into his own conduct that was the subject of widespread media attention. The evidence indicates that news of the obstruction investigation prompted the President to call McGahn and seek to have the Special Counsel removed. By mid-June, the Department of Justice had already cleared the Special Counsel's service and the President's advisors had told him that the claimed conflicts of interest were "silly" and did not provide a basis to remove the Special Counsel. On June 13, 2017, the Acting Attorney General testified before Congress that no good cause for removing the Special Counsel existed, and the President dictated a press statement to Sanders saying he had no intention of firing the Special Counsel. But the next day, the media reported that the President was under investigation for obstruction of justice and the Special Counsel was interviewing witnesses about events related to possible obstruction—spurring the President to write critical tweets about the Special Counsel's investigation. The President called McGahn at home that night and then called him on Saturday from Camp David. The evidence accordingly indicates that news that an obstruction investigation had been opened is what led the President to call McGahn to have the Special Counsel terminated.

There also is evidence that the President knew that he should not have made those calls to McGahn. The President made the calls to McGahn after McGahn had specifically told the President that the White House Counsel's Office—and McGahn himself—could not be involved in pressing conflicts claims and that the President should consult with his personal counsel if he wished to raise conflicts. Instead of relying on his personal counsel to submit the conflicts claims, the President sought to use his official powers to remove the Special Counsel. And after the media reported on the President's actions, he denied that he ever ordered McGahn to have the Special Counsel terminated and made repeated efforts to have McGahn deny the story, as discussed in Volume II, Section II.I, *infra*. Those denials are contrary to the evidence and suggest the President's awareness that the direction to McGahn could be seen as improper.

F.   **The President's Efforts to Curtail the Special Counsel Investigation**

Overview

Two days after the President directed McGahn to have the Special Counsel removed, the President made another attempt to affect the course of the Russia investigation. On June 19, 2017, the President met one-on-one with Corey Lewandowski in the Oval Office and dictated a message to be delivered to Attorney General Sessions that would have had the effect of limiting the Russia investigation to future election interference only. One month later, the President met again with Lewandowski and followed up on the request to have Sessions limit the scope of the Russia investigation. Lewandowski told the President the message would be delivered soon. Hours later, the President publicly criticized Sessions in an unplanned press interview, raising questions about Sessions's job security.

1.   The President Asks Corey Lewandowski to Deliver a Message to Sessions to Curtail the Special Counsel Investigation

On June 19, 2017, two days after the President directed McGahn to have the Special Counsel removed, the President met one-on-one in the Oval Office with his former campaign manager Corey Lewandowski.[603] Senior White House advisors described Lewandowski as a "devotee" of the President and said the relationship between the President and Lewandowski was "close."[604]

During the June 19 meeting, Lewandowski recalled that, after some small talk, the President brought up Sessions and criticized his recusal from the Russia investigation.[605] The President told Lewandowski that Sessions was weak and that if the President had known about the likelihood of recusal in advance, he would not have appointed Sessions.[606] The President then asked Lewandowski to deliver a message to Sessions and said "write this down."[607] This was the first time the President had asked Lewandowski to take dictation, and Lewandowski wrote as fast as possible to make sure he captured the content correctly.[608]

The President directed that Sessions should give a speech publicly announcing:

> I know that I recused myself from certain things having to do with specific areas. But our POTUS . . . is being treated very unfairly. He shouldn't have a Special Prosecutor/Counsel b/c he hasn't done anything wrong. I was on the campaign w/ him for nine months, there were no Russians involved with him. I know it for a fact b/c I was there. He didn't do anything wrong except he ran the greatest campaign in American history.[609]

The dictated message went on to state that Sessions would meet with the Special Counsel to limit his jurisdiction to future election interference:

> Now a group of people want to subvert the Constitution of the United States. I am going to meet with the Special Prosecutor to explain this is very unfair and let the Special Prosecutor move forward with investigating election meddling for future elections so that nothing can happen in future elections.[610]

---

[603] Lewandowski 4/6/18 302, at 2; SCR026_000201 (President's Daily Diary, 6/19/17).
Personal Privacy

[604] Kelly 8/2/18 302, at 7; Dearborn 6/20/18 302, at 1 (describing Lewandowski as a "comfort to the President" whose loyalty was appreciated). Kelly said that when he was Chief of Staff and the President had meetings with friends like Lewandowski, Kelly tried not to be there and to push the meetings to the residence to create distance from the West Wing. Kelly 8/2/18 302, at 7.

[605] Lewandowski 4/6/18 302, at 2.

[606] Lewandowski 4/6/18 302, at 2.

[607] Lewandowski 4/6/18 302, at 2.

[608] Lewandowski 4/6/18 302, at 3.

[609] Lewandowski 4/6/18 302, at 2-3; Lewandowski 6/19/17 Notes, at 1-2.

[610] Lewandowski 4/6/18 302, at 3; Lewandowski 6/19/17 Notes, at 3.

91

The President said that if Sessions delivered that statement he would be the "most popular guy in the country."[611] Lewandowski told the President he understood what the President wanted Sessions to do.[612]

Lewandowski wanted to pass the message to Sessions in person rather than over the phone.[613] He did not want to meet at the Department of Justice because he did not want a public log of his visit and did not want Sessions to have an advantage over him by meeting on what Lewandowski described as Sessions's turf.[614] Lewandowski called Sessions and arranged a meeting for the following evening at Lewandowski's office, but Sessions had to cancel due to a last minute conflict.[615] Shortly thereafter, Lewandowski left Washington, D.C., without having had an opportunity to meet with Sessions to convey the President's message.[616] Lewandowski stored the notes in a safe at his home, which he stated was his standard procedure with sensitive items.[617]

2. The President Follows Up with Lewandowski

Following his June meeting with the President, Lewandowski contacted Rick Dearborn, then a senior White House official, and asked if Dearborn could pass a message to Sessions.[618] Dearborn agreed without knowing what the message was, and Lewandowski later confirmed that Dearborn would meet with Sessions for dinner in late July and could deliver the message then.[619] Lewandowski recalled thinking that the President had asked him to pass the message because the President knew Lewandowski could be trusted, but Lewandowski believed Dearborn would be a better messenger because he had a longstanding relationship with Sessions and because Dearborn was in the government while Lewandowski was not.[620]

On July 19, 2017, the President again met with Lewandowski alone in the Oval Office.[621] In the preceding days, as described in Volume II, Section II.G, *infra*, emails and other information about the June 9, 2016 meeting between several Russians and Donald Trump Jr., Jared Kushner, and Paul Manafort had been publicly disclosed. In the July 19 meeting with Lewandowski, the

---

[611] Lewandowski 4/6/18 302, at 3; Lewandowski 6/19/17 Notes, at 4.

[612] Lewandowski 4/6/18 302, at 3.

[613] Lewandowski 4/6/18 302, at 3-4.

[614] Lewandowski 4/6/18 302, at 4.

[615] Lewandowski 4/6/18 302, at 4.

[616] Lewandowski 4/6/18 302, at 4.

[617] Lewandowski 4/6/18 302, at 4.

[618] Lewandowski 4/6/18 302, at 4; *see* Dearborn 6/20/18 302, at 3.

[619] Lewandowski 4/6/18 302, at 4-5.

[620] Lewandowski 4/6/18 302, at 4, 6.

[621] Lewandowski 4/6/18 302, at 5; SCR029b_000002-03 (6/5/18 Additional Response to Special Counsel Request for Certain Visitor Log Information).

President raised his previous request and asked if Lewandowski had talked to Sessions.[622] Lewandowski told the President that the message would be delivered soon.[623] Lewandowski recalled that the President told him that if Sessions did not meet with him, Lewandowski should tell Sessions he was fired.[624]

Immediately following the meeting with the President, Lewandowski saw Dearborn in the anteroom outside the Oval Office and gave him a typewritten version of the message the President had dictated to be delivered to Sessions.[625] Lewandowski told Dearborn that the notes were the message they had discussed, but Dearborn did not recall whether Lewandowski said the message was from the President.[626] The message "definitely raised an eyebrow" for Dearborn, and he recalled not wanting to ask where it came from or think further about doing anything with it.[627] Dearborn also said that being asked to serve as a messenger to Sessions made him uncomfortable.[628] He recalled later telling Lewandowski that he had handled the situation, but he did not actually follow through with delivering the message to Sessions, and he did not keep a copy of the typewritten notes Lewandowski had given him.[629]

3. The President Publicly Criticizes Sessions in a New York Times Interview

Within hours of the President's meeting with Lewandowski on July 19, 2017, the President gave an unplanned interview to the New York Times in which he criticized Sessions's decision to recuse from the Russia investigation.[630] The President said that "Sessions should have never recused himself, and if he was going to recuse himself, he should have told me before he took the job, and I would have picked somebody else."[631] Sessions's recusal, the President said, was "very unfair to the president. How do you take a job and then recuse yourself? If he would have recused himself before the job, I would have said, 'Thanks, Jeff, but I can't, you know, I'm not going to

---

[622] Lewandowski 4/6/18 302, at 5.

[623] Lewandowski 4/6/18 302, at 5.

[624] Lewandowski 4/6/18 302, at 6. Priebus vaguely recalled Lewandowski telling him that in approximately May or June 2017 the President had asked Lewandowski to get Sessions's resignation. Priebus recalled that Lewandowski described his reaction as something like, "What can I do? I'm not an employee of the administration. I'm a nobody." Priebus 4/3/18 302, at 6.

[625] Lewandowski 4/6/18 302, at 5. Lewandowski said he asked Hope Hicks to type the notes when he went in to the Oval Office, and he then retrieved the notes from her partway through his meeting with the President. Lewandowski 4/6/18 302, at 5.

[626] Lewandowski 4/6/18 302, at 5; Dearborn 6/20/18 302, at 3.

[627] Dearborn 6/20/18 302, at 3.

[628] Dearborn 6/20/18 302, at 3.

[629] Dearborn 6/20/18 302, at 3-4.

[630] Peter Baker et al., *Excerpts From The Times's Interview With Trump*, New York Times (July 19, 2017).

[631] Peter Baker et al., *Excerpts From The Times's Interview With Trump*, New York Times (July 19, 2017).

U.S. Department of Justice

~~Attorney Work Product // May Contain Material Protected Under Fed. R. Crim. P. 6(e)~~

take you.' It's extremely unfair, and that's a mild word, to the president."[632] Hicks, who was present for the interview, recalled trying to "throw [herself] between the reporters and [the President]" to stop parts of the interview, but the President "loved the interview."[633]

Later that day, Lewandowski met with Hicks and they discussed the President's New York Times interview.[634] Lewandowski recalled telling Hicks about the President's request that he meet with Sessions and joking with her about the idea of firing Sessions as a private citizen if Sessions would not meet with him.[635] As Hicks remembered the conversation, Lewandowski told her the President had recently asked him to meet with Sessions and deliver a message that he needed to do the "right thing" and resign.[636] While Hicks and Lewandowski were together, the President called Hicks and told her he was happy with how coverage of his New York Times interview criticizing Sessions was playing out.[637]

4. The President Orders Priebus to Demand Sessions's Resignation

Three days later, on July 21, 2017, the Washington Post reported that U.S. intelligence intercepts showed that Sessions had discussed campaign-related matters with the Russian ambassador, contrary to what Sessions had said publicly.[638] That evening, Priebus called Hunt to talk about whether Sessions might be fired or might resign.[639] Priebus had previously talked to Hunt when the media had reported on tensions between Sessions and the President, and, after speaking to Sessions, Hunt had told Priebus that the President would have to fire Sessions if he wanted to remove Sessions because Sessions was not going to quit.[640] According to Hunt, who took contemporaneous notes of the July 21 call, Hunt told Priebus that, as they had previously discussed, Sessions had no intention of resigning.[641] Hunt asked Priebus what the President would

---

[632] Peter Baker et al., *Excerpts From The Times's Interview With Trump*, New York Times (July 19, 2017).

[633] Hicks 12/8/17 302, at 23.

[634] Hicks 3/13/18 302, at 10; Lewandowski 4/6/18 302, at 6.

[635] Lewandowski 4/6/18 302, at 6.

[636] Hicks 3/13/18 302, at 10. Hicks thought that the President might be able to make a recess appointment of a new Attorney General because the Senate was about to go on recess. Hicks 3/13/18 302, at 10. Lewandowski recalled that in the afternoon of July 19, 2017, following his meeting with the President, he conducted research on recess appointments but did not share his research with the President. Lewandowski 4/6/18 302, at 7.

[637] Lewandowski 4/6/18 302, at 6.

[638] Adam Entous et al., *Sessions discussed Trump campaign-related matters with Russian ambassador, U.S. intelligence intercepts show*, Washington Post (July 21, 2017). The underlying events concerning the Sessions-Kislyak contacts are discussed in Volume I, Section IV.A.4.c, *supra*.

[639] Hunt 2/1/18 302, at 23.

[640] Hunt 2/1/18 302, at 23.

[641] Hunt 2/1/18 302, at 23-24; Hunt 7/21/17 Notes, at 1.

accomplish by firing Sessions, pointing out there was an investigation before and there would be an investigation after.[642]

Early the following morning, July 22, 2017, the President tweeted, "A new INTELLIGENCE LEAK from the Amazon Washington Post, this time against A.G. Jeff Sessions. These illegal leaks, like Comey's, must stop!"[643] Approximately one hour later, the President tweeted, "So many people are asking why isn't the A.G. or Special Council looking at the many Hillary Clinton or Comey crimes. 33,000 e-mails deleted?"[644] Later that morning, while aboard Marine One on the way to Norfolk, Virginia, the President told Priebus that he had to get Sessions to resign immediately.[645] The President said that the country had lost confidence in Sessions and the negative publicity was not tolerable.[646] According to contemporaneous notes taken by Priebus, the President told Priebus to say that he "need[ed] a letter of resignation on [his] desk immediately" and that Sessions had "no choice" but "must immediately resign."[647] Priebus replied that if they fired Sessions, they would never get a new Attorney General confirmed and that the Department of Justice and Congress would turn their backs on the President, but the President suggested he could make a recess appointment to replace Sessions.[648]

Priebus believed that the President's request was a problem, so he called McGahn and asked for advice, explaining that he did not want to pull the trigger on something that was "all wrong."[649] Although the President tied his desire for Sessions to resign to Sessions's negative press and poor performance in congressional testimony, Priebus believed that the President's desire to replace Sessions was driven by the President's hatred of Sessions's recusal from the Russia investigation.[650] McGahn told Priebus not to follow the President's order and said they should consult their personal counsel, with whom they had attorney-client privilege.[651] McGahn

---

[642] Hunt 2/1/18 302, at 23-24; Hunt 7/21/17 Notes, at 1-2.

[643] @realDonaldTrump 7/22/17 (6:33 a.m. ET) Tweet.

[644] @realDonaldTrump 7/22/17 (7:44 a.m. ET) Tweet. Three minutes later, the President tweeted, "What about all of the Clinton ties to Russia, including Podesta Company, Uranium deal, Russian Reset, big dollar speeches etc." @realDonaldTrump 7/22/17 (7:47 a.m. ET) Tweet.

[645] Priebus 1/18/18 302, at 13-14.

[646] Priebus 1/18/18 302, at 14; Priebus 4/3/18 302, at 4-5; see RP_000073 (Priebus 7/22/17 Notes).

[647] RP_000073 (Priebus 7/22/17 Notes).

[648] Priebus 4/3/18 302, at 5.

[649] Priebus 1/18/18 302, at 14; Priebus 4/3/18 302, at 4-5.

[650] Priebus 4/3/18 302, at 5.

[651] RP_000074 (Priebus 7/22/17 Notes); McGahn 12/14/17 302, at 11; Priebus 1/18/18 302, at 14. Priebus followed McGahn's advice and called his personal attorney to discuss the President's request because he thought it was the type of thing about which one would need to consult an attorney. Priebus 1/18/18 302, at 14.

U.S. Department of Justice

Attorney Work Product // May Contain Material Protected Under Fed. R. Crim. P. 6(e)

and Priebus discussed the possibility that they would both have to resign rather than carry out the President's order to fire Sessions.[652]

That afternoon, the President followed up with Priebus about demanding Sessions's resignation, using words to the effect of, "Did you get it? Are you working on it?"[653] Priebus said that he believed that his job depended on whether he followed the order to remove Sessions, although the President did not directly say so.[654] Even though Priebus did not intend to carry out the President's directive, he told the President he would get Sessions to resign.[655] Later in the day, Priebus called the President and explained that it would be a calamity if Sessions resigned because Priebus expected that Rosenstein and Associate Attorney General Rachel Brand would also resign and the President would be unable to get anyone else confirmed.[656] The President agreed to hold off on demanding Sessions's resignation until after the Sunday shows the next day, to prevent the shows from focusing on the firing.[657]

By the end of that weekend, Priebus recalled that the President relented and agreed not to ask Sessions to resign.[658] Over the next several days, the President tweeted about Sessions. On the morning of Monday, July 24, 2017, the President criticized Sessions for neglecting to investigate Clinton and called him "beleaguered."[659] On July 25, the President tweeted, "Attorney General Jeff Sessions has taken a VERY weak position on Hillary Clinton crimes (where are E-mails & DNC server) & Intel leakers!"[660] The following day, July 26, the President tweeted, "Why didn't A.G. Sessions replace Acting FBI Director Andrew McCabe, a Comey friend who was in charge of Clinton investigation."[661] According to Hunt, in light of the President's frequent public attacks, Sessions prepared another resignation letter and for the rest of the year carried it with him in his pocket every time he went to the White House.[662]

---

[652] McGahn 12/14/17 302, at 11; RP_000074 (Priebus 7/22/17 Notes) ("discuss resigning together").

[653] Priebus 1/18/18 302, at 14; Priebus 4/3/18 302, at 4.

[654] Priebus 4/3/18 302, at 4.

[655] Priebus 1/18/18 302, at 15.

[656] Priebus 1/18/18 302, at 15.

[657] Priebus 1/18/18 302, at 15.

[658] Priebus 1/18/18 302, at 15.

[659] @realDonaldTrump 7/24/17 (8:49 a.m. ET) Tweet ("So why aren't the Committees and investigators, and of course our beleaguered A.G., looking into Crooked Hillarys crimes & Russia relations?").

[660] @realDonaldTrump 7/25/17 (6:12 a.m. ET) Tweet. The President sent another tweet shortly before this one asking "where is the investigation A.G." @realDonaldTrump 7/25/17 (6:03 a.m. ET) Tweet.

[661] @realDonaldTrump 7/26/17 (9:48 a.m. ET) Tweet.

[662] Hunt 2/1/18 302, at 24-25.

U.S. Department of Justice

~~Attorney Work Product~~ // ~~May Contain Material Protected Under Fed. R. Crim. P. 6(e)~~

Analysis

In analyzing the President's efforts to have Lewandowski deliver a message directing Sessions to publicly announce that the Special Counsel investigation would be confined to future election interference, the following evidence is relevant to the elements of obstruction of justice:

a.   Obstructive act.   The President's effort to send Sessions a message through Lewandowski would qualify as an obstructive act if it would naturally obstruct the investigation and any grand jury proceedings that might flow from the inquiry.

The President sought to have Sessions announce that the President "shouldn't have a Special Prosecutor/Counsel" and that Sessions was going to "meet with the Special Prosecutor to explain this is very unfair and let the Special Prosecutor move forward with investigating election meddling for future elections so that nothing can happen in future elections." The President wanted Sessions to disregard his recusal from the investigation, which had followed from a formal DOJ ethics review, and have Sessions declare that he knew "for a fact" that "there were no Russians involved with the campaign" because he "was there." The President further directed that Sessions should explain that the President should not be subject to an investigation "because he hasn't done anything wrong." Taken together, the President's directives indicate that Sessions was being instructed to tell the Special Counsel to end the existing investigation into the President and his campaign, with the Special Counsel being permitted to "move forward with investigating election meddling for future elections."

b.   Nexus to an official proceeding.   As described above, by the time of the President's initial one-on-one meeting with Lewandowski on June 19, 2017, the existence of a grand jury investigation supervised by the Special Counsel was public knowledge.   By the time of the President's follow-up meeting with Lewandowski, ▮▮Grand Jury▮▮

▮▮▮▮▮▮▮▮▮▮▮▮▮▮▮▮▮▮▮▮▮▮▮▮▮▮▮▮ *See* Volume II, Section II.G, *infra.* To satisfy the nexus requirement, it would be necessary to show that limiting the Special Counsel's investigation would have the natural and probable effect of impeding that grand jury proceeding.

c.   Intent.   Substantial evidence indicates that the President's effort to have Sessions limit the scope of the Special Counsel's investigation to future election interference was intended to prevent further investigative scrutiny of the President's and his campaign's conduct.

As previously described, *see* Volume II, Section II.B, *supra,* the President knew that the Russia investigation was focused in part on his campaign, and he perceived allegations of Russian interference to cast doubt on the legitimacy of his election. The President further knew that the investigation had broadened to include his own conduct and whether he had obstructed justice. Those investigations would not proceed if the Special Counsel's jurisdiction were limited to future election interference only.

The timing and circumstances of the President's actions support the conclusion that he sought that result. The President's initial direction that Sessions should limit the Special Counsel's investigation came just two days after the President had ordered McGahn to have the Special Counsel removed, which itself followed public reports that the President was personally under

97

investigation for obstruction of justice. The sequence of those events raises an inference that after seeking to terminate the Special Counsel, the President sought to exclude his and his campaign's conduct from the investigation's scope. The President raised the matter with Lewandowski again on July 19, 2017, just days after emails and information about the June 9, 2016 meeting between Russians and senior campaign officials had been publicly disclosed, generating substantial media coverage and investigative interest.

The manner in which the President acted provides additional evidence of his intent. Rather than rely on official channels, the President met with Lewandowski alone in the Oval Office. The President selected a loyal "devotee" outside the White House to deliver the message, supporting an inference that he was working outside White House channels, including McGahn, who had previously resisted contacting the Department of Justice about the Special Counsel. The President also did not contact the Acting Attorney General, who had just testified publicly that there was no cause to remove the Special Counsel. Instead, the President tried to use Sessions to restrict and redirect the Special Counsel's investigation when Sessions was recused and could not properly take any action on it.

The July 19, 2017 events provide further evidence of the President's intent. The President followed up with Lewandowski in a separate one-on-one meeting one month after he first dictated the message for Sessions, demonstrating he still sought to pursue the request. And just hours after Lewandowski assured the President that the message would soon be delivered to Sessions, the President gave an unplanned interview to the New York Times in which he publicly attacked Sessions and raised questions about his job security. Four days later, on July 22, 2017, the President directed Priebus to obtain Sessions's resignation. That evidence could raise an inference that the President wanted Sessions to realize that his job might be on the line as he evaluated whether to comply with the President's direction that Sessions publicly announce that, notwithstanding his recusal, he was going to confine the Special Counsel's investigation to future election interference.

G. The President's Efforts to Prevent Disclosure of Emails About the June 9, 2016 Meeting Between Russians and Senior Campaign Officials

Overview

By June 2017, the President became aware of emails setting up the June 9, 2016 meeting between senior campaign officials and Russians who offered derogatory information on Hillary Clinton as "part of Russia and its government's support for Mr. Trump." On multiple occasions in late June and early July 2017, the President directed aides not to publicly disclose the emails, and he then dictated a statement about the meeting to be issued by Donald Trump Jr. describing the meeting as about adoption.

Evidence

1. The President Learns About the Existence of Emails Concerning the June 9, 2016 Trump Tower Meeting

In mid-June 2017—the same week that the President first asked Lewandowski to pass a message to Sessions—senior Administration officials became aware of emails exchanged during

98

U.S. Department of Justice

~~Attorney Work Product // May Contain Material Protected Under Fed. R. Crim. P. 6(e)~~

the campaign arranging a meeting between Donald Trump Jr., Paul Manafort, Jared Kushner, and a Russian attorney.[663] As described in Volume I, Section IV.A.5, *supra*, the emails stated that the "Crown [P]rosecutor of Russia" had offered "to provide the Trump campaign with some official documents and information that would incriminate Hillary and her dealings with Russia" as part of "Russia and its government's support for Mr. Trump."[664] Trump Jr. responded, "[I]f it's what you say I love it,"[665] and he, Kushner, and Manafort met with the Russian attorney and several other Russian individuals at Trump Tower on June 9, 2016.[666] At the meeting, the Russian attorney claimed that funds derived from illegal activities in Russia were provided to Hillary Clinton and other Democrats, and the Russian attorney then spoke about the Magnitsky Act, a 2012 U.S. statute that imposed financial and travel sanctions on Russian officials and that had resulted in a retaliatory ban in Russia on U.S. adoptions of Russian children.[667]

According to written answers submitted by the President in response to questions from this Office, the President had no recollection of learning of the meeting or the emails setting it up at the time the meeting occurred or at any other time before the election.[668]

The Trump Campaign had previously received a document request from SSCI that called for the production of various information, including, "[a] list and a description of all meetings" between any "individual affiliated with the Trump campaign" and "any individual formally or informally affiliated with the Russian government or Russian business interests which took place between June 16, 2015, and 12 pm on January 20, 2017," and associated records.[669] Trump Organization attorneys became aware of the June 9 meeting no later than the first week of June 2017, when they began interviewing the meeting participants, and the Trump Organization attorneys provided the emails setting up the meeting to the President's personal counsel.[670] Mark Corallo, who had been hired as a spokesman for the President's personal legal team, recalled that he learned about the June 9 meeting around June 21 or 22, 2017.[671] Priebus recalled learning about the June 9 meeting from Fox News host Sean Hannity in late June 2017.[672] Priebus notified one

---

[663] Hicks 3/13/18 302, at 1; Raffel 2/8/18 302, at 2.

[664] RG000061 (6/3/16 Email, Goldstone to Trump Jr.); @DonaldJTrumpJR 7/11/17 (11:01 a.m. ET) Tweet.

[665] RG000061 (6/3/16 Email, Trump Jr. to Goldstone); @DonaldJTrumpJR 7/11/17 (11:01 a.m. ET) Tweet.

[666] Samochornov 7/12/17 302, at 4.

[667] *See* Volume I, Section IV.A.5, *supra* (describing meeting in detail).

[668] Written Responses of Donald J. Trump (Nov. 20, 2018), at 8 (Response to Question I, Parts (a) through (c)). The President declined to answer questions about his knowledge of the June 9 meeting or other events after the election.

[669] DJTFP_SCO_PDF_00000001-02 (5/17/17 Letter, SSCI to Donald J. Trump for President, Inc.).

[670] Goldstone 2/8/18 302, at 12; 6/2/17 and 6/5/17 Emails, Goldstone & Garten; Raffel 2/8/18 302, at 3; Hicks 3/13/18 302, at 2.

[671] Corallo 2/15/18 302, at 3.

[672] Priebus 4/3/18 302, at 7.

of the President's personal attorneys, who told Priebus he was already working on it.[673] By late June, several advisors recalled receiving media inquiries that could relate to the June 9 meeting.[674]

2. The President Directs Communications Staff Not to Publicly Disclose Information About the June 9 Meeting

Communications advisors Hope Hicks and Josh Raffel recalled discussing with Jared Kushner and Ivanka Trump that the emails were damaging and would inevitably be leaked.[675] Hicks and Raffel advised that the best strategy was to proactively release the emails to the press.[676] On or about June 22, 2017, Hicks attended a meeting in the White House residence with the President, Kushner, and Ivanka Trump.[677] According to Hicks, Kushner said that he wanted to fill the President in on something that had been discovered in the documents he was to provide to the congressional committees involving a meeting with him, Manafort, and Trump Jr.[678] Kushner brought a folder of documents to the meeting and tried to show them to the President, but the President stopped Kushner and said he did not want to know about it, shutting the conversation down.[679]

On June 28, 2017, Hicks viewed the emails at Kushner's attorney's office.[680] She recalled being shocked by the emails because they looked "really bad."[681] The next day, Hicks spoke privately with the President to mention her concern about the emails, which she understood were soon going to be shared with Congress.[682] The President seemed upset because too many people knew about the emails and he told Hicks that just one lawyer should deal with the matter.[683] The President indicated that he did not think the emails would leak, but said they would leak if everyone had access to them.[684]

---

[673] Priebus 4/3/18 302, at 7.

[674] Corallo 2/15/18 302, at 3; Hicks 12/7/17 302, at 8; Raffel 2/8/18 302, at 3.

[675] Raffel 2/8/18 302, at 2-3; Hicks 3/13/18 302, at 2.

[676] Raffel 2/8/18 302, at 2-3, 5; Hicks 3/13/18 302, at 2; Hicks 12/7/17 302, at 8.

[677] Hicks 12/7/17 302, at 6-7; Hicks 3/13/18 302, at 1.

[678] Hicks 12/7/17 302, at 7; Hicks 3/13/18 302, at 1.

[679] Hicks 12/7/17 302, at 7; Hicks 3/13/18 302, at 1. Counsel for Ivanka Trump provided an attorney proffer that is consistent with Hicks's account and with the other events involving Ivanka Trump set forth in this section of the report. Kushner said that he did not recall talking to the President at this time about the June 9 meeting or the underlying emails. Kushner 4/11/18 302, at 30.

[680] Hicks 3/13/18 302, at 1-2.

[681] Hicks 3/13/18 302, at 2.

[682] Hicks 12/7/17 302, at 8.

[683] Hicks 3/13/18 302, at 2-3; Hicks 12/7/17 302, at 8.

[684] Hicks 12/7/17 302, at 8.

U.S. Department of Justice

~~Attorney Work Product // May Contain Material Protected Under Fed. R. Crim. P. 6(e)~~

Later that day, Hicks, Kushner, and Ivanka Trump went together to talk to the President.[685] Hicks recalled that Kushner told the President the June 9 meeting was not a big deal and was about Russian adoption, but that emails existed setting up the meeting.[686] Hicks said she wanted to get in front of the story and have Trump Jr. release the emails as part of an interview with "softball questions."[687] The President said he did not want to know about it and they should not go to the press.[688] Hicks warned the President that the emails were "really bad" and the story would be "massive" when it broke, but the President was insistent that he did not want to talk about it and said he did not want details.[689] Hicks recalled that the President asked Kushner when his document production was due.[690] Kushner responded that it would be a couple of weeks and the President said, "then leave it alone."[691] Hicks also recalled that the President said Kushner's attorney should give the emails to whomever he needed to give them to, but the President did not think they would be leaked to the press.[692] Raffel later heard from Hicks that the President had directed the group not to be proactive in disclosing the emails because the President believed they would not leak.[693]

3. The President Directs Trump Jr.'s Response to Press Inquiries About the June 9 Meeting

The following week, the President departed on an overseas trip for the G20 summit in Hamburg, Germany, accompanied by Hicks, Raffel, Kushner, and Ivanka Trump, among others.[694] On July 7, 2017, while the President was overseas, Hicks and Raffel learned that the New York Times was working on a story about the June 9 meeting.[695] The next day, Hicks told the President about the story and he directed her not to comment.[696] Hicks thought the President's reaction was odd because he usually considered not responding to the press to be the ultimate sin.[697] Later that day, Hicks and the President again spoke about the story.[698] Hicks recalled that the President asked

---

[685] Hicks 12/7/17 302, at 8; Hicks 3/13/18 302, at 2.

[686] Hicks 3/13/18 302, at 2; Hicks 12/7/17 302, at 9.

[687] Hicks 3/13/18 302, at 2-3.

[688] Hicks 3/13/18 302, at 2-3; Hicks 12/7/17 302, at 9.

[689] Hicks 3/13/18 302, at 3; Hicks 12/7/17 302, at 9.

[690] Hicks 3/13/18 302, at 3.

[691] Hicks 3/13/18 302, at 3.

[692] Hicks 12/7/17 302, at 9.

[693] Raffel 2/8/18 302, at 5.

[694] Raffel 2/8/18 302, at 6.

[695] Raffel 2/8/18 302, at 6-7; Hicks 3/13/18 302, at 3.

[696] Hicks 12/7/17 302, at 10; Hicks 3/13/18 302, at 3.

[697] Hicks 12/7/17 302, at 10.

[698] Hicks 3/13/18 302, at 3.

her what the meeting had been about, and she said that she had been told the meeting was about Russian adoption.[699] The President responded, "then just say that."[700]

On the flight home from the G20 on July 8, 2017, Hicks obtained a draft statement about the meeting to be released by Trump Jr. and brought it to the President.[701] The draft statement began with a reference to the information that was offered by the Russians in setting up the meeting: "I was asked to have a meeting by an acquaintance I knew from the 2013 Miss Universe pageant with an individual who I was told might have information helpful to the campaign."[702] Hicks again wanted to disclose the entire story, but the President directed that the statement not be issued because it said too much.[703] The President told Hicks to say only that Trump Jr. took a brief meeting and it was about Russian adoption.[704] After speaking with the President, Hicks texted Trump Jr. a revised statement on the June 9 meeting that read:

> It was a short meeting. I asked Jared and Paul to stop by. We discussed a program about the adoption of Russian children that was active and popular with American families years ago and was since ended by the Russian government, but it was not a campaign issue at that time and there was no follow up.[705]

Hicks's text concluded, "Are you ok with this? Attributed to you."[706] Trump Jr. responded by text message that he wanted to add the word "primarily" before "discussed" so that the statement would read, "We primarily discussed a program about the adoption of Russian children."[707] Trump Jr. texted that he wanted the change because "[t]hey started with some Hillary thing which was bs and some other nonsense which we shot down fast."[708] Hicks texted back, "I think that's right too but boss man worried it invites a lot of questions[.] [U]ltimately [d]efer to you and [your attorney] on that word Bc I know it's important and I think the mention of a campaign issue adds something to it in case we have to go further."[709] Trump Jr. responded, "If I don't have it in there it appears as though I'm lying later when they inevitably leak something."[710] Trump Jr.'s statement—adding

---

[699] Hicks 3/13/18 302, at 3; Hicks 12/7/17 302, at 10.

[700] Hicks 3/13/18 302, at 3; *see* Hicks 12/7/17 302, at 10.

[701] Hicks 3/13/18 302, at 4.

[702] Hicks 7/8/17 Notes.

[703] Hicks 3/13/18 302, at 4-5; Hicks 12/7/17 302, at 11.

[704] Hicks 12/7/17 302, at 11.

[705] SCR011a_000004 (7/8/17 Text Message, Hicks to Trump Jr.).

[706] SCR011a_000004 (7/8/17 Text Message, Hicks to Trump Jr.).

[707] SCR011a_000005 (7/8/17 Text Message, Trump Jr. to Hicks).

[708] SCR011a_000005 (7/8/17 Text Message, Trump Jr. to Hicks).

[709] SCR011a_000005 (7/8/17 Text Message, Hicks to Trump Jr.).

[710] SCR011a_000006 (7/8/17 Text Message, Trump Jr. to Hicks).

U.S. Department of Justice

Attorney Work Product // May Contain Material Protected Under Fed. R. Crim. P. 6(e)

the word "primarily" and making other minor additions—was then provided to the New York Times.[711] The full statement provided to the *Times* stated:

> It was a short introductory meeting. I asked Jared and Paul to stop by. We primarily discussed a program about the adoption of Russian children that was active and popular with American families years ago and was since ended by the Russian government, but it was not a campaign issue at the time and there was no follow up. I was asked to attend the meeting by an acquaintance, but was not told the name of the person I would be meeting with beforehand.[712]

The statement did not mention the offer of derogatory information about Clinton or any discussion of the Magnitsky Act or U.S. sanctions, which were the principal subjects of the meeting, as described in Volume I, Section IV.A.5, *supra*.

A short while later, while still on Air Force One, Hicks learned that Priebus knew about the emails, which further convinced her that additional information about the June 9 meeting would leak and the White House should be proactive and get in front of the story.[713] Hicks recalled again going to the President to urge him that they should be fully transparent about the June 9 meeting, but he again said no, telling Hicks, "You've given a statement. We're done."[714]

Later on the flight home, Hicks went to the President's cabin, where the President was on the phone with one of his personal attorneys.[715] At one point the President handed the phone to Hicks, and the attorney told Hicks that he had been working with Circa News on a separate story, and that she should not talk to the New York Times.[716]

4. The Media Reports on the June 9, 2016 Meeting

Before the President's flight home from the G20 landed, the New York Times published its story about the June 9, 2016 meeting.[717] In addition to the statement from Trump Jr., the Times story also quoted a statement from Corallo on behalf of the President's legal team suggesting that the meeting might have been a setup by individuals working with the firm that produced the Steele reporting.[718] Corallo also worked with Circa News on a story published an hour later that

---

[711] Hicks 3/13/18 302, at 6; *see* Jo Becker et al., *Trump Team Met With Lawyer Linked to Kremlin During Campaign*, New York Times (July 8, 2017).

[712] *See* Jo Becker et al., *Trump Team Met With Lawyer Linked to Kremlin During Campaign*, New York Times (July 8, 2017).

[713] Hicks 3/13/18 302, at 6; Raffel 2/8/18 302, at 9-10.

[714] Hicks 12/7/17 302, at 12; Raffel 2/8/18 302, at 10.

[715] Hicks 3/13/18 302, at 7.

[716] Hicks 3/13/18 302, at 7.

[717] *See* Jo Becker et al., *Trump Team Met With Lawyer Linked to Kremlin During Campaign*, New York Times (July 8, 2017); Raffel 2/8/18 302, at 10.

[718] *See* Jo Becker et al., *Trump Team Met With Lawyer Linked to Kremlin During Campaign*, New York Times (July 8, 2017).

103

questioned whether Democratic operatives had arranged the June 9 meeting to create the appearance of improper connections between Russia and Trump family members.[719] Hicks was upset about Corallo's public statement and called him that evening to say the President had not approved the statement.[720]

The next day, July 9, 2017, Hicks and the President called Corallo together and the President criticized Corallo for the statement he had released.[721] Corallo told the President the statement had been authorized and further observed that Trump Jr.'s statement was inaccurate and that a document existed that would contradict it.[722] Corallo said that he purposely used the term "document" to refer to the emails setting up the June 9 meeting because he did not know what the President knew about the emails.[723] Corallo recalled that when he referred to the "document" on the call with the President, Hicks responded that only a few people had access to it and said "it will never get out."[724] Corallo took contemporaneous notes of the call that say: "Also mention existence of doc. Hope says 'only a few people have it. It will never get out.'"[725] Hicks later told investigators that she had no memory of making that comment and had always believed the emails would eventually be leaked, but she might have been channeling the President on the phone call because it was clear to her throughout her conversations with the President that he did not think the emails would leak.[726]

On July 11, 2017, Trump Jr. posted redacted images of the emails setting up the June 9 meeting on Twitter; the New York Times reported that he did so "[a]fter being told that The Times was about to publish the content of the emails."[727] Later that day, the media reported that the President had been personally involved in preparing Trump Jr.'s initial statement to the New York Times that had claimed the meeting "primarily" concerned "a program about the adoption of Russian children."[728] Over the next several days, the President's personal counsel repeatedly and

---

[719] *See Donald Trump Jr. gathered members of campaign for meeting with Russian lawyer before election,* Circa News (July 8, 2017).

[720] Hicks 3/13/18 302, at 8; Corallo 2/15/18 302, at 6-7.

[721] Corallo 2/15/18 302, at 7.

[722] Corallo 2/15/18 302, at 7.

[723] Corallo 2/15/18 302, at 7-9.

[724] Corallo 2/15/18 302, at 8.

[725] Corallo 2/15/18 302, at 8; Corallo 7/9/17 Notes ("Sunday 9th – Hope calls w/ POTUS on line"). Corallo said he is "100% confident" that Hicks said "It will never get out" on the call. Corallo 2/15/18 302, at 9.

[726] Hicks 3/13/18 302, at 9.

[727] @DonaldJTrumpJR 7/11/17 (11:01 a.m. ET) Tweet; Jo Becker et al., *Russian Dirt on Clinton? 'I Love It,' Donald Trump Jr. Said,* New York Times (July 11, 2017).

[728] *See, e.g.,* Peter Baker & Maggie Haberman, *Rancor at White House as Russia Story Refuses to Let the Page Turn,* New York Times (July 11, 2017) (reporting that the President "signed off" on Trump Jr.'s statement).

U.S. Department of Justice

~~Attorney Work Product // May Contain Material Protected Under Fed. R. Crim. P. 6(e)~~

inaccurately denied that the President played any role in drafting Trump Jr.'s statement.[729] After consulting with the President on the issue, White House Press Secretary Sarah Sanders told the media that the President "certainly didn't dictate" the statement, but that "he weighed in, offered suggestions like any father would do."[730] Several months later, the President's personal counsel stated in a private communication to the Special Counsel's Office that "the President dictated a short but accurate response to the New York Times article on behalf of his son, Donald Trump, Jr."[731] The President later told the press that it was "irrelevant" whether he dictated the statement and said, "It's a statement to the New York Times. . . . That's not a statement to a high tribunal of judges."[732]

On July 12, 2017, the Special Counsel's Office **Grand Jury**   Trump Jr. **Grand Jury**   related to the June 9 meeting and those who attended the June 9 meeting.[733]

On July 19, 2017, the President had his follow-up meeting with Lewandowski and then met with reporters for the New York Times. In addition to criticizing Sessions in his Times interview, the President addressed the June 9, 2016 meeting and said he "didn't know anything about the meeting" at the time.[734] The President added, "As I've said—most other people, you know, when they call up and say, 'By the way, we have information on your opponent,' I think most politicians — I was just with a lot of people, they said . . . , 'Who wouldn't have taken a meeting like that?'"[735]

Analysis

In analyzing the President's actions regarding the disclosure of information about the June 9 meeting, the following evidence is relevant to the elements of obstruction of justice:

a.   Obstructive act. On at least three occasions between June 29, 2017, and July 9, 2017, the President directed Hicks and others not to publicly disclose information about the June

---

[729] See, e.g., David Wright, Trump lawyer: President was aware of "nothing", CNN (July 12, 2017) (quoting the President's personal attorney as saying, "I wasn't involved in the statement drafting at all nor was the President."); see also Good Morning America, ABC (July 12, 2017) ("The President didn't sign off on anything. . . . The President wasn't involved in that."); Meet the Press, NBC (July 16, 2017) ("I do want to be clear—the President was not involved in the drafting of the statement.").

[730] Sarah Sanders, White House Daily Briefing, C-SPAN (Aug. 1, 2017); Sanders 7/3/18 302, at 9 (the President told Sanders he "weighed in, as any father would" and knew she intended to tell the press what he said).

[731] 1/29/18 Letter, President's Personal Counsel to Special Counsel's Office, at 18.

[732] Remarks by President Trump in Press Gaggle (June 15, 2018).

[733] **Grand Jury**   .

[734] Peter Baker et al., Excerpts From The Times's Interview With Trump, New York Times (July 19, 2017).

[735] Peter Baker et al., Excerpts From The Times's Interview With Trump, New York Times (July 19, 2017).

105

9, 2016 meeting between senior campaign officials and a Russian attorney. On June 29, Hicks warned the President that the emails setting up the June 9 meeting were "really bad" and the story would be "massive" when it broke, but the President told her and Kushner to "leave it alone." Early on July 8, after Hicks told the President the New York Times was working on a story about the June 9 meeting, the President directed her not to comment, even though Hicks said that the President usually considered not responding to the press to be the ultimate sin. Later that day, the President rejected Trump Jr.'s draft statement that would have acknowledged that the meeting was with "an individual who I was told might have information helpful to the campaign." The President then dictated a statement to Hicks that said the meeting was about Russian adoption (which the President had twice been told was discussed at the meeting). The statement dictated by the President did not mention the offer of derogatory information about Clinton.

Each of these efforts by the President involved his communications team and was directed at the press. They would amount to obstructive acts only if the President, by taking these actions, sought to withhold information from or mislead congressional investigators or the Special Counsel. On May 17, 2017, the President's campaign received a document request from SSCI that clearly covered the June 9 meeting and underlying emails, and those documents also plainly would have been relevant to the Special Counsel's investigation.

But the evidence does not establish that the President took steps to prevent the emails or other information about the June 9 meeting from being provided to Congress or the Special Counsel. The series of discussions in which the President sought to limit access to the emails and prevent their public release occurred in the context of developing a press strategy. The only evidence we have of the President discussing the production of documents to Congress or the Special Counsel is the conversation on June 29, 2017, when Hicks recalled the President acknowledging that Kushner's attorney should provide emails related to the June 9 meeting to whomever he needed to give them to. We do not have evidence of what the President discussed with his own lawyers at that time.

b.   Nexus to an official proceeding. As described above, by the time of the President's attempts to prevent the public release of the emails regarding the June 9 meeting, the existence of a grand jury investigation supervised by the Special Counsel was public knowledge, and the President had been told that the emails were responsive to congressional inquiries. To satisfy the nexus requirement, however, it would be necessary to show that preventing the release of the emails to the public would have the natural and probable effect of impeding the grand jury proceeding or congressional inquiries. As noted above, the evidence does not establish that the President sought to prevent disclosure of the emails in those official proceedings.

c.   Intent. The evidence establishes the President's substantial involvement in the communications strategy related to information about his campaign's connections to Russia and his desire to minimize public disclosures about those connections. The President became aware of the emails no later than June 29, 2017, when he discussed them with Hicks and Kushner, and he could have been aware of them as early as June 2, 2017, when lawyers for the Trump Organization began interviewing witnesses who participated in the June 9 meeting. The President thereafter repeatedly rejected the advice of Hicks and other staffers to publicly release information about the June 9 meeting. The President expressed concern that multiple people had access to the emails and instructed Hicks that only one lawyer should deal with the matter. And the President

106

dictated a statement to be released by Trump Jr. in response to the first press accounts of the June 9 meeting that said the meeting was about adoption.

But as described above, the evidence does not establish that the President intended to prevent the Special Counsel's Office or Congress from obtaining the emails setting up the June 9 meeting or other information about that meeting. The statement recorded by Corallo—that the emails "will never get out"—can be explained as reflecting a belief that the emails would not be made public if the President's press strategy were followed, even if the emails were provided to Congress and the Special Counsel.

H. The President's Further Efforts to Have the Attorney General Take Over the Investigation

Overview

From summer 2017 through 2018, the President attempted to have Attorney General Sessions reverse his recusal, take control of the Special Counsel's investigation, and order an investigation of Hillary Clinton.

Evidence

1. The President Again Seeks to Have Sessions Reverse his Recusal

After returning Sessions's resignation letter at the end of May 2017, but before the President's July 19, 2017 New York Times interview in which he publicly criticized Sessions for recusing from the Russia investigation, the President took additional steps to have Sessions reverse his recusal. In particular, at some point after the May 17, 2017 appointment of the Special Counsel, Sessions recalled, the President called him at home and asked if Sessions would "unrecuse" himself.[736] According to Sessions, the President asked him to reverse his recusal so that Sessions could direct the Department of Justice to investigate and prosecute Hillary Clinton, and the "gist" of the conversation was that the President wanted Sessions to unrecuse from "all of it," including the Special Counsel's Russia investigation.[737] Sessions listened but did not respond, and he did not reverse his recusal or order an investigation of Clinton.[738]

In early July 2017, the President asked Staff Secretary Rob Porter what he thought of Associate Attorney General Rachel Brand.[739] Porter recalled that the President asked him if Brand was good, tough, and "on the team."[740] The President also asked if Porter thought Brand was interested in being responsible for the Special Counsel's investigation and whether she would want

---

[736] Sessions 1/17/18 302, at 15. That was the second time that the President asked Sessions to reverse his recusal from campaign-related investigations. *See* Volume II, Section II.C.1, *supra* (describing President's March 2017 request at Mar-a-Lago for Sessions to unrecuse).

[737] Sessions 1/17/18 302, at 15.

[738] Sessions 1/17/18 302, at 15.

[739] Porter 4/13/18 302, at 11; Porter 5/8/18 302, at 6.

[740] Porter 4/13/18 302, at 11; Porter 5/8/18 302, at 6.

to be Attorney General one day.[741] Because Porter knew Brand, the President asked him to sound her out about taking responsibility for the investigation and being Attorney General.[742] Contemporaneous notes taken by Porter show that the President told Porter to "Keep in touch with your friend," in reference to Brand.[743] Later, the President asked Porter a few times in passing whether he had spoken to Brand, but Porter did not reach out to her because he was uncomfortable with the task.[744] In asking him to reach out to Brand, Porter understood the President to want to find someone to end the Russia investigation or fire the Special Counsel, although the President never said so explicitly.[745] Porter did not contact Brand because he was sensitive to the implications of that action and did not want to be involved in a chain of events associated with an effort to end the investigation or fire the Special Counsel.[746]

McGahn recalled that during the summer of 2017, he and the President discussed the fact that if Sessions were no longer in his position the Special Counsel would report directly to a non-recused Attorney General.[747] McGahn told the President that things might not change much under a new Attorney General.[748] McGahn also recalled that in or around July 2017, the President frequently brought up his displeasure with Sessions.[749] Hicks recalled that the President viewed Sessions's recusal from the Russia investigation as an act of disloyalty.[750] In addition to criticizing Sessions's recusal, the President raised other concerns about Sessions and his job performance with McGahn and Hicks.[751]

---

[741] Porter 4/13/18 302, at 11; Porter 5/8/18 302, at 6. Because of Sessions's recusal, if Rosenstein were no longer in his position, Brand would, by default, become the DOJ official in charge of supervising the Special Counsel's investigation, and if both Sessions and Rosenstein were removed, Brand would be next in line to become Acting Attorney General for all DOJ matters. *See* 28 U.S.C. § 508.

[742] Porter 4/13/18 302, at 11; Porter 5/8/18 302, at 6.

[743] SC_RRP000020 (Porter 7/10/17 Notes).

[744] Porter 4/13/18 302, at 11-12.

[745] Porter 4/13/18 302, at 11-12.

[746] Porter 4/13/18 302, at 11-12. Brand confirmed that no one ever raised with her the prospect of taking over the Russia investigation or becoming Attorney General. Brand 1/29/19 302, at 2.

[747] McGahn 12/14/17 302, at 11.

[748] McGahn 12/14/17 302, at 11.

[749] McGahn 12/14/17 302, at 9.

[750] Hicks 3/13/18 302, at 10.

[751] McGahn 12/14/17 302, at 9; Hicks 3/13/18 302, at 10.

2. Additional Efforts to Have Sessions Unrecuse or Direct Investigations Covered by his Recusal

Later in 2017, the President continued to urge Sessions to reverse his recusal from campaign-related investigations and considered replacing Sessions with an Attorney General who would not be recused.

On October 16, 2017, the President met privately with Sessions and said that the Department of Justice was not investigating individuals and events that the President thought the Department should be investigating.[752] According to contemporaneous notes taken by Porter, who was at the meeting, the President mentioned Clinton's emails and said, "Don't have to tell us, just take [a] look."[753] Sessions did not offer any assurances or promises to the President that the Department of Justice would comply with that request.[754] Two days later, on October 18, 2017, the President tweeted, "Wow, FBI confirms report that James Comey drafted letter exonerating Crooked Hillary Clinton long before investigation was complete. Many people not interviewed, including Clinton herself. Comey stated under oath that he didn't do this-obviously a fix? Where is Justice Dept?"[755] On October 29, 2017, the President tweeted that there was "ANGER & UNITY" over a "lack of investigation" of Clinton and "the Comey fix," and concluded: "DO SOMETHING!"[756]

On December 6, 2017, five days after Flynn pleaded guilty to lying about his contacts with the Russian government, the President asked to speak with Sessions in the Oval Office at the end of a cabinet meeting.[757] During that Oval Office meeting, which Porter attended, the President again suggested that Sessions could "unrecuse," which Porter linked to taking back supervision of the Russia investigation and directing an investigation of Hillary Clinton.[758] According to contemporaneous notes taken by Porter, the President said, "I don't know if you could un-recuse yourself. You'd be a hero. Not telling you to do anything. Dershowitz says POTUS can get involved. Can order AG to investigate. I don't want to get involved. I'm not going to get involved. I'm not going to do anything or direct you to do anything. I just want to be treated fairly."[759] According to Porter's notes, Sessions responded, "We are taking steps; whole new leadership

---

[752] Porter 5/8/18 302, at 10.

[753] SC_RRP000024 (Porter 10/16/17 Notes); *see* Porter 5/8/18 302, at 10.

[754] Porter 5/8/18 302, at 10.

[755] @realDonaldTrump 10/18/17 (6:21 a.m. ET) Tweet; @realDonaldTrump 10/18/17 (6:27 a.m. ET) Tweet.

[756] @realDonaldTrump 10/29/17 (9:53 a.m. ET) Tweet; @realDonaldTrump 10/29/17 (10:02 a.m. ET) Tweet; @realDonaldTrump 10/29/17 (10:17 a.m. ET) Tweet.

[757] Porter 4/13/18 302, at 5-6; *see* SC_RRP000031 (Porter 12/6/17 Notes) ("12:45pm With the President, Gen. Kelly, and Sessions (who I pulled in after the Cabinet meeting)"); SC_RRP000033 (Porter 12/6/17 Notes) ("Post-cabinet meeting – POTUS asked me to get AG Sessions. Asked me to stay. Also COS Kelly.").

[758] Porter 5/8/18 302, at 12; Porter 4/13/18 302, at 5-6.

[759] SC_RRP000033 (Porter 12/6/17 Notes); *see* Porter 4/13/18 302, at 6; Porter 5/8/18 302, at 12.

team. Professionals; will operate according to the law."[760] Sessions also said, "I never saw anything that was improper," which Porter thought was noteworthy because it did not fit with the previous discussion about Clinton.[761] Porter understood Sessions to be reassuring the President that he was on the President's team.[762]

At the end of December, the President told the New York Times it was "too bad" that Sessions had recused himself from the Russia investigation.[763] When asked whether Holder had been a more loyal Attorney General to President Obama than Sessions was to him, the President said, "I don't want to get into loyalty, but I will tell you that, I will say this: Holder protected President Obama. Totally protected him. When you look at the things that they did, and Holder protected the president. And I have great respect for that, I'll be honest."[764] Later in January, the President brought up the idea of replacing Sessions and told Porter that he wanted to "clean house" at the Department of Justice.[765] In a meeting in the White House residence that Porter attended on January 27, 2018, Porter recalled that the President talked about the great attorneys he had in the past with successful win records, such as Roy Cohn and Jay Goldberg, and said that one of his biggest failings as President was that he had not surrounded himself with good attorneys, citing Sessions as an example.[766] The President raised Sessions's recusal and brought up and criticized the Special Counsel's investigation.[767]

Over the next several months, the President continued to criticize Sessions in tweets and media interviews and on several occasions appeared to publicly encourage him to take action in the Russia investigation despite his recusal.[768] On June 5, 2018, for example, the President

---

[760] SC_RRP000033 (Porter 12/6/17 Notes); *see* Porter 4/13/18 302, at 6.

[761] SC_RRP000033 (Porter 12/6/17 Notes); Porter 4/13/18 302, at 6.

[762] Porter 4/13/18 302, at 6-7.

[763] Michael S. Schmidt & Michael D. Shear, *Trump Says Russia Inquiry Makes U.S. "Look Very Bad"*, New York Times (Dec. 28, 2017).

[764] Michael S. Schmidt & Michael D. Shear, *Trump Says Russia Inquiry Makes U.S. "Look Very Bad"*, New York Times (Dec. 28, 2017).

[765] Porter 4/13/18 302, at 14.

[766] Porter 5/8/18 302, at 15. Contemporaneous notes Porter took of the conversation state, "Roy Cohn (14-0) / Jay Goldberg (12-0)." SC_RRP000047 (Porter 1/27/18 Notes).

[767] Porter 5/8/18 302, at 15-16.

[768] *See, e.g.*, @realDonaldTrump 2/28/18 (9:34 a.m. ET) Tweet ("Why is A.G. Jeff Sessions asking the Inspector General to investigate potentially massive FISA abuse. Will take forever, has no prosecutorial power and already late with reports on Comey etc. Isn't the I.G. an Obama guy? Why not use Justice Department lawyers? DISGRACEFUL!"); @realDonaldTrump 4/7/18 (4:52 p.m. ET) Tweet ("Lawmakers of the House Judiciary Committee are angrily accusing the Department of Justice of missing the Thursday Deadline for turning over UNREDACTED Documents relating to FISA abuse, FBI, Comey, Lynch, McCabe, Clinton Emails and much more. Slow walking – what is going on? BAD!"); @realDonaldTrump 4/22/18 (8:22 a.m. ET) Tweet ("'GOP Lawmakers asking Sessions to Investigate Comey and Hillary Clinton.' @FoxNews Good luck with that request!"); @realDonaldTrump 12/16/18 (3:37 p.m. ET) Tweet

U.S. Department of Justice

~~Attorney Work Product // May Contain Material Protected Under Fed. R. Crim. P. 6(e)~~

tweeted, "The Russian Witch Hunt Hoax continues, all because Jeff Sessions didn't tell me he was going to recuse himself. . . . I would have quickly picked someone else. So much time and money wasted, so many lives ruined . . . and Sessions knew better than most that there was No Collusion!"[769] On August 1, 2018, the President tweeted that "Attorney General Jeff Sessions should stop this Rigged Witch Hunt right now."[770] On August 23, 2018, the President publicly criticized Sessions in a press interview and suggested that prosecutions at the Department of Justice were politically motivated because Paul Manafort had been prosecuted but Democrats had not.[771] The President said, "I put in an Attorney General that never took control of the Justice Department, Jeff Sessions."[772] That day, Sessions issued a press statement that said, "I took control of the Department of Justice the day I was sworn in . . . . While I am Attorney General, the actions of the Department of Justice will not be improperly influenced by political considerations."[773] The next day, the President tweeted a response: "'Department of Justice will not be improperly influenced by political considerations.' Jeff, this is GREAT, what everyone wants, so look into all of the corruption on the 'other side' including deleted Emails, Comey lies & leaks, Mueller conflicts, McCabe, Strzok, Page, Ohr, FISA abuse, Christopher Steele & his phony and corrupt Dossier, the Clinton Foundation, illegal surveillance of Trump campaign, Russian collusion by Dems – and so much more. Open up the papers & documents without redaction? Come on Jeff, you can do it, the country is waiting!"[774]

On November 7, 2018, the day after the midterm elections, the President replaced Sessions with Sessions's chief of staff as Acting Attorney General.[775]

Analysis

In analyzing the President's efforts to have Sessions unrecuse himself and regain control of the Russia investigation, the following considerations and evidence are relevant to the elements of obstruction of justice:

a. Obstructive act. To determine if the President's efforts to have the Attorney General unrecuse could qualify as an obstructive act, it would be necessary to assess evidence on whether those actions would naturally impede the Russia investigation. That inquiry would take into account the supervisory role that the Attorney General, if unrecused, would play in the Russia investigation. It also would have to take into account that the Attorney General's recusal covered

---

("Jeff Sessions should be ashamed of himself for allowing this total HOAX to get started in the first place!").

[769] @realDonaldTrump 6/5/18 (7:31 a.m. ET) Tweet.

[770] @realDonaldTrump 8/1/18 (9:24 a.m. ET) Tweet.

[771] Fox & Friends Interview of President Trump, Fox News (Aug. 23, 2018).

[772] Fox & Friends Interview of President Trump, Fox News (Aug. 23, 2018).

[773] Sessions 8/23/18 Press Statement.

[774] @realDonaldTrump 8/24/18 (6:17 a.m. ET) Tweet; @realDonaldTrump 8/24/18 (6:28 a.m. ET) Tweet.

[775] @realDonaldTrump 11/7/18 (2:44 p.m. ET) Tweet.

U.S. Department of Justice

~~Attorney Work Product // May Contain Material Protected Under Fed. R. Crim. P. 6(e)~~

other campaign-related matters. The inquiry would not turn on what Attorney General Sessions would actually do if unrecused, but on whether the efforts to reverse his recusal would naturally have had the effect of impeding the Russia investigation.

On multiple occasions in 2017, the President spoke with Sessions about reversing his recusal so that he could take over the Russia investigation and begin an investigation and prosecution of Hillary Clinton. For example, in early summer 2017, Sessions recalled the President asking him to unrecuse, but Sessions did not take it as a directive. When the President raised the issue again in December 2017, the President said, as recorded by Porter, "Not telling you to do anything. . . . I'm not going to get involved. I'm not going to do anything or direct you to do anything. I just want to be treated fairly." The duration of the President's efforts—which spanned from March 2017 to August 2018—and the fact that the President repeatedly criticized Sessions in public and in private for failing to tell the President that he would have to recuse is relevant to assessing whether the President's efforts to have Sessions unrecuse could qualify as obstructive acts.

b. Nexus to an official proceeding. As described above, by mid-June 2017, the existence of a grand jury investigation supervised by the Special Counsel was public knowledge. In addition, in July 2017, a different grand jury supervised by the Special Counsel was empaneled in the District of Columbia, and the press reported on the existence of this grand jury in early August 2017.[776] Whether the conduct towards the Attorney General would have a foreseeable impact on those proceedings turns on much of the same evidence discussed above with respect to the obstructive-act element.

c. Intent. There is evidence that at least one purpose of the President's conduct toward Sessions was to have Sessions assume control over the Russia investigation and supervise it in a way that would restrict its scope. By the summer of 2017, the President was aware that the Special Counsel was investigating him personally for obstruction of justice. And in the wake of the disclosures of emails about the June 9 meeting between Russians and senior members of the campaign, see Volume II, Section II.G, supra, it was evident that the investigation into the campaign now included the President's son, son-in-law, and former campaign manager. The President had previously and unsuccessfully sought to have Sessions publicly announce that the Special Counsel investigation would be confined to future election interference. Yet Sessions remained recused. In December 2017, shortly after Flynn pleaded guilty, the President spoke to Sessions in the Oval Office with only Porter present and told Sessions that he would be a hero if he unrecused. Porter linked that request to the President's desire that Sessions take back supervision of the Russia investigation and direct an investigation of Hillary Clinton. The President said in that meeting that he "just want[ed] to be treated fairly," which could reflect his perception that it was unfair that he was being investigated while Hillary Clinton was not. But a principal effect of that act would be to restore supervision of the Russia investigation to the Attorney General—a position that the President frequently suggested should be occupied by someone like Eric Holder and Bobby Kennedy, who the President described as protecting their

---

[776] E.g., Del Quentin Wilbur & Byron Tau, Special Counsel Robert Mueller Impanels Washington Grand Jury in Russia Probe, Wall Street Journal (Aug. 3, 2017); Carol D. Leonnig et al., Special Counsel Mueller using grand jury in federal court in Washington as part of Russia investigation, Washington Post (Aug. 3, 2017).

presidents. A reasonable inference from those statements and the President's actions is that the President believed that an unrecused Attorney General would play a protective role and could shield the President from the ongoing Russia investigation.

I.   The President Orders McGahn to Deny that the President Tried to Fire the Special Counsel

Overview

In late January 2018, the media reported that in June 2017 the President had ordered McGahn to have the Special Counsel fired based on purported conflicts of interest but McGahn had refused, saying he would quit instead. After the story broke, the President, through his personal counsel and two aides, sought to have McGahn deny that he had been directed to remove the Special Counsel. Each time he was approached, McGahn responded that he would not refute the press accounts because they were accurate in reporting on the President's effort to have the Special Counsel removed. The President later personally met with McGahn in the Oval Office with only the Chief of Staff present and tried to get McGahn to say that the President never ordered him to fire the Special Counsel. McGahn refused and insisted his memory of the President's direction to remove the Special Counsel was accurate. In that same meeting, the President challenged McGahn for taking notes of his discussions with the President and asked why he had told Special Counsel investigators that he had been directed to have the Special Counsel removed.

Evidence

1.   The Press Reports that the President Tried to Fire the Special Counsel

On January 25, 2018, the New York Times reported that in June 2017, the President had ordered McGahn to have the Department of Justice fire the Special Counsel.[777] According to the article, "[a]mid the first wave of news media reports that Mr. Mueller was examining a possible obstruction case, the president began to argue that Mr. Mueller had three conflicts of interest that disqualified him from overseeing the investigation."[778] The article further reported that "[a]fter receiving the president's order to fire Mr. Mueller, the White House counsel . . . refused to ask the Justice Department to dismiss the special counsel, saying he would quit instead."[779] The article stated that the president "ultimately backed down after the White House counsel threatened to resign rather than carry out the directive."[780] After the article was published, the President

---

[777] Michael S. Schmidt & Maggie Haberman, *Trump Ordered Mueller Fired, but Backed Off When White House Counsel Threatened to Quit*, New York Times (Jan. 25. 2018).

[778] Michael S. Schmidt & Maggie Haberman, *Trump Ordered Mueller Fired, but Backed Off When White House Counsel Threatened to Quit*, New York Times (Jan. 25. 2018).

[779] Michael S. Schmidt & Maggie Haberman, *Trump Ordered Mueller Fired, but Backed Off When White House Counsel Threatened to Quit*, New York Times (Jan. 25. 2018).

[780] Michael S. Schmidt & Maggie Haberman, *Trump Ordered Mueller Fired, but Backed Off When White House Counsel Threatened to Quit*, New York Times (Jan. 25. 2018).

113

U.S. Department of Justice

~~Attorney Work Product~~ // ~~May Contain Material Protected Under Fed. R. Crim. P. 6(e)~~

dismissed the story when asked about it by reporters, saying, "Fake news, folks. Fake news. A typical New York Times fake story."[781]

The next day, the Washington Post reported on the same event but added that McGahn had not told the President directly that he intended to resign rather than carry out the directive to have the Special Counsel terminated.[782] In that respect, the Post story clarified the Times story, which could be read to suggest that McGahn had told the President of his intention to quit, causing the President to back down from the order to have the Special Counsel fired.[783]

2. The President Seeks to Have McGahn Dispute the Press Reports

On January 26, 2018, the President's personal counsel called McGahn's attorney and said that the President wanted McGahn to put out a statement denying that he had been asked to fire the Special Counsel and that he had threatened to quit in protest.[784] McGahn's attorney spoke with McGahn about that request and then called the President's personal counsel to relay that McGahn would not make a statement.[785] McGahn's attorney informed the President's personal counsel that the Times story was accurate in reporting that the President wanted the Special Counsel removed.[786] Accordingly, McGahn's attorney said, although the article was inaccurate in some other respects, McGahn could not comply with the President's request to dispute the story.[787] Hicks recalled relaying to the President that one of his attorneys had spoken to McGahn's attorney about the issue.[788]

---

[781] Sophie Tatum & Kara Scannell, *Trump denies he called for Mueller's firing*, CNN (Jan. 26, 2018); Michael S. Schmidt & Maggie Haberman, *Trump Ordered Mueller Fired, but Backed Off When White House Counsel Threatened to Quit*, New York Times (Jan. 25, 2018).

[782] The *Post* article stated, "Despite internal objections, Trump decided to assert that Mueller had unacceptable conflicts of interest and moved to remove him from his position. . . . In response, McGahn said he would not remain at the White House if Trump went through with the move. . . . McGahn did not deliver his resignation threat directly to Trump but was serious about his threat to leave." Rosalind S. Helderman & Josh Dawsey, *Trump moved to fire Mueller in June, bringing White House counsel to the brink of leaving*, Washington Post (Jan. 26, 2018).

[783] Rosalind S. Helderman & Josh Dawsey, *Trump moved to fire Mueller in June, bringing White House counsel to the brink of leaving*, Washington Post (Jan. 26, 2018); *see* McGahn 3/8/17 302, at 3-4.

[784] McGahn 3/8/18 302, at 3 (agent note).

[785] McGahn 3/8/18 302, at 3 (agent note).

[786] McGahn 3/8/18 302, at 3-4 (agent note).

[787] McGahn 3/8/18 302, at 4 (agent note).

[788] Hicks 3/13/18 302, at 11. Hicks also recalled that the President spoke on the phone that day with Chief of Staff John Kelly and that the President said Kelly told him that McGahn had totally refuted the story and was going to put out a statement. Hicks 3/13/18 302, at 11. But Kelly said that he did not speak to McGahn when the article came out and did not tell anyone he had done so. Kelly 8/2/18 302, at 1-2.

114

Also on January 26, 2017, Hicks recalled that the President asked Sanders to contact McGahn about the story.[789] McGahn told Sanders there was no need to respond and indicated that some of the article was accurate.[790] Consistent with that position, McGahn did not correct the *Times* story.

On February 4, 2018, Priebus appeared on Meet the Press and said he had not heard the President say that he wanted the Special Counsel fired.[791] After Priebus's appearance, the President called Priebus and said he did a great job on Meet the Press.[792] The President also told Priebus that the President had "never said any of those things about" the Special Counsel.[793]

The next day, on February 5, 2018, the President complained about the *Times* article to Porter.[794] The President told Porter that the article was "bullshit" and he had not sought to terminate the Special Counsel.[795] The President said that McGahn leaked to the media to make himself look good.[796] The President then directed Porter to tell McGahn to create a record to make clear that the President never directed McGahn to fire the Special Counsel.[797] Porter thought the matter should be handled by the White House communications office, but the President said he wanted McGahn to write a letter to the file "for our records" and wanted something beyond a press statement to demonstrate that the reporting was inaccurate.[798] The President referred to McGahn as a "lying bastard" and said that he wanted a record from him.[799] Porter recalled the President

---

[789] Hicks 3/13/18 302, at 11. Sanders did not recall whether the President asked her to speak to McGahn or if she did it on her own. Sanders 7/23/18 302, at 2.

[790] Sanders 7/23/18 302, at 1-2.

[791] Meet the Press Interview with Reince Priebus, NBC (Feb. 4, 2018).

[792] Priebus 4/3/18 302, at 10.

[793] Priebus 4/3/18 302, at 10.

[794] Porter 4/13/18 302, at 16-17. Porter did not recall the timing of this discussion with the President. Porter 4/13/18 302, at 17. Evidence indicates it was February 5, 2018. On the back of a pocket card dated February 5, 2018, Porter took notes that are consistent with his description of the discussion: "COS: (1) Letter from DM – Never threatened to quit – DJT never told him to fire M." SC_RRP000053 (Porter Undated Notes). Porter said it was possible he took the notes on a day other than February 5. Porter 4/13/18 302, at 17. But Porter also said that "COS" referred to matters he wanted to discuss with Chief of Staff Kelly, Porter 4/13/18 302, at 17, and Kelly took notes dated February 5, 2018, that state "POTUS – Don McGahn letter – Mueller + resigning." WH000017684 (Kelly 2/5/18 Notes). Kelly said he did not recall what the notes meant, but thought the President may have "mused" about having McGahn write a letter. Kelly 8/2/18 302, at 3. McGahn recalled that Porter spoke with him about the President's request about two weeks after the New York Times story was published, which is consistent with the discussion taking place on or about February 5. McGahn 3/8/18 302, at 4.

[795] Porter 4/13/18 302, at 17.

[796] Porter 4/13/18 302, at 17.

[797] Porter 4/13/18 302, at 17.

[798] Porter 4/13/18 302, at 17; Porter 5/8/18 302, at 18.

[799] Porter 4/13/18 302, at 17; Porter 5/8/18 302, at 18.

U.S. Department of Justice

Attorney Work Product // May Contain Material Protected Under Fed. R. Crim. P. 6(e)

saying something to the effect of, "If he doesn't write a letter, then maybe I'll have to get rid of him."[800]

Later that day, Porter spoke to McGahn to deliver the President's message.[801] Porter told McGahn that he had to write a letter to dispute that he was ever ordered to terminate the Special Counsel.[802] McGahn shrugged off the request, explaining that the media reports were true.[803] McGahn told Porter that the President had been insistent on firing the Special Counsel and that McGahn had planned to resign rather than carry out the order, although he had not personally told the President he intended to quit.[804] Porter told McGahn that the President suggested that McGahn would be fired if he did not write the letter.[805] McGahn dismissed the threat, saying that the optics would be terrible if the President followed through with firing him on that basis.[806] McGahn said he would not write the letter the President had requested.[807] Porter said that to his knowledge the issue of McGahn's letter never came up with the President again, but Porter did recall telling Kelly about his conversation with McGahn.[808]

The next day, on February 6, 2018, Kelly scheduled time for McGahn to meet with him and the President in the Oval Office to discuss the Times article.[809] The morning of the meeting, the President's personal counsel called McGahn's attorney and said that the President was going to be speaking with McGahn and McGahn could not resign no matter what happened in the meeting.[810]

The President began the Oval Office meeting by telling McGahn that the New York Times story did not "look good" and McGahn needed to correct it.[811] McGahn recalled the President said, "I never said to fire Mueller. I never said 'fire.' This story doesn't look good. You need to correct this. You're the White House counsel."[812]

---

[800] Porter 4/13/18 302, at 17.

[801] Porter 4/13/18 302, at 17; McGahn 3/8/18 302, at 4.

[802] Porter 4/13/18 302, at 17; McGahn 3/8/18 302, at 4.

[803] Porter 4/13/18 302, at 17; McGahn 3/8/18 302, at 4.

[804] Porter 4/13/18 302, at 17; McGahn 3/8/18 302, at 4.

[805] Porter 4/13/18 302, at 17; McGahn 3/8/18 302, at 4.

[806] Porter 4/13/18 302, at 17-18; McGahn 3/8/18 302, at 4.

[807] McGahn 3/8/18 302, at 4.

[808] Porter 4/13/18 302, at 18.

[809] McGahn 3/8/18 302, at 4; WH000017685 (Kelly 2/6/18 Notes). McGahn recalled that, before the Oval Office meeting, he told Kelly that he was not inclined to fix the article. McGahn 3/8/18 302, at 4.

[810] McGahn 3/8/18 302, at 5 (agent note); 2/26/19 Email, Counsel for Don McGahn to Special Counsel's Office (confirming February 6, 2018 date of call from the President's personal counsel).

[811] McGahn 3/8/18 302, at 4; Kelly 8/2/18 302, at 2.

[812] McGahn 3/8/18 302, at 4; Kelly 8/2/18 302, at 2.

In response, McGahn acknowledged that he had not told the President directly that he planned to resign, but said that the story was otherwise accurate.[813] The President asked McGahn, "Did I say the word 'fire'?"[814] McGahn responded, "What you said is, 'Call Rod [Rosenstein], tell Rod that Mueller has conflicts and can't be the Special Counsel.'"[815] The President responded, "I never said that."[816] The President said he merely wanted McGahn to raise the conflicts issue with Rosenstein and leave it to him to decide what to do.[817] McGahn told the President he did not understand the conversation that way and instead had heard, "Call Rod. There are conflicts. Mueller has to go."[818] The President asked McGahn whether he would "do a correction," and McGahn said no.[819] McGahn thought the President was testing his mettle to see how committed McGahn was to what happened.[820] Kelly described the meeting as "a little tense."[821]

The President also asked McGahn in the meeting why he had told Special Counsel's Office investigators that the President had told him to have the Special Counsel removed.[822] McGahn responded that he had to and that his conversations with the President were not protected by attorney-client privilege.[823] The President then asked, "What about these notes? Why do you take notes? Lawyers don't take notes. I never had a lawyer who took notes."[824] McGahn responded that he keeps notes because he is a "real lawyer" and explained that notes create a record and are not a bad thing.[825] The President said, "I've had a lot of great lawyers, like Roy Cohn. He did not take notes."[826]

After the Oval Office meeting concluded, Kelly recalled McGahn telling him that McGahn and the President "did have that conversation" about removing the Special Counsel.[827] McGahn recalled that Kelly said that he had pointed out to the President after the Oval Office that McGahn

---

[813] McGahn 3/8/18 302, at 4.

[814] McGahn 3/8/18 302, at 4; Kelly 8/2/18 302, at 2.

[815] McGahn 3/8/18 302, at 5.

[816] McGahn 3/8/18 302, at 5.

[817] McGahn 3/8/18 302, at 5.

[818] McGahn 3/8/18 302, at 5.

[819] McGahn 3/8/18 302, at 5; Kelly 8/2/18 302, at 2.

[820] McGahn 3/8/18 302, at 5.

[821] Kelly 8/2/18 302, at 2.

[822] McGahn 3/8/18 302, at 5.

[823] McGahn 3/8/18 302, at 5.

[824] McGahn 3/8/18 302, at 5. McGahn said the President was referring to Donaldson's notes, which the President thought of as McGahn's notes. McGahn 3/8/18 302, at 5.

[825] McGahn 3/8/18 302, at 5.

[826] McGahn 3/8/18 302, at 5.

[827] Kelly 8/2/18 302, at 2.

had not backed down and would not budge.[828] Following the Oval Office meeting, the President's personal counsel called McGahn's counsel and relayed that the President was "fine" with McGahn.[829]

Analysis

In analyzing the President's efforts to have McGahn deny that he had been ordered to have the Special Counsel removed, the following evidence is relevant to the elements of obstruction of justice:

a.   Obstructive act. The President's repeated efforts to get McGahn to create a record denying that the President had directed him to remove the Special Counsel would qualify as an obstructive act if it had the natural tendency to constrain McGahn from testifying truthfully or to undermine his credibility as a potential witness if he testified consistently with his memory, rather than with what the record said.

There is some evidence that at the time the New York Times and Washington Post stories were published in late January 2018, the President believed the stories were wrong and that he had never told McGahn to have Rosenstein remove the Special Counsel. The President correctly understood that McGahn had not told the President directly that he planned to resign. In addition, the President told Priebus and Porter that he had not sought to terminate the Special Counsel, and in the Oval Office meeting with McGahn, the President said, "I never said to fire Mueller. I never said 'fire.'" That evidence could indicate that the President was not attempting to persuade McGahn to change his story but was instead offering his own—but different—recollection of the substance of his June 2017 conversations with McGahn and McGahn's reaction to them.

Other evidence cuts against that understanding of the President's conduct. As previously described, see Volume II, Section II.E, supra, substantial evidence supports McGahn's account that the President had directed him to have the Special Counsel removed, including the timing and context of the President's directive; the manner in which McGahn reacted; and the fact that the President had been told the conflicts were insubstantial, were being considered by the Department of Justice, and should be raised with the President's personal counsel rather than brought to McGahn. In addition, the President's subsequent denials that he had told McGahn to have the Special Counsel removed were carefully worded. When first asked about the New York Times story, the President said, "Fake news, folks. Fake news. A typical New York Times fake story." And when the President spoke with McGahn in the Oval Office, he focused on whether he had used the word "fire," saying, "I never said to fire Mueller. I never said 'fire'" and "Did I say the word 'fire'?" The President's assertion in the Oval Office meeting that he had never directed McGahn to have the Special Counsel removed thus runs counter to the evidence.

In addition, even if the President sincerely disagreed with McGahn's memory of the June 17, 2017 events, the evidence indicates that the President knew by the time of the Oval Office

---

[828] McGahn 3/8/18 302, at 5. Kelly did not recall discussing the Oval Office meeting with the President after the fact. Kelly 8/2/18 302, at 2. Handwritten notes taken by Kelly state, "Don[:] Mueller discussion in June. - Bannon Priebus - came out okay." WH000017685 (Kelly 2/6/18 Notes).

[829] McGahn 3/8/18 302, at 5 (agent note).

meeting that McGahn's account differed and that McGahn was firm in his views. Shortly after the story broke, the President's counsel told McGahn's counsel that the President wanted McGahn to make a statement denying he had been asked to fire the Special Counsel, but McGahn responded through his counsel that that aspect of the story was accurate and he therefore could not comply with the President's request. The President then directed Sanders to tell McGahn to correct the story, but McGahn told her he would not do so because the story was accurate in reporting on the President's order. Consistent with that position, McGahn never issued a correction. More than a week later, the President brought up the issue again with Porter, made comments indicating the President thought McGahn had leaked the story, and directed Porter to have McGahn create a record denying that the President had tried to fire the Special Counsel. At that point, the President said he might "have to get rid of" McGahn if McGahn did not comply. McGahn again refused and told Porter, as he had told Sanders and as his counsel had told the President's counsel, that the President had in fact ordered him to have Rosenstein remove the Special Counsel. That evidence indicates that by the time of the Oval Office meeting the President was aware that McGahn did not think the story was false and did not want to issue a statement or create a written record denying facts that McGahn believed to be true. The President nevertheless persisted and asked McGahn to repudiate facts that McGahn had repeatedly said were accurate.

b.   Nexus to an official proceeding. By January 2018, the Special Counsel's use of a grand jury had been further confirmed by the return of several indictments. The President also was aware that the Special Counsel was investigating obstruction-related events because, among other reasons, on January 8, 2018, the Special Counsel's Office provided his counsel with a detailed list of topics for a possible interview with the President.[830] The President knew that McGahn had personal knowledge of many of the events the Special Counsel was investigating and that McGahn had already been interviewed by Special Counsel investigators. And in the Oval Office meeting, the President indicated he knew that McGahn had told the Special Counsel's Office about the President's effort to remove the Special Counsel. The President challenged McGahn for disclosing that information and for taking notes that he viewed as creating unnecessary legal exposure. That evidence indicates the President's awareness that the June 17, 2017 events were relevant to the Special Counsel's investigation and any grand jury investigation that might grow out of it.

To establish a nexus, it would be necessary to show that the President's actions would have the natural tendency to affect such a proceeding or that they would hinder, delay, or prevent the communication of information to investigators. Because McGahn had spoken to Special Counsel investigators before January 2018, the President could not have been seeking to influence his prior statements in those interviews. But because McGahn had repeatedly spoken to investigators and the obstruction inquiry was not complete, it was foreseeable that he would be interviewed again on obstruction-related topics. If the President were focused solely on a press strategy in seeking to have McGahn refute the New York Times article, a nexus to a proceeding or to further investigative interviews would not be shown. But the President's efforts to have McGahn write a letter "for our records" approximately ten days after the stories had come out—well past the typical

---

[830] 1/29/18 Letter, President's Personal Counsel to Special Counsel's Office, at 1-2 ("In our conversation of January 8, your office identified the following topics as areas you desired to address with the President in order to complete your investigation on the subjects of alleged collusion and obstruction of justice"; listing 16 topics).

U.S. Department of Justice

~~Attorney Work Product // May Contain Material Protected Under Fed. R. Crim. P. 6(e)~~

time to issue a correction for a news story—indicates the President was not focused solely on a press strategy, but instead likely contemplated the ongoing investigation and any proceedings arising from it.

      c.   Intent. Substantial evidence indicates that in repeatedly urging McGahn to dispute that he was ordered to have the Special Counsel terminated, the President acted for the purpose of influencing McGahn's account in order to deflect or prevent further scrutiny of the President's conduct towards the investigation.

      Several facts support that conclusion. The President made repeated attempts to get McGahn to change his story. As described above, by the time of the last attempt, the evidence suggests that the President had been told on multiple occasions that McGahn believed the President had ordered him to have the Special Counsel terminated. McGahn interpreted his encounter with the President in the Oval Office as an attempt to test his mettle and see how committed he was to his memory of what had occurred. The President had already laid the groundwork for pressing McGahn to alter his account by telling Porter that it might be necessary to fire McGahn if he did not deny the story, and Porter relayed that statement to McGahn. Additional evidence of the President's intent may be gleaned from the fact that his counsel was sufficiently alarmed by the prospect of the President's meeting with McGahn that he called McGahn's counsel and said that McGahn could not resign no matter what happened in the Oval Office that day. The President's counsel was well aware of McGahn's resolve not to issue what he believed to be a false account of events despite the President's request. Finally, as noted above, the President brought up the Special Counsel investigation in his Oval Office meeting with McGahn and criticized him for telling this Office about the June 17, 2017 events. The President's statements reflect his understanding—and his displeasure—that those events would be part of an obstruction-of-justice inquiry.

J.   **The President's Conduct Towards Flynn, Manafort, HOM**

Overview

      In addition to the interactions with McGahn described above, the President has taken other actions directed at possible witnesses in the Special Counsel's investigation, including Flynn, Manafort, HOM and as described in the next section, Cohen. When Flynn withdrew from a joint defense agreement with the President, the President's personal counsel stated that Flynn's actions would be viewed as reflecting "hostility" towards the President. During Manafort's prosecution and while the jury was deliberating, the President repeatedly stated that Manafort was being treated unfairly and made it known that Manafort could receive a pardon. Harm to Ongoing Matter

Evidence

1. Conduct Directed at Michael Flynn

      As previously noted, *see* Volume II, Section II.B, *supra*, the President asked for Flynn's resignation on February 13, 2017. Following Flynn's resignation, the President made positive public comments about Flynn, describing him as a "wonderful man," "a fine person," and a "very good person."[831] The President also privately asked advisors to pass messages to Flynn conveying that the President still cared about him and encouraging him to stay strong.[832]

In late November 2017, Flynn began to cooperate with this Office. On November 22, 2017, Flynn withdrew from a joint defense agreement he had with the President.[833] Flynn's counsel told the President's personal counsel and counsel for the White House that Flynn could no longer have confidential communications with the White House or the President.[834] Later that night, the President's personal counsel left a voicemail for Flynn's counsel that said:

> I understand your situation, but let me see if I can't state it in starker terms. . . . [I]t wouldn't surprise me if you've gone on to make a deal with . . . the government. . . . [I]f . . . there's information that implicates the President, then we've got a national security issue, . . . so, you know, . . . we need some kind of heads up. Um, just for the sake of protecting all our interests if we can. . . . [R]emember what we've always said about the President and his feelings toward Flynn and, that still remains . . . .[835]

On November 23, 2017, Flynn's attorneys returned the call from the President's personal counsel to acknowledge receipt of the voicemail.[836] Flynn's attorneys reiterated that they were no longer in a position to share information under any sort of privilege.[837] According to Flynn's attorneys, the President's personal counsel was indignant and vocal in his disagreement.[838] The President's personal counsel said that he interpreted what they said to him as a reflection of Flynn's

---

[831] *See, e.g.*, *Remarks by President Trump in Press Conference*, White House (Feb. 16, 2018) (stating that "Flynn is a fine person" and "I don't think [Flynn] did anything wrong. If anything, he did something right . . . You know, he was just doing his job"); *Interview of Donald J. Trump*, NBC (May 11, 2017) (stating that Flynn is a "very good person").

[832] *See* Priebus 1/18/17 302, at 9-10 (the President asked Priebus to contact Flynn the week he was terminated to convey that the President still cared about him and felt bad about what happened to him; Priebus thought the President did not want Flynn to have a problem with him); McFarland 12/22/17 302, at 18 (about a month or two after Flynn was terminated, the President asked McFarland to get in touch with Flynn and tell him that he was a good guy, he should stay strong, and the President felt bad for him); Flynn 1/19/18 302, at 9 (recalling the call from Priebus and an additional call from Hicks who said she wanted to relay on behalf of the President that the President hoped Flynn was okay); Christie 2/13/19 302, at 3 (describing a phone conversation between Kushner and Flynn the day after Flynn was fired where Kushner said, "You know the President respects you. The President cares about you. I'll get the President to send out a positive tweet about you later," and the President nodded his assent to Kushner's comment promising a tweet).

[833] Counsel for Flynn 3/1/18 302, at 1.

[834] Counsel for Flynn 3/1/18 302, at 1.

[835] 11/22/17 Voicemail Transcript, President's Personal Counsel to Counsel for Michael Flynn.

[836] Counsel for Flynn 3/1/18 302, at 1.

[837] Counsel for Flynn 3/1/18 302, at 1.

[838] Counsel for Flynn 3/1/18 302, at 1.

121

hostility towards the President and that he planned to inform his client of that interpretation.[839] Flynn's attorneys understood that statement to be an attempt to make them reconsider their position because the President's personal counsel believed that Flynn would be disturbed to know that such a message would be conveyed to the President.[840]

On December 1, 2017, Flynn pleaded guilty to making false statements pursuant to a cooperation agreement.[841] The next day, the President told the press that he was not concerned about what Flynn might tell the Special Counsel.[842] In response to a question about whether the President still stood behind Flynn, the President responded, "We'll see what happens."[843] Over the next several days, the President made public statements expressing sympathy for Flynn and indicating he had not been treated fairly.[844] On December 15, 2017, the President responded to a press inquiry about whether he was considering a pardon for Flynn by saying, "I don't want to talk about pardons for Michael Flynn yet. We'll see what happens. Let's see. I can say this: When you look at what's gone on with the FBI and with the Justice Department, people are very, very angry."[845]

2. Conduct Directed at Paul Manafort

On October 27, 2017, a grand jury in the District of Columbia indicted Manafort and former deputy campaign manager Richard Gates on multiple felony counts, and on February 22, 2018, a grand jury in the Eastern District of Virginia indicted Manafort and Gates on additional felony

---

[839] Counsel for Flynn 3/1/18 302, at 2. Because of attorney-client privilege issues, we did not seek to interview the President's personal counsel about the extent to which he discussed his statements to Flynn's attorneys with the President.

[840] Counsel for Flynn 3/1/18 302, at 2.

[841] Information, *United States v. Michael T. Flynn*, 1:17-cr-232 (D.D.C. Dec. 1, 2017), Doc. 1; Plea Agreement, *United States v. Michael T. Flynn*, 1:17-cr-232 (D.D.C. Dec. 1, 2017), Doc. 3.

[842] *President Trump Remarks on Tax Reform and Michael Flynn's Guilty Plea*, C-SPAN (Dec. 2, 2017).

[843] *President Trump Remarks on Tax Reform and Michael Flynn's Guilty Plea*, C-SPAN (Dec. 2, 2017).

[844] *See* @realDonaldTrump 12/2/17 (9:06 p.m. ET) Tweet ("So General Flynn lies to the FBI and his life is destroyed, while Crooked Hillary Clinton, on that now famous FBI holiday 'interrogation' with no swearing in and no recording, lies many times . . . and nothing happens to her? Rigged system, or just a double standard?"); President Trump Departure Remarks, C-SPAN (Dec. 4, 2017) ("Well, I feel badly for General Flynn. I feel very badly. He's led a very strong life. And I feel very badly.").

[845] *President Trump White House Departure*, C-SPAN (Dec. 15, 2017).

U.S. Department of Justice

~~Attorney Work Product // May Contain Material Protected Under Fed. R. Crim. P. 6(e)~~

counts.[846] The charges in both cases alleged criminal conduct by Manafort that began as early as 2005 and continued through 2018.[847]

In January 2018, Manafort told Gates that he had talked to the President's personal counsel and they were "going to take care of us."[848] Manafort told Gates it was stupid to plead, saying that he had been in touch with the President's personal counsel and repeating that they should "sit tight" and "we'll be taken care of."[849] Gates asked Manafort outright if anyone mentioned pardons and Manafort said no one used that word.[850]

As the proceedings against Manafort progressed in court, the President told Porter that he never liked Manafort and that Manafort did not know what he was doing on the campaign.[851] The President discussed with aides whether and in what way Manafort might be cooperating with the Special Counsel's investigation, and whether Manafort knew any information that would be harmful to the President.[852]

In public, the President made statements criticizing the prosecution and suggesting that Manafort was being treated unfairly. On June 15, 2018, before a scheduled court hearing that day on whether Manafort's bail should be revoked based on new charges that Manafort had tampered with witnesses while out on bail, the President told the press, "I feel badly about a lot of them

---

[846] Indictment, *United States v. Paul J. Manafort, Jr. and Richard W. Gates III*, 1:17-cr-201 (D.D.C. Oct, 27, 2017), Doc. 13 ("*Manafort and Gates D.D.C. Indictment*"); Indictment, *United States v. Paul J. Manafort, Jr. and Richard W. Gates III*, 1:18-cr-83 (E.D. Va. Feb. 22, 2018), Doc. 9 ("*Manafort and Gates E.D. Va. Indictment*")

[847] *Manafort and Gates* D.D.C. Indictment; *Manafort and Gates* E.D. Va. Indictment.

[848] Gates 4/18/18 302, at 4. In February 2018, Gates pleaded guilty, pursuant to a cooperation plea agreement, to a superseding criminal information charging him with conspiring to defraud and commit multiple offenses (*i.e.*, tax fraud, failure to report foreign bank accounts, and acting as an unregistered agent of a foreign principal) against the United States, as well as making false statements to our Office. Superseding Criminal Information, *United States v. Richard W. Gates III*, 1:17-cr-201 (D.D.C. Feb. 23, 2018), Doc. 195; Plea Agreement, *United States v. Richard W. Gates III*, 1:17-cr-201 (D.D.C. Feb. 23, 2018), Doc. 205. Gates has provided information and in-court testimony that the Office has deemed to be reliable.

[849] Gates 4/18/18 302, at 4.

[850] Gates 4/18/18 302, at 4. Manafort told this Office that he never told Gates that he had talked to the President's personal counsel or suggested that they would be taken care of. Manafort also said he hoped for a pardon but never discussed one with the President, although he noticed the President's public comments about pardons. Manafort 10/1/18 302, at 11. As explained in Volume I, Section IV.A.8, *supra*, Manafort entered into a plea agreement with our Office. The U.S. District Court for the District of Columbia determined that he breached the agreement by being untruthful in proffer sessions and before the grand jury. Order, *United States v. Manafort*, 1:17-cr-201 (D.D.C. Feb. 13, 2019), Doc. 503.

[851] Porter 5/8/18 302, at 11. Priebus recalled that the President never really liked Manafort. *See* Priebus 4/3/18 302, at 11. Hicks said that candidate Trump trusted Manafort's judgment while he worked on the Campaign, but she also once heard Trump tell Gates to keep an eye on Manafort. Hicks 3/13/18 302, at 16.

[852] Porter 5/8/18 302, at 11; McGahn 12/14/17 302, at 14.

U.S. Department of Justice

~~Attorney Work Product~~ // ~~May Contain Material Protected Under Fed. R. Crim. P. 6(e)~~

because I think a lot of it is very unfair. I mean, I look at some of them where they go back 12 years. Like Manafort has nothing to do with our campaign. But I feel so—I tell you, I feel a little badly about it. They went back 12 years to get things that he did 12 years ago? ... I feel badly for some people, because they've gone back 12 years to find things about somebody, and I don't think it's right."[853] In response to a question about whether he was considering a pardon for Manafort or other individuals involved in the Special Counsel's investigation, the President said, "I don't want to talk about that. No, I don't want to talk about that. ... But look, I do want to see people treated fairly. That's what it's all about." [854] Hours later, Manafort's bail was revoked and the President tweeted, "Wow, what a tough sentence for Paul Manafort, who has represented Ronald Reagan, Bob Dole and many other top political people and campaigns. Didn't know Manafort was the head of the Mob. What about Comey and Crooked Hillary and all the others? Very unfair!"[855]

Immediately following the revocation of Manafort's bail, the President's personal lawyer, Rudolph Giuliani, gave a series of interviews in which he raised the possibility of a pardon for Manafort. Giuliani told the New York Daily News that "[w]hen the whole thing is over, things might get cleaned up with some presidential pardons."[856] Giuliani also said in an interview that, although the President should not pardon anyone while the Special Counsel's investigation was ongoing, "when the investigation is concluded, he's kind of on his own, right?"[857] In a CNN interview two days later, Giuliani said, "I guess I should clarify this once and for all. ... The president has issued no pardons in this investigation. The president is not going to issue pardons in this investigation. ... When it's over, hey, he's the president of the United States. He retains his pardon power. Nobody is taking that away from him."[858] Giuliani rejected the suggestion that his and the President's comments could signal to defendants that they should not cooperate in a criminal prosecution because a pardon might follow, saying the comments were "certainly not intended that way."[859] Giuliani said the comments only acknowledged that an individual involved in the investigation would not be "excluded from [a pardon], if in fact the president and his advisors ... come to the conclusion that you have been treated unfairly."[860] Giuliani observed that pardons were not unusual in political investigations but said, "That doesn't mean they're going to happen

---

[853] Remarks by President Trump in Press Gaggle, White House (June 15, 2018).

[854] Remarks by President Trump in Press Gaggle, White House (June 15, 2018).

[855] @realDonaldTrump 6/15/18 (1:41 p.m. ET) Tweet.

[856] Chris Sommerfeldt, *Rudy Giuliani says Mueller probe 'might get cleaned up' with 'presidential pardons' in light of Paul Manafort going to jail*, New York Daily News (June 15, 2018).

[857] Sharon LaFraniere, *Judge Orders Paul Manafort Jailed Before Trial, Citing New Obstruction Charges*, New York Times (June 15, 2018) (quoting Giuliani).

[858] *State of the Union with Jake Tapper Transcript*, CNN (June 17, 2018); see Karoun Demirjian, *Giuliani suggests Trump may pardon Manafort after Mueller's probe*, Washington Post (June 17, 2018).

[859] *State of the Union with Jake Tapper Transcript*, CNN (June 17, 2018).

[860] *State of the Union with Jake Tapper Transcript*, CNN (June 17, 2018).

here. Doesn't mean that anybody should rely on it. . . . Big signal is, nobody has been pardoned yet."[861]

On July 31, 2018, Manafort's criminal trial began in the Eastern District of Virginia, generating substantial news coverage.[862] The next day, the President tweeted, "This is a terrible situation and Attorney General Jeff Sessions should stop this Rigged Witch Hunt right now, before it continues to stain our country any further. Bob Mueller is totally conflicted, and his 17 Angry Democrats that are doing his dirty work are a disgrace to USA!"[863] Minutes later, the President tweeted, "Paul Manafort worked for Ronald Reagan, Bob Dole and many other highly prominent and respected political leaders. He worked for me for a very short time. Why didn't government tell me that he was under investigation. These old charges have nothing to do with Collusion—a Hoax!"[864] Later in the day, the President tweeted, "Looking back on history, who was treated worse, Alfonse Capone, legendary mob boss, killer and 'Public Enemy Number One,' or Paul Manafort, political operative & Reagan/Dole darling, now serving solitary confinement—although convicted of nothing? Where is the Russian Collusion?"[865] The President's tweets about the Manafort trial were widely covered by the press.[866] When asked about the President's tweets, Sanders told the press, "Certainly, the President's been clear. He thinks Paul Manafort's been treated unfairly."[867]

On August 16, 2018, the Manafort case was submitted to the jury and deliberations began. At that time, Giuliani had recently suggested to reporters that the Special Counsel investigation needed to be "done in the next two or three weeks,"[868] and media stories reported that a Manafort acquittal would add to criticism that the Special Counsel investigation was not worth the time and expense, whereas a conviction could show that ending the investigation would be premature.[869]

---

[861] *State of the Union with Jake Tapper Transcript*, CNN (June 17, 2018).

[862] *See, e.g.*, Katelyn Polantz, *Takeaways from day one of the Paul Manafort trial*, CNN (July 31, 2018); Frank Bruni, *Paul Manafort's Trial Is Donald Trump's, Too*, New York Times Opinion (July 31, 2018); Rachel Weiner et al., *Paul Manafort trial Day 2: Witnesses describe extravagant clothing purchases, home remodels, lavish cars paid with wire transfers*, Washington Post (Aug. 1, 2018).

[863] @realDonaldTrump 8/1/18 (9:24 a.m. ET) Tweet. Later that day, when Sanders was asked about the President's tweet, she told reporters, "It's not an order. It's the President's opinion." Sarah Sanders, *White House Daily Briefing*, C-SPAN (Aug. 1, 2018).

[864] @realDonaldTrump 8/1/18 (9:34 a.m. ET) Tweet.

[865] @realDonaldTrump 8/1/18 (11:35 a.m. ET) Tweet.

[866] *See, e.g.*, Carol D. Leonnig et al., *Trump calls Manafort prosecution "a hoax," says Sessions should stop Mueller investigation "right now"*, Washington Post (Aug. 1, 2018); Louis Nelson, *Trump claims Manafort case has "nothing to do with collusion"*, Politico (Aug. 1. 2018).

[867] Sarah Sanders, *White House Daily Briefing*, C-SPAN (Aug. 1, 2018).

[868] Chris Strohm & Shannon Pettypiece, *Mueller Probe Doesn't Need to Shut Down Before Midterms, Officials Say*, Bloomberg (Aug. 15, 2018).

[869] *See, e.g.*, Katelyn Polantz et al., *Manafort jury ends first day of deliberations without a verdict*, CNN (Aug. 16, 2018); David Voreacos, *What Mueller's Manafort Case Means for the Trump Battle to*

On August 17, 2018, as jury deliberations continued, the President commented on the trial from the South Lawn of the White House. In an impromptu exchange with reporters that lasted approximately five minutes, the President twice called the Special Counsel's investigation a "rigged witch hunt."[870] When asked whether he would pardon Manafort if he was convicted, the President said, "I don't talk about that now. I don't talk about that."[871] The President then added, without being asked a further question, "I think the whole Manafort trial is very sad when you look at what's going on there. I think it's a very sad day for our country. He worked for me for a very short period of time. But you know what, he happens to be a very good person. And I think it's very sad what they've done to Paul Manafort."[872] The President did not take further questions.[873] In response to the President's statements, Manafort's attorney said, "Mr. Manafort really appreciates the support of President Trump."[874]

On August 21, 2018, the jury found Manafort guilty on eight felony counts. Also on August 21, Michael Cohen pleaded guilty to eight offenses, including a campaign-finance violation that he said had occurred "in coordination with, and at the direction of, a candidate for federal office."[875] The President reacted to Manafort's convictions that day by telling reporters, "Paul Manafort's a good man" and "it's a very sad thing that happened."[876] The President described the Special Counsel's investigation as "a witch hunt that ends in disgrace."[877] The next day, the President tweeted, "I feel very badly for Paul Manafort and his wonderful family. 'Justice' took a 12 year old tax case, among other things, applied tremendous pressure on him and, unlike Michael Cohen, he refused to 'break'—make up stories in order to get a 'deal.' Such respect for a brave man!"[878]

In a Fox News interview on August 22, 2018, the President said: "[Cohen] makes a better deal when he uses me, like everybody else. And one of the reasons I respect Paul Manafort so much is he went through that trial—you know they make up stories. People make up stories. This

Come, Bloomberg (Aug. 2, 2018); Gabby Morrongiello, *What a guilty verdict for Manafort would mean for Trump and Mueller*, Washington Examiner (Aug. 18, 2018).

[870] President Trump Remarks on John Brennan and Mueller Probe, C-SPAN (Aug. 17, 2018).

[871] President Trump Remarks on John Brennan and Mueller Probe, C-SPAN (Aug. 17, 2018).

[872] President Trump Remarks on John Brennan and Mueller Probe, C-SPAN (Aug. 17, 2018).

[873] President Trump Remarks on John Brennan and Mueller Probe, C-SPAN (Aug. 17, 2018).

[874] *Trump calls Manafort "very good person,"* All In with Chris Hayes (Aug. 17, 2018) (transcript); *Manafort lawyer: We appreciate Trump's support*, CNN (Aug. 17, 2018) (https://www.cnn.com/videos/politics/2018/08/17/paul-manafort-attorney-trump-jury-deliberations-schneider-lead-vpx.cnn).

[875] Transcript at 23, *United States v. Michael Cohen*, 1:18-cr-602 (S.D.N.Y. Aug. 21, 2018), Doc. 7 (*Cohen* 8/21/18 Transcript).

[876] *President Trump Remarks on Manafort Trial*, C-SPAN (Aug. 21, 2018).

[877] *President Trump Remarks on Manafort Trial*, C-SPAN (Aug. 21, 2018).

[878] @realDonaldTrump 8/22/18 (9:21 a.m. ET) Tweet.

whole thing about flipping, they call it, I know all about flipping."[879] The President said that flipping was "not fair" and "almost ought to be outlawed."[880] In response to a question about whether he was considering a pardon for Manafort, the President said, "I have great respect for what he's done, in terms of what he's gone through. . . . He worked for many, many people many, many years, and I would say what he did, some of the charges they threw against him, every consultant, every lobbyist in Washington probably does."[881] Giuliani told journalists that the President "really thinks Manafort has been horribly treated" and that he and the President had discussed the political fallout if the President pardoned Manafort.[882] The next day, Giuliani told the Washington Post that the President had asked his lawyers for advice on the possibility of a pardon for Manafort and other aides, and had been counseled against considering a pardon until the investigation concluded.[883]

On September 14, 2018, Manafort pleaded guilty to charges in the District of Columbia and signed a plea agreement that required him to cooperate with investigators.[884] Giuliani was reported to have publicly said that Manafort remained in a joint defense agreement with the President following Manafort's guilty plea and agreement to cooperate, and that Manafort's attorneys regularly briefed the President's lawyers on the topics discussed and the information Manafort had provided in interviews with the Special Counsel's Office.[885] On November 26, 2018, the Special Counsel's Office disclosed in a public court filing that Manafort had breached his plea agreement by lying about multiple subjects.[886] The next day, Giuliani said that the President had been "upset for weeks" about what he considered to be "the un-American, horrible treatment of

---

[879] *Fox & Friends Exclusive Interview with President Trump*, Fox News (Aug. 23, 2018) (recorded the previous day).

[880] *Fox & Friends Exclusive Interview with President Trump*, Fox News (Aug. 23, 2018) (recorded the previous day).

[881] *Fox & Friends Exclusive Interview with President Trump*, Fox News (Aug. 23, 2018) (recorded the previous day).

[882] Maggie Haberman & Katie Rogers, *"How Did We End Up Here?" Trump Wonders as the White House Soldiers On*, New York Times (Aug. 22, 2018).

[883] Carol D. Leonnig & Josh Dawsey, *Trump recently sought his lawyers' advice on possibility of pardoning Manafort, Giuliani says*, Washington Post (Aug. 23, 2018).

[884] Plea Agreement, *United States v. Paul J. Manafort, Jr.*, 1:17-cr-201 (D.D.C. Sept. 14, 2018), Doc. 422.

[885] Karen Freifeld & Nathan Layne, *Trump lawyer: Manafort said nothing damaging in Mueller interviews*, Reuters (Oct. 22, 2018); Michael S. Schmidt et al., *Manafort's Lawyer Said to Brief Trump Attorneys on What He Told Mueller*, New York Times (Nov. 27, 2018); Dana Bash, *Manafort team briefed Giuliani on Mueller meetings*, CNN, Posted 11/28/18, *available at* https://www.cnn.com/videos/politics/2018/11/28/manafort-lawyers-keeping-trump-lawyers-giuliani-updated-mueller-probe-bash-sot-nr-vpx.cnn; *see* Sean Hannity, *Interview with Rudy Giuliani*, Fox News (Sept. 14, 2018) (Giuliani: "[T]here was a quote put out by a source close to Manafort that the plea agreement has, and cooperation agreement has, nothing to do with the Trump campaign. . . . Now, I know that because I've been privy to a lot of facts I can't repeat.").

[886] Joint Status Report, *United States v. Paul J. Manafort, Jr.*, (D.D.C Nov. 26, 2018), Doc. 455.

U.S. Department of Justice

Attorney Work Product // May Contain Material Protected Under Fed. R. Crim. P. 6(e)

Manafort."[887] In an interview on November 28, 2018, the President suggested that it was "very brave" that Manafort did not "flip":

> If you told the truth, you go to jail. You know this flipping stuff is terrible. You flip and you lie and you get—the prosecutors will tell you 99 percent of the time they can get people to flip. It's rare that they can't. But I had three people: Manafort, Corsi—I don't know Corsi, but he refuses to say what they demanded.[888] Manafort, Corsi HOM . It's actually very brave.[889]

In response to a question about a potential pardon for Manafort, the President said, "It was never discussed, but I wouldn't take it off the table. Why would I take it off the table?"[890]

3. Harm to Ongoing Matter

Harm to Ongoing Matter

[891] Harm to Ongoing Matter
[892] Harm to Ongoing Matter

93

Harm to Ongoing Matter

[894] Harm to Ongoing Matter

---

[887] Stephen Collinson, *Trump appears consumed by Mueller investigation as details emerge*, CNN (Nov. 29, 2018).

[888] "Corsi" is a reference to Jerome Corsi, HOM who was involved in efforts to coordinate with WikiLeaks and Assange, and who stated publicly at that time that he had refused a plea offer from the Special Counsel's Office because he was "not going to sign a lie." Sara Murray & Eli Watkins, HOM *says he won't agree to plea deal*, CNN (Nov. 26, 2018).

[889] Marisa Schultz & Nikki Schwab, *Oval Office Interview with President Trump: Trump says pardon for Paul Manafort still a possibility,* New York Post (Nov. 28, 2018). That same day, the President tweeted: "While the disgusting Fake News is doing everything within their power not to report it that way, at least 3 major players are intimating that the Angry Mueller Gang of Dems is viciously telling witnesses to lie about facts & they will get relief. This is our Joseph McCarthy Era!" @realDonaldTrump 11/28/18 (8:39 a.m. ET) Tweet.

[890] Marisa Schultz & Nikki Schwab, *New York Post Oval Office Interview with President Trump: Trump says pardon for Paul Manafort still a possibility*, New York Post (Nov. 28, 2018).

[891] Harm to Ongoing Matter

[892] Harm to Ongoing Matter

[893] Harm to Ongoing Matter

[894] Harm to Ongoing Matter

128

Harm to Ongoing Matter

[95] Harm to Ongoing Matter

[96]

Harm to Ongoing Matter

Harm to Ongoing Matter

Harm to Ongoing Matter

[897]

[98] Harm to Ongoing Matter

[899]

Harm to Ongoing Matter

Harm to Ongoing Matter

[895] Harm to Ongoing Matter

[896] Harm to Ongoing Matter

[897] Harm to Ongoing Matter

[898] Harm to Ongoing Matter

[899] Harm to Ongoing Matter

129

Harm to Ongoing Matter

Harm to Ongoing Matter

Harm to Ongoing Matter

Harm to Ongoing Matter

Harm to Ongoing Matter

Harm to Ongoing Matter

Harm to Ongoing Matter

Harm to Ongoing Matter
Harm to Ongoing Matter

---

900 Harm to Ongoing Matter
901 Harm to Ongoing Matter

902 Harm to Ongoing Matter

903 Harm to Ongoing Matter

904 Harm to Ongoing Matter

905 Harm to Ongoing Matter

906 Harm to Ongoing Matter

907 Harm to Ongoing Matter
908 Harm to Ongoing Matter

394

Analysis

In analyzing the President's conduct towards Flynn, Manafort, HOM, the following evidence is relevant to the elements of obstruction of justice:

a.   Obstructive act. The President's actions towards witnesses in the Special Counsel's investigation would qualify as obstructive if they had the natural tendency to prevent particular witnesses from testifying truthfully, or otherwise would have the probable effect of influencing, delaying, or preventing their testimony to law enforcement.

With regard to Flynn, the President sent private and public messages to Flynn encouraging him to stay strong and conveying that the President still cared about him before he began to cooperate with the government. When Flynn's attorneys withdrew him from a joint defense agreement with the President, signaling that Flynn was potentially cooperating with the government, the President's personal counsel initially reminded Flynn's counsel of the President's warm feelings towards Flynn and said "that still remains." But when Flynn's counsel reiterated that Flynn could no longer share information under a joint defense agreement, the President's personal counsel stated that the decision would be interpreted as reflecting Flynn's hostility towards the President. That sequence of events could have had the potential to affect Flynn's decision to cooperate, as well as the extent of that cooperation. Because of privilege issues, however, we could not determine whether the President was personally involved in or knew about the specific message his counsel delivered to Flynn's counsel.

With respect to Manafort, there is evidence that the President's actions had the potential to influence Manafort's decision whether to cooperate with the government. The President and his personal counsel made repeated statements suggesting that a pardon was a possibility for Manafort, while also making it clear that the President did not want Manafort to "flip" and cooperate with the government. On June 15, 2018, the day the judge presiding over Manafort's D.C. case was considering whether to revoke his bail, the President said that he "felt badly" for Manafort and stated, "I think a lot of it is very unfair." And when asked about a pardon for Manafort, the President said, "I do want to see people treated fairly. That's what it's all about." Later that day, after Manafort's bail was revoked, the President called it a "tough sentence" that was "Very unfair!" Two days later, the President's personal counsel stated that individuals involved in the Special Counsel's investigation could receive a pardon "if in fact the [P]resident and his advisors . . . come to the conclusion that you have been treated unfairly"—using language that paralleled how the President had already described the treatment of Manafort. Those statements, combined with the President's commendation of Manafort for being a "brave man" who "refused to 'break',," suggested that a pardon was a more likely possibility if Manafort continued not to cooperate with the government. And while Manafort eventually pleaded guilty pursuant to a cooperation agreement, he was found to have violated the agreement by lying to investigators.

The President's public statements during the Manafort trial, including during jury deliberations, also had the potential to influence the trial jury. On the second day of trial, for example, the President called the prosecution a "terrible situation" and a "hoax" that "continues to stain our country" and referred to Manafort as a "Reagan/Dole darling" who was "serving solitary confinement" even though he was "convicted of nothing." Those statements were widely picked up by the press. While jurors were instructed not to watch or read news stories about the case and

131

395

U.S. Department of Justice

~~Attorney Work Product // May Contain Material Protected Under Fed. R. Crim. P. 6(e)~~

are presumed to follow those instructions, the President's statements during the trial generated substantial media coverage that could have reached jurors if they happened to see the statements or learned about them from others. And the President's statements during jury deliberations that Manafort "happens to be a very good person" and that "it's very sad what they've done to Paul Manafort" had the potential to influence jurors who learned of the statements, which the President made just as jurors were considering whether to convict or acquit Manafort.

Harm to Ongoing Matter

b.   <u>Nexus to an official proceeding</u>. The President's actions towards Flynn, Manafort, HOM appear to have been connected to pending or anticipated official proceedings involving each individual. The President's conduct towards Flynn HOM principally occurred when both were under criminal investigation by the Special Counsel's Office and press reports speculated about whether they would cooperate with the Special Counsel's investigation. And the President's conduct towards Manafort was directly connected to the official proceedings involving him. The President made statements about Manafort and the charges against him during Manafort's criminal trial. And the President's comments about the prospect of Manafort "flipping" occurred when it was clear the Special Counsel continued to oversee grand jury proceedings.

c.   <u>Intent</u>. Evidence concerning the President's intent related to Flynn as a potential witness is inconclusive. As previously noted, because of privilege issues we do not have evidence establishing whether the President knew about or was involved in his counsel's communications with Flynn's counsel stating that Flynn's decision to withdraw from the joint defense agreement and cooperate with the government would be viewed as reflecting "hostility" towards the President. And regardless of what the President's personal counsel communicated, the President continued to express sympathy for Flynn after he pleaded guilty pursuant to a cooperation agreement, stating that Flynn had "led a very strong life" and the President "fe[lt] very badly" about what had happened to him.

Evidence concerning the President's conduct towards Manafort indicates that the President intended to encourage Manafort to not cooperate with the government. Before Manafort was convicted, the President repeatedly stated that Manafort had been treated unfairly. One day after Manafort was convicted on eight felony charges and potentially faced a lengthy prison term, the President said that Manafort was "a brave man" for refusing to "break" and that "flipping" "almost ought to be outlawed." At the same time, although the President had privately told aides he did not like Manafort, he publicly called Manafort "a good man" and said he had a "wonderful family." And when the President was asked whether he was considering a pardon for Manafort, the President did not respond directly and instead said he had "great respect for what [Manafort]'s done, in terms of what he's gone through." The President added that "some of the charges they threw against him, every consultant, every lobbyist in Washington probably does." In light of the President's counsel's previous statements that the investigations "might get cleaned up with some presidential pardons" and that a pardon would be possible if the President "come[s] to the conclusion that you have been treated unfairly," the evidence supports the inference that the

President intended Manafort to believe that he could receive a pardon, which would make cooperation with the government as a means of obtaining a lesser sentence unnecessary.

We also examined the evidence of the President's intent in making public statements about Manafort at the beginning of his trial and when the jury was deliberating. Some evidence supports a conclusion that the President intended, at least in part, to influence the jury. The trial generated widespread publicity, and as the jury began to deliberate, commentators suggested that an acquittal would add to pressure to end the Special Counsel's investigation. By publicly stating on the second day of deliberations that Manafort "happens to be a very good person" and that "it's very sad what they've done to Paul Manafort" right after calling the Special Counsel's investigation a "rigged witch hunt," the President's statements could, if they reached jurors, have the natural tendency to engender sympathy for Manafort among jurors, and a factfinder could infer that the President intended that result. But there are alternative explanations for the President's comments, including that he genuinely felt sorry for Manafort or that his goal was not to influence the jury but to influence public opinion. The President's comments also could have been intended to continue sending a message to Manafort that a pardon was possible. As described above, the President made his comments about Manafort being "a very good person" immediately after declining to answer a question about whether he would pardon Manafort.

Harm to Ongoing Matter

133

U.S. Department of Justice

~~Attorney Work Product // May Contain Material Protected Under Fed. R. Crim. P. 6(e)~~

K.   The President's Conduct Involving Michael Cohen

Overview

The President's conduct involving Michael Cohen spans the full period of our investigation. During the campaign, Cohen pursued the Trump Tower Moscow project on behalf of the Trump Organization. Cohen briefed candidate Trump on the project numerous times, including discussing whether Trump should travel to Russia to advance the deal. After the media began questioning Trump's connections to Russia, Cohen promoted a "party line" that publicly distanced Trump from Russia and asserted he had no business there. Cohen continued to adhere to that party line in 2017, when Congress asked him to provide documents and testimony in its Russia investigation. In an attempt to minimize the President's connections to Russia, Cohen submitted a letter to Congress falsely stating that he only briefed Trump on the Trump Tower Moscow project three times, that he did not consider asking Trump to travel to Russia, that Cohen had not received a response to an outreach he made to the Russian government, and that the project ended in January 2016, before the first Republican caucus or primary. While working on the congressional statement, Cohen had extensive discussions with the President's personal counsel, who, according to Cohen, said that Cohen should not contradict the President and should keep the statement short and "tight." After the FBI searched Cohen's home and office in April 2018, the President publicly asserted that Cohen would not "flip" and privately passed messages of support to him. Cohen also discussed pardons with the President's personal counsel and believed that if he stayed on message, he would get a pardon or the President would do "something else" to make the investigation end. But after Cohen began cooperating with the government in July 2018, the President publicly criticized him, called him a "rat," and suggested his family members had committed crimes.

Evidence

1. Candidate Trump's Awareness of and Involvement in the Trump Tower Moscow Project

The President's interactions with Cohen as a witness took place against the background of the President's involvement in the Trump Tower Moscow project.

As described in detail in Volume I, Section IV.A.1, *supra*, from September 2015 until at least June 2016, the Trump Organization pursued a Trump Tower Moscow project in Russia, with negotiations conducted by Cohen, then-executive vice president of the Trump Organization and special counsel to Donald J. Trump.[909] The Trump Organization had previously and

---

[909] In August 2018 and November 2018, Cohen pleaded guilty to multiple crimes of deception, including making false statements to Congress about the Trump Tower Moscow project, as described later in this section. When Cohen first met with investigators from this Office, he repeated the same lies he told Congress about the Trump Tower Moscow project. Cohen 8/7/18 302, at 12-17. But after Cohen pleaded guilty to offenses in the Southern District of New York on August 21, 2018, he met with investigators again and corrected the record. The Office found Cohen's testimony in these subsequent proffer sessions to be consistent with and corroborated by other information obtained in the course of the Office's investigation. The Office's sentencing submission in Cohen's criminal case stated: "Starting with his second meeting with the [Special Counsel's Office] in September 2018, the defendant has accepted responsibility not only for

U.S. Department of Justice

~~Attorney Work Product // May Contain Material Protected Under Fed. R. Crim. P. 6(e)~~

unsuccessfully pursued a building project in Moscow.[910] According to Cohen, in approximately September 2015 he obtained internal approval from Trump to negotiate on behalf of the Trump Organization to have a Russian corporation build a tower in Moscow that licensed the Trump name and brand.[911] Cohen thereafter had numerous brief conversations with Trump about the project.[912] Cohen recalled that Trump wanted to be updated on any developments with Trump Tower Moscow and on several occasions brought the project up with Cohen to ask what was happening on it.[913] Cohen also discussed the project on multiple occasions with Donald Trump Jr. and Ivanka Trump.[914]

In the fall of 2015, Trump signed a Letter of Intent for the project that specified highly lucrative terms for the Trump Organization.[915] In December 2015, Felix Sater, who was handling negotiations between Cohen and the Russian corporation, asked Cohen for a copy of his and Trump's passports to facilitate travel to Russia to meet with government officials and possible financing partners.[916] Cohen recalled discussing the trip with Trump and requesting a copy of Trump's passport from Trump's personal secretary, Rhona Graff.[917]

By January 2016, Cohen had become frustrated that Sater had not set up a meeting with Russian government officials, so Cohen reached out directly by email to the office of Dmitry

---

his false statements concerning the [Trump Tower] Moscow Project, but also his broader efforts through public statements and testimony before Congress to minimize his role in, and what he knew about, contacts between the [Trump Organization] and Russian interests during the course of the campaign. . . . The information provided by Cohen about the [Trump Tower] Moscow Project in these proffer sessions is consistent with and corroborated by other information obtained in the course of the [Special Counsel's Office's] investigation. . . . The defendant, without prompting by the [Special Counsel's Office], also corrected other false and misleading statements that he had made concerning his outreach to and contacts with Russian officials during the course of the campaign." Gov't Sentencing Submission at 4, *United States v. Michael Cohen*, 1:18-cr-850 (S.D.N.Y. Dec. 7, 2018), Doc. 14. At Cohen's sentencing, our Office further explained that Cohen had "provided valuable information . . . while taking care and being careful to note what he knows and what he doesn't know." Transcript at 19, *United States v. Michael Cohen*, 1:18-cr-850 (S.D.N.Y. Dec. 12, 2018), Doc. 17 (*Cohen 12/12/18 Transcript*).

[910] *See* Volume I, Section IV.A.1, *supra* (noting that starting in at least 2013, several employees of the Trump Organization, including then-president of the organization Donald J. Trump, pursued a Trump Tower Moscow deal with several Russian counterparties).

[911] Cohen 9/12/18 302, at 1-4; Cohen 8/7/18 302, at 15.

[912] Cohen 9/12/18 302, at 2, 4.

[913] Cohen 9/12/18 302, at 4.

[914] Cohen 9/12/18 302, at 4, 10.

[915] MDC-H-000618-25 (10/28/15 Letter of Intent, signed by Donald J. Trump, Trump Acquisition, LLC and Andrey Rozov, I.C. Expert Investment Company); Cohen 9/12/18 302, at 3; Written Responses of Donald J. Trump (Nov. 20, 2018), at 15 (Response to Question III, Parts (a) through (g)).

[916] MDC-H-000600 (12/19/15 Email, Sater to Cohen).

[917] Cohen 9/12/18 302, at 5.

Peskov, who was Putin's deputy chief of staff and press secretary.[918] On January 20, 2016, Cohen received an email response from Elena Poliakova, Peskov's personal assistant, and phone records confirm that they then spoke for approximately twenty minutes, during which Cohen described the Trump Tower Moscow project and requested assistance in moving the project forward.[919] Cohen recalled briefing candidate Trump about the call soon afterwards.[920] Cohen told Trump he spoke with a woman he identified as "someone from the Kremlin," and Cohen reported that she was very professional and asked detailed questions about the project.[921] Cohen recalled telling Trump he wished the Trump Organization had assistants who were as competent as the woman from the Kremlin.[922]

Cohen thought his phone call renewed interest in the project.[923] The day after Cohen's call with Poliakova, Sater texted Cohen, asking him to "[c]all me when you have a few minutes to chat . . . It's about Putin they called today."[924] Sater told Cohen that the Russian government liked the project and on January 25, 2016, sent an invitation for Cohen to visit Moscow "for a working visit."[925] After the outreach from Sater, Cohen recalled telling Trump that he was waiting to hear back on moving the project forward.[926]

After January 2016, Cohen continued to have conversations with Sater about Trump Tower Moscow and continued to keep candidate Trump updated about those discussions and the status of the project.[927] Cohen recalled that he and Trump wanted Trump Tower Moscow to succeed and that Trump never discouraged him from working on the project because of the campaign.[928] In March or April 2016, Trump asked Cohen if anything was happening in Russia.[929] Cohen also

---

[918] *See* FS00004 (12/30/15 Text Message, Cohen to Sater); TRUMPORG_MC_000233 (1/11/16 Email, Cohen to pr_peskova@prpress.gof.ru); MDC-H-000690 (1/14/16 Email, Cohen to info@prpress.gov.ru); TRUMPORG_MC_000235 (1/16/16 Email, Cohen to pr_peskova@prpress.gov.ru).

[919] 1/20/16 Email, Poliakova to Cohen; Call Records of Michael Cohen. (Showing a 22-minute call on January 20, 2016, between Cohen and the number Poliakova provided in her email); Cohen 9/12/18 302, at 2-3. After the call, Cohen saved Poliakova's contact information in his Trump Organization Outlook contact list. 1/20/16 Cohen Microsoft Outlook Entry (6:22 a.m.).

[920] Cohen 11/20/18 302, at 5.

[921] Cohen 11/20/18 302, at 5-6; Cohen 11/12/18 302, at 4.

[922] Cohen 11/20/18 302, at 5.

[923] Cohen 9/12/18 302, at 5.

[924] FS00011 (1/21/16 Text Messages, Sater & Cohen).

[925] Cohen 9/12/18 302, at 5; 1/25/16 Email, Sater to Cohen (attachment).

[926] Cohen 11/20/18 302, at 5.

[927] Cohen 9/12/18 302, at 6. In later congressional testimony, Cohen stated that he briefed Trump on the project approximately six times after January 2016. *Hearing on Issues Related to Trump Organization Before the House Oversight and Reform Committee*, 116th Cong. (Feb. 27, 2019) (CQ Cong. Transcripts, at 24) (testimony of Michael Cohen).

[928] Cohen 9/12/18 302, at 6.

[929] Cohen 9/18/18 302, at 4.

recalled briefing Donald Trump Jr. in the spring—a conversation that Cohen said was not "idle chit chat" because Trump Tower Moscow was potentially a $1 billion deal.[930]

Cohen recalled that around May 2016, he again raised with candidate Trump the possibility of a trip to Russia to advance the Trump Tower Moscow project.[931] At that time, Cohen had received several texts from Sater seeking to arrange dates for such a trip.[932] On May 4, 2016, Sater wrote to Cohen, "I had a chat with Moscow. ASSUMING the trip does happen the question is before or after the convention. . . . . Obviously the premeeting trip (you only) can happen anytime you want but the 2 big guys [is] the question. I said I would confirm and revert."[933] Cohen responded, "My trip before Cleveland. Trump once he becomes the nominee after the convention."[934] On May 5, 2016, Sater followed up with a text that Cohen thought he probably read to Trump:

> Peskov would like to invite you as his guest to the St. Petersburg Forum which is Russia's Davos it's June 16-19. He wants to meet there with you and possibly introduce you to either Putin or Medvedev. . . . This is perfect. The entire business class of Russia will be there as well. He said anything you want to discuss including dates and subjects are on the table to discuss.[935]

Cohen recalled discussing the invitation to the St. Petersburg Economic Forum with candidate Trump and saying that Putin or Russian Prime Minister Dmitry Medvedev might be there.[936] Cohen remembered that Trump said that he would be willing to travel to Russia if Cohen could "lock and load" on the deal.[937] In June 2016, Cohen decided not to attend the St. Petersburg Economic Forum because Sater had not obtained a formal invitation for Cohen from Peskov.[938] Cohen said he had a quick conversation with Trump at that time but did not tell him that the project was over because he did not want Trump to complain that the deal was on-again-off-again if it were revived.[939]

During the summer of 2016, Cohen recalled that candidate Trump publicly claimed that he had nothing to do with Russia and then shortly afterwards privately checked with Cohen about the status of the Trump Tower Moscow project, which Cohen found "interesting."[940] At some point

---

[930] Cohen 9/12/18 302, at 10.

[931] Cohen 9/12/18 302, at 7.

[932] Cohen 9/12/18 302, at 7.

[933] FS00015 (5/4/16 Text Message, Sater to Cohen).

[934] FS00015 (5/4/16 Text Message, Cohen to Sater).

[935] FS00016-17 (5/5/16 Text Messages, Sater & Cohen).

[936] Cohen 9/12/18 302, at 7.

[937] Cohen 9/12/18 302, at 7.

[938] Cohen 9/12/18 302, at 7-8.

[939] Cohen 9/12/18 302, at 8.

[940] Cohen 3/19/19 302, at 2.

U.S. Department of Justice

~~Attorney Work Product // May Contain Material Protected Under Fed. R. Crim. P. 6(e)~~

that summer, Cohen recalled having a brief conversation with Trump in which Cohen said the Trump Tower Moscow project was going nowhere because the Russian development company had not secured a piece of property for the project.[941] Trump said that was "too bad," and Cohen did not recall talking with Trump about the project after that.[942] Cohen said that at no time during the campaign did Trump tell him not to pursue the project or that the project should be abandoned.[943]

2. Cohen Determines to Adhere to a "Party Line" Distancing Candidate Trump From Russia

As previously discussed, *see* Volume II, Section II.A, *supra*, when questions about possible Russian support for candidate Trump emerged during the 2016 presidential campaign, Trump denied having any personal, financial, or business connection to Russia, which Cohen described as the "party line" or "message" to follow for Trump and his senior advisors.[944]

After the election, the Trump Organization sought to formally close out certain deals in advance of the inauguration.[945] Cohen recalled that Trump Tower Moscow was on the list of deals to be closed out.[946] In approximately January 2017, Cohen began receiving inquiries from the media about Trump Tower Moscow, and he recalled speaking to the President-Elect when those inquiries came in.[947] Cohen was concerned that truthful answers about the Trump Tower Moscow project might not be consistent with the "message" that the President-Elect had no relationship with Russia.[948]

In an effort to "stay on message," Cohen told a New York Times reporter that the Trump Tower Moscow deal was not feasible and had ended in January 2016.[949] Cohen recalled that this was part of a "script" or talking points he had developed with President-Elect Trump and others to

---

[941] Cohen 3/19/19 302, at 2. Cohen could not recall the precise timing of this conversation, but said he thought it occurred in June or July 2016. Cohen recalled that the conversation happened at some point after candidate Trump was publicly stating that he had nothing to do with Russia. Cohen 3/19/19 302, at 2.

[942] Cohen 3/19/19 302, at 2.

[943] Cohen 3/19/19 302, at 2.

[944] Cohen 11/20/18 302, at 1; Cohen 9/18/18 302, at 3, 5; Cohen 9/12/18 302, at 9.

[945] Cohen 9/18/18 302, at 1-2; *see also* Rtskhiladze 4/4/18 302, at 8-9.

[946] Cohen 9/18/18 302, at 1-2.

[947] Cohen 9/18/18 302, at 3.

[948] Cohen 11/20/18 302, at 4.

[949] Cohen 9/18/18 302, at 5. The article was published on February 19, 2017, and reported that Sater and Cohen had been working on plan for a Trump Tower Moscow "as recently as the fall of 2015" but had come to a halt because of the presidential campaign. Consistent with Cohen's intended party line message, the article stated, "Cohen said the Trump Organization had received a letter of intent for a project in Moscow from a Russian real estate developer at that time but determined that the project was not feasible." Megan Twohey & Scott Shane, *A Back-Channel Plan for Ukraine and Russia, Courtesy of Trump Associates*, New York Times (Feb. 19, 2017).

402

U.S. Department of Justice

~~Attorney Work Product~~ // ~~May Contain Material Protected Under Fed. R. Crim. P. 6(e)~~

dismiss the idea of a substantial connection between Trump and Russia.[950] Cohen said that he discussed the talking points with Trump but that he did not explicitly tell Trump he thought they were untrue because Trump already knew they were untrue.[951] Cohen thought it was important to say the deal was done in January 2016, rather than acknowledge that talks continued in May and June 2016, because it limited the period when candidate Trump could be alleged to have a relationship with Russia to an early point in the campaign, before Trump had become the party's presumptive nominee.[952]

3. Cohen Submits False Statements to Congress Minimizing the Trump Tower Moscow Project in Accordance with the Party Line

In early May 2017, Cohen received requests from Congress to provide testimony and documents in connection with congressional investigations of Russian interference in the 2016 election.[953] At that time, Cohen understood Congress's interest in him to be focused on the allegations in the Steele reporting concerning a meeting Cohen allegedly had with Russian officials in Prague during the campaign.[954] Cohen had never traveled to Prague and was not concerned about those allegations, which he believed were provably false.[955] On May 18, 2017, Cohen met with the President to discuss the request from Congress, and the President instructed Cohen that he should cooperate because there was nothing there.[956]

Cohen eventually entered into a joint defense agreement (JDA) with the President and other individuals who were part of the Russia investigation.[957] In the months leading up to his congressional testimony, Cohen frequently spoke with the President's personal counsel.[958] Cohen

---

[950] Cohen 9/18/18 302, at 5-6.

[951] Cohen 9/18/18 302, at 6.

[952] Cohen 9/12/18 302, at 10.

[953] P-SCO-000000328 (5/9/17 Letter, HPSCI to Cohen); P-SCO-000000331 (5/12/17 Letter, SSCI to Cohen).

[954] Cohen 11/20/18 302, at 2-3.

[955] Cohen 11/20/18 302, at 2-3.

[956] Cohen 11/12/18 302, at 2; Cohen 11/20/19 302, at 3.

[957] Cohen 11/12/18 302, at 2.

[958] Cohen 11/12/18 302, at 2-3; Cohen 11/20/18, at 2-6. Cohen told investigators about his conversations with the President's personal counsel after waiving any privilege of his own and after this Office advised his counsel not to provide any communications that would be covered by any other privilege, including communications protected by a joint defense or common interest privilege. As a result, most of what Cohen told us about his conversations with the President's personal counsel concerned what Cohen had communicated to the President's personal counsel, and not what was said in response. Cohen described certain statements made by the President's personal counsel, however, that are set forth in this section. Cohen and his counsel were better positioned than this Office to evaluate whether any privilege protected those statements because they had knowledge of the scope of their joint defense agreement and access to privileged communications that may have provided context for evaluating the statements they shared. After interviewing Cohen about these matters, we asked the President's personal counsel if he wished to provide information to us about his conversations with Cohen related to Cohen's congressional testimony about

said that in those conversations the President's personal counsel would sometimes say that he had just been with the President.[959] Cohen recalled that the President's personal counsel told him the JDA was working well together and assured him that there was nothing there and if they stayed on message the investigations would come to an end soon.[960] At that time, Cohen's legal bills were being paid by the Trump Organization,[961] and Cohen was told not to worry because the investigations would be over by summer or fall of 2017.[962] Cohen said that the President's personal counsel also conveyed that, as part of the JDA, Cohen was protected, which he would not be if he "went rogue."[963] Cohen recalled that the President's personal counsel reminded him that "the President loves you" and told him that if he stayed on message, the President had his back.[964]

In August 2017, Cohen began drafting a statement about Trump Tower Moscow to submit to Congress along with his document production.[965] The final version of the statement contained several false statements about the project.[966] First, although the Trump Organization continued to pursue the project until at least June 2016, the statement said, "The proposal was under consideration at the Trump Organization from September 2015 until the end of January 2016. By the end of January 2016, I determined that the proposal was not feasible for a variety of business reasons and should not be pursued further. Based on my business determinations, the Trump Organization abandoned the proposal."[967] Second, although Cohen and candidate Trump had discussed possible travel to Russia by Trump to pursue the venture, the statement said, "Despite overtures by Mr. Sater, I never considered asking Mr. Trump to travel to Russia in connection with this proposal. I told Mr. Sater that Mr. Trump would not travel to Russia unless there was a definitive agreement in place."[968] Third, although Cohen had regularly briefed Trump on the status

---

Trump Tower Moscow. The President's personal counsel declined and, through his own counsel, indicated that he could not disaggregate information he had obtained from Cohen from information he had obtained from other parties in the JDA. In view of the admonition this Office gave to Cohen's counsel to withhold communications that could be covered by privilege, the President's personal counsel's uncertainty about the provenance of his own knowledge, the burden on a privilege holder to establish the elements to support a claim of privilege, and the substance of the statements themselves, we have included relevant statements Cohen provided in this report. If the statements were to be used in a context beyond this report, further analysis could be warranted.

[959] Cohen 11/20/18 302, at 6.

[960] Cohen 11/20/18 302, at 2, 4.

[961] Cohen 11/20/18 302, at 4.

[962] Cohen 9/18/18 302, at 8; Cohen 11/20/18 302, at 3-4.

[963] Cohen 11/20/18 302, at 4.

[964] Cohen 9/18/18 302, at 11; Cohen 11/20/18 302, at 2.

[965] P-SCO-000003680 and P-SCO-0000003687 (8/16/17 Email and Attachment, Michael Cohen's Counsel to Cohen). Cohen said it was not his idea to write a letter to Congress about Trump Tower Moscow. Cohen 9/18/18 302, at 7.

[966] P-SCO-00009478 (Statement of Michael D. Cohen, Esq. (Aug. 28, 2017)).

[967] P-SCO-00009478 (Statement of Michael D. Cohen, Esq. (Aug. 28, 2017)).

[968] P-SCO-00009478 (Statement of Michael D. Cohen, Esq. (Aug. 28, 2017)).

of the project and had numerous conversations about it, the statement said, "Mr. Trump was never in contact with anyone about this proposal other than me on three occasions, including signing a non-binding letter of intent in 2015."[969] Fourth, although Cohen's outreach to Peskov in January 2016 had resulted in a lengthy phone call with a representative from the Kremlin, the statement said that Cohen did "not recall any response to my email [to Peskov], nor any other contacts by me with Mr. Peskov or other Russian government officials about the proposal."[970]

Cohen's statement was circulated in advance to, and edited by, members of the JDA.[971] Before the statement was finalized, early drafts contained a sentence stating, "The building project led me to make limited contacts with Russian government officials."[972] In the final version of the statement, that line was deleted.[973] Cohen thought he was told that it was a decision of the JDA to take out that sentence, and he did not push back on the deletion.[974] Cohen recalled that he told the President's personal counsel that he would not contest a decision of the JDA.[975]

Cohen also recalled that in drafting his statement for Congress, he spoke with the President's personal counsel about a different issue that connected candidate Trump to Russia: Cohen's efforts to set up a meeting between Trump and Putin in New York during the 2015 United Nations General Assembly.[976] In September 2015, Cohen had suggested the meeting to Trump, who told Cohen to reach out to Putin's office about it.[977] Cohen spoke and emailed with a Russian official about a possible meeting, and recalled that Trump asked him multiple times for updates on the proposed meeting with Putin.[978] When Cohen called the Russian official a second time, she told him it would not follow proper protocol for Putin to meet with Trump, and Cohen relayed that

---

[969] P-SCO-00009478 (Statement of Michael D. Cohen, Esq. (Aug. 28, 2017)).

[970] P-SCO-00009478 (Statement of Michael D. Cohen, Esq. (Aug. 28, 2017)).

[971] Cohen 9/12/18 302, at 8-9. Cohen also testified in Congress that the President's counsel reviewed and edited the statement. *Hearing on Issues Related to Trump Organization Before the House Oversight and Reform Committee*, 116th Cong. (Feb. 27, 2019) (CQ Cong. Transcripts, at 24-25) (testimony by Michael Cohen). Because of concerns about the common interest privilege, we did not obtain or review all drafts of Cohen's statement. Based on the drafts that were released through this Office's filter process, it appears that the substance of the four principal false statements described above were contained in an early draft prepared by Cohen and his counsel. P-SCO-0000003680 and P-SCO-0000003687 (8/16/17 Email and Attachment, Cohen's counsel to Cohen).

[972] P-SCO-0000003687 (8/16/17 Draft Statement of Michael Cohen); Cohen 11/20/18 302, at 4.

[973] Cohen 11/20/18 302, at 4. A different line stating that Cohen did "not recall any response to my email [to Peskov in January 2016], nor any other contacts by me with Mr. Peskov or other Russian government officials about the proposal" remained in the draft. *See* P-SCO-0000009478 (Statement of Michael D. Cohen, Esq. (Aug. 28, 2017)).

[974] Cohen 11/20/18 302, at 4.

[975] Cohen 11/20/18 302, at 5.

[976] Cohen 9/18/18 302, at 10-11.

[977] Cohen 9/18/18 302, at 11; Cohen 11/12/18 302, at 4.

[978] Cohen 9/18/18 302, at 11; Cohen 11/12/18 302, at 5.

message to Trump.[979] Cohen anticipated he might be asked questions about the proposed Trump-Putin meeting when he testified before Congress because he had talked about the potential meeting on Sean Hannity's radio show.[980] Cohen recalled explaining to the President's personal counsel the "whole story" of the attempt to set up a meeting between Trump and Putin and Trump's role in it.[981] Cohen recalled that he and the President's personal counsel talked about keeping Trump out of the narrative, and the President's personal counsel told Cohen the story was not relevant and should not be included in his statement to Congress.[982]

Cohen said that his "agenda" in submitting the statement to Congress with false representations about the Trump Tower Moscow project was to minimize links between the project and the President, give the false impression that the project had ended before the first presidential primaries, and shut down further inquiry into Trump Tower Moscow, with the aim of limiting the ongoing Russia investigations.[983] Cohen said he wanted to protect the President and be loyal to him by not contradicting anything the President had said.[984] Cohen recalled he was concerned that if he told the truth about getting a response from the Kremlin or speaking to candidate Trump about travel to Russia to pursue the project, he would contradict the message that no connection existed between Trump and Russia, and he rationalized his decision to provide false testimony because the deal never happened.[985] He was not concerned that the story would be contradicted by individuals who knew it was false because he was sticking to the party line adhered to by the whole group.[986] Cohen wanted the support of the President and the White House, and he believed that following the party line would help put an end to the Special Counsel and congressional investigations.[987]

Between August 18, 2017, when the statement was in an initial draft stage, and August 28, 2017, when the statement was submitted to Congress, phone records reflect that Cohen spoke with the President's personal counsel almost daily.[988] On August 27, 2017, the day before Cohen

---

[979] Cohen 11/12/18 302, at 5.

[980] Cohen 9/18/18 302, at 11.

[981] Cohen 3/19/19 302, at 2.

[982] Cohen 3/19/19 302, at 2; *see* Cohen 9/18/18 302, at 11 (recalling that he was told that if he stayed on message and kept the President out of the narrative, the President would have his back).

[983] Cohen 9/12/18 302, at 8; Information at 4-5, *United States v. Michael Cohen*, 1:18-cr-850 (S.D.N.Y. Nov. 29, 2018), Doc. 2 (*Cohen* Information).

[984] Cohen 11/20/18 302, at 4.

[985] Cohen 11/20/18 302, at 4; Cohen 11/12/18 302, at 2-3, 4, 6.

[986] Cohen 9/12/18 302, at 9.

[987] Cohen 9/12/18 302, at 8-9.

[988] Cohen 11/12/18 302, at 2-3; Cohen 11/20/18 302, at 5; Call Records of Michael Cohen (Reflecting three contacts on August 18, 2017 (24 seconds; 5 minutes 25 seconds; and 10 minutes 58 seconds); two contacts on August 19 (23 seconds and 24 minutes 26 seconds); three contacts on August 23 (8 seconds; 20 minutes 33 seconds; and 5 minutes 8 seconds); one contact on August 24 (11 minutes 59 seconds); 14 contacts on August 27 (28 seconds; 4 minutes 37 seconds; 1 minute 16 seconds; 1 minutes 35

U.S. Department of Justice

~~Attorney Work Product // May Contain Material Protected Under Fed. R. Crim. P. 6(e)~~

submitted the statement to Congress, Cohen and the President's personal counsel had numerous contacts by phone, including calls lasting three, four, six, eleven, and eighteen minutes.[989] Cohen recalled telling the President's personal counsel, who did not have first-hand knowledge of the project, that there was more detail on Trump Tower Moscow that was not in the statement, including that there were more communications with Russia and more communications with candidate Trump than the statement reflected.[990] Cohen stated that the President's personal counsel responded that it was not necessary to elaborate or include those details because the project did not progress and that Cohen should keep his statement short and "tight" and the matter would soon come to an end.[991] Cohen recalled that the President's personal counsel said "his client" appreciated Cohen, that Cohen should stay on message and not contradict the President, that there was no need to muddy the water, and that it was time to move on.[992] Cohen said he agreed because it was what he was expected to do.[993] After Cohen later pleaded guilty to making false statements to Congress about the Trump Tower Moscow project, this Office sought to speak with the President's personal counsel about these conversations with Cohen, but counsel declined, citing potential privilege concerns.[994]

At the same time that Cohen finalized his written submission to Congress, he served as a source for a Washington Post story published on August 27, 2017, that reported in depth for the first time that the Trump Organization was "pursuing a plan to develop a massive Trump Tower in Moscow" at the same time as candidate Trump was "running for president in late 2015 and early 2016."[995] The article reported that "the project was abandoned at the end of January 2016, just before the presidential primaries began, several people familiar with the proposal said."[996] Cohen recalled that in speaking to the Post, he held to the false story that negotiations for the deal ceased in January 2016.[997]

---

seconds; 6 minutes 16 seconds; 1 minutes 10 seconds; 3 minutes 5 seconds; 18 minutes 55 seconds; 4 minutes 56 seconds; 11 minutes 6 seconds; 8 seconds; 3 seconds; 2 seconds; 2 seconds).

[989] Cohen 11/20/18 302, at 5; Call Records of Michael Cohen. (Reflecting 14 contacts on August 27, 2017 (28 seconds; 4 minutes 37 seconds; 1 minute 16 seconds; 1 minutes 35 seconds; 6 minutes 16 seconds; 1 minutes 10 seconds; 3 minutes 5 seconds; 18 minutes 55 seconds; 4 minutes 56 seconds; 11 minutes 6 seconds; 8 seconds; 3 seconds; 2 seconds; 2 seconds)).

[990] Cohen 11/20/18 302, at 5.

[991] Cohen 11/20/18 302, at 5. Cohen also vaguely recalled telling the President's personal counsel that he spoke with a woman from the Kremlin and that the President's personal counsel responded to the effect of "so what?" because the deal never happened. Cohen 11/20/18 302, at 5.

[992] Cohen 11/20/18 302, at 5.

[993] Cohen 11/20/18 302, at 5.

[994] 2/8/19 email, Counsel for personal counsel to the President to Special Counsel's Office.

[995] Cohen 9/18/18 302, at 7; Carol D. Leonnig et al., *Trump's business sought deal on a Trump Tower in Moscow while he ran for president*, Washington Post (Aug. 27, 2017).

[996] Carol D. Leonnig et al., *Trump's business sought deal on a Trump Tower in Moscow while he ran for president*, Washington Post (Aug. 27, 2017).

[997] Cohen 9/18/18 302, at 7.

On August 28, 2017, Cohen submitted his statement about the Trump Tower Moscow project to Congress.[998] Cohen did not recall talking to the President about the specifics of what the statement said or what Cohen would later testify to about Trump Tower Moscow.[999] He recalled speaking to the President more generally about how he planned to stay on message in his testimony.[1000] On September 19, 2017, in anticipation of his impending testimony, Cohen orchestrated the public release of his opening remarks to Congress, which criticized the allegations in the Steele material and claimed that the Trump Tower Moscow project "was terminated in January of 2016; which occurred before the Iowa caucus and months before the very first primary."[1001] Cohen said the release of his opening remarks was intended to shape the narrative and let other people who might be witnesses know what Cohen was saying so they could follow the same message.[1002] Cohen said his decision was meant to mirror Jared Kushner's decision to release a statement in advance of Kushner's congressional testimony, which the President's personal counsel had told Cohen the President liked.[1003] Cohen recalled that on September 20, 2017, after Cohen's opening remarks had been printed by the media, the President's personal counsel told him that the President was pleased with the Trump Tower Moscow statement that had gone out.[1004]

On October 24 and 25, 2017, Cohen testified before Congress and repeated the false statements he had included in his written statement about Trump Tower Moscow.[1005] Phone records show that Cohen spoke with the President's personal counsel immediately after his testimony on both days.[1006]

4. The President Sends Messages of Support to Cohen

In January 2018, the media reported that Cohen had arranged a $130,000 payment during the campaign to prevent a woman from publicly discussing an alleged sexual encounter she had

---

[998] P-SCO-000009477 - 9478 (8/28/17 Letter and Attachment, Cohen to SSCI).

[999] Cohen 11/12/18 302, at 2; Cohen 9/12/18 302, at 9.

[1000] Cohen 9/12/18 302, at 9.

[1001] Cohen 9/18/18 302, at 7; *see, e.g., READ: Michael Cohen's statement to the Senate intelligence committee*, CNN (Sept. 19, 2017).

[1002] Cohen 9/18/18 302, at 7.

[1003] Cohen 9/18/18 302, at 7; Cohen 11/20/18 302, at 6.

[1004] Cohen 11/20/18 302, at 6. Phone records show that the President's personal counsel called Cohen on the morning of September 20, 2017, and they spoke for approximately 11 minutes, and that they had two more contacts that day, one of which lasted approximately 18 minutes. Call Records of Michael Cohen. (Reflecting three contacts on September 20, 2017, with calls lasting for 11 minutes 3 seconds; 2 seconds; and 18 minutes 38 seconds).

[1005] *Cohen* Information, at 4; Executive Session, Permanent Select Committee on Intelligence, U.S. House of Representatives, Interview of Michael Cohen (Oct. 24, 2017), at 10-11, 117-119.

[1006] Call Records of Michael Cohen. (Reflecting two contacts on October 24, 2017 (12 minutes 8 seconds and 8 minutes 27 seconds) and three contacts on October 25, 2017 (1 second; 4 minutes 6 seconds; and 6 minutes 6 seconds)).

144

with the President before he ran for office.[1007] This Office did not investigate Cohen's campaign-period payments to women.[1008] However, those events, as described here, are potentially relevant to the President's and his personal counsel's interactions with Cohen as a witness who later began to cooperate with the government.

On February 13, 2018, Cohen released a statement to news organizations that stated, "In a private transaction in 2016, I used my own personal funds to facilitate a payment of $130,000 to [the woman]. Neither the Trump Organization nor the Trump campaign was a party to the transaction with [the woman], and neither reimbursed me for the payment, either directly or indirectly."[1009] In congressional testimony on February 27, 2019, Cohen testified that he had discussed what to say about the payment with the President and that the President had directed Cohen to say that the President "was not knowledgeable . . . of [Cohen's] actions" in making the payment.[1010] On February 19, 2018, the day after the New York Times wrote a detailed story attributing the payment to Cohen and describing Cohen as the President's "fixer," Cohen received a text message from the President's personal counsel that stated, "Client says thanks for what you do."[1011]

On April 9, 2018, FBI agents working with the U.S. Attorney's Office for the Southern District of New York executed search warrants on Cohen's home, hotel room, and office.[1012] That day, the President spoke to reporters and said that he had "just heard that they broke into the office of one of my personal attorneys—a good man."[1013] The President called the searches "a real disgrace" and said, "It's an attack on our country, in a true sense. It's an attack on what we all

---

[1007] *See, e.g.*, Michael Rothfeld & Joe Palazzolo, *Trump Lawyer Arranged $130,000 Payment for Adult-Film Star's Silence*, Wall Street Journal (Jan. 12, 2018).

[1008] The Office was authorized to investigate Cohen's establishment and use of Essential Consultants LLC, which Cohen created to facilitate the $130,000 payment during the campaign, based on evidence that the entity received funds from Russian-backed entities. Cohen's use of Essential Consultants to facilitate the $130,000 payment to the woman during the campaign was part of the Office's referral of certain Cohen-related matters to the U.S. Attorney's Office for the Southern District of New York.

[1009] *See, e.g.*, Mark Berman, *Longtime Trump attorney says he made $130,000 payment to Stormy Daniels with his money*, Washington Post (Feb. 14, 2018).

[1010] *Hearing on Issues Related to Trump Organization Before the House Oversight and Reform Committee*, 116th Cong. (Feb. 27, 2019) (CQ Cong. Transcripts, at 147-148) (testimony of Michael Cohen). Toll records show that Cohen was connected to a White House phone number for approximately five minutes on January 19, 2018, and for approximately seven minutes on January 30, 2018, and that Cohen called Melania Trump's cell phone several times between January 26, 2018, and January 30, 2018. Call Records of Michael Cohen.

[1011] 2/19/18 Text Message, President's personal counsel to Cohen; *see* Jim Rutenberg et al., *Tools of Trump's Fixer: Payouts, Intimidation and the Tabloids*, New York Times (Feb. 18, 2018).

[1012] Gov't Opp. to Def. Mot. for Temp. Restraining Order, *In the Matter of Search Warrants Executed on April 9, 2018*, 18-mj-3161 (S.D.N.Y. Apr. 13, 2018), Doc. 1 ("On April 9, 2018, agents from the New York field office of the Federal Bureau of Investigation . . . executed search warrants for Michael Cohen's residence, hotel room, office, safety deposit box, and electronic devices.").

[1013] Remarks by President Trump Before Meeting with Senior Military Leadership, White House (Apr. 9, 2018).

U.S. Department of Justice

~~Attorney Work Product // May Contain Material Protected Under Fed. R. Crim. P. 6(e)~~

stand for."[1014] Cohen said that after the searches he was concerned that he was "an open book," that he did not want issues arising from the payments to women to "come out," and that his false statements to Congress were "a big concern."[1015]

A few days after the searches, the President called Cohen.[1016] According to Cohen, the President said he wanted to "check in" and asked if Cohen was okay, and the President encouraged Cohen to "hang in there" and "stay strong."[1017] Cohen also recalled that following the searches he heard from individuals who were in touch with the President and relayed to Cohen the President's support for him.[1018] Cohen recalled that ██ PP ███████, a friend of the President's, reached out to say that he was with "the Boss" in Mar-a-Lago and the President had said "he loves you" and not to worry.[1019] Cohen recalled that ██ Personal Privacy ██████████ for the Trump Organization, told him, "the boss loves you."[1020] And Cohen said that ██ PP ████, a friend of the President's, told him, "everyone knows the boss has your back."[1021]

On or about April 17, 2018, Cohen began speaking with an attorney, Robert Costello, who had a close relationship with Rudolph Giuliani, one of the President's personal lawyers.[1022] Costello told Cohen that he had a "back channel of communication" to Giuliani, and that Giuliani had said the "channel" was "crucial" and "must be maintained."[1023] On April 20, 2018, the New York Times published an article about the President's relationship with and treatment of Cohen.[1024] The President responded with a series of tweets predicting that Cohen would not "flip":

> The New York Times and a third rate reporter . . . are going out of their way to destroy Michael Cohen and his relationship with me in the hope that he will 'flip.' They use non-existent 'sources' and a drunk/drugged up loser who hates Michael, a fine person with a wonderful family. Michael is a businessman for his own account/lawyer who I have always liked & respected. Most people will flip if the Government lets them out of trouble, even

---

[1014] Remarks by President Trump Before Meeting with Senior Military Leadership, White House (Apr. 9, 2018).

[1015] Cohen, 10/17/18 302, at 11.

[1016] Cohen 3/19/19 302, at 4.

[1017] Cohen 3/19/19 302, at 4.

[1018] Cohen 9/12/18 302, at 11.

[1019] Cohen 9/12/18 302, at 11.

[1020] Cohen 9/12/18 302, at 11.

[1021] Cohen 9/12/18 302, at 11.

[1022] 4/17/18 Email, Citron to Cohen; 4/19/18 Email, Costello to Cohen; MC-SCO-001 (7/7/18 redacted billing statement from Davidoff, Hutcher & Citron to Cohen).

[1023] 4/21/18 Email, Costello to Cohen.

[1024] See Maggie Haberman et al., *Michael Cohen Has Said He Would Take a Bullet for Trump. Maybe Not Anymore.*, New York Times (Apr. 20, 2018).

if it means lying or making up stories. Sorry, I don't see Michael doing that despite the horrible Witch Hunt and the dishonest media![1025]

In an email that day to Cohen, Costello wrote that he had spoken with Giuliani.[1026] Costello told Cohen the conversation was "Very Very Positive[.] You are 'loved'. . . they are in our corner. . . . Sleep well tonight[], you have friends in high places."[1027]

Cohen said that following these messages he believed he had the support of the White House if he continued to toe the party line, and he determined to stay on message and be part of the team.[1028] At the time, Cohen's understood that his legal fees were still being paid by the Trump Organization, which he said was important to him.[1029] Cohen believed he needed the power of the President to take care of him, so he needed to defend the President and stay on message.[1030]

Cohen also recalled speaking with the President's personal counsel about pardons after the searches of his home and office had occurred, at a time when the media had reported that pardon discussions were occurring at the White House.[1031] Cohen told the President's personal counsel he had been a loyal lawyer and servant, and he said that after the searches he was in an uncomfortable position and wanted to know what was in it for him.[1032] According to Cohen, the President's personal counsel responded that Cohen should stay on message, that the investigation was a witch hunt, and that everything would be fine.[1033] Cohen understood based on this conversation and previous conversations about pardons with the President's personal counsel that as long as he stayed on message, he would be taken care of by the President, either through a pardon or through the investigation being shut down.[1034]

[1025] @realDonaldTrump 4/21/18 (9:10 a.m. ET) Tweets.

[1026] 4/21/18 Email, Costello to Cohen.

[1027] 4/21/18 Email, Costello to Cohen. **Harm to Ongoing Matter**

[1028] Cohen 9/12/18 302, at 11.

[1029] Cohen 9/12/18 302, at 10.

[1030] Cohen 9/12/18 302, at 10.

[1031] Cohen 11/20/18 302, at 7. At a White House press briefing on April 23, 2018, in response to a question about whether the White House had "close[d] the door one way or the other on the President pardoning Michael Cohen," Sanders said, "It's hard to close the door on something that hasn't taken place. I don't like to discuss or comment on hypothetical situations that may or may not ever happen. I would refer you to personal attorneys to comment on anything specific regarding that case, but we don't have anything at this point." Sarah Sanders, *White House Daily Briefing*, C-SPAN (Apr. 23, 2018).

[1032] Cohen 11/20/18 302, at 7; Cohen 3/19/19 302, at 3.

[1033] Cohen 3/19/19 302, at 3.

[1034] Cohen 3/19/19 302, at 3-4.

U.S. Department of Justice

~~Attorney Work Product // May Contain Material Protected Under Fed. R. Crim. P. 6(e)~~

On April 24, 2018, the President responded to a reporter's inquiry whether he would consider a pardon for Cohen with, "Stupid question."[1035] On June 8, 2018, the President said he "hadn't even thought about" pardons for Manafort or Cohen, and continued, "It's far too early to be thinking about that. They haven't been convicted of anything. There's nothing to pardon."[1036] And on June 15, 2018, the President expressed sympathy for Cohen, Manafort, and Flynn in a press interview and said, "I feel badly about a lot of them, because I think a lot of it is very unfair."[1037]

5. The President's Conduct After Cohen Began Cooperating with the Government

On July 2, 2018, ABC News reported based on an "exclusive" interview with Cohen that Cohen "strongly signaled his willingness to cooperate with special counsel Robert Mueller and federal prosecutors in the Southern District of New York—even if that puts President Trump in jeopardy."[1038] That week, the media reported that Cohen had added an attorney to his legal team who previously had worked as a legal advisor to President Bill Clinton.[1039]

Beginning on July 20, 2018, the media reported on the existence of a recording Cohen had made of a conversation he had with candidate Trump about a payment made to a second woman who said she had had an affair with Trump.[1040] On July 21, 2018, the President responded: "Inconceivable that the government would break into a lawyer's office (early in the morning)— almost unheard of. Even more inconceivable that a lawyer would tape a client—totally unheard of & perhaps illegal. The good news is that your favorite President did nothing wrong!"[1041] On July 27, 2018, after the media reported that Cohen was willing to inform investigators that Donald Trump Jr. told his father about the June 9, 2016 meeting to get "dirt" on Hillary Clinton,[1042] the President tweeted: "[S]o the Fake News doesn't waste my time with dumb questions, NO, I did NOT know of the meeting with my son, Don jr. Sounds to me like someone is trying to make up

---

[1035] Remarks by President Trump and President Macron of France Before Restricted Bilateral Meeting, The White House (Apr. 24, 2018).

[1036] *President Donald Trump Holds Media Availability Before Departing for the G-7 Summit*, CQ Newsmaker Transcripts (June 8, 2018).

[1037] Remarks by President Trump in Press Gaggle, The White House (June 15, 2018).

[1038] *EXCLUSIVE: Michael Cohen says family and country, not President Trump, is his 'first loyalty'*, ABC (July 2, 2018). Cohen said in the interview, "To be crystal clear, my wife, my daughter and my son, and this country have my first loyalty."

[1039] *See e.g.*, Darren Samuelsohn, *Michael Cohen hires Clinton scandal veteran Lanny Davis*, Politico (July 5, 2018).

[1040] *See, e.g.*, Matt Apuzzo et al., *Michael Cohen Secretly Taped Trump Discussing Payment to Playboy Model*, New York Times (July 20, 2018).

[1041] @realDonaldTrump 7/21/18 (8:10 a.m. ET) Tweet.

[1042] *See, e.g.*, Jim Sciutto, *Cuomo Prime Time Transcript*, CNN (July 26, 2018).

stories in order to get himself out of an unrelated jam (Taxi cabs maybe?). He even retained Bill and Crooked Hillary's lawyer. Gee, I wonder if they helped him make the choice!"[1043]

On August 21, 2018, Cohen pleaded guilty in the Southern District of New York to eight felony charges, including two counts of campaign-finance violations based on the payments he had made during the final weeks of the campaign to women who said they had affairs with the President.[1044] During the plea hearing, Cohen stated that he had worked "at the direction of" the candidate in making those payments.[1045] The next day, the President contrasted Cohen's cooperation with Manafort's refusal to cooperate, tweeting, "I feel very badly for Paul Manafort and his wonderful family. 'Justice' took a 12 year old tax case, among other things, applied tremendous pressure on him and, unlike Michael Cohen, he refused to 'break'—make up stories in order to get a 'deal.' Such respect for a brave man!"[1046]

On September 17, 2018, this Office submitted written questions to the President that included questions about the Trump Tower Moscow project and attached Cohen's written statement to Congress and the Letter of Intent signed by the President.[1047] Among other issues, the questions asked the President to describe the timing and substance of discussions he had with Cohen about the project, whether they discussed a potential trip to Russia, and whether the President "at any time direct[ed] or suggest[ed] that discussions about the Trump Moscow project should cease," or whether the President was "informed at any time that the project had been abandoned."[1048]

On November 20, 2018, the President submitted written responses that did not answer those questions about Trump Tower Moscow directly and did not provide any information about the timing of the candidate's discussions with Cohen about the project or whether he participated in any discussions about the project being abandoned or no longer pursued.[1049] Instead, the President's answers stated in relevant part:

> I had few conversations with Mr. Cohen on this subject. As I recall, they were brief, and they were not memorable. I was not enthused about the proposal, and I do not recall any discussion of travel to Russia in connection with it. I do not remember discussing it with

---

[1043] @realDonaldTrump 7/27/18 (7:26 a.m. ET) Tweet; @realDonaldTrump 7/27/18 (7:38 a.m. ET) Tweet; @realDonaldTrump 7/27/18 (7:56 a.m. ET) Tweet. At the time of these tweets, the press had reported that Cohen's financial interests in taxi cab medallions were being scrutinized by investigators. *See, e.g.,* Matt Apuzzo et al., *Michael Cohen Secretly Taped Trump Discussing Payment to Playboy Model,* New York Times (July 20, 2018).

[1044] *Cohen* Information.

[1045] *Cohen* 8/21/18 Transcript, at 23.

[1046] @realDonaldTrump 8/22/18 (9:21 a.m. ET) Tweet.

[1047] 9/17/18 Letter, Special Counsel's Office to President's Personal Counsel (attaching written questions for the President, with attachments).

[1048] 9/17/18 Letter, Special Counsel's Office to President's Personal Counsel (attaching written questions for the President), Question III, Parts (a) through (g).

[1049] Written Responses of Donald J. Trump (Nov. 20, 2018).

149

anyone else at the Trump Organization, although it is possible. I do not recall being aware at the time of any communications between Mr. Cohen and Felix Sater and any Russian government official regarding the Letter of Intent.[1050]

On November 29, 2018, Cohen pleaded guilty to making false statements to Congress based on his statements about the Trump Tower Moscow project.[1051] In a plea agreement with this Office, Cohen agreed to "provide truthful information regarding any and all matters as to which this Office deems relevant."[1052] Later on November 29, after Cohen's guilty plea had become public, the President spoke to reporters about the Trump Tower Moscow project, saying:

> I decided not to do the project. . . . I decided ultimately not to do it. There would have been nothing wrong if I did do it. If I did do it, there would have been nothing wrong. That was my business. . . . It was an option that I decided not to do. . . . I decided not to do it. The primary reason . . . I was focused on running for President. . . . I was running my business while I was campaigning. There was a good chance that I wouldn't have won, in which case I would've gone back into the business. And why should I lose lots of opportunities?[1053]

The President also said that Cohen was "a weak person. And by being weak, unlike other people that you watch—he is a weak person. And what he's trying to do is get a reduced sentence. So he's lying about a project that everybody knew about."[1054] The President also brought up Cohen's written submission to Congress regarding the Trump Tower Moscow project: "So here's the story: Go back and look at the paper that Michael Cohen wrote before he testified in the House and/or Senate. It talked about his position."[1055] The President added, "Even if [Cohen] was right, it doesn't matter because I was allowed to do whatever I wanted during the campaign."[1056]

In light of the President's public statements following Cohen's guilty plea that he "decided not to do the project," this Office again sought information from the President about whether he participated in any discussions about the project being abandoned or no longer pursued, including when he "decided not to do the project," who he spoke to about that decision, and what motivated

---

[1050] Written Responses of Donald J. Trump (Nov. 20, 2018), at 15 (Response to Question III, Parts (a) through (g)).

[1051] *Cohen* Information; *Cohen* 8/21/18 Transcript.

[1052] Plea Agreement at 4, *United States v. Michael Cohen*, 1:18-cr-850 (S.D.N.Y. Nov. 29, 2018).

[1053] *President Trump Departure Remarks*, C-SPAN (Nov. 29, 2018). In contrast to the President's remarks following Cohen's guilty plea, Cohen's August 28, 2017 statement to Congress stated that Cohen, not the President, "decided to abandon the proposal" in late January 2016; that Cohen "did not ask or brief Mr. Trump . . . before I made the decision to terminate further work on the proposal"; and that the decision to abandon the proposal was "unrelated" to the Campaign. P-SCO-000009477 (Statement of Michael D. Cohen, Esq. (Aug. 28, 2017)).

[1054] *President Trump Departure Remarks*, C-SPAN (Nov. 29, 2018).

[1055] *President Trump Departure Remarks*, C-SPAN (Nov. 29, 2018).

[1056] *President Trump Departure Remarks*, C-SPAN (Nov. 29, 2018).

the decision.[1057] The Office also again asked for the timing of the President's discussions with Cohen about Trump Tower Moscow and asked him to specify "what period of the campaign" he was involved in discussions concerning the project.[1058] In response, the President's personal counsel declined to provide additional information from the President and stated that "the President has fully answered the questions at issue."[1059]

In the weeks following Cohen's plea and agreement to provide assistance to this Office, the President repeatedly implied that Cohen's family members were guilty of crimes. On December 3, 2018, after Cohen had filed his sentencing memorandum, the President tweeted, "'Michael Cohen asks judge for no Prison Time.' You mean he can do all of the TERRIBLE, unrelated to Trump, things having to do with fraud, big loans, Taxis, etc., and not serve a long prison term? He makes up stories to get a GREAT & ALREADY reduced deal for himself, and *get his wife and father-in-law (who has the money?) off Scott Free*. He lied for this outcome and should, in my opinion, serve a full and complete sentence."[1060] **Harm to Ongoing Matter**

[1061]

On December 12, 2018, Cohen was sentenced to three years of imprisonment.[1062] The next day, the President sent a series of tweets that said:

> I never directed Michael Cohen to break the law. . . . Those charges were just agreed to by him in order to embarrass the president and get a much reduced prison sentence, which he did—including the fact that *his family was temporarily let off the hook*. As a lawyer, Michael has great liability to me![1063]

On December 16, 2018, the President tweeted, "Remember, Michael Cohen only became a 'Rat' after the FBI did something which was absolutely unthinkable & unheard of until the Witch Hunt was illegally started. They BROKE INTO AN ATTORNEY'S OFFICE! Why didn't they break into the DNC to get the Server, or Crooked's office?"[1064]

In January 2019, after the media reported that Cohen would provide public testimony in a congressional hearing, the President made additional public comments suggesting that Cohen's

---

[1057] 1/23/19 Letter, Special Counsel's Office to President's Personal Counsel.

[1058] 1/23/19 Letter, Special Counsel's Office to President's Personal Counsel.

[1059] 2/6/19 Letter, President's Personal Counsel to Special Counsel's Office.

[1060] @realDonaldTrump 12/3/18 (10:24 a.m. ET and 10:29 a.m. ET) Tweets (emphasis added).

[1061] @realDonaldTrump 12/3/18 (10:48 a.m. ET) Tweet.

[1062] *Cohen* 12/12/18 Transcript.

[1063] @realDonaldTrump 12/13/18 (8:17 a.m. ET, 8:25 a.m. ET, and 8:39 a.m. ET) Tweets (emphasis added).

[1064] @realDonaldTrump 12/16/18 (9:39 a.m. ET) Tweet.

family members had committed crimes. In an interview on Fox on January 12, 2019, the President was asked whether he was worried about Cohen's testimony and responded:

> [I]n order to get his sentence reduced, [Cohen] says "I have an idea, I'll ah, tell—I'll give you some information on the president." Well, there is no information. But *he should give information maybe on his father-in-law because that's the one that people want to look at because where does that money—that's the money in the family. And I guess he didn't want to talk about his father-in-law,* he's trying to get his sentence reduced. So it's ah, pretty sad. You know, it's weak and it's very sad to watch a thing like that.[1065]

On January 18, 2019, the President tweeted, "Kevin Corke, @FoxNews 'Don't forget, Michael Cohen has already been convicted of perjury and fraud, and as recently as this week, the Wall Street Journal has suggested that he may have stolen tens of thousands of dollars. . . .' Lying to reduce his jail time! *Watch father-in-law!*"[1066]

On January 23, 2019, Cohen postponed his congressional testimony, citing threats against his family.[1067] The next day, the President tweeted, "So interesting that bad lawyer Michael Cohen, who sadly will not be testifying before Congress, is using the lawyer of Crooked Hillary Clinton to represent him—Gee, how did that happen?"[1068]

Also in January 2019, Giuliani gave press interviews that appeared to confirm Cohen's account that the Trump Organization pursued the Trump Tower Moscow project well past January 2016. Giuliani stated that "it's our understanding that [discussions about the Trump Moscow project] went on throughout 2016. Weren't a lot of them, but there were conversations. Can't be sure of the exact date. But the president can remember having conversations with him about it. . . . The president also remembers—yeah, probably up—could be up to as far as October, November."[1069] In an interview with the New York Times, Giuliani quoted the President as saying that the discussions regarding the Trump Moscow project were "going on from the day I announced to the day I won."[1070] On January 21, 2019, Giuliani issued a statement that said: "My recent statements about discussions during the 2016 campaign between Michael Cohen and candidate Donald Trump about a potential Trump Moscow 'project' were hypothetical and not based on conversations I had with the president."[1071]

[1065] *Jeanine Pirro Interview with President Trump*, Fox News (Jan. 12, 2019) (emphasis added).

[1066] @realDonaldTrump 1/18/19 (10:02 a.m. ET) Tweet (emphasis added).

[1067] Statement by Lanny Davis, Cohen's personal counsel (Jan. 23, 2019).

[1068] @realDonaldTrump 1/24/19 (7:48 a.m. ET) Tweet.

[1069] Meet the Press Interview with Rudy Giuliani, NBC (Jan. 20, 2019).

[1070] Mark Mazzetti et al., *Moscow Skyscraper Talks Continued Through "the Day I Won,"* Trump Is Said to Acknowledge, New York Times (Jan. 20, 2019).

[1071] Maggie Haberman, *Giuliani Says His Moscow Trump Tower Comments Were "Hypothetical"*, New York Times (Jan. 21, 2019). In a letter to this Office, the President's counsel stated that Giuliani's public comments "were not intended to suggest nor did they reflect knowledge of the existence or timing

Analysis

In analyzing the President's conduct related to Cohen, the following evidence is relevant to the elements of obstruction of justice.

a.   Obstructive act. We gathered evidence of the President's conduct related to Cohen on two issues: (i) whether the President or others aided or participated in Cohen's false statements to Congress, and (ii) whether the President took actions that would have the natural tendency to prevent Cohen from providing truthful information to the government.

i.   First, with regard to Cohen's false statements to Congress, while there is evidence, described below, that the President knew Cohen provided false testimony to Congress about the Trump Tower Moscow project, the evidence available to us does not establish that the President directed or aided Cohen's false testimony.

Cohen said that his statements to Congress followed a "party line" that developed within the campaign to align with the President's public statements distancing the President from Russia. Cohen also recalled that, in speaking with the President in advance of testifying, he made it clear that he would stay on message—which Cohen believed they both understood would require false testimony. But Cohen said that he and the President did not explicitly discuss whether Cohen's testimony about the Trump Tower Moscow project would be or was false, and the President did not direct him to provide false testimony. Cohen also said he did not tell the President about the specifics of his planned testimony. During the time when his statement to Congress was being drafted and circulated to members of the JDA, Cohen did not speak directly to the President about the statement, but rather communicated with the President's personal counsel—as corroborated by phone records showing extensive communications between Cohen and the President's personal counsel before Cohen submitted his statement and when he testified before Congress.

Cohen recalled that in his discussions with the President's personal counsel on August 27, 2017—the day before Cohen's statement was submitted to Congress—Cohen said that there were more communications with Russia and more communications with candidate Trump than the statement reflected. Cohen recalled expressing some concern at that time. According to Cohen, the President's personal counsel—who did not have first-hand knowledge of the project—responded by saying that there was no need to muddy the water, that it was unnecessary to include those details because the project did not take place, and that Cohen should keep his statement short and tight, not elaborate, stay on message, and not contradict the President. Cohen's recollection of the content of those conversations is consistent with direction about the substance of Cohen's draft statement that appeared to come from members of the JDA. For example, Cohen omitted any reference to his outreach to Russian government officials to set up a meeting between Trump and Putin during the United Nations General Assembly, and Cohen believed it was a decision of

---

of conversations beyond that contained in the President's [written responses to the Special Counsel's Office]." 2/6/19 Letter, President's Personal Counsel to Special Counsel's Office.

the JDA to delete the sentence, "The building project led me to make limited contacts with Russian government officials."

The President's personal counsel declined to provide us with his account of his conversations with Cohen, and there is no evidence available to us that indicates that the President was aware of the information Cohen provided to the President's personal counsel. The President's conversations with his personal counsel were presumptively protected by attorney-client privilege, and we did not seek to obtain the contents of any such communications. The absence of evidence about the President and his counsel's conversations about the drafting of Cohen's statement precludes us from assessing what, if any, role the President played.

        ii.   Second, we considered whether the President took actions that would have the natural tendency to prevent Cohen from providing truthful information to criminal investigators or to Congress.

Before Cohen began to cooperate with the government, the President publicly and privately urged Cohen to stay on message and not "flip." Cohen recalled the President's personal counsel telling him that he would be protected so long as he did not go "rogue." In the days and weeks that followed the April 2018 searches of Cohen's home and office, the President told reporters that Cohen was a "good man" and said he was "a fine person with a wonderful family . . . who I have always liked & respected." Privately, the President told Cohen to "hang in there" and "stay strong." People who were close to both Cohen and the President passed messages to Cohen that "the President loves you," "the boss loves you," and "everyone knows the boss has your back." Through the President's personal counsel, the President also had previously told Cohen "thanks for what you do" after Cohen provided information to the media about payments to women that, according to Cohen, both Cohen and the President knew was false. At that time, the Trump Organization continued to pay Cohen's legal fees, which was important to Cohen. Cohen also recalled discussing the possibility of a pardon with the President's personal counsel, who told him to stay on message and everything would be fine. The President indicated in his public statements that a pardon had not been ruled out, and also stated publicly that "[m]ost people will flip if the Government lets them out of trouble" but that he "d[idn't] see Michael doing that."

After it was reported that Cohen intended to cooperate with the government, however, the President accused Cohen of "mak[ing] up stories in order to get himself out of an unrelated jam (Taxi cabs maybe?)," called Cohen a "rat," and on multiple occasions publicly suggested that Cohen's family members had committed crimes. The evidence concerning this sequence of events could support an inference that the President used inducements in the form of positive messages in an effort to get Cohen not to cooperate, and then turned to attacks and intimidation to deter the provision of information or undermine Cohen's credibility once Cohen began cooperating.

        b.   <u>Nexus to an official proceeding</u>. The President's relevant conduct towards Cohen occurred when the President knew the Special Counsel's Office, Congress, and the U.S. Attorney's Office for the Southern District of New York were investigating Cohen's conduct. The President acknowledged through his public statements and tweets that Cohen potentially could cooperate with the government investigations.

c.   Intent.   In analyzing the President's intent in his actions towards Cohen as a potential witness, there is evidence that could support the inference that the President intended to discourage Cohen from cooperating with the government because Cohen's information would shed adverse light on the President's campaign-period conduct and statements.

i.   Cohen's false congressional testimony about the Trump Tower Moscow project was designed to minimize connections between the President and Russia and to help limit the congressional and DOJ Russia investigations—a goal that was in the President's interest, as reflected by the President's own statements. During and after the campaign, the President made repeated statements that he had "no business" in Russia and said that there were "no deals that could happen in Russia, because we've stayed away."   As Cohen knew, and as he recalled communicating to the President during the campaign, Cohen's pursuit of the Trump Tower Moscow project cast doubt on the accuracy or completeness of these statements.

In connection with his guilty plea, Cohen admitted that he had multiple conversations with candidate Trump to give him status updates about the Trump Tower Moscow project, that the conversations continued through at least June 2016, and that he discussed with Trump possible travel to Russia to pursue the project. The conversations were not off-hand, according to Cohen, because the project had the potential to be so lucrative. In addition, text messages to and from Cohen and other records further establish that Cohen's efforts to advance the project did not end in January 2016 and that in May and June 2016, Cohen was considering the timing for possible trips to Russia by him and Trump in connection with the project.

The evidence could support an inference that the President was aware of these facts at the time of Cohen's false statements to Congress. Cohen discussed the project with the President in early 2017 following media inquiries. Cohen recalled that on September 20, 2017, the day after he released to the public his opening remarks to Congress—which said the project "was terminated in January of 2016"—the President's personal counsel told him the President was pleased with what Cohen had said about Trump Tower Moscow. And after Cohen's guilty plea, the President told reporters that he had ultimately decided not to do the project, which supports the inference that he remained aware of his own involvement in the project and the period during the Campaign in which the project was being pursued.

ii.   The President's public remarks following Cohen's guilty plea also suggest that the President may have been concerned about what Cohen told investigators about the Trump Tower Moscow project. At the time the President submitted written answers to questions from this Office about the project and other subjects, the media had reported that Cohen was cooperating with the government but Cohen had not yet pleaded guilty to making false statements to Congress. Accordingly, it was not publicly known what information about the project Cohen had provided to the government. In his written answers, the President did not provide details about the timing and substance of his discussions with Cohen about the project and gave no indication that he had decided to no longer pursue the project. Yet after Cohen pleaded guilty, the President publicly stated that he had personally made the decision to abandon the project. The President then declined to clarify the seeming discrepancy to our Office or answer additional questions. The content and timing of the President's provision of information about his knowledge and actions regarding the Trump Tower Moscow project is evidence that the President may have been concerned about the information that Cohen could provide as a witness.

155

iii.   The President's concern about Cohen cooperating may have been directed at the Southern District of New York investigation into other aspects of the President's dealings with Cohen rather than an investigation of Trump Tower Moscow. There also is some evidence that the President's concern about Cohen cooperating was based on the President's stated belief that Cohen would provide false testimony against the President in an attempt to obtain a lesser sentence for his unrelated criminal conduct. The President tweeted that Manafort, unlike Cohen, refused to "break" and "make up stories in order to get a 'deal.'" And after Cohen pleaded guilty to making false statements to Congress, the President said, "what [Cohen]'s trying to do is get a reduced sentence. So he's lying about a project that everybody knew about." But the President also appeared to defend the underlying conduct, saying, "Even if [Cohen] was right, it doesn't matter because I was allowed to do whatever I wanted during the campaign." As described above, there is evidence that the President knew that Cohen had made false statements about the Trump Tower Moscow project and that Cohen did so to protect the President and minimize the President's connections to Russia during the campaign.

iv.   Finally, the President's statements insinuating that members of Cohen's family committed crimes after Cohen began cooperating with the government could be viewed as an effort to retaliate against Cohen and chill further testimony adverse to the President by Cohen or others. It is possible that the President believes, as reflected in his tweets, that Cohen "ma[d]e[] up stories" in order to get a deal for himself and "get his wife and father-in-law . . . off Scott Free." It also is possible that the President's mention of Cohen's wife and father-in-law were not intended to affect Cohen as a witness but rather were part of a public-relations strategy aimed at discrediting Cohen and deflecting attention away from the President on Cohen-related matters. But the President's suggestion that Cohen's family members committed crimes happened more than once, including just before Cohen was sentenced (at the same time as the President stated that Cohen "should, in my opinion, serve a full and complete sentence") and again just before Cohen was scheduled to testify before Congress. The timing of the statements supports an inference that they were intended at least in part to discourage Cohen from further cooperation.

L.   Overarching Factual Issues

Although this report does not contain a traditional prosecution decision or declination decision, the evidence supports several general conclusions relevant to analysis of the facts concerning the President's course of conduct.

1. Three features of this case render it atypical compared to the heartland obstruction-of-justice prosecutions brought by the Department of Justice.

First, the conduct involved actions by the President. Some of the conduct did not implicate the President's constitutional authority and raises garden-variety obstruction-of-justice issues. Other events we investigated, however, drew upon the President's Article II authority, which raised constitutional issues that we address in Volume II, Section III.B, *infra*. A factual analysis of that conduct would have to take into account both that the President's acts were facially lawful and that his position as head of the Executive Branch provides him with unique and powerful means of influencing official proceedings, subordinate officers, and potential witnesses.

156

420

Second, many obstruction cases involve the attempted or actual cover-up of an underlying crime. Personal criminal conduct can furnish strong evidence that the individual had an improper obstructive purpose, *see, e.g., United States v. Willoughby*, 860 F.2d 15, 24 (2d Cir. 1988), or that he contemplated an effect on an official proceeding, *see, e.g., United States v. Binday*, 804 F.3d 558, 591 (2d Cir. 2015). But proof of such a crime is not an element of an obstruction offense. *See United States v. Greer*, 872 F.3d 790, 798 (6th Cir. 2017) (stating, in applying the obstruction sentencing guideline, that "obstruction of a criminal investigation is punishable even if the prosecution is ultimately unsuccessful or even if the investigation ultimately reveals no underlying crime"). Obstruction of justice can be motivated by a desire to protect non-criminal personal interests, to protect against investigations where underlying criminal liability falls into a gray area, or to avoid personal embarrassment. The injury to the integrity of the justice system is the same regardless of whether a person committed an underlying wrong.

In this investigation, the evidence does not establish that the President was involved in an underlying crime related to Russian election interference. But the evidence does point to a range of other possible personal motives animating the President's conduct. These include concerns that continued investigation would call into question the legitimacy of his election and potential uncertainty about whether certain events—such as advance notice of WikiLeaks's release of hacked information or the June 9, 2016 meeting between senior campaign officials and Russians—could be seen as criminal activity by the President, his campaign, or his family.

Third, many of the President's acts directed at witnesses, including discouragement of cooperation with the government and suggestions of possible future pardons, occurred in public view. While it may be more difficult to establish that public-facing acts were motivated by a corrupt intent, the President's power to influence actions, persons, and events is enhanced by his unique ability to attract attention through use of mass communications. And no principle of law excludes public acts from the scope of obstruction statutes. If the likely effect of the acts is to intimidate witnesses or alter their testimony, the justice system's integrity is equally threatened.

2. Although the events we investigated involved discrete acts—*e.g.*, the President's statement to Comey about the Flynn investigation, his termination of Comey, and his efforts to remove the Special Counsel—it is important to view the President's pattern of conduct as a whole. That pattern sheds light on the nature of the President's acts and the inferences that can be drawn about his intent.

a. Our investigation found multiple acts by the President that were capable of exerting undue influence over law enforcement investigations, including the Russian-interference and obstruction investigations. The incidents were often carried out through one-on-one meetings in which the President sought to use his official power outside of usual channels. These actions ranged from efforts to remove the Special Counsel and to reverse the effect of the Attorney General's recusal; to the attempted use of official power to limit the scope of the investigation; to direct and indirect contacts with witnesses with the potential to influence their testimony. Viewing the acts collectively can help to illuminate their significance. For example, the President's direction to McGahn to have the Special Counsel removed was followed almost immediately by his direction to Lewandowski to tell the Attorney General to limit the scope of the Russia investigation to prospective election-interference only—a temporal connection that suggests that both acts were taken with a related purpose with respect to the investigation.

157

The President's efforts to influence the investigation were mostly unsuccessful, but that is largely because the persons who surrounded the President declined to carry out orders or accede to his requests. Comey did not end the investigation of Flynn, which ultimately resulted in Flynn's prosecution and conviction for lying to the FBI. McGahn did not tell the Acting Attorney General that the Special Counsel must be removed, but was instead prepared to resign over the President's order. Lewandowski and Dearborn did not deliver the President's message to Sessions that he should confine the Russia investigation to future election meddling only. And McGahn refused to recede from his recollections about events surrounding the President's direction to have the Special Counsel removed, despite the President's multiple demands that he do so. Consistent with that pattern, the evidence we obtained would not support potential obstruction charges against the President's aides and associates beyond those already filed.

b. In considering the full scope of the conduct we investigated, the President's actions can be divided into two distinct phases reflecting a possible shift in the President's motives. In the first phase, before the President fired Comey, the President had been assured that the FBI had not opened an investigation of him personally. The President deemed it critically important to make public that he was not under investigation, and he included that information in his termination letter to Comey after other efforts to have that information disclosed were unsuccessful.

Soon after he fired Comey, however, the President became aware that investigators were conducting an obstruction-of-justice inquiry into his own conduct. That awareness marked a significant change in the President's conduct and the start of a second phase of action. The President launched public attacks on the investigation and individuals involved in it who could possess evidence adverse to the President, while in private, the President engaged in a series of targeted efforts to control the investigation. For instance, the President attempted to remove the Special Counsel; he sought to have Attorney General Sessions unrecuse himself and limit the investigation; he sought to prevent public disclosure of information about the June 9, 2016 meeting between Russians and campaign officials; and he used public forums to attack potential witnesses who might offer adverse information and to praise witnesses who declined to cooperate with the government. Judgments about the nature of the President's motives during each phase would be informed by the totality of the evidence.

III. LEGAL DEFENSES TO THE APPLICATION OF OBSTRUCTION-OF-JUSTICE STATUTES TO THE PRESIDENT

The President's personal counsel has written to this Office to advance statutory and constitutional defenses to the potential application of the obstruction-of-justice statutes to the President's conduct.[1072] As a statutory matter, the President's counsel has argued that a core obstruction-of-justice statute, 18 U.S.C. § 1512(c)(2), does not cover the President's actions.[1073] As a constitutional matter, the President's counsel argued that the President cannot obstruct justice by exercising his constitutional authority to close Department of Justice investigations or terminate the FBI Director.[1074] Under that view, any statute that restricts the President's exercise of those powers would impermissibly intrude on the President's constitutional role. The President's counsel has conceded that the President may be subject to criminal laws that do not directly involve exercises of his Article II authority, such as laws prohibiting bribing witnesses or suborning perjury.[1075] But counsel has made a categorical argument that "the President's exercise of his constitutional authority here to terminate an FBI Director and to close investigations cannot constitutionally constitute obstruction of justice."[1076]

In analyzing counsel's statutory arguments, we concluded that the President's proposed interpretation of Section 1512(c)(2) is contrary to the litigating position of the Department of Justice and is not supported by principles of statutory construction.

As for the constitutional arguments, we recognized that the Department of Justice and the courts have not definitively resolved these constitutional issues. We therefore analyzed the President's position through the framework of Supreme Court precedent addressing the separation of powers. Under that framework, we concluded, Article II of the Constitution does not categorically and permanently immunize the President from potential liability for the conduct that we investigated. Rather, our analysis led us to conclude that the obstruction-of-justice statutes can

---

[1072] 6/23/17 Letter, President's Personal Counsel to Special Counsel's Office; *see also* 1/29/18 Letter, President's Personal Counsel to Special Counsel's Office; 2/6/18 Letter, President's Personal Counsel to Special Counsel's Office; 8/8/18 Letter, President's Personal Counsel to Special Counsel's Office, at 4.

[1073] 2/6/18 Letter, President's Personal Counsel to Special Counsel's Office, at 2-9. Counsel has also noted that other potentially applicable obstruction statutes, such as 18 U.S.C. § 1505, protect only pending proceedings. 6/23/17 Letter, President's Personal Counsel to Special Counsel's Office, at 7-8. Section 1512(c)(2) is not limited to pending proceedings, but also applies to future proceedings that the person contemplated. *See* Volume II, Section III.A, *supra*.

[1074] 6/23/17 Letter, President's Personal Counsel to Special Counsel's Office, at 1 ("[T]he President cannot obstruct . . . by simply exercising these inherent Constitutional powers.").

[1075] 6/23/17 Letter, President's Personal Counsel to Special Counsel's Office, at 2 n. 1.

[1076] 6/23/17 Letter, President's Personal Counsel to Special Counsel's Office, at 2 n.1 (dashes omitted); *see also* 8/8/18 Letter, President's Personal Counsel to Special Counsel's Office, at 4 ("[T]he obstruction-of-justice statutes cannot be read so expansively as to create potential liability based on facially lawful acts undertaken by the President in furtherance of his core Article II discretionary authority to remove principal officers or carry out the prosecution function.").

validly prohibit a President's corrupt efforts to use his official powers to curtail, end, or interfere with an investigation.

A.   Statutory Defenses to the Application of Obstruction-Of-Justice Provisions to the Conduct Under Investigation

The obstruction-of-justice statute most readily applicable to our investigation is 18 U.S.C. § 1512(c)(2). Section 1512(c) provides:

> (c) Whoever corruptly—
>
>> (1) alters, destroys, mutilates, or conceals a record, document, or other object, or attempts to do so, with the intent to impair the object's integrity or availability for use in an official proceeding; or
>>
>> (2) otherwise obstructs, influences, or impedes any official proceeding, or attempts to do so,
>
> shall be fined under this title or imprisoned not more than 20 years, or both.

The Department of Justice has taken the position that Section 1512(c)(2) states a broad, independent, and unqualified prohibition on obstruction of justice.[1077] While defendants have argued that subsection (c)(2) should be read to cover only acts that would impair the availability or integrity of evidence because that is subsection (c)(1)'s focus, strong arguments weigh against that proposed limitation. The text of Section 1512(c)(2) confirms that its sweep is not tethered to Section 1512(c)(1); courts have so interpreted it; its history does not counsel otherwise; and no principle of statutory construction dictates a contrary view. On its face, therefore, Section 1512(c)(2) applies to all corrupt means of obstructing a proceeding, pending or contemplated— including by improper exercises of official power. In addition, other statutory provisions that are potentially applicable to certain conduct we investigated broadly prohibit obstruction of proceedings that are pending before courts, grand juries, and Congress. *See* 18 U.S.C. §§ 1503, 1505. Congress has also specifically prohibited witness tampering. *See* 18 U.S.C. § 1512(b).

1. The Text of Section 1512(c)(2) Prohibits a Broad Range of Obstructive Acts

Several textual features of Section 1512(c)(2) support the conclusion that the provision broadly prohibits corrupt means of obstructing justice and is not limited by the more specific prohibitions in Section 1512(c)(1), which focus on evidence impairment.

First, the text of Section 1512(c)(2) is unqualified: it reaches acts that "obstruct[], influence[], or impede[] any official proceeding" when committed "corruptly." Nothing in Section 1512(c)(2)'s text limits the provision to acts that would impair the integrity or availability of evidence for use in an official proceeding. In contrast, Section 1512(c)(1) explicitly includes the requirement that the defendant act "with the intent to impair the object's integrity or availability

---

[1077] *See* U.S. Br., *United States v. Kumar*, Nos. 06–5482–cr(L), 06–5654–cr(CON) (2d Cir. filed Oct. 26, 2007), at pp. 15-28; *United States v. Singleton*, Nos. H-04-CR-514SS, H-06-cr-80 (S.D. Tex. filed June 5, 2006).

160

U.S. Department of Justice

Attorney Work Product // May Contain Material Protected Under Fed. R. Crim. P. 6(e)

for use in an official proceeding," a requirement that Congress also included in two other sections of Section 1512. *See* 18 U.S.C. §§ 1512(a)(2)(B)(ii) (use of physical force with intent to cause a person to destroy an object "with intent to impair the integrity or availability of the object for use in an official proceeding"); 1512(b)(2)(B) (use of intimidation, threats, corrupt persuasion, or misleading conduct with intent to cause a person to destroy an object "with intent to impair the integrity or availability of the object for use in an official proceeding"). But no comparable intent or conduct element focused on evidence impairment appears in Section 1512(c)(2). The intent element in Section 1512(c)(2) comes from the word "corruptly." *See, e.g., United States v. McKibbins*, 656 F.3d 707, 711 (7th Cir. 2011) ("The intent element is important because the word 'corruptly' is what serves to separate criminal and innocent acts of obstruction.") (internal quotation marks omitted). And the conduct element in Section 1512(c)(2) is "obstruct[ing], influenc[ing], or imped[ing]" a proceeding. Congress is presumed to have acted intentionally in the disparate inclusion and exclusion of evidence-impairment language. *See Loughrin v. United States*, 573 U.S. 351, 358 (2014) ("[W]hen 'Congress includes particular language in one section of a statute but omits it in another'—let alone in the very next provision—this Court 'presume[s]' that Congress intended a difference in meaning") (quoting *Russello v. United States*, 464 U.S. 16, 23 (1983)); *accord Digital Realty Trust, Inc. v. Somers*, 138 S. Ct. 767, 777 (2018).

Second, the structure of Section 1512 supports the conclusion that Section 1512(c)(2) defines an independent offense. Section 1512(c)(2) delineates a complete crime with different elements from Section 1512(c)(1)—and each subsection of Section 1512(c) contains its own "attempt" prohibition, underscoring that they are independent prohibitions. The two subsections of Section 1512(c) are connected by the conjunction "or," indicating that each provides an alternative basis for criminal liability. *See Loughrin*, 573 U.S. at 357 ("ordinary use [of 'or'] is almost always disjunctive, that is, the words it connects are to be given separate meanings") (internal quotation marks omitted). In *Loughrin*, for example, the Supreme Court relied on the use of the word "or" to hold that adjacent and overlapping subsections of the bank fraud statute, 18 U.S.C. § 1344, state distinct offenses and that subsection 1344(2) therefore should not be interpreted to contain an additional element specified only in subsection 1344(1). *Id.*; *see also Shaw v. United States*, 137 S. Ct. 462, 465-469 (2016) (recognizing that the subsections of the bank fraud statute "overlap substantially" but identifying distinct circumstances covered by each).[1078] And here, as in *Loughrin*, Section 1512(c)'s "two clauses have separate numbers, line breaks before, between, and after them, and equivalent indentation—thus placing the clauses visually on an equal footing and indicating that they have separate meanings." 573 U.S. at 359.

Third, the introductory word "otherwise" in Section 1512(c)(2) signals that the provision covers obstructive acts that are different from those listed in Section 1512(c)(1). *See* Black's Law Dictionary 1101 (6th ed. 1990) ("otherwise" means "in a different manner; in another way, or in other ways"); *see also, e.g.*, American Heritage College Dictionary Online ("1. In another way;

[1078] The Office of Legal Counsel recently relied on several of the same interpretive principles in concluding that language that appeared in the first clause of the Wire Act, 18 U.S.C. § 1084, restricting its prohibition against certain betting or wagering activities to "any sporting event or contest," did not apply to the second clause of the same statute, which reaches other betting or wagering activities. *See Reconsidering Whether the Wire Act Applies to Non-Sports Gambling* (Nov. 2, 2018), slip op. 7 (relying on plain language); *id.* at 11 (finding it not "tenable to read into the second clause the qualifier 'on any sporting event or contest' that appears in the first clause"); *id.* at 12 (relying on *Digital Realty*).

161

differently; 2. Under other circumstances"); *see also Gooch v. United States*, 297 U.S. 124, 128 (1936) (characterizing "otherwise" as a "broad term" and holding that a statutory prohibition on kidnapping "for ransom or reward or otherwise" is not limited by the words "ransom" and "reward" to kidnappings for pecuniary benefits); *Collazos v. United States*, 368 F.3d 190, 200 (2d Cir. 2004) (construing "otherwise" in 28 U.S.C. § 2466(1)(C) to reach beyond the "specific examples" listed in prior subsections, thereby covering the "myriad means that human ingenuity might devise to permit a person to avoid the jurisdiction of a court"); *cf. Begay v. United States*, 553 U.S. 137, 144 (2006) (recognizing that "otherwise" is defined to mean "in a different way or manner," and holding that the word "otherwise" introducing the residual clause in the Armed Career Criminal Act, 18 U.S.C. § 924(e)(2)(B)(ii), can, but need not necessarily, "refer to a crime that is similar to the listed examples in some respects but different in others").[1079] The purpose of the word "otherwise" in Section 1512(c)(2) is therefore to clarify that the provision covers obstructive acts *other* than the destruction of physical evidence with the intent to impair its integrity or availability, which is the conduct addressed in Section 1512(c)(1). The word "otherwise" does not signal that Section 1512(c)(2) has less breadth in covering obstructive conduct than the language of the provision implies.

2. Judicial Decisions Support a Broad Reading of Section 1512(c)(2)

Courts have not limited Section 1512(c)(2) to conduct that impairs evidence, but instead have read it to cover obstructive acts in any form.

As one court explained, "[t]his expansive subsection operates as a catch-all to cover 'otherwise' obstructive behavior that might not constitute a more specific offense like document destruction, which is listed in (c)(1)." *United States v. Volpendesto*, 746 F.3d 273, 286 (7th Cir. 2014) (some quotation marks omitted). For example, in *United States v. Ring*, 628 F. Supp. 2d 195 (D.D.C. 2009), the court rejected the argument that "§ 1512(c)(2)'s reference to conduct that 'otherwise obstructs, influences, or impedes any official proceeding' is limited to conduct that is similar to the type of conduct proscribed by subsection (c)(1)—namely, conduct that impairs the integrity or availability of 'record[s], documents[s], or other object[s] for use in an official proceeding." *Id.* at 224. The court explained that "the meaning of § 1512(c)(2) is plain on its face." *Id.* (alternations in original). And courts have upheld convictions under Section 1512(c)(2) that did not involve evidence impairment, but instead resulted from conduct that more broadly thwarted arrests or investigations. *See, e.g., United States v. Martinez*, 862 F.3d 223, 238 (2d Cir. 2017) (police officer tipped off suspects about issuance of arrest warrants before "outstanding warrants could be executed, thereby potentially interfering with an ongoing grand jury proceeding"); *United States v. Ahrensfield*, 698 F.3d 1310, 1324-1326 (10th Cir. 2012) (officer disclosed existence of an undercover investigation to its target); *United States v. Phillips*, 583 F.3d 1261, 1265 (10th Cir. 2009) (defendant disclosed identity of an undercover officer thus preventing him from making controlled purchases from methamphetamine dealers). Those cases illustrate that Section 1512(c)(2) applies to corrupt acts—including by public officials—that frustrate the

---

[1079] In *Sykes v. United States*, 564 U.S. 1, 15 (2011), the Supreme Court substantially abandoned *Begay*'s reading of the residual clause, and in *Johnson v. United States*, 135 S. Ct. 2551 (2015), the Court invalidated the residual clause as unconstitutionally vague. *Begay*'s analysis of the word "otherwise" is thus of limited value.

commencement or conduct of a proceeding, and not just to acts that make evidence unavailable or impair its integrity.

Section 1512(c)(2)'s breadth is reinforced by the similarity of its language to the omnibus clause of 18 U.S.C. § 1503, which covers anyone who "corruptly . . . obstructs, or impedes, or endeavors to influence, obstruct, or impede, the due administration of justice." That clause of Section 1503 follows two more specific clauses that protect jurors, judges, and court officers. The omnibus clause has nevertheless been construed to be "far more general in scope than the earlier clauses of the statute." *United States v. Aguilar*, 515 U.S. 593, 599 (1995). "The omnibus clause is essentially a catch-all provision which generally prohibits conduct that interferes with the due administration of justice." *United States v. Brenson*, 104 F.3d 1267, 1275 (11th Cir. 1997). Courts have accordingly given it a "non-restrictive reading." *United States v. Kumar*, 617 F.3d 612, 620 (2d Cir. 2010); *id.* at 620 n.7 (collecting cases from the Third, Fourth, Sixth, Seventh, and Eleventh Circuits). As one court has explained, the omnibus clause "prohibits acts that are similar in result, rather than manner, to the conduct described in the first part of the statute." *United States v. Howard*, 569 F.2d 1331, 1333 (5th Cir. 1978). While the specific clauses "forbid certain means of obstructing justice . . . the omnibus clause aims at obstruction of justice itself, regardless of the means used to reach that result." *Id.* (collecting cases). Given the similarity of Section 1512(c)(2) to Section 1503's omnibus clause, Congress would have expected Section 1512(c)(2) to cover acts that produced a similar result to the evidence-impairment provisions—*i.e.*, the result of obstructing justice—rather than covering only acts that were similar in manner. Read this way, Section 1512(c)(2) serves a distinct function in the federal obstruction-of-justice statutes: it captures corrupt conduct, other than document destruction, that has the natural tendency to obstruct contemplated as well as pending proceedings.

Section 1512(c)(2) overlaps with other obstruction statutes, but it does not render them superfluous. Section 1503, for example, which covers pending grand jury and judicial proceedings, and Section 1505, which covers pending administrative and congressional proceedings, reach "*endeavors* to influence, obstruct, or impede" the proceedings—a broader test for inchoate violations than Section 1512(c)(2)'s "attempt" standard, which requires a substantial step towards a completed offense. *See United States v. Sampson*, 898 F.3d 287, 302 (2d Cir. 2018) ("[E]fforts to witness tamper that rise to the level of an 'endeavor' yet fall short of an 'attempt' cannot be prosecuted under § 1512."); *United States v. Leisure*, 844 F.2d 1347, 1366-1367 (8th Cir. 1988) (collecting cases recognizing the difference between the "endeavor" and "attempt" standards). And 18 U.S.C. § 1519, which prohibits destruction of documents or records in contemplation of an investigation or proceeding, does not require the "nexus" showing under *Aguilar*, which Section 1512(c)(2) demands. *See, e.g.*, *United States v. Yielding*, 657 F.3d 688, 712 (8th Cir. 2011) ("The requisite knowledge and intent [under Section 1519] can be present even if the accused lacks knowledge that he is likely to succeed in obstructing the matter."); *United States v. Gray*, 642 F.3d 371, 376-377 (2d Cir. 2011) ("[I]n enacting § 1519, Congress rejected any requirement that the government prove a link between a defendant's conduct and an imminent or pending official proceeding."). The existence of even "substantial" overlap is not "uncommon" in criminal statutes. *Loughrin*, 573 U.S. at 359 n.4; *see Shaw*, 137 S. Ct. at 458-469; *Aguilar*, 515 U.S. at 616 (Scalia, J., dissenting) ("The fact that there is now some overlap between § 1503 and § 1512 is no more intolerable than the fact that there is some overlap between the omnibus clause of § 1503 and the other provisions of § 1503 itself."). But given that Sections 1503, 1505, and

163

U.S. Department of Justice

~~Attorney Work Product // May Contain Material Protected Under Fed. R. Crim. P. 6(e)~~

1519 each reach conduct that Section 1512(c)(2) does not, the overlap provides no reason to give Section 1512(c)(2) an artificially limited construction. *See Shaw*, 137 S. Ct. at 469.[1080]

> 3. The Legislative History of Section 1512(c)(2) Does Not Justify Narrowing Its Text

"Given the straightforward statutory command" in Section 1512(c)(2), "there is no reason to resort to legislative history." *United States v. Gonzales*, 520 U.S. 1, 6 (1997). In any event, the legislative history of Section 1512(c)(2) is not a reason to impose extratextual limitations on its reach.

Congress enacted Section 1512(c)(2) as part the Sarbanes-Oxley Act of 2002, Pub. L. No. 107-204, Tit. XI, § 1102, 116 Stat. 807. The relevant section of the statute was entitled "Tampering with a Record *or Otherwise Impeding an Official Proceeding*." 116 Stat. 807 (emphasis added). That title indicates that Congress intended the two clauses to have independent effect. Section 1512(c) was added as a floor amendment in the Senate and explained as closing a certain "loophole" with respect to "document shredding." *See* 148 Cong. Rec. S6545 (July 10, 2002) (Sen. Lott); *id.* at S6549-S6550 (Sen. Hatch). But those explanations do not limit the enacted text. *See Pittston Coal Group v. Sebben*, 488 U.S. 105, 115 (1988) ("[I]t is not the law that a statute can have no effects which are not explicitly mentioned in its legislative history."); *see also Encino Motorcars, LLC v. Navarro*, 138 S. Ct. 1134, 1143 (2018) ("Even if Congress did not foresee all of the applications of the statute, that is no reason not to give the statutory text a fair reading."). The floor statements thus cannot detract from the meaning of the enacted text. *See Barnhart v. Sigmon Coal Co.*, 534 U.S. 438, 457 (2002) ("Floor statements from two Senators cannot amend the clear and unambiguous language of a statute. We see no reason to give greater weight to the views of two Senators than to the collective votes of both Houses, which are memorialized in the unambiguous statutory text."). That principle has particular force where one of the proponents of the amendment to Section 1512 introduced his remarks as only "briefly elaborat[ing] on some of the specific provisions contained in this bill." 148 Cong. Rec. S6550 (Sen. Hatch).

Indeed, the language Congress used in Section 1512(c)(2)—prohibiting "corruptly . . . obstruct[ing], influenc[ing], or imped[ing] any official proceeding" or attempting to do so— parallels a provision that Congress considered years earlier in a bill designed to strengthen protections against witness tampering and obstruction of justice. While the earlier provision is not a direct antecedent of Section 1512(c)(2), Congress's understanding of the broad scope of the

---

[1080] The Supreme Court's decision in *Marinello v. United States*, 138 S. Ct. 1101 (2018), does not support imposing a non-textual limitation on Section 1512(c)(2). *Marinello* interpreted the tax obstruction statute, 26 U.S.C. § 7212(a), to require "a 'nexus' between the defendant's conduct and a particular administrative proceeding." *Id.* at 1109. The Court adopted that construction in light of the similar interpretation given to "other obstruction provisions," *id.* (citing *Aguilar* and *Arthur Andersen*), as well as considerations of context, legislative history, structure of the criminal tax laws, fair warning, and lenity. *Id.* at 1106-1108. The type of "nexus" element the Court adopted in *Marinello* already applies under Section 1512(c)(2), and the remaining considerations the Court cited do not justify reading into Section 1512(c)(2) language that is not there. *See Bates v. United States*, 522 U.S. 23, 29 (1997) (the Court "ordinarily resist[s] reading words or elements into a statute that do not appear on its face.").

U.S. Department of Justice

~~Attorney Work Product // May Contain Material Protected Under Fed. R. Crim. P. 6(e)~~

earlier provision is instructive. Recognizing that "the proper administration of justice may be impeded or thwarted" by a "variety of corrupt methods . . . limited only by the imagination of the criminally inclined," S. Rep. No. 532, 97th Cong., 2d Sess. 17-18 (1982), Congress considered a bill that would have amended Section 1512 by making it a crime, *inter alia*, when a person "corruptly . . . influences, obstructs, or impedes . . . [t]he enforcement and prosecution of federal law," "administration of a law under which an official proceeding is being or may be conducted," or the "exercise of a Federal legislative power of inquiry." *Id.* at 17-19 (quoting S. 2420).

The Senate Committee explained that:

> [T]he purpose of preventing an obstruction of or miscarriage of justice cannot be fully carried out by a simple enumeration of the commonly prosecuted obstruction offenses. There must also be protection against the rare type of conduct that is the product of the inventive criminal mind and which also thwarts justice.

Id. at 18. The report gave examples of conduct "actually prosecuted under the current residual clause [in 18 U.S.C. § 1503], which would probably not be covered in this series [of provisions] without a residual clause." *Id.* One prominent example was "[a] conspiracy to cover up the Watergate burglary and its aftermath by having the Central Intelligence Agency seek to interfere with an ongoing FBI investigation of the burglary." *Id.* (citing *United States v. Haldeman*, 559 F.2d 31 (D.C. Cir. 1976)). The report therefore indicates a congressional awareness not only that residual-clause language resembling Section 1512(c)(2) broadly covers a wide variety of obstructive conduct, but also that such language reaches the improper use of governmental processes to obstruct justice—specifically, the Watergate cover-up orchestrated by White House officials including the President himself. *See Haldeman*, 559 F.3d at 51, 86-87, 120-129, 162.[1081]

> 4. <u>General Principles of Statutory Construction Do Not Suggest That Section 1512(c)(2) is Inapplicable to the Conduct in this Investigation</u>

The requirement of fair warning in criminal law, the interest in avoiding due process concerns in potentially vague statutes, and the rule of lenity do not justify narrowing the reach of Section 1512(c)(2)'s text.[1082]

a. As with other criminal laws, the Supreme Court has "exercised restraint" in interpreting obstruction-of-justice provisions, both out of respect for Congress's role in defining crimes and in the interest of providing individuals with "fair warning" of what a criminal statute prohibits. *Marinello v. United States*, 138 S. Ct. 1101, 1106 (2018); *Arthur Andersen*, 544 U.S. at 703;

[1081] The Senate ultimately accepted the House version of the bill, which excluded an omnibus clause. *See United States v. Poindexter*, 951 F.2d 369, 382-383 (D.C. Cir. 1991) (tracing history of the proposed omnibus provision in the witness-protection legislation). During the floor debate on the bill, Senator Heinz, one of the initiators and primary backers of the legislation, explained that the omnibus clause was beyond the scope of the witness-protection measure at issue and likely "duplicative" of other obstruction laws, 128 Cong. Rec. 26,810 (1982) (Sen. Heinz), presumably referring to Sections 1503 and 1505.

[1082] In a separate section addressing considerations unique to the presidency, we consider principles of statutory construction relevant in that context. *See* Volume II, Section III.B.1, *infra*.

Aguilar, 515 U.S. at 599-602. In several obstruction cases, the Court has imposed a nexus test that requires that the wrongful conduct targeted by the provision be sufficiently connected to an official proceeding to ensure the requisite culpability. *Marinello*, 138 S. Ct. at 1109; *Arthur Andersen*, 544 U.S. at 707-708; *Aguilar*, 515 U.S. at 600-602. Section 1512(c)(2) has been interpreted to require a similar nexus. *See, e.g.*, *United States v. Young*, 916 F.3d 368, 386 (4th Cir. 2019); *United States v. Petruk*, 781 F.3d 438, 445 (8th Cir. 2015); *United States v. Phillips*, 583 F.3d 1261, 1264 (10th Cir. 2009); *United States v. Reich*, 479 F.3d 179, 186 (2d Cir. 2007). To satisfy the nexus requirement, the government must show as an objective matter that a defendant acted "in a manner that is likely to obstruct justice," such that the statute "excludes defendants who have an evil purpose but use means that would only unnaturally and improbably be successful." *Aguilar*, 515 U.S. at 601-602 (internal quotation marks omitted); *see id.* at 599 ("the endeavor must have the natural and probable effect of interfering with the due administration of justice") (internal quotation marks omitted). The government must also show as a subjective matter that the actor "contemplated a particular, foreseeable proceeding." *Petruk*, 781 F.3d at 445. Those requirements alleviate fair-warning concerns by ensuring that obstructive conduct has a close enough connection to existing or future proceedings to implicate the dangers targeted by the obstruction laws and that the individual actually has the obstructive result in mind.

b. Courts also seek to construe statutes to avoid due process vagueness concerns. *See, e.g.*, *McDonnell v. United States*, 136 S. Ct. 2355, 2373 (2016); *Skilling v. United States*, 561 U.S. 358, 368, 402-404 (2010). Vagueness doctrine requires that a statute define a crime "with sufficient definiteness that ordinary people can understand what conduct is prohibited" and "in a manner that does not encourage arbitrary and discriminatory enforcement." *Id.* at 402-403 (internal quotation marks omitted). The obstruction statutes' requirement of acting "corruptly" satisfies that test.

"Acting 'corruptly' within the meaning of § 1512(c)(2) means acting with an improper purpose and to engage in conduct knowingly and dishonestly with the specific intent to subvert, impede or obstruct" the relevant proceeding. *United States v. Gordon*, 710 F.3d 1124, 1151 (10th Cir. 2013) (some quotation marks omitted). The majority opinion in *Aguilar* did not address the defendant's vagueness challenge to the word "corruptly," 515 U.S. at 600 n. 1, but Justice Scalia's separate opinion did reach that issue and would have rejected the challenge, *id.* at 616-617 (Scalia, J., joined by Kennedy and Thomas, JJ., concurring in part and dissenting in part). "Statutory language need not be colloquial," Justice Scalia explained, and "the term 'corruptly' in criminal laws has a longstanding and well-accepted meaning. It denotes an act done with an intent to give some advantage inconsistent with official duty and the rights of others." *Id.* at 616 (internal quotation marks omitted; citing lower court authority and legal dictionaries). Justice Scalia added that "in the context of obstructing jury proceedings, any claim of ignorance of wrongdoing is incredible." *Id.* at 617. Lower courts have also rejected vagueness challenges to the word "corruptly." *See, e.g.*, *United States v. Edwards*, 869 F.3d 490, 501-502 (7th Cir. 2017); *United States v. Brenson*, 104 F.3d 1267, 1280-1281 (11th Cir. 1997); *United States v. Howard*, 569 F.2d 1331, 1336 n.9 (5th Cir. 1978). This well-established intent standard precludes the need to limit the obstruction statutes to only certain kinds of inherently wrongful conduct.[1083]

[1083] In *United States v. Poindexter*, 951 F.2d 369 (D.C. Cir. 1991), the court of appeals found the term "corruptly" in 18 U.S.C. § 1505 vague as applied to a person who provided false information to Congress. After suggesting that the word "corruptly" was vague on its face, 951 F.2d at 378, the court

166

c. Finally, the rule of lenity does not justify treating Section 1512(c)(2) as a prohibition on evidence impairment, as opposed to an omnibus clause. The rule of lenity is an interpretive principle that resolves ambiguity in criminal laws in favor of the less-severe construction. *Cleveland v. United States*, 531 U.S. 12, 25 (2000). "[A]s [the Court has] repeatedly emphasized," however, the rule of lenity applies only if, "after considering text, structure, history and purpose, there remains a grievous ambiguity or uncertainty in the statute such that the Court must simply guess as to what Congress intended." *Abramski v. United States*, 573 U.S. 169, 188 n.10 (2014) (internal quotation marks omitted). The rule has been cited, for example, in adopting a narrow meaning of "tangible object" in an obstruction statute when the prohibition's title, history, and list of prohibited acts indicated a focus on destruction of records. *See Yates v. United States*, 135 S. Ct. 1074, 1088 (2015) (plurality opinion) (interpreting "tangible object" in the phrase "record, document, or tangible object" in 18 U.S.C. § 1519 to mean an item capable of recording or preserving information). Here, as discussed above, the text, structure, and history of Section 1512(c)(2) leaves no "grievous ambiguity" about the statute's meaning. Section 1512(c)(2) defines a structurally independent general prohibition on obstruction of official proceedings.

5. Other Obstruction Statutes Might Apply to the Conduct in this Investigation

Regardless whether Section 1512(c)(2) covers all corrupt acts that obstruct, influence, or impede pending or contemplated proceedings, other statutes would apply to such conduct in pending proceedings, provided that the remaining statutory elements are satisfied. As discussed above, the omnibus clause in 18 U.S.C. § 1503(a) applies generally to obstruction of pending judicial and grand proceedings.[1084] *See Aguilar*, 515 U.S. at 598 (noting that the clause is "far more general in scope" than preceding provisions). Section 1503(a)'s protections extend to witness tampering and to other obstructive conduct that has a nexus to pending proceedings. *See Sampson*, 898 F.3d at 298-303 & n.6 (collecting cases from eight circuits holding that Section 1503 covers witness-related obstructive conduct, and cabining prior circuit authority). And Section 1505 broadly criminalizes obstructive conduct aimed at pending agency and congressional proceedings.[1085] *See, e.g., United States v. Rainey*, 757 F.3d 234, 241-247 (5th Cir. 2014).

---

concluded that the statute did not clearly apply to corrupt conduct by the person himself and the "core" conduct to which Section 1505 could constitutionally be applied was one person influencing another person to violate a legal duty. *Id*. at 379-386. Congress later enacted a provision overturning that result by providing that "[a]s used in [S]ection 1505, the term 'corruptly' means acting with an improper purpose, personally or by influencing another, including by making a false or misleading statement, or withholding, concealing, altering, or destroying a document or other information." 18 U.S.C. § 1515(b). Other courts have declined to follow *Poindexter* either by limiting it to Section 1505 and the specific conduct at issue in that case, *see Brenson*, 104 F.3d at 1280-1281; reading it as narrowly limited to certain types of conduct, *see United States v. Morrison*, 98 F.3d 619, 629-630 (D.C. Cir. 1996); or by noting that it predated *Arthur Andersen*'s interpretation of the term "corruptly," *see Edwards*, 869 F.3d at 501-502.

[1084] Section 1503(a) provides for criminal punishment of:

> Whoever . . . corruptly or by threats or force, or by any threatening letter or communication, influences, obstructs, or impedes, or endeavors to influence, obstruct, or impede, the due administration of justice.

[1085] Section 1505 provides for criminal punishment of:

167

Finally, 18 U.S.C. § 1512(b)(3) criminalizes tampering with witnesses to prevent the communication of information about a crime to law enforcement. The nexus inquiry articulated in *Aguilar*—that an individual has "knowledge that his actions are likely to affect the judicial proceeding," 515 U.S. at 599—does not apply to Section 1512(b)(3). *See United States v. Byrne*, 435 F.3d 16, 24-25 (1st Cir. 2006). The nexus inquiry turns instead on the actor's intent to prevent communications to a federal law enforcement official. *See Fowler v. United States*, 563 U.S. 668, 673-678 (2011).

*   *   *

In sum, in light of the breadth of Section 1512(c)(2) and the other obstruction statutes, an argument that the conduct at issue in this investigation falls outside the scope of the obstruction laws lacks merit.

B. Constitutional Defenses to Applying Obstruction-Of-Justice Statutes to Presidential Conduct

The President has broad discretion to direct criminal investigations. The Constitution vests the "executive Power" in the President and enjoins him to "take Care that the Laws be faithfully executed." U.S. CONST. ART II, §§ 1, 3. Those powers and duties form the foundation of prosecutorial discretion. *See United States v. Armstrong*, 517 U.S. 456, 464 (1996) (Attorney General and United States Attorneys "have this latitude because they are designated by statute as the President's delegates to help him discharge his constitutional responsibility to 'take Care that the Laws be faithfully executed.'"). The President also has authority to appoint officers of the United States and to remove those whom he has appointed. U.S. CONST. ART II, § 2, cl. 2 (granting authority to the President to appoint all officers with the advice and consent of the Senate, but providing that Congress may vest the appointment of inferior officers in the President alone, the heads of departments, or the courts of law); *see also Free Enterprise Fund v. Public Company Accounting Oversight Board*, 561 U.S. 477, 492-493, 509 (2010) (describing removal authority as flowing from the President's "responsibility to take care that the laws be faithfully executed").

Although the President has broad authority under Article II, that authority coexists with Congress's Article I power to enact laws that protect congressional proceedings, federal investigations, the courts, and grand juries against corrupt efforts to undermine their functions. Usually, those constitutional powers function in harmony, with the President enforcing the criminal laws under Article II to protect against corrupt obstructive acts. But when the President's official actions come into conflict with the prohibitions in the obstruction statutes, any constitutional tension is reconciled through separation-of-powers analysis.

Whoever corruptly . . . influences, obstructs, or impedes or endeavors to influence, obstruct, or impede the due and proper administration of the law under which any pending proceeding is being had before any department or agency of the United States, or the due and proper exercise of the power of inquiry under which any inquiry or investigation is being had by either House, or any committee of either House or any joint committee of the Congress.

168

The President's counsel has argued that "the President's exercise of his constitutional authority . . . to terminate an FBI Director and to close investigations . . . cannot constitutionally constitute obstruction of justice."[1086] As noted above, no Department of Justice position or Supreme Court precedent directly resolved this issue. We did not find counsel's contention, however, to accord with our reading of the Supreme Court authority addressing separation-of-powers issues. Applying the Court's framework for analysis, we concluded that Congress can validly regulate the President's exercise of official duties to prohibit actions motivated by a corrupt intent to obstruct justice. The limited effect on presidential power that results from that restriction would not impermissibly undermine the President's ability to perform his Article II functions.

1. The Requirement of a Clear Statement to Apply Statutes to Presidential Conduct Does Not Limit the Obstruction Statutes

Before addressing Article II issues directly, we consider one threshold statutory-construction principle that is unique to the presidency: "The principle that general statutes must be read as not applying to the President if they do not expressly apply where application would arguably limit the President's constitutional role." OLC, *Application of 28 U.S.C. § 458 to Presidential Appointments of Federal Judges*, 19 Op. O.L.C. 350, 352 (1995). This "clear statement rule," *id.*, has its source in two principles: statutes should be construed to avoid serious constitutional questions, and Congress should not be assumed to have altered the constitutional separation of powers without clear assurance that it intended that result. OLC, *The Constitutional Separation of Powers Between the President and Congress*, 20 Op. O.L.C. 124, 178 (1996).

The Supreme Court has applied that clear-statement rule in several cases. In one leading case, the Court construed the Administrative Procedure Act, 5 U.S.C. § 701 *et seq.*, not to apply to judicial review of presidential action. *Franklin v. Massachusetts*, 505 U.S. 788, 800-801 (1992). The Court explained that it "would require an express statement by Congress before assuming it intended the President's performance of his statutory duties to be reviewed for abuse of discretion." *Id.* at 801. In another case, the Court interpreted the word "utilized" in the Federal Advisory Committee Act (FACA), 5 U.S.C. App., to apply only to the use of advisory committees established directly or indirectly by the government, thereby excluding the American Bar Association's advice to the Department of Justice about federal judicial candidates. *Public Citizen v. United States Department of Justice*, 491 U.S. 440, 455, 462-467 (1989). The Court explained that a broader interpretation of the term "utilized" in FACA would raise serious questions whether the statute "infringed unduly on the President's Article II power to nominate federal judges and violated the doctrine of separation of powers." *Id.* at 466-467. Another case found that an established canon of statutory construction applied with "special force" to provisions that would impinge on the President's foreign-affairs powers if construed broadly. *Sale v. Haitian Centers Council*, 509 U.S. 155, 188 (1993) (applying the presumption against extraterritorial application to construe the Refugee Act of 1980 as not governing in an overseas context where it could affect "foreign and military affairs for which the President has unique responsibility"). *See Application*

[1086] 6/23/17 Letter, President's Personal Counsel to Special Counsel's Office, at 2 n. 1.

of 28 U.S.C. § 458 to Presidential Appointments of Federal Judges, 19 Op. O.L.C. at 353-354 (discussing *Franklin, Public Citizen*, and *Sale*).

The Department of Justice has relied on this clear-statement principle to interpret certain statutes as not applying to the President at all, similar to the approach taken in *Franklin. See, e.g.*, Memorandum for Richard T. Burress, Office of the President, from Laurence H. Silberman, Deputy Attorney General, *Re: Conflict of Interest Problems Arising out of the President's Nomination of Nelson A. Rockefeller to be Vice President under the Twenty-Fifth Amendment to the Constitution*, at 2, 5 (Aug. 28, 1974) (criminal conflict-of-interest statute, 18 U.S.C. § 208, does not apply to the President). Other OLC opinions interpret statutory text not to apply to certain presidential or executive actions because of constitutional concerns. *See Application of 28 U.S.C. § 458 to Presidential Appointments of Federal Judges*, 19 Op. O.L.C. at 350-357 (consanguinity limitations on court appointments, 28 U.S.C. § 458, found inapplicable to "presidential appointments of judges to the federal judiciary"); *Constraints Imposed by 18 U.S.C. § 1913 on Lobbying Efforts*, 13 Op. O.L.C. 300, 304-306 (1989) (limitation on the use of appropriated funds for certain lobbying programs found inapplicable to certain communications by the President and executive officials).

But OLC has also recognized that this clear-statement rule "does not apply with respect to a statute that raises no separation of powers questions were it to be applied to the President," such as the federal bribery statute, 18 U.S.C. § 201. *Application of 28 U.S.C. § 458 to Presidential Appointments of Federal Judges*, 19 Op. O.L.C. at 357 n.11. OLC explained that "[a]pplication of § 201 raises no separation of powers question, let alone a serious one," because [t]he Constitution confers no power in the President to receive bribes." *Id.* In support of that conclusion, OLC noted constitutional provisions that forbid increases in the President's compensation while in office, "which is what a bribe would function to do," *id.* (citing U.S. CONST. ART. II, § 1, cl. 7), and the express constitutional power of "Congress to impeach [and convict] a President for, *inter alia*, bribery," *id.* (citing U.S. CONST. ART II, § 4).

Under OLC's analysis, Congress can permissibly criminalize certain obstructive conduct by the President, such as suborning perjury, intimidating witnesses, or fabricating evidence, because those prohibitions raise no separation-of-powers questions. *See Application of 28 U.S.C. § 458 to Presidential Appointments of Federal Judges*, 19 Op. O.L.C. at 357 n.11. The Constitution does not authorize the President to engage in such conduct, and those actions would transgress the President's duty to "take Care that the Laws be faithfully executed." U.S. CONST. ART II, §§ 3. In view of those clearly permissible applications of the obstruction statutes to the President, *Franklin*'s holding that the President is entirely excluded from a statute absent a clear statement would not apply in this context.

A more limited application of a clear-statement rule to exclude from the obstruction statutes only certain acts by the President—for example, removing prosecutors or ending investigations for corrupt reasons—would be difficult to implement as a matter of statutory interpretation. It is not obvious how a clear-statement rule would apply to an omnibus provision like Section 1512(c)(2) to exclude corruptly motivated obstructive acts only when carried out in the President's conduct of office. No statutory term could easily bear that specialized meaning. For example, the word "corruptly" has a well-established meaning that does not exclude exercises of official power for corrupt ends. Indeed, an established definition states that "corruptly" means action with an

170

434

U.S. Department of Justice

~~Attorney Work Product // May Contain Material Protected Under Fed. R. Crim. P. 6(e)~~

intent to secure an improper advantage "*inconsistent with official duty* and the rights of others." BALLENTINE'S LAW DICTIONARY 276 (3d ed. 1969) (emphasis added). And it would be contrary to ordinary rules of statutory construction to adopt an unconventional meaning of a statutory term only when applied to the President. *See United States v. Santos*, 553 U.S. 507, 522 (2008) (plurality opinion of Scalia, J.) (rejecting proposal to "giv[e] the same word, in the same statutory provision, different meanings in different factual contexts"); *cf. Public Citizen*, 491 U.S. at 462-467 (giving the term "utilized" in the FACA a uniform meaning to avoid constitutional questions). Nor could such an exclusion draw on a separate and established background interpretive presumption, such as the presumption against extraterritoriality applied in *Sale*. The principle that courts will construe a statute to avoid serious constitutional questions "is not a license for the judiciary to rewrite language enacted by the legislature." *Salinas v. United States*, 522 U.S. 52, 59-60 (1997). "It is one thing to acknowledge and accept . . . well defined (or even newly enunciated), generally applicable, background principles of assumed legislative intent. It is quite another to espouse the broad proposition that criminal statutes do not have to be read as broadly as they are written, but are subject to case-by-case exceptions." *Brogan v. United States*, 522 U.S. 398, 406 (1998*)*.

When a proposed construction "would thus function as an extra-textual limit on [a statute's] compass," thereby preventing the statute "from applying to a host of cases falling within its clear terms," *Loughrin*, 573 U.S. at 357, it is doubtful that the construction would reflect Congress's intent. That is particularly so with respect to obstruction statutes, which "have been given a broad and all-inclusive meaning." *Rainey*, 757 F.3d at 245 (discussing Sections 1503 and 1505) (internal quotation marks omitted). Accordingly, since no established principle of interpretation would exclude the presidential conduct we have investigated from statutes such as Sections 1503, 1505, 1512(b), and 1512(c)(2), we proceed to examine the separation-of-powers issues that could be raised as an Article II defense to the application of those statutes.

> 2. Separation-of-Powers Principles Support the Conclusion that Congress May Validly Prohibit Corrupt Obstructive Acts Carried Out Through the President's Official Powers

When Congress imposes a limitation on the exercise of Article II powers, the limitation's validity depends on whether the measure "disrupts the balance between the coordinate branches." *Nixon v. Administrator of General Services*, 433 U.S. 425, 443 (1977). "Even when a branch does not arrogate power to itself, . . . the separation-of-powers doctrine requires that a branch not impair another in the performance of its constitutional duties." *Loving v. United States*, 517 U.S. 748, 757 (1996). The "separation of powers does not mean," however, "that the branches 'ought to have no partial agency in, or no controul over the acts of each other.'" *Clinton v. Jones*, 520 U.S. 681, 703 (1997) (quoting James Madison, The Federalist No. 47, pp. 325–326 (J. Cooke ed. 1961) (emphasis omitted)). In this context, a balancing test applies to assess separation-of-powers issues. Applying that test here, we concluded that Congress can validly make obstruction-of-justice statutes applicable to corruptly motivated official acts of the President without impermissibly undermining his Article II functions.

a. The Supreme Court's Separation-of-Powers Balancing Test Applies In This Context

A congressionally imposed limitation on presidential action is assessed to determine "the extent to which it prevents the Executive Branch from accomplishing its constitutionally assigned functions," and, if the "potential for disruption is present[,] . . . whether that impact is justified by an overriding need to promote objectives within the constitutional authority of Congress." *Administrator of General Services*, 433 U.S. at 443; *see Nixon v. Fitzgerald*, 457 U.S. 731,753-754 (1982); *United States v. Nixon*, 418 U.S. 683, 706-707 (1974). That balancing test applies to a congressional regulation of presidential power through the obstruction-of-justice laws. [1087]

When an Article II power has not been "explicitly assigned by the text of the Constitution to be within the sole province of the President, but rather was thought to be encompassed within the general grant to the President of the 'executive Power,'" the Court has balanced competing constitutional considerations. *Public Citizen*, 491 U.S. at 484 (Kennedy, J., concurring in the judgment, joined by Rehnquist, C.J., and O'Connor, J.). As Justice Kennedy noted in *Public Citizen*, the Court has applied a balancing test to restrictions on "the President's power to remove Executive officers, a power [that] . . . is not conferred by any explicit provision in the text of the Constitution (as is the appointment power), but rather is inferred to be a necessary part of the grant of the 'executive Power.'" *Id.* (citing *Morrison v. Olson*, 487 U.S. 654, 694 (1988), and *Myers v. United States*, 272 U.S. 52, 115–116 (1926)). Consistent with that statement, *Morrison* sustained a good-cause limitation on the removal of an inferior officer with defined prosecutorial responsibilities after determining that the limitation did not impermissibly undermine the President's ability to perform his Article II functions. 487 U.S. at 691-693, 695-696. The Court has also evaluated other general executive-power claims through a balancing test. For example, the Court evaluated the President's claim of an absolute privilege for presidential communications about his official acts by balancing that interest against the Judicial Branch's need for evidence in a criminal case. *United States v. Nixon, supra* (recognizing a qualified constitutional privilege for presidential communications on official matters). The Court has also upheld a law that provided for archival access to presidential records despite a claim of absolute presidential privilege over the records. *Administrator of General Services*, 433 U.S. at 443-445, 451-455. The analysis in those cases supports applying a balancing test to assess the constitutionality of applying the obstruction-of-justice statutes to presidential exercises of executive power.

Only in a few instances has the Court applied a different framework. When the President's power is "both 'exclusive' and 'conclusive' on the issue," Congress is precluded from regulating its exercise. *Zivotofsky v. Kerry*, 135 S. Ct. 2076, 2084 (2015). In *Zivotofsky*, for example, the Court followed "Justice Jackson's familiar tripartite framework" in *Youngstown Sheet & Tube Co. v. Sawyer*, 343 U.S. 579, 635-638 (1952) (Jackson, J., concurring), and held that the President's

---

[1087] OLC applied such a balancing test in concluding that the President is not subject to criminal prosecution while in office, relying on many of the same precedents discussed in this section. *See A Sitting President's Amenability to Indictment and Criminal Prosecution*, 24 Op. O.L.C. 222, 237-238, 244-245 (2000) (relying on, *inter alia*, *United States v. Nixon*, *Nixon v. Fitzgerald*, and *Clinton v. Jones*, and quoting the legal standard from *Administrator of General Services v. Nixon* that is applied in the text). OLC recognized that "[t]he balancing analysis" it had initially relied on in finding that a sitting President is immune from prosecution had "been adopted as the appropriate mode of analysis by the Court." *Id.* at 244.

172

authority to recognize foreign nations is exclusive. *Id.* at 2083, 2094. *See also Public Citizen* 491 U.S. at 485-486 (Kennedy, J., concurring in the judgment) (citing the power to grant pardons under U.S. CONST., ART. II, § 2, cl. 1, and the Presentment Clauses for legislation, U.S. CONST., ART. I, § 7, Cls. 2, 3, as examples of exclusive presidential powers by virtue of constitutional text).

But even when a power is exclusive, "Congress' powers, and its central role in making laws, give it substantial authority regarding many of the policy determinations that precede and follow" the President's act. *Zivotofsky*, 135 S. Ct. at 2087. For example, although the President's power to grant pardons is exclusive and not subject to congressional regulation, *see United States v. Klein*, 80 U.S. (13 Wall.) 128, 147-148 (1872), Congress has the authority to prohibit the corrupt use of "anything of value" to influence the testimony of another person in a judicial, congressional, or agency proceeding, 18 U.S.C. § 201(b)(3)—which would include the offer or promise of a pardon to induce a person to testify falsely or not to testify at all. The offer of a pardon would precede the act of pardoning and thus be within Congress's power to regulate even if the pardon itself is not. Just as the Speech or Debate Clause, U.S. CONST. ART. I, § 6, cl.1, absolutely protects legislative acts, but not a legislator's "taking or agreeing to take money for a promise to act in a certain way . . . for it is taking the bribe, not performance of the illicit compact, that is a criminal act," *United States v. Brewster*, 408 U.S. 501, 526 (1972) (emphasis omitted), the promise of a pardon to corruptly influence testimony would not be a constitutionally immunized act. The application of obstruction statutes to such promises therefore would raise no serious separation-of-powers issue.

b. The Effect of Obstruction-of-Justice Statutes on the President's Capacity to Perform His Article II Responsibilities is Limited

Under the Supreme Court's balancing test for analyzing separation-of-powers issues, the first task is to assess the degree to which applying obstruction-of-justice statutes to presidential actions affects the President's ability to carry out his Article II responsibilities. *Administrator of General Services*, 433 U.S. at 443. As discussed above, applying obstruction-of-justice statutes to presidential conduct that does not involve the President's conduct of office—such as influencing the testimony of witnesses—is constitutionally unproblematic. The President has no more right than other citizens to impede official proceedings by corruptly influencing witness testimony. The conduct would be equally improper whether effectuated through direct efforts to produce false testimony or suppress the truth, or through the actual, threatened, or promised use of official powers to achieve the same result.

The President's action in curtailing criminal investigations or prosecutions, or discharging law enforcement officials, raises different questions. Each type of action involves the exercise of executive discretion in furtherance of the President's duty to "take Care that the Laws be faithfully executed." U.S. CONST., ART. II, § 3. Congress may not supplant the President's exercise of executive power to supervise prosecutions or to remove officers who occupy law enforcement positions. *See Bowsher v. Synar*, 478 U.S. 714, 726-727 (1986) ("Congress cannot reserve for itself the power of removal of an officer charged with the execution of the laws except by impeachment. . . . [Because t]he structure of the Constitution does not permit Congress to execute the laws, . . . [t]his kind of congressional control over the execution of the laws . . . is constitutionally impermissible."). Yet the obstruction-of-justice statutes do not aggrandize power in Congress or usurp executive authority. Instead, they impose a discrete limitation on conduct

173

U.S. Department of Justice

~~Attorney Work Product // May Contain Material Protected Under Fed. R. Crim. P. 6(e)~~

only when it is taken with the "corrupt" intent to obstruct justice. The obstruction statutes thus would restrict presidential action only by prohibiting the President from acting to obstruct official proceedings for the improper purpose of protecting his own interests. *See* Volume II, Section III.A.3, *supra*.

The direct effect on the President's freedom of action would correspondingly be a limited one. A preclusion of "corrupt" official action is not a major intrusion on Article II powers. For example, the proper supervision of criminal law does not demand freedom for the President to act with the intention of shielding himself from criminal punishment, avoiding financial liability, or preventing personal embarrassment. To the contrary, a statute that prohibits official action undertaken for such personal purposes furthers, rather than hinders, the impartial and evenhanded administration of the law. And the Constitution does not mandate that the President have unfettered authority to direct investigations or prosecutions, with no limits whatsoever, in order to carry out his Article II functions. *See Heckler v. Chaney*, 470 U.S. 821, 833 (1985) ("Congress may limit an agency's exercise of enforcement power if it wishes, either by setting substantive priorities, or by otherwise circumscribing an agency's power to discriminate among issues or cases it will pursue."); *United States v. Nixon*, 418 U.S. at 707 ("[t]o read the Art. II powers of the President as providing an absolute privilege [to withhold confidential communications from a criminal trial]. . . would upset the constitutional balance of 'a workable government' and gravely impair the role of the courts under Art. III").

Nor must the President have unfettered authority to remove all Executive Branch officials involved in the execution of the laws. The Constitution establishes that Congress has legislative authority to structure the Executive Branch by authorizing Congress to create executive departments and officer positions and to specify how inferior officers are appointed. *E.g.*, U.S. CONST., ART. I, § 8, cl. 18 (Necessary and Proper Clause); ART. II, § 2, cl. 1 (Opinions Clause); ART. II, § 2, cl. 2 (Appointments Clause); *see Free Enterprise Fund*, 561 U.S. at 499. While the President's removal power is an important means of ensuring that officers faithfully execute the law, Congress has a recognized authority to place certain limits on removal. *Id.* at 493-495.

The President's removal powers are at their zenith with respect to principal officers—that is, officers who must be appointed by the President and who report to him directly. *See Free Enterprise Fund*, 561 U.S. at 493, 500. The President's "exclusive and illimitable power of removal" of those principal officers furthers "the President's ability to ensure that the laws are faithfully executed." *Id.* at 493, 498 (internal quotation marks omitted); *Myers*, 272 U.S. at 627. Thus, "there are some 'purely executive' officials who must be removable by the President at will if he is able to accomplish his constitutional role." *Morrison*, 487 U.S. at 690; *Myers*, 272 U.S. at 134 (the President's "cabinet officers must do his will," and "[t]he moment that he loses confidence in the intelligence, ability, judgment, or loyalty of any one of them, he must have the power to remove him without delay"); *cf. Humphrey's Executor v. United States*, 295 U.S. 602 (1935) (Congress has the power to create independent agencies headed by principal officers removable only for good cause). In light of those constitutional precedents, it may be that the obstruction statutes could not be constitutionally applied to limit the removal of a cabinet officer such as the Attorney General. *See* 5 U.S.C. § 101; 28 U.S.C. § 503. In that context, at least absent circumstances showing that the President was clearly attempting to thwart accountability for personal conduct while evading ordinary political checks and balances, even the highly limited

174

regulation imposed by the obstruction statutes could possibly intrude too deeply on the President's freedom to select and supervise the members of his cabinet.

The removal of inferior officers, in contrast, need not necessarily be at will for the President to fulfill his constitutionally assigned role in managing the Executive Branch. "[I]nferior officers are officers whose work is directed and supervised at some level by other officers appointed by the President with the Senate's consent." *Free Enterprise Fund*, 561 U.S. at 510 (quoting *Edmond v. United States*, 520 U.S. 651, 663 (1997)) (internal quotation marks omitted). The Supreme Court has long recognized Congress's authority to place for-cause limitations on the President's removal of "inferior Officers" whose appointment may be vested in the head of a department. U.S. CONST. ART. II, § 2, cl. 2. *See United States v. Perkins*, 116 U.S. 483, 485 (1886) ("The constitutional authority in Congress to thus vest the appointment [of inferior officers in the heads of departments] implies authority to limit, restrict, and regulate the removal by such laws as Congress may enact in relation to the officers so appointed") (quoting lower court decision); *Morrison*, 487 U.S. at 689 n. 27 (citing *Perkins*); *accord id.* at 723-724 & n.4 (Scalia, J., dissenting) (recognizing that *Perkins* is "established" law); *see also Free Enterprise Fund*, 561 U.S. at 493-495 (citing *Perkins* and *Morrison*). The category of inferior officers includes both the FBI Director and the Special Counsel, each of whom reports to the Attorney General. *See* 28 U.S.C. §§ 509, 515(a), 531; 28 C.F.R. Part 600. Their work is thus "directed and supervised" by a presidentially-appointed, Senate-confirmed officer. *See In re: Grand Jury Investigation*, ___ F.3d ___, 2019 WL 921692, at *3-*4 (D.C. Cir. Feb. 26, 2019) (holding that the Special Counsel is an "inferior officer" for constitutional purposes).

Where the Constitution permits Congress to impose a good-cause limitation on the removal of an Executive Branch officer, the Constitution should equally permit Congress to bar removal for the corrupt purpose of obstructing justice. Limiting the range of permissible reasons for removal to exclude a "corrupt" purpose imposes a lesser restraint on the President than requiring an affirmative showing of good cause. It follows that for such inferior officers, Congress may constitutionally restrict the President's removal authority if that authority was exercised for the corrupt purpose of obstructing justice. And even if a particular inferior officer's position might be of such importance to the execution of the laws that the President must have at-will removal authority, the obstruction-of-justice statutes could still be constitutionally applied to forbid removal for a corrupt reason.[1088] A narrow and discrete limitation on removal that precluded corrupt action would leave ample room for all other considerations, including disagreement over policy or loss of confidence in the officer's judgment or commitment. A corrupt-purpose prohibition therefore would not undermine the President's ability to perform his Article II functions. Accordingly, because the separation-of-powers question is "whether the removal restrictions are of such a nature that they impede the President's ability to perform his constitutional duty," *Morrison*, 487 U.S. at 691, a restriction on removing an inferior officer for a

---

[1088] Although the FBI director is an inferior officer, he is appointed by the President and removable by him at will, *see* 28 U.S.C. § 532 note, and it is not clear that Congress could constitutionally provide the FBI director with good-cause tenure protection. *See* OLC, *Constitutionality of Legislation Extending the Term of the FBI Director*, 2011 WL 2566125, at *3 (O.L.C. June 20, 2011) ("tenure protection for an officer with the FBI Director's broad investigative, administrative, and policymaking responsibilities would raise a serious constitutional question whether Congress had 'impede[d] the President's ability to perform his constitutional duty' to take care that the laws be faithfully executed") (quoting *Morrison*, 487 U.S. at 691).

corrupt reason—a reason grounded in achieving personal rather than official ends—does not seriously hinder the President's performance of his duties. The President retains broad latitude to supervise investigations and remove officials, circumscribed in this context only by the requirement that he not act for corrupt personal purposes.[1089]

c. Congress Has Power to Protect Congressional, Grand Jury, and Judicial Proceedings Against Corrupt Acts from Any Source

Where a law imposes a burden on the President's performance of Article II functions, separation-of-powers analysis considers whether the statutory measure "is justified by an overriding need to promote objectives within the constitutional authority of Congress." *Administrator of General Services*, 433 U.S. at 443. Here, Congress enacted the obstruction-of-justice statutes to protect, among other things, the integrity of its own proceedings, grand jury investigations, and federal criminal trials. Those objectives are within Congress's authority and serve strong governmental interests.

i. Congress has Article I authority to define generally applicable criminal law and apply it to all persons—including the President. Congress clearly has authority to protect its own legislative functions against corrupt efforts designed to impede legitimate fact-gathering and lawmaking efforts. *See Watkins v. United States*, 354 U.S. 178, 187, 206-207 (1957); *Chapman v. United States*, 5 App. D.C. 122, 130 (1895). Congress also has authority to establish a system of federal courts, which includes the power to protect the judiciary against obstructive acts. *See* U.S. CONST. ART. I, § 8, cls. 9, 18 ("The Congress shall have Power . . . To constitute Tribunals inferior to the supreme Court" and "To make all Laws which shall be necessary and proper for carrying into Execution the foregoing powers"). The long lineage of the obstruction-of-justice statutes, which can be traced to at least 1831, attests to the necessity for that protection. *See An Act Declaratory of the Law Concerning Contempts of Court*, 4 Stat. 487-488 § 2 (1831) (making it a crime if "any person or persons shall corruptly . . . endeavor to influence, intimidate, or impede any juror, witness, or officer, in any court of the United States, in the discharge of his duty, or shall, corruptly . . . obstruct, or impede, or endeavor to obstruct or impede, the due administration of justice therein").

ii. The Article III courts have an equally strong interest in being protected against obstructive acts, whatever their source. As the Supreme Court explained in *United States v. Nixon*, a "primary constitutional duty of the Judicial Branch" is "to do justice in criminal prosecutions." 418 U.S. at 707; *accord Cheney v. United States District Court for the District of Columbia*, 542 U.S. 367, 384 (2004). In *Nixon*, the Court rejected the President's claim of absolute executive privilege because "the allowance of the privilege to withhold evidence that is demonstrably

---

[1089] The obstruction statutes do not disqualify the President from acting in a case simply because he has a personal interest in it or because his own conduct may be at issue. As the Department of Justice has made clear, a claim of a conflict of interest, standing alone, cannot deprive the President of the ability to fulfill his constitutional function. *See, e.g.*, OLC, *Application of 28 U.S.C. § 458 to Presidential Appointments of Federal Judges*, 19 O.L.C. Op. at 356 (citing Memorandum for Richard T. Burress, Office of the President, from Laurence H. Silberman, Deputy Attorney General, *Re: Conflict of Interest Problems Arising out of the President's Nomination of Nelson A. Rockefeller to be Vice President under the Twenty-Fifth Amendment to the Constitution*, at 2, 5 (Aug. 28, 1974)).

U.S. Department of Justice

~~Attorney Work Product // May Contain Material Protected Under Fed. R. Crim. P. 6(e)~~

relevant in a criminal trial would cut deeply into the guarantee of due process of law and gravely impair the basic function of the courts." 407 U.S. at 712. As *Nixon* illustrates, the need to safeguard judicial integrity is a compelling constitutional interest. *See id.* at 709 (noting that the denial of full disclosure of the facts surrounding relevant presidential communications threatens "[t]he very integrity of the judicial system and public confidence in the system").

iii. Finally, the grand jury cannot achieve its constitutional purpose absent protection from corrupt acts. Serious federal criminal charges generally reach the Article III courts based on an indictment issued by a grand jury. *Cobbledick v. United States*, 309 U.S. 323, 327 (1940) ("The Constitution itself makes the grand jury a part of the judicial process."). And the grand jury's function is enshrined in the Fifth Amendment. U.S. CONST. AMEND. V. ("[n]o person shall be held to answer" for a serious crime "unless on a presentment or indictment of a Grand Jury"). "[T]he whole theory of [the grand jury's] function is that it belongs to no branch of the institutional government, serving as a kind of buffer or referee between the Government and the people," *United States v. Williams*, 504 U.S. 36, 47 (1992), "pledged to indict no one because of prejudice and to free no one because of special favor." *Costello v. United States*, 350 U.S. 359, 362 (1956). If the grand jury were not protected against corrupt interference from all persons, its function as an independent charging body would be thwarted. And an impartial grand jury investigation to determine whether probable cause exists to indict is vital to the criminal justice process.

*   *   *

The final step in the constitutional balancing process is to assess whether the separation-of-powers doctrine permits Congress to take action within its constitutional authority notwithstanding the potential impact on Article II functions. *See Administrator of General Services*, 433 U.S. at 443; *see also Morrison*, 487 U.S. at 691-693, 695-696; *United States v. Nixon*, 418 U.S. at 711-712. In the case of the obstruction-of-justice statutes, our assessment of the weighing of interests leads us to conclude that Congress has the authority to impose the limited restrictions contained in those statutes on the President's official conduct to protect the integrity of important functions of other branches of government.

A general ban on corrupt action does not unduly intrude on the President's responsibility to "take Care that the Laws be faithfully executed." U.S. CONST. ART II, §§ 3.[1090] To the contrary, the concept of "faithful execution" connotes the use of power in the interest of the public, not in the office holder's personal interests. *See* 1 Samuel Johnson, *A Dictionary of the English Language* 763 (1755) ("faithfully" def. 3: "[w]ith strict adherence to duty and allegiance"). And immunizing the President from the generally applicable criminal prohibition against corrupt obstruction of official proceedings would seriously impair Congress's power to enact laws "to promote objectives within [its] constitutional authority," *Administrator of General Services*, 433 U.S. at 425—*i.e.*, protecting the integrity of its own proceedings and the proceedings of Article III courts and grand juries.

[1090] As noted above, the President's selection and removal of principal executive officers may have a unique constitutional status.

Accordingly, based on the analysis above, we were not persuaded by the argument that the President has blanket constitutional immunity to engage in acts that would corruptly obstruct justice through the exercise of otherwise-valid Article II powers. [1091]

3. Ascertaining Whether the President Violated the Obstruction Statutes Would Not Chill his Performance of his Article II Duties

Applying the obstruction statutes to the President's official conduct would involve determining as a factual matter whether he engaged in an obstructive act, whether the act had a nexus to official proceedings, and whether he was motivated by corrupt intent. But applying those standards to the President's official conduct should not hinder his ability to perform his Article II duties. *Cf. Nixon v. Fitzgerald*, 457 U.S. at 752-753 & n.32 (taking into account chilling effect on the President in adopting a constitutional rule of presidential immunity from private civil damages action based on official duties). Several safeguards would prevent a chilling effect: the existence of settled legal standards, the presumption of regularity in prosecutorial actions, and the existence of evidentiary limitations on probing the President's motives. And historical experience confirms that no impermissible chill should exist.

a. As an initial matter, the term "corruptly" sets a demanding standard. It requires a concrete showing that a person acted with an intent to obtain an "improper advantage for [him]self or someone else, inconsistent with official duty and the rights of others." BALLENTINE'S LAW DICTIONARY 276 (3d ed. 1969); *see United States v. Pasha*, 797 F.3d 1122, 1132 (D.C. Cir. 2015); *Aguilar*, 515 U.S. at 616 (Scalia, J., concurring in part and dissenting in part). That standard parallels the President's constitutional obligation to ensure the faithful execution of the laws. And virtually everything that the President does in the routine conduct of office will have a clear governmental purpose and will not be contrary to his official duty. Accordingly, the President has no reason to be chilled in those actions because, in virtually all instances, there will be no credible basis for suspecting a corrupt personal motive.

That point is illustrated by examples of conduct that would and would not satisfy the stringent corrupt-motive standard. Direct or indirect action by the President to end a criminal investigation into his own or his family members' conduct to protect against personal embarrassment or legal liability would constitute a core example of corruptly motivated conduct. So too would action to halt an enforcement proceeding that directly and adversely affected the President's financial interests for the purpose of protecting those interests. In those examples,

---

[1091] A possible remedy through impeachment for abuses of power would not substitute for potential criminal liability after a President leaves office. Impeachment would remove a President from office, but would not address the underlying culpability of the conduct or serve the usual purposes of the criminal law. Indeed, the Impeachment Judgment Clause recognizes that criminal law plays an independent role in addressing an official's conduct, distinct from the political remedy of impeachment. *See* U.S. CONST. ART. I, § 3, cl. 7. Impeachment is also a drastic and rarely invoked remedy, and Congress is not restricted to relying only on impeachment, rather than making criminal law applicable to a former President, as OLC has recognized. *A Sitting President's Amenability to Indictment and Criminal Prosecution*, 24 Op. O.L.C. at 255 ("Recognizing an immunity from prosecution for a sitting President would not preclude such prosecution once the President's term is over or he is otherwise removed from office by resignation or impeachment.").

official power is being used for the purpose of protecting the President's personal interests. In contrast, the President's actions to serve political or policy interests would not qualify as corrupt. The President's role as head of the government necessarily requires him to take into account political factors in making policy decisions that affect law-enforcement actions and proceedings. For instance, the President's decision to curtail a law-enforcement investigation to avoid international friction would not implicate the obstruction-of-justice statutes. The criminal law does not seek to regulate the consideration of such political or policy factors in the conduct of government. And when legitimate interests animate the President's conduct, those interests will almost invariably be readily identifiable based on objective factors. Because the President's conduct in those instances will obviously fall outside the zone of obstruction law, no chilling concern should arise.

b. There is also no reason to believe that investigations, let alone prosecutions, would occur except in highly unusual circumstances when a credible factual basis exists to believe that obstruction occurred. Prosecutorial action enjoys a presumption of regularity: absent "clear evidence to the contrary, courts presume that [prosecutors] have properly discharged their official duties." *Armstrong*, 517 U.S. at 464 (*quoting United States v. Chemical Foundation, Inc.*, 272 U.S. 1, 14–15 (1926)). The presumption of prosecutorial regularity would provide even greater protection to the President than exists in routine cases given the prominence and sensitivity of any matter involving the President and the likelihood that such matters will be subject to thorough and careful review at the most senior levels of the Department of Justice. Under OLC's opinion that a sitting President is entitled to immunity from indictment, only a successor Administration would be able to prosecute a former President. But that consideration does not suggest that a President would have any basis for fearing abusive investigations or prosecutions after leaving office. There are "obvious political checks" against initiating a baseless investigation or prosecution of a former President. *See Administrator of General Services*, 433 U.S. at 448 (considering political checks in separation-of-powers analysis). And the Attorney General holds "the power to conduct the criminal litigation of the United States Government," *United States v. Nixon*, 418 U.S. at 694 (citing 28 U.S.C. § 516), which provides a strong institutional safeguard against politicized investigations or prosecutions. [1092]

[1092] Similar institutional safeguards protect Department of Justice officers and line prosecutors against unfounded investigations into prosecutorial acts. Prosecutors are generally barred from participating in matters implicating their personal interests, *see* 28 C.F.R. § 45.2, and are instructed not to be influenced by their "own professional or personal circumstances," Justice Manual § 9-27.260, so prosecutors would not frequently be in a position to take action that could be perceived as corrupt and personally motivated. And if such cases arise, criminal investigation would be conducted by responsible officials at the Department of Justice, who can be presumed to refrain from pursuing an investigation absent a credible factual basis. Those facts distinguish the criminal context from the common-law rule of prosecutorial immunity, which protects against the threat of suit by "a defendant [who] often will transform his resentment at being prosecuted into the ascription of improper and malicious actions." *Imbler v. Pachtman*, 424 U.S. 409, 425 (1976). As the Supreme Court has noted, the existence of civil immunity does not justify criminal immunity. *See O'Shea v. Littleton*, 414 U.S. 488, 503 (1974) ("Whatever may be the case with respect to civil liability generally, . . . we have never held that the performance of the duties of judicial, legislative, or executive officers, requires or contemplates the immunization of otherwise criminal deprivation of constitutional rights.") (citations omitted).

These considerations distinguish the Supreme Court's holding in *Nixon v. Fitzgerald* that, in part because inquiries into the President's motives would be "highly intrusive," the President is absolutely immune from private civil damages actions based on his official conduct. 457 U.S. at 756-757. As *Fitzgerald* recognized, "there is a lesser public interest in actions for civil damages than, for example, in criminal prosecutions." *Fitzgerald*, 457 U.S. at 754 n.37; *see Cheney*, 542 U.S. at 384. And private actions are not subject to the institutional protections of an action under the supervision of the Attorney General and subject to a presumption of regularity. *Armstrong*, 517 U.S. at 464.

c. In the rare cases in which a substantial and credible basis justifies conducting an investigation of the President, the process of examining his motivations to determine whether he acted for a corrupt purpose need not have a chilling effect. Ascertaining the President's motivations would turn on any explanation he provided to justify his actions, the advice he received, the circumstances surrounding the actions, and the regularity or irregularity of the process he employed to make decisions. But grand juries and courts would not have automatic access to confidential presidential communications on those matters; rather, they could be presented in official proceedings only on a showing of sufficient need. *Nixon*, 418 U.S. at 712; *In re Sealed Case*, 121 F.3d 729, 754, 756-757 (D.C. Cir. 1997); *see also Administrator of General Services*, 433 U.S. at 448-449 (former President can invoke presidential communications privilege, although successor's failure to support the claim "detracts from [its] weight").

In any event, probing the President's intent in a criminal matter is unquestionably constitutional in at least one context: the offense of bribery turns on the corrupt intent to receive a thing of value in return for being influenced in official action. 18 U.S.C. § 201(b)(2). There can be no serious argument against the President's potential criminal liability for bribery offenses, notwithstanding the need to ascertain his purpose and intent. *See* U.S. CONST. ART. I, § 3; ART. II, § 4; *see also Application of 28 U.S.C. § 458 to Presidential Appointments of Federal Judges*, 19 Op. O.L.C. at 357 n.11 ("Application of § 201[to the President] raises no separation of powers issue, let alone a serious one.").

d. Finally, history provides no reason to believe that any asserted chilling effect justifies exempting the President from the obstruction laws. As a historical matter, Presidents have very seldom been the subjects of grand jury investigations. And it is rarer still for circumstances to raise even the possibility of a corrupt personal motive for arguably obstructive action through the President's use of official power. Accordingly, the President's conduct of office should not be chilled based on hypothetical concerns about the possible application of a corrupt-motive standard in this context.

* * *

In sum, contrary to the position taken by the President's counsel, we concluded that, in light of the Supreme Court precedent governing separation-of-powers issues, we had a valid basis for investigating the conduct at issue in this report. In our view, the application of the obstruction statutes would not impermissibly burden the President's performance of his Article II function to supervise prosecutorial conduct or to remove inferior law-enforcement officers. And the protection of the criminal justice system from corrupt acts by any person—including the President—accords with the fundamental principle of our government that "[n]o [person] in this

180

U.S. Department of Justice

Attorney Work Product // May Contain Material Protected Under Fed. R. Crim. P. 6(e)

country is so high that he is above the law." *United States v. Lee*, 106 U.S. 196, 220 (1882); *see also Clinton v. Jones*, 520 U.S. at 697; *United States v. Nixon, supra.*

U.S. Department of Justice
~~Attorney Work Product // May Contain Material Protected Under Fed. R. Crim. P. 6(e)~~

IV. CONCLUSION

Because we determined not to make a traditional prosecutorial judgment, we did not draw ultimate conclusions about the President's conduct. The evidence we obtained about the President's actions and intent presents difficult issues that would need to be resolved if we were making a traditional prosecutorial judgment. At the same time, if we had confidence after a thorough investigation of the facts that the President clearly did not commit obstruction of justice, we would so state. Based on the facts and the applicable legal standards, we are unable to reach that judgment. Accordingly, while this report does not conclude that the President committed a crime, it also does not exonerate him.

Appendix A

U.S. Department of Justice

~~Attorney Work Product // May Contain Material Protected Under Fed. R. Crim. P. 6(e)~~

Office of the Deputy Attorney General
Washington, D.C. 20530

ORDER NO. 3915-2017

APPOINTMENT OF SPECIAL COUNSEL
TO INVESTIGATE RUSSIAN INTERFERENCE WITH THE
2016 PRESIDENTIAL ELECTION AND RELATED MATTERS

By virtue of the authority vested in me as Acting Attorney General, including 28 U.S.C. §§ 509, 510, and 515, in order to discharge my responsibility to provide supervision and management of the Department of Justice, and to ensure a full and thorough investigation of the Russian government's efforts to interfere in the 2016 presidential election, I hereby order as follows:

(a)   Robert S. Mueller III is appointed to serve as Special Counsel for the United States Department of Justice.

(b)   The Special Counsel is authorized to conduct the investigation confirmed by then-FBI Director James B. Comey in testimony before the House Permanent Select Committee on Intelligence on March 20, 2017, including:

    (i)   any links and/or coordination between the Russian government and individuals associated with the campaign of President Donald Trump; and

    (ii)   any matters that arose or may arise directly from the investigation; and

    (iii)   any other matters within the scope of 28 C.F.R. § 600.4(a).

(c)   If the Special Counsel believes it is necessary and appropriate, the Special Counsel is authorized to prosecute federal crimes arising from the investigation of these matters.

(d)   Sections 600.4 through 600.10 of Title 28 of the Code of Federal Regulations are applicable to the Special Counsel.

_5/17/17_
Date

Rod J. Rosenstein
Acting Attorney General

A-1

Appendix B

APPENDIX B: GLOSSARY

The following glossary contains names and brief descriptions of individuals and entities referenced in the two volumes of this report. It is not intended to be comprehensive and is intended only to assist a reader in the reading the rest of the report.

Referenced Persons

Agalarov, Aras	Russian real-estate developer (owner of the Crocus Group); met Donald Trump in connection with the Miss Universe pageant and helped arrange the June 9, 2016 meeting at Trump Tower between Natalia Veselnitskaya and Trump Campaign officials.
Agalarov, Emin	Performer, executive vice president of Crocus Group, and son of Aras Agalarov; helped arrange the June 9, 2016 meeting at Trump Tower between Natalia Veselnitskaya and Trump Campaign officials.
Akhmetov, Rinat	Former member in the Ukrainian parliament who hired Paul Manafort to conduct work for Ukrainian political party, the Party of Regions.
Akhmetshin, Rinat	U.S. lobbyist and associate of Natalia Veselnitskaya who attended the June 9, 2016 meeting at Trump Tower between Veselnitskaya and Trump Campaign officials.
Aslanov, Dzheykhun (Jay)	Head of U.S. department of the Internet Research Agency, which engaged in an "active measures" social media campaign to interfere in the 2016 U.S. presidential election.
Assange, Julian	Founder of WikiLeaks, which in 2016 posted on the internet documents stolen from entities and individuals affiliated with the Democratic Party.
Aven, Petr	Chairman of the board of Alfa-Bank who attempted outreach to the Presidential Transition Team in connection with anticipated post-election sanctions.
Bannon, Stephen (Steve)	White House chief strategist and senior counselor to President Trump (Jan. 2017 – Aug. 2017); chief executive of the Trump Campaign.
Baranov, Andrey	Director of investor relations at Russian state-owned oil company, Rosneft, and associate of Carter Page.
Berkowitz, Avi	Assistant to Jared Kushner.
Boente, Dana	Acting Attorney General (Jan. 2017 – Feb. 2017); Acting Deputy Attorney General (Feb. 2017 – Apr. 2017).
Bogacheva, Anna	Internet Research Agency employee who worked on "active measures" social media campaign to interfere in in the 2016 U.S. presidential election; traveled to the United States under false pretenses in 2014.
Bossert, Thomas (Tom)	Former homeland security advisor to the President who also served as a senior official on the Presidential Transition Team.

Boyarkin, Viktor	Employee of Russian oligarch Oleg Deripaska.
Boyd, Charles	Chairman of the board of directors at the Center for the National Interest, a U.S.-based think tank with operations in and connections to Russia.
Boyko, Yuriy	Member of the Ukrainian political party Opposition Bloc and member of the Ukrainian parliament.
Brand, Rachel	Associate Attorney General (May 2017 – Feb. 2018).
Browder, William (Bill)	Founder of Hermitage Capital Management who lobbied in favor of the Magnitsky Act, which imposed financial and travel sanctions on Russian officials.
Bulatov, Alexander	Russian intelligence official who associated with Carter Page in 2008.
Burchik, Mikhail	Executive director of the Internet Research Agency, which engaged in an "active measures" social media campaign to interfere in the 2016 U.S. presidential election.
Burck, William	Personal attorney to Don McGahn, White House Counsel.
Burnham, James	Attorney in the White House Counsel's Office who attended January 2017 meetings between Sally Yates and Donald McGahn.
Burt, Richard	Former U.S. ambassador who had done work Alfa-Bank and was a board member of the Center for the National Interest.
Bystrov, Mikhail	General director of the Internet Research Agency, which engaged in an "active measures" social media campaign to interfere in the 2016 U.S. presidential election.
Calamari, Matt	Chief operating officer for the Trump Organization.
Caputo, Michael	Trump Campaign advisor.
Chaika, Yuri	Prosecutor general of the Russian Federation who also maintained a relationship with Aras Agalarov.
Christie, Chris	Former Governor of New Jersey.
Clapper, James	Director of National Intelligence (Aug. 2010 – Jan. 2017).
Clovis, Samuel Jr.	Chief policy advisor and national co-chair of the Trump Campaign.
Coats, Dan	Director of National Intelligence.
Cobb, Ty	Special Counsel to the President (July 2017 – May 2018).
Cohen, Michael	Former vice president to the Trump Organization and special counsel to Donald Trump who spearheaded an effort to build a Trump-branded property in Moscow. He admitted to lying to Congress about the project.
Comey, James Jr.	Director of the Federal Bureau of Investigation (Sept. 4, 2013 – May 9, 2017).

B-2

Conway, Kellyanne	Counselor to President Trump and manager of the Trump Campaign.
Corallo, Mark	Spokesman for President Trump's personal legal team (June 2017 – July 2017).
Corsi, Jerome	Author and political commentator who formerly worked for WorldNetDaily and InfoWars. ▉Harm to Ongoing Matter▉
Costello, Robert	Attorney who represented he had a close relationship with Rudolph Giuliani, the President's personal counsel.
Credico, Randolph (Randy)	Radio talk show host who interviewed Julian Assange in 2016. ▉ Harm to Ongoing Matter ▉
Davis, Richard (Rick) Jr.	Partner with Pegasus Sustainable Century Merchant Bank, business partner of Paul Manafort, and co-founder of the Davis Manafort lobbying firm.
Dearborn, Rick	Former White House deputy chief of staff for policy who previously served as chief of staff to Senator Jeff Sessions.
Dempsey, Michael	Office of Director of National Intelligence official who recalled discussions with Dan Coats after Coats's meeting with President Trump on March 22, 2017.
Denman, Diana	Delegate to 2016 Republican National Convention who proposed a platform plank amendment that included armed support for Ukraine.
Deripaska, Oleg	Russian businessman with ties to Vladimir Putin who hired Paul Manafort for consulting work between 2005 and 2009.
Dhillon, Uttam	Attorney in the White House Counsel's Office (Jan. 2017 – June 2018).
Dmitriev, Kirill	Head of the Russian Direct Investment Fund (RDIF); met with Erik Prince in the Seychelles in January 2017 and, separately, drafted a U.S.-Russia reconciliation plan with Rick Gerson.
Donaldson, Annie	Chief of staff to White House Counsel Donald McGahn (Jan. 2017 – Dec. 2018).
Dvorkovich, Arkady	Deputy prime minister of the Russian Federation and chairman of the board of directors of the New Economic School in Moscow. He met with Carter Page twice in 2016.
Dvoskin, Evgeney	Executive of Genbank in Crimea and associate of Felix Sater.
Eisenberg, John	Attorney in the White House Counsel's Office and legal counsel for the National Security Council.
Erchova, Lana (a/k/a Lana Alexander)	Ex-wife of Dmitry Klokov who emailed Ivanka Trump to introduce Klokov to the Trump Campaign in the fall of 2015.

U.S. Department of Justice

~~Attorney Work Product // May Contain Material Protected Under Fed. R. Crim. P. 6(e)~~

Fabrizio, Anthony (Tony)	Partner at the research and consulting firm Fabrizio, Lee & Associates. He was a pollster for the Trump Campaign and worked with Paul Manafort on Ukraine-related polling after the election.
Fishbein, Jason	Attorney who performed worked for Julian Assange and also sent WikiLeaks a password for an unlaunched website PutinTrump.org on September 20, 2016.
Flynn, Michael G. (a/k/a Michael Flynn Jr.)	Son of Michael T. Flynn, National Security Advisor (Jan. 20, 2017 – Feb. 13, 2017).
Flynn, Michael T.	National Security Advisor (Jan. 20, 2017 – Feb. 13, 2017), Director of the Defense Intelligence Agency (July 2012 – Aug. 7, 2014), and Trump Campaign advisor. He pleaded guilty to lying to the FBI about communications with Ambassador Sergey Kislyak in December 2016.
Foresman, Robert (Bob)	Investment banker who sought meetings with the Trump Campaign in spring 2016 to discuss Russian foreign policy, and after the election met with Michael Flynn.
Futerfas, Alan	Outside counsel for the Trump Organization and subsequently personal counsel for Donald Trump Jr.
Garten, Alan	General counsel of the Trump Organization.
Gates, Richard (Rick) III	Deputy campaign manager for Trump Campaign, Trump Inaugural Committee deputy chairman, and longtime employee of Paul Manafort. He pleaded guilty to conspiring to defraud the United States and violate U.S. laws, as well as making false statements to the FBI.
Gerson, Richard (Rick)	New York hedge fund manager and associate of Jared Kushner. During the transition period, he worked with Kirill Dmitriev on a proposal for reconciliation between the United States and Russia.
Gistaro, Edward	Deputy Director of National Intelligence for Intelligence Integration.
Glassner, Michael	Political director of the Trump Campaign who helped introduce George Papadopoulos to others in the Trump Campaign.
Goldstone, Robert	Publicist for Emin Agalarov who contacted Donald Trump Jr. to arrange the June 9, 2016 meeting at Trump Tower between Natalia Veselnitskaya and Trump Campaign officials.
Gordon, Jeffrey (J.D.)	National security advisor to the Trump Campaign involved in changes to the Republican party platform and who communicated with Russian Ambassador Sergey Kislyak at the Republican National Convention.
Gorkov, Sergey	Chairman of Vnesheconombank (VEB), a Russian state-owned bank, who met with Jared Kushner during the transition period.
Graff, Rhona	Senior vice-president and executive assistant to Donald J. Trump at the Trump Organization.

HOM **Harm to Ongoing Matter**

Hawker, Jonathan	Public relations consultant at FTI Consulting; worked with Davis Manafort International LLC on public relations campaign in Ukraine.
Heilbrunn, Jacob	Editor of the National Interest, the periodical that officially hosted candidate Trump's April 2016 foreign policy speech.
Hicks, Hope	White House communications director (Aug. 2017 – Mar. 2018) and press secretary for the Trump Campaign.
Holt, Lester	NBC News anchor who interviewed President Trump on May 11, 2017.
Hunt, Jody	Chief of staff to Attorney General Jeff Sessions (Feb. 2017 – Oct. 2017).
Ivanov, Igor	President of the Russian International Affairs Council and former Russian foreign minister. Ivan Timofeev told George Papadopoulos that Ivanov advised on arranging a "Moscow visit" for the Trump Campaign.
Ivanov, Sergei	Special representative of Vladimir Putin, former Russian deputy prime minister, and former FSB deputy director. In January 2016, Michael Cohen emailed the Kremlin requesting to speak to Ivanov.
Kasowitz, Marc	President Trump's personal counsel (May 2017 – July 2017).
Katsyv, Denis	Son of Peter Katsyv; owner of Russian company Prevezon Holdings Ltd. and associate of Natalia Veselnitskaya.
Katsyv, Peter	Russian businessman and father of Denis Katsyv.

HOM **Harm to Ongoing Matter**

Kaveladze, Irakli (Ike)	Vice president at Crocus Group and Aras Agalarov's deputy in the United States. He participated in the June 9, 2016 meeting at Trump Tower between Natalia Veselnitskaya and Trump Campaign officials.
Kaverzina, Irina	Employee of the Internet Research Agency, which engaged in an "active measures" social media campaign to interfere in the 2016 U.S. presidential election.
Kelly, John	White House chief of staff (July 2017 – Jan. 2019).
Khalilzad, Zalmay	U.S. special representative to Afghanistan and former U.S. ambassador. He met with Senator Jeff Sessions during foreign policy dinners put together through the Center for the National Interest.
Kilimnik, Konstantin	Russian-Ukrainian political consultant and long-time employee of Paul Manafort assessed by the FBI to have ties to Russian intelligence.
Kislyak, Sergey	Former Russian ambassador to the United States and current Russian senator from Mordovia.
Klimentov, Denis	Employee of the New Economic School who informed high-ranking Russian government officials of Carter Page's July 2016 visit to Moscow.

U.S. Department of Justice

~~Attorney Work Product // May Contain Material Protected Under Fed. R. Crim. P. 6(e)~~

Klimentov, Dmitri	Brother of Denis Klimentov who contacted Kremlin press secretary Dmitri Peskov about Carter Page's July 2016 visit to Moscow.
Klokov, Dmitry	Executive for PJSC Federal Grid Company of Unified Energy System and former aide to Russia's minister of energy. He communicated with Michael Cohen about a possible meeting between Vladimir Putin and candidate Trump.
Kobyakov, Anton	Advisor to Vladimir Putin and member of the Roscongress Foundation who invited candidate Trump to the St. Petersburg International Economic Forum.
Krickovic, Andrej	Professor at the Higher School of Economics who recommended that Carter Page give a July 2016 commencement address in Moscow.
Krylova, Aleksandra	Internet Research Agency employee who worked on "active measures" social media campaign to interfere in the 2016 U.S. presidential election; traveled to the United States under false pretenses in 2014.
Kushner, Jared	President Trump's son-in-law and senior advisor to the President.
Kuznetsov, Sergey	Russian government official at the Russian Embassy to the United States who transmitted Vladimir Putin's congratulations to President-Elect Trump for his electoral victory on November 9, 2016.
Landrum, Pete	Advisor to Senator Jeff Sessions who attended the September 2016 meeting between Sessions and Russian Ambassador Sergey Kislyak.
Lavrov, Sergey	Russian minister of foreign affairs and former permanent representative of Russia to the United Nations.
Ledeen, Barbara	Senate staffer and associate of Michael Flynn who sought to obtain Hillary Clinton emails during the 2016 U.S. presidential campaign period.
Ledeen, Michael	Member of the Presidential Transition Team who advised on foreign policy and national security matters.
Ledgett, Richard	Deputy director of the National Security Agency (Jan. 2014 – Apr. 2017); present when President Trump called Michael Rogers on March 26, 2017.
Lewandowski, Corey	Campaign manager for the Trump Campaign (Jan. 2015 – June 2016).
Luff, Sandra	Legislative director for Senator Jeff Sessions; attended a September 2016 meeting between Sessions and Russian Ambassador Sergey Kislyak.
Lyovochkin, Serhiy	Member of Ukrainian parliament and member of Ukrainian political party, Opposition Bloc Party.
Magnitsky, Sergei	Russian tax specialist who alleged Russian government corruption and died in Russian police custody in 2009. His death prompted passage of

the Magnitsky Act, which imposed financial and travel sanctions on Russian officials.

Malloch, Theodore (Ted) — Chief executive officer of Global Fiduciary Governance and the Roosevelt Group. He was a London-based associate of Jerome Corsi.

Manafort, Paul Jr. — Trump campaign member (March 2016 – Aug. 2016) and chairman and chief strategist (May 2016 – Aug. 2016).

Mashburn, John — Trump administration official and former policy director to the Trump Campaign.

McCabe, Andrew — Acting director of the FBI (May 2017 – Aug. 2017); deputy director of the FBI (Feb. 2016 – Jan. 2018).

McCord, Mary — Acting Assistant Attorney General (Oct. 2016 – May 2017).

McFarland, Kathleen (K.T.) — Deputy White House National Security Advisor (Jan. 2017 – May 2017).

McGahn, Donald (Don) — White House Counsel (Jan. 2017 – Oct. 2018).

Medvedev, Dmitry — Prime Minister of Russia.

Melnik, Yuriy — Spokesperson for the Russian Embassy in Washington, D.C., who connected with George Papadopoulos on social media.

Mifsud, Joseph — Maltese national and former London-based professor who, immediately after returning from Moscow in April 2016, told George Papadopoulos that the Russians had "dirt" in the form of thousands of Clinton emails.

Miller, Matt — Trump Campaign staff member who was present at the meeting of the National Security and Defense Platform Subcommittee in July 2016.

Miller, Stephen — Senior advisor to the President.

Millian, Sergei — Founder of the Russian American Chamber of Commerce who met with George Papadopoulos during the campaign.

Mnuchin, Steven — Secretary of the Treasury.

HOM — Harm to Ongoing Matter .

Müller-Maguhn, Andrew — Member of hacker association Chaos Computer Club and associate of Julian Assange, founder of WikiLeaks.

Nader, George — Advisor to the United Arab Emirates's Crown Prince who arranged a meeting between Kirill Dmitriev and Erik Prince during the transition period.

Netyksho, Viktor — Russian military officer in command of a unit involved in Russian hack-and-release operations to interfere in the 2016 U.S. presidential election.

U.S. Department of Justice

~~Attorney Work Product~~ // ~~May Contain Material Protected Under Fed. R. Crim. P. 6(e)~~

Oganov, Georgiy	Advisor to Oleg Deripaska and a board member of investment company Basic Element. He met with Paul Manafort in Spain in early 2017.
Oknyansky, Henry (a/k/a Henry Greenberg)	Florida-based Russian individual who claimed to have derogatory information pertaining to Hillary Clinton. He met with Roger Stone in May 2016.
Page, Carter	Foreign policy advisor to the Trump Campaign who advocated pro-Russian views and made July 2016 and December 2016 visits to Moscow.
Papadopoulos, George	Foreign policy advisor to the Trump Campaign who received information from Joseph Mifsud that Russians had "dirt" in the form of thousands of Clinton emails. He pleaded guilty to lying to the FBI about his contact with Mifsud.
Parscale, Bradley	Digital media director for the 2016 Trump Campaign.
Patten, William (Sam) Jr.	Lobbyist and business partner of Konstantin Kilimnik.
Peskov, Dmitry	Deputy chief of staff of and press secretary for the Russian presidential administration.
Phares, Walid	Foreign policy advisor to the Trump Campaign and co-secretary general of the Transatlantic Parliamentary Group on Counterterrorism (TAG).
Pinedo, Richard	U.S. person who pleaded guilty to a single-count information of identity fraud.
Podesta, John Jr.	Clinton campaign chairman whose email account was hacked by the GRU. WikiLeaks released his stolen emails during the 2016 campaign.
Podobnyy, Victor	Russian intelligence officer who interacted with Carter Page while operating inside the United States; later charged in 2015 with conspiring to act as an unregistered agent of Russia.
Poliakova, Elena	Personal assistant to Dmitry Peskov who responded to Michael Cohen's outreach about the Trump Tower Moscow project in January 2016.
Polonskaya, Olga	Russian national introduced to George Papadopoulos by Joseph Mifsud as an individual with connections to Vladimir Putin.
Pompeo, Michael	U.S. Secretary of State; director of the Central Intelligence Agency (Jan. 2017 – Apr. 2018).
Porter, Robert	White House staff secretary (Jan. 2017 – Feb. 2018).
Priebus, Reince	White House chief of staff (Jan. 2017 – July 2017); chair of the Republican National Committee (Jan. 2011 – Jan. 2017).
Prigozhin, Yevgeniy	Head of Russian companies Concord Catering and Concord Management and Consulting; supported and financed the Internet Research Agency, which engaged in an "active measures" social media campaign to interfere in the 2016 U.S. presidential election.

Prikhodko, Sergei	First deputy head of the Russian Government Office and former Russian deputy prime minister. In January 2016, he invited candidate Trump to the St. Petersburg International Economic Forum.
Prince, Erik	Businessman and Trump Campaign supporter who met with Presidential Transition Team officials after the election and traveled to the Seychelles to meet with Kirill Dmitriev in January 2017.
Raffel, Josh	White House communications advisor (Apr. 2017 – Feb. 2018).
Rasin, Alexei	Ukrainian associate of Henry Oknyansky who claimed to possess derogatory information regarding Hillary Clinton.
Rogers, Michael	Director of the National Security Agency (Apr. 2014 – May 2018).
Rosenstein, Rod	Deputy Attorney General (Apr. 2017 – present); Acting Attorney General for the Russian election interference investigation (May 2017 – Nov. 2018).
Rozov, Andrei	Chairman of I.C. Expert Investment Company, a Russian real-estate development corporation that signed a letter of intent for the Trump Tower Moscow project in 2015.
Rtskhiladze, Giorgi	Executive of the Silk Road Transatlantic Alliance, LLC who communicated with Cohen about a Trump Tower Moscow proposal.
Ruddy, Christopher	Chief executive of Newsmax Media and associate of President Trump.
Rybicki, James	FBI chief of staff (May 2015 – Feb. 2018).
Samochornov, Anatoli	Translator who worked with Natalia Veselnitskaya and attended a June 9, 2016 meeting at Trump Tower between Veselnitskaya and Trump Campaign officials.
Sanders, Sarah Huckabee	White House press secretary (July 2017 – present).
Sater, Felix	Real-estate advisor who worked with Michael Cohen to pursue a Trump Tower Moscow project.
Saunders, Paul J.	Executive with the Center for the National Interest who worked on outlines and logistics of candidate Trump's April 2016 foreign policy speech.
Sechin, Igor	Executive chairman of Rosneft, a Russian-stated owned oil company.
Sessions, Jefferson III (Jeff)	Attorney General (Feb. 2017 – Nov. 2018); U.S. Senator (Jan. 1997 – Feb. 2017); head of the Trump Campaign's foreign policy advisory team.
Shoygu, Sergey	Russian Minister of Defense.
Simes, Dimitri	President and chief executive officer of the Center for the National Interest.

Smith, Peter	Investment banker active in Republican politics who sought to obtain Hillary Clinton emails during the 2016 U.S. presidential campaign period.
Spicer, Sean	White House press secretary and communications director (Jan. 2017 – July 2017).
Stone, Roger	Advisor to the Trump Campaign **Harm to Ongoing Matter**
Tillerson, Rex	U.S. Secretary of State (Feb. 2017 – Mar. 2018).
Timofeev, Ivan	Director of programs at the Russian International Affairs Council and program director of the Valdai Discussion Club who communicated in 2016 with George Papadopoulos, attempting to arrange a meeting between the Russian government and the Trump Campaign.
Trump, Donald Jr.	President Trump's son; trustee and executive vice president of the Trump Organization; helped arrange and attended the June 9, 2016 meeting at Trump Tower between Natalia Veselnitskaya and Trump Campaign officials.
Trump, Eric	President Trump's son; trustee and executive vice president of the Trump Organization.
Trump, Ivanka	President Trump's daughter; advisor to the President and former executive vice president of the Trump Organization.
Ushakov, Yuri Viktorovich	Aide to Vladimir Putin and former Russian ambassador to the United States; identified to the Presidential Transition Team as the proposed channel to the Russian government.
Vaino, Anton	Chief of staff to Russian president Vladimir Putin.
Van der Zwaan, Alexander	Former attorney at Skadden, Arps, Slate, Meagher & Flom, LLP; worked with Paul Manafort and Rick Gates.
Vargas, Catherine	Executive assistant to Jared Kushner.
Vasilchenko, Gleb	Internet Research Agency employee who engaged in an "active measures" social media campaign to interfere in the 2016 U.S. presidential election.
Veselnitskaya, Natalia	Russian attorney who advocated for the repeal of the Magnitsky Act and was the principal speaker at the June 9, 2016 meeting at Trump Tower with Trump Campaign officials.
Weber, Shlomo	Rector of the New Economic School (NES) in Moscow who invited Carter Page to speak at NES commencement in July 2016.
Yanukovych, Viktor	Former president of Ukraine who had worked with Paul Manafort.

U.S. Department of Justice

~~Attorney Work Product~~ // ~~May Contain Material Protected Under Fed. R. Crim. P. 6(e)~~

Yates, Sally	Acting Attorney General (Jan. 20, 2017 – Jan. 30, 2017); Deputy Attorney General (Jan. 10, 2015 – Jan. 30, 2017).
Yatsenko, Sergey	Deputy chief financial officer of Gazprom, a Russian state-owned energy company, and associate of Carter Page.
Zakharova, Maria	Director of the Russian Ministry of Foreign Affair's Information and Press Department who received notification of Carter Page's speech in July 2016 from Denis Klimentov.
Zayed al Nahyan, Mohammed bin	Crown Prince of Abu Dhabi and deputy supreme commander of the United Arab Emirates (UAE) armed forces.

Entities and Organizations

Alfa-Bank	Russia's largest commercial bank, which is headed by Petr Aven.
Center for the National Interest (CNI)	U.S.-based think tank with expertise in and connections to Russia. CNI's publication, the National Interest, hosted candidate Trump's foreign policy speech in April 2016.
Concord	Umbrella term for Concord Management and Consulting, LLC and Concord Catering, which are Russian companies controlled by Yevgeniy Prigozhin.
Crocus Group or Crocus International	A Russian real-estate and property development company that, in 2013, hosted the Miss Universe Pageant, and from 2013 through 2014, worked with the Trump Organization on a Trump Moscow project.
DCLeaks	Fictitious online persona operated by the GRU that released stolen documents during the 2016 U.S. presidential campaign period.
Democratic Congressional Campaign Committee	Political committee working to elect Democrats to the House of Representatives; hacked by the GRU in April 2016.
Democratic National Committee	Formal governing body for the Democratic Party; hacked by the GRU in April 2016.
Duma	Lower House of the national legislature of the Russian Federation.
Gazprom	Russian oil and gas company majority-owned by the Russian government.
Global Energy Capital, LLC	Investment and management firm founded by Carter Page.
Global Partners in Diplomacy	Event hosted in partnership with the U.S. Department of State and the Republican National Convention. In 2016, Jeff Sessions and J.D. Gordon delivered speeches at the event and interacted with Russian Ambassador Sergey Kislyak.

Guccifer 2.0	Fictitious online persona operated by the GRU that released stolen documents during the 2016 U.S. presidential campaign period.
I.C. Expert Investment Company	Russian real-estate and development corporation that signed a letter of intent with a Trump Organization subsidiary to develop a Trump Moscow property.
Internet Research Agency (IRA)	Russian entity based in Saint Petersburg and funded by Concord that engaged in an "active measures" social media campaign to interfere in the 2016 U.S. presidential election.
KLS Research LLC	Business established by an associate of and at the direction of Peter Smith to further Smith's search for Hillary Clinton emails.
Kremlin	Official residence of the president of the Russian Federation; it is used colloquially to refer to the office of the president or the Russian government.
LetterOne	Company that includes Petr Aven and Richard Burt as board members. During a board meeting in December 2016, Aven asked for Burt's help to make contact with the Presidential Transition Team.
Link Campus University	University in Rome, Italy, where George Papadopoulos was introduced to Joseph Mifsud.
London Centre of International Law Practice (LCILP)	International law advisory organization in London that employed Joseph Mifsud and George Papadopoulos.
Main Intelligence Directorate of the General Staff (GRU)	Russian Federation's military intelligence agency.
New Economic School in Moscow (NES)	Moscow-based school that invited Carter Page to speak at its July 2016 commencement ceremony.
Opposition Bloc	Ukrainian political party that incorporated members of the defunct Party of Regions.
Party of Regions	Ukrainian political party of former President Yanukovych. It was generally understood to align with Russian policies.
Pericles Emerging Market Partners LLP	Company registered in the Cayman Islands by Paul Manafort and his business partner Rick Davis. Oleg Deripaska invested in the fund.
Prevezon Holdings Ltd.	Russian company that was a defendant in a U.S. civil action alleging the laundering of proceeds from fraud exposed by Sergei Magnitsky.
Roscongress Foundation	Russian entity that organized the St. Petersburg International Economic Forum.
Rosneft	Russian state-owned oil and energy company.
Russian Direct Investment Fund	Sovereign wealth fund established by the Russian Government in 2011 and headed by Kirill Dmitriev.

Russian International Affairs Council	Russia-based nonprofit established by Russian government decree. It is associated with the Ministry of Foreign Affairs, and its members include Ivan Timofeev, Dmitry Peskov, and Petr Aven.
Silk Road Group	Privately held investment company that entered into a licensing agreement to build a Trump-branded hotel in Georgia.
St. Petersburg International Economic Forum	Annual event held in Russia and attended by prominent Russian politicians and businessmen.
Tatneft	Russian energy company.
Transatlantic Parliamentary Group on Counterterrorism	European group that sponsored a summit between European Parliament lawmakers and U.S. persons. George Papadopoulos, Sam Clovis, and Walid Phares attended the TAG summit in July 2016.
Unit 26165 (GRU)	GRU military cyber unit dedicated to targeting military, political, governmental, and non-governmental organizations outside of Russia. It engaged in computer intrusions of U.S. persons and organizations, as well as the subsequent release of the stolen data, in order to interfere in the 2016 U.S. presidential election.
Unit 74455 (GRU)	GRU military unit with multiple departments that engaged in cyber operations. It engaged in computer intrusions of U.S. persons and organizations, as well as the subsequent release of the stolen data, in order to interfere in the 2016 U.S. presidential election.
Valdai Discussion Club	Group that holds a conference attended by Russian government officials, including President Putin.
WikiLeaks	Organization founded by Julian Assange that posts information online, including data stolen from private, corporate, and U.S. Government entities. Released data stolen by the GRU during the 2016 U.S. presidential election.

Index of Acronyms

CNI	Center for the National Interest
DCCC	Democratic Congressional Campaign Committee
DNC	Democratic National Committee
FBI	Federal Bureau of Investigation
FSB	Russian Federal Security Service
GEC	Global Energy Capital, LLC
GRU	Russian Federation's Main Intelligence Directorate of the General Staff
HPSCI	U.S. House of Representatives Permanent Select Committee on Intelligence
HRC	Hillary Rodham Clinton
IRA	Internet Research Agency
LCILP	London Centre of International Law Practice
NATO	North Atlantic Treaty Organization
NES	New Economic School
NSA	National Security Agency
ODNI	Office of the Director of National Intelligence
PTT	Presidential Transition Team
RDIF	Russian Direct Investment Fund
RIAC	Russian International Affairs Council
SBOE	State boards of elections
SCO	Special Counsel's Office
SJC	U.S. Senate Judiciary Committee
SSCI	U.S. Senate Select Committee on Intelligence
TAG	Transatlantic Parliamentary Group on Counterterrorism
VEB	Vnesheconombank

Appendix C

U.S. Department of Justice

~~Attorney Work Product~~ // ~~May Contain Material Protected Under Fed. R. Crim. P. 6(e)~~

APPENDIX C

INTRODUCTORY NOTE

The President provided written responses through his personal counsel to questions submitted to him by the Special Counsel's Office. We first explain the process that led to the submission of written questions and then attach the President's responses.

Beginning in December 2017, this Office sought for more than a year to interview the President on topics relevant to both Russian-election interference and obstruction-of-justice. We advised counsel that the President was a "subject" of the investigation under the definition of the Justice Manual—"a person whose conduct is within the scope of the grand jury's investigation." Justice Manual § 9-11.151 (2018). We also advised counsel that "[a]n interview with the President is vital to our investigation" and that this Office had "carefully considered the constitutional and other arguments raised by . . . counsel, and they d[id] not provide us with reason to forgo seeking an interview."[1] We additionally stated that "it is in the interest of the Presidency and the public for an interview to take place" and offered "numerous accommodations to aid the President's preparation and avoid surprise."[2] After extensive discussions with the Department of Justice about the Special Counsel's objective of securing the President's testimony, these accommodations included the submissions of written questions to the President on certain Russia-related topics.[3]

We received the President's written responses in late November 2018.[4] In December 2018, we informed counsel of the insufficiency of those responses in several respects.[5] We noted, among other things, that the President stated on more than 30 occasions that he "does not 'recall' or 'remember' or have an 'independent recollection'" of information called for by the questions.[6] Other answers were "incomplete or imprecise."[7] The written responses, we informed counsel, "demonstrate the inadequacy of the written format, as we have had no opportunity to ask follow-up questions that would ensure complete answers and potentially refresh your client's recollection or clarify the extent or nature of his lack of recollection."[8] We again requested an in-person interview, limited to certain topics, advising the President's counsel that "[t]his is the President's

---

[1] 5/16/18 Letter, Special Counsel to the President's Personal Counsel, at 1.

[2] 5/16/18 Letter, Special Counsels's Office to the President's Personal Counsel, at 1; see 7/30/18 Letter, Special Counsel's Office to the President's Personal Counsel, at 1 (describing accommodations).

[3] 9/17/18 Letter, Special Counsel's Office to the President's Personal Counsel, at 1 (submitting written questions).

[4] 11/20/18 Letter, President's Personal Counsel to the Special Counsel's Office (transmitting written responses of Donald J. Trump).

[5] 12/3/18 Letter, Special Counsel's Office to the President's Personal Counsel, at 3.

[6] 12/3/18 Letter, Special Counsel's Office to the President's Personal Counsel, at 3.

[7] 12/3/18 Letter, Special Counsel's Office to the President's Personal Counsel, at 3; see (noting, "for example," that the President "did not answer whether he had at any time directed or suggested that discussions about the Trump Moscow Project should cease . . . but he has since made public comments about that topic").

[8] 12/3/18 Letter, Special Counsel's Office to the President's Personal Counsel, at 3.

opportunity to voluntarily provide us with information for us to evaluate in the context of all of the evidence we have gathered."[9] The President declined.[10]

Recognizing that the President would not be interviewed voluntarily, we considered whether to issue a subpoena for his testimony. We viewed the written answers to be inadequate. But at that point, our investigation had made significant progress and had produced substantial evidence for our report. We thus weighed the costs of potentially lengthy constitutional litigation, with resulting delay in finishing our investigation, against the anticipated benefits for our investigation and report. As explained in Volume II, Section II.B., we determined that the substantial quantity of information we had obtained from other sources allowed us to draw relevant factual conclusions on intent and credibility, which are often inferred from circumstantial evidence and assessed without direct testimony from the subject of the investigation.

*   *   *

---

[9] 12/3/18 Letter, Special Counsel to the President's Personal Counsel.

[10] 12/12/18 Letter, President's Personal Counsel to the Special Counsel's Office, at 2.

[11] Grand Jury

[12] Grand Jury

U.S. Department of Justice

~~Attorney Work Product // May Contain Material Protected Under Fed. R. Crim. P. 6(e)~~

WRITTEN QUESTIONS TO BE ANSWERED UNDER OATH BY PRESIDENT DONALD J. TRUMP

I. **June 9, 2016 Meeting at Trump Tower**

    a. When did you first learn that Donald Trump, Jr., Paul Manafort, or Jared Kushner was considering participating in a meeting in June 2016 concerning potentially negative information about Hillary Clinton? Describe who you learned the information from and the substance of the discussion.

    b. Attached to this document as Exhibit A is a series of emails from June 2016 between, among others, Donald Trump, Jr. and Rob Goldstone. In addition to the emails reflected in Exhibit A, Donald Trump, Jr. had other communications with Rob Goldstone and Emin Agalarov between June 3, 2016, and June 9, 2016.

        i. Did Mr. Trump, Jr. or anyone else tell you about or show you any of these communications? If yes, describe who discussed the communications with you, when, and the substance of the discussion(s).

        ii. When did you first see or learn about all or any part of the emails reflected in Exhibit A?

        iii. When did you first learn that the proposed meeting involved or was described as being part of Russia and its government's support for your candidacy?

        iv. Did you suggest to or direct anyone not to discuss or release publicly all or any portion of the emails reflected in Exhibit A? If yes, describe who you communicated with, when, the substance of the communication(s), and why you took that action.

    c. On June 9, 2016, Donald Trump, Jr., Paul Manafort, and Jared Kushner attended a meeting at Trump Tower with several individuals, including a Russian lawyer, Natalia Veselnitskaya (the "June 9 meeting").

        i. Other than as set forth in your answers to I.a and I.b, what, if anything, were you told about the possibility of this meeting taking place, or the scheduling of such a meeting? Describe who you discussed this with, when, and what you were informed about the meeting.

        ii. When did you learn that some of the individuals attending the June 9 meeting were Russian or had any affiliation with any part of the Russian government? Describe who you learned this information from and the substance of the discussion(s).

        iii. What were you told about what was discussed at the June 9 meeting? Describe each conversation in which you were told about what was discussed at the meeting, who the conversation was with, when it occurred, and the substance of the statements they made about the meeting.

U.S. Department of Justice

~~Attorney Work Product // May Contain Material Protected Under Fed. R. Crim. P. 6(e)~~

    iv. Were you told that the June 9 meeting was about, in whole or in part, adoption and/or the Magnitsky Act? If yes, describe who you had that discussion with, when, and the substance of the discussion.

d. For the period June 6, 2016 through June 9, 2016, for what portion of each day were you in Trump Tower?
    i. Did you speak or meet with Donald Trump, Jr., Paul Manafort, or Jared Kushner on June 9, 2016? If yes, did any portion of any of those conversations or meetings include any reference to any aspect of the June 9 meeting? If yes, describe who you spoke with and the substance of the conversation.

e. Did you communicate directly or indirectly with any member or representative of the Agalarov family after June 3, 2016? If yes, describe who you spoke with, when, and the substance of the communication.

f. Did you learn of any communications between Donald Trump, Jr., Paul Manafort, or Jared Kushner and any member or representative of the Agalarov family, Natalia Veselnitskaya, Rob Goldstone, or any Russian official or contact that took place after June 9, 2016 and concerned the June 9 meeting or efforts by Russia to assist the campaign? If yes, describe who you learned this information from, when, and the substance of what you learned.

g. On June 7, 2016, you gave a speech in which you said, in part, "I am going to give a major speech on probably Monday of next week and we're going to be discussing all of the things that have taken place with the Clintons."
    i. Why did you make that statement?
    ii. What information did you plan to share with respect to the Clintons?
    iii. What did you believe the source(s) of that information would be?
    iv. Did you expect any of the information to have come from the June 9 meeting?
    v. Did anyone help draft the speech that you were referring to? If so, who?
    vi. Why did you ultimately not give the speech you referenced on June 7, 2016?

h. Did any person or entity inform you during the campaign that Vladimir Putin or the Russian government supported your candidacy or opposed the candidacy of Hillary Clinton? If yes, describe the source(s) of the information, when you were informed, and the content of such discussion(s).

i. Did any person or entity inform you during the campaign that any foreign government or foreign leader, other than Russia or Vladimir Putin, had provided, wished to provide, or offered to provide tangible support to your campaign, including by way of offering to provide negative information on Hillary Clinton? If

U.S. Department of Justice

~~Attorney Work Product~~ // ~~May Contain Material Protected Under Fed. R. Crim. P. 6(e)~~

yes, describe the source(s) of the information, when you were informed, and the content of such discussion(s).

II. **Russian Hacking / Russian Efforts Using Social Media / WikiLeaks**

a. On June 14, 2016, it was publicly reported that computer hackers had penetrated the computer network of the Democratic National Committee (DNC) and that Russian intelligence was behind the unauthorized access, or hack. Prior to June 14, 2016, were you provided any information about any potential or actual hacking of the computer systems or email accounts of the DNC, the Democratic Congressional Campaign Committee (DCCC), the Clinton Campaign, Hillary Clinton, or individuals associated with the Clinton campaign? If yes, describe who provided this information, when, and the substance of the information.

b. On July 22, 2016, WikiLeaks released nearly 20,000 emails sent or received by Democratic party officials.
   i. Prior to the July 22, 2016 release, were you aware from any source that WikiLeaks, Guccifer 2.0, DCLeaks, or Russians had or potentially had possession of or planned to release emails or information that could help your campaign or hurt the Clinton campaign? If yes, describe who you discussed this issue with, when, and the substance of the discussion(s).
   ii. After the release of emails by WikiLeaks on July 22, 2016, were you told that WikiLeaks possessed or might possess additional information that could be released during the campaign? If yes, describe who provided this information, when, and what you were told.

c. Are you aware of any communications during the campaign, directly or indirectly, between Roger Stone, Donald Trump, Jr., Paul Manafort, or Rick Gates and (a) WikiLeaks, (b) Julian Assange, (c) other representatives of WikiLeaks, (d) Guccifer 2.0, (e) representatives of Guccifer 2.0, or (f) representatives of DCLeaks? If yes, describe who provided you with this information, when you learned of the communications, and what you know about those communications.

d. On July 27, 2016, you stated at a press conference: "Russia, if you're listening, I hope you're able to find the 30,000 emails that are missing. I think you will probably be rewarded mightily by our press."
   i. Why did you make that request of Russia, as opposed to any other country, entity, or individual?
   ii. In advance of making that statement, what discussions, if any, did you have with anyone else about the substance of the statement?
   iii. Were you told at any time before or after you made that statement that Russia was attempting to infiltrate or hack computer systems or email accounts of Hillary Clinton or her campaign? If yes, describe who provided this information, when, and what you were told.

e. On October 7, 2016, emails hacked from the account of John Podesta were released by WikiLeaks.
   i. Where were you on October 7, 2016?
   ii. Were you told at any time in advance of, or on the day of, the October 7 release that WikiLeaks possessed or might possess emails related to John Podesta? If yes, describe who told you this, when, and what you were told.
   iii. Are you aware of anyone associated with you or your campaign, including Roger Stone, reaching out to WikiLeaks, either directly or through an intermediary, on or about October 7, 2016? If yes, identify the person and describe the substance of the conversations or contacts.

f. Were you told of anyone associated with you or your campaign, including Roger Stone, having any discussions, directly or indirectly, with WikiLeaks, Guccifer 2.0, or DCLeaks regarding the content or timing of release of hacked emails? If yes, describe who had such contacts, how you became aware of the contacts, when you became aware of the contacts, and the substance of the contacts.

g. From June 1, 2016 through the end of the campaign, how frequently did you communicate with Roger Stone? Describe the nature of your communication(s) with Mr. Stone.
   i. During that time period, what efforts did Mr. Stone tell you he was making to assist your campaign, and what requests, if any, did you make of Mr. Stone?
   ii. Did Mr. Stone ever discuss WikiLeaks with you or, as far as you were aware, with anyone else associated with the campaign? If yes, describe what you were told, from whom, and when.
   iii. Did Mr. Stone at any time inform you about contacts he had with WikiLeaks or any intermediary of WikiLeaks, or about forthcoming releases of information? If yes, describe what Stone told you and when.

h. Did you have any discussions prior to January 20, 2017, regarding a potential pardon or other action to benefit Julian Assange? If yes, describe who you had the discussion(s) with, when, and the content of the discussion(s).

i. Were you aware of any efforts by foreign individuals or companies, including those in Russia, to assist your campaign through the use of social media postings or the organization of rallies? If yes, identify who you discussed such assistance with, when, and the content of the discussion(s).

III. **The Trump Organization Moscow Project**

a. In October 2015, a "Letter of Intent," a copy of which is attached as Exhibit B, was signed for a proposed Trump Organization project in Moscow (the "Trump Moscow project").

     i. When were you first informed of discussions about the Trump Moscow project? By whom? What were you told about the project?

     ii. Did you sign the letter of intent?

b. In a statement provided to Congress, attached as Exhibit C, Michael Cohen stated: "To the best of my knowledge, Mr. Trump was never in contact with anyone about this proposal other than me on three occasions, including signing a non-binding letter of intent in 2015." Describe all discussions you had with Mr. Cohen, or anyone else associated with the Trump Organization, about the Trump Moscow project, including who you spoke with, when, and the substance of the discussion(s).

c. Did you learn of any communications between Michael Cohen or Felix Sater and any Russian government officials, including officials in the office of Dmitry Peskov, regarding the Trump Moscow project? If so, identify who provided this information to you, when, and the substance of what you learned.

d. Did you have any discussions between June 2015 and June 2016 regarding a potential trip to Russia by you and/or Michael Cohen for reasons related to the Trump Moscow project? If yes, describe who you spoke with, when, and the substance of the discussion(s).

e. Did you at any time direct or suggest that discussions about the Trump Moscow project should cease, or were you informed at any time that the project had been abandoned? If yes, describe who you spoke with, when, the substance of the discussion(s), and why that decision was made.

f. Did you have any discussions regarding what information would be provided publicly or in response to investigative inquiries about potential or actual investments or business deals the Trump Organization had in Russia, including the Trump Moscow project? If yes, describe who you spoke with, when, and the substance of the discussion(s).

g. Aside from the Trump Moscow project, did you or the Trump Organization have any other prospective or actual business interests, investments, or arrangements with Russia or any Russian interest or Russian individual during the campaign? If yes, describe the business interests, investments, or arrangements.

IV. Contacts with Russia and Russia-Related Issues During the Campaign

a. Prior to mid-August 2016, did you become aware that Paul Manafort had ties to the Ukrainian government? If yes, describe who you learned this information from, when, and the substance of what you were told. Did Mr. Manafort's connections to the Ukrainian or Russian governments play any role in your decision to have him join your campaign? If yes, describe that role.

b. Were you aware that Paul Manafort offered briefings on the progress of your campaign to Oleg Deripaska? If yes, describe who you learned this information from, when, the substance of what you were told, what you understood the purpose was of sharing such information with Mr. Deripaska, and how you responded to learning this information.

c. Were you aware of whether Paul Manafort or anyone else associated with your campaign sent or directed others to send internal Trump campaign information to any person located in Ukraine or Russia or associated with the Ukrainian or Russian governments? If yes, identify who provided you with this information, when, the substance of the discussion(s), what you understood the purpose was of sharing the internal campaign information, and how you responded to learning this information.

d. Did Paul Manafort communicate to you, directly or indirectly, any positions Ukraine or Russia would want the U.S. to support? If yes, describe when he communicated those positions to you and the substance of those communications.

e. During the campaign, were you told about efforts by Russian officials to meet with you or senior members of your campaign? If yes, describe who you had conversations with on this topic, when, and what you were told.

f. What role, if any, did you have in changing the Republican Party platform regarding arming Ukraine during the Republican National Convention? Prior to the convention, what information did you have about this platform provision? After the platform provision was changed, who told you about the change, when did they tell you, what were you told about why it was changed, and who was involved?

g. On July 27, 2016, in response to a question about whether you would recognize Crimea as Russian territory and lift sanctions on Russia, you said: "We'll be looking at that. Yeah, we'll be looking." Did you intend to communicate by that statement or at any other time during the campaign a willingness to lift sanctions and/or recognize Russia's annexation of Crimea if you were elected?

    i. What consideration did you give to lifting sanctions and/or recognizing Russia's annexation of Crimea if you were elected? Describe who you spoke with about this topic, when, the substance of the discussion(s).

V.   Contacts with Russia and Russia-Related Issues During the Transition

a. Were you asked to attend the World Chess Championship gala on November 10, 2016? If yes, who asked you to attend, when were you asked, and what were you told about about why your presence was requested?

    i. Did you attend any part of the event? If yes, describe any interactions you had with any Russians or representatives of the Russian government at the event.

b. Following the Obama Administration's imposition of sanctions on Russia in December 2016 ("Russia sanctions"), did you discuss with Lieutenant General (LTG) Michael Flynn, K.T. McFarland, Steve Bannon, Reince Priebus, Jared Kushner, Erik Prince, or anyone else associated with the transition what should be communicated to the Russian government regarding the sanctions? If yes, describe who you spoke with about this issue, when, and the substance of the discussion(s).

c. On December 29 and December 31, 2016, LTG Flynn had conversations with Russian Ambassador Sergey Kislyak about the Russia sanctions and Russia's response to the Russia sanctions.

    i. Did you direct or suggest that LTG Flynn have discussions with anyone from the Russian government about the Russia sanctions?

    ii. Were you told in advance of LTG Flynn's December 29, 2016 conversation that he was going to be speaking with Ambassador Kislyak? If yes, describe who told you this information, when, and what you were told. If no, when and from whom did you learn of LTG Flynn's December 29, 2016 conversation with Ambassador Kislyak?

    iii. When did you learn of LTG Flynn and Ambassador Kislyak's call on December 31, 2016? Who told you and what were you told?

    iv. When did you learn that sanctions were discussed in the December 29 and December 31, 2016 calls between LTG Flynn and Ambassador Kislyak? Who told you and what were you told?

d. At any time between December 31, 2016, and January 20, 2017, did anyone tell you or suggest to you that Russia's decision not to impose reciprocal sanctions was attributable in any way to LTG Flynn's communications with Ambassador Kislyak? If yes, identify who provided you with this information, when, and the substance of what you were told.

e. On January 12, 2017, the Washington Post published a column that stated that LTG Flynn phoned Ambassador Kislyak several times on December 29, 2016. After learning of the column, did you direct or suggest to anyone that LTG Flynn should deny that he discussed sanctions with Ambassador Kislyak? If yes, who did you make this suggestion or direction to, when, what did you say, and why did you take this step?

    i. After learning of the column, did you have any conversations with LTG Flynn about his conversations with Ambassador Kislyak in December 2016? If yes, describe when those discussions occurred and the content of the discussions.

f. Were you told about a meeting between Jared Kushner and Sergei Gorkov that took place in December 2016?

    i. If yes, describe who you spoke with, when, the substance of the discussion(s), and what you understood was the purpose of the meeting.

g. Were you told about a meeting or meetings between Erik Prince and Kirill Dmitriev or any other representative from the Russian government that took place in January 2017?

    i. If yes, describe who you spoke with, when, the substance of the discussion(s), and what you understood was the purpose of the meeting(s).

h. Prior to January 20, 2017, did you talk to Steve Bannon, Jared Kushner, or any other individual associated with the transition regarding establishing an unofficial line of communication with Russia? If yes, describe who you spoke with, when, the substance of the discussion(s), and what you understood was the purpose of such an unofficial line of communication.

U.S. Department of Justice

~~Attorney Work Product // May Contain Material Protected Under Fed. R. Crim. P. 6(e)~~

RESPONSES OF PRESIDENT DONALD J. TRUMP

I.   **June 9, 2016 Meeting at Trump Tower**

a.   When did you first learn that Donald Trump, Jr., Paul Manafort, or Jared Kushner was considering participating in a meeting in June 2016 concerning potentially negative information about Hillary Clinton? Describe who you learned the information from and the substance of the discussion.

b.   Attached to this document as Exhibit A is a series of emails from June 2016 between, among others, Donald Trump, Jr. and Rob Goldstone. In addition to the emails reflected in Exhibit A, Donald Trump, Jr. had other communications with Rob Goldstone and Emin Agalarov between June 3, 2016, and June 9, 2016.

    i.   Did Mr. Trump, Jr. or anyone else tell you about or show you any of these communications? If yes, describe who discussed the communications with you, when, and the substance of the discussion(s).

    ii.   When did you first see or learn about all or any part of the emails reflected in Exhibit A?

    iii. When did you first learn that the proposed meeting involved or was described as being part of Russia and its government's support for your candidacy?

    iv.   Did you suggest to or direct anyone not to discuss or release publicly all or any portion of the emails reflected in Exhibit A? If yes, describe who you communicated with, when, the substance of the communication(s), and why you took that action.

c.   On June 9, 2016, Donald Trump, Jr., Paul Manafort, and Jared Kushner attended a meeting at Trump Tower with several individuals, including a Russian lawyer, Natalia Veselnitskaya (the "June 9 meeting").

    i.   Other than as set forth in your answers to I.a and I.b, what, if anything, were you told about the possibility of this meeting taking place, or the scheduling of such a meeting? Describe who you discussed this with, when, and what you were informed about the meeting.

    ii.   When did you learn that some of the individuals attending the June 9 meeting were Russian or had any affiliation with any part of the Russian government? Describe who you learned this information from and the substance of the discussion(s).

6

    iii.   What were you told about what was discussed at the June 9 meeting? Describe each conversation in which you were told about what was discussed at the meeting, who the conversation was with, when it occurred, and the substance of the statements they made about the meeting.

    iv.   Were you told that the June 9 meeting was about, in whole or in part, adoption and/or the Magnitsky Act? If yes, describe who you had that discussion with, when, and the substance of the discussion.

d.   For the period June 6, 2016 through June 9, 2016, for what portion of each day were you in Trump Tower?

    i.   Did you speak or meet with Donald Trump, Jr., Paul Manafort, or Jared Kushner on June 9, 2016? If yes, did any portion of any of those conversations or meetings include any reference to any aspect of the June 9 meeting? If yes, describe who you spoke with and the substance of the conversation.

e.   Did you communicate directly or indirectly with any member or representative of the Agalarov family after June 3, 2016? If yes, describe who you spoke with, when, and the substance of the communication.

f.   Did you learn of any communications between Donald Trump, Jr., Paul Manafort, or Jared Kushner and any member or representative of the Agalarov family, Natalia Veselnitskaya, Rob Goldstone, or any Russian official or contact that took place after June 9, 2016 and concerned the June 9 meeting or efforts by Russia to assist the campaign? If yes, describe who you learned this information from, when, and the substance of what you learned.

g.   On June 7, 2016, you gave a speech in which you said, in part, "I am going to give a major speech on probably Monday of next week and we're going to be discussing all of the things that have taken place with the Clintons."

    i.   Why did you make that statement?

    ii.   What information did you plan to share with respect to the Clintons?

    iii.   What did you believe the source(s) of that information would be?

    iv.   Did you expect any of the information to have come from the June 9 meeting?

    v.   Did anyone help draft the speech that you were referring to? If so, who?

    vi.   Why did you ultimately not give the speech you referenced on June 7, 2016?

h.   Did any person or entity inform you during the campaign that Vladimir Putin or the Russian

7

U.S. Department of Justice

~~Attorney Work Product // May Contain Material Protected Under Fed. R. Crim. P. 6(e)~~

government supported your candidacy or opposed the candidacy of Hillary Clinton? If yes, describe the source(s) of the information, when you were informed, and the content of such discussion(s).

i.   Did any person or entity inform you during the campaign that any foreign government or foreign leader, other than Russia or Vladimir Putin, had provided, wished to provide, or offered to provide tangible support to your campaign, including by way of offering to provide negative information on Hillary Clinton? If yes, describe the source(s) of the information, when you were informed, and the content of such discussion(s).

Response to Question I, Parts (a) through (c)

I have no recollection of learning at the time that Donald Trump, Jr., Paul Manafort, or Jared Kushner was considering participating in a meeting in June 2016 concerning potentially negative information about Hillary Clinton. Nor do I recall learning during the campaign that the June 9, 2016 meeting had taken place, that the referenced emails existed, or that Donald J. Trump, Jr., had other communications with Emin Agalarov or Robert Goldstone between June 3, 2016 and June 9, 2016.

Response to Question I, Part (d)

I have no independent recollection of what portion of these four days in June of 2016 I spent in Trump Tower. This was one of many busy months during a fast-paced campaign, as the primary season was ending and we were preparing for the general election campaign.

I am now aware that my Campaign's calendar indicates that I was in New York City from June 6 – 9, 2016. Calendars kept in my Trump Tower office reflect that I had various calls and meetings scheduled for each of these days. While those calls and meetings may or may not actually have taken place, they do indicate that I was in Trump Tower during a portion of each of these working days, and I have no reason to doubt that I was. When I was in New York City, I stayed at my Trump Tower apartment.

My Trump Organization desk calendar also reflects that I was outside Trump Tower during portions of these days. The June 7, 2016 calendar indicates I was scheduled to leave Trump Tower in the early evening for Westchester where I gave remarks after winning the California, New Jersey, New Mexico, Montana, and South Dakota Republican primaries held that day. The June 8, 2016 calendar indicates a scheduled departure in late afternoon to attend a ceremony at my son's school. The June 9, 2016 calendar indicates I was scheduled to attend midday meetings and a fundraising luncheon at the Four Seasons Hotel. At this point, I do not remember on what dates these events occurred, but I do not currently have a reason to doubt that they took place as scheduled on my calendar.

Widely available media reports, including television footage, also shed light on my activities during these days. For example, I am aware that my June 7, 2016 victory remarks at the Trump

8

National Golf Club in Briarcliff Manor, New York, were recorded and published by the media. I remember winning those primaries and generally recall delivering remarks that evening.

At this point in time, I do not remember whether I spoke or met with Donald Trump, Jr., Paul Manafort, or Jared Kushner on June 9, 2016. My desk calendar indicates I was scheduled to meet with Paul Manafort on the morning of June 9, but I do not recall if that meeting took place. It was more than two years ago, at a time when I had many calls and interactions daily.

Response to Question I, Part (e)

I have no independent recollection of any communications I had with the Agalarov family or anyone I understood to be a representative of the Agalarov family after June 3, 2016 and before the end of the campaign. While preparing to respond to these questions, I have become aware of written communications with the Agalarovs during the campaign that were sent, received, and largely authored by my staff and which I understand have already been produced to you.

In general, the documents include congratulatory letters on my campaign victories, emails about a painting Emin and Aras Agalarov arranged to have delivered to Trump Tower as a birthday present, and emails regarding delivery of a book written by Aras Agalarov. The documents reflect that the deliveries were screened by the Secret Service.

Response to Question I, Part (f)

I do not recall being aware during the campaign of communications between Donald Trump, Jr., Paul Manafort, or Jared Kushner and any member or representative of the Agalarov family, Robert Goldstone, Natalia Veselnitskaya (whose name I was not familiar with), or anyone I understood to be a Russian official.

Response to Question I, Part (g)

In remarks I delivered the night I won the California, New Jersey, New Mexico, Montana, and South Dakota Republican primaries, I said, "I am going to give a major speech on probably Monday of next week and we're going to be discussing all of the things that have taken place with the Clintons." In general, I expected to give a speech referencing the publicly available, negative information about the Clintons, including, for example, Mrs. Clinton's failed policies, the Clintons' use of the State Department to further their interests and the interests of the Clinton Foundation, Mrs. Clinton's improper use of a private server for State Department business, the destruction of 33,000 emails on that server, and Mrs. Clinton's temperamental unsuitability for the office of President.

In the course of preparing to respond to your questions, I have become aware that the Campaign documents already produced to you reflect the drafting, evolution, and sources of information for the speech I expected to give "probably" on the Monday following my June 7, 2016 comments. These documents generally show that the text of the speech was initially drafted by Campaign staff

9

with input from various outside advisors and was based on publicly available material, including, in particular, information from the book *Clinton Cash* by Peter Schweizer.

The Pulse Nightclub terrorist attack took place in the early morning hours of Sunday, June 12, 2016. In light of that tragedy, I gave a speech directed more specifically to national security and terrorism than to the Clintons. That speech was delivered at the Saint Anselm College Institute of Politics in Manchester, New Hampshire, and, as reported, opened with the following:

> This was going to be a speech on Hillary Clinton and how bad a President, especially in these times of Radical Islamic Terrorism, she would be. Even her former Secret Service Agent, who has seen her under pressure and in times of stress, has stated that she lacks the temperament and integrity to be president. There will be plenty of opportunity to discuss these important issues at a later time, and I will deliver that speech soon. But today there is only one thing to discuss: the growing threat of terrorism inside of our borders.

I continued to speak about Mrs. Clinton's failings throughout the campaign, using the information prepared for inclusion in the speech to which I referred on June 7, 2016.

Response to Question I, Part (h)

I have no recollection of being told during the campaign that Vladimir Putin or the Russian government "supported" my candidacy or "opposed" the candidacy of Hillary Clinton. However, I was aware of some reports indicating that President Putin had made complimentary statements about me.

Response to Question I, Part (i)

I have no recollection of being told during the campaign that any foreign government or foreign leader had provided, wished to provide, or offered to provide tangible support to my campaign.

II. Russian Hacking / Russian Efforts Using Social Media / WikiLeaks

a.   On June 14, 2016, it was publicly reported that computer hackers had penetrated the computer network of the Democratic National Committee (DNC) and that Russian intelligence was behind the unauthorized access, or hack. Prior to June 14, 2016, were you provided any information about any potential or actual hacking of the computer systems or email accounts of the DNC, the Democratic Congressional Campaign Committee (DCCC), the Clinton Campaign, Hillary Clinton, or individuals associated with the Clinton campaign? If yes, describe who provided this information, when, and the substance of the information.

10

b. On July 22, 2016, WikiLeaks released nearly 20,000 emails sent or received by Democratic party officials.

  i. Prior to the July 22, 2016 release, were you aware from any source that WikiLeaks, Guccifer 2.0, DCLeaks, or Russians had or potentially had possession of or planned to release emails or information that could help your campaign or hurt the Clinton campaign? If yes, describe who you discussed this issue with, when, and the substance of the discussion(s).

  ii. After the release of emails by WikiLeaks on July 22, 2016, were you told that WikiLeaks possessed or might possess additional information that could be released during the campaign? If yes, describe who provided this information, when, and what you were told.

c. Are you aware of any communications during the campaign, directly or indirectly, between Roger Stone, Donald Trump, Jr., Paul Manafort, or Rick Gates and (a) WikiLeaks, (b) Julian Assange, (c) other representatives of WikiLeaks, (d) Guccifer 2.0, (e) representatives of Guccifer 2.0, or (f) representatives of DCLeaks? If yes, describe who provided you with this information, when you learned of the communications, and what you know about those communications.

d. On July 27, 2016, you stated at a press conference: "Russia, if you're listening, I hope you're able to find the 30,000 emails that are missing. I think you will probably be rewarded mightily by our press."

  i. Why did you make that request of Russia, as opposed to any other country, entity, or individual?

  ii. In advance of making that statement, what discussions, if any, did you have with anyone else about the substance of the statement?

  iii. Were you told at any time before or after you made that statement that Russia was attempting to infiltrate or hack computer systems or email accounts of Hillary Clinton or her campaign? If yes, describe who provided this information, when, and what you were told.

e. On October 7, 2016, emails hacked from the account of John Podesta were released by WikiLeaks.

  i. Where were you on October 7, 2016?

  ii. Were you told at any time in advance of, or on the day of, the October 7 release that WikiLeaks possessed or might possess emails related to John Podesta? If yes, describe who told you this, when, and what you were told.

11

iii.   Are you aware of anyone associated with you or your campaign, including Roger Stone, reaching out to WikiLeaks, either directly or through an intermediary, on or about October 7, 2016? If yes, identify the person and describe the substance of the conversations or contacts.

f.   Were you told of anyone associated with you or your campaign, including Roger Stone, having any discussions, directly or indirectly, with WikiLeaks, Guccifer 2.0, or DCLeaks regarding the content or timing of release of hacked emails? If yes, describe who had such contacts, how you became aware of the contacts, when you became aware of the contacts, and the substance of the contacts.

g.   From June 1, 2016 through the end of the campaign, how frequently did you communicate with Roger Stone? Describe the nature of your communication(s) with Mr. Stone.

i.   During that time period, what efforts did Mr. Stone tell you he was making to assist your campaign, and what requests, if any, did you make of Mr. Stone?

ii.   Did Mr. Stone ever discuss WikiLeaks with you or, as far as you were aware, with anyone else associated with the campaign? If yes, describe what you were told, from whom, and when.

iii.   Did Mr. Stone at anytime inform you about contacts he had with WikiLeaks or any intermediary of WikiLeaks, or about forthcoming releases of information? If yes, describe what Stone told you and when.

h.   Did you have any discussions prior to January 20, 2017, regarding a potential pardon or other action to benefit Julian Assange? If yes, describe who you had the discussion(s) with, when, and the content of the discussion(s).

i.   Were you aware of any efforts by foreign individuals or companies, including those in Russia, to assist your campaign through the use of social media postings or the organization of rallies? If yes, identify who you discussed such assistance with, when, and the content of the discussion(s).

Response to Question II, Part (a)

I do not remember the date on which it was publicly reported that the DNC had been hacked, but my best recollection is that I learned of the hacking at or shortly after the time it became the subject of media reporting. I do not recall being provided any information during the campaign about the hacking of any of the named entities or individuals before it became the subject of media reporting.

12

U.S. Department of Justice
~~Attorney Work Product // May Contain Material Protected Under Fed. R. Crim. P. 6(e)~~

Response to Question II, Part (b)

I recall that in the months leading up to the election there was considerable media reporting about the possible hacking and release of campaign-related information and there was a lot of talk about this matter. At the time, I was generally aware of these media reports and may have discussed these issues with my campaign staff or others, but at this point in time – more than two years later – I have no recollection of any particular conversation, when it occurred, or who the participants were.

Response to Question II, Part (c)

I do not recall being aware during the campaign of any communications between the individuals named in Question II (c) and anyone I understood to be a representative of WikiLeaks or any of the other individuals or entities referred to in the question.

Response to Question II, Part (d)

I made the statement quoted in Question II (d) in jest and sarcastically, as was apparent to any objective observer. The context of the statement is evident in the full reading or viewing of the July 27, 2016 press conference, and I refer you to the publicly available transcript and video of that press conference. I do not recall having any discussion about the substance of the statement in advance of the press conference. I do not recall being told during the campaign of any efforts by Russia to infiltrate or hack the computer systems or email accounts of Hillary Clinton or her campaign prior to them becoming the subject of media reporting and I have no recollection of any particular conversation in that regard.

Response to Question II, Part (e)

I was in Trump Tower in New York City on October 7, 2016. I have no recollection of being told that WikiLeaks possessed or might possess emails related to John Podesta before the release of Mr. Podesta's emails was reported by the media. Likewise, I have no recollection of being told that Roger Stone, anyone acting as an intermediary for Roger Stone, or anyone associated with my campaign had communicated with WikiLeaks on October 7, 2016.

Response to Question II, Part (f)

I do not recall being told during the campaign that Roger Stone or anyone associated with my campaign had discussions with any of the entities named in the question regarding the content or timing of release of hacked emails.

Response to Question II, Part (g)

I spoke by telephone with Roger Stone from time to time during the campaign. I have no recollection of the specifics of any conversations I had with Mr. Stone between June 1, 2016 and

13

November 8, 2016. I do not recall discussing WikiLeaks with him, nor do I recall being aware of Mr. Stone having discussed WikiLeaks with individuals associated with my campaign, although I was aware that WikiLeaks was the subject of media reporting and campaign-related discussion at the time.

Response to Question II, Part (h)

I do not recall having had any discussion during the campaign regarding a pardon or action to benefit Julian Assange.

Response to Question II, Part (i)

I do not recall being aware during the campaign of specific efforts by foreign individuals or companies to assist my campaign through the use of social media postings or the organization of rallies.

III.   The Trump Organization Moscow Project

a.   In October 2015, a "Letter of Intent," a copy of which is attached as Exhibit B, was signed for a proposed Trump Organization project in Moscow (the "Trump Moscow project").

   i.   When were you first informed of discussions about the Trump Moscow project? By whom? What were you told about the project?

   ii.   Did you sign the letter of intent?

b.   In a statement provided to Congress, attached as Exhibit C, Michael Cohen stated: "To the best of my knowledge, Mr. Trump was never in contact with anyone about this proposal other than me on three occasions, including signing a non-binding letter of intent in 2015." Describe all discussions you had with Mr. Cohen, or anyone else associated with the Trump Organization, about the Trump Moscow project, including who you spoke with, when, and the substance of the discussion(s).

c.   Did you learn of any communications between Michael Cohen or Felix Sater and any Russian government officials, including officials in the office of Dmitry Peskov, regarding the Trump Moscow project? If so, identify who provided this information to you, when, and the substance of what you learned.

d.   Did you have any discussions between June 2015 and June 2016 regarding a potential trip to Russia by you and/or Michael Cohen for reasons related to the Trump Moscow project? If yes, describe who you spoke with, when, and the substance of the discussion(s).

e.   Did you at any time direct or suggest that discussions about the Trump Moscow project

14

should cease, or were you informed at any time that the project had been abandoned? If yes, describe who you spoke with, when, the substance of the discussion(s), and why that decision was made.

f.   Did you have any discussions regarding what information would be provided publicly or in response to investigative inquiries about potential or actual investments or business deals the Trump Organization had in Russia, including the Trump Moscow project? If yes, describe who you spoke with, when, and the substance of the discussion(s).

g.   Aside from the Trump Moscow project, did you or the Trump Organization have any other prospective or actual business interests, investments, or arrangements with Russia or any Russian interest or Russian individual during the campaign? If yes, describe the business interests, investments, or arrangements.

Response to Question III, Parts (a) through (g)

Sometime in 2015, Michael Cohen suggested to me the possibility of a Trump Organization project in Moscow. As I recall, Mr. Cohen described this as a proposed project of a general type we have done in the past in a variety of locations. I signed the non-binding Letter of Intent attached to your questions as Exhibit B which required no equity or expenditure on our end and was consistent with our ongoing efforts to expand into significant markets around the world.

I had few conversations with Mr. Cohen on this subject. As I recall, they were brief, and they were not memorable. I was not enthused about the proposal, and I do not recall any discussion of travel to Russia in connection with it. I do not remember discussing it with anyone else at the Trump Organization, although it is possible. I do not recall being aware at the time of any communications between Mr. Cohen or Felix Sater and any Russian government official regarding the Letter of Intent. In the course of preparing to respond to your questions, I have become aware that Mr. Cohen sent an email regarding the Letter of Intent to "Mr. Peskov" at a general, public email account, which should show there was no meaningful relationship with people in power in Russia. I understand those documents already have been provided to you.

I vaguely remember press inquiries and media reporting during the campaign about whether the Trump Organization had business dealings in Russia. I may have spoken with campaign staff or Trump Organization employees regarding responses to requests for information, but I have no current recollection of any particular conversation, with whom I may have spoken, when, or the substance of any conversation. As I recall, neither I nor the Trump Organization had any projects or proposed projects in Russia during the campaign other than the Letter of Intent.

IV.   Contacts with Russia and Russia-Related Issues During the Campaign

a.   Prior to mid-August 2016, did you become aware that Paul Manafort had ties to the Ukrainian government? If yes, describe who you learned this information from, when, and the substance of what you were told. Did Mr. Manafort's connections to the Ukrainian or

15

Russian governments play any role in your decision to have him join your campaign? If yes, describe that role.

b.   Were you aware that Paul Manafort offered briefings on the progress of your campaign to Oleg Deripaska? If yes, describe who you learned this information from, when, the substance of what you were told, what you understood the purpose was of sharing such information with Mr. Deripaska, and how you responded to learning this information.

c.   Were you aware of whether Paul Manafort or anyone else associated with your campaign sent or directed others to send internal Trump campaign information to any person located in Ukraine or Russia or associated with the Ukrainian or Russian governments? If yes, identify who provided you with this information, when, the substance of the discussion(s), what you understood the purpose was of sharing the internal campaign information, and how you responded to learning this information.

d.   Did Paul Manafort communicate to you, directly or indirectly, any positions Ukraine or Russia would want the U.S. to support? If yes, describe when he communicated those positions to you and the substance of those communications.

e.   During the campaign, were you told about efforts by Russian officials to meet with you or senior members of your campaign? If yes, describe who you had conversations with on this topic, when, and what you were told.

f.   What role, if any, did you have in changing the Republican Party platform regarding arming Ukraine during the Republican National Convention? Prior to the convention, what information did you have about this platform provision? After the platform provision was changed, who told you about the change, when did they tell you, what were you told about why it was changed, and who was involved?

g.   On July 27, 2016, in response to a question about whether you would recognize Crimea as Russian territory and lift sanctions on Russia, you said: "We'll be looking at that. Yeah, we'll be looking." Did you intend to communicate by that statement or at any other time during the campaign a willingness to lift sanctions and/or recognize Russia's annexation of Crimea if you were elected?

   i.   What consideration did you give to lifting sanctions and/or recognizing Russia's annexation of Crimea if you were elected? Describe who you spoke with about this topic, when, the substance of the discussion(s).

Response to Question IV, Parts (a) through (d)

Mr. Manafort was hired primarily because of his delegate work for prior presidential candidates, including Gerald Ford, Ronald Reagan, George H.W. Bush, and Bob Dole. I knew that Mr. Manafort had done international consulting work and, at some time before Mr. Manafort left the

16

campaign, I learned that he was somehow involved with individuals concerning Ukraine, but I do not remember the specifics of what I knew at the time.

I had no knowledge of Mr. Manafort offering briefings on the progress of my campaign to an individual named Oleg Deripaska, nor do I remember being aware of Mr. Manafort or anyone else associated with my campaign sending or directing others to send internal Trump Campaign information to anyone I knew to be in Ukraine or Russia at the time or to anyone I understood to be a Ukrainian or Russian government employee or official. I do not remember Mr. Manafort communicating to me any particular positions Ukraine or Russia would want the United States to support.

Response to Question IV, Part (e)

I do not recall being told during the campaign of efforts by Russian officials to meet with me or with senior members of my campaign. In the process of preparing to respond to these questions, I became aware that on March 17, 2016, my assistant at the Trump Organization, Rhona Graff, received an email from a Sergei Prikhodko, who identified himself as Deputy Prime Minister of the Russian Federation, Foundation Roscongress, inviting me to participate in the St. Petersburg International Economic Forum to be held in June 2016. The documents show that Ms. Graff prepared for my signature a brief response declining the invitation. I understand these documents already have been produced to you.

Response to Question IV, Part (f)

I have no recollection of the details of what, when, or from what source I first learned about the change to the platform amendment regarding arming Ukraine, but I generally recall learning of the issue as part of media reporting. I do not recall being involved in changing the language to the amendment.

Response to Question IV, Part (g)

My statement did not communicate any position.

V.   Contacts with Russia and Russia-Related Issues During the Transition

a.   Were you asked to attend the World Chess Championship gala on November 10, 2016? If yes, who asked you to attend, when were you asked, and what were you told about about [sic] why your presence was requested?

    i.   Did you attend any part of the event? If yes, describe any interactions you had with any Russians or representatives of the Russian government at the event.

17

Response to Question V, Part (a)

I do not remember having been asked to attend the World Chess Championship gala, and I did not attend the event. During the course of preparing to respond to these questions, I have become aware of documents indicating that in March of 2016, the president of the World Chess Federation invited the Trump Organization to host, at Trump Tower, the 2016 World Chess Championship Match to be held in New York in November 2016. I have also become aware that in November 2016, there were press inquiries to my staff regarding whether I had plans to attend the tournament, which was not being held at Trump Tower. I understand these documents have already been provided to you.

Executed on **NOVEMBER 20**, 2018

DONALD J. TRUMP
President of the United States

Appendix D

U.S. Department of Justice

~~Attorney Work Product // May Contain Material Protected Under Fed. R. Crim. P. 6(e)~~

APPENDIX D

SPECIAL COUNSEL'S OFFICE TRANSFERRED, REFERRED, AND COMPLETED CASES

This appendix identifies matters transferred or referred by the Special Counsel's Office, as well as cases prosecuted by the Office that are now completed.

A. Transfers

The Special Counsel's Office has concluded its investigation into links and coordination between the Russian government and individuals associated with the Trump Campaign. Certain matters assigned to the Office by the Acting Attorney General have not fully concluded as of the date of this report. After consultation with the Office of the Deputy Attorney General, the Office has transferred responsibility for those matters to other components of the Department of Justice and the FBI. Those transfers include:

1. United States v. Bijan Rafiekian and Kamil Ekim Alptekin

   U.S. Attorney's Office for the Eastern District of Virginia
   (Awaiting trial)

   The Acting Attorney General authorized the Special Counsel to investigate, among other things, possible criminal conduct by Michael Flynn in acting as an unregistered agent for the Government of Turkey. *See* August 2, 2017 Memorandum from Rod J. Rosenstein to Robert S. Mueller, III. The Acting Attorney General later confirmed the Special Counsel's authority to investigate Rafiekian and Alptekin because they "may have been jointly involved" with Flynn in FARA-related crimes. *See* October 20, 2017 Memorandum from Associate Deputy Attorney General Scott Schools to Deputy Attorney General Rod J. Rosenstein.

   On December 1, 2017, Flynn pleaded guilty to an Information charging him with making false statements to the FBI about his contacts with the Russian ambassador to the United States. As part of that plea, Flynn agreed to a Statement of the Offense in which he acknowledged that the Foreign Agents Registration Act (FARA) documents he filed on March 7, 2017 "contained materially false statements and omissions." Flynn's plea occurred before the Special Counsel had made a final decision on whether to charge Rafiekian or Alptekin. On March 27, 2018, after consultation with the Office of the Deputy Attorney General, the Special Counsel's Office referred the investigation of Rafiekian and Alptekin to the National Security Division (NSD) for any action it deemed appropriate. The Special Counsel's Office determined the referral was appropriate because the investigation of Flynn had been completed, and that investigation had provided the rationale for the Office's investigation of Rafiekian and Alptekin. At NSD's request, the Eastern District of Virginia continued the investigation of Rafiekian and Alptekin.

2. United States v. Michael Flynn

   U.S. Attorney's Office for the District of Columbia
   (Awaiting sentencing)

495

3. United States v. Richard Gates

   U.S. Attorney's Office for the District of Columbia
   (Awaiting sentencing)

4. United States v. Internet Research Agency, et al. (Russian Social Media Campaign)

   U.S. Attorney's Office for the District of Columbia
   National Security Division
   (Post-indictment, pre-arrest & pre-trial[1])

5. United States v. Konstantin Kilimnik

   U.S. Attorney's Office for the District of Columbia
   (Post-indictment, pre-arrest)

6. United States v. Paul Manafort

   U.S. Attorney's Office for the District of Columbia
   U.S. Attorney's Office for the Eastern District of Virginia
   (Post-conviction)

7. United States v. Viktor Netyksho, et al. (Russian Hacking Operations)

   U.S. Attorney's Office for the Western District of Pennsylvania
   National Security Division
   (Post-indictment, pre-arrest)

8. United States v. William Samuel Patten

   U.S. Attorney's Office for the District of Columbia
   (Awaiting sentencing)

The Acting Attorney General authorized the Special Counsel to investigate aspects of Patten's conduct that related to another matter that was under investigation by the Office. The investigation uncovered evidence of a crime; the U.S. Attorney's Office for the District of Columbia handled the prosecution of Patten.

9. Harm to Ongoing Matter

   (Investigation ongoing)

The Acting Attorney General authorized the Special Counsel to investigate, among other things, crime or crimes arising out of payments Paul Manafort received from the Ukrainian government before and during the tenure of President Viktor Yanukovych. *See* August 2, 2017 Memorandum from Rod J. Rosenstein to Robert S. Mueller, III. The Acting Attorney General

---

[1] One defendant, Concord Management & Consulting LLC, appeared through counsel and is in pre-trial litigation.

later confirmed the Special Counsel's authority to investigate ███Harm to Ongoing Matter███

██

On October 27, 2017, Paul Manafort and Richard Gates were charged in the District of Columbia with various crimes (including FARA) in connection with work they performed for Russia-backed political entities in Ukraine. On February 22, 2018, Manafort and Gates were charged in the Eastern District of Virginia with various other crimes in connection with the payments they received for work performed for Russia-backed political entities in Ukraine. During the course of its ███HOM███, the Special Counsel's Office developed substantial evidence with respect to individuals and entities that wer ███Harm to Ongoing Matter███

██████████.[2] On February 23, 2018, Gates pleaded guilty in the District of Columbia to a multi-object conspiracy and to making false statements; the remaining charges against Gates were dismissed.[3] Thereafter, in consultation with the Office of the Deputy Attorney General, the Special Counsel's Office closed the ███Harm to Ongoing Matter███ and referred them ███HOM███ for further investigation as it deemed appropriate. The Office based its decision to close those matters on its mandate, the indictments of Manafort, Gates's plea, and its determination as to how best to allocate its resources, among other reasons; ███████████████ At ███Harm to Ongoing Matter███ continued the investigation of those closed matters.

10. United States v. Roger Stone

> *U.S. Attorney's Office for the District of Columbia*
> (Awaiting trial)

11. ███Harm to Ongoing Matter███

███████████████████████████████████

(Investigation ongoing)

B. Referrals

During the course of the investigation, the Office periodically identified evidence of potential criminal activity that was outside the scope of the Special Counsel's jurisdiction established by the Acting Attorney General. After consultation with the Office of the Deputy Attorney General, the Office referred that evidence to appropriate law enforcement authorities, principally other components of the Department of Justice and the FBI. Those referrals, listed

---

[2] ███Harm to Ongoing Matter███

███████████████████████████████████

[3] Manafort was ultimately convicted at trial in the Eastern District of Virginia and pleaded guilty in the District of Columbia. *See* Vol. I, Section IV.A.8. The trial and plea happened after the transfer decision described here.

alphabetically by subject, are summarized below.

1. HOM

Harm to Ongoing Matter

2. Michael Cohen

During the course of the investigation, the Special Counsel's Office uncovered evidence of potential wire fraud and FECA violations pertaining to Michael Cohen. That evidence was referred to the U.S. Attorney's Office for the Southern District of New York and the FBI's New York Field Office.

3. HOM

Harm to Ongoing Matter

4. HOM

Harm to Ongoing Matter

5. Gregory Craig HOM Skadden, Arps, Slate, Meagher & Flom LLP

During the course of the FARA investigation of Paul Manafort and Rick Gates, the Special Counsel's Office uncovered evidence of potential FARA violations pertaining to HOM Gregory Craig, Skadden, Arps, Slate, Meagher & Flom LLP (Skadden), and their work on behalf of the government of Ukraine.

After consultation with the NSD, the evidence regarding Craig HOM was referred to NSD, and NSD elected to partner with the U.S. Attorney's Office for the Southern District of New York and the FBI's New York Field Office. NSD later elected to partner on the Craig matter with the U.S. Attorney's Office for the District of Columbia. NSD retained and handled issues relating to Skadden itself.

6. HOM

Harm to Ongoing Matter

498

Harm to Ongoing Matter

7. HOM

Harm to Ongoing Matter

8. HOM

Harm to Ongoing Matter

9. HOM

Harm to Ongoing Matter

10. HOM

Harm to Ongoing Matter

11. HOM

Harm to Ongoing Matter

12. HOM

Harm to Ongoing Matter

13. HOM

Harm to Ongoing Matter

U.S. Department of Justice

Attorney Work Product // May Contain Material Protected Under Fed. R. Crim. P. 6(e)

Harm to Ongoing Matter

14. HOM

Harm to Ongoing Matter

Harm to Ongoing Matter

C. Completed Prosecutions

In three cases prosecuted by the Special Counsel's Office, the defendants have completed or are about to complete their terms of imprisonment. Because no further proceedings are likely in any case, responsibility for them has not been transferred to any other office or component.

1. United States v. George Papadopoulos

    Post-conviction, Completed term of imprisonment (December 7, 2018)

2. United States v. Alex van der Zwaan

    Post-conviction, Completed term of imprisonment (June 4, 2018)

3. United States v. Richard Pinedo

    Post-conviction, Currently in Residential Reentry Center (release date May 13, 2019)

500

D-6

Mueller and Trump:
Born to Wealth, Raised to Lead.
Then, Sharply Different Choices

---

by Marc Fisher and Sari Horwitz
of *The Washington Post*

They are the sons of wealth, brought up in families accustomed to power. They were raised to show and demand respect, and they were raised to lead.

They rose to positions of enormous authority, the president of the United States and the special counsel chosen to investigate him. They dress more formally than most of those around them; both sport meticulously coifed hair. They have won unusual loyalty from those who believe in them. They attended elite all-male private schools, were accomplished high school athletes and went on to Ivy League colleges. As young men, each was deeply affected by the death of a man he admired greatly.

Yet Robert Swan Mueller III and Donald John Trump, born 22 months apart in New York City, also can seem to come from different planets. One is courtly and crisp, the other blustery and brash. One turned away from the path to greater wealth, while the other spent half a century exploring every possible avenue to add to his assets.

At pivotal points in their lives, they made sharply divergent choices—as students, as draft-age men facing the dilemma of the Vietnam War, as ambitious alpha males deciding where to focus their energies.

Now, they face each other in a slow-moving, long-running confrontation that could end in anything from deeper political discord to a fatal blow to this presidency. For the two-plus years of the Russia investigation, Trump, 72, and Mueller, 74, have behaved much as they have throughout their lives: As the president fumed about a "witch hunt" and took his frustrations to his supporters, the special counsel remained publicly mute, speaking through inquiries, indictments and, finally, a report.

The months flipped by, and the showdown loomed: Mueller and Trump, the war hero and the draft avoider, two men who rise early and live mainly at the office, two men who find relief on the golf course. They circled each other, speaking different languages. One railed against the idea that there were facts to uncover; the other hewed to his career-long belief that the facts would out and the facts would resolve doubts.

Their aides spoke in fits and starts about whether and when the two would meet, and in the end, they communicated only through written questions and answers, keeping to their missions, one loudly, the other in silence, neither knowing how this dramatic and divisive chapter of American history would end.

FROM PRINCETON TO THE MARINES

Mueller was born to a social rank that barely exists anymore, a cosseted WASP elite of northeastern families who sent their sons to New England prep schools built with generations of inherited wealth.

Mueller's father was an executive at DuPont, part of a family firmly planted in the country's plutocracy. Mueller, who grew up in Princeton, N.J., and the Philadelphia Main Line, was sent to St. Paul's School in New Hampshire, where the Astor, Vanderbilt and Mellon families educated their boys. At the Episcopal school, Mueller became captain of the soccer, ice hockey and lacrosse teams. He played ice hockey with classmate John F. Kerry, a future secretary of state and one of three St. Paul's alumni who would run for president.

Mueller epitomized the tradition of "the muscular Christian" at the top prep schools, the archetype of the strong boy who embodies "values of kindness, respect and integrity," said Maxwell King, 73, a classmate at St. Paul's. "Bob was a very strong figure in our class. . . . He was thought of as somebody you could count on to be thoughtful about everybody on the team and to have very high standards."

King, a former editor of the Philadelphia Inquirer who runs the Pittsburgh Foundation, said Mueller "had a good sense of humor, but he wasn't smartass at all. He was serious, but in a way that everybody liked him and liked being around him."

Mueller was, from early on, a role model. As a group of boys gathered one day at the Tuck, a snack shop at St. Paul's, a student made a derogatory comment about someone who wasn't there. "Bob said he didn't want to hear that," King said. "I mean, we all said disparaging things about each other face to face. But saying something about someone who wasn't there was something that Bob was uncomfortable with, and he let it be known and just walked out."

At Princeton, which his father also had attended, Mueller was accepted into one of the most socially exclusive eating clubs, where he often was seen before dinner playing bridge by the sitting-room fireplace. Mueller had planned to go to medical school, but as a classmate who studied with him recalled, organic chemistry got the better of him. Mueller pronounced himself defeated by the subject; he realized he would not be a doctor.

Just a few weeks after he finished Princeton with a degree in politics in 1966, Mueller enlisted in the Marine Corps, a rare choice for an Ivy League graduate at a time when many young men were casting about for ways to avoid the draft. Mueller, who declined to be interviewed, has often said he was inspired to join the Marines by his lacrosse teammate David Hackett, who had graduated from Princeton a year earlier and gone off to fight in Vietnam.

"As we were graduating, we . . . faced the decision of how to respond to the war in Vietnam," Mueller said in a speech in 2017. "And a number of [Hackett's] friends and teammates joined the Marine Corps because of him, as did I." In April 1967, as he led his platoon in evacuating fallen Marines from a battleground, Hackett was shot in the back of the head by a North Vietnamese sniper. Mueller to this day speaks of Hackett's death as a turning point, as the event that pushed him to a career of public service.

Before beginning his military training, and while recovering from a knee injury, Mueller studied international relations at New York University. Then he started Officer Candidates School at Quantico, Va., where he excelled, although he did get a D in delegation. Mueller followed that, according to military records, by going through the Army's grueling Ranger School and Airborne School—unusual training for a Marine, signaling that he was going places.

By November 1968, he was leading a rifle platoon in the jungles of Vietnam.

OFF TO MILITARY SCHOOL

Like Mueller, Trump was raised in rare comfort. The Trumps had a family chef and chauffeur, but they never considered themselves part of the country's ruling class. Theirs was immigrant stock, from Germany and Scotland, hardy entrepreneurs who tackled the new land with a blitz of new businesses—restaurants, hotels and, finally, real estate.

The president's father, Fred Trump, made his fortune himself, building middle-class housing for the union workers and civil servants of New York's outer boroughs. Even after he'd established himself as one of the city's biggest builders, Fred Trump still toiled in the trenches, taking young Donald along on weekends when they went door to door at Trump Village in Brooklyn, collecting rent.

Donald Trump grew up in a 23-room manse in Queens, a faux Southern plantation house with a Cadillac limousine in the driveway. He attended private school from kindergarten on; his focus in school, Trump told The Washington Post in 2016, was "creating mischief, because, for some reason, I liked to stir things up and I liked to test people. . . . It wasn't malicious so much as it was aggressive."

In second grade, he said, he punched his music teacher in the face.

He got into trouble often. Before eighth grade started, his father sent him to military school.

At New York Military Academy, where the rules were so strictly enforced that a desperate cadet was said to have leaped into the Hudson River in an attempted escape, Trump thrived. Although he ate in a mess hall instead of being served steaks by the family cook, and although he slept in a barracks rather than his own room in a mansion, he for the first time took pride in his grades. He won medals for neatness and order.

He also won notice from fellow cadets for touting his father's wealth and boasting to friends that "I'm going to be famous one day."

Trump competed to become a cadet leader and enjoyed wielding authority. As a junior supply sergeant in E Company, he ordered that a cadet be struck on the backside as punishment for breaking formation. Another time, while inspecting dorm rooms, Trump saw cadet Ted Levine's unmade bed and blew up, ripping off the sheets and tossing them on the floor, Levine said. Levine threw a combat boot at Trump and hit him with a broomstick. Trump, infuriated, grabbed Levine and tried to push him out a second-story window, Levine said.

Promoted to captain of A Company, Trump won respect from some of the other boys, who said they never wanted to disappoint him. Trump introduced them to a world of fun, setting up a tanning salon in his dorm room, bringing beautiful women to campus and leading the baseball team to victory.

But other cadets said Trump tried to break boys who didn't bend to his will. During Trump's senior year, when one of his sergeants shoved a new cadet against a wall for not standing at attention quickly enough, Trump was relieved of his duty in the barracks, said Lee Ains, the student who was shoved.

Trump denied being demoted, saying he was actually moved up. "You don't get elevated if you partake in hazing," he told The Washington Post in 2016. He was put in charge of a drill team that would perform in New York City's Columbus Day Parade.

FLEETING VICTORIES AND FIERY RETREATS

Mutter's Ridge was a killing ground, a craggy hellscape in Quang Tri province where the Marines had been fighting for years, setting up and abandoning bases as they tried over and over to assert control of one of the main routes the North Vietnamese used to infiltrate the South.

Year after year, the ridge, hard by the demilitarized zone that separated North from South, was the scene of fierce assaults, fleeting victories and fiery retreats.

On Dec. 11, 1968, Mueller led a platoon of Marines into an eight-hour battle around an extensive complex of North Vietnamese army bunkers. The enemy hit Mueller's men with a "heavy volume of small arms, automatic weapons, and grenade launcher fire," according to a Marine Corps account.

As his platoon suffered heavy casualties, "Second Lieutenant Mueller fearlessly moved from one position to another, directing the accurate counterfire of his men and shouting words of encouragement to them," the account said.

Mueller set up a defensive perimeter and "with complete disregard for his own safety, he then skillfully supervised the evacuation of casualties from the hazardous fire area," as the Marines put it. Mueller led a team across the smoldering terrain and into a North Vietnamese–controlled area to recover a mortally wounded Marine. For that, he earned a Bronze Star Medal with "V" distinction for combat valor. He was promoted to first lieutenant.

Four months later, the North Vietnamese attacked a squad of about a dozen Marines from Mueller's platoon. Responding to the ambush, Mueller led the rest of his men to assist the Marines under assault. They pushed ahead against heavy fire, and Mueller was shot in the thigh.

"Although seriously wounded during the fire fight, he resolutely maintained his position and, ably directing the fire of his platoon, was instrumental in defeating the North Vietnamese Army force," said the citation on the medal Mueller received.

His year in Vietnam was a turning point, friends said. "He never speaks to that horror and what he did," said Thomas B. Wilner, a longtime friend and Washington lawyer.

A lifelong friend said that after Vietnam, Mueller "went from being this affable, good guy, good athlete" to having the "backbone and the steel that he has today." But Mueller doesn't talk about those harrowing months in the jungle. "That is not his style. He doesn't brag about himself."

DRAFT DEFERMENTS

The country felt as though it were coming apart at the seams. At the University of Pennsylvania, where Trump had transferred after two years at Fordham University in the Bronx, protests against the Vietnam War grew larger and more insistent. There were sit-ins, candlelight vigils, demonstrations against university contracts with the military—a metastasizing culture of conflict as a new generation pushed back against war, segregation, dress codes and curfews.

Trump took part in none of that. Nor did he pay much attention to his coursework, fellow students said. He was already spending nearly as much time working for his father's real estate business in New York as he was on campus in Philadelphia. He said he spent many of his off-hours while at school scouring the neighborhood for apartments to buy so he could rent them to students.

Trump never burned a draft card, but he never enlisted either. He benefited from five draft deferments between 1964 and 1968—four for being a college student and one for a medical disqualification.

Trump has said he had bone spurs in his foot. During his presidential campaign, Trump said he could not recall which foot had the spurs. Later, his campaign said he had them in both heels. At another point, a campaign statement said that in 1969, Trump was fit for service and "had his draft number been selected, he would have proudly served." His draft lottery number was 356 out of 366—high enough that he almost certainly would have been spared from mandatory service.

"MUELLER, HOMICIDE"

Mueller spent the first two decades of his legal career putting bad guys behind bars. He worked as a prosecutor in San Francisco and Boston. And in Washington, he headed the Justice Department's criminal division as an assistant attorney general under President George H. W. Bush, supervising high-profile cases such as the prosecution of Panamanian dictator Manuel Antonio Noriega and the terrorist bombing of Pan Am Flight 103.

But by 1995, he was ensconced in the $400,000-a-year luxury of a white-collar litigation job in the Washington office of a Boston law firm, Hale and Dorr. It was not a happy time.

"He hated it," said Wilner, the longtime friend. "He couldn't stand selling his services to defend people he thought might be guilty. . . . There was no hesitation for Bob in leaving a lucrative job to . . . do what he thought was helping make the world a better place."

So one day, Mueller called the District's local prosecutor, U.S. Attorney Eric H. Holder Jr., and asked for a job, not handling the office's big national cases but working the line, prosecuting homicides on the streets of Washington. He wanted no title, no supervisory position. He told Holder that he was shaken by all of the killings in Washington, then the nation's murder capital, and that he just wanted to try homicide cases.

"I was taken aback," Holder recalled. He reminded Mueller that coming to work at the "Triple Nickel"—as the prosecutors' office at 555 Fourth Street NW was called—would mean a pay cut of more than 75 percent, a big step down in stature and a daunting job. The District, plagued with a crack cocaine epidemic and about 400 homicides a year, was a nightmare for prosecutors, who faced huge caseloads and witnesses who often were too scared to talk.

Mueller said he knew what he was getting into. Holder hired him but insisted on giving him a title—senior litigation counsel—and eventually made him head of the homicide section. Day to day, though, Mueller was "just a line guy," Holder said. "He would be in those parts of Washington that were most affected by the violence. . . . He would be interviewing people at crime scenes, going to people's homes to build cases, working with street cops."

He got a kick out of answering his phone, "Mueller, Homicide."

"I love everything about investigations," Mueller said years later in an interview with UVA Lawyer, the magazine of the University of Virginia School of Law, where he earned his law degree. "I love the forensics. I love the fingerprints and the bullet casings and all the rest."

He led the prosecution of high-profile cases including the grisly murders in 1997 of three workers in a Starbucks coffee shop in Georgetown. D.C. Police were not thrilled about the idea, but Mueller brought in a star FBI agent to work on the investigation. Three years after the killings, a D.C. man was sentenced to life in prison without parole.

"If it wasn't for [Mueller], that case would never have been solved," said former longtime homicide detective James Trainum, who worked with Mueller on the case. "With his quiet demeanor, he just kind of waded in and diplomatically parted the waters."

Through the decades, Mueller has often said that what matters even more than the content of one's work is "how we do it," as he put it in a commencement address in 2013. "You are only as good as your word. You can be smart, aggressive, articulate and indeed persuasive, but if you are not honest, your reputation will suffer, and once lost, a good reputation can never be regained."

TOUGH ENOUGH TO MAKE IT

Trump was determined to push beyond his father's realm in New York's outer boroughs and make it big in Manhattan. He had neither time nor patience for climbing the ladder rung by rung. He believed in big, bold leaps, even if that meant breaking with tradition or rules.

"The key to the way I promote is bravado," he wrote in "Trump: The Art of the Deal," his best-selling book. "I play to people's fantasies. People may not always think big themselves, but they can still get very excited by those who do. That's why a little hyperbole never hurts."

It was Trump's older brother, Fred Jr., who was originally supposed to take over the family business. But Freddy, mild-mannered and, in Donald's view, not tough enough to make it, struggled to live up to his father's demands. Freddy left the family company to become an airline pilot, but he began drinking excessively. In 1981, at age 43, he died of a heart attack following years of alcoholism. Donald had adored his brother, and now he resolved never to drink alcohol and always to remember a lesson he drew from Freddy's failure: "To keep my guard up one hundred percent. . . . Life is a series of battles ending in victory or defeat," he said at the time. "You just can't let people make a sucker out of you."

In contrast to his brother, Donald Trump was determined to do whatever it took to "be a killer," as his father had repeatedly insisted. While working on his first hotel project in 1976, Trump persuaded a New York Times reporter to profile him as "a major New York builder," even though he had never built a thing and had no financing.

He touted his ties to power. In the mid-1970s, seeking to buy New York's World Trade Center, Trump had lunch with Peter C. Goldmark Jr., the head of New York's Port Authority, which owned the twin towers. "You wouldn't last in your job very long if Governor [Hugh] Carey decided you weren't doing the right thing," Trump said, according to Goldmark. "You should know I have a lot of weight in Albany."

Goldmark said he ended the discussion after that. Trump denied Goldmark's account, saying, "I really don't talk that way."

Trump's knack for drawing attention sometimes embarrassed or persuaded the powers that were to cede to his demands. When city politicians who opposed granting Trump a tax incentive called a news conference outside the shuttered Commodore Hotel, Trump showed up and threatened to abandon the project if the city didn't give him tax relief.

Trump had prepared for the event by directing his workers to replace the clean boards that covered the once-grand building's windows with dirty scrap wood, accentuating the decrepit state of the midtown eyesore. The dramatic flourish had the desired effect. Trump got the exemption. He beat the system.

G-MAN

After Mueller did a stint as U.S. attorney in San Francisco, President George W. Bush nominated him to direct the FBI. He was sworn in on Sept. 4, 2001, one week before the planes hit the twin towers.

For the next 12 years, in both Republican and Democratic administrations, Mueller led the FBI through one of the most difficult periods in its history. The bureau shifted from a domestic law enforcement agency largely focused on criminal threats to a global intelligence organization reoriented to fight terrorism.

Although more terrorist attacks were feared, Mueller was intent on protecting civil liberties, according to those who worked with him. "He didn't allow FBI agents in the post-9/11 era to engage in interrogation techniques that he thought were inconsistent with American law and tradition," said Holder, who, as President Barack Obama's attorney general, was his boss once again.

Mueller worked around the clock, traveling from his Georgetown home to FBI headquarters in a black SUV that arrived shortly after 6 a.m. for morning security briefings, heading back late at night. He wore a traditional J. Edgar Hoover–era G-man uniform: dark suit, red or blue tie and white shirt—always white.

"He won't wear a blue shirt," Wilner said. "He is so straight, he always wears a white shirt. He's a pain in the ass in many ways because he is so straight. . . . He's conscious that he's a public figure, and he doesn't want anything to compromise his integrity. Even a blue shirt."

Around the building, some privately dubbed him "Bobby Three Sticks," a reference to both the Roman numeral at the end of his name and the three-finger Boy Scout salute. No one dared use the nickname in his presence, former Justice Department officials said.

Mueller usually avoided the limelight. He frustrated his speech-writers by crossing out every "I" in speeches they wrote for him. It wasn't about him, he told them: "It's about the organization."

FAMILY AND POLITICS

Mueller burrowed into the bureaucracy and won allies by eschewing publicity. Trump charged into one industry after another, from casino gambling to steaks to for-profit education and finally to politics. The only through line in his career was his own celebrity—the power and allure of his name.

In nearly every possible way, from their family relations to their political involvement, the two men have presented themselves in opposite ways.

Three months after he graduated from college, Mueller married his girlfriend, Ann Standish, whose ancestors had come to the United States on the Mayflower. The couple, who met at a party when they were 17, have two daughters. One of them has spina bifida, and at one point, Mueller took a job in the U.S. attorney's office in Boston in part to be near the treatment she needed.

Throughout the investigation and earlier stages of his career, Mueller asked reporters not to discuss his family life; Trump for decades regularly sought coverage of his love life by gossip columnists, and talked about his dates and bedroom activities with radio host Howard Stern.

Trump has five children by three wives, each of them newcomers to New York City, two from Central Europe and one from a small town in Georgia. None was born to privilege. Like his father before him, Trump was distant from his children when they were very young but grew close once they were mature enough to learn the family business and join him on his daily rounds.

Mueller is a lifelong Republican who has worked for administrations of both parties; Trump was raised in a Republican home by a father who spent many weekends visiting the Democratic clubs of Brooklyn, building relationships with the politicians who might help him get his projects built.

For four decades, Trump toyed with the idea of entering politics. He changed his party registration seven times between 1999 and 2012—he was a Democrat twice, a Republican three times and an independent. In 2000, he briefly ran for president under the Reform Party banner. Once, when asked in a television interview why he was a Republican, he said, "I have no idea."

A FRIENDLY CONVERSATION

In the Rose Garden on June 21, 2013, Obama announced that James B. Comey would replace Mueller as FBI director. "Like the Marine that he's always been, Bob never took his eyes off his mission," Obama said. "It's a tribute to Bob's trademark humility that most Americans probably wouldn't recognize him on the street, but all of us are better because of his service."

Four years later, in May of 2017, the new president invited Mueller back to the White House. President Trump had abruptly fired Comey and now, at the suggestion of Attorney General Jeff Sessions, Mueller was coming in to talk about his former job. On his way into the Oval Office, Mueller met then–chief strategist Stephen K. Bannon, a former Navy officer, and teased him for letting his daughter go to West Point.

Mueller and Trump spoke for about 30 minutes, according to a person familiar with the interview. It was a friendly conversation but seemed almost pro forma because Mueller made it clear from the start that he was unlikely to take the job he had held for 12 years.

Trump liked Mueller, according to the person. "He thought he was smart and tough," a type Trump admires more than almost any other.

The question became moot within days, as Deputy Attorney General Rod J. Rosenstein appointed Mueller as the special counsel to investigate whether the Trump campaign coordinated with Russian officials during the 2016 campaign.

Trump heard the news and asked one of his aides, "Wasn't that guy just in here interviewing for the FBI?"

This is an updated version of an article that appeared in The Washington Post *on February 23, 2018.*

Glossary of Legal Terms

attorney general: The top law enforcement official in the United States, and the head of the Justice Department.

conspiracy to defraud the United States: A legal charge used against people thought to have worked together to commit fraud against the US government in some way, such as by impeding the functions of the Federal Election Commission or another government agency. The special counsel's office made use of this charge against former Trump campaign officials Paul Manafort and Rick Gates, and against the Russian organization that engineered a social media campaign to influence the 2016 election. This is the technical charge that pundits likely mean when they colloquially refer to "collusion," which envisions a conspiracy between Russians and Americans to defraud the US election system.

criminal information: A way of charging someone with a crime that is generally used when a person is expected to plead guilty. The criminal information, which is sometimes scant on details, lays out the legal violations of which a person is accused, and the person then pleads guilty to those violations. The document is filed by prosecutors without the use of a grand jury.

deputy attorney general: The No. 2 official in the Justice Department, who effectively serves as the department's chief operating officer and is assumed to be in charge of matters from which the attorney general is recused.

executive privilege: A murky power of the president that allows him to withhold information from the other branches of government on the grounds that it is privileged. Trump's legal team weighed

515

invoking the concept to stop the special counsel from making public certain findings that would include information covered by executive privilege.

false statements: The criminal charge for lying to government investigators. The special counsel's office used this extensively against people who lied during interviews. It is also illegal to give false testimony to Congress.

5K1 letter: A letter prosecutors file to a judge that details how a defendant has cooperated in an investigation so the judge can consider a lesser sentence. The letters are coveted by defendants. The term *5K1* refers to section 5K1.1 of the US Sentencing Guidelines, which describes how a judge can impose a lesser sentence on cooperators.

Foreign Agents Registration Act: A law requiring people who do political and public relations work for foreign governments or political parties to influence events in the United States to register with the Justice Department.

forfeiture: Property or money a person is required to give up because it was used in or derived from criminal activity.

grand jury: A group of citizens before whom prosecutors call witnesses and present evidence in secret. The grand jury then votes on whether the information is sufficient to bring charges, in the form of an indictment, against a person in a criminal case. An accused person does not get to bring a defense attorney to a grand jury, which is highly deferential to prosecutors.

immunity: A guarantee a person won't be prosecuted. Importantly, there is a difference between *full immunity*, where prosecutors agree not to prosecute someone for a particular crime, and *use immunity*, where a person talks to prosecutors on the condition that nothing the person says during that conversation can be used against the person.

indictment: A document that outlines the specific criminal charges against a person. It is returned by a grand jury after a prosecutor presents evidence showing there is probable cause, or reasonable grounds, to believe that a crime was committed in the case.

material (to an investigation): A legal term that essentially means "relevant."

money laundering: Concealing the origin of funds that were obtained illegally.

obstruction of justice: Taking steps with the intention of interfering with a legal or judicial process.

proffer session: A meeting between prosecutors and a suspect in a criminal investigation in which the suspect agrees to talk on the condition that nothing from the interview can be used in a future prosecution. Such sessions often come in the advanced stages of plea negotiations, when the suspect is offering to admit guilt to certain crimes in exchange for leniency.

sentencing memorandum: A document filed in court in advance of a person's sentencing hearing that lays out details of the case and advocates for a punishment. Both prosecutors and defense attorneys file sentencing memorandums to advance their respective arguments and provide context about the defendant's actions to a judge, who imposes a sentence.

speaking indictment: An indictment that reveals more detail than is necessary to support the charges, so that prosecutors can reveal to the public information that might otherwise not be disclosed. Mueller seemed to use this practice especially in his indictments of Russians, who are unlikely to ever come to the United States to face trial.

special counsel: A lawyer appointed by the attorney general—or the acting attorney general, if the attorney general is recused—to lead an independent law enforcement investigation of a particular matter. The role of special counsel is defined by regulations adopted by the Justice Department, after a statute that allowed for the appointment of independent counsels was allowed to expire in 1999. A special counsel is not subject to daily Justice Department supervision, but unlike under the independent counsel law, the attorney general retains some supervisory powers over the special counsel. For instance, the special counsel must notify the attorney general of significant actions, and the attorney general can veto those actions if they are out of step with Justice Department norms.

statement of offense: A court document, generally filed when someone is pleading guilty, that details the specific conduct to which the person is admitting.

treason: Giving aid and comfort to enemies of the United States. As a criminal matter, treason has been limited to acts to assist countries against whom Congress has declared war or authorized the use of force.

The Key Documents
in the Special Counsel's Investigation,
Arranged in Chronological Order,
with Introductions by *The Washington Post*

Special Counsel Robert S. Mueller III ran one of the highest-profile investigations in US history and said almost nothing about it to the media. Throughout his work, Mueller never gave a public press conference, and his spokesman offered a simple "No comment" to almost every story with which he was presented.

Instead, Mueller and his team spoke in court documents, laying out in detailed indictments and other filings what they had found, and who they believed had committed crimes. Legal experts said Mueller's "speaking indictments" appeared designed not just to make criminal cases against individual defendants but to educate the country about the evidence his team had gathered.

Following is a limited selection of some of the most important documents of the Mueller investigation, which lay bare how the special counsel penetrated the inner workings of Russian hacking and social media influence operations and charged a host of Trump allies with a variety of wrongdoing.

1. Appointment Order, Acting Attorney General Rod J. Rosenstein, May 17, 2017

Robert S. Mueller III became special counsel on May 17, 2017, when Deputy Attorney General Rod J. Rosenstein affixed his signature to this single page of open-ended instructions. The document's brevity belies its significance: Rosenstein had just set in motion one of the most important investigations in US history, one that would explore whether the president's campaign had worked with a foreign power to get him elected, and whether the president had then worked to thwart law enforcement's effort to figure out what happened.

Rosenstein's order gave Mueller wide latitude. The Vietnam veteran and former FBI director was assigned to take over the inquiry into possible coordination between the Russian government and the Trump campaign, as well as "any matters that arose or may arise directly from the investigation." That appeared to be a reference to an investigation—already opened at the time of Mueller's appointment though not yet publicly confirmed—into whether President Trump had sought to obstruct justice. Rosenstein would issue a more detailed memo a few months later providing a more specific description of Mueller's authority, and noting that his first order was "worded categorically in order to permit its public release without confirming specific investigations involving specific individuals."

Note to the Reader:

The Rod Rosenstein appointment letter was included in the *Report On The Investigation Into Russian Interference In The 2016 Presidential Election* as Appendix A and also appears in that context in this volume on page 449.

ORDER NO. 3915-2017

APPOINTMENT OF SPECIAL COUNSEL
TO INVESTIGATE RUSSIAN INTERFERENCE WITH THE
2016 PRESIDENTIAL ELECTION AND RELATED MATTERS

By virtue of the authority vested in me as Acting Attorney General, including 28 U.S.C. §§ 509, 510, and 515, in order to discharge my responsibility to provide supervision and management of the Department of Justice, and to ensure a full and thorough investigation of the Russian government's efforts to interfere in the 2016 presidential election, I hereby order as follows:

(a)   Robert S. Mueller III is appointed to serve as Special Counsel for the United States Department of Justice.

(b)   The Special Counsel is authorized to conduct the investigation confirmed by then-FBI Director James B. Comey in testimony before the House Permanent Select Committee on Intelligence on March 20, 2017, including:

(i)   any links and/or coordination between the Russian government and individuals associated with the campaign of President Donald Trump; and

(ii)   any matters that arose or may arise directly from the investigation; and

(iii)   any other matters within the scope of 28 C.F.R. § 600.4(a).

(c)   If the Special Counsel believes it is necessary and appropriate, the Special Counsel is authorized to prosecute federal crimes arising from the investigation of these matters.

(d)   Sections 600.4 through 600.10 of Title 28 of the Code of Federal Regulations are applicable to the Special Counsel.

_5/17/17_
Date

Rod J. Rosenstein
Acting Attorney General

2. Statement of the Offense, *US v. George Papadopoulos* (US District Court for the District of Columbia, October 5, 2017)

Few people had ever heard of George Papadopoulos, a former campaign adviser to Donald Trump, when the special counsel's office announced on October 30, 2017, that he had pleaded guilty three weeks earlier to lying to the FBI. Papadopoulos's plea was an early indication of just how much Robert S. Mueller III was doing and learning in total secrecy. After all, Papadopoulos had been arrested at Washington Dulles International Airport in July and walked unnoticed into court to enter his guilty plea in early October, with not a word leaking to the public.

This document outlines the nature of Papadopoulos's lies to the FBI, who first knocked on the energy consultant's Chicago door in January 2017 to ask him about Russia. Prosecutors revealed key information about the Trump team's flirtation with Russia during the campaign. Papadopoulos acknowledged that he worked to downplay his Russia contacts to the FBI to protect Donald Trump. In fact, soon after he was named a volunteer adviser to the campaign in March 2016, Papadopoulos had been befriended by "an overseas professor" who informed him that the Russians held dirt on Democrat Hillary Clinton in the form of thousands of emails.

The professor—who has been identified as Maltese academic Joseph Mifsud—introduced Papadopoulos to a "female Russian national," who falsely told the young aide she was Vladimir Putin's niece, and a man described as a "Russian national connected to the Russian Ministry of Foreign Affairs." Papadopoulos communicated extensively with the woman and the Russian man, think tank director Ivan Timofeev—working with the two and with Mifsud to try to organize a meeting between Trump campaign staff and Russians, perhaps even a face-to-face Trump-Putin encounter. Timofeev has said his think tank's interactions with Papadopoulos were routine academic outreach. Mifsud has confirmed that he is the professor referenced in the document but denied wrongdoing or any knowledge that Russia held Clinton emails.

The document also explained to the public that these Russian interactions were hardly a secret to Trump's most senior aides. Among those Papadopoulos told of his efforts were his "campaign supervisor"—later identified as Trump campaign cochair Sam Clovis—as well as campaign manager Corey Lewandowski (referred to as a "high-ranking campaign official") and campaign chairman Paul Manafort ("another high-ranking campaign official.") According to the document, Papadopoulos even informed Trump, announcing to the candidate at a March 31, 2016, meeting in Washington, DC, that he could help arrange a meeting for him with Putin.

UNITED STATES DISTRICT COURT
FOR THE DISTRICT OF COLUMBIA

UNITED STATES OF AMERICA	Criminal No.: 17 G. 182 (RDM) SEALED
v.	Violation: 18 U.S.C. § 1001 (False Statements)
GEORGE PAPADOPOULOS,	**FILED**
Defendant.	OCT - 5 2017
	Clerk, District and Bankruptcy Courts

STATEMENT OF THE OFFENSE

Pursuant to Federal Rule of Criminal Procedure 11, the United States of America and the defendant, GEORGE PAPADOPOULOS, stipulate and agree that the following facts are true and accurate. These facts do not constitute all of the facts known to the parties concerning the charged offense; they are being submitted to demonstrate that sufficient facts exist that the defendant committed the offense to which he is pleading guilty.

I.   Overview

1.   The defendant, GEORGE PAPADOPOULOS, who served as a foreign policy advisor for the presidential campaign of Donald J. Trump (the "Campaign"), made material false statements and material omissions during an interview with the Federal Bureau of Investigation ("FBI") that took place on January 27, 2017. At the time of the interview, the FBI had an open investigation into the Russian government's efforts to interfere in the 2016 presidential election, including the nature of any links between individuals associated with the Campaign and the Russian government, and whether there was any coordination between the Campaign and Russia's efforts. The FBI opened and coordinated the investigation in Washington, D.C.

2.   Defendant PAPADOPOULOS made the following material false statements and material omissions to the FBI:

525

      a.   Defendant PAPADOPOULOS claimed that his interactions with an overseas professor, who defendant PAPADOPOULOS understood to have substantial connections to Russian government officials, occurred before defendant PAPADOPOULOS became a foreign policy adviser to the Campaign. Defendant PAPADOPOULOS acknowledged that the professor had told him about the Russians possessing "dirt" on then-candidate Hillary Clinton in the form of "thousands of emails," but stated multiple times that he learned that information prior to joining the Campaign. In truth and in fact, however, defendant PAPADOPOULOS learned he would be an advisor to the Campaign in early March, and met the professor on or about March 14, 2016; the professor only took interest in defendant PAPADOPOULOS because of his status with the Campaign; and the professor told defendant PAPADOPOULOS about the "thousands of emails" on or about April 26, 2016, when defendant PAPADOPOULOS had been a foreign policy adviser to the Campaign for over a month.

      b.   Defendant PAPADOPOULOS further told the investigating agents that the professor was "a nothing" and "just a guy talk[ing] up connections or something." In truth and in fact, however, defendant PAPADOPOULOS understood that the professor had substantial connections to Russian government officials (and had met with some of those officials in Moscow immediately prior to telling defendant PAPADOPOULOS about the "thousands of emails") and, over a period of months, defendant PAPADOPOULOS repeatedly sought to use the professor's Russian connections in an effort to arrange a meeting between the Campaign and Russian government officials.

      c.   Defendant PAPADOPOULOS claimed he met a certain female Russian national before he joined the Campaign and that their communications consisted of emails such as, "'Hi, how are you?'" In truth and in fact, however, defendant PAPADOPOULOS met the

526

female Russian national on or about March 24, 2016, after he had become an adviser to the

Campaign; he believed that she had connections to Russian government officials; and he sought

to use her Russian connections over a period of months in an effort to arrange a meeting between

the Campaign and Russian government officials.

3.   Through his false statements and omissions, defendant PAPADOPOULOS

impeded the FBI's ongoing investigation into the existence of any links or coordination between

individuals associated with the Campaign and the Russian government's efforts to interfere with

the 2016 presidential election.

II.   Timeline of Selected Events

PAPADOPOULOS's Role on the Campaign

4.   In early March 2016, defendant PAPADOPOULOS learned he would be a foreign

policy advisor for the Campaign. Defendant PAPADOPOULOS was living in London, England,

at the time. Based on a conversation that took place on or about March 6, 2016, with a

supervisory campaign official (the "Campaign Supervisor"), defendant PAPADOPOULOS

understood that a principal foreign policy focus of the Campaign was an improved U.S.

relationship with Russia.

PAPADOPOULOS's Introduction to the Professor and the Female Russian National

5.   On or about March 14, 2016, while traveling in Italy, defendant

PAPADOPOULOS met an individual who was a professor based in London (the "Professor").

Initially, the Professor seemed uninterested in defendant PAPADOPOULOS. However, after

defendant PAPADOPOULOS informed the Professor about his joining the Campaign, the

Professor appeared to take great interest in defendant PAPADOPOULOS. Defendant

PAPADOPOULOS was interested in the Professor because, among other reasons, the Professor

3

527

claimed to have substantial connections with Russian government officials, which defendant PAPADOPOULOS thought could increase his importance as a policy advisor to the Campaign.

6. On or about March 21, 2016, the Campaign told *The Washington Post* that defendant PAPADOPOULOS was one of five named foreign policy advisors for the Campaign.

7. On or about March 24, 2016, defendant PAPADOPOULOS met with the Professor in London. The Professor brought with him a female Russian national (the "Female Russian National"), introduced to defendant PAPADOPOULOS as a relative of Russian President Vladimir Putin with connections to senior Russian government officials.

PAPADOPOULOS Pursues His Contacts with the Professor and the Female Russian National

8. Following his March 24, 2016 meeting with the Professor and the Female Russian National, defendant PAPADOPOULOS emailed the Campaign Supervisor and several members of the Campaign's foreign policy team and stated that he had just met with his "good friend" the Professor, who had introduced him to the Female Russian National (described by defendant PAPADOPOULOS in the email as "Putin's niece") and the Russian Ambassador in London.[1] Defendant PAPADOPOULOS stated that the topic of their discussion was "to arrange a meeting between us and the Russian leadership to discuss U.S.-Russia ties under President Trump." The Campaign Supervisor responded that he would "work it through the campaign," but that no commitments should be made at that point. The Campaign Supervisor added: "Great work."

9. On or about March 31, 2016, defendant PAPADOPOULOS attended a "national security meeting" in Washington, D.C., with then-candidate Trump and other foreign policy

---

[1] Defendant PAPADOPOULOS later learned that the Female Russian National was not in fact a relative of President Putin. In addition, while defendant PAPADOPOULOS expected that the Professor and the Female Russian National would introduce him to the Russian Ambassador in London, they never did.

advisors for the Campaign. When defendant PAPADOPOULOS introduced himself to the group, he stated, in sum and substance, that he had connections that could help arrange a meeting between then-candidate Trump and President Putin.

10.   After his trip to Washington, D.C., defendant PAPADOPOULOS worked with the Professor and the Female Russian National to arrange a meeting between the Campaign and the Russian government, and took steps to advise the Campaign of his progress.

a.   In early April 2016, defendant PAPADOPOULOS sent multiple emails to other members of the Campaign's foreign policy team regarding his contacts with "the Russians" and his "outreach to Russia."

b.   On or about April 10, 2016, defendant PAPADOPOULOS emailed the Female Russian National, who responded the next day, on or about April 11, 2016, that she "would be very pleased to support your initiatives between our two countries." Defendant PAPADOPOULOS then asked the Female Russian National, in an email cc'ing the Professor, about setting up "a potential foreign policy trip to Russia."

c.   The Professor responded to defendant PAPADOPOULOS's email later that day, on or about April 11, 2016: "This is already been agreed. I am flying to Moscow on the 18th for a Valdai meeting, plus other meetings at the Duma." The Duma is a Russian government legislative assembly.

d.   The Female Russian National responded: "I have already alerted my personal links to our conversation and your request. . . . As mentioned we are all very excited by the possibility of a good relationship with Mr. Trump. The Russian Federation would love to welcome him once his candidature would be officially announced."

5

The Professor Introduces PAPADOPOULOS to a Russian National Connected to the Russian Ministry of Foreign Affairs

11.   On or about April 18, 2016, the Professor introduced defendant

PAPADOPOULOS over email to an individual in Moscow (the "Russian MFA Connection")

who told defendant PAPADOPOULOS he had connections to the Russian Ministry of Foreign

Affairs ("MFA"). The MFA is the executive entity in Russia responsible for Russian foreign

relations. Over the next several weeks, defendant PAPADOPOULOS and the Russian MFA

Connection had multiple conversations over Skype and email about setting "the groundwork" for

a "potential" meeting between the Campaign and Russian government officials.

12.   On or about April 22, 2016, the Russian MFA Connection sent defendant

PAPADOPOULOS an email thanking him "for an extensive talk" and proposing "to meet in

London or in Moscow." Defendant PAPADOPOULOS replied by suggesting that "we set one

up here in London with the Ambassador as well to discuss a process moving forward."

13.   On or about April 25, 2016, defendant PAPADOPOULOS emailed a senior

policy advisor for the Campaign (the "Senior Policy Advisor"): "The Russian government has an

open invitation by Putin for Mr. Trump to meet him when he is ready []. The advantage of being

in London is that these governments tend to speak a bit more openly in 'neutral' cities."

PAPADOPOULOS Learns that the Russians Have "Dirt" on Clinton

14.   On or about April 26, 2016, defendant PAPADOPOULOS met the Professor for

breakfast at a London hotel. During this meeting, the Professor told defendant

PAPADOPOULOS that he had just returned from a trip to Moscow where he had met with high-

level Russian government officials. The Professor told defendant PAPADOPOULOS that on

that trip he (the Professor) learned that the Russians had obtained "dirt" on then-candidate

Clinton. The Professor told defendant PAPADOPOULOS, as defendant PAPADOPOULOS

6

530

later described to the FBI, that "They [the Russians] have dirt on her"; "the Russians had emails of Clinton"; "they have thousands of emails."

15.   Following that conversation, defendant PAPADOPOULOS continued to correspond with Campaign officials, and continued to communicate with the Professor and the Russian MFA Connection, in an effort to arrange a meeting between the Campaign and the Russian government.

   a.   For example, the day after his meeting at the hotel with the Professor, on or about April 27, 2016, defendant PAPADOPOULOS emailed the Senior Policy Advisor: "Have some interesting messages coming in from Moscow about a trip when the time is right."

   b.   Also on or about April 27, 2016, defendant PAPADOPOULOS emailed a high-ranking official of the Campaign (the "High-Ranking Campaign Official") "to discuss Russia's interest in hosting Mr. Trump. Have been receiving a lot of calls over the last month about Putin wanting to host him and the team when the time is right."

   c.   On or about April 30, 2016, defendant PAPADOPOULOS thanked the Professor for his "critical help" in arranging a meeting between the Campaign and the Russian government, and remarked: "It's history making if it happens."

PAPADOPOULOS Shares Information from the Russian MFA Connection

16.   On or about May 4, 2016, the Russian MFA Connection sent an email (the "May 4 MFA Email") to defendant PAPADOPOULOS and the Professor that stated: "I have just talked to my colleagues from the MFA. The[y] are open for cooperation. One of the options is to make a meeting for you at the North America Desk, if you are in Moscow." Defendant PAPADOPOULOS responded that he was "[g]lad the MFA is interested." Defendant PAPADOPOULOS forwarded the May 4 MFA Email to the High-Ranking Campaign Official,

adding: "What do you think? Is this something we want to move forward with?" The next day, on or about May 5, 2016, defendant PAPADOPOULOS had a phone call with the Campaign Supervisor, and then forwarded the May 4 MFA Email to him, adding to the top of the email: "Russia updates."

17.   On or about May 13, 2016, the Professor emailed defendant PAPADOPOULOS with "an update" of what they had discussed in their "recent conversations," including: "We will continue to liaise through you with the Russian counterparts in terms of what is needed for a high level meeting of Mr. Trump with the Russian Federation."

18.   The next day, on or about May 14, 2016, defendant PAPADOPOULOS emailed the High-Ranking Campaign Official and stated that the "Russian government[] ha[s] also relayed to me that they are interested in hosting Mr. Trump."

19.   On or about May 21, 2016, defendant PAPADOPOULOS emailed another high-ranking Campaign official, with the subject line "Request from Russia to meet Mr. Trump." The email included the May 4 MFA Email and added: "Russia has been eager to meet Mr. Trump for quite sometime and have been reaching out to me to discuss."[2]

20.   On or about June 1, 2016, defendant PAPADOPOULOS emailed the High-Ranking Campaign Official and asked about Russia. The High-Ranking Campaign Official referred him to the Campaign Supervisor because "[h]e is running point." Defendant PAPADOPOULOS then emailed the Campaign Supervisor, with the subject line "Re: Messages from Russia": "I have the Russian MFA asking me if Mr. Trump is interested in visiting Russia

---

[2]   The government notes that the official forwarded defendant PAPADOPOULOS's email to another Campaign official (without including defendant PAPADOPOULOS) and stated: "Let[']s discuss. We need someone to communicate that DT is not doing these trips. It should be someone low level in the campaign so as not to send any signal."

8

at some point. Wanted to pass this info along to you for you to decide what's best to do with it and what message I should send (or to ignore)."

21.   From mid-June through mid-August 2016, PAPADOPOULOS pursued an "off the record" meeting between one or more Campaign representatives and "members of president putin's office and the mfa."

      a.   For example, on or about June 19, 2016, after several email and Skype exchanges with the Russian MFA Connection, defendant PAPADOPOULOS emailed the High-Ranking Campaign Official, with the subject line "New message from Russia": "The Russian ministry of foreign affairs messaged and said that if Mr. Trump is unable to make it to Russia, if a campaign rep (me or someone else) can make it for meetings? I am willing to make the trip off the record if it's in the interest of Mr. Trump and the campaign to meet specific people."

      b.   After several weeks of further communications regarding a potential "off the record" meeting with Russian officials, on or about August 15, 2016, the Campaign Supervisor told defendant PAPADOPOULOS that "I would encourage you" and another foreign policy advisor to the Campaign to "make the trip[], if it is feasible."

      c.   The trip proposed by defendant PAPADOPOULOS did not take place.

III.   *The Defendant's False Statements to the FBI*

22.   On or about January 27, 2017, defendant PAPADOPOULOS agreed to be interviewed by agents from the FBI.

23.   The agents informed defendant PAPADOPOULOS that the FBI was investigating interference by the Russian government in the 2016 presidential election and whether any individuals related to the Campaign were involved. The agents further informed defendant PAPADOPOULOS that he needed to be truthful and warned that he could get "in trouble" if he

9

lied. The agents also advised him that lying to them "is a federal offense." They confirmed that the interview was "completely voluntary."

24.   During the course of the interview, defendant PAPADOPOULOS made numerous false statements and omitted material facts regarding the conduct and communications described above, and, in particular, lied about the extent, timing, and nature of his communications with the Professor, the Female Russian National, and the Russian MFA Connection.

>   *False Statement: PAPADOPOULOS Met the Professor and Learned About*
>   *Russian "Dirt" Before He Joined the Campaign*

25.   During his interview with the FBI, defendant PAPADOPOULOS acknowledged that he met the Professor and that the Professor told him the Russians had "dirt" on then-candidate Clinton in the form of "thousands of emails," but defendant PAPADOPOULOS stated multiple times that those communications occurred prior to when he joined the Campaign. Defendant PAPADOPOULOS told the FBI: "This isn't like he [the Professor]'s messaging me while I'm in April with Trump"; "I wasn't even on the Trump team, that wasn't even on the radar"; "I wasn't even on Trump's orbit[] at this time"; and "This was a year ago, this was before I even got with Trump." He also said it was a "very strange coincidence" to be told of the "dirt" before he started working for the Campaign.

26.   In truth and in fact, however, and as set forth above, defendant PAPADOPOULOS met the Professor for the first time on or about March 14, 2016, after defendant PAPADOPOULOS had already learned he would be a foreign policy advisor for the Campaign; the Professor showed interest in defendant PAPADOPOULOS only after learning of his role on the Campaign; and the Professor told defendant PAPADOPOULOS about the Russians possessing "dirt" on then-candidate Clinton in late April 2016, more than a month after defendant PAPADOPOULOS had joined the Campaign.

False Statement: PAPADOPOULOS's Contacts with the Professor Were Inconsequential

27.   During his interview with the FBI, defendant PAPADOPOULOS also made false statements in an effort to minimize the extent and importance of his communications with the Professor. For example, defendant PAPADOPOULOS stated that "[the Professor]'s a nothing," that he thought the Professor was "just a guy talk[ing] up connections or something," and that he believed the Professor was "BS'ing to be completely honest with you."

28.   In truth and in fact, however, defendant PAPADOPOULOS understood the Professor to have substantial connections to high-level Russian government officials and that the Professor spoke with some of those officials in Moscow before telling defendant PAPADOPOULOS about the "dirt." Defendant PAPADOPOULOS also engaged in extensive communications over a period of months with the Professor regarding foreign policy issues for the Campaign, including efforts to arrange a "history making" meeting between the Campaign and Russian government officials.

29.   In addition, defendant PAPADOPOULOS failed to inform investigators that the Professor had introduced him to the Russian MFA Connection, despite being asked if he had met with Russian nationals or "[a]nyone with a Russian accent" during the Campaign. Indeed, while defendant PAPADOPOULOS told the FBI that he was involved in meetings and did "shuttle diplomacy" with officials from several other countries during the Campaign, he omitted the entire course of conduct with the Professor and the Russian MFA Connection regarding his efforts to establish meetings between the Campaign and Russian government officials.

11

False Statement: PAPADOPOULOS Met the Female Russian National Before He Joined the Campaign, and His Contacts with Her Were Inconsequential

30.   During his interview with the FBI, defendant PAPADOPOULOS also falsely claimed that he met the Female Russian National before he joined the Campaign, and falsely told the FBI that he had "no" relationship at all with the Female Russian National. He stated that the extent of their communications was her sending emails – "Just, 'Hi, how are you?'" "That's it."

31.   In truth and in fact, however, defendant PAPADOPOULOS met the Female Russian National on or about March 24, 2016, after he had joined the Campaign; he believed that the Female Russian National had connections to high-level Russian government officials and could help him arrange a potential foreign policy trip to Russia; and during the Campaign he emailed and spoke over Skype on numerous occasions with the Female Russian National about the potential foreign policy trip to Russia.

IV.   *Events Following PAPADOPOULOS's January 27, 2017 Interview with the FBI*

32.   The FBI interviewed defendant PAPADOPOULOS again on February 16, 2017. His counsel was present for the interview. During the interview, defendant PAPADOPOULOS reiterated his purported willingness to cooperate with the FBI's investigation.

33.   The next day, on or about February 17, 2017, defendant PAPADOPOULOS deactivated his Facebook account, which he had maintained since approximately August 2005 and which contained information about communications he had with the Professor and the Russian MFA Connection. Shortly after he deactivated his account, PAPADOPOULOS created a new Facebook account that did not contain the communications with the Professor and the Russian MFA Connection.

34.   On or about February 23, 2017, defendant PAPADOPOULOS ceased using his cell phone number and began using a new number.

35.   On July 27, 2017, defendant PAPADOPOULOS was arrested upon his arrival at Dulles International Airport. Following his arrest, defendant PAPADOPOULOS met with the Government on numerous occasions to provide information and answer questions.

ROBERT S. MUELLER, III
Special Counsel

By: _____
Jeannie S. Rhee
Andrew D. Goldstein
Aaron S.J. Zelinsky
The Special Counsel's Office

13

DEFENDANT'S ACCEPTANCE

The preceding statement is a summary, made for the purpose of providing the Court with a factual basis for my guilty plea to the charge against me. It does not include all of the facts known to me regarding this offense. I make this statement knowingly and voluntarily and because I am, in fact, guilty of the crime charged. No threats have been made to me nor am I under the influence of anything that could impede my ability to understand this Statement of the Offense fully.

I have read every word of this Statement of the Offense, or have had it read to me. Pursuant to Federal Rule of Criminal Procedure 11, after consulting with my attorney, I agree and stipulate to this Statement of the Offense, and declare under penalty of perjury that it is true and correct.

Date: 10/5/17

George Papadopoulos
Defendant

ATTORNEY'S ACKNOWLEDGMENT

I have read this Statement of the Offense, and have reviewed it with my client fully. I concur in my client's desire to adopt and stipulate to this Statement of the Offense as true and accurate.

Date: 10/5/17

Thomas M. Breen
Robert W. Stanley
Attorneys for Defendant

14

538

3. Statement of the Offense,
US v. Michael T. Flynn
(US District Court for the District
of Columbia, December 1, 2017)

On December 28, 2016, as his eight years in office came to a close, President Obama imposed new sanctions on Russia as punishment for its interference in the 2016 presidential election. Uncharacteristically, Russian president Vladimir Putin announced that he would take no immediate retaliation. President-elect Donald Trump tweeted that Putin's move was "very smart."

Putin's restraint sparked confusion in Washington—until *The Washington Post* reported that Trump's designated national security adviser, Michael T. Flynn, spoke several times with Russian ambassador Sergey Kislyak on the day the new sanctions were announced. At first, Flynn insisted that the two had exchanged pleasantries and had not discussed the sanctions. Flynn offered that story to the public, privately to Vice President Pence—and, four days after Trump was inaugurated, to FBI agents sent to the White House to interview him about his Kislyak interactions. Flynn's statements were false.

After the *Post* reported that Flynn had in fact talked sanctions with Kislyak, he resigned his White House job on February 14, 2017, after just twenty-four days in office. And ten months later, on December 1, he pleaded guilty to misleading the FBI and agreed to cooperate with Special Counsel Robert S. Mueller III. This six-page statement of offense outlines exactly how Flynn lied. He agreed that he had asked Kislyak not to escalate the situation with the United States and had been told by Kislyak the next day that Putin's restraint was a direct response to Flynn's request. When Flynn resigned, Trump had said he had no idea that Flynn had talked to Kislyak about sanctions. But this document revealed that Flynn, who was traveling in the Dominican Republic at the time, had called a "senior official of the presidential transition team"—later identified as Flynn's deputy K. T. McFarland—before speaking with Kislyak to strategize what Flynn should say about sanctions. McFarland was spending the holidays with other senior officials and Trump at the president-elect's Florida club.

Flynn also agreed that he lied to the FBI about another contact with Kislyak, a December 2016 phone call in which Flynn asked if Russia would delay or vote against a proposed United Nations resolution critical of Israel. Flynn said he made this call at the direction of a "very senior member of the presidential transition team," identified later as Trump's son-in-law, Jared Kushner. Flynn also agreed that he had submitted false information to the Department of Justice as he belatedly registered as a foreign lobbyist for work he conducted during the campaign to benefit the Turkish government.

Flynn was the highest-ranking Trump official to plead guilty and agree to assist Mueller, whose prosecutors praised Flynn's cooperation as he sat for nineteen interviews over the following year. But at a stunning hearing in December 2018, US District Court judge Emmet G. Sullivan reminded the country of Flynn's fall as he conducted secret work for a foreign government and lied to federal agents on the grounds of the White House: "Arguably," Sullivan told Flynn, "you sold your country out."

**UNITED STATES DISTRICT COURT
FOR THE DISTRICT OF COLUMBIA**

UNITED STATES OF AMERICA	Criminal No.:
v.	Violation: 18 U.S.C. § 1001 (False Statements)
MICHAEL T. FLYNN,	
Defendant.	

STATEMENT OF THE OFFENSE

Pursuant to Federal Rule of Criminal Procedure 11, the United States of America and the defendant, MICHAEL T. FLYNN, stipulate and agree that the following facts are true and accurate. These facts do not constitute all of the facts known to the parties concerning the charged offense; they are being submitted to demonstrate that sufficient facts exist that the defendant committed the offense to which he is pleading guilty.

1.   The defendant, MICHAEL T. FLYNN, who served as a surrogate and national security advisor for the presidential campaign of Donald J. Trump ("Campaign"), as a senior member of President-Elect Trump's Transition Team ("Presidential Transition Team"), and as the National Security Advisor to President Trump, made materially false statements and omissions during an interview with the Federal Bureau of Investigation ("FBI") on January 24, 2017, in Washington, D.C. At the time of the interview, the FBI had an open investigation into the Government of Russia's ("Russia") efforts to interfere in the 2016 presidential election, including the nature of any links between individuals associated with the Campaign and Russia, and whether there was any coordination between the Campaign and Russia's efforts.

2.   FLYNN's false statements and omissions impeded and otherwise had a material impact on the FBI's ongoing investigation into the existence of any links or coordination

541

between individuals associated with the Campaign and Russia's efforts to interfere with the 2016

presidential election.

False Statements Regarding FLYNN's Request to the Russian Ambassador that Russia
Refrain from Escalating the Situation in Response to U.S. Sanctions against Russia

3.   On or about January 24, 2017, FLYNN agreed to be interviewed by agents from

the FBI ("January 24 voluntary interview"). During the interview, FLYNN falsely stated that he

did not ask Russia's Ambassador to the United States ("Russian Ambassador") to refrain from

escalating the situation in response to sanctions that the United States had imposed against

Russia. FLYNN also falsely stated that he did not remember a follow-up conversation in which

the Russian Ambassador stated that Russia had chosen to moderate its response to those

sanctions as a result of FLYNN's request. In truth and in fact, however, FLYNN then and there

knew that the following had occurred:

        a.   On or about December 28, 2016, then-President Barack Obama signed

Executive Order 13757, which was to take effect the following day. The

executive order announced sanctions against Russia in response to that

government's actions intended to interfere with the 2016 presidential

election ("U.S. Sanctions").

        b.   On or about December 28, 2016, the Russian Ambassador contacted

FLYNN.

        c.   On or about December 29, 2016, FLYNN called a senior official of the

Presidential Transition Team ("PTT official"), who was with other senior

members of the Presidential Transition Team at the Mar-a-Lago resort in

Palm Beach, Florida, to discuss what, if anything, to communicate to the

Russian Ambassador about the U.S. Sanctions. On that call, FLYNN and

2

the PTT official discussed the U.S. Sanctions, including the potential impact of those sanctions on the incoming administration's foreign policy goals. The PTT official and FLYNN also discussed that the members of the Presidential Transition Team at Mar-a-Lago did not want Russia to escalate the situation.

d.   Immediately after his phone call with the PTT official, FLYNN called the Russian Ambassador and requested that Russia not escalate the situation and only respond to the U.S. Sanctions in a reciprocal manner.

e.   Shortly after his phone call with the Russian Ambassador, FLYNN spoke with the PTT official to report on the substance of his call with the Russian Ambassador, including their discussion of the U.S. Sanctions.

f.   On or about December 30, 2016, Russian President Vladimir Putin released a statement indicating that Russia would not take retaliatory measures in response to the U.S. Sanctions at that time.

g.   On or about December 31, 2016, the Russian Ambassador called FLYNN and informed him that Russia had chosen not to retaliate in response to FLYNN's request.

h.   After his phone call with the Russian Ambassador, FLYNN spoke with senior members of the Presidential Transition Team about FLYNN's conversations with the Russian Ambassador regarding the U.S. Sanctions and Russia's decision not to escalate the situation.

543

False Statements Regarding FLYNN's Request that Foreign Officials Vote Against or Delay a United Nations Security Council Resolution

4.   During the January 24 voluntary interview, FLYNN made additional false statements about calls he made to Russia and several other countries regarding a resolution submitted by Egypt to the United Nations Security Council on December 21, 2016. Specifically FLYNN falsely stated that he only asked the countries' positions on the vote, and that he did not request that any of the countries take any particular action on the resolution. FLYNN also falsely stated that the Russian Ambassador never described to him Russia's response to FLYNN's request regarding the resolution. In truth and in fact, however, FLYNN then and there knew that the following had occurred:

a.   On or about December 21, 2016, Egypt submitted a resolution to the United Nations Security Council on the issue of Israeli settlements ("resolution"). The United Nations Security Council was scheduled to vote on the resolution the following day.

b.   On or about December 22, 2016, a very senior member of the Presidential Transition Team directed FLYNN to contact officials from foreign governments, including Russia, to learn where each government stood on the resolution and to influence those governments to delay the vote or defeat the resolution.

c.   On or about December 22, 2016, FLYNN contacted the Russian Ambassador about the pending vote. FLYNN informed the Russian Ambassador about the incoming administration's opposition to the resolution, and requested that Russia vote against or delay the resolution.

544   4

d. On or about December 23, 2016, FLYNN again spoke with the Russian Ambassador, who informed FLYNN that if it came to a vote Russia would not vote against the resolution.

Other False Statements Regarding FLYNN's Contacts with Foreign Governments

5. On March 7, 2017, FLYNN filed multiple documents with the Department of Justice pursuant to the Foreign Agents Registration Act ("FARA") pertaining to a project performed by him and his company, the Flynn Intel Group, Inc. ("FIG"), for the principal benefit of the Republic of Turkey ("Turkey project"). In the FARA filings, FLYNN made materially false statements and omissions, including by falsely stating that (a) FIG did not know whether or the extent to which the Republic of Turkey was involved in the Turkey project, (b) the Turkey project was focused on improving U.S. business organizations' confidence regarding doing business in Turkey, and (c) an op-ed by FLYNN published in *The Hill* on November 8, 2016, was written at his own initiative; and by omitting that officials from the Republic of Turkey provided supervision and direction over the Turkey project.

ROBERT S. MUELLER, III
Special Counsel

By:

Brandon L. Van Grack
Zainab N. Ahmad
Senior Assistant Special Counsels
The Special Counsel's Office

5

545

DEFENDANT'S ACCEPTANCE

The preceding statement is a summary, made for the purpose of providing the Court with a factual basis for my guilty plea to the charge against me. It does not include all of the facts known to me regarding this offense. I make this statement knowingly and voluntarily and because I am, in fact, guilty of the crime charged. No threats have been made to me nor am I under the influence of anything that could impede my ability to understand this Statement of the Offense fully.

I have read every word of this Statement of the Offense, or have had it read to me. Pursuant to Federal Rule of Criminal Procedure 11, after consulting with my attorneys, I agree and stipulate to this Statement of the Offense, and declare under penalty of perjury that it is true and correct.

Date: 11/30/17

Michael T. Flynn
Defendant

ATTORNEYS' ACKNOWLEDGMENT

I have read this Statement of the Offense, and have reviewed it with my client fully. I concur in my client's desire to adopt and stipulate to this Statement of the Offense as true and accurate.

Date: 11/30/17

Robert K. Kelner
Attorney for Defendant

Stephen P. Anthony
Attorney for Defendant

546

6

4. Indictment in
US v. Internet Research Agency et al.
(US District Court for the District
of Columbia, February 16, 2018)

Robert S. Mueller III's first major strike against the Russians accused of election interference came in February 2018, when he filed this thirty-seven-page indictment detailing how the Internet Research Agency—a small company based in St. Petersburg, Russia—had engineered a massive online propaganda effort to push voters toward Donald Trump and away from his rival, Democratic presidential nominee Hillary Clinton.

The social media plot was hatched in 2014, before most Americans had begun to think about the presidential election. According to the indictment, by the spring of 2016, these Russians had decided they would support Trump and work to damage Clinton.

The indictment was remarkable in its specificity, revealing that investigators had access to the group's internal communications, including an email from September 2017 in which one charged employee of the company wrote to a family member, "The FBI busted our work (not a joke)." The special counsel also alleged that these Russians worked off-line as well, asserting that three of those charged visited ten states to gather intelligence about US politics.

The group had online conversations with Americans, who became unwitting pawns, the special counsel alleged. The Russians persuaded Americans to hold rallies in support of Trump and paid for costumes and other materials so rallies could feature Americans dressed as Clinton in a prison jumpsuit.

At this stage, the special counsel notably did not accuse the Russian government of wrongdoing, nor did the indictment detail any Russian hacking. That would come later in a similarly detailed indictment, in which Mueller took aim at the Russian military intelligence unit believed to have hacked the emails of Clinton's campaign chairman, John Podesta, and the Democratic National Committee.

One of the named defendants in the case, Yevgeniy Prigozhin, who prosecutors alleged help fund the effort, told a Russian state news agency that he was not upset to be charged. A company connected to Prigozhin that was also named in the indictment has denied the charges and hired US lawyers to fight the case in court.

IN THE UNITED STATES DISTRICT COURT
FOR THE DISTRICT OF COLUMBIA

UNITED STATES OF AMERICA   *

     *   CRIMINAL NO.

      v.   *

     *   (18 U.S.C. §§ 2, 371, 1349, 1028A)

INTERNET RESEARCH AGENCY LLC   *
   A/K/A MEDIASINTEZ LLC A/K/A   *
   GLAVSET LLC A/K/A MIXINFO   *
   LLC A/K/A AZIMUT LLC A/K/A   *
   NOVINFO LLC,   *
CONCORD MANAGEMENT AND   *
   CONSULTING LLC,   *
CONCORD CATERING,   *
YEVGENIY VIKTOROVICH   *
   PRIGOZHIN,   *
MIKHAIL IVANOVICH BYSTROV,   *
MIKHAIL LEONIDOVICH BURCHIK   *
   A/K/A MIKHAIL ABRAMOV,   *
ALEKSANDRA YURYEVNA   *
   KRYLOVA,   *
ANNA VLADISLAVOVNA   *
   BOGACHEVA,   *
SERGEY PAVLOVICH POLOZOV,   *
MARIA ANATOLYEVNA BOVDA   *
   A/K/A MARIA ANATOLYEVNA   *
   BELYAEVA,   *
ROBERT SERGEYEVICH BOVDA,   *
DZHEYKHUN NASIMI OGLY   *
   ASLANOV A/K/A JAYHOON   *
   ASLANOV A/K/A JAY ASLANOV,   *
VADIM VLADIMIROVICH   *
   PODKOPAEV,   *
GLEB IGOREVICH VASILCHENKO,   *
IRINA VIKTOROVNA KAVERZINA,   *
   and   *
VLADIMIR VENKOV.   *******

     Defendants.

549

INDICTMENT

The Grand Jury for the District of Columbia charges:

Introduction

1.   The United States of America, through its departments and agencies, regulates the activities

of foreign individuals and entities in and affecting the United States in order to prevent, disclose,

and counteract improper foreign influence on U.S. elections and on the U.S. political system. U.S.

law bans foreign nationals from making certain expenditures or financial disbursements for the

purpose of influencing federal elections. U.S. law also bars agents of any foreign entity from

engaging in political activities within the United States without first registering with the Attorney

General. And U.S. law requires certain foreign nationals seeking entry to the United States to

obtain a visa by providing truthful and accurate information to the government. Various federal

agencies, including the Federal Election Commission, the U.S. Department of Justice, and the U.S.

Department of State, are charged with enforcing these laws.

2.   Defendant INTERNET RESEARCH AGENCY LLC ("ORGANIZATION") is a Russian

organization engaged in operations to interfere with elections and political processes. Defendants

MIKHAIL IVANOVICH BYSTROV, MIKHAIL LEONIDOVICH BURCHIK, ALEKSANDRA

YURYEVNA KRYLOVA, ANNA VLADISLAVOVNA BOGACHEVA, SERGEY PAVLOVICH

POLOZOV, MARIA ANATOLYEVNA BOVDA, ROBERT SERGEYEVICH BOVDA,

DZHEYKHUN NASIMI OGLY ASLANOV, VADIM VLADIMIROVICH PODKOPAEV, GLEB

IGOREVICH VASILCHENKO, IRINA VIKTOROVNA KAVERZINA, and VLADIMIR

VENKOV worked in various capacities to carry out Defendant ORGANIZATION's interference

operations targeting the United States. From in or around 2014 to the present, Defendants

knowingly and intentionally conspired with each other (and with persons known and unknown to

2

550

the Grand Jury) to defraud the United States by impairing, obstructing, and defeating the lawful functions of the government through fraud and deceit for the purpose of interfering with the U.S. political and electoral processes, including the presidential election of 2016.

3.   Beginning as early as 2014, Defendant ORGANIZATION began operations to interfere with the U.S. political system, including the 2016 U.S. presidential election.   Defendant ORGANIZATION received funding for its operations from Defendant YEVGENIY VIKTOROVICH PRIGOZHIN and companies he controlled, including Defendants CONCORD MANAGEMENT AND CONSULTING LLC and CONCORD CATERING (collectively "CONCORD"). Defendants CONCORD and PRIGOZHIN spent significant funds to further the ORGANIZATION's operations and to pay the remaining Defendants, along with other uncharged ORGANIZATION employees, salaries and bonuses for their work at the ORGANIZATION.

4.   Defendants, posing as U.S. persons and creating false U.S. personas, operated social media pages and groups designed to attract U.S. audiences. These groups and pages, which addressed divisive U.S. political and social issues, falsely claimed to be controlled by U.S. activists when, in fact, they were controlled by Defendants. Defendants also used the stolen identities of real U.S. persons to post on ORGANIZATION-controlled social media accounts. Over time, these social media accounts became Defendants' means to reach significant numbers of Americans for purposes of interfering with the U.S. political system, including the presidential election of 2016.

5.   Certain Defendants traveled to the United States under false pretenses for the purpose of collecting intelligence to inform Defendants' operations. Defendants also procured and used computer infrastructure, based partly in the United States, to hide the Russian origin of their activities and to avoid detection by U.S. regulators and law enforcement.

6.   Defendant ORGANIZATION had a strategic goal to sow discord in the U.S. political system, including the 2016 U.S. presidential election. Defendants posted derogatory information about a number of candidates, and by early to mid-2016, Defendants' operations included supporting the presidential campaign of then-candidate Donald J. Trump ("Trump Campaign") and disparaging Hillary Clinton. Defendants made various expenditures to carry out those activities, including buying political advertisements on social media in the names of U.S. persons and entities. Defendants also staged political rallies inside the United States, and while posing as U.S. grassroots entities and U.S. persons, and without revealing their Russian identities and ORGANIZATION affiliation, solicited and compensated real U.S. persons to promote or disparage candidates. Some Defendants, posing as U.S. persons and without revealing their Russian association, communicated with unwitting individuals associated with the Trump Campaign and with other political activists to seek to coordinate political activities.

7.   In order to carry out their activities to interfere in U.S. political and electoral processes without detection of their Russian affiliation, Defendants conspired to obstruct the lawful functions of the United States government through fraud and deceit, including by making expenditures in connection with the 2016 U.S. presidential election without proper regulatory disclosure; failing to register as foreign agents carrying out political activities within the United States; and obtaining visas through false and fraudulent statements.

COUNT ONE

(Conspiracy to Defraud the United States)

8.   Paragraphs 1 through 7 of this Indictment are re-alleged and incorporated by reference as if fully set forth herein.

9.   From in or around 2014 to the present, in the District of Columbia and elsewhere,

4

552

Defendants, together with others known and unknown to the Grand Jury, knowingly and intentionally conspired to defraud the United States by impairing, obstructing, and defeating the lawful functions of the Federal Election Commission, the U.S. Department of Justice, and the U.S. Department of State in administering federal requirements for disclosure of foreign involvement in certain domestic activities.

Defendants

10.   Defendant INTERNET RESEARCH AGENCY LLC (Агентство Интернет Исследований) is a Russian organization engaged in political and electoral interference operations. In or around July 2013, the ORGANIZATION registered with the Russian government as a Russian corporate entity. Beginning in or around June 2014, the ORGANIZATION obscured its conduct by operating through a number of Russian entities, including Internet Research LLC, MediaSintez LLC, GlavSet LLC, MixInfo LLC, Azimut LLC, and NovInfo LLC. Starting in or around 2014, the ORGANIZATION occupied an office at 55 Savushkina Street in St. Petersburg, Russia. That location became one of the ORGANIZATION's operational hubs from which Defendants and other co-conspirators carried out their activities to interfere in the U.S. political system, including the 2016 U.S. presidential election.

a.   The ORGANIZATION employed hundreds of individuals for its online operations, ranging from creators of fictitious personas to technical and administrative support. The ORGANIZATION's annual budget totaled the equivalent of millions of U.S. dollars.

b.   The ORGANIZATION was headed by a management group and organized into departments, including: a graphics department; a data analysis department; a search-engine optimization ("SEO") department; an information-technology ("IT")

5

553

department to maintain the digital infrastructure used in the ORGANIZATION's operations; and a finance department to budget and allocate funding.

c.   The ORGANIZATION sought, in part, to conduct what it called "information warfare against the United States of America" through fictitious U.S. personas on social media platforms and other Internet-based media.

d.   By in or around April 2014, the ORGANIZATION formed a department that went by various names but was at times referred to as the "translator project." This project focused on the U.S. population and conducted operations on social media platforms such as YouTube, Facebook, Instagram, and Twitter. By approximately July 2016, more than eighty ORGANIZATION employees were assigned to the translator project.

e.   By in or around May 2014, the ORGANIZATION's strategy included interfering with the 2016 U.S. presidential election, with the stated goal of "spread[ing] distrust towards the candidates and the political system in general."

11.   Defendants CONCORD MANAGEMENT AND CONSULTING LLC (Конкорд Менеджмент и Консалтинг) and CONCORD CATERING are related Russian entities with various Russian government contracts. CONCORD was the ORGANIZATION's primary source of funding for its interference operations. CONCORD controlled funding, recommended personnel, and oversaw ORGANIZATION activities through reporting and interaction with ORGANIZATION management.

a.   CONCORD funded the ORGANIZATION as part of a larger CONCORD-funded interference operation that it referred to as "Project Lakhta." Project Lakhta had multiple components, some involving domestic audiences within the Russian

6

Federation and others targeting foreign audiences in various countries, including the United States.

b.   By in or around September 2016, the ORGANIZATION's monthly budget for Project Lakhta submitted to CONCORD exceeded 73 million Russian rubles (over 1,250,000 U.S. dollars), including approximately one million rubles in bonus payments.

c.   To conceal its involvement, CONCORD labeled the monies paid to the ORGANIZATION for Project Lakhta as payments related to software support and development. To further conceal the source of funds, CONCORD distributed monies to the ORGANIZATION through approximately fourteen bank accounts held in the names of CONCORD affiliates, including Glavnaya Liniya LLC, Merkuriy LLC, Obshchepit LLC, Potentsial LLC, RSP LLC, ASP LLC, MTTs LLC, Kompleksservis LLC, SPb Kulinariya LLC, Almira LLC, Pishchevik LLC, Galant LLC, Rayteks LLC, and Standart LLC.

12.   Defendant YEVGENIY VIKTOROVICH PRIGOZHIN (Пригожин Евгений Викторович) is a Russian national who controlled CONCORD.

a.   PRIGOZHIN approved and supported the ORGANIZATION's operations, and Defendants and their co-conspirators were aware of PRIGOZHIN's role.

b.   For example, on or about May 29, 2016, Defendants and their co-conspirators, through an ORGANIZATION-controlled social media account, arranged for a real U.S. person to stand in front of the White House in the District of Columbia under false pretenses to hold a sign that read "Happy 55th Birthday Dear Boss." Defendants and their co-conspirators informed the real U.S. person that the sign

7

was for someone who "is a leader here and our boss . . . our funder." PRIGOZHIN's Russian passport identifies his date of birth as June 1, 1961.

13.   Defendant MIKHAIL IVANOVICH BYSTROV (Быстров Михаил Иванович) joined the ORGANIZATION by at least in or around February 2014.

a.   By approximately April 2014, BYSTROV was the general director, the ORGANIZATION's highest-ranking position. BYSTROV subsequently served as the head of various other entities used by the ORGANIZATION to mask its activities, including, for example, Glavset LLC, where he was listed as that entity's general director.

b.   In or around 2015 and 2016, BYSTROV frequently communicated with PRIGOZHIN about Project Lakhta's overall operations, including through regularly scheduled in-person meetings.

14.   Defendant MIKHAIL LEONIDOVICH BURCHIK (Бурчик Михаил Леонидович) A/K/A MIKHAIL ABRAMOV joined the ORGANIZATION by at least in or around October 2013.   By approximately March 2014, BURCHIK was the executive director, the ORGANIZATION's second-highest ranking position.   Throughout the ORGANIZATION's operations to interfere in the U.S political system, including the 2016 U.S. presidential election, BURCHIK was a manager involved in operational planning, infrastructure, and personnel. In or around 2016, BURCHIK also had in-person meetings with PRIGOZHIN.

15.   Defendant ALEKSANDRA YURYEVNA KRYLOVA (Крылова Александра Юрьевна) worked for the ORGANIZATION from at least in or around September 2013 to at least in or around November 2014. By approximately April 2014, KRYLOVA served as director and was the ORGANIZATION's third-highest ranking employee. In 2014, KRYLOVA traveled to the United

States under false pretenses for the purpose of collecting intelligence to inform the ORGANIZATION's operations.

16.   Defendant SERGEY PAVLOVICH POLOZOV (Полозов Сергей Павлович) worked for the ORGANIZATION from at least in or around April 2014 to at least in or around October 2016. POLOZOV served as the manager of the IT department and oversaw the procurement of U.S. servers and other computer infrastructure that masked the ORGANIZATION's Russian location when conducting operations within the United States.

17.   Defendant ANNA VLADISLAVOVNA BOGACHEVA (Богачева Анна Владиславовна) worked for the ORGANIZATION from at least in or around April 2014 to at least in or around July 2014. BOGACHEVA served on the translator project and oversaw the project's data analysis group. BOGACHEVA also traveled to the United States under false pretenses for the purpose of collecting intelligence to inform the ORGANIZATION's operations.

18.   Defendant MARIA ANATOLYEVNA BOVDA (Бовда Мария Анатольевна) A/K/A MARIA ANATOLYEVNA BELYAEVA ("M. BOVDA") worked for the ORGANIZATION from at least in or around November 2013 to at least in or around October 2014. M. BOVDA served as the head of the translator project, among other positions.

19.   Defendant ROBERT SERGEYEVICH BOVDA (Бовда Роберт Сергеевич) ("R. BOVDA") worked for the ORGANIZATION from at least in or around November 2013 to at least in or around October 2014. R. BOVDA served as the deputy head of the translator project, among other positions. R. BOVDA attempted to travel to the United States under false pretenses for the purpose of collecting intelligence to inform the ORGANIZATION's operations but could not obtain the necessary visa.

20.   Defendant DZHEYKHUN NASIMI OGLY ASLANOV (Асланов Джейхун Насими Оглы) A/K/A JAYHOON ASLANOV A/K/A JAY ASLANOV joined the ORGANIZATION by at least in or around September 2014. ASLANOV served as head of the translator project and oversaw many of the operations targeting the 2016 U.S. presidential election. ASLANOV was also listed as the general director of Azimut LLC, an entity used to move funds from CONCORD to the ORGANIZATION.

21.   Defendant VADIM VLADIMIROVICH PODKOPAEV (Подкопаев Вадим Владимирович) joined the ORGANIZATION by at least in or around June 2014. PODKOPAEV served as an analyst on the translator project and was responsible for conducting U.S.-focused research and drafting social media content for the ORGANIZATION.

22.   Defendant GLEB IGOREVICH VASILCHENKO (Васильченко Глеб Игоревич) worked for the ORGANIZATION from at least in or around August 2014 to at least in or around September 2016. VASILCHENKO was responsible for posting, monitoring, and updating the social media content of many ORGANIZATION-controlled accounts while posing as U.S. persons or U.S. grassroots organizations. VASILCHENKO later served as the head of two sub-groups focused on operations to interfere in the U.S. political system, including the 2016 U.S. presidential election.

23.   Defendant IRINA VIKTOROVNA KAVERZINA (Каверзина Ирина Викторовна) joined the ORGANIZATION by at least in or around October 2014. KAVERZINA served on the translator project and operated multiple U.S. personas that she used to post, monitor, and update social media content for the ORGANIZATION.

24.   Defendant VLADIMIR VENKOV (Венков Владимир) joined the ORGANIZATION by at least in or around March 2015. VENKOV served on the translator project and operated multiple

10

558

U.S. personas, which he used to post, monitor, and update social media content for the ORGANIZATION.

Federal Regulatory Agencies

25.   The Federal Election Commission is a federal agency that administers the Federal Election Campaign Act ("FECA"). Among other things, FECA prohibits foreign nationals from making any contributions, expenditures, independent expenditures, or disbursements for electioneering communications. FECA also requires that individuals or entities who make certain independent expenditures in federal elections report those expenditures to the Federal Election Commission. The reporting requirements permit the Federal Election Commission to fulfill its statutory duties of providing the American public with accurate data about the financial activities of individuals and entities supporting federal candidates, and enforcing FECA's limits and prohibitions, including the ban on foreign expenditures.

26.   The U.S. Department of Justice administers the Foreign Agent Registration Act ("FARA"). FARA establishes a registration, reporting, and disclosure regime for agents of foreign principals (which includes foreign non-government individuals and entities) so that the U.S. government and the people of the United States are informed of the source of information and the identity of persons attempting to influence U.S. public opinion, policy, and law. FARA requires, among other things, that persons subject to its requirements submit periodic registration statements containing truthful information about their activities and the income earned from them. Disclosure of the required information allows the federal government and the American people to evaluate the statements and activities of such persons in light of their function as foreign agents.

27.   The U.S. Department of State is the federal agency responsible for the issuance of non-immigrant visas to foreign individuals who need a visa to enter the United States. Foreign

11

559

individuals who are required to obtain a visa must, among other things, provide truthful information in response to questions on the visa application form, including information about their employment and the purpose of their visit to the United States.

Object of the Conspiracy

28.   The conspiracy had as its object impairing, obstructing, and defeating the lawful governmental functions of the United States by dishonest means in order to enable the Defendants to interfere with U.S. political and electoral processes, including the 2016 U.S. presidential election.

Manner and Means of the Conspiracy

Intelligence-Gathering to Inform U.S. Operations

29.   Starting at least in or around 2014, Defendants and their co-conspirators began to track and study groups on U.S. social media sites dedicated to U.S. politics and social issues. In order to gauge the performance of various groups on social media sites, the ORGANIZATION tracked certain metrics like the group's size, the frequency of content placed by the group, and the level of audience engagement with that content, such as the average number of comments or responses to a post.

30.   Defendants and their co-conspirators also traveled, and attempted to travel, to the United States under false pretenses in order to collect intelligence for their interference operations.

    a.   KRYLOVA and BOGACHEVA, together with other Defendants and co-conspirators, planned travel itineraries, purchased equipment (such as cameras, SIM cards, and drop phones), and discussed security measures (including "evacuation scenarios") for Defendants who traveled to the United States.

    b.   To enter the United States, KRYLOVA, BOGACHEVA, R. BOVDA, and another co-conspirator applied to the U.S. Department of State for visas to travel. During

12

560

their application process, KRYLOVA, BOGACHEVA, R. BOVDA, and their co-conspirator falsely claimed they were traveling for personal reasons and did not fully disclose their place of employment to hide the fact that they worked for the ORGANIZATION.

c. Only KRYLOVA and BOGACHEVA received visas, and from approximately June 4, 2014 through June 26, 2014, KRYLOVA and BOGACHEVA traveled in and around the United States, including stops in Nevada, California, New Mexico, Colorado, Illinois, Michigan, Louisiana, Texas, and New York to gather intelligence. After the trip, KRYLOVA and BURCHIK exchanged an intelligence report regarding the trip.

d. Another co-conspirator who worked for the ORGANIZATION traveled to Atlanta, Georgia from approximately November 26, 2014 through November 30, 2014. Following the trip, the co-conspirator provided POLOZOV a summary of his trip's itinerary and expenses.

31. In order to collect additional intelligence, Defendants and their co-conspirators posed as U.S. persons and contacted U.S. political and social activists. For example, starting in or around June 2016, Defendants and their co-conspirators, posing online as U.S. persons, communicated with a real U.S. person affiliated with a Texas-based grassroots organization. During the exchange, Defendants and their co-conspirators learned from the real U.S. person that they should focus their activities on "purple states like Colorado, Virginia & Florida." After that exchange, Defendants and their co-conspirators commonly referred to targeting "purple states" in directing their efforts.

13

561

Use of U.S. Social Media Platforms

32.   Defendants and their co-conspirators, through fraud and deceit, created hundreds of social media accounts and used them to develop certain fictitious U.S. personas into "leader[s] of public opinion" in the United States.

33.   ORGANIZATION employees, referred to as "specialists," were tasked to create social media accounts that appeared to be operated by U.S. persons. The specialists were divided into day-shift and night-shift hours and instructed to make posts in accordance with the appropriate U.S. time zone. The ORGANIZATION also circulated lists of U.S. holidays so that specialists could develop and post appropriate account activity. Specialists were instructed to write about topics germane to the United States such as U.S. foreign policy and U.S. economic issues. Specialists were directed to create "political intensity through supporting radical groups, users dissatisfied with [the] social and economic situation and oppositional social movements."

34.   Defendants and their co-conspirators also created thematic group pages on social media sites, particularly on the social media platforms Facebook and Instagram. ORGANIZATION-controlled pages addressed a range of issues, including: immigration (with group names including "Secured Borders"); the Black Lives Matter movement (with group names including "Blacktivist"); religion (with group names including "United Muslims of America" and "Army of Jesus"); and certain geographic regions within the United States (with group names including "South United" and "Heart of Texas"). By 2016, the size of many ORGANIZATION-controlled groups had grown to hundreds of thousands of online followers.

35.   Starting at least in or around 2015, Defendants and their co-conspirators began to purchase advertisements on online social media sites to promote ORGANIZATION-controlled social media groups, spending thousands of U.S. dollars every month. These expenditures were included in the budgets the ORGANIZATION submitted to CONCORD.

14

36. Defendants and their co-conspirators also created and controlled numerous Twitter accounts designed to appear as if U.S. persons or groups controlled them. For example, the ORGANIZATION created and controlled the Twitter account "Tennessee GOP," which used the handle @TEN_GOP. The @TEN_GOP account falsely claimed to be controlled by a U.S. state political party. Over time, the @TEN_GOP account attracted more than 100,000 online followers.

37. To measure the impact of their online social media operations, Defendants and their co-conspirators tracked the performance of content they posted over social media. They tracked the size of the online U.S. audiences reached through posts, different types of engagement with the posts (such as likes, comments, and reposts), changes in audience size, and other metrics. Defendants and their co-conspirators received and maintained metrics reports on certain group pages and individualized posts.

38. Defendants and their co-conspirators also regularly evaluated the content posted by specialists (sometimes referred to as "content analysis") to ensure they appeared authentic—as if operated by U.S. persons. Specialists received feedback and directions to improve the quality of their posts. Defendants and their co-conspirators issued or received guidance on: ratios of text, graphics, and video to use in posts; the number of accounts to operate; and the role of each account (for example, differentiating a main account from which to post information and auxiliary accounts to promote a main account through links and reposts).

Use of U.S. Computer Infrastructure

39. To hide their Russian identities and ORGANIZATION affiliation, Defendants and their co-conspirators—particularly POLOZOV and the ORGANIZATION's IT department—purchased space on computer servers located inside the United States in order to set up virtual private networks ("VPNs"). Defendants and their co-conspirators connected from Russia to the U.S.-

15

based infrastructure by way of these VPNs and conducted activity inside the United States—including accessing online social media accounts, opening new accounts, and communicating with real U.S. persons—while masking the Russian origin and control of the activity.

40.   Defendants and their co-conspirators also registered and controlled hundreds of web-based email accounts hosted by U.S. email providers under false names so as to appear to be U.S. persons and groups. From these accounts, Defendants and their co-conspirators registered or linked to online social media accounts in order to monitor them; posed as U.S. persons when requesting assistance from real U.S. persons; contacted media outlets in order to promote activities inside the United States; and conducted other operations, such as those set forth below.

Use of Stolen U.S. Identities

41.   In or around 2016, Defendants and their co-conspirators also used, possessed, and transferred, without lawful authority, the social security numbers and dates of birth of real U.S. persons without those persons' knowledge or consent. Using these means of identification, Defendants and their co-conspirators opened accounts at PayPal, a digital payment service provider; created false means of identification, including fake driver's licenses; and posted on ORGANIZATION-controlled social media accounts using the identities of these U.S. victims. Defendants and their co-conspirators also obtained, and attempted to obtain, false identification documents to use as proof of identity in connection with maintaining accounts and purchasing advertisements on social media sites.

Actions Targeting the 2016 U.S. Presidential Election

42.   By approximately May 2014, Defendants and their co-conspirators discussed efforts to interfere in the 2016 U.S. presidential election. Defendants and their co-conspirators began to monitor U.S. social media accounts and other sources of information about the 2016 U.S. presidential election.

564

43.   By 2016, Defendants and their co-conspirators used their fictitious online personas to interfere with the 2016 U.S. presidential election. They engaged in operations primarily intended to communicate derogatory information about Hillary Clinton, to denigrate other candidates such as Ted Cruz and Marco Rubio, and to support Bernie Sanders and then-candidate Donald Trump.

a.   On or about February 10, 2016, Defendants and their co-conspirators internally circulated an outline of themes for future content to be posted to ORGANIZATION-controlled social media accounts. Specialists were instructed to post content that focused on "politics in the USA" and to "use any opportunity to criticize Hillary and the rest (except Sanders and Trump—we support them)."

b.   On or about September 14, 2016, in an internal review of an ORGANIZATION-created and controlled Facebook group called "Secured Borders," the account specialist was criticized for having a "low number of posts dedicated to criticizing Hillary Clinton" and was told "it is imperative to intensify criticizing Hillary Clinton" in future posts.

44.   Certain ORGANIZATION-produced materials about the 2016 U.S. presidential election used election-related hashtags, including: "#Trump2016," "#TrumpTrain," "#MAGA," "#IWontProtectHillary," and "#Hillary4Prison." Defendants and their co-conspirators also established additional online social media accounts dedicated to the 2016 U.S. presidential election, including the Twitter account "March for Trump" and Facebook accounts "Clinton FRAUDation" and "Trumpsters United."

45.   Defendants and their co-conspirators also used false U.S. personas to communicate with unwitting members, volunteers, and supporters of the Trump Campaign involved in local community outreach, as well as grassroots groups that supported then-candidate Trump. These

17

565

individuals and entities at times distributed the ORGANIZATION's materials through their own accounts via retweets, reposts, and similar means. Defendants and their co-conspirators then monitored the propagation of content through such participants.

46.   In or around the latter half of 2016, Defendants and their co-conspirators, through their ORGANIZATION-controlled personas, began to encourage U.S. minority groups not to vote in the 2016 U.S. presidential election or to vote for a third-party U.S. presidential candidate.

   a.   On or about October 16, 2016, Defendants and their co-conspirators used the ORGANIZATION-controlled Instagram account "Woke Blacks" to post the following message: "[A] particular hype and hatred for Trump is misleading the people and forcing Blacks to vote Killary. We cannot resort to the lesser of two devils. Then we'd surely be better off without voting AT ALL."

   b.   On or about November 3, 2016, Defendants and their co-conspirators purchased an advertisement to promote a post on the ORGANIZATION-controlled Instagram account "Blacktivist" that read in part: "Choose peace and vote for Jill Stein. Trust me, it's not a wasted vote."

   c.   By in or around early November 2016, Defendants and their co-conspirators used the ORGANIZATION-controlled "United Muslims of America" social media accounts to post anti-vote messages such as: "American Muslims [are] boycotting elections today, most of the American Muslim voters refuse to vote for Hillary Clinton because she wants to continue the war on Muslims in the middle east and voted yes for invading Iraq."

47.   Starting in or around the summer of 2016, Defendants and their co-conspirators also began to promote allegations of voter fraud by the Democratic Party through their fictitious U.S. personas

18

and groups on social media. Defendants and their co-conspirators purchased advertisements on Facebook to further promote the allegations.

 a. On or about August 4, 2016, Defendants and their co-conspirators began purchasing advertisements that promoted a post on the ORGANIZATION-controlled Facebook account "Stop A.I." The post alleged that "Hillary Clinton has already committed voter fraud during the Democrat Iowa Caucus."

 b. On or about August 11, 2016, Defendants and their co-conspirators posted that allegations of voter fraud were being investigated in North Carolina on the ORGANIZATION-controlled Twitter account @TEN_GOP.

 c. On or about November 2, 2016, Defendants and their co-conspirators used the same account to post allegations of "#VoterFraud by counting tens of thousands of ineligible mail in Hillary votes being reported in Broward County, Florida."

Political Advertisements

48. From at least April 2016 through November 2016, Defendants and their co-conspirators, while concealing their Russian identities and ORGANIZATION affiliation through false personas, began to produce, purchase, and post advertisements on U.S. social media and other online sites expressly advocating for the election of then-candidate Trump or expressly opposing Clinton. Defendants and their co-conspirators did not report their expenditures to the Federal Election Commission, or register as foreign agents with the U.S. Department of Justice.

49. To pay for the political advertisements, Defendants and their co-conspirators established various Russian bank accounts and credit cards, often registered in the names of fictitious U.S. personas created and used by the ORGANIZATION on social media. Defendants and their co-conspirators also paid for other political advertisements using PayPal accounts.

19

567

50.   The political advertisements included the following:

Approximate Date	Excerpt of Advertisement
April 6, 2016	"You know, a great number of black people support us saying that #HillaryClintonIsNotMyPresident"
April 7, 2016	"I say no to Hillary Clinton / I say no to manipulation"
April 19, 2016	"JOIN our #HillaryClintonForPrison2016"
May 10, 2016	"Donald wants to defeat terrorism . . . Hillary wants to sponsor it"
May 19, 2016	"Vote Republican, vote Trump, and support the Second Amendment!"
May 24, 2016	"Hillary Clinton Doesn't Deserve the Black Vote"
June 7, 2016	"Trump is our only hope for a better future!"
June 30, 2016	"#NeverHillary #HillaryForPrison #Hillary4Prison #HillaryForPrison2016 #Trump2016 #Trump #Trump4President"
July 20, 2016	"Ohio Wants Hillary 4 Prison"
August 4, 2016	"Hillary Clinton has already committed voter fraud during the Democrat Iowa Caucus."
August 10, 2016	"We cannot trust Hillary to take care of our veterans!"
October 14, 2016	"Among all the candidates Donald Trump is the one and only who can defend the police from terrorists."
October 19, 2016	"Hillary is a Satan, and her crimes and lies had proved just how evil she is."

Staging U.S. Political Rallies in the United States

51.   Starting in approximately June 2016, Defendants and their co-conspirators organized and coordinated political rallies in the United States. To conceal the fact that they were based in Russia, Defendants and their co-conspirators promoted these rallies while pretending to be U.S. grassroots activists who were located in the United States but unable to meet or participate in person.

20

568

Defendants and their co-conspirators did not register as foreign agents with the U.S. Department of Justice.

52.   In order to build attendance for the rallies, Defendants and their co-conspirators promoted the events through public posts on their false U.S. persona social media accounts. In addition, Defendants and their co-conspirators contacted administrators of large social media groups focused on U.S. politics and requested that they advertise the rallies.

53.   In or around late June 2016, Defendants and their co-conspirators used the Facebook group "United Muslims of America" to promote a rally called "Support Hillary. Save American Muslims" held on July 9, 2016 in the District of Columbia. Defendants and their co-conspirators recruited a real U.S. person to hold a sign depicting Clinton and a quote attributed to her stating "I think Sharia Law will be a powerful new direction of freedom." Within three weeks, on or about July 26, 2016, Defendants and their co-conspirators posted on the same Facebook page that Muslim voters were "between Hillary Clinton and a hard place."

54.   In or around June and July 2016, Defendants and their co-conspirators used the Facebook group "Being Patriotic," the Twitter account @March_for_Trump, and other ORGANIZATION accounts to organize two political rallies in New York. The first rally was called "March for Trump" and held on June 25, 2016. The second rally was called "Down with Hillary" and held on July 23, 2016.

      a.   In or around June through July 2016, Defendants and their co-conspirators purchased advertisements on Facebook to promote the "March for Trump" and "Down with Hillary" rallies.

      b.   Defendants and their co-conspirators used false U.S. personas to send individualized messages to real U.S. persons to request that they participate in and

21

help organize the rally. To assist their efforts, Defendants and their co-conspirators, through false U.S. personas, offered money to certain U.S. persons to cover rally expenses.

c.   On or about June 5, 2016, Defendants and their co-conspirators, while posing as a U.S. grassroots activist, used the account @March_for_Trump to contact a volunteer for the Trump Campaign in New York. The volunteer agreed to provide signs for the "March for Trump" rally.

55.   In or around late July 2016, Defendants and their co-conspirators used the Facebook group "Being Patriotic," the Twitter account @March_for_Trump, and other false U.S. personas to organize a series of coordinated rallies in Florida. The rallies were collectively referred to as "Florida Goes Trump" and held on August 20, 2016.

a.   In or around August 2016, Defendants and their co-conspirators used false U.S. personas to communicate with Trump Campaign staff involved in local community outreach about the "Florida Goes Trump" rallies.

b.   Defendants and their co-conspirators purchased advertisements on Facebook and Instagram to promote the "Florida Goes Trump" rallies.

c.   Defendants and their co-conspirators also used false U.S. personas to contact multiple grassroots groups supporting then-candidate Trump in an unofficial capacity. Many of these groups agreed to participate in the "Florida Goes Trump" rallies and serve as local coordinators.

d.   Defendants and their co-conspirators also used false U.S. personas to ask real U.S. persons to participate in the "Florida Goes Trump" rallies. Defendants and their co-conspirators asked certain of these individuals to perform tasks at the rallies.

22

570

For example, Defendants and their co-conspirators asked one U.S. person to build a cage on a flatbed truck and another U.S. person to wear a costume portraying Clinton in a prison uniform. Defendants and their co-conspirators paid these individuals to complete the requests.

56.   After the rallies in Florida, Defendants and their co-conspirators used false U.S. personas to organize and coordinate U.S. political rallies supporting then-candidate Trump in New York and Pennsylvania. Defendants and their co-conspirators used the same techniques to build and promote these rallies as they had in Florida, including: buying Facebook advertisements; paying U.S. persons to participate in, or perform certain tasks at, the rallies; and communicating with real U.S. persons and grassroots organizations supporting then-candidate Trump.

57.   After the election of Donald Trump in or around November 2016, Defendants and their co-conspirators used false U.S. personas to organize and coordinate U.S. political rallies in support of then president-elect Trump, while simultaneously using other false U.S. personas to organize and coordinate U.S. political rallies protesting the results of the 2016 U.S. presidential election. For example, in or around November 2016, Defendants and their co-conspirators organized a rally in New York through one ORGANIZATION-controlled group designed to "show your support for President-Elect Donald Trump" held on or about November 12, 2016. At the same time, Defendants and their co-conspirators, through another ORGANIZATION-controlled group, organized a rally in New York called "Trump is NOT my President" held on or about November 12, 2016. Similarly, Defendants and their co-conspirators organized a rally entitled "Charlotte Against Trump" in Charlotte, North Carolina, held on or about November 19, 2016.

23

Destruction of Evidence

58.   In order to avoid detection and impede investigation by U.S. authorities of Defendants'

operations, Defendants and their co-conspirators deleted and destroyed data, including emails,

social media accounts, and other evidence of their activities.

a.   Beginning in or around June 2014, and continuing into June 2015, public reporting

began to identify operations conducted by the ORGANIZATION in the United

States. In response, Defendants and their co-conspirators deleted email accounts

used to conduct their operations.

b.   Beginning in or around September 2017, U.S. social media companies, starting

with Facebook, publicly reported that they had identified Russian expenditures on

their platforms to fund political and social advertisements. Facebook's initial

disclosure of the Russian purchases occurred on or about September 6, 2017, and

included a statement that Facebook had "shared [its] findings with US authorities

investigating these issues."

c.   Media reporting on or about the same day as Facebook's disclosure referred to

Facebook working with investigators for the Special Counsel's Office of the U.S.

Department of Justice, which had been charged with investigating the Russian

government's efforts to interfere in the 2016 presidential election.

d.   Defendants and their co-conspirators thereafter destroyed evidence for the purpose

of impeding the investigation. On or about September 13, 2017, KAVERZINA

wrote in an email to a family member: "We had a slight crisis here at work: the

FBI busted our activity (not a joke). So, I got preoccupied with covering tracks

together with the colleagues." KAVERZINA further wrote, "I created all these

pictures and posts, and the Americans believed that it was written by their people."

24

572

Overt Acts

59.   In furtherance of the Conspiracy and to effect its illegal object, Defendants and their co-conspirators committed the following overt acts in connection with the staging of U.S. political rallies, as well as those as set forth in paragraphs 1 through 7, 9 through 27, and 29 through 58, which are re-alleged and incorporated by reference as though fully set forth herein.

60.   On or about June 1, 2016, Defendants and their co-conspirators created and purchased Facebook advertisements for their "March for Trump" rally.

61.   On or about June 4, 2016, Defendants and their co-conspirators used allforusa@yahoo.com, the email address of a false U.S. persona, to send out press releases for the "March for Trump" rally to New York media outlets.

62.   On or about June 23, 2016, Defendants and their co-conspirators used the Facebook account registered under a false U.S. persona "Matt Skiber" to contact a real U.S. person to serve as a recruiter for the "March for Trump" rally, offering to "give you money to print posters and get a megaphone."

63.   On or about June 24, 2016, Defendants and their co-conspirators purchased advertisements on Facebook to promote the "Support Hillary. Save American Muslims" rally.

64.   On or about July 5, 2016, Defendants and their co-conspirators ordered posters for the "Support Hillary. Save American Muslims" rally, including the poster with the quote attributed to Clinton that read "I think Sharia Law will be a powerful new direction of freedom."

65.   On or about July 8, 2016, Defendants and their co-conspirators communicated with a real U.S. person about the posters they had ordered for the "Support Hillary. Save American Muslims" rally.

66.   On or about July 12, 2016, Defendants and their co-conspirators created and purchased Facebook advertisements for the "Down With Hillary" rally in New York.

67.   On or about July 23, 2016, Defendants and their co-conspirators used the email address of a false U.S. persona, joshmilton024@gmail.com, to send out press releases to over thirty media outlets promoting the "Down With Hillary" rally at Trump Tower in New York City.

68.   On or about July 28, 2016, Defendants and their co-conspirators posted a series of tweets through the false U.S. persona account @March_for_Trump stating that "[w]e're currently planning a series of rallies across the state of Florida" and seeking volunteers to assist.

69.   On or about August 2, 2016, Defendants and their co-conspirators used the false U.S. persona "Matt Skiber" Facebook account to send a private message to a real Facebook account, "Florida for Trump," set up to assist then-candidate Trump in the state of Florida. In the first message, Defendants and their co-conspirators wrote:

> Hi there! I'm a member of Being Patriotic online community. Listen, we've got an idea. Florida is still a purple state and we need to paint it red. If we lose Florida, we lose America. We can't let it happen, right? What about organizing a YUGE pro-Trump flash mob in every Florida town? We are currently reaching out to local activists and we've got the folks who are okay to be in charge of organizing their events almost everywhere in FL. However, we still need your support. What do you think about that? Are you in?

70.   On or about August 2, 2016, and August 3, 2016, Defendants and their co-conspirators, through the use of a stolen identity of a real U.S. person, T.W., sent emails to certain grassroots groups located in Florida that stated in part:

> My name is [T.W.] and I represent a conservative patriot community named as "Being Patriotic." . . . So we're gonna organize a flash mob across Florida to support Mr. Trump. We clearly understand that the elections winner will be predestined by purple states. And we must win Florida. . . . We got a lot of volunteers in ~25 locations and it's just the beginning. We're currently choosing venues for each

26

574

location and recruiting more activists. This is why we ask you to spread this info and participate in the flash mob.

71.   On or about August 4, 2016, Defendants and their co-conspirators created and purchased Facebook advertisements for the "Florida Goes Trump" rally. The advertisements reached over 59,000 Facebook users in Florida, and over 8,300 Facebook users responded to the advertisements by clicking on it, which routed users to the ORGANIZATION's "Being Patriotic" page.

72.   Beginning on or about August 5, 2016, Defendants and their co-conspirators used the false U.S. persona @March_for_Trump Twitter account to recruit and later pay a real U.S. person to wear a costume portraying Clinton in a prison uniform at a rally in West Palm Beach.

73.   Beginning on or about August 11, 2016, Defendants and their co-conspirators used the false U.S. persona "Matt Skiber" Facebook account to recruit a real U.S. person to acquire signs and a costume depicting Clinton in a prison uniform.

74.   On or about August 15, 2016, Defendants and their co-conspirators received an email at one of their false U.S. persona accounts from a real U.S. person, a Florida-based political activist identified as the "Chair for the Trump Campaign" in a particular Florida county. The activist identified two additional sites in Florida for possible rallies. Defendants and their co-conspirators subsequently used their false U.S. persona accounts to communicate with the activist about logistics and an additional rally in Florida.

75.   On or about August 16, 2016, Defendants and their co-conspirators used a false U.S. persona Instagram account connected to the ORGANIZATION-created group "Tea Party News" to purchase advertisements for the "Florida Goes Trump" rally.

76.   On or about August 18, 2016, the real "Florida for Trump" Facebook account responded to the false U.S. persona "Matt Skiber" account with instructions to contact a member of the Trump Campaign ("Campaign Official 1") involved in the campaign's Florida operations and provided

Campaign Official 1's email address at the campaign domain donaldtrump.com. On approximately the same day, Defendants and their co-conspirators used the email address of a false U.S. persona, joshmilton024@gmail.com, to send an email to Campaign Official 1 at that donaldtrump.com email account, which read in part:

> Hello [Campaign Official 1], [w]e are organizing a state-wide event in Florida on August, 20 to support Mr. Trump. Let us introduce ourselves first. "Being Patriotic" is a grassroots conservative online movement trying to unite people offline. . . . [W]e gained a huge lot of followers and decided to somehow help Mr. Trump get elected. You know, simple yelling on the Internet is not enough. There should be real action. We organized rallies in New York before. Now we're focusing on purple states such as Florida.

The email also identified thirteen "confirmed locations" in Florida for the rallies and requested the campaign provide "assistance in each location."

77.   On or about August 18, 2016, Defendants and their co-conspirators sent money via interstate wire to another real U.S. person recruited by the ORGANIZATION, using one of their false U.S. personas, to build a cage large enough to hold an actress depicting Clinton in a prison uniform.

78.   On or about August 19, 2016, a supporter of the Trump Campaign sent a message to the ORGANIZATION-controlled "March for Trump" Twitter account about a member of the Trump Campaign ("Campaign Official 2") who was involved in the campaign's Florida operations and provided Campaign Official 2's email address at the domain donaldtrump.com. On or about the same day, Defendants and their co-conspirators used the false U.S. persona joshmilton024@gmail.com account to send an email to Campaign Official 2 at that donaldtrump.com email account.

79.   On or about August 19, 2016, the real "Florida for Trump" Facebook account sent another message to the false U.S. persona "Matt Skiber" account to contact a member of the Trump

28

Campaign ("Campaign Official 3") involved in the campaign's Florida operations. On or about August 20, 2016, Defendants and their co-conspirators used the "Matt Skiber" Facebook account to contact Campaign Official 3.

80. On or about August 19, 2016, Defendants and their co-conspirators used the false U.S. persona "Matt Skiber" account to write to the real U.S. person affiliated with a Texas-based grassroots organization who previously had advised the false persona to focus on "purple states like Colorado, Virginia & Florida." Defendants and their co-conspirators told that U.S. person, "We were thinking about your recommendation to focus on purple states and this is what we're organizing in FL." Defendants and their co-conspirators then sent a link to the Facebook event page for the Florida rallies and asked that person to send the information to Tea Party members in Florida. The real U.S. person stated that he/she would share among his/her own social media contacts, who would pass on the information.

81. On or about August 24, 2016, Defendants and their co-conspirators updated an internal ORGANIZATION list of over 100 real U.S. persons contacted through ORGANIZATION-controlled false U.S. persona accounts and tracked to monitor recruitment efforts and requests. The list included contact information for the U.S. persons, a summary of their political views, and activities they had been asked to perform by Defendants and their co-conspirators.

82. On or about August 31, 2016, Defendants and their co-conspirators, using a U.S. persona, spoke by telephone with a real U.S. person affiliated with a grassroots group in Florida. That individual requested assistance in organizing a rally in Miami, Florida. On or about September 9, 2016, Defendants and their co-conspirators sent the group an interstate wire to pay for materials needed for the Florida rally on or about September 11, 2016.

29

83.   On or about August 31, 2016, Defendants and their co-conspirators created and purchased Facebook advertisements for a rally they organized and scheduled in New York for September 11, 2016.

84.   On or about September 9, 2016, Defendants and their co-conspirators, through a false U.S. persona, contacted the real U.S. person who had impersonated Clinton at the West Palm Beach rally. Defendants and their co-conspirators sent that U.S. person money via interstate wire as an inducement to travel from Florida to New York and to dress in costume at another rally they organized.

85.   On or about September 22, 2016, Defendants and their co-conspirators created and purchased Facebook advertisements for a series of rallies they organized in Pennsylvania called "Miners for Trump" and scheduled for October 2, 2016.

All in violation of Title 18, United States Code, Section 371.

COUNT TWO

(Conspiracy to Commit Wire Fraud and Bank Fraud)

86.   Paragraphs 1 through 7, 9 through 27, and 29 through 85 of this Indictment are re-alleged and incorporated by reference as if fully set forth herein.

87.   From in or around 2016 through present, in the District of Columbia and elsewhere, Defendants INTERNET RESEARCH AGENCY LLC, DZHEYKHUN NASIMI OGLY ASLANOV, and GLEB IGOREVICH VASILCHENKO, together with others known and unknown to the Grand Jury, knowingly and intentionally conspired to commit certain offenses against the United States, to wit:

    a.   to knowingly, having devised and intending to devise a scheme and artifice to defraud, and to obtain money and property by means of false and fraudulent

578

pretenses, representations, and promises, transmit and cause to be transmitted, by means of wire communications in interstate and foreign commerce, writings, signs, signals, pictures, and sounds, for the purposes of executing such scheme and artifice, in violation of Title 18, United States Code, Section 1343; and

b.   to knowingly execute and attempt to execute a scheme and artifice to defraud a federally insured financial institution, and to obtain monies, funds, credits, assets, securities and other property from said financial institution by means of false and fraudulent pretenses, representations, and promises, all in violation of Title 18, United States Code, Section 1344.

Object of the Conspiracy

88.   The conspiracy had as its object the opening of accounts under false names at U.S. financial institutions and a digital payments company in order to receive and send money into and out of the United States to support the ORGANIZATION's operations in the United States and for self-enrichment.

Manner and Means of the Conspiracy

89.   Beginning in at least 2016, Defendants and their co-conspirators used, without lawful authority, the social security numbers, home addresses, and birth dates of real U.S. persons without their knowledge or consent. Using these means of stolen identification, Defendants and their co-conspirators opened accounts at a federally insured U.S. financial institution ("Bank 1"), including the following accounts:

31

Approximate Date	Account Name	Means of Identification
June 16, 2016	T.B.	Social Security Number Date of Birth
July 21, 2016	A.R.	Social Security Number Date of Birth
July 27, 2016	T.C.	Social Security Number Date of Birth
August 2, 2016	T.W.	Social Security Number Date of Birth

90.   Defendants and their co-conspirators also used, without lawful authority, the social security numbers, home addresses, and birth dates of real U.S. persons to open accounts at PayPal, a digital payments company, including the following accounts:

Approximate Date	Initials of Identity Theft Victim	Means of Identification
June 16, 2016	T.B.	Social Security Number Date of Birth
July 21, 2016	A.R.	Social Security Number Date of Birth
August 2, 2016	T.W.	Social Security Number Date of Birth
November 11, 2016	J.W.	Home Address
January 18, 2017	V.S.	Social Security Number

Defendants and their co-conspirators also established other accounts at PayPal in the names of false and fictitious U.S. personas. Some personas used to register PayPal accounts were the same as the false U.S. personas used in connection with the ORGANIZATION's social media accounts.

91.   Defendants and their co-conspirators purchased credit card and bank account numbers from online sellers for the unlawful purpose of evading security measures at PayPal, which used account numbers to verify a user's identity. Many of the bank account numbers purchased by Defendants

32

580

and their co-conspirators were created using the stolen identities of real U.S. persons. After purchasing the accounts, Defendants and their co-conspirators submitted these bank account numbers to PayPal.

92.   On or about the dates identified below, Defendants and their co-conspirators obtained and used the following fraudulent bank account numbers for the purpose of evading PayPal's security measures:

Approximate Date	Card/Bank Account Number	Financial Institution	Email Used to Acquire Account Number
June 13, 2016	xxxxxxxxx8902	Bank 2	wemakeweather@gmail.com
June 16, 2016	xxxxxx8731	Bank 1	allforusa@yahoo.com
July 21, 2016	xxxxxx2215	Bank 3	antwan_8@yahoo.com
August 2, 2016	xxxxxx5707	Bank 1	xtimwaltersx@gmail.com
October 18, 2016	xxxxxxxxx5792	Bank 4	unitedvetsofamerica@gmail.com
October 18, 2016	xxxxxxxxx4743	Bank 4	patriototus@gmail.com
November 11, 2016	xxxxxxxxx2427	Bank 4	beautifullelly@gmail.com
November 11, 2016	xxxxxxxxx7587	Bank 5	staceyredneck@gmail.com
November 11, 2016	xxxxxxxx7590	Bank 5	ihatecrime1@gmail.com
November 11, 2016	xxxxxxxx1780	Bank 6	staceyredneck@gmail.com
November 11, 2016	xxxxxxxx1762	Bank 6	ihatecrime1@gmail.com
December 13, 2016	xxxxxxxx6168	Bank 6	thetaylorbrooks@aol.com
March 30, 2017	xxxxxxxxx6316	Bank 3	wokeaztec@outlook.com
March 30, 2017	xxxxxx9512	Bank 3	wokeaztec@outlook.com

33

93.   Additionally, and in order to maintain their accounts at PayPal and elsewhere, including online cryptocurrency exchanges, Defendants and their co-conspirators purchased and obtained false identification documents, including fake U.S. driver's licenses. Some false identification documents obtained by Defendants and their co-conspirators used the stolen identities of real U.S. persons, including U.S. persons T.W. and J.W.

94.   After opening the accounts at Bank 1 and PayPal, Defendants and their co-conspirators used them to receive and send money for a variety of purposes, including to pay for certain ORGANIZATION expenses. Some PayPal accounts were used to purchase advertisements on Facebook promoting ORGANIZATION-controlled social media accounts. The accounts were also used to pay other ORGANIZATION-related expenses such as buttons, flags, and banners for rallies.

95.   Defendants and their co-conspirators also used the accounts to receive money from real U.S. persons in exchange for posting promotions and advertisements on the ORGANIZATION-controlled social media pages. Defendants and their co-conspirators typically charged certain U.S. merchants and U.S. social media sites between 25 and 50 U.S. dollars per post for promotional content on their popular false U.S. persona accounts, including Being Patriotic, Defend the 2nd, and Blacktivist.

All in violation of Title 18, United States Code, Section 1349.

COUNTS THREE THROUGH EIGHT

(Aggravated Identity Theft)

96.   Paragraphs 1 through 7, 9 through 27, and 29 through 85, and 89 through 95 of this Indictment are re-alleged and incorporated by reference as if fully set forth herein.

97.   On or about the dates specified below, in the District of Columbia and elsewhere,

34

582

Defendants INTERNET RESEARCH AGENCY LLC, DZHEYKHUN NASIMI OGLY ASLANOV, GLEB IGOREVICH VASILCHENKO, IRINA VIKTOROVNA KAVERZINA, and VLADIMIR VENKOV did knowingly transfer, possess, and use, without lawful authority, a means of identification of another person during and in relation to a felony violation enumerated in 18 U.S.C. § 1028A(c), to wit, wire fraud and bank fraud, knowing that the means of identification belonged to another real person:

Count	Approximate Date	Initials of Identity Theft Victim	Means of Identification
3	June 16, 2016	T.B.	Social Security Number Date of Birth
4	July 21, 2016	A.R.	Social Security Number Date of Birth
5	July 27, 2016	T.C.	Social Security Number Date of Birth
6	August 2, 2016	T.W.	Social Security Number Date of Birth
7	January 18, 2017	V.S.	Social Security Number
8	May 19, 2017	J.W.	Home Address Date of Birth

All in violation of Title 18, United States Code, Sections 1028A(a)(1) and 2.

FORFEITURE ALLEGATION

98.   Pursuant to Federal Rule of Criminal Procedure 32.2, notice is hereby given to Defendants that the United States will seek forfeiture as part of any sentence in accordance with Title 18, United States Code, Sections 981(a)(1)(C) and 982(a)(2), and Title 28, United States Code, Section 2461(c), in the event of Defendants' convictions under Count Two of this Indictment. Upon conviction of the offense charged in Count Two, Defendants INTERNET RESEARCH AGENCY LLC, DZHEYKHUN NASIMI OGLY ASLANOV, and GLEB IGOREVICH VASILCHENKO

583

shall forfeit to the United States any property, real or personal, which constitutes or is derived from proceeds traceable to the offense of conviction. Upon conviction of the offenses charged in Counts Three through Eight, Defendants INTERNET RESEARCH AGENCY LLC, DZHEYKHUN NASIMI OGLY ASLANOV, GLEB IGOREVICH VASILCHENKO, IRINA VIKTOROVNA KAVERZINA, and VLADIMIR VENKOV shall forfeit to the United States any property, real or personal, which constitutes or is derived from proceeds traceable to the offense(s) of conviction. Notice is further given that, upon conviction, the United States intends to seek a judgment against each Defendant for a sum of money representing the property described in this paragraph, as applicable to each Defendant (to be offset by the forfeiture of any specific property).

Substitute Assets

99.   If any of the property described above as being subject to forfeiture, as a result of any act or omission of any defendant --

      a.   cannot be located upon the exercise of due diligence;

      b.   has been transferred or sold to, or deposited with, a third party;

      c.   has been placed beyond the jurisdiction of the court;

      d.   has been substantially diminished in value; or

      e.   has been commingled with other property that cannot be subdivided without difficulty;

it is the intent of the United States of America, pursuant to Title 18, United States Code, Section

982(b) and Title 28, United States Code, Section 2461(c), incorporating Title 21, United States

Code, Section 853, to seek forfeiture of any other property of said Defendant.

(18 U.S.C. §§ 981(a)(1)(C) and 982; 28 U.S.C. § 2461(c))

Robert S. Mueller, III
Special Counsel
U.S. Department of Justice

A TRUE BILL:

_____
Foreperson

Date: February ___, 2018

37

5. Indictment in
US v. Viktor Borisovich Netyksho et al.
(US District Court for the District
of Columbia, July 13, 2018)

At the core of the Russia investigation was always the 2016 hacking and publishing of emails from the Democratic National Committee and Hillary Clinton campaign chairman John Podesta. In January 2017, US officials attributed the attack to Russia and said the operation was personally directed by President Vladimir Putin. It was left to Robert S. Mueller III to sort out the specifics and determine if any Americans shared blame.

A little more than a year into his investigation, Mueller made this much clear: he knew exactly who carried out the hack, and how they did it. In this twenty-nine-page indictment of a dozen officers of the Russian military intelligence, known as the GRU, Mueller described in granular detail how the group hacked the emails, then laundered the stolen messages through fake online personas so they could be shared to influence voters.

Notably, Mueller did not include any Americans in the indictment, and he similarly spared the antisecrecy organization WikiLeaks, which is identified in the document only as "Organization 1."

Mueller did, however, describe an online conversation between the GRU, posing as a person called Guccifer 2.0, and a "person who was in regular contact with senior members of the presidential campaign of Donald J. Trump." Roger Stone has acknowledged that description refers to him.

Mueller also revealed a detail that—even if it was mere coincidence—seemed remarkable. On July 27, 2016, Trump gave a press conference declaring his hope that missing Hillary Clinton emails would be found and made public, saying, "Russia, if you're listening, I hope you're able to find the thirty thousand emails that are missing." Russia seemed to spring into action. According to Mueller's indictment, "on or about" that same day, those involved in the hacking tried "to spearphish for the first time email accounts at a domain hosted by a third-party provider and used by Clinton's personal office."

The indictment alleged, "At or around the same time they also targeted seventy-six email addresses at the domain for the Clinton campaign."

The Russian officers named in the indictment have not responded to the allegations.

IN THE UNITED STATES DISTRICT COURT
FOR THE DISTRICT OF COLUMBIA

UNITED STATES OF AMERICA	*
	* CRIMINAL NO.
v.	*
	*
	* (18 U.S.C. §§ 2, 371, 1030, 1028A, 1956,
VIKTOR BORISOVICH NETYKSHO,	* and 3551 et seq.)
BORIS ALEKSEYEVICH ANTONOV,	*
DMITRIY SERGEYEVICH BADIN,	*
IVAN SERGEYEVICH YERMAKOV,	*
ALEKSEY VIKTOROVICH	*
LUKASHEV,	*
SERGEY ALEKSANDROVICH	*
MORGACHEV,	*
NIKOLAY YURYEVICH KOZACHEK,	*
PAVEL VYACHESLAVOVICH	*
YERSHOV,	*
ARTEM ANDREYEVICH	*
MALYSHEV,	*
ALEKSANDR VLADIMIROVICH	*
OSADCHUK,	*
ALEKSEY ALEKSANDROVICH	*
POTEMKIN, and	*
ANATOLIY SERGEYEVICH	*
KOVALEV,	*
	*
Defendants.	*
	*

****

INDICTMENT

The Grand Jury for the District of Columbia charges:

COUNT ONE
(Conspiracy to Commit an Offense Against the United States)

1.   In or around 2016, the Russian Federation ("Russia") operated a military intelligence agency called the Main Intelligence Directorate of the General Staff ("GRU"). The GRU had multiple units, including Units 26165 and 74455, engaged in cyber operations that involved the staged releases of documents stolen through computer intrusions. These units conducted large-scale cyber operations to interfere with the 2016 U.S. presidential election.

589

2.   Defendants VIKTOR BORISOVICH NETYKSHO, BORIS ALEKSEYEVICH ANTONOV, DMITRIY SERGEYEVICH BADIN, IVAN SERGEYEVICH YERMAKOV, ALEKSEY VIKTOROVICH LUKASHEV, SERGEY ALEKSANDROVICH MORGACHEV, NIKOLAY YURYEVICH KOZACHEK, PAVEL VYACHESLAVOVICH YERSHOV, ARTEM ANDREYEVICH MALYSHEV, ALEKSANDR VLADIMIROVICH OSADCHUK, and ALEKSEY ALEKSANDROVICH POTEMKIN were GRU officers who knowingly and intentionally conspired with each other, and with persons known and unknown to the Grand Jury (collectively the "Conspirators"), to gain unauthorized access (to "hack") into the computers of U.S. persons and entities involved in the 2016 U.S. presidential election, steal documents from those computers, and stage releases of the stolen documents to interfere with the 2016 U.S. presidential election.

3.   Starting in at least March 2016, the Conspirators used a variety of means to hack the email accounts of volunteers and employees of the U.S. presidential campaign of Hillary Clinton (the "Clinton Campaign"), including the email account of the Clinton Campaign's chairman.

4.   By in or around April 2016, the Conspirators also hacked into the computer networks of the Democratic Congressional Campaign Committee ("DCCC") and the Democratic National Committee ("DNC"). The Conspirators covertly monitored the computers of dozens of DCCC and DNC employees, implanted hundreds of files containing malicious computer code ("malware"), and stole emails and other documents from the DCCC and DNC.

5.   By in or around April 2016, the Conspirators began to plan the release of materials stolen from the Clinton Campaign, DCCC, and DNC.

6.   Beginning in or around June 2016, the Conspirators staged and released tens of thousands of the stolen emails and documents. They did so using fictitious online personas, including

2

"DCLeaks" and "Guccifer 2.0."

7.   The Conspirators also used the Guccifer 2.0 persona to release additional stolen documents through a website maintained by an organization ("Organization 1"), that had previously posted documents stolen from U.S. persons, entities, and the U.S. government.   The Conspirators continued their U.S. election-interference operations through in or around November 2016.

8.   To hide their connections to Russia and the Russian government, the Conspirators used false identities and made false statements about their identities. To further avoid detection, the Conspirators used a network of computers located across the world, including in the United States, and paid for this infrastructure using cryptocurrency.

Defendants

9.   Defendant VIKTOR BORISOVICH NETYKSHO (Нетыкшо Виктор Борисович) was the Russian military officer in command of Unit 26165, located at 20 Komsomolskiy Prospekt, Moscow, Russia. Unit 26165 had primary responsibility for hacking the DCCC and DNC, as well as the email accounts of individuals affiliated with the Clinton Campaign.

10.   Defendant BORIS ALEKSEYEVICH ANTONOV (Антонов Борис Алексеевич) was a Major in the Russian military assigned to Unit 26165. ANTONOV oversaw a department within Unit 26165 dedicated to targeting military, political, governmental, and non-governmental organizations with spearphishing emails and other computer intrusion activity. ANTONOV held the title "Head of Department." In or around 2016, ANTONOV supervised other co-conspirators who targeted the DCCC, DNC, and individuals affiliated with the Clinton Campaign.

11.   Defendant DMITRIY SERGEYEVICH BADIN (Бадин Дмитрий Сергеевич) was a Russian military officer assigned to Unit 26165 who held the title "Assistant Head of Department." In or around 2016, BADIN, along with ANTONOV, supervised other co-conspirators who targeted the DCCC, DNC, and individuals affiliated with the Clinton Campaign.

3

591

12.   Defendant IVAN SERGEYEVICH YERMAKOV (Ермаков Иван Сергеевич) was a Russian military officer assigned to ANTONOV's department within Unit 26165. Since in or around 2010, YERMAKOV used various online personas, including "Kate S. Milton," "James McMorgans," and "Karen W. Millen," to conduct hacking operations on behalf of Unit 26165. In or around March 2016, YERMAKOV participated in hacking at least two email accounts from which campaign-related documents were released through DCLeaks. In or around May 2016, YERMAKOV also participated in hacking the DNC email server and stealing DNC emails that were later released through Organization 1.

13.   Defendant ALEKSEY VIKTOROVICH LUKASHEV (Лукашев Алексей Викторович) was a Senior Lieutenant in the Russian military assigned to ANTONOV's department within Unit 26165. LUKASHEV used various online personas, including "Den Katenberg" and "Yuliana Martynova." In or around 2016, LUKASHEV sent spearphishing emails to members of the Clinton Campaign and affiliated individuals, including the chairman of the Clinton Campaign.

14.   Defendant SERGEY ALEKSANDROVICH MORGACHEV (Моргачев Сергей Александрович) was a Lieutenant Colonel in the Russian military assigned to Unit 26165. MORGACHEV oversaw a department within Unit 26165 dedicated to developing and managing malware, including a hacking tool used by the GRU known as "X-Agent." During the hacking of the DCCC and DNC networks, MORGACHEV supervised the co-conspirators who developed and monitored the X-Agent malware implanted on those computers.

15.   Defendant NIKOLAY YURYEVICH KOZACHEK (Козачек Николай Юрьевич) was a Lieutenant Captain in the Russian military assigned to MORGACHEV's department within Unit 26165. KOZACHEK used a variety of monikers, including "kazak" and "blablabla1234565." KOZACHEK developed, customized, and monitored X-Agent malware used to hack the DCCC

4

and DNC networks beginning in or around April 2016.

16.   Defendant PAVEL VYACHESLAVOVICH YERSHOV (Ершов Павел Вячеславович) was a Russian military officer assigned to MORGACHEV's department within Unit 26165. In or around 2016, YERSHOV assisted KOZACHEK and other co-conspirators in testing and customizing X-Agent malware before actual deployment and use.

17.   Defendant ARTEM ANDREYEVICH MALYSHEV (Малышев Артём Андреевич) was a Second Lieutenant in the Russian military assigned to MORGACHEV's department within Unit 26165. MALYSHEV used a variety of monikers, including "djangomagicdev" and "realblatr." In or around 2016, MALYSHEV monitored X-Agent malware implanted on the DCCC and DNC networks.

18.   Defendant ALEKSANDR VLADIMIROVICH OSADCHUK (Осадчук Александр Владимирович) was a Colonel in the Russian military and the commanding officer of Unit 74455. Unit 74455 was located at 22 Kirova Street, Khimki, Moscow, a building referred to within the GRU as the "Tower." Unit 74455 assisted in the release of stolen documents through the DCLeaks and Guccifer 2.0 personas, the promotion of those releases, and the publication of anti-Clinton content on social media accounts operated by the GRU.

19.   Defendant ALEKSEY ALEKSANDROVICH POTEMKIN (Потемкин Алексей Александрович) was an officer in the Russian military assigned to Unit 74455. POTEMKIN was a supervisor in a department within Unit 74455 responsible for the administration of computer infrastructure used in cyber operations. Infrastructure and social media accounts administered by POTEMKIN's department were used, among other things, to assist in the release of stolen documents through the DCLeaks and Guccifer 2.0 personas.

5

Object of the Conspiracy

20.   The object of the conspiracy was to hack into the computers of U.S. persons and entities involved in the 2016 U.S. presidential election, steal documents from those computers, and stage releases of the stolen documents to interfere with the 2016 U.S. presidential election.

Manner and Means of the Conspiracy

Spearphishing Operations

21.   ANTONOV, BADIN, YERMAKOV, LUKASHEV, and their co-conspirators targeted victims using a technique known as spearphishing to steal victims' passwords or otherwise gain access to their computers. Beginning by at least March 2016, the Conspirators targeted over 300 individuals affiliated with the Clinton Campaign, DCCC, and DNC.

a.   For example, on or about March 19, 2016, LUKASHEV and his co-conspirators created and sent a spearphishing email to the chairman of the Clinton Campaign. LUKASHEV used the account "john356gh" at an online service that abbreviated lengthy website addresses (referred to as a "URL-shortening service"). LUKASHEV used the account to mask a link contained in the spearphishing email, which directed the recipient to a GRU-created website. LUKASHEV altered the appearance of the sender email address in order to make it look like the email was a security notification from Google (a technique known as "spoofing"), instructing the user to change his password by clicking the embedded link. Those instructions were followed. On or about March 21, 2016, LUKASHEV, YERMAKOV, and their co-conspirators stole the contents of the chairman's email account, which consisted of over 50,000 emails.

b.   Starting on or about March 19, 2016, LUKASHEV and his co-conspirators sent spearphishing emails to the personal accounts of other individuals affiliated with

6

594

the Clinton Campaign, including its campaign manager and a senior foreign policy advisor. On or about March 25, 2016, LUKASHEV used the same john356gh account to mask additional links included in spearphishing emails sent to numerous individuals affiliated with the Clinton Campaign, including Victims 1 and 2. LUKASHEV sent these emails from the Russia-based email account hi.mymail@yandex.com that he spoofed to appear to be from Google.

c.   On or about March 28, 2016, YERMAKOV researched the names of Victims 1 and 2 and their association with Clinton on various social media sites. Through their spearphishing operations, LUKASHEV, YERMAKOV, and their co-conspirators successfully stole email credentials and thousands of emails from numerous individuals affiliated with the Clinton Campaign. Many of these stolen emails, including those from Victims 1 and 2, were later released by the Conspirators through DCLeaks.

d.   On or about April 6, 2016, the Conspirators created an email account in the name (with a one-letter deviation from the actual spelling) of a known member of the Clinton Campaign. The Conspirators then used that account to send spearphishing emails to the work accounts of more than thirty different Clinton Campaign employees. In the spearphishing emails, LUKASHEV and his co-conspirators embedded a link purporting to direct the recipient to a document titled "hillary-clinton-favorable-rating.xlsx." In fact, this link directed the recipients' computers to a GRU-created website.

22.   The Conspirators spearphished individuals affiliated with the Clinton Campaign throughout the summer of 2016. For example, on or about July 27, 2016, the Conspirators

7

595

attempted after hours to spearphish for the first time email accounts at a domain hosted by a third-party provider and used by Clinton's personal office. At or around the same time, they also targeted seventy-six email addresses at the domain for the Clinton Campaign.

Hacking into the DCCC Network

23. Beginning in or around March 2016, the Conspirators, in addition to their spearphishing efforts, researched the DCCC and DNC computer networks to identify technical specifications and vulnerabilities.

    a. For example, beginning on or about March 15, 2016, YERMAKOV ran a technical query for the DNC's internet protocol configurations to identify connected devices.

    b. On or about the same day, YERMAKOV searched for open-source information about the DNC network, the Democratic Party, and Hillary Clinton.

    c. On or about April 7, 2016, YERMAKOV ran a technical query for the DCCC's internet protocol configurations to identify connected devices.

24. By in or around April 2016, within days of YERMAKOV's searches regarding the DCCC, the Conspirators hacked into the DCCC computer network. Once they gained access, they installed and managed different types of malware to explore the DCCC network and steal data.

    a. On or about April 12, 2016, the Conspirators used the stolen credentials of a DCCC Employee ("DCCC Employee 1") to access the DCCC network. DCCC Employee 1 had received a spearphishing email from the Conspirators on or about April 6, 2016, and entered her password after clicking on the link.

    b. Between in or around April 2016 and June 2016, the Conspirators installed multiple versions of their X-Agent malware on at least ten DCCC computers, which allowed them to monitor individual employees' computer activity, steal passwords, and maintain access to the DCCC network.

8

596

c.   X-Agent malware implanted on the DCCC network transmitted information from the victims' computers to a GRU-leased server located in Arizona. The Conspirators referred to this server as their "AMS" panel. KOZACHEK, MALYSHEV, and their co-conspirators logged into the AMS panel to use X-Agent's keylog and screenshot functions in the course of monitoring and surveilling activity on the DCCC computers. The keylog function allowed the Conspirators to capture keystrokes entered by DCCC employees. The screenshot function allowed the Conspirators to take pictures of the DCCC employees' computer screens.

d.   For example, on or about April 14, 2016, the Conspirators repeatedly activated X-Agent's keylog and screenshot functions to surveil DCCC Employee 1's computer activity over the course of eight hours. During that time, the Conspirators captured DCCC Employee 1's communications with co-workers and the passwords she entered while working on fundraising and voter outreach projects. Similarly, on or about April 22, 2016, the Conspirators activated X-Agent's keylog and screenshot functions to capture the discussions of another DCCC Employee ("DCCC Employee 2") about the DCCC's finances, as well as her individual banking information and other personal topics.

25.   On or about April 19, 2016, KOZACHEK, YERSHOV, and their co-conspirators remotely configured an overseas computer to relay communications between X-Agent malware and the AMS panel and then tested X-Agent's ability to connect to this computer. The Conspirators referred to this computer as a "middle server." The middle server acted as a proxy to obscure the connection between malware at the DCCC and the Conspirators' AMS panel. On or about April

9

597

20, 2016, the Conspirators directed X-Agent malware on the DCCC computers to connect to this middle server and receive directions from the Conspirators.

Hacking into the DNC Network

26.   On or about April 18, 2016, the Conspirators hacked into the DNC's computers through their access to the DCCC network. The Conspirators then installed and managed different types of malware (as they did in the DCCC network) to explore the DNC network and steal documents.

   a.   On or about April 18, 2016, the Conspirators activated X-Agent's keylog and screenshot functions to steal credentials of a DCCC employee who was authorized to access the DNC network. The Conspirators hacked into the DNC network from the DCCC network using stolen credentials. By in or around June 2016, they gained access to approximately thirty-three DNC computers.

   b.   In or around April 2016, the Conspirators installed X-Agent malware on the DNC network, including the same versions installed on the DCCC network. MALYSHEV and his co-conspirators monitored the X-Agent malware from the AMS panel and captured data from the victim computers. The AMS panel collected thousands of keylog and screenshot results from the DCCC and DNC computers, such as a screenshot and keystroke capture of DCCC Employee 2 viewing the DCCC's online banking information.

Theft of DCCC and DNC Documents

27.   The Conspirators searched for and identified computers within the DCCC and DNC networks that stored information related to the 2016 U.S. presidential election. For example, on or about April 15, 2016, the Conspirators searched one hacked DCCC computer for terms that included "hillary," "cruz," and "trump." The Conspirators also copied select DCCC folders, including "Benghazi Investigations." The Conspirators targeted computers containing information

10

such as opposition research and field operation plans for the 2016 elections.

28.   To enable them to steal a large number of documents at once without detection, the Conspirators used a publicly available tool to gather and compress multiple documents on the DCCC and DNC networks. The Conspirators then used other GRU malware, known as "X-Tunnel," to move the stolen documents outside the DCCC and DNC networks through encrypted channels.

      a.   For example, on or about April 22, 2016, the Conspirators compressed gigabytes of data from DNC computers, including opposition research. The Conspirators later moved the compressed DNC data using X-Tunnel to a GRU-leased computer located in Illinois.

      b.   On or about April 28, 2016, the Conspirators connected to and tested the same computer located in Illinois. Later that day, the Conspirators used X-Tunnel to connect to that computer to steal additional documents from the DCCC network.

29.   Between on or about May 25, 2016 and June 1, 2016, the Conspirators hacked the DNC Microsoft Exchange Server and stole thousands of emails from the work accounts of DNC employees. During that time, YERMAKOV researched PowerShell commands related to accessing and managing the Microsoft Exchange Server.

30.   On or about May 30, 2016, MALYSHEV accessed the AMS panel in order to upgrade custom AMS software on the server. That day, the AMS panel received updates from approximately thirteen different X-Agent malware implants on DCCC and DNC computers.

31.   During the hacking of the DCCC and DNC networks, the Conspirators covered their tracks by intentionally deleting logs and computer files. For example, on or about May 13, 2016, the Conspirators cleared the event logs from a DNC computer. On or about June 20, 2016, the

Conspirators deleted logs from the AMS panel that documented their activities on the panel, including the login history.

Efforts to Remain on the DCCC and DNC Networks

32.   Despite the Conspirators' efforts to hide their activity, beginning in or around May 2016, both the DCCC and DNC became aware that they had been hacked and hired a security company ("Company 1") to identify the extent of the intrusions. By in or around June 2016, Company 1 took steps to exclude intruders from the networks. Despite these efforts, a Linux-based version of X-Agent, programmed to communicate with the GRU-registered domain linuxkrnl.net, remained on the DNC network until in or around October 2016.

33.   In response to Company 1's efforts, the Conspirators took countermeasures to maintain access to the DCCC and DNC networks.

    a.   On or about May 31, 2016, YERMAKOV searched for open-source information about Company 1 and its reporting on X-Agent and X-Tunnel. On or about June 1, 2016, the Conspirators attempted to delete traces of their presence on the DCCC network using the computer program CCleaner.

    b.   On or about June 14, 2016, the Conspirators registered the domain actblues.com, which mimicked the domain of a political fundraising platform that included a DCCC donations page. Shortly thereafter, the Conspirators used stolen DCCC credentials to modify the DCCC website and redirect visitors to the actblues.com domain.

    c.   On or about June 20, 2016, after Company 1 had disabled X-Agent on the DCCC network, the Conspirators spent over seven hours unsuccessfully trying to connect to X-Agent. The Conspirators also tried to access the DCCC network using previously stolen credentials.

12

600

34.   In or around September 2016, the Conspirators also successfully gained access to DNC computers hosted on a third-party cloud-computing service. These computers contained test applications related to the DNC's analytics. After conducting reconnaissance, the Conspirators gathered data by creating backups, or "snapshots," of the DNC's cloud-based systems using the cloud provider's own technology. The Conspirators then moved the snapshots to cloud-based accounts they had registered with the same service, thereby stealing the data from the DNC.

Stolen Documents Released through DCLeaks

35.   More than a month before the release of any documents, the Conspirators constructed the online persona DCLeaks to release and publicize stolen election-related documents. On or about April 19, 2016, after attempting to register the domain electionleaks.com, the Conspirators registered the domain dcleaks.com through a service that anonymized the registrant. The funds used to pay for the dcleaks.com domain originated from an account at an online cryptocurrency service that the Conspirators also used to fund the lease of a virtual private server registered with the operational email account dirbinsaabol@mail.com. The dirbinsaabol email account was also used to register the john356gh URL-shortening account used by LUKASHEV to spearphish the Clinton Campaign chairman and other campaign-related individuals.

36.   On or about June 8, 2016, the Conspirators launched the public website dcleaks.com, which they used to release stolen emails. Before it shut down in or around March 2017, the site received over one million page views. The Conspirators falsely claimed on the site that DCLeaks was started by a group of "American hacktivists," when in fact it was started by the Conspirators.

37.   Starting in or around June 2016 and continuing through the 2016 U.S. presidential election, the Conspirators used DCLeaks to release emails stolen from individuals affiliated with the Clinton Campaign. The Conspirators also released documents they had stolen in other spearphishing operations, including those they had conducted in 2015 that collected emails from individuals

13

affiliated with the Republican Party.

38.   On or about June 8, 2016, and at approximately the same time that the dcleaks.com website was launched, the Conspirators created a DCLeaks Facebook page using a preexisting social media account under the fictitious name "Alice Donovan."   In addition to the DCLeaks Facebook page, the Conspirators used other social media accounts in the names of fictitious U.S. persons such as "Jason Scott" and "Richard Gingrey" to promote the DCLeaks website. The Conspirators accessed these accounts from computers managed by POTEMKIN and his co-conspirators.

39.   On or about June 8, 2016, the Conspirators created the Twitter account @dcleaks_. The Conspirators operated the @dcleaks_ Twitter account from the same computer used for other efforts to interfere with the 2016 U.S. presidential election. For example, the Conspirators used the same computer to operate the Twitter account @BaltimoreIsWhr, through which they encouraged U.S. audiences to "[j]oin our flash mob" opposing Clinton and to post images with the hashtag #BlacksAgainstHillary.

Stolen Documents Released through Guccifer 2.0

40.   On or about June 14, 2016, the DNC—through Company 1—publicly announced that it had been hacked by Russian government actors. In response, the Conspirators created the online persona Guccifer 2.0 and falsely claimed to be a lone Romanian hacker to undermine the allegations of Russian responsibility for the intrusion.

41.   On or about June 15, 2016, the Conspirators logged into a Moscow-based server used and managed by Unit 74455 and, between 4:19 PM and 4:56 PM Moscow Standard Time, searched for certain words and phrases, including:

14

602

Search Term(s)
"some hundred sheets"
"some hundreds of sheets"
dcleaks
illuminati
широко известный перевод [widely known translation]
"worldwide known"
"think twice about"
"company's competence"

42.   Later that day, at 7:02 PM Moscow Standard Time, the online persona Guccifer 2.0

published its first post on a blog site created through WordPress. Titled "DNC's servers hacked

by a lone hacker," the post used numerous English words and phrases that the Conspirators had

searched for earlier that day (bolded below):

> **Worldwide known** cyber security company [Company 1] announced that
> the Democratic National Committee (DNC) servers had been hacked by
> "sophisticated" hacker groups.
>
> I'm very pleased the company appreciated my skills so highly))) [. . .]
>
> Here are just a few docs from many thousands I extracted when hacking
> into DNC's network. [. . .]
>
> **Some hundred sheets**! This's a serious case, isn't it? [. . .]
>
> I guess [Company 1] customers should **think twice about company's
> competence**.
>
> F[***] the **Illuminati** and their conspiracies!!!!!!!!! F[***]
> [Company 1]!!!!!!!!!

43.   Between in or around June 2016 and October 2016, the Conspirators used Guccifer 2.0 to

release documents through WordPress that they had stolen from the DCCC and DNC. The

Conspirators, posing as Guccifer 2.0, also shared stolen documents with certain individuals.

      a.   On or about August 15, 2016, the Conspirators, posing as Guccifer 2.0, received a

15

request for stolen documents from a candidate for the U.S. Congress. The Conspirators responded using the Guccifer 2.0 persona and sent the candidate stolen documents related to the candidate's opponent.

b.   On or about August 22, 2016, the Conspirators, posing as Guccifer 2.0, transferred approximately 2.5 gigabytes of data stolen from the DCCC to a then-registered state lobbyist and online source of political news. The stolen data included donor records and personal identifying information for more than 2,000 Democratic donors.

c.   On or about August 22, 2016, the Conspirators, posing as Guccifer 2.0, sent a reporter stolen documents pertaining to the Black Lives Matter movement. The reporter responded by discussing when to release the documents and offering to write an article about their release.

44.   The Conspirators, posing as Guccifer 2.0, also communicated with U.S. persons about the release of stolen documents. On or about August 15, 2016, the Conspirators, posing as Guccifer 2.0, wrote to a person who was in regular contact with senior members of the presidential campaign of Donald J. Trump, "thank u for writing back . . . do u find anyt[h]ing interesting in the docs i posted?" On or about August 17, 2016, the Conspirators added, "please tell me if i can help u anyhow . . . it would be a great pleasure to me." On or about September 9, 2016, the Conspirators, again posing as Guccifer 2.0, referred to a stolen DCCC document posted online and asked the person, "what do u think of the info on the turnout model for the democrats entire presidential campaign." The person responded, "[p]retty standard."

45.   The Conspirators conducted operations as Guccifer 2.0 and DCLeaks using overlapping computer infrastructure and financing.

a.   For example, between on or about March 14, 2016 and April 28, 2016, the

16

604

Conspirators used the same pool of bitcoin funds to purchase a virtual private network ("VPN") account and to lease a server in Malaysia. In or around June 2016, the Conspirators used the Malaysian server to host the dcleaks.com website. On or about July 6, 2016, the Conspirators used the VPN to log into the @Guccifer_2 Twitter account. The Conspirators opened that VPN account from the same server that was also used to register malicious domains for the hacking of the DCCC and DNC networks.

b.   On or about June 27, 2016, the Conspirators, posing as Guccifer 2.0, contacted a U.S. reporter with an offer to provide stolen emails from "Hillary Clinton's staff." The Conspirators then sent the reporter the password to access a nonpublic, password-protected portion of dcleaks.com containing emails stolen from Victim 1 by LUKASHEV, YERMAKOV, and their co-conspirators in or around March 2016.

46.   On or about January 12, 2017, the Conspirators published a statement on the Guccifer 2.0 WordPress blog, falsely claiming that the intrusions and release of stolen documents had "totally no relation to the Russian government."

Use of Organization 1

47.   In order to expand their interference in the 2016 U.S. presidential election, the Conspirators transferred many of the documents they stole from the DNC and the chairman of the Clinton Campaign to Organization 1. The Conspirators, posing as Guccifer 2.0, discussed the release of the stolen documents and the timing of those releases with Organization 1 to heighten their impact on the 2016 U.S. presidential election.

a.   On or about June 22, 2016, Organization 1 sent a private message to Guccifer 2.0 to "[s]end any new material [stolen from the DNC] here for us to review and it will

17

605

have a much higher impact than what you are doing." On or about July 6, 2016, Organization 1 added, "if you have anything hillary related we want it in the next tweo [*sic*] days prefable [*sic*] because the DNC [Democratic National Convention] is approaching and she will solidify bernie supporters behind her after." The Conspirators responded, "ok . . . i see." Organization 1 explained, "we think trump has only a 25% chance of winning against hillary . . . so conflict between bernie and hillary is interesting."

b.   After failed attempts to transfer the stolen documents starting in late June 2016, on or about July 14, 2016, the Conspirators, posing as Guccifer 2.0, sent Organization 1 an email with an attachment titled "wk dnc link1.txt.gpg." The Conspirators explained to Organization 1 that the encrypted file contained instructions on how to access an online archive of stolen DNC documents. On or about July 18, 2016, Organization 1 confirmed it had "the 1Gb or so archive" and would make a release of the stolen documents "this week."

48.   On or about July 22, 2016, Organization 1 released over 20,000 emails and other documents stolen from the DNC network by the Conspirators. This release occurred approximately three days before the start of the Democratic National Convention. Organization 1 did not disclose Guccifer 2.0's role in providing them. The latest-in-time email released through Organization 1 was dated on or about May 25, 2016, approximately the same day the Conspirators hacked the DNC Microsoft Exchange Server.

49.   On or about October 7, 2016, Organization 1 released the first set of emails from the chairman of the Clinton Campaign that had been stolen by LUKASHEV and his co-conspirators. Between on or about October 7, 2016 and November 7, 2016, Organization 1 released

18

606

approximately thirty-three tranches of documents that had been stolen from the chairman of the Clinton Campaign. In total, over 50,000 stolen documents were released.

Statutory Allegations

50.   Paragraphs 1 through 49 of this Indictment are re-alleged and incorporated by reference as if fully set forth herein.

51.   From at least in or around March 2016 through November 2016, in the District of Columbia and elsewhere, Defendants NETYKSHO, ANTONOV, BADIN, YERMAKOV, LUKASHEV, MORGACHEV, KOZACHEK, YERSHOV, MALYSHEV, OSADCHUK, and POTEMKIN, together with others known and unknown to the Grand Jury, knowingly and intentionally conspired to commit offenses against the United States, namely:

a.   To knowingly access a computer without authorization and exceed authorized access to a computer, and to obtain thereby information from a protected computer, where the value of the information obtained exceeded $5,000, in violation of Title 18, United States Code, Sections 1030(a)(2)(C) and 1030(c)(2)(B); and

b.   To knowingly cause the transmission of a program, information, code, and command, and as a result of such conduct, to intentionally cause damage without authorization to a protected computer, and where the offense did cause and, if completed, would have caused, loss aggregating $5,000 in value to at least one person during a one-year period from a related course of conduct affecting a protected computer, and damage affecting at least ten protected computers during a one-year period, in violation of Title 18, United States Code, Sections 1030(a)(5)(A) and 1030(c)(4)(B).

52.   In furtherance of the Conspiracy and to effect its illegal objects, the Conspirators committed the overt acts set forth in paragraphs 1 through 19, 21 through 49, 55, and 57 through

607

64, which are re-alleged and incorporated by reference as if fully set forth herein.

53.   In furtherance of the Conspiracy, and as set forth in paragraphs 1 through 19, 21 through 49, 55, and 57 through 64, the Conspirators knowingly falsely registered a domain name and knowingly used that domain name in the course of committing an offense, namely, the Conspirators registered domains, including dcleaks.com and actblues.com, with false names and addresses, and used those domains in the course of committing the felony offense charged in Count One.

All in violation of Title 18, United States Code, Sections 371 and 3559(g)(1).

COUNTS TWO THROUGH NINE
(Aggravated Identity Theft)

54.   Paragraphs 1 through 19, 21 through 49, and 57 through 64 of this Indictment are re-alleged and incorporated by reference as if fully set forth herein.

55.   On or about the dates specified below, in the District of Columbia and elsewhere, Defendants VIKTOR BORISOVICH NETYKSHO, BORIS ALEKSEYEVICH ANTONOV, DMITRIY SERGEYEVICH BADIN, IVAN SERGEYEVICH YERMAKOV, ALEKSEY VIKTOROVICH LUKASHEV, SERGEY ALEKSANDROVICH MORGACHEV, NIKOLAY YURYEVICH KOZACHEK, PAVEL VYACHESLAVOVICH YERSHOV, ARTEM ANDREYEVICH MALYSHEV, ALEKSANDR VLADIMIROVICH OSADCHUK, and ALEKSEY ALEKSANDROVICH POTEMKIN did knowingly transfer, possess, and use, without lawful authority, a means of identification of another person during and in relation to a felony violation enumerated in Title 18, United States Code, Section 1028A(c), namely, computer fraud in violation of Title 18, United States Code, Sections 1030(a)(2)(C) and 1030(c)(2)(B), knowing that the means of identification belonged to another real person:

20

608

Count	Approximate Date	Victim	Means of Identification
2	March 21, 2016	Victim 3	Username and password for personal email account
3	March 25, 2016	Victim 1	Username and password for personal email account
4	April 12, 2016	Victim 4	Username and password for DCCC computer network
5	April 15, 2016	Victim 5	Username and password for DCCC computer network
6	April 18, 2016	Victim 6	Username and password for DCCC computer network
7	May 10, 2016	Victim 7	Username and password for DNC computer network
8	June 2, 2016	Victim 2	Username and password for personal email account
9	July 6, 2016	Victim 8	Username and password for personal email account

All in violation of Title 18, United States Code, Sections 1028A(a)(1) and 2.

COUNT TEN
(Conspiracy to Launder Money)

56.   Paragraphs 1 through 19, 21 through 49, and 55 are re-alleged and incorporated by reference as if fully set forth herein.

57.   To facilitate the purchase of infrastructure used in their hacking activity—including hacking into the computers of U.S. persons and entities involved in the 2016 U.S. presidential election and releasing the stolen documents—the Defendants conspired to launder the equivalent of more than $95,000 through a web of transactions structured to capitalize on the perceived anonymity of cryptocurrencies such as bitcoin.

58.   Although the Conspirators caused transactions to be conducted in a variety of currencies, including U.S. dollars, they principally used bitcoin when purchasing servers, registering domains, and otherwise making payments in furtherance of hacking activity. Many of these payments were

21

609

processed by companies located in the United States that provided payment processing services to hosting companies, domain registrars, and other vendors both international and domestic. The use of bitcoin allowed the Conspirators to avoid direct relationships with traditional financial institutions, allowing them to evade greater scrutiny of their identities and sources of funds.

59.   All bitcoin transactions are added to a public ledger called the Blockchain, but the Blockchain identifies the parties to each transaction only by alpha-numeric identifiers known as bitcoin addresses. To further avoid creating a centralized paper trail of all of their purchases, the Conspirators purchased infrastructure using hundreds of different email accounts, in some cases using a new account for each purchase. The Conspirators used fictitious names and addresses in order to obscure their identities and their links to Russia and the Russian government. For example, the dcleaks.com domain was registered and paid for using the fictitious name "Carrie Feehan" and an address in New York. In some cases, as part of the payment process, the Conspirators provided vendors with nonsensical addresses such as "usa Denver AZ," "gfhgh ghfhgfh fdgfdg WA," and "1 2 dwd District of Columbia."

60.   The Conspirators used several dedicated email accounts to track basic bitcoin transaction information and to facilitate bitcoin payments to vendors. One of these dedicated accounts, registered with the username "gfadel47," received hundreds of bitcoin payment requests from approximately 100 different email accounts. For example, on or about February 1, 2016, the gfadel47 account received the instruction to "[p]lease send *exactly* **0.026043** bitcoin to" a certain thirty-four character bitcoin address. Shortly thereafter, a transaction matching those exact instructions was added to the Blockchain.

61.   On occasion, the Conspirators facilitated bitcoin payments using the same computers that they used to conduct their hacking activity, including to create and send test spearphishing emails.

22

610

Additionally, one of these dedicated accounts was used by the Conspirators in or around 2015 to renew the registration of a domain (linuxkrnl.net) encoded in certain X-Agent malware installed on the DNC network.

62.   The Conspirators funded the purchase of computer infrastructure for their hacking activity in part by "mining" bitcoin. Individuals and entities can mine bitcoin by allowing their computing power to be used to verify and record payments on the bitcoin public ledger, a service for which they are rewarded with freshly-minted bitcoin. The pool of bitcoin generated from the GRU's mining activity was used, for example, to pay a Romanian company to register the domain dcleaks.com through a payment processing company located in the United States.

63.   In addition to mining bitcoin, the Conspirators acquired bitcoin through a variety of means designed to obscure the origin of the funds. This included purchasing bitcoin through peer-to-peer exchanges, moving funds through other digital currencies, and using pre-paid cards. They also enlisted the assistance of one or more third-party exchangers who facilitated layered transactions through digital currency exchange platforms providing heightened anonymity.

64.   The Conspirators used the same funding structure—and in some cases, the very same pool of funds—to purchase key accounts, servers, and domains used in their election-related hacking activity.

    a.   The bitcoin mining operation that funded the registration payment for dcleaks.com also sent newly-minted bitcoin to a bitcoin address controlled by "Daniel Farell," the persona that was used to renew the domain linuxkrnl.net. The bitcoin mining operation also funded, through the same bitcoin address, the purchase of servers and domains used in the GRU's spearphishing operations, including accounts-qooqle.com and account-gooogle.com.

23

611

b.   On or about March 14, 2016, using funds in a bitcoin address, the Conspirators purchased a VPN account, which they later used to log into the @Guccifer_2 Twitter account. The remaining funds from that bitcoin address were then used on or about April 28, 2016, to lease a Malaysian server that hosted the dcleaks.com website.

c.   The Conspirators used a different set of fictitious names (including "Ward DeClaur" and "Mike Long") to send bitcoin to a U.S. company in order to lease a server used to administer X-Tunnel malware implanted on the DCCC and DNC networks, and to lease two servers used to hack the DNC's cloud network.

Statutory Allegations

65.   From at least in or around 2015 through 2016, within the District of Columbia and elsewhere, Defendants VIKTOR BORISOVICH NETYKSHO, BORIS ALEKSEYEVICH ANTONOV, DMITRIY SERGEYEVICH BADIN, IVAN SERGEYEVICH YERMAKOV, ALEKSEY VIKTOROVICH LUKASHEV, SERGEY ALEKSANDROVICH MORGACHEV, NIKOLAY YURYEVICH KOZACHEK, PAVEL VYACHESLAVOVICH YERSHOV, ARTEM ANDREYEVICH MALYSHEV, ALEKSANDR VLADIMIROVICH OSADCHUK, and ALEKSEY ALEKSANDROVICH POTEMKIN, together with others, known and unknown to the Grand Jury, did knowingly and intentionally conspire to transport, transmit, and transfer monetary instruments and funds to a place in the United States from and through a place outside the United States and from a place in the United States to and through a place outside the United States, with the intent to promote the carrying on of specified unlawful activity, namely, a violation of Title 18, United States Code, Section 1030, contrary to Title 18, United States Code, Section 1956(a)(2)(A).

All in violation of Title 18, United States Code, Section 1956(h).

24

612

COUNT ELEVEN
(Conspiracy to Commit an Offense Against the United States)

66.   Paragraphs 1 through 8 of this Indictment are re-alleged and incorporated by reference as if fully set forth herein.

Defendants

67.   Paragraph 18 of this Indictment relating to ALEKSANDR VLADIMIROVICH OSADCHUK is re-alleged and incorporated by reference as if fully set forth herein.

68.   Defendant ANATOLIY SERGEYEVICH KOVALEV (Ковалев Анатолий Сергеевич) was an officer in the Russian military assigned to Unit 74455 who worked in the GRU's 22 Kirova Street building (the Tower).

69.   Defendants OSADCHUK and KOVALEV were GRU officers who knowingly and intentionally conspired with each other and with persons, known and unknown to the Grand Jury, to hack into the computers of U.S. persons and entities responsible for the administration of 2016 U.S. elections, such as state boards of elections, secretaries of state, and U.S. companies that supplied software and other technology related to the administration of U.S. elections.

Object of the Conspiracy

70.   The object of the conspiracy was to hack into protected computers of persons and entities charged with the administration of the 2016 U.S. elections in order to access those computers and steal voter data and other information stored on those computers.

Manner and Means of the Conspiracy

71.   In or around June 2016, KOVALEV and his co-conspirators researched domains used by U.S. state boards of elections, secretaries of state, and other election-related entities for website vulnerabilities. KOVALEV and his co-conspirators also searched for state political party email addresses, including filtered queries for email addresses listed on state Republican Party websites.

25

613

72.   In or around July 2016, KOVALEV and his co-conspirators hacked the website of a state board of elections ("SBOE 1") and stole information related to approximately 500,000 voters, including names, addresses, partial social security numbers, dates of birth, and driver's license numbers.

73.   In or around August 2016, KOVALEV and his co-conspirators hacked into the computers of a U.S. vendor ("Vendor 1") that supplied software used to verify voter registration information for the 2016 U.S. elections.   KOVALEV and his co-conspirators used some of the same infrastructure to hack into Vendor 1 that they had used to hack into SBOE 1.

74.   In or around August 2016, the Federal Bureau of Investigation issued an alert about the hacking of SBOE 1 and identified some of the infrastructure that was used to conduct the hacking. In response, KOVALEV deleted his search history.   KOVALEV and his co-conspirators also deleted records from accounts used in their operations targeting state boards of elections and similar election-related entities.

75.   In or around October 2016, KOVALEV and his co-conspirators further targeted state and county offices responsible for administering the 2016 U.S. elections.   For example, on or about October 28, 2016, KOVALEV and his co-conspirators visited the websites of certain counties in Georgia, Iowa, and Florida to identify vulnerabilities.

76.   In or around November 2016 and prior to the 2016 U.S. presidential election, KOVALEV and his co-conspirators used an email account designed to look like a Vendor 1 email address to send over 100 spearphishing emails to organizations and personnel involved in administering elections in numerous Florida counties.   The spearphishing emails contained malware that the Conspirators embedded into Word documents bearing Vendor 1's logo.

Statutory Allegations

77.   Between in or around June 2016 and November 2016, in the District of Columbia and

26

614

elsewhere, Defendants OSADCHUK and KOVALEV, together with others known and unknown to the Grand Jury, knowingly and intentionally conspired to commit offenses against the United States, namely:

a.   To knowingly access a computer without authorization and exceed authorized access to a computer, and to obtain thereby information from a protected computer, where the value of the information obtained exceeded $5,000, in violation of Title 18, United States Code, Sections 1030(a)(2)(C) and 1030(c)(2)(B); and

b.   To knowingly cause the transmission of a program, information, code, and command, and as a result of such conduct, to intentionally cause damage without authorization to a protected computer, and where the offense did cause and, if completed, would have caused, loss aggregating $5,000 in value to at least one person during a one-year period from a related course of conduct affecting a protected computer, and damage affecting at least ten protected computers during a one-year period, in violation of Title 18, United States Code, Sections 1030(a)(5)(A) and 1030(c)(4)(B).

78.   In furtherance of the Conspiracy and to effect its illegal objects, OSADCHUK, KOVALEV, and their co-conspirators committed the overt acts set forth in paragraphs 67 through 69 and 71 through 76, which are re-alleged and incorporated by reference as if fully set forth herein.

All in violation of Title 18, United States Code, Section 371.

FORFEITURE ALLEGATION

79.   Pursuant to Federal Rule of Criminal Procedure 32.2, notice is hereby given to Defendants that the United States will seek forfeiture as part of any sentence in the event of Defendants' convictions under Counts One, Ten, and Eleven of this Indictment. Pursuant to Title 18, United

615

States Code, Sections 982(a)(2) and 1030(i), upon conviction of the offenses charged in Counts

One and Eleven, Defendants NETYKSHO, ANTONOV, BADIN, YERMAKOV, LUKASHEV,

MORGACHEV, KOZACHEK, YERSHOV, MALYSHEV, OSADCHUK, POTEMKIN, and

KOVALEV shall forfeit to the United States any property, real or personal, which constitutes or

is derived from proceeds obtained directly or indirectly as a result of such violation, and any

personal property that was used or intended to be used to commit or to facilitate the commission

of such offense. Pursuant to Title 18, United States Code, Section 982(a)(1), upon conviction of

the offense charged in Count Ten, Defendants NETYKSHO, ANTONOV, BADIN,

YERMAKOV, LUKASHEV, MORGACHEV, KOZACHEK, YERSHOV, MALYSHEV,

OSADCHUK, and POTEMKIN shall forfeit to the United States any property, real or personal,

involved in such offense, and any property traceable to such property. Notice is further given that,

upon conviction, the United States intends to seek a judgment against each Defendant for a sum

of money representing the property described in this paragraph, as applicable to each Defendant

(to be offset by the forfeiture of any specific property).

Substitute Assets

80.   If any of the property described above as being subject to forfeiture, as a result of any act or

omission of any Defendant --

   a.   cannot be located upon the exercise of due diligence;

   b.   has been transferred or sold to, or deposited with, a third party;

   c.   has been placed beyond the jurisdiction of the court;

   d.   has been substantially diminished in value; or

   e.   has been commingled with other property that cannot be subdivided without

          difficulty;

it is the intent of the United States of America, pursuant to Title 18, United States Code, Section

616

982(b) and Title 28, United States Code, Section 2461(c), incorporating Title 21, United States Code, Section 853, to seek forfeiture of any other property of said Defendant.

Pursuant to 18 U.S.C. §§ 982 and 1030(i); 28 U.S.C. § 2461(c).

Robert S. Mueller, III
Special Counsel
U.S. Department of Justice

A TRUE BILL:

_____
Foreperson

Date: July 13, 2018

6. Statement of the Offenses and Other Acts, *US v. Paul J. Manafort, Jr.* (US District Court for the District of Columbia, September 14, 2018)

Paul Manafort's legal travails formed the longest-running legal saga in the special counsel investigation. He was charged in federal court in Washington, DC, on October 30, 2017, with crimes related to his work as a political consultant in Ukraine, then charged again in February 2018 in Virginia, where he lived, with additional allegations, including that he filed fraudulent loan applications to banks. Accused of trying to reach out to witnesses to coach them on his defense, he was tossed in jail in June 2018, then tried in Virginia and convicted on eight felony counts. Finally, averting a second trial, he pleaded guilty in September 2018 to charges brought in Washington.

This twenty-four-page statement of offenses describes all of Paul Manafort's crimes. He agreed that he conspired against the United States by illegally laundering through offshore accounts the $60 million he earned working in Ukraine from 2006 to 2016. He evaded $15 million in US taxes by failing to properly inform the IRS of those accounts and by lying to his own accountants and tax preparers. He failed to register as a foreign lobbyist while helping his Ukrainian clients press their views in Washington and, when questioned, submitted false information to the Department of Justice about his work.

Manafort had helped Viktor Yanukovych get elected president of Ukraine in 2010, but after Yanukovych rejected a plan to move his country toward membership in the European Union, he was ousted from office by public protests and fled to Russia. Manafort's Ukrainian gravy train dried up. Unable to continue supporting his lavish lifestyle, Manafort conceded that he committed bank fraud by lying on loan applications. After he was charged by Robert S. Mueller III, Manafort attempted to try to tamper with witnesses, in partnership with a longtime Russian associate, Konstantin Kilimnik. (Kilimnik, who lives in Moscow, has ties to Russian intelligence, according to Mueller. Kilimnik was also charged in the effort to tamper with witnesses.) He's in Russia and has not publicly addressed the obstruction charge, though court documents show that Manafort told prosecutors that Kilimnik didn't think he had suborned perjury and thought it was "crazy" that he was indicted.

The conduct outlined by Mueller painted a devastating portrait of Donald Trump's campaign chairman. Manafort had volunteered to work for Trump for free but was drowning in debt at the time. He appeared eager to use his campaign role to angle for money from his wealthy patrons in Ukraine and Russia, working in concert with an alleged Russian intelligence asset. His service for Trump coincided with the ramp-up of Russians intervention in the US election and a ratcheting-up of Trump's pro-Russia campaign rhetoric. For all those reasons, Manafort's decision to plead guilty and cooperate with Mueller was seen as a potential turning point for the special counsel. But in December 2018, Mueller announced yet one more twist. His team said Manafort, after sitting for twelve interviews and two sessions with the grand jury, had breached his plea agreement: they said he was still lying about matters important to the investigation.

FILED

IN THE UNITED STATES DISTRICT COURT
FOR THE DISTRICT OF COLUMBIA

SEP 1 4 2018

Clerk, U.S. District & Bankruptcy
Courts for the District of Columbia

UNITED STATES OF AMERICA	*	
	*	CRIMINAL NO. 17-201-1 (ABJ)
	*	
v.	*	Violations: 18 U.S.C. § 371
	*	(Conspiracy Against the United States
	*	and Conspiracy to Obstruct Justice)
PAUL J. MANAFORT, JR.,	*	
	*	
Defendant.	*	

****

STATEMENT OF THE OFFENSES AND OTHER ACTS

Pursuant to the Federal Rules of Criminal Procedure 11, the United States and the

defendant PAUL J. MANAFORT, JR. (MANAFORT) stipulate and agree that the following

facts are true and accurate. These facts do not constitute all of the facts known to the parties

concerning the charged offense and covered conduct. This statement is being submitted by the

parties to demonstrate that sufficient facts exist to establish that the defendant committed the

offenses to which he is pleading guilty.

Count 1: Conspiracy Against the United States (18 U.S.C. § 371)

1.   At all relevant times herein, MANAFORT was an owner of Davis Manafort Partners, Inc.

(DMP) or DMP International, LLC (DMI) or both. MANAFORT engaged in a variety of criminal

schemes, and knowingly, intentionally, and willfully conspired with Richard W. Gates, Konstantin

Kilimnik, and others to carry out the criminal schemes that make up Counts One and Two of the

Information, as more fully set forth below.

A. FARA Conspiracy
22 U.S.C. §§ 612 and 618(a)(1)

MANAFORT's Lobbying in the United States on Behalf of the Government of Ukraine

Page **1** of **24**

621

2.   MANAFORT knew it was illegal to lobby government officials and engage in public relations activities (hereinafter collectively referred to as lobbying) in the United States on behalf of a foreign government or political party, without registering with the United States Government under the Foreign Agents Registration Act.   MANAFORT knew he was lobbying in the United States for the Government of Ukraine, President Viktor F. Yanukovych, the Party of Regions, and the Opposition Bloc (the latter two being political parties in Ukraine), and thus he was supposed to submit a written registration statement to the United States Department of Justice. MANAFORT knew that the filing was required to disclose the name of the foreign country, all the financial payments to the lobbyist, and the specific steps undertaken for the foreign country in the United States, among other information.

3.   MANAFORT knew that Ukraine had a strong interest in the United States' taking economic and policy positions favorable to Ukraine, including not imposing sanctions on Ukraine. MANAFORT also knew that the trial and treatment of President Yanukovych's political rival, former Prime Minister Yulia Tymoshenko, was strongly condemned by leading United States executive and legislative branch officials, and was a major hurdle to improving United States and Ukraine relations.

4.   From 2006 until 2015, MANAFORT led a multi-million dollar lobbying campaign in the United States at the direction of the Government of Ukraine, President Yanukovych, the Party of Regions, and the Opposition Bloc.   MANAFORT intentionally did so without registering and providing the disclosures required by law.

5.   As part of the lobbying scheme, MANAFORT hired numerous firms and people to assist in his lobbying campaign in the United States. He hired Companies A, B, C, D, and E, and Law Firm A, among others, to participate in what he described to President Yanukovych in writing as a global

"Engage Ukraine" lobbying campaign that he devised and led. These companies and law firm were paid the equivalent of over \$11 million for their Ukraine work.

6.   MANAFORT viewed secrecy for himself and for the actions of his lobbyists as integral to the effectiveness of the lobbying offensive he orchestrated for Ukraine. Filing under the Foreign Agents Registration Act would have thwarted the secrecy MANAFORT sought in order to conduct an effective campaign for Ukraine to influence both American leaders and the American public.

7.   MANAFORT took steps to avoid any of these firms and people disclosing their lobbying efforts under the Foreign Agents Registration Act. As one example, even though MANAFORT engaged Company E in 2007 to lobby in the United States for the Government of Ukraine, MANAFORT tried to dissuade Company E from filing under the Foreign Agents Registration Act. Only after MANAFORT ceased to use Company E in the fall of 2007 did Company E disclose its work for Ukraine, in a belated filing under the Act in 2008.

8.   MANAFORT took other measures to keep the Ukraine lobbying as secret as possible. For example, MANAFORT, in written communications on or about May 16, 2013, directed his lobbyists (including Persons D1 and D2, who worked for Company D) to write and disseminate within the United States news stories that alleged that Tymoshenko had paid for the murder of a Ukrainian official. MANAFORT stated that it should be "push[ed]" "[w]ith no fingerprints." "It is very important we have no connection." MANAFORT stated that "[m]y goal is to plant some stink on Tymo." Person D1 objected to the plan, but ultimately Persons D1 and D2 complied with MANAFORT's direction. The Foreign Agents Registration Act required MANAFORT to disclose such lobbying, as MANAFORT knew. He did not.

The Hapsburg Group and Company D

9.   As part of the lobbying scheme, starting in 2011, MANAFORT secretly retained Company

D and a group of four former European heads of state and senior officials (including a former Austrian Chancellor, Italian Prime Minister, and Polish President) to lobby in the United States and Europe on behalf of Ukraine. The former politicians, called the Hapsburg Group by MANAFORT, appeared to be providing solely their independent assessments of Government of Ukraine policies, when in fact they were paid by Ukraine. MANAFORT explained in an "EYES ONLY" memorandum in or about June 2012 that his purpose was to "assemble a small group of high-level European infuencial [sic] champions and politically credible friends who can act informally and without any visible relationship with the Government of Ukraine."

10.   Through MANAFORT, the Government of Ukraine retained an additional group of lobbyists (Company D and Persons D1 and D2). In addition to lobbying itself, Company D secretly served as intermediaries between the Hapsburg Group and MANAFORT and the Government of Ukraine. In or about 2012 through 2013, MANAFORT directed more than the equivalent of 700,000 euros to be wired from at least three of his offshore accounts to the benefit of Company D to pay secretly for its services.

11.   All four Hapsburg Group members, at the direction, and with the direct assistance, of MANAFORT, advocated positions favorable to Ukraine in meetings with United States lawmakers, interviews with United States journalists, and ghost written op-eds in American publications. In or about 2012 through 2014, MANAFORT directed more than 2 million euros to be wired from at least four of his offshore accounts to pay secretly the Hapsburg Group. To avoid European taxation, the contract with the Hapsburg Group falsely stated that none of its work would take place in Europe.

12.   One of the Hapsburg Group members, a former Polish President, was also a representative of the European Parliament with oversight responsibility for Ukraine. MANAFORT solicited that

624

official to provide MANAFORT inside information about the European Parliament's views and actions toward Ukraine and to take actions favorable to Ukraine. MANAFORT also used this Hapsburg Group member's current European Parliament position to Ukraine's advantage in his lobbying efforts in the United States. In the fall of 2012, the United States Senate was considering and ultimately passed a resolution critical of President Yanukovych's treatment of former Prime Minister Tymoshenko. MANAFORT engaged in an all-out campaign to try to kill or delay the passage of this resolution. Among the steps he took was having the Hapsburg Group members reach out to United States Senators, as well as directing Companies A and B to have private conversations with Senators to lobby them to place a "hold" on the resolution. MANAFORT told his lobbyists to stress to the Senators that the former Polish President who was advocating against the resolution was currently a designated representative of the President of the European Parliament, to give extra clout to his supposedly independent judgment against the Senate resolution. MANAFORT never revealed to the Senators or to the American public that any of these lobbyists or Hapsburg Group members were paid by Ukraine.

13.   In another example, on May 16, 2013, another member of the Hapsburg Group lobbied in the United States for Ukraine. The Hapsburg Group member accompanied his country's prime minister to the Oval Office and met with the President and Vice President of the United States, as well as senior United States officials in the executive and legislative branches. In written communications sent to MANAFORT, Person D1 reported that the Hapsburg Group member delivered the message of not letting "Russians Steal Ukraine from the West." The Foreign Agents Registration Act required MANAFORT to disclose such lobbying, as MANAFORT knew. He did not.

Law Firm Report and Tymoshenko

14.   As another part of the lobbying scheme, in 2012, on behalf of President Yanukovych and the Government of Ukraine's Ministry of Justice, MANAFORT solicited a United States law firm to write a report evaluating the trial of Yanukovych's political opponent Yulia Tymoshenko. MANAFORT caused Ukraine to hire the law firm so that its report could be used in the United States and elsewhere to defend the Tymoshenko criminal trial and argue that President Yanukovych and Ukraine had not engaged in selective prosecution.

15.   MANAFORT retained a public relations firm (Company C) to prepare a media roll-out plan for the law firm report. MANAFORT used one of his offshore accounts to pay Company C the equivalent of more than $1 million for its services.

16.   MANAFORT worked closely with Company C to develop a detailed written lobbying plan in connection with what MANAFORT termed the "selling" of the report. This campaign included getting the law firm's report "seeded" to the press in the United States—that is, to leak the report ahead of its official release to a prominent United States newspaper and then use that initial article to influence reporting globally. As part of the roll-out plan, on the report's issuance on December 13, 2012, MANAFORT arranged to have the law firm disseminate hard copies of the report to numerous government officials, including senior United States executive and legislative branch officials.

17.   MANAFORT reported on the law firm's work on the report and Company C's lobbying plan to President Yanukovych and other representatives of the Government of Ukraine. For example, in a July 27, 2012 memorandum to President Yanukovych's Chief of Staff, MANAFORT reported on "the global rollout strategy for the [law firm's] legal report, and provide[d] a detailed plan of action[]" which included step-by-step lobbying outreach in the United States.

18.   MANAFORT directed lobbyists to tout the report as showing that President Yanukovych

had not selectively prosecuted Tymoshenko. But in November 2012 MANAFORT had been told privately in writing by the law firm that the evidence of Tymoshenko's criminal intent "is virtually non-existent" and that it was unclear even among legal experts that Tymoshenko lacked power to engage in the conduct central to the Ukraine criminal case. These facts, known by MANAFORT, were not disclosed to the public.

19.   MANAFORT knew that the report also did not disclose that the law firm, in addition to being retained to write the report, was retained to represent Ukraine itself, including in connection with the Tymoshenko case and to provide training to the trial team prosecuting Tymoshenko.

20.   MANAFORT also knew that the Government of Ukraine did not want to disclose how much the report cost. More than $4.6 million was paid to the law firm for its work. MANAFORT used one of his offshore accounts to funnel $4 million to pay the law firm, a fact that MANAFORT did not disclose to the public. Instead, the Government of Ukraine reported falsely that the report cost just $12,000.

21.   MANAFORT and others knew that the actual cost of the report and the scope of the law firm's work would undermine the report's being perceived as an independent assessment and thus being an effective lobbying tool for MANAFORT to use to support the incarceration of President Yanukovych's political opponent.

22.   In addition to the law firm report, MANAFORT took other steps on behalf of the Government of Ukraine to tarnish Tymoshenko in the United States. In addition to disseminating stories about her soliciting murder, noted above, in October 2012, MANAFORT orchestrated a scheme to have, as he wrote in a contemporaneous communication, "[O]bama jews" put pressure on the Administration to disavow Tymoshenko and support Yanukovych. MANAFORT sought to undermine United States support for Tymoshenko by spreading stories in the United States that

627

a senior Cabinet official (who had been a prominent critic of Yanukovych's treatment of Tymoshenko) was supporting anti-Semitism because the official supported Tymoshenko, who in turn had formed a political alliance with a Ukraine party that espoused anti-Semitic views. MANAFORT coordinated privately with a senior Israeli government official to issue a written statement publicizing this story. MANAFORT then, with secret advance knowledge of that Israeli statement, worked to disseminate this story in the United States, writing to Person D1 "I have someone pushing it on the NY Post. Bada bing bada boom." MANAFORT sought to have the Administration understand that "the Jewish community will take this out on Obama on election day if he does nothing." MANAFORT then told his United States lobbyist to inform the Administration that Ukraine had worked to prevent the Administration's presidential opponent from including damaging language in the Israeli statement, so as not to harm the Administration, and thus further ingratiate Yanukovych with the Administration.

<u>Company A and Company B</u>

23.   As a third part of the lobbying scheme, in February 2012, MANAFORT solicited two Washington, D.C. lobbying firms (Company A and Company B) to lobby in the United States on behalf of President Yanukovych, the Party of Regions and the Government of Ukraine. For instance, in early 2012 at the inception of the relationship, Company B wrote in an email to its team about a "potential representation for the Ukraine," having been contacted "at the suggestion of Paul Manafort who has been working on the current PM elections."

24.   MANAFORT arranged to pay Companies A and B over $2 million from his offshore accounts for their United States lobbying work for Ukraine.

25.   MANAFORT provided direction to Companies A and B in their lobbying efforts, including providing support for numerous United States visits by numerous senior Ukrainian officials.

Companies A and B, at MANAFORT's direction, engaged in extensive United States lobbying. Among other things, they lobbied dozens of Members of Congress, their staff, and White House and State Department officials about Ukraine sanctions, the validity of Ukraine elections, and the propriety of President Yanukovych's imprisoning Tymoshenko, his presidential rival.

26.   In addition, with the assistance of Company A, MANAFORT also personally lobbied in the United States. He drafted and edited numerous ghost-written op-eds for publication in United States newspapers. He also personally met in March 2013 in Washington, D.C., with a Member of Congress who was on a subcommittee that had Ukraine within its purview. After the meeting, MANAFORT prepared a report for President Yanukovych that the meeting "went well" and reported a series of positive developments for Ukraine from the meeting.

27.   Indeed, MANAFORT repeatedly communicated in person and in writing with President Yanukovych and his staff about the lobbying activities of Companies A and B and he tasked the companies to prepare assessments of their work so he, in turn, could brief President Yanukovych. For instance, MANAFORT wrote President Yanukovych a memorandum dated April 8, 2012, in which he provided an update on the lobbying firms' activities "since the inception of the project a few weeks ago. It is my intention to provide you with a weekly update moving forward." In November 2012, Gates wrote to Companies A and B that the firms needed to prepare an assessment of their past and prospective lobbying efforts so the "President" could be briefed by "Paul" "on what Ukraine has done well and what it can do better as we move into 2013." The resulting memorandum from Companies A and B, with input from Gates, noted among other things that the "client" had not been as successful as hoped given that it had an Embassy in Washington.

28.   To distance their United States lobbying work from the Government of Ukraine, and to avoid having to register as agents of Ukraine under the Foreign Agents Registration Act,

MANAFORT with others arranged for Companies A and B to be engaged by a newly-formed Brussels entity called the European Centre for the Modern Ukraine (the Centre), instead of directly by the Government of Ukraine.

29.   MANAFORT described the Centre as "the Brussels NGO that we have formed" to coordinate lobbying for Ukraine. The Centre was founded by a Ukraine Party of Regions member and Ukraine First Vice-Prime Minister. The head of its Board was another member of the Party of Regions, who became the Ukraine Foreign Minister.

30.   In spite of these ties to Ukraine, MANAFORT and others arranged for the Centre to represent falsely that it was not "directly or indirectly supervised, directed, [or] controlled" in whole or in major part by the Government of Ukraine or the Party of Regions. MANAFORT knew that the false and misleading representations would lead Companies A and B not to register their activities pursuant to the Foreign Agents Registration Act.

31.   Despite the Centre being the ostensible client of Companies A and B, MANAFORT knew that the Centre did not direct or oversee their work. The firms received direction from MANAFORT and his subordinate Gates, on behalf of the Government of Ukraine.

32.   As MANAFORT knows from giving directions to Companies A and B, and from the discovery material provided herein, various employees of Companies A and B understood that they were receiving direction from MANAFORT and President Yanukovych, not the Centre, which was not even operational when Companies A and B began lobbying for Ukraine. MANAFORT, Gates, and employees of both Companies A and B referred to the client in ways that made clear they knew it was Ukraine, for instance noting that the "client" had an Embassy in Washington D.C. The head of Company B told his team to think the President of Ukraine "is the client." As a Company A employee noted to another company employee: the lobbying for the

630

Centre was "in name only. [Y]ou've gotta see through the nonsense of that[.]" "It's like Alice in Wonderland." An employee of Company B described the Centre as a fig leaf, and the Centre's written certification that it was not related to the Party of Regions as "a fig leaf on a fig leaf," referring to the Centre in an email as the "European hot dog stand for a Modern Ukraine."

<u>Conspiring to Obstruct Justice: False and Misleading Submissions to the Department of Justice</u>

33.   In September 2016, after numerous press reports concerning MANAFORT had appeared in August, the Department of Justice National Security Division informed MANAFORT, Gates, and DMI in writing that it sought to determine whether they had acted as agents of a foreign principal under the Foreign Agents Registration Act, without registering. In November 2016 and February 2017, MANAFORT and Gates conspired to knowingly and intentionally cause false and misleading letters to be submitted to the Department of Justice, through his unwitting legal counsel. The letters, both of which were approved by MANAFORT before they were submitted by his counsel, represented falsely, among other things, that:

a.   DMI's "efforts on behalf of the Party of Regions" "did not include meetings or outreach within the U.S.";

b.   MANAFORT did not "recall meeting with or conducting outreach to U.S. government officials or U.S. media outlets on behalf of the [Centre], nor do they recall being party to, arranging, or facilitating any such communications. Rather, it is the recollection and understanding of Messrs. Gates and Manafort that such communications would have been facilitated and conducted by the [Centre's] U.S. consultants, as directed by the [Centre]. . . .";

c.   MANAFORT had merely served as a means of introduction of Company A and Company B to the Centre and provided the Centre with a list of "potential U.S.-based consultants—including [Company A] and [Company B]—for the [Centre's] reference and further consideration."

    d.   DMI "does not retain communications beyond thirty days" and as a result of this policy, a "search has returned no responsive documents." The November 2016 letter attached a one-page, undated document that purported to be a DMI "Email Retention Policy."

34.   In fact, MANAFORT had: selected Companies A and B; engaged in weekly scheduled calls and frequent emails with Companies A and B to provide them directions as to specific lobbying steps that should be taken; sought and received detailed oral and written reports from these firms on the lobbying work they had performed; communicated with Yanukovych to brief him on their lobbying efforts; both congratulated and reprimanded Companies A and B on their lobbying work; communicated directly with United States officials in connection with this work; and paid the lobbying firms over $2.5 million from offshore accounts he controlled, among other things.

35.   Although MANAFORT had represented to the Department of Justice in November 2016 and February 2017 that he had no relevant documents, in fact MANAFORT had numerous incriminating documents in his possession, as he knew at the time. The Federal Bureau of Investigation conducted a court-authorized search of MANAFORT'S home in Virginia in the summer of 2017. The documents attached hereto as Government Exhibits 503, 504, 517, 532, 594, 604, 606, 616, 691, 692, 697, 706 and 708, among numerous others, were all documents that MANAFORT had in his possession (and were found in the search) and all pre-dated the November 2016 letter.

B. Money Laundering Conspiracy

36.   In or around and between 2006 and 2016, MANAFORT, together with others,   did

knowingly and intentionally conspire (a) to conduct financial transactions, affecting interstate and foreign commerce, which involved the proceeds of specified unlawful activity, to wit, felony violations of FARA in violation of Title 22, United States Code, Sections 612 and 618, knowing that the property involved in the financial transactions represented proceeds of some form of unlawful activity, with intent to engage in conduct constituting a violation of sections 7201 and 7206 of the Internal Revenue Code of 1986; and (b) to transport, transmit, and transfer monetary instruments and funds from places outside the United States to and through places in the United States and from places in the United States to and through places outside the United States, with the intent to promote the carrying on of specified unlawful activity, to wit: a felony violation of FARA, in violation of Title 22, United States Code, Sections 612 and 618, contrary to Title 18, United States Code, Section 1956(a)(1)(A)(ii) and (a)(2)(A).

37.   MANAFORT caused the following transfers to be made, knowing that they were being made to entities to carry on activities that were required to be timely reported under the Foreign Agents Registration Act, but were not:

Payee	Date	Payer	Originating Bank Account	Country of... Origin	Destination	Amount (USD)
Company A	8/2/2012	Bletilla Ventures Ltd.	Bank of Cyprus Account -0480	Cyprus	US	$270,000.00
	10/10/2012	Bletilla Ventures Ltd.	Bank of Cyprus Account -0480	Cyprus	US	$90,000.00
	11/16/2012	Bletilla Ventures Ltd.	Bank of Cyprus Account -0480	Cyprus	US	$120,000.00
	11/20/2012	Bletilla Ventures Ltd.	Bank of Cyprus Account -0480	Cyprus	US	$182,968.07
	12/21/2012	Bletilla Ventures Ltd.	Bank of Cyprus Account -0480	Cyprus	US	$25,000.00
	3/15/2013	Bletilla Ventures Ltd.	Hellenic Bank Account -2501	Cyprus	US	$90,000.00
	9/18/2013	Global Endeavour Inc.	Loyal Bank Limited Account -1840	SVG*	US	$135,937.37

Payee	Date	Payer	Originating Bank Account	Country of... Origin	Country of... Destination	Amount (USD)
	10/31/2013	Jeunet Ltd.	Loyal Bank Limited Account -4978	SVG*	US	$167,689.40
	3/28/2014	Jeunet Ltd.	Loyal Bank Limited Account -4978	SVG*	US	$135,639.65
	4/3/2014	Jeunet Ltd.	Loyal Bank Limited Account -4978	SVG*	US	$82,979.93
Total Company A Transfers						**$1,300,214.42**
Company B	5/30/2012	Bletilla Ventures Ltd.	Bank of Cyprus Account -0480	Cyprus	US	$130,000.00
	8/2/2012	Bletilla Ventures Ltd.	Bank of Cyprus Account -0480	Cyprus	US	$195,000.00
	10/10/2012	Bletilla Ventures Ltd.	Bank of Cyprus Account -0480	Cyprus	US	$130,000.00
	11/16/2012	Bletilla Ventures Ltd.	Bank of Cyprus Account -0480	Cyprus	US	$50,000.00
	12/21/2012	Bletilla Ventures Ltd.	Bank of Cyprus Account -0480	Cyprus	US	$54,649.51
	3/15/2013	Bletilla Ventures Ltd.	Hellenic Bank Account -2501	Cyprus	US	$150,000.00
	9/3/2013	Jeunet Ltd.	Loyal Bank Limited Account -4978	SVG*	US	$175,857.51
	10/31/2013	Jeunet Ltd.	Loyal Bank Limited Account -4978	SVG*	US	$195,857.51
	3/12/2014	Jeunet Ltd.	Loyal Bank Limited Account -4978	SVG*	US	$26,891.78
	3/21/2014	Jeunet Ltd.	Loyal Bank Limited Account -4978	SVG*	US	$138,026.00
	4/15/2014	Jeunet Ltd.	Loyal Bank Limited Account -4978	SVG*	US	$4,728.81
	4/25/2014	Jeunet Ltd.	Loyal Bank Limited Account -4978	SVG*	US	$4,739.23
Total Company B Transfers						**$1,255,750.35**

Payee	Date	Payer	Originating Bank Account	Country of... Origin	Destination	Amount (USD)
Law Firm A	4/19/2012	Black Sea View Limited	Bank of Cyprus Account -7412	Cyprus	US	$2,000,000.00
	5/30/2012	Black Sea View Limited	Bank of Cyprus Account -7412	Cyprus	US	$1,000,000.00
	7/13/2012	Black Sea View Limited	Bank of Cyprus Account -7412	Cyprus	US	$1,000,000.00
Total Law Firm A Transfers						**$4,000,000.00**
TOTAL TRANSFERS						**$6,555,964.77**

* SVG refers to St. Vincent and the Grenadines.

C. Tax and Foreign Bank Account Conspiracy
26 U.S.C. § 7206(1)
31 U.S.C. §§ 5314 and 5322(a)

38.   From 2008 through 2014, MANAFORT caused millions of dollars of wire transfers to be made from offshore nominee accounts, without paying taxes on that income. The payments were made for goods, services, and real estate. MANAFORT also hid income by denominating various overseas payments as "loans," thereby evading payment of any taxes on that income by MANAFORT.

39.   MANAFORT directly and through Gates repeatedly misled his bookkeeper and tax accountants, including by not disclosing Manafort's overseas accounts and income. Further, MANAFORT and Gates, acting at Manafort's instruction, classified overseas payments made to MANAFORT falsely as "loans" to avoid incurring additional taxes on the income.

40.   MANAFORT owned and controlled a range of foreign bank accounts in Cyprus, the Grenadines, and the United Kingdom. MANAFORT directly and through Gates maintained these accounts, including by managing them and by making substantial transfers from the accounts to both himself and vendors for personal items for him and his family. MANAFORT was aware that many of these accounts held well in excess of $10,000 in the aggregate at some point during each year in which they existed. MANAFORT did not report the accounts' existence to his bookkeeper

and his tax preparers in an effort to hide them, and to allow him to avoid disclosing their existence on an FBAR filing.

41.   MANAFORT was aware at the time that it was illegal to hide income from the Internal Revenue Service (IRS) by failing to account for reportable income on his income tax returns. MANAFORT was also aware that it was illegal to fail to report information to the IRS regarding the existence of foreign bank accounts, as required by Schedule B of the IRS Form 1040. MANAFORT also understood at the time that a U.S. person who had a financial interest in, or signature or other authority over, a bank account or other financial account in a foreign country, which exceeded $10,000 in any one year (at any time during that year), was required to report the account to the Department of the Treasury. MANAFORT also understood, after 2010, that the failure to make such a report constituted a crime.

42.   Knowing the existence of his reportable foreign accounts and hidden income, MANAFORT knowingly, intentionally, and willfully filed and conspired to file false tax returns from 2006-2015 in that he said he did not have reportable foreign bank accounts when he knew that he did, he did not report income that he knew he in fact had earned, and he did not file Foreign Bank Account Reports. MANAFORT failed to report over $15 million in income during the period 2010-2014.

FORFEITURE

43.   The following assets constitute or were derived from proceeds of MANAFORT's conspiracy to violate the Foreign Agents Registration Act and/or they constitute property involved in MANAFORT's conspiracy to launder money in violation of 18 U.S.C. § 1956 or are traceable thereto and/or they represent substitute assets for such property which has been made unavailable for forfeiture by the acts or omissions of MANAFORT:

    a)   The real property and premises commonly known as 377 Union Street, Brooklyn, New

York 11231 (Block 429, Lot 65), including all appurtenances, improvements, and attachments thereon, and any property traceable thereto;

b) The real property and premises commonly known as 29 Howard Street, #4D, New York, New York 10013 (Block 209, Lot 1104), including all appurtenances, improvements, and attachments thereon, and any property traceable thereto;

c) The real property and premises commonly known as 174 Jobs Lane, Water Mill, New York 11976, including all appurtenances, improvements, and attachments thereon, and any property traceable thereto;

d) All funds held in account number XXXXXX0969 at The Federal Savings Bank, and any property traceable thereto;

e) All funds seized from account number XXXXXX1388 at Capital One N.A. and any property traceable thereto;

f) All funds seized from account number XXXXXX9952 at The Federal Savings Bank and any property traceable thereto;

g) Northwestern Mutual Universal Life Insurance Policy   and any property traceable thereto;

h) The real property and premises commonly known as 123 Baxter Street, #5D, New York, New York 10016 in lieu of 1046 N. Edgewood Street; and

i) The real property and premises commonly known as 721 Fifth Avenue, #43G, New York, New York 10022 in lieu of all funds from account number   at Charles Schwab & Co. Inc., and any property traceable thereto.

Count Two: Witness Tampering Conspiracy (18 U.S.C. § 371)

44.   From in or about and between February 23, 2018, and April 2018, both dates being approximate and inclusive, within the District of Columbia and elsewhere, the defendant PAUL J.

MANAFORT, JR., together with others, including Konstantin Kilimnik, knowingly and intentionally conspired to corruptly persuade another person, to wit: Persons D1 and D2, with intent to influence, delay and prevent the testimony of any person in an official proceeding, in violation of 18 U.S.C. § 1512(b)(1). The facts set forth with respect to Count One are incorporated herein.

45.   On February 22, 2018, MANAFORT was charged in the District of Columbia in a Superseding Indictment that for the first time included allegations about the Hapsburg Group and MANAFORT's use of that group to lobby illegally in the United States in violation of the Foreign Agent Registration Act. MANAFORT knew that the Act prescribed only United States lobbying. Immediately after February 22, 2018, MANAFORT began reaching out directly and indirectly to Persons D1 and D2 to induce them to say falsely that they did not work in the United States as part of the lobbying campaign, even though MANAFORT then and there well knew that they did lobby in the United States.

46.   MANAFORT committed the following overt acts directly and through his conspirators.

Date/Time*	Sender	Receiver	Event
MANAFORT contacted Person D1 by phone and a messaging application:			
2/24/2018; 15:51 (UTC)	MANAFORT	Person D1	Phone call (attempted): No duration.
2/24/2018; 15:51 (UTC)	MANAFORT	Person D1	Phone call: 1 min, 24 second call.
2/24/2018; 15:53 (UTC)	MANAFORT	Person D1	Text: "This is paul"
2/25/2018; 18:41 (UTC)	MANAFORT	Person D1	Phone call (attempted): No duration.
2/26/2018; 23:56 (UTC)	MANAFORT	Person D1	Text: "http://www.businessinsider.com/former-european-leaders-manafort-hapsburg-group-2018-2?r=UK&IR=T"

Date/Time*	Sender	Receiver	Event
2/26/2018; 23:57 (UTC)	MANAFORT	Person D1	Text: "We should talk. I have made clear that they worked in Europe."
2/27/2018; 11:03 (UTC)	MANAFORT	Person D1	Phone call (attempted): No duration.
2/27/2018; 11:31 (UTC)	MANAFORT	Person D1	Phone call (attempted): No duration.
Kilimnik contacted Person D2 a messaging application, sending four messages:			
2/28/2018; 01:49 (CEST)	Kilimnik	Person D2	"[Person D2], hi! How are you? Hope you are doing fine. ;))"
2/28/2018; 01:51 (CEST)	Kilimnik	Person D2	"My friend P is trying to reach [Person D1] to brief him on what's going on."
2/28/2018; 01:51 (CEST)	Kilimnik	Person D2	"If you have a chance to mention this to [Person D1] - would be great"
2/28/2018; 01:53 (CEST)	Kilimnik	Person D2	"Basically P wants to give him a quick summary that he says to everybody (which is true) that our friends never lobbied in the US, and the purpose of the program was EU"
Kilimnik contacted Person D2 using a different messaging application, sending five messages:			
2/28/2018; 06:01 (CEST)	Kilimnik	Person D2	"Hey, how are you? This is K."
2/28/2018; 06:01(CEST)	Kilimnik	Person D2	"Hope you are doing fine."
2/28/2018; 06:01 (CEST)	Kilimnik	Person D2	"My friend P is trying to reach [Person D1] to brief him on what's going on"
2/28/2018; 06:02 (CEST)	Kilimnik	Person D2	"Basically P wants to give him a quick summary that he says to everybody (which is true) that our friends never lobbied in the US, and the purpose of the program was EU"

Date/Time*	Sender	Receiver	Event
2/28/2018; 06:03 (CEST)	Kilimnik	Person D2	"If you have a chance to mention this to [First Initial of Person D1's Name]. - it would be great. It would be good to get them connected to discuss in person. P is his friend."
Kilimnik contacted Person D2 using two different applications, sending three messages:			
4/4/2018; 08:53 (CEST)	Kilimnik	Person D2	"Hey. This is Konstantin. My friend P asked me again to help connect him with [Person D1]. Can you help?"
4/4/2018; 08:54 (CEST)	Kilimnik	Person D2	"Hey. My friend P has asked me again if there is any way to help connect him through [Person D1]"
4/4/2018; 08:54 (CEST)	Kilimnik	Person D2	"I tried him on all numbers."
Kilimnik contacted Person D1 using a messaging application:			
4/4/2018; 13:00 (UTC)	Kilimnik	Person D1	"Hi. This is K. My friend P is looking for ways to connect to you to pass you several messages. Can we arrange that."

*UTC and CEST refer to Coordinated Universal Time and Central European Summer Time, respectively.

Other Acts

I.   Bank/Bank Fraud Conspiracy
18 U.S.C. §§ 1344 and 1349

Bank Fraud Conspiracy / Citizens Bank / $3.4 million loan
(Charged as Count 24 in the Eastern District of Virginia Superseding Indictment)

47.   Between December 2015 and March 2016, MANAFORT conspired to intentionally defraud Citizens Bank in connection with his application for a mortgage for approximately $3.4 million. The mortgage related to a condominium on Howard Street in the Soho neighborhood of Manhattan, New York. During the course of the conspiracy, MANAFORT made and caused to be made, a series of false and fraudulent representations to the bank in order to secure the loan, including the

following: (a) MANAFORT falsely represented the amount of debt he had by failing to disclose on his loan application the existence of a mortgage on his Union Street property (from Genesis Capital); (b) MANAFORT caused an insurance broker to provide Citizens Bank false information, namely, an outdated insurance report that did not list the Union Street loan (from Genesis Capital); (c) MANAFORT falsely stated that a $1.5 million Peranova loan had been forgiven in 2015; and (d) MANAFORT falsely represented to the lender and its agents that the Howard Street property was a secondary home used as such by his daughter and son-in-law and was not held as a rental property. These statements were material to Citizens Bank.

48.   Citizens Bank was a financial institution chartered by the United States.

Bank Fraud Conspiracy / Banc of California / $1 million loan
(Charged as Count 26 in the Eastern District of Virginia Superseding Indictment)

49.   In approximately February 2016, MANAFORT conspired to intentionally defraud Banc of California in connection with his application for a business loan. During the course of the conspiracy, MANAFORT made and caused to be made a series of false and fraudulent representations to the bank, including the following: (a) the submission of a false statement of assets and liabilities that failed to disclose a loan on the Union Street property (from Genesis Capital) and misrepresented, among other things, the amount of the mortgage on the Howard Street property; and (b) the submission of a doctored 2015 DMI profit and loss statement (P&L) that overstated DMI's 2015 income by more than $4 million. These statements were material to Banc of California.

50.   Banc of California was a financial institution chartered by the United States.

Bank Fraud Conspiracy / Citizens Bank / $5.5 million loan
(Charged as Count 28 in the Eastern District of Virginia Superseding Indictment)

51.   Between December 2015 and March 2016, MANAFORT conspired to intentionally

defraud Citizens Bank in connection with his application for a mortgage for approximately $5.5

million on a property at Union Street in Brooklyn, New York. During the course of the

conspiracy, MANAFORT made or caused to be made a series of false and fraudulent material

representations to the bank in order to secure the loan, including the following: (a) the

submission of a false statement of assets and liabilities that hid a prior loan on the Union Street

property (from Genesis Capital), among other liabilities; and (b) the submission of a falsified

2016 DMI P&L that overstated DMI's income by more than $2 million.

Bank Fraud/Bank Fraud Conspiracy / The Federal Savings Bank / $9.5 million loan & $6.5
million loan
(Charged in Counts 29, 30, 31 & 32 in the Eastern District of Virginia Superseding Indictment)

52.   Between April 2016 and January 2017, MANAFORT conspired to intentionally defraud,

and did defraud, The Federal Savings Bank in connection with his applications for the following

two loans: (a) a loan for approximately $9.5 million related to various properties, including a

house in Bridgehampton, New York, and (b) a loan for approximately $6.5 million related to his

Union Street property.   During the course of the fraudulent scheme, MANAFORT made and

caused to be made a series of false and fraudulent material representations to the bank in order to

secure both loans, including the following: (a) MANAFORT provided the bank with doctored

P&Ls for DMI for both 2015 and 2016, overstating its income by millions of dollars; and (b)

MANAFORT falsely represented to The Federal Savings Bank that he had lent his credit card to

a friend who had incurred more than $200,000 in charges relating to the purchase of Yankee

tickets.

53.   Both loans were extended by The Federal Savings Bank.

642

54.   The Federal Savings Bank was a financial institution chartered by the United States.

                                                ROBERT S. MUELLER, III
                                                Special Counsel

                              By:

                                                Andrew Weissmann
                                                Jeannie S. Rhee
                                                Greg D. Andres
                                                Kyle R. Freeny
                                                Senior/Assistant Special Counsels

643

DEFENDANT'S ACCEPTANCE

I have read every page of this Agreement and have discussed it with my attorneys Kevin Downing, Thomas Zehnle, and Richard Westling. I am fully satisfied with the legal representation by them, who I have chosen to represent me herein. Nothing about the quality of the representation of other counsel is affecting my decision herein to plead guilty. I fully understand this Agreement and agree to it without reservation. I do this voluntarily and of my own free will, intending to be legally bound. No threats have been made to me nor am I under the influence of anything that could impede my ability to understand this Agreement fully. I am pleading guilty because I am in fact guilty of the offense identified in this Agreement.

I reaffirm that absolutely no promises, agreements, understandings, or conditions have been made or entered into in connection with my decision to plead guilty except those set forth in this Agreement. I am satisfied with the legal services provided by my attorneys in connection with this Agreement and matters related to it.

Date: _9-14-18_   _Paul J. Manfort_
                                   Paul J. Manafort, Jr.
                                   Defendant

ATTORNEYS' ACKNOWLEDGMENT

I have read every page of this Agreement, reviewed this Agreement with my client, Paul J. Manafort, and fully discussed the provisions of this Agreement with my client. These pages accurately and completely set forth the entire Agreement. I concur in my client's desire to plead guilty as set forth in this Agreement.

Date: _9-14-18_   _[signature]_
                                   Kevin M. Downing
                                   Richard W. Westling
                                   Thomas E. Zehnle
                                   Attorneys for Defendant

7. Criminal Information,
US v. Michael Cohen
(US District Court for the Southern
District of New York, November 29, 2018)

Of all Trump's allies to cooperate with the special counsel's investigation, perhaps the most interesting was Michael Cohen, the president's personal lawyer. Fierce loyalty to Trump was long what defined Cohen, who considered himself more fixer and protector than legal adviser.

But as investigators dove into Cohen's personal finances—finding criminal tax and bank fraud that could subject him to significant prison time—Trump's fixer turned into another problem for the president. Cohen ultimately pleaded guilty in multiple cases—one in which he agreed to facilitating hush-money payments to help the president cover up alleged affairs, and another in which he admitted lying to Congress about a possible Trump business project in Moscow. He began cooperating with the special counsel's team.

Cohen's lie to Congress, detailed in this criminal information, was remarkable. It showed he had been willing to deceive the public—and then commit a crime—to keep secret the timing of his dealings with the Kremlin. Cohen admitted that he had told Congress work on the Moscow project ended in January 2016—in fact, it lasted until June 2016, after Trump had sealed up the Republican nomination for president. Cohen also conceded he had direct contact with a Kremlin official to request help with the project, speaking by phone to an assistant to Dmitry Peskov, a powerful Putin aide. The document indicates the assistant took notes and promised she would follow up with others in Russia. Peskov has said Russian officials gave it routine business consideration.

The document described Trump as "Individual 1" and the Trump Organization as a "Manhattan-based real estate company."

The special counsel's office would reveal in a later court filing that Cohen met with its investigators seven times and provided information "on core topics under investigation" that was deemed "credible and consistent with other evidence." Prosecutors wrote that they believed the motive for his lying to Congress was to "minimize links" between the Moscow project and Trump.

That was worrisome for Trump. Cohen, one of Trump's closest confidants, was talking frequently to the office investigating Trump. And while he might have been able to attack Cohen's credibility— Cohen, after all, was an admitted liar—the special counsel's office had cryptically hinted they had evidence to back up what the president's fixer was saying.

UNITED STATES DISTRICT COURT
SOUTHERN DISTRICT OF NEW YORK

- - - - - - - - - - - - - - - - - - x

UNITED STATES OF AMERICA   :

         - v. -   :

MICHAEL COHEN,   :

              Defendant.   :

                                  :

- - - - - - - - - - - - - - - - - - x

INFORMATION

18 Cr.

18 CRIM 850

The Special Counsel charges:

Background

The Defendant

1.   From in or around 2007 through in or around January 2017, MICHAEL COHEN, the defendant, was an attorney and employee of a Manhattan-based real estate company (the "Company"). COHEN held the title of "Executive Vice President" and "Special Counsel" to the owner of the Company ("Individual 1").

False Statements to the U.S. Congress

2.   On or about January 13, 2017, the U.S. Senate Select Committee on Intelligence ("SSCI") announced that it would conduct an investigation into Russian election interference and possible links between Russia and individuals associated with political campaigns. On or about January 25, 2017, the House of Representatives Permanent Select Committee on Intelligence ("HPSCI") announced that it also was conducting an investigation

into Russian election interference and possible links between Russia and individuals associated with political campaigns.

3. On or about August 28, 2017, COHEN caused a two-page letter to be sent on his behalf to SSCI and HPSCI. The letter addressed his efforts at the Company to pursue a branded property in Moscow, Russia (the "Moscow Project"). COHEN stated the purpose of the letter was "to provide the Committee with additional information regarding the proposal," referring to the Moscow Project.

4. In the letter to SSCI and HPSCI, COHEN knowingly and deliberately made the following false representations:

a. **The Moscow Project ended in January 2016 and was not discussed extensively with others in the Company.** "The proposal was under consideration at the [Company] from September 2015 until the end of January 2016. By the end of January 2016, I determined that the proposal was not feasible for a variety of business reasons and should not be pursued further. Based on my business determinations, the [Company] abandoned the [Moscow Project] proposal. . . . To the best of my knowledge, [Individual 1] was never in contact with anyone about this proposal other than me on three occasions. . . . I did not ask or brief [Individual

2

1], or any of his family, before I made the decision to terminate further work on the proposal."

b. **COHEN never agreed to travel to Russia in connection with the Moscow Project and "never considered" asking Individual 1 to travel for the project.** "I primarily communicated with the Moscow-based development company . . . through a U.S. citizen third-party intermediary, [Individual 2]. . . . [Individual 2] constantly asked me to travel to Moscow as part of his efforts to push forward the discussion of the proposal. I ultimately determined that the proposal was not feasible and never agreed to make a trip to Russia. . . . Despite overtures by [Individual 2], I never considered asking [Individual 1] to travel to Russia in connection with this proposal."

c. **COHEN did not recall any Russian government response or contact about the Moscow Project.** "In mid-January 2016, [Individual 2] suggested that I send an email to [Russian Official 1], the Press Secretary for the President of Russia, since the proposal would require approvals within the Russian government that had not been issued. Those permissions were never provided. I decided to abandon the proposal less than two weeks

3

later for business reasons and do not recall any response to my email, nor any other contacts by me with [Russian Official 1] or other Russian government officials about the proposal."

5. On or about September 19, 2017, COHEN was scheduled to appear before SSCI accompanied by counsel. In prepared remarks released to the public, COHEN stated, "I assume we will discuss the rejected proposal to build a [Company-branded] property in Moscow that was terminated in January of 2016; which occurred before the Iowa caucus and months before the very first primary. This was solely a real estate deal and nothing more. I was doing my job. I would ask that the two-page statement about the Moscow proposal that I sent to the Committee in August be incorporated into and attached to this transcript."

6. On or about October 25, 2017, COHEN gave testimony to SSCI, which included testimony about the Moscow Project consistent with his prepared remarks and his two-page statement.

7. In truth and in fact, and as COHEN well knew, COHEN's representations about the Moscow Project he made to SSCI and HPSCI were false and misleading. COHEN made the false statements to (1) minimize links between the Moscow Project and Individual 1 and (2) give the false impression that the Moscow Project ended before "the Iowa caucus and . . . the very first primary," in hopes of

4

limiting the ongoing Russia investigations. COHEN attempted to
conceal or minimize through his false statements the following
facts:

a. **The Moscow Project was discussed multiple times within
the Company and did not end in January 2016.** Instead,
as late as approximately June 2016, COHEN and
Individual 2 discussed efforts to obtain Russian
governmental approval for the Moscow Project. COHEN
discussed the status and progress of the Moscow
Project with Individual 1 on more than the three
occasions COHEN claimed to the Committee, and he
briefed family members of Individual 1 within the
Company about the project.

b. **COHEN agreed to travel to Russia in connection with
the Moscow Project and took steps in contemplation of
Individual 1's possible travel to Russia.** COHEN and
Individual 2 discussed on multiple occasions
traveling to Russia to pursue the Moscow Project.

i. COHEN asked Individual 1 about the possibility
of Individual 1 traveling to Russia in
connection with the Moscow Project, and asked a
senior campaign official about potential
business travel to Russia.

5

ii. On or about May 4, 2016, Individual 2 wrote to COHEN, "I had a chat with Moscow. ASSUMING the trip does happen the question is before or after the convention . . . Obviously the pre-meeting trip (you only) can happen anytime you want but the 2 big guys where [sic] the question. I said I would confirm and revert." COHEN responded, "My trip before Cleveland. [Individual 1] once he becomes the nominee after the convention."

iii. On or about May 5, 2016, Individual 2 followed up with COHEN and wrote, "[Russian Official 1] would like to invite you as his guest to the St. Petersburg Forum which is Russia's Davos it's June 16-19. He wants to meet there with you and possibly introduce you to either [the President of Russia] or [the Prime Minister of Russia], as they are not sure if 1 or both will be there. . . . He said anything you want to discuss including dates and subjects are on the table to discuss."

6

    iv.   On or about May 6, 2016, Individual 2 asked COHEN to confirm those dates would work for him to travel. COHEN wrote back, "Works for me."

    v.   From on or about June 9 to June 14, 2016, Individual 2 sent numerous messages to COHEN about the travel, including forms for COHEN to complete. However, on or about June 14, 2016, COHEN met Individual 2 in the lobby of the Company's headquarters to inform Individual 2 he would not be traveling at that time.

c. **COHEN did recall that in or around January 2016, COHEN received a response from the office of Russian Official 1, the Press Secretary for the President of Russia, and spoke to a member of that office about the Moscow Project.**

    i.   On or about January 14, 2016, COHEN emailed Russian Official 1's office asking for assistance in connection with the Moscow Project. On or about January 16, 2016, COHEN emailed Russian Official 1's office again, said he was trying to reach another high-level Russian official, and asked for someone who spoke English to contact him.

7

ii. On or about January 20, 2016, COHEN received an email from the personal assistant to Russian Official 1 ("Assistant 1"), stating that she had been trying to reach COHEN and requesting that he call her using a Moscow-based phone number she provided.

iii. Shortly after receiving the email, COHEN called Assistant 1 and spoke to her for approximately 20 minutes. On that call, COHEN described his position at the Company and outlined the proposed Moscow Project, including the Russian development company with which the Company had partnered. COHEN requested assistance in moving the project forward, both in securing land to build the proposed tower and financing the construction. Assistant 1 asked detailed questions and took notes, stating that she would follow up with others in Russia.

iv. The day after COHEN's call with Assistant 1, Individual 2 contacted him, asking for a call. Individual 2 wrote to COHEN, "It's about [the President of Russia] they called today."

8

COUNT 1
(False Statements)

8.   Paragraphs 1 through 7 of this Information are re-alleged and incorporated by reference as if fully set forth herein.

9.   On or about August 28, 2017, the defendant MICHAEL COHEN, in the District of Columbia and elsewhere, in a matter within the jurisdiction of the legislative branch of the Government of the United States, knowingly and willfully made a materially false, fictitious, and fraudulent statement and representation, to wit, COHEN caused to be submitted a written statement to SSCI containing material false statements about the Moscow Project, including false statements about the timing of the Moscow Project, discussions with people in the Company and in Russia about the Moscow Project, and contemplated travel to Russia in connection with the Moscow Project.

(Title 18, United States Code, Section 1001(a)(2).)

_____
ROBERT S. MUELLER, III
Special Counsel

9

UNITED STATES DISTRICT COURT
SOUTHERN DISTRICT OF NEW YORK

UNITED STATES OF AMERICA

- v. -

MICHAEL COHEN,

Defendant.

INFORMATION

18 Cr. __

ROBERT S. MUELLER, III
SPECIAL COUNSEL

8. Transcript of Sentencing Hearing, *US v. Michael Cohen* (US District Court for the Southern District of New York, December 12, 2018)

Michael Cohen, Donald Trump's personal lawyer, had admitted arranging secret payoffs to women to keep quiet about alleged affairs with Trump, and to lying about a Trump business project in Moscow that was pursued during the heart of Trump's campaign. On a cold, windy day in December 2018, he stood before a federal judge in Manhattan to hear what punishment he would receive for those crimes.

The sentencing hearing, which is captured word for word in this transcript, was remarkable. Cohen, in a charcoal suit and light blue tie, sniffed and fought back tears as he pleaded for leniency from Judge William H. Pauley III. Cohen said he had felt duty bound to cover up Trump's "dirty deeds," and in some ways his life was beginning anew, now that he was free from the "personal and mental incarceration" that came from working for Trump.

A prosecutor from the US Attorney's Office in Manhattan blasted Cohen for his personal wrongdoing. A special counsel's office lawyer was gentler, noting that Cohen had been "helpful" to the special counsel's probe.

Pauley sentenced Cohen to three years behind bars, along with nearly $2 million in financial penalties, crediting Cohen for his cooperation but rejecting Cohen's bid to avoid prison entirely.

"While Mr. Cohen has taken steps to mitigate his criminal conduct by pleading guilty and volunteering useful information to prosecutors, that does not wipe the slate clean," Pauley said.

ICCQCOHs

1 UNITED STATES DISTRICT COURT
   SOUTHERN DISTRICT OF NEW YORK
2 ------------------------------x
   UNITED STATES OF AMERICA
3   v.   18 CR 602 (WHP)
                                            18 CR 850 (WHP)
4   Sentence

   MICHAEL COHEN
5
                Defendant
6 ------------------------------x

7   New York, N.Y.
                                            December 12, 2018
8   11:00 a.m.

9 Before:
                    HON. WILLIAM H. PAULEY III
10   District Judge

11
                          APPEARANCES
12 ROBERT KHUZAMI
        Acting United States Attorney for the
13   Southern District of New York
   NICOLAS ROOS
14 THOMAS McKAY
   RACHEL MAIMIN
15 ANDREA GRISWOLD
        Assistant United States Attorneys
16

17 UNITED STATES DEPARTMENT OF JUSTICE
        Special Counsel's Office
18 JEANNIE S. RHEE
   ANDREW D. GOLDSTEIN
19 L. RUSH ATKINSON
        Assistant United States Attorneys
20

21 PETRILLO KLEIN & BOXER LLP
        Attorneys for Defendant
22 GUY PETRILLO
   AMY LESTER
23
   -Also Present-
24 HEATHER D'AGOSTINO, FBI
   MICKEY ROBINSON, FBI
25

1   (Case called)

2   DEPUTY CLERK: Appearances for the United States

3   Attorney's Office.

4   MR. ROOS: For the United States Attorney's Office,

5   good morning.

6   Nicks Roos, Thomas McKay, Rachel Maimin and Andrea

7   Griswold.

8   DEPUTY CLERK: Appearances for Special Counsel's

9   Office.

10   MS. RHEE: Jeannie Rhee on behalf of Special Counsel's

11 Office. I'm joined here today by Andrew Goldstein and Rush

12 Atkinson. Also in the courtroom in the back, we're joined by

13 FBI Heather D'Agostino and Mickey Robinson.

14   DEPUTY CLERK: Appearances for the defendant.

15   MR. PETRILLO: Good morning, your Honor.

16   Guy Petrillo and Amy Lester for Michael Cohen.

17   THE COURT: Good morning to all of you, and I note the

18 presence of the defendant, Mr. Cohen, at counsel table.

19   This matter is on for sentencing. Are the parties

20 ready to proceed?

21   MR. ROOS: Yes, your Honor.

22   MR. PETRILLO: Yes, your Honor.

23   MS. RHEE: Yes, your Honor.

24   THE COURT: First, Mr. Petrillo, have you reviewed

25 with your client the presentence investigation report?

1   MR. PETRILLO: I have, your Honor.

2   THE COURT: Are there any factual matters set forth in

3 the report that you believe warrant modification or correction?

4   MR. PETRILLO: Not at this time, your Honor. Thank

5 you.

6   THE COURT: Mr. Roos, are there any factual matters

7 set forth in the presentence report that the government

8 believes warrant modification or correction?

9   MR. ROOS: No, your Honor.

10   THE COURT: What about the Special Counsel's Office?

11   MS. RHEE: No, your Honor.

12   THE COURT: Very well.

13   MR. PETRILLO: Your Honor, just to confirm, did the

14 Court receive our letter of last night?

15   THE COURT: I did.

16   MR. PETRILLO: Very well.

17   THE COURT: I did.

18   Now, the parties here, before I hear from them, have a

19 difference of opinion concerning the guidelines calculation,

20 and, in particular, the grouping analysis for 18 CR 602.

21   Defense counsel argues that the tax evasion counts are

22 not closely related to the other counts and, therefore, should

23 not be grouped together. The government counters that Section

24 3D1.2 specifically enumerates guidelines that are to be

25 grouped, which include Section 2T1.1 for the tax evasion

1 counts, Section 2B1.1 for the false statement count, and

2 Section 2C1.8 for the illegal campaign contributions counts.

3   This Court finds the government's argument to be

4 correct as a matter of law where the offense levels are

5 principally determined by the amount of loss. *See United*

6 *States v. Gordon*, 291 F.3d 181, 192 (2d.Cir 2002).

7   Accordingly, this Court makes the following guidelines

8 calculations: Grouping all eight counts of 18 CR 602 together,

9 the base offense level is 7. Because the loss here exceeded

10 $1.5 million, but was less than $3.5 million, an increase of 16

11 levels is warranted.

12   Further, because the offense involved the use of

13 sophisticated means, including Mr. Cohen's creation of shell

14 companies and fake invoices, a further two-level enhancement is

15 appropriate.

16   Finally, because Mr. Cohen used special skills as a

17 licensed attorney to facilitate the commission and concealment

18 of these offenses, a further two-level enhancement is

19 warranted. Thus, the adjusted offense level for group one,

20 that is, the counts charged in 18 CR 602, is 27.

21   Now, Mr. Cohen pled guilty to these crimes in a timely

22 manner before me and, accordingly, I grant him a three-level

23 reduction for acceptance of responsibility. Thus, his total

24 offense level is 24. The defendant has no prior criminal

25 convictions, and, therefore, his Criminal History Category is a

1 I. With a total offense level of 24 and a Criminal History

2 Category of I, Mr. Cohen's guideline range is 51 to 63 months

3 of imprisonment on the eight charges of income tax evasion,

4 making false statements to a banking institution, and the two

5 campaign finance crimes.

6   Now, with respect to Mr. Cohen's plea to making false

7 statements to Congress, that is separately grouped and has a

8 base offense level of 6. This Court agrees with the Special

9 Counsel's Office and Mr. Cohen that no enhancements are

10 appropriate. Mr. Cohen pled guilty to this crime before my

11 colleague, Judge Carter, and, accordingly, I grant him a

12 two-level reduction for acceptance of responsibility on this

13 offense. So, with a total offense level of 4 and a Criminal

14 History Category of I, his guidelines range for making false

15 statements to Congress is zero to six months of imprisonment.

16 Accordingly, no multiple account adjustment applies.

17   And so with the guidelines calculation resolved, I

18 will hear now from the parties.

19   Mr. Petrillo, do you wish to be heard on behalf of

20 Mr. Cohen?

21   MR. PETRILLO: I do, your Honor. Thank you.

22   Your Honor, may it please the Court, thank you.

23   My partner, Amy Lester, and I have the privilege of

24 representing Michael Cohen and the honor of having met some of

25 the members of his family who are present here today. The

1 group is larger than I've met, but it includes his mother and

2 father, his mother-in-law and his father-in-law, his wife and

3 children, and his brother and sisters, along with a niece and a

4 cousin.

5   Your Honor, we have made a sentencing submission with

6 numerous letters in support of the character of Mr. Cohen, and

7 it would not be our purpose today to repeat all of what we have

8 already written. Rather, unless your Honor would like me to

9 proceed otherwise, I would like first to address the remarkable

10 nature and significance of the life decision made by Mr. Cohen

11 to cooperate with the DOJ Special Counsel and the relevance

12 and, respectfully, the importance of that cooperation, not only

13 to this specific man and your Honor's evaluation of this

14 specific man, but also to the Court's consideration of how

15 Mr. Cohen's cooperation promotes respect for law and the

16 courage of the individual to stand up to power and influence.

17   When Mr. Cohen authorized us to contact the Special

18 Counsel's Office in July, he did so to offer his relevant

19 knowledge to the investigation knowing that he would face as a

20 result when his offer became public a barrage of attack by the

21 President. He knew that the President might shut down the

22 investigation, and he knew that there might come a time when he

23 would appear in court, and there would be no Special Counsel to

24 stand up for him, as there is today.

25   He moved forward nonetheless. So it is true, as has

1   been pointed out by the government, that part of what Mr. Cohen

2   did in coming forward is similar to what many folks who are

3   expecting criminal charges do in that expectation. At that

4   time he acknowledged that it was more than possible that his

5   case might proceed from mere investigation to charges and that

6   his offer to assist could help him in some fashion should there

7   be charges and should there be a proceeding. But it is also

8   the case that his decision was an importantly different

9   decision from the usual decision to cooperate. He came forward

10 to offer evidence against the most powerful person in our

11 country. He did so not knowing what the result would be, not

12 knowing how the politics would play out, and not knowing

13 whether the Special Counsel would even survive, nor could he

14 anticipate the full measure of attack that has been made

15 against him; not only by the President, who continues to say

16 that people like Mr. Cohen who cooperate with the Special

17 Counsel are weaklings and those who hold fast and clam up are

18 heroes, but also attacks by partisans and by citizens who

19 happen to be aligned with the President. And those attacks

20 have included threats against him and his family.

21   So, respectfully, this is not a standard case of

22 cooperation. The cooperation here should be viewed under a

23 non-standard or in a non-standard framework. The SCO's

24 investigation, the Special Counsel's investigation is of the

25 utmost national significance, no less than seen 40 plus years

1 ago in the days of Watergate. In the light of that reality,

2 respectfully, your Honor, it is important that others in

3 Mr. Cohen's position who provide assistance to this historic

4 inquiry take renewed courage from this proceeding, and that law

5 enforcement and the promotion of respect for law also receive a

6 boost from what happens here today. Mr. Cohen would want me to

7 say that he's always respected law enforcement. He's always

8 supported it.

9 　　　　In the plea agreement with the Special Counsel, the

10 Special Counsel committed, subject to conditions that have been

11 fully satisfied, to bring to your Honor's attention for

12 sentencing purposes in both cases the nature and extent of

13 Mr. Cohen's cooperation with that office. The Special Counsel

14 says Mr. Cohen has gone to significant lengths to assist the

15 investigation, providing information on core topics under

16 investigation, and is committed to continue to assist.

17 　　　　The office says the information provided has been

18 credible and consistent with other evidence obtained in its

19 investigation. The office further says that it has been useful

20 cooperation in four specific respects that are detailed in the

21 Special Counsel letter to the Court. And, finally, Mr. Cohen,

22 according to the Special Counsel, has made substantial and

23 significant efforts to remediate his own misconduct, accept

24 responsibility for his actions, and assist the Special

25 Counsel's investigation.

1   Even the Southern District which has submitted a

2 somewhat sharp memo, which I will comment on in a few minutes,

3 to the Court, agrees that Mr. Cohen's assistance to the Special

4 Counsel was significant. That's at page 17 of its memo. And

5 that his provision of information to law enforcement in matters

6 of national interest is deserving of credit. And that's at

7 page 37 of the memo.

8   Your Honor, in this exceptionally important matter,

9 Mr. Cohen's cooperation is overwhelmingly the factor, we

10 submit, that should substantially mitigate his sentence, and

11 his action stands in profound contrast to the decision of some

12 others not to cooperate and allegedly to double deal while

13 pretending to cooperate.

14   But that's not all. We also ask the Court

15 respectfully that it consider Mr. Cohen's life of good works as

16 it considers the sentence in this case. As we set forth in our

17 memo, and as supported by the letters sent with the memo, he

18 has been a prodigious fundraiser for the St. Jude's Children's

19 Hospital.

20   He has been the key figure at a Manhattan private

21 school in the raising of funds committed to financial aid for

22 students without means to attend and who otherwise would not be

23 able to attend absent his efforts.

24   He has done likewise impressive fundraising for

25 Operation Smile and assisted the Weatherford Foundation with

1 active personal efforts to advance the role model program of

2 that athletes' organization.

3 Your Honor has read, I have no doubt, of the aid and

4 assistance Mr. Cohen provides regularly to children and friends

5 when they need to find medical care and stands by them in their

6 times of illness and hard times.

7 Whatever millions of words are said and written about

8 Mr. Cohen, and certainly he's in the paper every day, and on TV

9 there's coverage, sometimes it appears 24/7, this is a man of

10 generous spirit and the submissions to the Court demonstrate

11 that.

12 There is some mention in the Southern District's memo

13 regarding emphasis on his own contributions financially, but I

14 don't find it in our memo. The crux of what we're saying is

15 that he puts himself out to raise money for very, very

16 worthwhile organizations. He puts his whole body into it, and

17 this is a man whose first instinct is to help.

18 When it comes to Mr. Cohen's capacity to follow

19 through in his commitment to lead a good and law-abiding life,

20 I would also like to underscore what the Court has been

21 informed of by several members of the bar. All portray a man

22 of integrity and honorable intentions and care for the

23 underserved, a man who does not engage in sharp business

24 practices.

25 To be sure, the Southern District points out that like

1   many clients that lawyers meet from time to time, Mr. Cohen has

2   occasionally erupted in frustration at what he perceives to be

3   wrongs. For example, as the Southern District points out, he

4   became very angry when a bank refused to focus on a transaction

5   that would have allowed him to sell his taxi medallions at a

6   time when doing so would have been lucrative, waited so long

7   before they approved the transactions, that the transaction

8   melted away as the market dipped. He expressed frustration,

9   and that is cited in the Southern District's memo as evidence

10   of a bad character. I have so many clients who come into my

11   office on a regular basis frustrated with life. That's an

12   immature and meaningless observation in my view as to his

13   character. It's simplistic and it's unfair.

14   Mr. Alpstein says, a lawyer who's worked with

15   Mr. Cohen on transactions, "Every seller of a transaction on

16   which I've represented Michael would say without equivocation

17   that Michael was and is an honest, responsible, and fair

18   businessman."

19   The man is 52 years old. There's a long record of how

20   he has conducted himself in business and with financial

21   institutions. No bank has ever lost money dealing with Michael

22   Cohen. I'll say that again: No bank has ever lost money

23   dealing with Michael Cohen. No friend in need has ever been

24   turned away.

25   Your Honor, we addressed the offense conduct, and I

1   had not planned to say more than a few words about it until I

2   read the Southern District's memo, and I just want to say few

3   words in response to the memo. And I don't want to belabor it;

4   I know that you've read all the materials. No one is saying,

5   least of all, Michael Cohen, or has said that a false statement

6   to a bank is other than serious. In this case, we simply made

7   the point that the home equity line of credit as to which the

8   application was false was ten times oversecured at the time of

9   the application and that no money damage resulted. Does that

10 make it right? No. It does not make it right. But it puts

11 the conduct into some kind of proportion.

12   No one is saying, least of us, Michael Cohen, that tax

13 evasion of any kind is other than serious. The speaking

14 information in this case, however, says that the crux of the

15 conduct was failing to identify deposits as income to an

16 accountant who received bank statements. Does that make it

17 right? No. It doesn't make it right. But it puts in

18 proportion and points out that the Court here is not dealing

19 with a mastermind of tax deception.

20   Ms. Lester and I were given three to four days to

21 speak to the tax charges in this case before they were filed.

22 They were not specified. When asked questions about what they

23 entailed, I was met with stony silence and no realistic

24 opportunity to meet with the tax division, as is common. I

25 believe that we would have had a very strong chance of

1   diverting the case from the criminal track had we had that

2   opportunity.

3   But life is tough and Michael Cohen accepts that. We

4   accept it. Our point is not to explain the conduct away. Our

5   point is to say that the offense is well within the heartland

6   of cases that are routinely treated in a non-criminal context,

7   solely so that your Honor can consider the punishment aspect

8   associated with the criminal tax evasion that has been

9   admitted, and that no one is trying to push away as someone

0   else's fault.

1   I will say very little on the campaign charges, the

2   campaign finance charges, and the statement to the legislature.

3   I do want to point out what Mr. Gerber, a lawyer in New York,

4   writes to the Court. He's a former member of the grievance

5   committee, and he's written on behalf of Mr. Cohen that he's

6   seen many attorneys succumb to the wishes of a particularly

7   persuasive client. "Mr. Cohen," he writes, "had a client whose

8   extraordinary power of persuasion got him elected to the

9   highest office in the land." Again, the conduct is quite

0   serious, but Mr. Gerber's experience is certainly worthy of

1   note, as the Court takes into account the human element of what

2   happened here.

3   Based on all these factors, your Honor, most

4   importantly cooperation, good works, and the nature of the

5   offenses, we respectfully submit that the case calls for a full

1 consideration of mercy as your Honor sentences our client,

2 Michael Cohen.

3   A few words on what the Southern District has

4 submitted. It is not the case that Mr. Cohen has declined to

5 answer questions from the Southern District or from our duly

6 authorized U.S. Attorney's Offices, state law enforcement

7 entities, and Congress. He's ready to do that. He is wary of

8 a long-term cooperation agreement for personal reasons and

9 because he wants both to remove himself and to remove his

10 family from the glare of the cameras and try to work his way

11 and their way back from an abnormal life. The period of such

12 an agreement would be indeterminate. The press is overwhelming

13 in this case. But none of this is to say he will not make

14 himself available for questioning on investigated matters, and

15 indeed, as you know, he's already met with the Southern

16 District on one of those matters.

17   But it's also unfair and it's mere innuendo that

18 Mr. Cohen would not describe his own misconduct, as the

19 government says twice, "if any." I know the Court is aware

20 that search warrants were executed in this case. As a result,

21 all of his papers, computers, devices, phones, and recordings

22 were seized and dozens of agents, and at least four Assistant

23 U.S. Attorneys and supervisors questioned dozens and dozens of

24 witnesses and reviewed the evidence. They know what is there.

25 He pled to what he pled to, and the plea agreement immunized

1 him for the conduct that the plea agreement immunized him for.

2 When the government repeats twice that Mr. Cohen declined to

3 disclose his prior bad acts "if any," they come forward with

4 nothing to suggest that they don't know everything already,

5 much less that there's anything there.

6   At the end of the day, it's not that important, your

7 Honor. I just don't think it's fair. I don't really

8 understand the strident tone of the memo, and trying to put it

9 into context, I'm looking at the beginning of the case. First,

0 an unwillingness to delineate charges, a claim that I should

1 already know what they are. A few days to respond once three

2 categories of alleged offenses were set forth. And then after

3 the plea, a courthouse press conference on a plea of guilty. I

4 submit, your Honor, that no other defendant would be treated in

5 this fashion on these offenses, but Mr. Cohen had the

6 misfortune to have been counsel to the President.

7   This rush to charge and media display suggest,

8 respectfully, that the Court should take with a healthy grain

9 of salt the contentions by the Southern District of New York

0 that Mr. Cohen left them at the altar of a Southern District

1 cooperation agreement. Rather, he made a personal and rational

2 decision that he would respond truthfully to any investigative

3 topic, but that it was not in his or his family's interest to

4 remain in the constant glare and under the requirements of a

5 cooperation agreement which could go on for months and months

1   and years and years. And he sat down with Southern, and they

2   found him "forthright and credible." Page 15.

3   The rules of the Southern District of New York as to

4   how every case of cooperation should proceed, of course, were

5   given to us by the minor gods and woe unto those who fail to

6   follow their scriptures, but they don't mean that they work in

7   every situation, no matter the facts, no matter the

8   circumstances. They don't mean the prosecutor is always right

9   about how the standard procedure will play out.

10   And, effectively, your Honor, the Southern District

11 would have this Court penalize Mr. Cohen because he did not

12 follow their standard form agreement and procedure even though

13 he cooperated with the Special Counsel, provided them with

14 forthright and credible information, and offered, and hereby

15 offers, to respond to any other questions, and they would do it

16 without putting forth anything to suggest that there's any

17 there there by way of prior bad acts. This approach, your

18 Honor, is erroneous. It's error to consider what they are

19 asking you to consider. It's fundamentally unfair for a

20 prosecutor to ask a Court to sentence a defendant on

21 hypothetical facts and circumstances rather than based on the

22 facts and circumstances that the Court actually knows. Those

23 facts and circumstances do not present a mystery of the kind

24 that the office's memorandum seeks to suggest. I don't know

25 what's behind it, and it's peculiar in a context in which a

1 sibling office of the DOJ agrees that Mr. Cohen cooperated as

2 set forth in the plea agreement and as reported to your Honor

3 in the Special Counsel's letter.

4 I'm not going to overly speculate about what's going

5 on here. I think the Court has as much experience as I in

6 these matters, but I would suggest that power to the Southern

7 District if they want to make a bigger case than they've

8 already made, God bless them. And maybe there's a little bit

9 of pride involved here in not being at the center of attention.

0 Who knows? Maybe all those articles about a big financial

1 fraud case and a big taxi medallion case followed by these

2 pleas is somehow disappointing. It's not for me to say.

3 We respectfully request, your Honor, a variance under

4 the guidelines and the exercise of leniency in the imposition

5 of sentence on Mr. Cohen, and we request that on behalf of our

6 client and his family. He has done, Michael has, a good deal

7 to help, not only the Special Counsel but a lot of people. He

8 is a very good man.

9 Thank you.

0 THE COURT: Thank you, Mr. Petrillo.

1 Ms. Rhee, does the Special Counsel's Office wish to be

2 heard?

3 MS. RHEE: Yes, your Honor.

4 Thank you, your Honor. On behalf of the Special

5 Counsel's Office, our remarks will be brief. We rely, and we

1   speak primarily through our written submission which has

2   already been submitted to this Court. In supplement to that,

3   we just have two discrete, important points that we want to

4   highlight for the Court's attention.

5   The first is that the offense that Mr. Cohen pled to

6   in 18 CR 850 was a serious criminal violation. As Mr. Petrillo

7   alluded to, the subject at issue here that Mr. Cohen actively

8   misled Congress about was an issue of national importance and

9   interest, and Mr. Cohen intentionally repeated many of the

10 false statements to us at the Special Counsel's Office

11 initially when we met with him in July. And those false

12 statements were intended to limit ongoing investigations into

13 Russian interference in a U.S. presidential election, and the

14 question of any links or coordination between a campaign and a

15 foreign government. Our submission elucidates why those lies

16 were material, why those lies were consequential.

17   But what we really want to leave with the Court today

18 for the Court's consideration is Mr. Cohen's interactions with

19 the Special Counsel's Office since that initial voluntary

20 interview in July. The government has agreed with Mr. Cohen to

21 bring his assistance to your attention for due consideration at

22 this sentencing, and what we want to say about that is that

23 Mr. Cohen has endeavored from his second session with us in

24 September of this year going forward to this day, he has

25 endeavored to account for his criminal misconduct in numerous

ways. He has fully accepted responsibility for the lies that
he told Congress. He has provided our office with credible and
reliable information about core Russia-related issues under
investigation and within the purview of the Special Counsel's
Office. There is only so much that we can say about the
particulars at this time given our ongoing investigation, but
we hope that we have sufficiently outlined for the Court that
they were ranging, and that they were helpful.

Finally, your Honor, what we want to highlight for
this Court is that one of the things that we and the Special
Counsel's Office have most appreciated about Mr. Cohen's
assistance is that he has provided valuable information,
investigative information, to us while taking care and being
careful to note what he knows and what he doesn't know. Rather
than inflate the value of any information that he has brought
forward to us in what he had to provide, Mr. Cohen has sought
to tell us the truth, and that is of utmost value to us as we
seek in our office to determine what in fact occurred.

And so we want to highlight that for the Court and to
underscore what we set out in our submission about the value,
the nature, the reliability, and the credibility of Mr. Cohen's
assistance.

THE COURT: Thank you, Ms. Rhee.

MS. RHEE: Thank you, your Honor.

THE COURT: Mr. Roos, does the United States

1 Attorney's Office wish to be heard?

2 MR. ROOS: Yes, your Honor. Thank you.

3 Your Honor, I'd like to start where Mr. Petrillo

4 ended, which is to share a few words about the information that

5 Mr. Cohen provided to law enforcement and the credit that is

6 appropriate.

7 Now, we agree that Mr. Cohen's decision to provide

8 information to the Special Counsel's Office in matters of

9 national interest is deserving of credit, and we defer to SCO's

10 description of Mr. Cohen's assistance to them and in their

11 investigation. We don't dispute any of that assessment or the

12 assessment, frankly, that defense counsel has made.

13 But for the reasons that we've detailed in our

14 sentencing memorandum, any downward variance that Mr. Cohen

15 receives should be modest. Any successful assistance Mr. Cohen

16 provided was in the context of a case where the guidelines

17 range is zero to six months. It's within the context of the

18 Special Counsel Office's case.

19 But here, he is facing three additional categories of

20 crimes, eight total charges, and didn't come anywhere close to

21 assisting this office in an investigation. There is no mystery

22 about this. No one is attempting to penalize Mr. Cohen for not

23 cooperating. Quite the opposite, there is no obligation to

24 cooperate, but for all the hypothesizing that Mr. Petrillo has

25 done, Mr. Cohen can't have it both ways. There is a standard

1   way in which this office conducts cooperation. Your Honor is

2   familiar with it. There is no reason, no matter the

3   significance or the nature of the case, whether or not it

4   receives public attention, for us to depart from that practice.

5   We've treated Mr. Cohen just the way we treat every other

6   defendant that deals with the United States Attorney's Office.

7   Now, Mr. Cohen, he chose not to pursue the path of

8   full cooperation. He didn't provide substantial assistance to

9   the government in this investigation, and he doesn't have a 5K

10   letter. And for these reasons, our view is that a significant

11   variance, the variance urged by the defendant isn't warranted

12   here. To do so would send the wrong message. It would send

13   the message that a defendant who chooses a different path, a

14   selective cooperation on only particular subjects can receive

15   the credit that so many defendants seek when they expose

16   themselves completely to the government.

17   Now, I'd like to touch on two points, two of the

18   3553(a) factors that in the government's view are so important

19   here, and they really go to what Mr. Petrillo said about the

20   nature and the seriousness of these offenses.

21   So, first, the defendant pled guilty to four crimes

22   here, your Honor, and Mr. Petrillo, he identified areas in

23   which certain crimes in their view may not be as serious, but

24   he pled guilty to four different crimes, and your Honor is

25   sentencing Mr. Cohen not only on four different charges but

1 four separate crimes. Each of those charges is itself serious.

2 Each merits punishment in its own right. Each cause a distinct

3 harm, and taken together there is a compounding effect.

4 Collectively, the charges portray a pattern of deception, of

5 brazenness, and of greed that manifested in multiple aspects of

6 Mr. Cohen's professional life.

7   In particular, Mr. Cohen's conduct related to the

8 election is serious because of the tremendous societal cost

9 associated with the campaign finance crimes and the lies to

10 Congress. Mr. Cohen committed these deceptive acts to protect

11 the political campaign from allegations of impropriety, and, by

12 his own admission, he committed the campaign finance crimes for

13 the purpose of influencing the election.

14   He also, quite brazenly, stole millions of dollars in

15 income from the IRS. And on this subject, defense counsel

16 describes the ways in which this is really nothing more than a

17 civil matter. But that is not the case, your Honor. These tax

18 crimes went on for at least five years. They involve millions

19 of dollars of income that was deliberately not reported to the

20 IRS. This is not a case of an assessed tax not being paid.

21 It's something quite different. It was deliberate, it was

22 willful, and that's what the defendant's plea reflects.

23   Now, together these crimes implicate core defining

24 parts of our democracy: Government funded by the people, free

25 and transparent elections. And in committing these crimes,

1   Mr. Cohen has eroded faith in the electoral process and

2   compromised the rule of law. And so just as he asks for

3   leniency because of what he claims he's done for the republic,

4   the same can be true in the way in which he's undermined it.

5   All of these facts, your Honor, favor a substantial custodial

6   sentence.

7   But the second reason why a substantial custodial

8   sentence is warranted here is because of the need to promote

9   deterrence. And when it comes to Mr. Cohen, his training and

10 experience as an attorney should have been a deterrent to his

11 own criminal conduct. Instead, he used his legal license in

12 furtherance of his crimes, and that is a significant point that

13 should be taken into consideration in sentencing. A

14 substantial sentence would serve as a deterrent to future

15 criminal conduct by this particular defendant.

16   But more importantly, your Honor, a substantial

17 sentence would also serve as a general deterrent to future

18 criminal conduct by individuals like Mr. Cohen. This is

19 particularly important in the context of tax evasion and the

20 campaign's finance crimes, crimes that are difficult to detect,

21 that are so frequently orchestrated through private

22 transactions kept secret from the public. The unfairness here

23 is not to Mr. Cohen. It's to the public. Particularly in

24 light of the public interest in this case, a meaningful

25 sentence of imprisonment, one that sends a message, an

1   appropriate message about the seriousness of these crimes is

2   appropriate. That sort of message must be sent in this case,

3   that even powerful and privileged individuals cannot violate

4   these laws with impunity.

5   Unless the Court has any questions for the government,

6   we otherwise rest on our submission

7   THE COURT: Thank you, Mr. Roos.

8   MR. PETRILLO: Just a point of clarification, your

9   Honor, if I may.

10   THE COURT: Yes. Go ahead, Mr. Petrillo.

11   MR. PETRILLO: I just want to be clear because I

12 wasn't sure whether Mr. Roos affirmed or failed to affirm that

13 the government; that is, the Southern District, by a letter

14 dated November 29 in this case captioned with this case number

15 that is the first plea before your Honor, agreed that the

16 defendant's provision of information to the Special Counsel is

17 a factor to be considered by the Court under Title 18

18 U.S. Code, Section 3553(a) in the first case, not just the

19 second case. And I wasn't sure whether I heard properly that

20 Mr. Roos was delineating between the two cases. I may just

21 have misheard, but I want to make sure it's clear.

22   MR. ROOS: Your Honor, if I may?

23   THE COURT: You may.

24   MR. ROOS: I believe this was the first point I

25 addressed, but to clarify any confusion, the government's view

1   is that the defendant provided information that was valuable to

2   the Special Counsel's Office. We don't dispute that. And

3   that's the reason why the government is seeking or recommends a

4   modest variance in this case as opposed to seeking a guideline

5   sentence. So I guess the answer to Mr. Petrillo's question is

6   yes.

7   THE COURT: All right. Thank you.

8   Mr. Petrillo, does your client wish to address the

9   Court before sentence is imposed?

10 MR. PETRILLO: He does, your Honor, and he's asked me

11 just to clarify because he heard -- and, again, I may have

12 heard it incorrectly, that -- the amount of restitution in this

13 case; that is, the amount due and owing to the IRS is

14 approximately $1.393 million, and he's under the impression the

15 Court may have said that the guidelines range started where it

16 did because the loss amount was one and a half million. And he

17 just wanted to make sure that that point was entered into the

18 record. It doesn't change our position on the guidelines

19 though, and I am only noting it for the record.

20 And Mr. Cohen would like to be heard, your Honor.

21 THE COURT: Fine. I'll hear from Mr. Cohen now.

22 THE DEFENDANT: Your Honor, stand here or to the

23 podium?

24 THE COURT: I think it would be best to take the

25 podium.

1   THE DEFENDANT: Thank you, your Honor.

2   I stand before your Honor humbly and painfully aware

3   that we are here today for one reason: Because of my actions

4   that I pled guilty to on August 21, and as well on November 29.

5   I take full responsibility for each act that I pled

6   guilty to, the personal ones to me and those involving the

7   President of the United States of America. Viktor Frankl in

8   his book, "Man's Search for Meaning," he wrote, "There are

9   forces beyond your control that can take away everything you

10   possess except one thing, your freedom to choose how you will

11   respond to the situation."

12   Your Honor, this may seem hard to believe, but today

13   is one of the most meaningful days of my life. The irony is

14   today is the day I am getting my freedom back as you sit at the

15   bench and you contemplate my fate.

16   I have been living in a personal and mental

17   incarceration ever since the fateful day that I accepted the

18   offer to work for a famous real estate mogul whose business

19   acumen I truly admired. In fact, I now know that there is

20   little to be admired. I want to be clear. I blame myself for

21   the conduct which has brought me here today, and it was my own

22   weakness, and a blind loyalty to this man that led me to choose

23   a path of darkness over light. It is for these reasons I chose

24   to participate in the elicit act of the President rather than

25   to listen to my own inner voice which should have warned me

1   that the campaign finance violations that I later pled guilty

2   to were insidious.

3   Recently, the President Tweeted a statement calling me

4   weak, and he was correct, but for a much different reason than

5   he was implying. It was because time and time again I felt it

6   was my duty to cover up his dirty deeds rather than to listen

7   to my own inner voice and my moral compass. My weakness can be

8   characterized as a blind loyalty to Donald Trump, and I was

9   weak for not having the strength to question and to refuse his

10   demands. I have already spent years living a personal and

11   mental incarceration, which no matter what is decided today,

12   owning this mistake will free me to be once more the person I

13   really am.

14   Your Honor, I love my family more than anything in the

15   world: My dad who is here today, my mom, my in-laws, siblings,

16   love of my life, my wife Laura, my pride and joy, my daughter

17   Samantha, my son, Jake. There is no sentence that could

18   supersede the suffering that I live with on a daily basis,

19   knowing that my actions have brought undeserved pain and shame

20   upon my family. I deserve that pain. They do not.

21   I also stand before my children, for them to see their

22   father taking responsibility for his mistakes, mistakes that

23   have forced them to bear a shameful spotlight which they have

24   done nothing to deserve, and this breaks my heart. For me, the

25   greatest punishment has been seeing the unbearable pain that my

1   actions and my associations have brought to my entire family.

2   My mom, my dad, this isn't what they deserve to see in their

3   older age, especially when as a child they emphasized to all of

4   us the difference between right and wrong. And I'm sorry.

5   I believed during this process that there were only

6   two things I could do to minimize the pain to my family: Admit

7   my guilt and move these proceedings along. This is why I did

8   not enter into a cooperation agreement. I have elected to be

9   sentenced without asking for adjournment. I have given

10   information during countless hours of meetings with prosecutors

11   that have been cited as substantial, meaningful and credible.

12   I have chosen this unorthodox path because the faster I am

13   sentenced, the sooner I can return to my family, be the father

14   I want to be, the husband I want to be, and a productive member

15   of society again. I do not need a cooperation agreement to be

16   in place to do the right thing. And I will continue to

17   cooperate with government, offering as much information as I

18   truthfully possess.

19   I stand behind my statement that I made to George

20   Stephanopoulos, that my wife, my daughter, my son have my first

21   loyalty and always will. I put family and country first. My

22   departure as a loyal soldier to the President bears a very

23   hefty price.

24   For months now the President of the United States, one

25   of the most powerful men in the world, publicly mocks me,

1   calling me a rat and a liar, and insists that the Court

2   sentence me to the absolute maximum time in prison. Not only

3   is this improper; it creates a false sense that the President

4   can weigh in on the outcome of judicial proceedings that

5   implicate him. Despite being vilified by the press and

6   inundated with character assassinations over the past almost

7   two years, I still stand today, and I am committed to proving

8   my integrity and ensuring that history will not remember me as

9   the villain of his story. I now know that every action I take

10 in the future has to be well thought out and with honorable

11 intention because I wish to leave no room for future mistakes

12 in my life.

13   And so I beseech your Honor to consider this path that

14 I am currently taking when sentencing me today. And I want to

15 apologize to my entire family for what my actions have put them

16 through. My family has suffered immeasurably in the home and

17 the world outside. I know I have let them all down, and it

18 will be my life's work to make it right, and to become the best

19 version of myself.

20   Most all, I want to apologize to the people of the

21 United States. You deserve to know the truth and lying to you

22 was unjust. I want to thank you, your Honor, for all the time

23 I'm sure you've committed to this matter and the consideration

24 that you have given to my future.

25   Again, I want to thank my family, my friends, many who

1 are here today, who are with me, especially all the people who

2 wrote letters on my behalf. In addition, I would like to thank

3 the tens of thousands of strangers who despite not knowing me

4 at all, not knowing me personally have shown kindness and

5 empathy in writing letters to me and offering support and

6 prayer. And I thank you, your Honor, I am truly sorry, and I

7 promise I will be better.

8   THE COURT: You may be seated, Mr. Cohen.

9   THE DEFENDANT: Thank you.

10   THE COURT: The defendant, Michael Cohen, comes before

11 this Court, having pled guilty to five counts of income tax

12 evasion, one count of making false statements to a banking

13 institution, one count of causing an unlawful corporate

14 contribution, and one count of an excessive campaign

15 contribution in the 18 CR 602 criminal case, and one count of

16 making false statements to the U.S. Congress in 18 CR 850.

17 Each of these crimes is a serious offense against the United

18 States.

19   Now, I've reviewed the revised presentence

20 investigation report, and I adopt the findings of fact in that

21 report as my own. I will cause the report to be docketed and

22 filed under seal as part of the record in each of these cases.

23 I have also reviewed all of the memoranda submitted by counsel

24 for the parties and the letters submitted on Mr. Cohen's

25 behalf.

1   I previously reviewed the guidelines with all of you.

2   Suffice it to say at this juncture that with respect to the

3   first case, the guidelines range is 51 to 63 months of

4   imprisonment, and the guideline range on the second case is

5   zero to six months of imprisonment. Of course, the Sentencing

6   Guidelines should be the starting point and the initial

7   benchmark.

8   Turning to the 3553(a) factors, the question for this

9   Court is what is the appropriate and just sentence for these

10   crimes and this defendant. Mr. Cohen pled guilty to a

11   veritable smorgasbord of fraudulent conduct: Willful tax

12   evasion, making false statements to a financial institution,

13   illegal campaign contributions, and making false statements to

14   Congress. Each of the crimes involved deception and each

15   appears to have been motivated by personal greed and ambition.

16   His extensive criminal conduct also has broader public

17   consequences. Mr. Cohen evaded more than $1.3 million in

18   personal income taxes for the tax years 2012 through 2016. He

19   willfully failed to report $4 million earned through various

20   streams of income from leasing taxi medallions to consulting

21   fees and brokerage commissions. As Justice Oliver Wendell

22   Holmes famously said, "Taxes are the price we pay for a

23   civilized society."

24   Now, Mr. Cohen also made a series of false statements

25   to financial institutions regarding his liabilities and monthly

SOUTHERN DISTRICT REPORTERS, P.C.
(212) 805-0300

1 expenses so that he would be approved for a $500,000 home

2 equity line of credit.

3   Further, Mr. Cohen committed two campaign finance

4 crimes on the eve of the 2016 presidential election with the

5 intent to influence the outcome of that election. He made or

6 facilitated payments to silence two women who threatened to go

7 public with details of purported extramarital affairs, and

8 Mr. Cohen admitted that he did so in coordination with and at

9 the direction of Individual One.

10   Finally, in a separate criminal proceeding filed by

11 the Special Counsel's Office, Mr. Cohen admitted that he made

12 false statements about a proposed business project in Moscow to

13 congressional committees investigating possible interference by

14 the Russian government with the 2016 presidential election.

15 Each of these crimes standing alone warrant serious punishment.

16   The financial harms are readily ascertainable.

17 Mr. Cohen's tax evasion offenses cheated the federal government

18 out of $1,393,858. His deception caused a bank to approve a

19 $500,000 line of credit he did not deserve. And even his

20 campaign finance crimes may be measured by the amount of

21 unlawful contributions: The $150,000 hush money payment that

22 he coordinated, and the $130,000 hush money payment that he

23 funneled from his home equity loan through a shell corporation.

24   While this is his first conviction, the magnitude,

25 breadth, and duration of his criminal conduct requires specific

1   deterrence. Tax and campaign finance prosecutions are rare,

2   but unlike the mine-run tax evasion or campaign finance

3   violation, Mr. Cohen's crimes implicate a far more insidious

4   harm to our democratic institutions, especially in view of his

5   subsequent plea to making false statements to Congress. Thus,

6   the need for general deterrence is amplified in this case.

7   Now, Mr. Cohen had a comfortable childhood and enjoyed

8   all the privileges of growing up in a close-knit, upper class

9   suburb on Long Island. He and his siblings had loving parents

10 who worked hard to provide everything for their children. He

11 graduated from law school and practiced law in various law

12 firms until the Trump organization hired him as an attorney in

13 2007. Thereafter, his entire professional life apparently

14 revolved around the Trump organization. He thrived on his

15 access to wealthy and powerful people, and he became one

16 himself.

17   The letters submitted on his behalf reveal a man

18 dedicated to his family and generous with his time and money to

19 help people in his own orbit. A number of individuals have

20 written to me describing how Mr. Cohen came to their aid

21 without seeking anything in return. Of course, that kind of

22 generosity is laudable. But somewhere along the way Mr. Cohen

23 appears to have lost his moral compass and sought instead to

24 monetize his new-found influence. That trajectory,

25 unfortunately, has led him to this courtroom today.

1   While Mr. Cohen does not have a formal cooperation

2   agreement with the United States Attorney's Office, he has

3   nevertheless met with prosecutors on a number of occasions.

4   The Special Counsel's Office notes that he has voluntarily

5   provided information "about his own conduct and that of others

6   on core topics under investigation" by the Special Counsel and

7   that the information he has provided has been "relevant and

8   useful."Further, the Special Counsel urges that any sentence

9   imposed in connection with 18 CR 850 should be concurrent to

10   any sentence imposed in the earlier case.

11   While the United States Attorney's Office acknowledges

12   that Mr. Cohen's assistance to the Special Counsel's Office was

13   "significant" and warrants a modest variance from the

14   guidelines range, they contend that it should not approach the

15   type of credit typically given to cooperating witnesses in this

16   district.

17   However, cooperation, even when it is not the product

18   of a formal agreement, should be encouraged where information

19   is provided that advances criminal investigations. Our system

20   of justice would be less robust without the use of cooperating

21   witnesses to assist law enforcement.

22   Based on the submissions of the parties, this Court

23   agrees that Mr. Cohen should receive some credit for providing

24   assistance to the Special Counsel's Office. While Mr. Cohen

25   pledges to assist the Special Counsel's Office in further

1   investigations, that is not a matter that this Court can

2   consider now.

3   There is an acute need for the sentence here to

4   reflect the seriousness of the offenses and to promote respect

5   for the law. As a lawyer, Mr. Cohen should have known better.

6   Tax evasion undercuts the government's ability to provide

7   essential services on which we all depend. False statements to

8   banking institutions undermine the integrity of our financial

9   system. Campaign finance violations threaten the fairness of

10 elections, and false statements to Congress interfere with the

11 fact-finding process in matters of national importance.

12   While Mr. Cohen has taken steps to mitigate his

13 criminal conduct by pleading guilty and volunteering useful

14 information to prosecutors, that does not wipe the slate clean.

15 Mr. Cohen selected the information he disclosed to the

16 government. This Court cannot agree with the defendant's

17 assertion that no jail time is warranted. In fact, this Court

18 firmly believes that a significant term of imprisonment is

19 fully justified in this highly publicized case to send a

20 message to those who contemplate avoiding their taxes, evading

21 campaign finance laws or lying to financial institutions or

22 Congress. Our democratic institutions depend on the honesty of

23 our citizenry in dealing with the government. And so it is

24 against that backdrop that I am prepared to sentence the

25 defendant.

1   Mr. Cohen I'd ask, sir, that you stand at this time.

2   Mr. Cohen, it's my judgment, sir, that on 18 CR 602

3 that you be sentenced to a term of 36 months of imprisonment to

4 be followed by three years of supervised release on each count

5 to be served concurrently with the sentence that I will impose

6 in a moment on 18 CR 850. I'm imposing all of the standard

7 conditions of supervised release and the following special

8 condition: That you provide the probation department with

9 access to any requested financial information.

10   Further, I'm going to enter an order of forfeiture in

11 this case in the amount of $500,000, and I'm going to enter an

12 order for restitution in the amount of $1,393,858. I am also

13 going to impose a fine of $50,000, and the mandatory special

14 assessment of $800.

15   Now, with respect to 18 CR 850, I sentence you to two

16 months of imprisonment to be served concurrently with the term

17 imposed in 18 CR 602 to be followed by three years of

18 supervised release, also to be served concurrently with the

19 term imposed in 18 CR 602, and with all of the standard

20 conditions of supervised release.

21   In this case with respect to 18 CR 850, I am also

22 going to impose a $50,000 fine in that case to recognize the

23 gravity of the harm of lying to Congress in matters of national

24 importance. And, once again, I will impose the mandatory

25 special assessment in that case of $100.

Just to be clear, the sentence in the earlier case is concurrent on all counts in that information.

And so, Mr. Cohen, this constitutes the sentence of this Court. I advise you that to the extent you have not previously waived your right to appeal, you have the right to appeal. I advise you further that if you cannot afford counsel, counsel will be provided to you free of cost. Mr. Petrillo has done a superb job in navigating you through this matter and bringing the sentencing submissions before the Court. I'm confident that he and Ms. Lester will advise you further with respect to your appellate rights. You may be seated, sir.

Are there any further applications at this time?

MR. ROOS: Not from the government, your Honor.

THE COURT: Ms. Rhee.

MS. RHEE: Your Honor, the Special Counsel's Office would just like to confirm that there will be a separate $50,000 fine.

THE COURT: Yes.

MS. RHEE: Not to run concurrently.

THE COURT: No, it's a separate fine. It's a separate harm, and the guidelines in my view do not recognize the gravity of the offense of making false statements to Congress.

MS. RHEE: Thank you for the clarification.

THE COURT: Mr. Petrillo.

1   MR. PETRILLO: Your Honor, if you would, would the

2 Court give consideration to voluntary surrender by the

3 defendant and consider recommending the designation of

4 Otisville as the place of imprisonment?

5   THE COURT: I will make that recommendation, and I

6 will allow for a voluntary surrender in this case. What

7 surrender date are you seeking?

8   MR. PETRILLO: I don't have one particularly in mind,

9 but from past experience it seems to take about 10 or 12 weeks

10 for the BOP to --

11   THE COURT: Right. Is March 6 all right? And if for

12 some reason you've not been notified of a designated

13 institution, just write a short note to me, and I will put the

14 surrender date over.

15   MR. PETRILLO: Very well.

16   THE COURT: Go ahead.

17   MR. PETRILLO: I have one other thing for the record

18 that doesn't require a ruling, but as you know, under *United*

19 *States v. Ganais* in the Second Circuit, it's incumbent upon the

20 defendant to demand his property back post a search procedure

21 as part of protecting his rights under the Fourth Amendment.

22 And so for the record, I'd like to make that demand and thus

23 have no confusion as to where that stands.

24   THE COURT: All right. I'm confident there will be

25 further briefing with respect to that matter after this

ICCQCOHs

1 proceeding is concluded, and I will await receipt of some

2 submission.

3   This matter is concluded.   Have a good afternoon

4   (Adjourned)

9. Indictment in
US v. Roger Jason Stone, Jr.
(US District Court for the District
of Columbia, January 24, 2019)

Perhaps the most colorful character in the special counsel investigation was Roger Stone, a longtime Republican political operative and Donald Trump friend who sports a tattoo of Richard Nixon on his back. Stone, who publicly cheered on WikiLeaks as the organization released hacked Democrats' emails during the presidential campaign, had said for months he would be charged by Robert S. Mueller III. On January 24, 2019, his prediction came true.

And early the next day, a team of FBI agents—armed and wearing bulletproof vests—knocked on the door of Stone's Florida home and took him into custody. The special counsel had secured this seven-count indictment against the sixty-six-year-old political operative, alleging that Stone had tried to thwart congressional inquiries into Russian interference in the election. He was charged with lying to Congress, obstruction, and witness tampering.

Stone vowed to plead not guilty and fight the charges.

The indictment alleged that Stone attempted to keep lawmakers from uncovering his efforts to get information about WikiLeaks' release of the hacked emails, after it was publicly alleged the hacking was done by the Russian government. It noted pointedly that a senior Trump campaign official "was directed" to contact Stone about WikiLeaks' releases and possible "damaging information" the group had about Hillary Clinton's campaign. Prosecutors identified WikiLeaks only as "Organization 1." It was unclear who the senior campaign official is.

"STONE thereafter told the Trump Campaign about potential future releases of damaging material by Organization 1," the indictment alleged.

The indictment detailed in particular Stone's communication with Steve Bannon, who was then Trump's chief strategist and is identified in the indictment as a "high-ranking Trump Campaign official," as well as two of Stone's associates—Jerome Corsi, a conservative writer identified in the indictment as "Person 1," and Randy Credico, a New York comedian and radio host identified in the indictment as "Person 2." By prosecutors' telling, Stone had tried through Credico and Corsi to get information from WikiLeaks and its founder, Julian Assange, though he would later tell lawmakers falsely he had no records about that.

Corsi's lawyers confirmed he is Person 1 in the indictment but noted it "does not accuse Dr. Corsi of any wrongdoing and indeed this is the case." Lawyers for Bannon and Credico declined to comment. All three were identified by people familiar with the case, and communications described in the indictment match their publicly known communications.

While the indictment did not charge Stone with conspiring with Russia, the allegations suggest that the campaign was willing to seek out and use messages hacked by a foreign state as political ammunition. And it provided lively anecdotes about how Stone sought to stymie investigators' work. For example, it alleged that in November 2017, Stone told Credico to "[s]tonewall" after the House Intelligence Committee sought his testimony. The next month, he invoked a character from the Mafia movie *The Godfather: Part II*, who, during a congressional hearing, told lawmakers, "I don't know nothin' about that."

"And if you turned over anything to the FBI you're a fool," Stone told Credico, according to the indictment.

IN THE UNITED STATES DISTRICT COURT
FOR THE DISTRICT OF COLUMBIA

UNITED STATES OF AMERICA	*	CRIMINAL NO.
	*	
v.	*	Grand Jury Original
	*	
ROGER JASON STONE, JR.,	*	18 U.S.C. §§ 1001, 1505, 1512, 2
	*	
Defendant.	*	
	*	
	*	
	*	
	*******	

se: 1:19-cr-00018
igned To : Judge Amy B Jackson
ign. Date : 01/24/2019
cription: INDICTMENT (B)
ated Case: 18cr215 (ABJ)

INDICTMENT

The Grand Jury for the District of Columbia charges:

Introduction

1.   By in or around May 2016, the Democratic National Committee ("DNC") and the Democratic Congressional Campaign Committee ("DCCC") became aware that their computer systems had been compromised by unauthorized intrusions and hired a security company ("Company 1") to identify the extent of the intrusions.

2.   On or about June 14, 2016, the DNC—through Company 1—publicly announced that it had been hacked by Russian government actors.

3.   From in or around July 2016 through in or around November 2016, an organization ("Organization 1"), which had previously posted documents stolen by others from U.S. persons, entities, and the U.S. government, released tens of thousands of documents stolen from the DNC and the personal email account of the chairman of the U.S. presidential campaign of Hillary Clinton ("Clinton Campaign").

a. On or about July 22, 2016, Organization 1 released documents stolen from the DNC.

b. Between on or about October 7, 2016 and on or about November 7, 2016, Organization 1 released approximately 33 tranches of documents that had been stolen from the personal email account of the Clinton Campaign chairman, totaling over 50,000 stolen documents.

4. ROGER JASON STONE, JR. was a political consultant who worked for decades in U.S. politics and on U.S. political campaigns. STONE was an official on the U.S. presidential campaign of Donald J. Trump ("Trump Campaign") until in or around August 2015, and maintained regular contact with and publicly supported the Trump Campaign through the 2016 election.

5. During the summer of 2016, STONE spoke to senior Trump Campaign officials about Organization 1 and information it might have had that would be damaging to the Clinton Campaign. STONE was contacted by senior Trump Campaign officials to inquire about future releases by Organization 1.

6. By in or around early August 2016, STONE was claiming both publicly and privately to have communicated with Organization 1. By in or around mid-August 2016, Organization 1 made a public statement denying direct communication with STONE. Thereafter, STONE said that his communication with Organization 1 had occurred through a person STONE described as a "mutual friend," "go-between," and "intermediary." STONE also continued to communicate with members of the Trump Campaign about Organization 1 and its intended future releases.

7. After the 2016 U.S. presidential election, the U.S. House of Representatives Permanent Select Committee on Intelligence ("HPSCI"), the U.S. Senate Select Committee on Intelligence ("SSCI"), and the Federal Bureau of Investigation ("FBI") opened or announced their respective

2

investigations into Russian interference in the 2016 U.S. presidential election, which included investigating STONE's claims of contact with Organization 1.

8.   In response, STONE took steps to obstruct these investigations. Among other steps to obstruct the investigations, STONE:

a.   Made multiple false statements to HPSCI about his interactions regarding Organization 1, and falsely denied possessing records that contained evidence of these interactions; and

b.   Attempted to persuade a witness to provide false testimony to and withhold pertinent information from the investigations.

Other Relevant Individuals

9.   Person 1 was a political commentator who worked with an online media publication during the 2016 U.S. presidential campaign. Person 1 spoke regularly with STONE throughout the campaign, including about the release of stolen documents by Organization 1.

10.   Person 2 was a radio host who had known STONE for more than a decade. In testimony before HPSCI on or about September 26, 2017, STONE described Person 2 (without naming him) as an "intermediary," "go-between," and "mutual friend" to the head of Organization 1. In a follow-up letter to HPSCI dated October 13, 2017, STONE identified Person 2 by name and claimed Person 2 was the "gentleman who confirmed for Mr. Stone" that the head of Organization 1 had "'[e]mails related to Hillary Clinton which are pending publication.'"

Background
STONE's Communications About Organization 1 During the Campaign

11.   By in or around June and July 2016, STONE informed senior Trump Campaign officials that he had information indicating Organization 1 had documents whose release would be

3

703

damaging to the Clinton Campaign. The head of Organization 1 was located at all relevant times at the Ecuadorian Embassy in London, United Kingdom.

12.   After the July 22, 2016 release of stolen DNC emails by Organization 1, a senior Trump Campaign official was directed to contact STONE about any additional releases and what other damaging information Organization 1 had regarding the Clinton Campaign. STONE thereafter told the Trump Campaign about potential future releases of damaging material by Organization 1.

13.   STONE also corresponded with associates about contacting Organization 1 in order to obtain additional emails damaging to the Clinton Campaign.

a.   On or about July 25, 2016, STONE sent an email to Person 1 with the subject line, "Get to [the head of Organization 1]." The body of the message read, "Get to [the head of Organization 1] [a]t Ecuadorian Embassy in London and get the pending [Organization 1] emails . . . they deal with Foundation, allegedly." On or about the same day, Person 1 forwarded STONE's email to an associate who lived in the United Kingdom and was a supporter of the Trump Campaign.

b.   On or about July 31, 2016, STONE emailed Person 1 with the subject line, "Call me MON." The body of the email read in part that Person 1's associate in the United Kingdom "should see [the head of Organization 1]."

c.   On or about August 2, 2016, Person 1 emailed STONE. Person 1 wrote that he was currently in Europe and planned to return in or around mid-August. Person 1 stated in part, "Word is friend in embassy plans 2 more dumps. One shortly after I'm back. 2nd in Oct. Impact planned to be very damaging." The phrase "friend in embassy" referred to the head of Organization 1. Person 1 added in the same email, "Time to let more than [the Clinton Campaign chairman] to be exposed as in bed w

4

704

enemy if they are not ready to drop HRC. That appears to be the game hackers are now about. Would not hurt to start suggesting HRC old, memory bad, has stroke – neither he nor she well. I expect that much of next dump focus, setting stage for Foundation debacle."

14.   Starting in early August 2016, after receiving the August 2, 2016 email from Person 1, STONE made repeated statements about information he claimed to have learned from the head of Organization 1.

    a.   On or about August 8, 2016, STONE attended a public event at which he stated, "I actually have communicated with [the head of Organization 1]. I believe the next tranche of his documents pertain to the Clinton Foundation, but there's no telling what the October surprise may be."

    b.   On or about August 12, 2016, STONE stated during an interview that he was "in communication with [the head of Organization 1]" but was "not at liberty to discuss what I have."

    c.   On or about August 16, 2016, STONE stated during an interview that "it became known on this program that I have had some back-channel communication with [Organization 1] and [the head of Organization 1]." In a second interview on or about the same day, STONE stated that he "communicated with [the head of Organization 1]" and that they had a "mutual acquaintance who is a fine gentleman."

    d.   On or about August 18, 2016, STONE stated during a television interview that he had communicated with the head of Organization 1 through an "intermediary, somebody who is a mutual friend."

5

705

    e.   On or about August 23, 2016, Person 2 asked STONE during a radio interview, "You've been in touch indirectly with [the head of Organization 1]. . . . Can you give us any kind of insight? Is there an October surprise happening?" STONE responded, "Well, first of all, I don't want to intimate in any way that I control or have influence with [the head of Organization 1] because I do not. . . . We have a mutual friend, somebody we both trust and therefore I am a recipient of pretty good information."

15.   Beginning on or about August 19, 2016, STONE exchanged written communications, including by text message and email, with Person 2 about Organization 1 and what the head of Organization 1 planned to do.

    a.   On or about August 19, 2016, Person 2 sent a text message to STONE that read in part, "I'm going to have [the head of Organization 1] on my show next Thursday." On or about August 21, 2016, Person 2 sent another text message to STONE, writing in part, "I have [the head of Organization 1] on Thursday so I'm completely tied up on that day."

    b.   On or about August 25, 2016, the head of Organization 1 was a guest on Person 2's radio show for the first time. On or about August 26, 2016, Person 2 sent a text message to STONE that stated, "[the head of Organization 1] talk[ed] about you last night." STONE asked what the head of Organization 1 said, to which Person 2 responded, "He didn't say anything bad we were talking about how the Press is trying to make it look like you and he are in cahoots."

    c.   On or about August 27, 2016, Person 2 sent text messages to STONE that said, "We are working on a [head of Organization 1] radio show," and that he (Person 2) was "in charge" of the project. In a text message sent later that day, Person 2 added, "[The head of Organization 1] has kryptonite on Hillary."

d. On or about September 18, 2016, STONE sent a text message to Person 2 that said, "I am e-mailing u a request to pass on to [the head of Organization 1]." Person 2 responded "Ok," and added in a later text message, "[j]ust remember do not name me as your connection to [the head of Organization 1] you had one before that you referred to."

i. On or about the same day, September 18, 2016, STONE emailed Person 2 an article with allegations against then-candidate Clinton related to her service as Secretary of State. STONE stated, "Please ask [the head of Organization 1] for any State or HRC e-mail from August 10 to August 30—particularly on August 20, 2011 that mention [the subject of the article] or confirm this narrative."

ii. On or about September 19, 2016, STONE texted Person 2 again, writing, "Pass my message . . . to [the head of Organization 1]." Person 2 responded, "I did." On or about September 20, 2016, Person 2 forwarded the request to a friend who was an attorney with the ability to contact the head of Organization 1. Person 2 blind-copied STONE on the forwarded email.

e. On or about September 30, 2016, Person 2 sent STONE via text message a photograph of Person 2 standing outside the Ecuadorian Embassy in London where the head of Organization 1 was located.

7

f.   On or about October 1, 2016, which was a Saturday, Person 2 sent STONE text messages that stated, "big news Wednesday . . . now pretend u don't know me . . . Hillary's campaign will die this week." In the days preceding these messages, the press had reported that the head of Organization 1 planned to make a public announcement on or about Tuesday, October 4, 2016, which was reported to be the ten-year anniversary of the founding of Organization 1.

g.   On or about October 2, 2016, STONE emailed Person 2, with the subject line "WTF?," a link to an article reporting that Organization 1 was canceling its "highly anticipated Tuesday announcement due to security concerns." Person 2 responded to STONE, "head fake."

h.   On or about the same day, October 2, 2016, STONE texted Person 2 and asked, "Did [the head of Organization 1] back off." On or about October 3, 2016, Person 2 initially responded, "I can't tal[k] about it." After further exchanges with STONE, Person 2 said, "I think it[']s on for tomorrow." Person 2 added later that day, "Off the Record Hillary and her people are doing a full-court press they [*sic*] keep [the head of Organization 1] from making the next dump . . . That's all I can tell you on this line . . . Please leave my name out of it."

16.   In or around October 2016, STONE made statements about Organization 1's future releases, including statements similar to those that Person 2 made to him. For example:

a.   On or about October 3, 2016, STONE wrote to a supporter involved with the Trump Campaign, "Spoke to my friend in London last night. The payload is still coming."

b.   Also on or about October 3, 2016, STONE received an email from a reporter who had connections to a high-ranking Trump Campaign official that asked, "[the head

8

of Organization 1] – what's he got? Hope it's good." STONE responded in part, "It is. I'd tell [the high-ranking Trump Campaign official] but he doesn't call me back."

c.   On or about October 4, 2016, the head of Organization 1 held a press conference but did not release any new materials pertaining to the Clinton Campaign. Shortly afterwards, STONE received an email from the high-ranking Trump Campaign official asking about the status of future releases by Organization 1. STONE answered that the head of Organization 1 had a "[s]erious security concern" but that Organization 1 would release "a load every week going forward."

d.   Later that day, on or about October 4, 2016, the supporter involved with the Trump Campaign asked STONE via text message if he had "hear[d] anymore from London." STONE replied, "Yes - want to talk on a secure line - got Whatsapp?" STONE subsequently told the supporter that more material would be released and that it would be damaging to the Clinton Campaign.

17.   On or about October 7, 2016, Organization 1 released the first set of emails stolen from the Clinton Campaign chairman. Shortly after Organization 1's release, an associate of the high-ranking Trump Campaign official sent a text message to STONE that read "well done." In subsequent conversations with senior Trump Campaign officials, STONE claimed credit for having correctly predicted the October 7, 2016 release.

The Investigations

18.   In or around 2017, government officials publicly disclosed investigations into Russian interference in the 2016 U.S. presidential election and possible links to individuals associated with the campaigns.

9

a.   On or about January 13, 2017, the chairman and vice chairman of SSCI announced the committee would conduct an inquiry that would investigate, among other things, any intelligence regarding links between Russia and individuals associated with political campaigns, as well as Russian cyber activity and other "active measures" directed against the United States in connection with the 2016 election.

b.   On or about January 25, 2017, the chairman and ranking member of HPSCI announced that HPSCI had been conducting an inquiry similar to SSCI's.

c.   On or about March 20, 2017, the then-director of the FBI testified at a HPSCI hearing and publicly disclosed that the FBI was investigating Russian interference in the 2016 election and possible links and coordination between the Trump Campaign and the Russian government.

d.   By in or around August 2017, news reports stated that a federal grand jury had opened an investigation into matters relating to Russian government efforts to interfere in the 2016 election, including possible links and coordination between the Trump Campaign and the Russian government.

STONE's False Testimony to HPSCI

19.   In or around May 2017, HPSCI sent a letter requesting that STONE voluntarily appear before the committee and produce:

> Any documents, records, electronically stored information including e-mail, communication, recordings, data and tangible things (including, but not limited to, graphs, charts, photographs, images and other documents) regardless of form, other than those widely available (e.g., newspaper articles) that reasonably could lead to the discovery of any facts within the investigation's publicly-announced parameters.

On or about May 22, 2017, STONE caused a letter to be submitted to HPSCI stating that "Mr.

10

Stone has no documents, records, or electronically stored information, regardless of form, other than those widely available that reasonably could lead to the discovery of any facts within the investigation's publicly-announced parameters."

20.   On or about September 26, 2017, STONE testified before HPSCI in Washington, D.C. as part of the committee's ongoing investigation. In his opening statement, STONE stated, "These hearings are largely based on a yet unproven allegation that the Russian state is responsible for the hacking of the DNC and [the Clinton Campaign chairman] and the transfer of that information to [Organization 1]." STONE further stated that "[m]embers of this Committee" had made certain "assertions against me which must be rebutted here today," which included "[t]he charge that I knew in advance about, and predicted, the hacking of Clinton campaign chairman['s] email, [and] that I had advanced knowledge of the source or actual content of the [Organization 1] disclosures regarding Hillary Clinton."

21.   In the course of his HPSCI testimony, STONE made deliberately false and misleading statements to the committee concerning, among other things, his possession of documents pertinent to HPSCI's investigation; the source for his early August 2016 statements about Organization 1; requests he made for information from the head of Organization 1; his communications with his identified intermediary; and his communications with the Trump Campaign about Organization 1.

STONE's False and Misleading Testimony About His Possession of Documents Pertinent to HPSCI's Investigation

22.   During his HPSCI testimony, STONE was asked, "So you have no emails to anyone concerning the allegations of hacked documents . . . or any discussions you have had with third parties about [the head of Organization 1]? You have no emails, no texts, no documents whatsoever, any kind of that nature?" STONE falsely and misleadingly answered, "That is correct.

11

711

Not to my knowledge."

23.   In truth and in fact, STONE had sent and received numerous emails and text messages during the 2016 campaign in which he discussed Organization 1, its head, and its possession of hacked emails. At the time of his false testimony, STONE was still in possession of many of these emails and text messages, including:

a.   The email from STONE to Person 1 on or about July 25, 2016 that read in part, "Get to [the head of Organization 1] [a]t Ecuadorian Embassy in London and get the pending [Organization 1] emails . . . they deal with Foundation, allegedly.";

b.   The email from STONE to Person 1 on or about July 31, 2016 that said an associate of Person 1 "should see [the head of Organization 1].";

c.   The email from Person 1 to STONE on or about August 2, 2016 that stated in part, "Word is friend in embassy plans 2 more dumps. One shortly after I'm back. 2nd in Oct. Impact planned to be very damaging.";

d.   Dozens of text messages and emails, beginning on or about August 19, 2016 and continuing through the election, between STONE and Person 2 in which they discussed Organization 1 and the head of Organization 1;

e.   The email from STONE on or about October 3, 2016 to the supporter involved with the Trump Campaign, which read in part, "Spoke to my friend in London last night. The payload is still coming."; and

f.   The emails on or about October 4, 2016 between STONE and the high-ranking member of the Trump Campaign, including STONE's statement that Organization 1 would release "a load every week going forward."

24.   By falsely claiming that he had no emails or text messages in his possession that referred

to the head of Organization 1, STONE avoided providing a basis for HPSCI to subpoena records

in his possession that could have shown that other aspects of his testimony were false and

misleading.

STONE's False and Misleading Testimony About His Early August 2016 Statements

25.   During his HPSCI testimony on or about September 26, 2017, STONE was asked to

explain his statements in early August 2016 about being in contact with the head of Organization 1.

STONE was specifically asked about his statement on or about August 8, 2016 that "I've actually

communicated with [the head of Organization 1]," as well as his statement on or about August 12,

2016 that he was "in communication with [the head of Organization 1]" but was "not at liberty to

discuss what I have."

26.   STONE responded that his public references to having a means of contacting Organization

1 referred exclusively to his contact with a journalist, who STONE described as a "go-between, as

an intermediary, as a mutual friend" of the head of Organization 1. STONE stated that he asked

this individual, his intermediary, "to confirm what [the head of Organization 1] ha[d] tweeted,

himself, on July 21st, that he ha[d] the Clinton emails and that he [would] publish them." STONE

further stated that the intermediary "was someone I knew had interviewed [the head of

Organization 1]. And I merely wanted confirmation of what he had tweeted on the 21st." STONE

declined to tell HPSCI the name of this "intermediary" but provided a description in his testimony

that was consistent with Person 2.

27.   On or about October 13, 2017, STONE caused a letter to be submitted to HPSCI that

identified Person 2 by name as the "gentleman who confirmed for Mr. Stone" that the head of

Organization 1 had "'[e]mails related to Hillary Clinton which are pending publication.'"

13

713

28.   STONE's explanation of his August 2016 statements about communicating with the head

of Organization 1 was false and misleading. In truth and in fact, the first time Person 2 interviewed

the head of Organization 1 was on or about August 25, 2016, after STONE made his August 8 and

August 12, 2016 public statements. Similarly, at the time STONE made his August 2016

statements, STONE had directed Person 1—not Person 2—to contact the head of Organization 1.

And Person 1—not Person 2—had told STONE in advance of STONE's August 8 and August 12,

2016 public statements that "[w]ord is friend in embassy plans 2 more dumps," including one in

October. At no time did STONE identify Person 1 to HPSCI as another individual STONE

contacted to serve as a "go-between," "intermediary," or other source of information from

Organization 1. STONE also never disclosed his exchanges with Person 1 when answering

HPSCI's questioning about STONE's August 8 and August 12, 2016 statements.

STONE's False and Misleading Testimony About Requests He Made for Information from the Head of Organization 1

29.   During his HPSCI testimony, STONE was asked, "[W]hat was the extent of the

communication with [the intermediary]?" STONE replied, "I asked him to confirm . . . that the

tweet of [the head of Organization 1] of the 21st was accurate, that they did in fact have . . . Hillary

Clinton emails and that they would release them." STONE was then asked, "Did you ask [the

intermediary] to communicate anything else to [the head of Organization 1]?" STONE falsely and

misleadingly responded, "I did not." STONE was then asked, "Did you ask [the intermediary] to

do anything on your own behalf?" STONE falsely and misleadingly responded, "I did not."

30.   In truth and in fact, STONE directed both Person 1 and Person 2 to pass on requests to the

head of Organization 1 for documents that STONE believed would be damaging to the Clinton

Campaign. For example:

     a.   As described above, on or about July 25, 2016, STONE sent Person 1 an email that read, "Get to [the head of Organization 1] [a]t Ecuadorian Embassy in London and get the pending [Organization 1] emails . . . they deal with Foundation, allegedly."

b. On or about September 18, 2016, STONE sent a text message to Person 2 that said, "I am e-mailing u a request to pass on to [the head of Organization 1]," and then emailed Person 2 an article with allegations against then-candidate Clinton related to her service as Secretary of State. STONE added, "Please ask [the head of Organization 1] for any State or HRC e-mail from August 10 to August 30— particularly on August 20, 2011 that mention [the subject of the article] or confirm this narrative."

c. On or about September 19, 2016, STONE texted Person 2 again, writing "Pass my message . . . to [the head of Organization 1]." Person 2 responded, "I did," and the next day Person 2, on an email blind-copied to STONE, forwarded the request to an attorney who had the ability to contact the head of Organization 1.

STONE's False and Misleading Testimony About Communications with His Identified Intermediary

31. During his HPSCI testimony, STONE was asked repeatedly about his communications with the person he identified as his intermediary. STONE falsely and misleadingly stated that he had never communicated with his intermediary in writing in any way. During one exchange, STONE falsely and misleadingly claimed only to have spoken with the intermediary telephonically:

> Q: [H]ow did you communicate with the intermediary?
>
> A: Over the phone.
>
> Q: And did you have any other means of communicating with the intermediary?
>
> A: No.
>
> Q: No text messages, no – none of the list, right?

15

A: No.

Later during his testimony, STONE again falsely denied ever communicating with his intermediary in writing:

    Q: So you never communicated with your intermediary in writing in any way?

    A: No.

    Q: Never emailed him or texted him?

    A: He's not an email guy.

    Q: So all your conversations with him were in person or over the phone.

    A: Correct.

32.   In truth and in fact, as described above, STONE and Person 2 (who STONE identified to HPSCI as his intermediary) engaged in frequent written communication by email and text message. STONE also engaged in frequent written communication by email and text message with Person 1, who also provided STONE with information regarding Organization 1.

33.   Written communications between STONE and Person 1 and between STONE and Person 2 continued through STONE's HPSCI testimony. Indeed, on or about September 26, 2017—the day that STONE testified before HPSCI and denied having ever sent or received emails or text messages from Person 2—STONE and Person 2 exchanged over thirty text messages.

34.   Certain electronic messages between STONE and Person 1 and between STONE and Person 2 would have been material to HPSCI. For example:

    a.   In or around July 2016, STONE emailed Person 1 to "get to" the head of Organization 1 and obtain the pending emails.

    b.   In or around September 2016, STONE sent messages directing Person 2 to pass a request to the head of Organization 1.

    c.   On or about January 6, 2017, Person 2 sent STONE an email that had the subject

16

line "Back channel bs." In the email, Person 2 wrote, "Well I have put together timelines[] and you [] said you have a back-channel way back a month before I had [the head of Organization 1] on my show . . . I have never had a conversation with [the head of Organization 1] other than my radio show . . . I have pieced it all together . . . so you may as well tell the truth that you had no back-channel or there's the guy you were talking about early August."

STONE's False and Misleading Testimony About Communications with the Trump Campaign

35.   During his HPSCI testimony, STONE was asked, "did you discuss your conversations with the intermediary with anyone involved in the Trump campaign?" STONE falsely and misleadingly answered, "I did not." In truth and in fact, and as described above, STONE spoke to multiple individuals involved in the Trump Campaign about what he claimed to have learned from his intermediary to Organization 1, including the following:

    a.   On multiple occasions, STONE told senior Trump Campaign officials about materials possessed by Organization 1 and the timing of future releases.

    b.   On or about October 3, 2016, STONE wrote to a supporter involved with the Trump Campaign, "Spoke to my friend in London last night. The payload is still coming."

    c.   On or about October 4, 2016, STONE told a high-ranking Trump Campaign official that the head of Organization 1 had a "[s]erious security concern" but would release "a load every week going forward."

Attempts to Prevent Person 2 from Contradicting STONE's False Statements to HPSCI

36.   On or about October 19, 2017, STONE sent Person 2 an excerpt of his letter to HPSCI that identified Person 2 as his "intermediary" to Organization 1. STONE urged Person 2, if asked by HPSCI, to falsely confirm what STONE had previously testified to, including that it was Person 2

who provided STONE with the basis for STONE's early August 2016 statements about contact with Organization 1. Person 2 repeatedly told STONE that his testimony was false and told him to correct his testimony to HPSCI. STONE did not do so. STONE then engaged in a prolonged effort to prevent Person 2 from contradicting STONE's false statements to HPSCI.

37.   In or around November 2017, Person 2 received a request from HPSCI to testify voluntarily before the committee. After being contacted by HPSCI, Person 2 spoke and texted repeatedly with STONE. In these discussions, STONE sought to have Person 2 testify falsely either that Person 2 was the identified intermediary or that Person 2 could not remember what he had told STONE. Alternatively, STONE sought to have Person 2 invoke his Fifth Amendment right against self-incrimination. For example:

a.   On or about November 19, 2017, in a text message to STONE, Person 2 said that his lawyer wanted to see him (Person 2). STONE responded, "'Stonewall it. Plead the fifth. Anything to save the plan' . . . Richard Nixon." On or about November 20, 2017, Person 2 informed HPSCI that he declined HPSCI's request for a voluntary interview.

b.   On or about November 21, 2017, Person 2 texted STONE, "I was told that the house committee lawyer told my lawyer that I will be getting a subpoena." STONE responded, "That was the point at which your lawyers should have told them you would assert your 5th Amendment rights if compelled to appear."

c.   On or about November 28, 2017, Person 2 received a subpoena compelling his testimony before HPSCI. Person 2 informed STONE of the subpoena.

d.   On or about November 30, 2017, STONE asked Person 1 to write publicly about Person 2. Person 1 responded, "Are you sure you want to make something out of

718

this now? Why not wait to see what [Person 2] does. You may be defending yourself too much—raising new questions that will fuel new inquiries. This may be a time to say less, not more." STONE responded by telling Person 1 that Person 2 "will take the 5th—but let's hold a day."

e.   On multiple occasions, including on or about December 1, 2017, STONE told Person 2 that Person 2 should do a "Frank Pentangeli" before HPSCI in order to avoid contradicting STONE's testimony. Frank Pentangeli is a character in the film *The Godfather: Part II*, which both STONE and Person 2 had discussed, who testifies before a congressional committee and in that testimony claims not to know critical information that he does in fact know.

f.   On or about December 1, 2017, STONE texted Person 2, "And if you turned over anything to the FBI you're a fool." Later that day, Person 2 texted STONE, "You need to amend your testimony before I testify on the 15th." STONE responded, "If you testify you're a fool. Because of tromp I could never get away with a certain [sic] my Fifth Amendment rights but you can. I guarantee you you are the one who gets indicted for perjury if you're stupid enough to testify."

38.   On or about December 12, 2017, Person 2 informed HPSCI that he intended to assert his Fifth Amendment privilege against self-incrimination if required to appear by subpoena. Person 2 invoked his Fifth Amendment privilege in part to avoid providing evidence that would show STONE's previous testimony to Congress was false.

39.   Following Person 2's invocation of his Fifth Amendment privilege not to testify before HPSCI, STONE and Person 2 continued to have discussions about the various investigations into Russian interference in the 2016 election and what information Person 2 would provide to

investigators.   During these conversations, STONE repeatedly made statements intended to prevent Person 2 from cooperating with the investigations. For example:

a.   On or about December 24, 2017, Person 2 texted STONE, "I met [the head of Organization 1] for f[i]rst time this yea[r] sept 7 . . . docs prove that. . . . You should be honest w fbi . . . there was no back channel . . . be honest." STONE replied approximately two minutes later, "I'm not talking to the FBI and if your smart you won't either."

b.   On or about April 9, 2018, STONE wrote in an email to Person 2, "You are a rat. A stoolie. You backstab your friends-run your mouth my lawyers are dying Rip you to shreds."   STONE also said he would "take that dog away from you," referring to Person 2's dog. On or about the same day, STONE wrote to Person 2, "I am so ready. Let's get it on. Prepare to die [expletive]."

c.   On or about May 21, 2018, Person 2 wrote in an email to STONE, "You should have just been honest with the house Intel committee . . . you've opened yourself up to perjury charges like an idiot." STONE responded, "You are so full of [expletive]. You got nothing. Keep running your mouth and I'll file a bar complaint against your friend [the attorney who had the ability to contact the head of Organization 1]."

COUNT ONE
(Obstruction of Proceeding)

40.   Paragraphs 1 through 39 of this Indictment are re-alleged and incorporated by reference as if fully set forth herein.

41.   From in or around May 2017 through at least December 2017, within the District of Columbia and elsewhere, the defendant ROGER JASON STONE, JR., corruptly influenced, obstructed, impeded, and endeavored to influence, obstruct, and impede the due and proper exercise of the power of inquiry under which any inquiry and investigation is being had by either House, and any committee of either House and any joint committee of the Congress, to wit: STONE testified falsely and misleadingly at a HPSCI hearing in or around September 2017; STONE failed to turn over and lied about the existence of responsive records to HPSCI's requests about documents; STONE submitted and caused to be submitted a letter to HPSCI falsely and misleadingly describing communications with Person 2; and STONE attempted to have Person 2 testify falsely before HPSCI or prevent him from testifying.

All in violation of Title 18, United States Code, Sections 1505 and 2.

21

COUNTS TWO THROUGH SIX
(False Statements)

42.   Paragraphs 1 through 39 of this Indictment are re-alleged and incorporated by reference as if fully set forth herein.

43.   On or about September 26, 2017, within the District of Columbia and elsewhere, in a matter within the jurisdiction of the legislative branch of the Government of the United States, the defendant ROGER JASON STONE, JR., knowingly and willfully made and caused to be made materially false, fictitious, and fraudulent statements and representations, to wit:

Count	False Statement
2	STONE testified falsely that he did not have emails with third parties about the head of Organization 1, and that he did not have any documents, emails, or text messages that refer to the head of Organization 1.
3	STONE testified falsely that his August 2016 references to being in contact with the head of Organization 1 were references to communications with a single "go-between," "mutual friend," and "intermediary," who STONE identified as Person 2.
4	STONE testified falsely that he did not ask the person he referred to as his "go-between," "mutual friend," and "intermediary," to communicate anything to the head of Organization 1 and did not ask the intermediary to do anything on STONE's behalf.
5	STONE testified falsely that he and the person he referred to as his "go-between," "mutual friend," and "intermediary" did not communicate via text message or email about Organization 1.
6	STONE testified falsely that he had never discussed his conversations with the person he referred to as his "go-between," "mutual friend," and "intermediary" with anyone involved in the Trump Campaign.

All in violation of Title 18, United States Code, Sections 1001(a)(2) and 2.

COUNT SEVEN
(Witness Tampering)

44.   Paragraphs 1 through 39 of this Indictment are re-alleged and incorporated by reference as if fully set forth herein.

45.   Between in or around September 2017 and present, within the District of Columbia and elsewhere, the defendant ROGER JASON STONE, JR., knowingly and intentionally corruptly persuaded and attempted to corruptly persuade another person, to wit: Person 2, with intent to influence, delay, and prevent the testimony of any person in an official proceeding.

All in violation of Title 18, United States Code, Section 1512(b)(1).

Robert S. Mueller, III
Special Counsel
U.S. Department of Justice

A TRUE BILL:

Foreperson

Date: January 24, 2019

23

10. Letter from Attorney General William P. Barr to US Senate and House Judiciary Committees, March 24, 2019

On Friday, March 22, 2019, just before a sudden hailstorm descended upon Washington, DC, a security officer from Robert S. Mueller III's office arrived at the Justice Department to deliver the final report from the special counsel. The investigation was over.

Attorney General William P. Barr broke the news in a mere one-page letter to lawmakers in which he said he would work on giving them Mueller's "principal conclusions" before the weekend was out. About forty-eight hours later, he made good on his promise, giving them this four-page summary of the special counsel's top-line findings.

The letter was a political windfall for President Trump. No one else would be indicted, Barr wrote, and Mueller did not find that Trump or anyone associated with his campaign had conspired with Russia to interfere in the election. That offered the president strong support for his constant refrain of "no collusion."

Further, Barr wrote, Mueller had declined to make a prosecutorial judgment on the question of whether Trump obstructed justice, but instead had described the facts he had found and noted "while this report does not conclude that the President committed a crime, it also does not exonerate him." Barr wrote that he and Deputy Attorney General Rod J. Rosenstein reviewed the question themselves and determined the evidence was "not sufficient to establish that the President committed an obstruction-of-justice offense."

Trump seized on the letter to declare he had been vindicated, and he and his allies turned their fire on those who had launched the investigation in the first place and the journalists and commentators who had covered it aggressively. Democrats, meanwhile, attacked Barr for offering an opinion they felt no one had asked for and pressed the attorney general to release Mueller's entire report—which they hoped might offer unflattering information for the president.

Polling had shown that people's views of Mueller's investigation split sharply on partisan lines, and the reaction to Barr's letter confirmed that his findings would be assessed through political lenses. The attorney general's summary shifted the battle from the law enforcement arena to Congress, with no sign that the country's sharp divide over Trump was likely to abate any time soon.

The Attorney General
Washington, D.C.

March 24, 2019

The Honorable Lindsey Graham
Chairman, Committee on the Judiciary
United States Senate
290 Russell Senate Office Building
Washington, D.C. 20510

The Honorable Jerrold Nadler
Chairman, Committee on the Judiciary
United States House of Representatives
2132 Rayburn House Office Building
Washington, D.C. 20515

The Honorable Dianne Feinstein
Ranking Member, Committee on the Judiciary
United States Senate
331 Hart Senate Office Building
Washington, D.C. 20510

The Honorable Doug Collins
Ranking Member, Committee on the Judiciary
United States House of Representatives
1504 Longworth House Office Building
Washington, D.C. 20515

Dear Chairman Graham, Chairman Nadler, Ranking Member Feinstein, and Ranking Member Collins:

As a supplement to the notification provided on Friday, March 22, 2019, I am writing today to advise you of the principal conclusions reached by Special Counsel Robert S. Mueller III and to inform you about the status of my initial review of the report he has prepared.

The Special Counsel's Report

On Friday, the Special Counsel submitted to me a "confidential report explaining the prosecution or declination decisions" he has reached, as required by 28 C.F.R. § 600.8(c). This report is entitled "Report on the Investigation into Russian Interference in the 2016 Presidential Election." Although my review is ongoing, I believe that it is in the public interest to describe the report and to summarize the principal conclusions reached by the Special Counsel and the results of his investigation.

The report explains that the Special Counsel and his staff thoroughly investigated allegations that members of the presidential campaign of Donald J. Trump, and others associated with it, conspired with the Russian government in its efforts to interfere in the 2016 U.S. presidential election, or sought to obstruct the related federal investigations. In the report, the Special Counsel noted that, in completing his investigation, he employed 19 lawyers who were assisted by a team of approximately 40 FBI agents, intelligence analysts, forensic accountants, and other professional staff. The Special Counsel issued more than 2,800 subpoenas, executed nearly 500 search warrants, obtained more than 230 orders for communication records, issued almost 50 orders authorizing use of pen registers, made 13 requests to foreign governments for evidence, and interviewed approximately 500 witnesses.

1

The Special Counsel obtained a number of indictments and convictions of individuals and entities in connection with his investigation, all of which have been publicly disclosed. During the course of his investigation, the Special Counsel also referred several matters to other offices for further action. The report does not recommend any further indictments, nor did the Special Counsel obtain any sealed indictments that have yet to be made public. Below, I summarize the principal conclusions set out in the Special Counsel's report.

Russian Interference in the 2016 U.S. Presidential Election. The Special Counsel's report is divided into two parts. The first describes the results of the Special Counsel's investigation into Russia's interference in the 2016 U.S. presidential election. The report outlines the Russian effort to influence the election and documents crimes committed by persons associated with the Russian government in connection with those efforts. The report further explains that a primary consideration for the Special Counsel's investigation was whether any Americans – including individuals associated with the Trump campaign – joined the Russian conspiracies to influence the election, which would be a federal crime. The Special Counsel's investigation did not find that the Trump campaign or anyone associated with it conspired or coordinated with Russia in its efforts to influence the 2016 U.S. presidential election. As the report states: "[T]he investigation did not establish that members of the Trump Campaign conspired or coordinated with the Russian government in its election interference activities."[1]

The Special Counsel's investigation determined that there were two main Russian efforts to influence the 2016 election. The first involved attempts by a Russian organization, the Internet Research Agency (IRA), to conduct disinformation and social media operations in the United States designed to sow social discord, eventually with the aim of interfering with the election. As noted above, the Special Counsel did not find that any U.S. person or Trump campaign official or associate conspired or knowingly coordinated with the IRA in its efforts, although the Special Counsel brought criminal charges against a number of Russian nationals and entities in connection with these activities.

The second element involved the Russian government's efforts to conduct computer hacking operations designed to gather and disseminate information to influence the election. The Special Counsel found that Russian government actors successfully hacked into computers and obtained emails from persons affiliated with the Clinton campaign and Democratic Party organizations, and publicly disseminated those materials through various intermediaries, including WikiLeaks. Based on these activities, the Special Counsel brought criminal charges against a number of Russian military officers for conspiring to hack into computers in the United States for purposes of influencing the election. But as noted above, the Special Counsel did not find that the Trump campaign, or anyone associated with it, conspired or coordinated with the Russian government in these efforts, despite multiple offers from Russian-affiliated individuals to assist the Trump campaign.

---

[1] In assessing potential conspiracy charges, the Special Counsel also considered whether members of the Trump campaign "coordinated" with Russian election interference activities. The Special Counsel defined "coordination" as an "agreement—tacit or express—between the Trump Campaign and the Russian government on election interference."

2

Obstruction of Justice. The report's second part addresses a number of actions by the President – most of which have been the subject of public reporting – that the Special Counsel investigated as potentially raising obstruction-of-justice concerns. After making a "thorough factual investigation" into these matters, the Special Counsel considered whether to evaluate the conduct under Department standards governing prosecution and declination decisions but ultimately determined not to make a traditional prosecutorial judgment. The Special Counsel therefore did not draw a conclusion – one way or the other – as to whether the examined conduct constituted obstruction. Instead, for each of the relevant actions investigated, the report sets out evidence on both sides of the question and leaves unresolved what the Special Counsel views as "difficult issues" of law and fact concerning whether the President's actions and intent could be viewed as obstruction. The Special Counsel states that "while this report does not conclude that the President committed a crime, it also does not exonerate him."

The Special Counsel's decision to describe the facts of his obstruction investigation without reaching any legal conclusions leaves it to the Attorney General to determine whether the conduct described in the report constitutes a crime. Over the course of the investigation, the Special Counsel's office engaged in discussions with certain Department officials regarding many of the legal and factual matters at issue in the Special Counsel's obstruction investigation. After reviewing the Special Counsel's final report on these issues; consulting with Department officials, including the Office of Legal Counsel; and applying the principles of federal prosecution that guide our charging decisions, Deputy Attorney General Rod Rosenstein and I have concluded that the evidence developed during the Special Counsel's investigation is not sufficient to establish that the President committed an obstruction-of-justice offense. Our determination was made without regard to, and is not based on, the constitutional considerations that surround the indictment and criminal prosecution of a sitting president.[2]

In making this determination, we noted that the Special Counsel recognized that "the evidence does not establish that the President was involved in an underlying crime related to Russian election interference," and that, while not determinative, the absence of such evidence bears upon the President's intent with respect to obstruction. Generally speaking, to obtain and sustain an obstruction conviction, the government would need to prove beyond a reasonable doubt that a person, acting with corrupt intent, engaged in obstructive conduct with a sufficient nexus to a pending or contemplated proceeding. In cataloguing the President's actions, many of which took place in public view, the report identifies no actions that, in our judgment, constitute obstructive conduct, had a nexus to a pending or contemplated proceeding, and were done with corrupt intent, each of which, under the Department's principles of federal prosecution guiding charging decisions, would need to be proven beyond a reasonable doubt to establish an obstruction-of-justice offense.

Status of the Department's Review

The relevant regulations contemplate that the Special Counsel's report will be a "confidential report" to the Attorney General. *See* Office of Special Counsel, 64 Fed. Reg. 37,038,

---

[2] *See A Sitting President's Amenability to Indictment and Criminal Prosecution*, 24 Op. O.L.C. 222 (2000).

37,040-41 (July 9, 1999). As I have previously stated, however, I am mindful of the public interest in this matter. For that reason, my goal and intent is to release as much of the Special Counsel's report as I can consistent with applicable law, regulations, and Departmental policies.

Based on my discussions with the Special Counsel and my initial review, it is apparent that the report contains material that is or could be subject to Federal Rule of Criminal Procedure 6(e), which imposes restrictions on the use and disclosure of information relating to "matter[s] occurring before [a] grand jury." Fed. R. Crim. P. 6(e)(2)(B). Rule 6(e) generally limits disclosure of certain grand jury information in a criminal investigation and prosecution. *Id*. Disclosure of 6(e) material beyond the strict limits set forth in the rule is a crime in certain circumstances. *See, e.g.*, 18 U.S.C. § 401(3). This restriction protects the integrity of grand jury proceedings and ensures that the unique and invaluable investigative powers of a grand jury are used strictly for their intended criminal justice function.

Given these restrictions, the schedule for processing the report depends in part on how quickly the Department can identify the 6(e) material that by law cannot be made public. I have requested the assistance of the Special Counsel in identifying all 6(e) information contained in the report as quickly as possible. Separately, I also must identify any information that could impact other ongoing matters, including those that the Special Counsel has referred to other offices. As soon as that process is complete, I will be in a position to move forward expeditiously in determining what can be released in light of applicable law, regulations, and Departmental policies.

* * *

As I observed in my initial notification, the Special Counsel regulations provide that "the Attorney General may determine that public release of" notifications to your respective Committees "would be in the public interest." 28 C.F.R. § 600.9(c). I have so determined, and I will disclose this letter to the public after delivering it to you.

Sincerely,

William P. Barr
Attorney General

4

11. Letter from Special Counsel Robert S. Mueller III to Attorney General William P. Barr, March 27, 2019

Attorney General William P. Barr's four-page letter from March 24, 2019, summarizing the "principal conclusions" of the investigation by Special Counsel Robert S. Mueller III, shaped public opinion of the report for more than three weeks, while the Department of Justice prepared the still-confidential document for release.

With the publication of a redacted version of Mueller's report on April 18, some critics raised concerns that Barr had not accurately described key elements of Mueller's conclusions. Only in May did the public learn that Mueller himself had shared this view. On March 27—three days after the release of Barr's letter—Mueller sent this confidential missive to the attorney general, arguing that Barr had failed to "fully capture the context, nature, and substance" of Mueller's work.

Mueller's letter went on to ask that Barr immediately publish the executive summaries of the report and its two volumes that his team had prepared in order to better educate the public about the scope of their work. Barr declined, preferring to prepare the entire report for release all at once.

In testimony to the Senate Judiciary Committee on May 1, Barr termed the letter "snitty" and suggested it perhaps reflected the views of Mueller's staff rather than the special counsel himself. He claimed that in a phone call following the submission of the letter, Mueller had assured him that he did not believe Barr's letter had been inaccurate but was merely distressed by media coverage of it. Mueller's letter

732 The Washington Post

had not referenced the media. As had been his practice throughout the investigation, Mueller declined to publicly comment or expand on his letter. The dispute intensified pressure from congressional Democrats to hold a hearing with the special counsel, so he could explain his views in his own words.

U.S. Department of Justice

The Special Counsel's Office

Washington, D.C. 20530

March 27, 2019   *Recieved*
                   OAG
                   March 28, 2019

The Honorable William P. Barr
Attorney General of the United States
Department of Justice
Washington, D.C.

Re: <u>Report of the Special Counsel on the Investigation Into Russian Interference in the 2016 Presidential Election and Obstruction of Justice (March 2019)</u>

Dear Attorney General Barr:

I previously sent you a letter dated March 25, 2019, that enclosed the introduction and executive summary for each volume of the Special Counsel's report marked with redactions to remove any information that potentially could be protected by Federal Rule of Criminal Procedure 6(e); that concerned declination decisions; or that related to a charged case. We also had marked an additional two sentences for review and have now confirmed that these sentences can be released publicly.

Accordingly, the enclosed documents are in a form that can be released to the public consistent with legal requirements and Department policies. I am requesting that you provide these materials to Congress and authorize their public release at this time.

As we stated in our meeting of March 5 and reiterated to the Department early in the afternoon of March 24, the introductions and executive summaries of our two-volume report accurately summarize this Office's work and conclusions. The summary letter the Department sent to Congress and released to the public late in the afternoon of March 24 did not fully capture the context, nature, and substance of this Office's work and conclusions. We communicated that concern to the Department on the morning of March 25. There is now public confusion about critical aspects of the results of our investigation. This threatens to undermine a central purpose for which the Department appointed the Special Counsel: to assure full public confidence in the outcome of the investigations. *See* Department of Justice, Press Release (May 17, 2017).

While we understand that the Department is reviewing the full report to determine what is appropriate for public release—a process that our Office is working with you to complete—that process need not delay release of the enclosed materials. Release at this time would alleviate the misunderstandings that have arisen and would answer congressional and public questions about the nature and outcome of our investigation. It would also accord with the standard for public release of notifications to Congress cited in your letter. *See* 28 C.F.R. § 609(c) ("the Attorney General may determine that public release" of congressional notifications "would be in the public interest").

Sincerely yours,

Robert S. Mueller, III
Special Counsel

Enclosures

About the Authors

Rosalind S. Helderman is an investigative reporter for the national political staff of *The Washington Post*. A reporter for the *Post* since 2001, Rosalind has helped cover two presidential elections and the US Congress, as well as local news in Virginia and Maryland. She was part of a team of reporters awarded the Pulitzer Prize in 2018 for coverage of Donald Trump and Russia and is a two-time recipient of the Polk Award for investigative reporting. She grew up in Nashville, Tennessee, and is a graduate of Harvard University.

Matt Zapotosky is a national security reporter who covers the Justice Department and the FBI for *The Washington Post*. He covered the special counsel investigation since its inception and was part of the *Post*'s team that won a Polk Award for stories on Donald Trump and Russia. Matt has been at the *Post* since 2008 and spent much of his career covering law enforcement and the court system in Maryland and Virginia. He grew up in Toledo, Ohio, and is a graduate of Ohio University.